HISTORY OF THE GREENBACKS

A HISTORY OF THE GREENBACKS

WITH SPECIAL REFERENCE TO THE ECONOMIC
CONSEQUENCES OF THEIR ISSUE: 1862–65

BY

WESLEY CLAIR MITCHELL

THE UNIVERSITY OF CHICAGO PRESS
Chicago and London

THE UNIVERSITY OF CHICAGO PRESS, CHICAGO 60637
The University of Chicago Press, Ltd., London W.C. 1

TO J. W. M. AND L. M. M.

PREFACE

APOLOGIES must be made both for the bulkiness and for the fragmentary character of the following monograph. These defects are due to the same cause: an attempt to utilize all the well-authenticated statistical material bearing upon the subjects treated. The amount of labor entailed by this attempt was so large that I have been unable to carry the discussion beyond the first four years in the history of the greenbacks. Even within this brief period two important topics are passed over. Nothing is said of the effects of the greenbacks upon foreign trade, and no comparisons are made between American and foreign experiences with paper money. The former topic is omitted from lack of time to get the refractory statistical data relating to it into significant shape; indeed, my dealings with the figures incline me to doubt whether any other than a speculative treatment is feasible. As for the latter topic, I soon discovered that foreign comparisons presented too large a subject to be dealt with as a side issue in such a monograph as the present. Moreover, the consequences of the abandonment of the specie standard in which I have been most interested are such as can be traced only when one has much fuller information regarding prices, wages, and the like than are available to the student of foreign experiments with inconvertible paper currencies.

All of the statistical data employed in the course of the discussion are presented at length in the Appendix in such form that they can be readily verified, or employed in new combinations. The tables have passed through the hands of two computers. While I can hardly hope that no errors of transcription, computation, or printing remain uncorrected, I should be surprised to find any of sufficient consequence to affect the validity of the conclusions drawn.

Four of the chapters have appeared at various dates as articles in the *Journal of Political Economy*, and one has been reprinted in *Sound Currency* and the *Report of the Indianapolis Monetary Commission*. Three of these articles have been entirely rewritten, and the fourth has been carefully revised.

Professor J. Laurence Laughlin and Dr. Herbert J. Davenport, of the University of Chicago, and Professor T. S. Adams, of the University of Wisconsin, have read different parts of the book and made valuable suggestions and criticisms. Miss Maude L. Radford, of University College, Chicago, has looked over all the chapters and done what she could to amend crudities of expression. My thanks are also due to the late Professor Charles F. Dunbar, and to Colonel Carroll D. Wright, for answers to troublesome inquiries by letter.

W. C. M.

UNIVERSITY OF CALIFORNIA.

TABLE OF CONTENTS

TABLE OF CONTENTS

STATISTICAL APPENDICES

TABLE OF CONTENTS

PART I
HISTORY OF THE LEGAL-TENDER ACTS

CHAPTER I

THE SUSPENSION OF SPECIE PAYMENTS

I. STATE OF THE FINANCES, MARCH, 1861

On the day after his inauguration President Lincoln sent to the Senate the nomination of Salmon P. Chase, of Ohio, as secretary of the treasury. Political considerations were of chief weight in determining this appointment. Mr. Lincoln perceived that the support of the various elements of which the young Republican party was compounded would be necessary to secure the success of his administration. So Seward, the recognized leader of the radical wing of the party, was made secretary of state; and Chase, the most prominent representative of the conservative wing composed of anti-slavery Democrats, became secretary of the treasury.[1]

In addition to political availability, Mr. Lincoln thought Chase possessed peculiar personal qualifications for the

---

[1] *Cf.* NICOLAY AND HAY, *Abraham Lincoln, A History* (New York, 1890), Vol. III, p. 354.

3

position. True, his thirty years' connection with the Cincinnati bar, and the term in the Senate and two terms as governor of Ohio, that constituted his experience of public affairs, had brought him little familiarity with fiscal questions. But they had shown that he had a clear intellect, administrative ability, and untiring industry. And, above all, they had given him a name for strict integrity that would be of especial weight in gaining the public confidence indispensable to success in the management of the then discredited treasury. Though Mr. Chase brought with him little knowledge of financial administration, his mind was deeply impressed with certain financial theories. From his former Democratic affiliations he had imbibed the "hard-money" principles of Jackson and Benton and their dislike for paper currencies. Personal observation of the unsound methods of banking then prevalent in the western states had strengthened these convictions and inspired in him an indiscriminating distrust of the issues of all banks whatsoever. The early suspension of specie payments and issue of an irredeemable currency of legal tender paper in the Civil War occurred, then, under the administration of a secretary of the treasury who cherished a strong predilection for metallic money.[1]

It was with great reluctance that Mr. Chase resigned his seat in the Senate to undertake the arduous task of managing the treasury in the face of threatening war.[2] The diffi-

---

[1] Three considerable biographies of Chase have been published, one by ROBERT B. WARDEN, *An Account of the Private Life and Public Services of Salmon Portland Chase*, Cincinnati, 1874; 8vo, pp. xxiii + 838 (valuable chiefly for copious extracts from Mr. Chase's private papers); the second by J. W. SCHUCKERS, *Life and Public Services of S. P. Chase*, New York, 1874; 8vo, pp. xv + 669; the third by PROFESSOR A. B. HART, *Salmon Portland Chase* ("American Statesmen" Series), Boston and New York, 1899; 8vo, pp. xi + 465. See also HUGH McCULLOCH, *Men and Measures of Half a Century* (New York, 1888), chap. xvi, and W. M. EVARTS, *Eulogy on Chase*, appended to SCHUCKERS's *Life*.

[2] *Cf.* Chase's letter to the governor of Ohio, SCHUCKERS, *op. cit.*, p. 207, and letter of F. A. Conkling to E. G. Spaulding, October 17, 1875, in SPAULDING, *History of the Legal Tender Paper Money Issued during the Great Rebellion*, 2d ed. (Buffalo, 1875), Appendix, p. 84.

culties of his position were increased by the disorganized condition in which the federal finances had been left by the preceding administration. When Mr. Buchanan was inaugurated his secretary of the treasury, Howell Cobb, of Georgia, found himself embarrassed by a redundant revenue, to reduce which Congress had just passed the tariff act of March, 1857, lowering the duties upon imports. Unfortunately the financial crisis of 1857 and the commencement of the Mormon troubles followed hard upon the date when the new tariff took effect; the one, in conjunction with the new tariff, decreased the treasury receipts from customs by a quarter, the other increased the expenses of the War Department. So, instead of a surplus the fiscal year 1858 presented a deficit in the revenue.[1]

To meet the shortage Congress authorized the issue of $20,000,000 of one-year treasury notes.[2] As the deficit recurred the next year, a fifteen-year loan of $20,000,000 was made;[3] and in March, 1859, when the one-year treasury notes began to fall due, it was necessary to extend their term to July, 1860.[4] Even by that time the financial situation had not improved sufficiently to enable the government to pay the notes out of revenue, and another loan of $21,000,000 had to be authorized to procure the necessary funds.[5]

Early in September, 1860, Secretary Cobb invited bids for $10,000,000 of this loan, a sum sufficient to meet the notes coming due before January, 1861. When the bids were opened, October 22, it was found that the whole sum had been taken at par or at a small premium. Payment of the subscriptions was to be made thirty days later. But in

---

1 *Report of the Secretary of the Treasury*, December, 1858, pp. 3, 4.

2 Act of December 23, 1857, 11 *Statutes at Large*, p. 257.

3 Act of June 14, 1858, *ibid.*, p. 365.   4 Act of March 3, 1859, *ibid.*, p. 430.

5 Act of June 22, 1860, 12 *Statutes at Large*, p. 79.

November Mr. Lincoln's election was followed by threats of secession from the southern press. A sudden business revulsion resulted, for everyone was anxious to prepare his affairs for the coming storm.[1] The subscribers to the loan were timid and embarrassed. To encourage them, Cobb offered an additional thirty days for making payments to all who would deposit one-half of their bids on the appointed day. Though most of the bidders accepted the offer, some preferred to forfeit the 1 per cent. deposits sent in with the bids rather than to take the bonds. From the $10,000,000 offered the treasury realized only $7,022,000.[2]

Convinced by this ill-success that an attempt to negotiate the remaining $11,000,000 of the loan would fail, Cobb requested Congress to substitute treasury notes for the bonds and to pledge the public lands unconditionally for their redemption. Further, he asked authority for a new loan of $10,000,000 to supply the deficit in the revenues due to the contraction of business.[3] Six days after sending this report to Congress Cobb resigned, giving as his reason that Georgia required his services.[4] Going home, he entered the campaign to persuade his state to secede, and a little later became vice-president of the Confederacy.

President Buchanan appointed as Cobb's successor Philip F. Thomas, of Maryland. Despite the change in secretaries, Congress acted on the second of Cobb's recommendations by authorizing the issue of $10,000,000 of one-year treasury notes at par to those bidders who would accept the lowest rates of interest.[5] The day after the act was approved,

[1] *Report of the Secretary of the Treasury*, December, 1860, p. 7; *cf.* W. G. SUMNER, *A History of American Currency* (New York, 1875), p. 189.

[2] *Report of the Secretary of the Treasury*, December, 1860, pp. 8, 9, and 480–83; *Senate Executive Document No. 2*, p. 11, 37th Cong., 1st Sess.

[3] *Report of the Secretary of the Treasury*, December, 1860, p. 9.

[4] E. McPHERSON, *Political History of the Rebellion*, 4th ed. (Washington, 1882), p. 28.

[5] Act of December 17, 1860, 12 *Statutes at Large*, p. 121.

Thomas invited proposals for one-half of this loan. The response showed how low the national credit had sunk; $1,831,000 was offered at 12 per cent. or less; $465,000 more at rates between 15 and 36 per cent. All offers at 12 per cent. or under were accepted.[1]

To explain why the government was compelled to pay such high rates of interest is not difficult. Public confidence in the Buchanan administration was shaken; particularly, confidence in the management of the Treasury Department which for four years had been contracting debts to meet annually recurring deficits. The check to business following the election in November had intensified the uneasiness. One secretary of the treasury had resigned to aid the secession movement; his successor was distrusted as a southern sympathizer. South Carolina had already adopted the ordinance of secession; other states were on the eve of following her example. At Washington there was disorganization and indecision. Under such circumstances it was natural that there should be hesitation in New York about lending to the government.

But the needs of the government were imperative. The full amount of the five millions offered was required to meet the treasury notes and interest on the debt due January 1. Foreseeing the failure of the public subscription, Mr. Cisco, the head of the subtreasury at New York, induced the New York banks to take at 12 per cent. interest whatever part of the $5,000,000 might not be bid for. Their offer was accepted by Secretary Thomas.[2] After the banks had paid a part of the money into the treasury they became convinced that Thomas intended "to transfer the money into the confederate region where it would be captured." Accordingly, they withheld payment of the

[1] H. R. Miscellaneous Document No. 20, p. 3, 36th Cong., 2d Sess.

[2] Ibid., loc. cit.

next instalment and sent representatives to confer with Mr. Buchanan.[1] The result was that Thomas resigned, ostensibly because he could not agree with the president "in the measures . . . . adopted in reference to the . . . . condition of things in South Carolina."[2] He was succeeded January 11 by General John A. Dix—a man who commanded the full confidence of the North—and the balance of the loan was paid.

Dix found the treasury empty, $350,000 of unpaid warrants accumulated, and a deficit in the revenue which was expected to reach nearly $27,000,000 by the end of June.[3] To meet immediate requirements he offered the remaining half of the $10,000,000 treasury-note loan authorized the preceding December. An improvement in the credit of the government was indicated by the fact that whereas 12 per cent. interest had been paid for the first $5,000,000, the second was borrowed at an average rate of $10\frac{5}{8}$ per cent.[4]

But the sum thus realized did not last long and further borrowing became necessary. Judging from Cobb's failure that it would be impossible to negotiate the balance of the $21,000,000 loan of June 22, 1860, under the terms of the law which forbade the sale of stock below par, Dix applied to Congress to authorize a new bond issue. He even suggested calling on the states to return the $28,000,000 of surplus revenue deposited with them in 1836.[5] Congress, however, would only pass a $25,000,000 loan act.[6] Dix then urged

[1] Correspondence between Mr. George S. Coe, one of the bankers concerned, and E. G. Spaulding, in H. KING, *Turning on the Light* (Philadelphia, 1895), pp. 186–9.

[2] Letter of resignation, G. T. CURTIS, *Life of James Buchanan* (New York, 1883), Vol. II, p. 404.

[3] *Cf.* Dix's letter to the chairman of the Committee on Ways and Means, *H. R. Miscellaneous Document No. 20*, 36th Cong., 2d Sess.

[4] *Cf.* J. J. KNOX, *United States Notes*, 2d ed. (London, 1885), p. 76.

[5] *H. R. Miscellaneous Document No. 20*, p. 6, 36th Cong., 2d Sess.

[6] Act of February 8, 1861, 12 *Statutes at Large*, p. 129. The bonds were to bear 6 per cent. interest and " to be reimbursed within a period not beyond twenty years and not less than ten years."—Sec. 2.

that the states be permitted to add the pledge of their faith to that of the federal government for the repayment of the loan; but the House refused to consider a bill for this purpose.[1] Nevertheless, when bids for $8,000,000 of the new loan were invited in February, the whole sum was subscribed on terms that made the average rate of interest 6.63 per cent., indicating a further improvement in the national credit.[2]

Such small loans, however, could afford but temporary relief. The real difficulty was the insufficient revenue. To stop the necessity of borrowing by increasing the treasury receipts was the nominal purpose of the last important law passed during the Buchanan administration. Bills to raise duties on imports had been presented at every session of Congress since 1858; but all had failed of adoption, until, shortly before the presidential election of 1860, the Morrill tariff act passed the House. It was not taken up by the Senate until the following session, and even then its progress for a time was blocked. But finally, after many of the southern senators had left Washington, it was passed and became a law two days before the close of Mr. Buchanan's term.[3]

As a revenue measure the new schedule was foredoomed to failure. The heaviest duties were levied on articles largely produced in the United States; sugar and molasses were lightly taxed, while coffee, tea, and wool worth less than 18 cents per pound, were entirely free. Revenue was thus sacrificed to protection. During the quarter, January-March, the customs receipts were $9,800,000; in the succeeding three

[1] *Congressional Globe*, 36th Cong., 2d Sess., pp. 871, 872.

[2] Bids were received for $14,460,250 at the rates ranging from 75 to 96.10. Of these bids $8,006,000 were accepted, all below 90.15 being refused.—*Senate Executive Document No. 2*, pp. 19–30, 37th Cong., 1st Sess. The average rate was 90.478.—BAYLEY, *National Loans of the United States*, p. 151.

[3] Act of March 2, 1861, 12 *Statutes at Large*, p. 178. *Cf.* F. W. TAUSSIG, *Tariff History of the United States*, 2d ed. (New York, 1893), p. 158. Sec. 1 of the act authorized a loan of $10,000,000.

months, when the new tariff was in effect, they were $5,500,-
000—a decrease of over 40 per cent.[1] Thus, instead of
improving the position of the treasury, the new tariff served
only to increase the financial embarrassment.[2]

II.   CHASE'S ADMINISTRATION OF THE TREASURY, MARCH TO
JUNE, 1861

It was at a time, then, when the revenue of the government was insufficient to pay its expenses even on a peace
footing, and when distrust and frequent borrowing had much
impaired its credit, that Mr. Chase, with small experience of
financial operations, undertook to raise the means for waging
a most expensive war.   From April to June the ordinary
receipts of the treasury were $5,800,000, its expenditures
$23,500,000.[3]   To fill the deficit there was but one recourse —
borrowing.   Disadvantageous as were the terms on which
the recent loans had been made, it was to a new loan that
Mr. Chase was forced to resort.

On the whole, he was in a more favorable position for
borrowing than Cobb, Thomas, or Dix had been.   True, the
political situation had become more grave.   Mississippi,
Florida, Alabama, Georgia, Louisiana, and Texas had followed South Carolina's example in seceding from the Union,
and when the new administration was installed at Washington it saw itself confronted by a rival government in Mont-
gomery.   But to offset this, Buchanan, who had become
thoroughly discredited in the North, had given place to

[1] *Report of the Secretary of the Treasury*, December, 1861, p. 30.

[2] On the condition of the finances at the commencement of the Civil War, *cf.*
R. J. WALKER, *American Finances and Resources* (London, 1864); VON HOCK, *Die
Finanzen und die Finanzgeschichte der Vereinigten Staaten* (Stuttgart, 1867), pp.
437–40; M. B. FIELD, *Memories of Many Men and of Some Women* (London, 1874),
pp. 250–52; JOHN SHERMAN, *Recollections of Forty Years in the House, Senate and
Cabinet* (Chicago, 1895), Vol. I, pp. 251–4; KNOX, *op. cit.*, pp. 70–83; J. G. BLAINE,
Twenty Years of Congress (Norwich, Conn., 1884), Vol. I, pp. 396–401; A. S. BOLLES,
Financial History of the United States from 1861 to 1885 (New York, 1886), pp. 4–6.

[3] *Report of the Secretary of the Treasury*, December, 1861, pp. 30–32.

Lincoln, in whom the people reposed greater confidence. In raising his first loan Mr. Chase had the benefit of this feeling. Moreover, the credit of the government was improved by a temporary increase of revenue. The Morrill tariff act, approved March 2, was to go into operation April 1. Importers took advantage of the intervening thirty days to pass their goods through the custom-houses as rapidly as possible in order to escape payment of the higher duties imposed by the new schedule, thus increasing the receipts from customs for the months of February and March.[1]

Under the existing laws the secretary had authority to borrow some $41,000,000. (1) Of the $21,000,000 loan of June 22, 1860, Cobb had negotiated $7,022,000, leaving a balance of $13,978,000 which could be issued in 6 per cent. twenty-year bonds — a resource available under the law, however, only when the bonds could be sold at par. (2) The two $5,000,000 treasury-note loans raised by Secretaries Thomas and Dix had exhausted the authority to borrow under the act of December 17, 1860 ; but (3) Dix had issued only $8,006,000 of the $25,000,000 of 6 per cent. stock provided for by the act of February 8, 1861. The disposal of the remainder of this stock — $16,994,000 — was not hampered by the customary provision forbidding sales below par. (4) Finally, the opening sections of the Morrill tariff act authorized a loan of $10,000,000 upon 6 per cent. ten-twenty-year bonds at par, or upon 6 per cent. treasury notes ; but the proceeds of this loan could not be applied to the service of the current fiscal year which would end June 30, 1861. However, this act made the authority to borrow, existing under other laws, more available, by permitting the president "to substitute treasury notes of equal amount for the whole or any part of any of the loans for which he is now by law authorized to

[1] Cf. American Annual Cyclopædia, 1861, p. 296, and Hunt's Merchants' Magazine, Vol. XLIV, p. 666.

contract and issue bonds." The treasury notes so issued were to bear interest at 6 per cent., be receivable for government dues, convertible at par into 6 per cent. bonds, and could be made redeemable at any time within two years; but, like the bonds, they could not be issued to creditors or sold for coin at less than par.[1]

Mr. Chase began by advertising, on March 22, $8,000,000 of the 6 per cent. stock which, under the act of February 8, could be sold to the highest bidder.[2] Ten days were allowed for making proposals. When the bids were opened, April 2, it was found that the loan had been subscribed three times over at rates ranging from 85 to par.[3] This indicated an encouraging improvement in the credit of the government, for the offers for an equal amount of the same stocks made to General Dix less than two months before varied from 75 to 96.10 and amounted to $14,460,250, as compared with $27,182,000. But Mr. Chase thought the treasury notes, which he had authority to issue in lieu of the bonds, could be sold at better prices.[4] Consequently he accepted only the bids at 94 and above, amounting to $3,099,000, and on April 6 invited bids for the balance — $4,901,000 — in treasury notes.[5] Unfortunately, the departure of the expedition to relieve Fort Sumter became known in the meantime. The news created much uneasiness, and when the bids were opened April 11, but one-fifth of the sum had been taken. Financiers who were interested in the success of the loan procured a delay, however,

----

[1] Act of March 2, 1861, Sec. 4, 12 *Statutes at Large*, p. 178. On Chase's authority to borrow, see his report of July 4, 1861, *Senate Executive Document No. 2*, p. 11, 37th Cong., 1st Sess.

[2] *Senate Executive Document No. 2*, p. 31, 37th Cong., 1st Sess.

[3] Schedule of bids, *ibid.*, pp. 32-49.

[4] Since the treasury notes bore 6 per cent. interest and were receivable for all government dues, large importers derived a profit from investing in them the money held in readiness for the payment of customs duties. *Cf. American Annual Cyclopædia*, 1861, p. 297.

[5] *Senate Executive Document No. 2*, pp. 11 and 50, 37th Cong., 1st Sess.

and by dint of their efforts subscriptions were secured for $5,340,000, of which sum $2,500,000 were taken by a single New York bank.[1]

The means thus provided were soon exhausted by the large government disbursements, and it became necessary to borrow again. On May 11 the balance of the 6 per cent. stock of the February loan — $8,994,000 — was advertised for sale.[2] Bids came in very slowly, and a failure of the subscription seemed probable. Such an event would have seriously affected the price of all government securities. In self-defense, the Chamber of Commerce of New York and the banks of New York and Boston came to the aid of the treasury. A card was issued signed among others by J. J. Astor, August Belmont, James Gallatin, A. T. Stewart, Moses Taylor, and George S. Coe, calling attention to the government loans and inviting "all capitalists and moneyed institutions to avail themselves of these opportunities for investment."[3] To give the committees appointed by the chamber and the banks more time to secure subscriptions, Mr. Chase postponed the opening of the bids four days, and also offered to consider bids for treasury notes at par in place of bonds, should that form of security be preferred by any subscriber.[4] Finally, bids ranging from 60 to 93 were obtained for $7,441,000 of the stock, and bids at par for $1,684,000 of the treasury notes. All the latter bids were accepted, and of the former all those at 85 or above — an amount of $7,310,000.[5] From this loan of $8,994,000 the treasury realized the sum of $7,922,553.45.[6]

[1] *Ibid.*, p. 51. Of course only $4,901,000 of the bids — the amount advertised — were accepted. The treasury realized $7,814,809.80 from $8,000,000 of securities sold. — *Ibid.*, p. 11. See *American Annual Cyclopædia*, 1861, p. 296, on the difficulty experienced in negotiating the treasury notes.

[2] *Senate Executive Document No. 2*, p. 52, 37th Cong., 1st Sess.

[3] *American Annual Cyclopædia*, 1861, p. 297; *cf.* "Federal Finances Examined" (anon.), *Hunt's Merchants' Magazine*, Vol. XLVII, p. 504; and *ibid.*, Vol. XLIV, p. 791.

[4] *Senate Executive Document No. 2*, p. 53, 37th Cong., 1st Sess.

[5] *Ibid.*, pp. 58 and 60.   [6] *Ibid.*, p. 11.

Requiring still more money, the secretary asked for proposals for the balance of the 6 per cent. twenty-year loan of June 22, 1860, amounting to $13,978,000.[1] As 6 per cent. government bonds could then be bought in the market at 84, the offer of this stock which the act forbade to be sold below par was a mere formality; but, by advertising the bonds, Mr. Chase complied with the terms of the law, and was enabled to issue treasury notes for the full sum.[2] Three bids, aggregating $12,000, were received; but they had been made under misapprehension and were withdrawn.[3] On account of this loan, however, Mr. Chase issued, by the end of June, $2,584,550 in treasury notes at par.[4]

Finally, just before Congress met, the treasury was again in need. Five million dollars were required to carry it along until new means of securing funds could be devised. As the two-year treasury notes were selling at a discount of 2 to $2\frac{1}{2}$ per cent., they were not directly available. But the banks agreed to advance the amount required for sixty days and take 6 per cent. treasury notes as collateral security.[5]

Two points in this review of the operations of the secretary of the treasury from March to July are of significance:

1. When hostilities opened the federal government was receiving less than a quarter of its revenue from taxation; for the remaining three-quarters it was depending upon hand-to-mouth borrowing.[6] From March 7, 1861, when Mr. Chase was installed, to July 1, there had been an addition of $14,-412,529.40 to the public debt.[7]

[1] *Senate Executive Document No. 2*, 37th Cong., 1st Sess., p. 11.

[2] *Cf. Appleton's Annual Cyclopædia*, 1861, p. 297.

[3] *Senate Executive Document No. 2*, p. 11, 37th Cong., 1st Sess.

[4] Of this sum $1,710,650 was sold for coin, and $873,900 was paid to creditors.—*Ibid.*, pp. 60–62.

[5] *Cf. American Annual Cyclopædia*, 1861, p. 297; and *Hunt's Merchants' Magazine*, Vol. XLVII, p. 505.

[6] From April to June, 1861, the receipts from customs, sales of public land, and miscellaneous sources, were $5,800,000, from loans $17,600,000.—*Report of the Secretary of the Treasury*, December, 1861, p. 30.

[7] *Senate Executive Document No. 2*, p. 18, 37th Cong., 1st Sess.

2. Mr. Chase had of his own accord inaugurated the policy of issuing interest-bearing treasury notes running one or two years, in preference to long-time bonds, whenever they would fetch a higher price, disregarding the fact that such a course exposed the treasury to the danger of being called upon to redeem its notes while hard pressed for funds to meet current demands.[1]

III. FINANCIAL LEGISLATION OF THE EXTRA SESSION OF CONGRESS

Such was the situation when Congress convened in extra session July 4. Emphasizing the need of extraordinary measures, President Lincoln's message recommended that "at least 400,000 men and $400,000,000" be placed "at the control of the government."[2] The financial program of the administration was outlined in a report submitted by Secretary Chase.[3]

It was estimated that the government would require $320,-000,000 to meet the expenditures of the coming twelve months. Of this sum the secretary thought that "not less than $80,000,000 should be provided by taxation, and that $240,-000,000 should be sought through loans." The $80,000,-000 would defray the expenses of a peace footing, estimated at $66,000,000, the interest on the public debt, $9,000,000, and provide an annual sinking fund of $5,000,000. By revising the Morrill tariff, Chase thought the customs could be made to yield a revenue of $57,000,000. An additional $3,000,000 from sales of public lands would leave $20,000,-000 of the $80,000,000 to be raised by direct tax or by internal duties as Congress might decide.

To secure $240,000,000 by borrowing new loans to the

[1] Mr. James Gallatin, president of the Gallatin Bank of New York, advised strongly against this policy. See his *Two Letters to the Hon. S. P. Chase*, etc., New York, 1861.

[2] *Lincoln's Complete Works*, ed. NICOLAY AND HAY, Vol. II, p. 60.

[3] *Senate Executive Document No. 2*, 37th Cong., 1st Sess.

full amount would be necessary; for the $21,393,450 which
the secretary still had authority to borrow under existing
laws[1] was available only when creditors were willing to
accept payment in 6 per cent. treasury notes at par, which,
Mr. Chase admitted, was "not to be expected." He suggested (1) a national loan of $100,000,000 in 7.3 per cent.
treasury notes, running three years; (2) a loan of like amount
in 7 per cent., thirty-year bonds; (3) the issue of not over
$50,000,000 of 3.65 per cent. one-year treasury notes to
meet any need unprovided for by the proceeds of taxation
and the other loans. But, said Mr. Chase, "the greatest
care will . . . . be requisite to prevent the degradation of
such issues into an irredeemable paper currency, than which
no more certainly fatal expedient for impoverishing the
masses and discrediting the government of any country can
well be devised."[2]

If Secretary Chase erred in thus proposing at the outset
to rely upon borrowing to secure three-quarters of the means
for waging the war because he doubted the readiness of the
people to submit to heavy taxation, Congress was neither
wiser nor bolder than he. With his report were submitted
drafts of bills embodying its suggestions.[3] After one hour's
debate, entirely taken up by Mr. Vallandigham in an attack
upon the policy of the president, the House passed the
$250,000,000 loan bill by a vote of 150 to 5.[4] In the Senate
a few verbal amendments were made;[5] these were quickly
concurred in by the House,[6] and eight days after its introduction the bill was approved by the president.[7]

[1] The issue of $2,584,550 treasury notes under the act of June 22, 1860 (p. 12,
above), had reduced the balance of that loan remaining to be borrowed to $11,393,450.
Besides this there was the $10,000,000 loan authorized by the act of March 2, 1861.
—Senate Executive Document No. 2, p. 12, 37th Cong., 1st Sess.

[2] Ibid., p. 14.   [3] Ibid., pp. 65 ff. and 71 ff.

[4] Congressional Globe, 37th Cong., 1st Sess., p. 61.

[5] Ibid., pp. 109 and 127.   [6] Ibid., p. 147.

[7] 12 Statutes at Large, p. 259. Act of July 17, 1861.

So hurriedly, indeed, was the work done that a supplementary act had immediately to be passed.[1] Together, these two laws authorized the secretary to borrow $250,000,000,[2] for which he could issue in such proportions as he might deem advisable, (1) 7 per cent. twenty-year bonds at par; (2) 6 per cent. twenty-year bonds "at any rate not less than the equivalent of par for the bonds bearing 7 per centum interest;" (3) 7.3 per cent. three-year treasury notes, fundable in 6 per. cent. twenty-year bonds; or (4) treasury notes, either bearing interest at 3.65 per cent. and payable in one year, or bearing no interest and payable on demand. These demand notes were to be receivable for all public dues and of denominations as low as $5; but their issues were not to exceed $50,000,000. Finally, 6 per cent. treasury notes, "payable at any time not exceeding twelve months from date," might be issued to the amount of $20,000,000. To facilitate the negotiation of the loan, it was provided that any part, not above $100,000,000, might be borrowed abroad, and the principal and interest made payable in Europe; and that the secretary might "deposit any of the moneys obtained on any of the loans . . . . in such solvent specie-paying banks as he may select."

Legislative indorsement was also promptly given to Secretary Chase's suggestion of increased taxation. August 5 a revenue act was approved which (1) raised the tariff by

---

[1] *Ibid.*, p. 313. Act of August 5, 1861.

[2] The amount of securities, however, that might be issued under these acts was not definitely limited; for Sec. 1 of the act of August 5 provided that holders of the three-year 7.30 notes might exchange them for 6 per cent. twenty-year bonds. —12 *Statutes at Large*, p. 313. The total issues under the acts were as follows:

6 per cent. bonds - - - - - -	$189,321,350
Demand treasury notes, no interest -	60,030,000
7.30 treasury notes - - - - -	139,999,750
	$389,351,100

R. A. BAYLEY, *National Loans of the United States*, p. 78. Of the 6 per cent. bonds only $50,000,000 was sold for money; the remainder, $139,321,350, was issued in exchange for 7.30 notes.—*Ibid.*, p. 153.

imposing duties on tea, coffee, sugar, and molasses —
important revenue articles admitted free or at low rates by
the Morrill act;[1] (2) apportioned between the states a direct
tax of $20,000,000, of which, however, there was small
hope of collecting the quotas of the disloyal states, amounting to $5,000,000; (3) levied a tax of 3 per cent. upon the
excess of incomes above $800.[2] While certain features of
this scheme of taxation encountered opposition, members of
Congress evinced a striking readiness to waive objections and
vote for any bill that the administration and the leaders of
the houses held to be a "war necessity." [3]

The striking feature of the plan of finance thus recommended at the commencement of the war by the secretary
of the treasury, and adopted by Congress, was the reliance
upon borrowing to meet all the extraordinary military and
naval expenditures. The taxes imposed were expected to
yield revenue sufficient only to defray the ordinary expenses
of government, to pay interest on the public debt, and to
provide a small sinking fund. Nothing shows more forcibly
the inadequacy of this policy than the quickness with which
the necessity for increased taxation made itself apparent.
The heavy expenses of the months following the adjournment of the extra session begot a general conviction that a
firmer foundation for the financial operations of the government was indispensable. When Congress reassembled in
December it was met by a strong popular demand for a vigorous tax policy. "The country presents," said the Boston
Advertiser, "the spectacle of a people praying to be taxed." [4]
An examination of the newspapers of the time shows how

---

[1] *Cf.* "Comparative Rates of Duty, 1842-61," *Hunt's Merchants' Magazine*,
Vol. XLV, pp. 506, 507.

[2] 12 *Statutes at Large*, p. 292.

[3] As examples of this disposition see the remarks of Senators McDougall, of
California, and Wilkinson, of Minnesota.— *Congressional Globe*, 37th Cong., 1st Sess.,
p. 399.

[4] February 4, 1862.

literally this was true.[1] Urged forward by public opinion, the same Congress that had in August deemed $80,000,000 a sufficient revenue to raise by taxation, resolved in January with but six dissenting votes in both branches, to levy taxes that would " secure an annual revenue of not less than $150,-000,000." [2] Mr. Chase, also, took a firmer stand, advocating in his report of December, 1861, an increase of the customs duties on tea, coffee, and sugar, and direct taxation aggregating $50,000,000.[3] With increasing experience his appreciation of the " great importance" of raising the " largest possible amount " of revenue by taxation became keener. " It is hardly too much," he declared to Congress in 1863, " perhaps hardly enough, to say that every dollar raised [by taxation] for extraordinary expenditures or reduction of debt is worth two in the increased value of national securities." [4] In the same report he explained his failure to recommend heavy taxation to the extra session of Congress in July, 1861, by pleading the impossibility of foreseeing at that time the magnitude and length of the war.[5]

IV.   THE $150,000,000 BANK LOAN

While these bills were pending in Congress and before the resources provided by them could be availed of, it was necessary to provide funds for the immediate wants of the

---

[1] Cf. New York Times, June 20 and July 23, 1861, and ·January 13, 1862; New York Herald, December 31, 1861, and January 7, 8, and 9, 1862; New York Tribune, June 26, 1861, and February 3, 1862; New York Commercial Advertiser, January 3, 11, and February 26, 1862; Springfield (Mass.) Republican, January 7, 15, and 21, 1862; Boston Daily Advertiser, January 11, 13, and 24, 1862; Boston Journal, January 8, 1862; Boston Post, January 28, 1862; Philadelphia Press, January 18 and February 5, 1862; National Intelligencer (Washington), January 11, 1862.   Cf. the letters urging heavy taxation received by the Ways and Means Committee, SPAULDING, op. cit., pp. 23, 24; Speech, ROSCOE CONKLING, Congressional Globe, 37th Cong., 2d Sess., p. 633; " Memorial of the New York Chamber of Commerce," Senate Miscellaneous Document No. 95, 37th Cong., 2d Sess., and EDWARD EVERETT in Atlantic Monthly, March, 1862, Vol. IX, pp. 393-7.

[2] Congressional Globe, 37th Cong., 2d Sess., pp. 344, 349, 376.

[3] Report of the Secretary of the Treasury, December, 1861, pp. 13 and 15.

[4] Ibid., 1863, p. 12.   [5] Ibid., p. 10.   Cf. chap. ii, p. 72, below.

treasury. Mr. Chase accomplished this by issuing "for
payment to public creditors or for advances of cash," $14,-
000,000 in two-year 6 per cent. treasury notes, and $13,-
000,000 in 6 per cent. notes running but 60 days.[1]

This, however, was but a temporary makeshift and the
more serious task remained of providing for the regular and
continuous expenses of the war. For this purpose the
secretary at once set about negotiating a large loan under
the ample powers conferred upon him by the extra session
of Congress. Borrowing abroad was out of the question;
for European capitalists were unwilling to lend.[2] Reliance
upon a popular loan seemed hazardous, not only because of
the ill success of recent ventures, but also because the
market for bonds was stocked with the securities of several
states which were negotiating war loans.[3] Circumstances
seemed, then, to indicate the banks as the most available
source from which to obtain means.

Fortunately the course of events had been such as to
render the banks, at least in the northern Atlantic states,
unusually strong. In the previous November the sudden
panic following Mr. Lincoln's election had caused the banks
to curtail discounts. A severe pressure for money followed
and a suspension of specie payments was averted in New
York only by the combination of bank reserves and the

[1] *Report of the Secretary of the Treasury*, December, 1861, p. 8. These issues were
made in accordance with the acts of June 22, 1860 (12 *Statutes at Large*, p. 79), and
March 2, 1861 (*ibid.*, p. 178).

[2] "It is utterly out of the question, in our judgment," said the London *Economist*
of August 24, 1861, "that the Americans can obtain, either at home or in Europe, anything like the extravagant sums they are asking for. Europe won't lend them;
America cannot."—*Economist*, 1861, pp. 927, 928. *Cf.* BLAINE, *Twenty Years of Congress*, Vol. I, pp. 409, 410.

[3] New York and Pennsylvania had authorized loans of $3,000,000 each; Connecti-
cut, New Jersey, Indiana and Ohio loans of $2,000,000; Massachusetts, Maine, Illinois,
and New York city had each offered loans of $1,000,000, Iowa of $800,000, Michigan of
$500,000, and Rhode Island of $100,000.—*Bankers' Magazine* (New York), Vol. XVI,
"Notes on the Money Market," and APPLETON'S *American Annual Cyclopædia* for
1861, pp. 297, 307, 308.

issue of clearing-house certificates.[1] But most of the paper held by the banks was good; liquidation proceeded favorably and the threatened danger passed. The acute pressure was followed by general stagnation. In the unsettled state of the country there was a general disposition to avoid new undertakings and to keep old ones on a most conservative basis. The result was that the banks could make no new loans.[2]

During the winter difficulty was experienced in making collections in the southern states. In the spring many firms resorted to intentional failures to rid themselves of northern obligations,[3] and in May a law was enacted directing that such debts should be paid, not to the creditors, but into the Confederate treasury.[4] The cessation of remittances from the South caused in May and June a series of failures affecting especially large jobbing houses.[5] But, owing to the very conservative nature of the business that had been done in the preceding half year, the crash did not become

[1] *Bankers' Magazine* (New York), Vol. XV, p. 500; *Hunt's Merchants' Magazine*, Vol. XLIV, pp. 75–92, 196, and 327; SUMNER, *History of American Currency*, New York, 1875, p. 189; DUNBAR, *Chapters on the Theory and History of Banking*, New York, 1891, pp. 68–73. The Boston banks rejected the use of clearing-house certificates, but allowed 50 per cent. of balances at the clearing house to be paid in a bank's own notes.—DUNBAR, *op. cit.*, p. 79; *cf.* "Report of the Massachusetts Bank Commissioners," *Executive Document No. 25*, pp. 48–50, 37th Cong., 3d Sess.

[2] "Inactivity, or increasing stagnation," wrote Mr. James Gallatin to Chase in March, "is the characteristic of our business affairs."—*Two Letters to the Honorable S. P. Chase* (New York, 1861), p. 5; *cf. Hunt's Merchants' Magazine*, Vol. XLIV, pp. 787 ff.

[3] *Hunt's Merchants' Magazine*, Vol. XLVI, p. 316; *American Annual Cyclopædia*, 1861, p. 313.

[4] See text of the act in *American Annual Cyclopædia*, 1861, p. 310; J. C. SCHWAB, *The Confederate States of America* (New York, 1901), p. 113.

[5] *Hunt's Merchants' Magazine*, Vol. XLV, p. 105. The indebtedness of the South to the North was estimated on the basis of R. G. Dun & Company's annual circular for 1861 at $300,000,000.—*Ibid.*, Vol. XLVI, p. 317. The losses of northern creditors were usually reckoned at $200,000,000. *Cf.* "Report of the Massachusetts Bank Commissioners," October, 1861; *Executive Document No. 25*, p. 50, 37th Cong., 3d Sess.; New York *Tribune*, September 18, 1861; President's Message, December 3, 1861, in *A. Lincoln, Complete Works*, ed. NICOLAY AND HAY, Vol. II, p. 99. Schwab considers this estimate exaggerated, *op. cit.*, p. 111.

general.   It had the effect, however, of making the times
yet more dull; the transactions of the New York clearing
house declined from $129,000,000 in the second week of
March, to $80,000,000 in the corresponding week of August.[1]
The banks were not seriously weakened by the failures,[2] but
found it still more difficult to lend their capital.   From
December, 1860, to August, 1861, bank loans in New York
diminished $23,000,000; in Boston the fall from January
to July was $2,000,000 and in Philadelphia $3,000,000.[3]

This decrease of loans was accompanied by a slight
decline in circulation, a more decided increase in deposits,
and a marked gain in the amount of specie held.   Small
imports — due partly to the Morrill tariff, but chiefly to the
depression of trade — and heavy exports of grain — the
result of good crops at home and poor crops abroad —
combined to turn the balance of payment toward the United
States.[4]   During the spring and summer months sterling
exchange sold from two to three points below par in New
York.[5]   Not only was the usual drain of specie to Europe
stopped, but the current was kept flowing in this direction,
so that, though the receipts from California declined and
considerable amounts were sent into the interior, specie accumulated in the vaults of the New York banks to an unprece-

[1] See table of clearings in *H. R. Executive Document No. 25*, p. 107, 37th Cong.,
3d Sess.

[2] The Massachusetts commissioners stated in October that the losses of the
Boston banks by the repudiation of southern debts would not exceed in amount the
undivided profits on hand.—*Executive Document No. 25*, p. 50, 37th Cong., 3d Sess.

[3] See table, p. 30, below.

[4] So large was the exportation of breadstuffs during the summer and autumn of
1861 that it more than offset the effect of the blockade in decreasing shipments of
cotton.   The movement is somewhat concealed by the usual statements of commerce
by years ending June 30; but appears clearly in the official table of imports and
exports of merchandise at the port of New York by months.   From January to April
imports exceeded exports, but from May to December there was an excess of exports,
amounting to five million dollars in June, two in July, two in August, four in
September, five in October, six in November, and six in December.— See tables in
Hunt's Merchants' Magazine, Vol. XLVI, pp. 277-81.

[5] *Bankers' Magazine* (New York), Vol. XVI, p. 736.

dented degree.   August 17 the ratio of the specie held by the associated banks of New York to their deposits and circulation was 50 per cent.; for Boston it was 27, and for Philadelphia 39 per cent.[1]   Thus the banks were unusually strong; but they were making little profit because the stagnation of trade gave them few opportunities of lending to business men.

Consequently, when Mr. Chase appealed to them to assist the government, the banks were both able and willing to render efficient aid.   A conference of representatives of the New York, Boston, and Philadelphia banks,[2] held August 10–17 in New York, at the secretary's invitation, drew up in consultation with him a "plan for assisting the United States government."[3]   Fifty million dollars was to be advanced to the treasury by the associated banks of the three cities.   In return they were to receive at par a like amount of treasury notes running three years and bearing interest at 7.30 per cent.   Further, the banks were given the option of taking a second $50,000,000 of the notes on the same terms October 15, and a third $50,000,000 December 15.[4]   Mr. Chase considered the plan highly advantageous to the government.   In the face of war he was borrowing money at "a rate of interest only 1.3 per cent. higher than the ordinary rate of 6 per cent."   Besides he received $50,000,000 immediately to meet the pressing

[1] See table, p. 30, below.

[2] "It was greatly desired," said one of the most prominent of the New York bankers, "to include also the banks of the West, but it was found impracticable to secure the co-operation of the state banks of Ohio and Indiana; and the state banks of Missouri, the only other organization under a compacted system, were surrounded by combatants."—Letter of George S. Coe to E. G. Spaulding, October 8, 1875, Spaulding, *op. cit.*, Appendix, p. 90.

[3] *Report of the Secretary of the Treasury*, December, 1861, pp. 8, 9.   A detailed account of the conference is given by A. S. Bolles in *Lippincott's Monthly Magazine*, Vol. XXXVIII, pp. 200–206; reprinted in *Bankers' Magazine*, Vol. XLI, pp. 363–7.

[4] For text of this agreement see *Bankers' Magazine* (New York), Vol. XVI, pp. 162, 163.

demands upon the treasury.[1]   To the banks the plan offered profitable employment for their idle capital.[2]

The banks which thus undertook to lend the government $150,000,000 in four months' time had an aggregate capital of but $120,000,000.   Although unusually strong in specie at the time the agreement was made, their combined coin reserves amounted only to $63,200,000.[3]   This sum would hardly more than pay the first instalment of the loan.   To prevent its being exhausted at the very beginning, it was necessary that the banks should be able to replace very rapidly the specie which they paid to the government. They counted on doing this in two ways: First, they would sell the securities received from the goverment to the public for cash.   It was part of the agreement that the treasury should help in this by opening public subscriptions to the loan in all parts of the country.   Second, the specie given to the government would be speedily paid out again in disbursements for the immense purchases of war supplies.   The coin would thus be restored to the channels of trade, and naturally flow again into the banks.

If the banks could collect specie in these two ways as rapidly as they paid it out to the government, they could continue to supply the treasury with funds indefinitely.   But the moment even a brief delay occurred in the return of specie to the banks trouble would come.   The reserves would be depleted by the drafts of the treasury, and suspension would be inevitable.   Such a delay would happen if anything occurred to make the public slow in buying the

[1] Chase's letter to Trowbridge, WARDEN, op. cit., pp. 386-8.

[2] At first the banks decided to divide the $50,000,000 among themselves in proportion to their respective capitals.   This would have given the fifty-four New York banks $29,500,000, the forty-six Boston banks $15,500,000, and the nineteen Philadelphia banks $5,000,000.   But the Boston banks finally decided that they could not take more than $10,000,000; so that the New York institutions had to make up their subscriptions to $35,000,000.—Hunt's Merchants' Magazine, Vol. XLV, p. 331.

[3] See table, p. 30, below.

7.30 treasury notes from the banks, or to interrupt the government's payments of specie out of the subtreasury, or to prevent men from depositing again in the banks the coin received from the government.   The situation, both of the banks and of the treasury, was thus very precarious.   The plan might work well in fair weather, but in the first storm it was likely to collapse.   Mr. Chase, however, seems to have been unconscious that danger lurked in the scheme.

At the very outset the banks encountered an unforeseen obstacle.   The independent subtreasury system required all dues to the United States to be paid into the treasury in coin.[1]   This would compel the banks to send the specie lent the government to the subtreasuries, there to lie in the vaults until paid out in disbursements to public creditors. But provision had been made by Congress with the special intent of removing this difficulty.[2]   The law of August 5 had relaxed the rigor of the subtreasury system so far as to permit the secretary "to deposit any of the moneys obtained on any of the loans . . . . in such solvent, specie-paying banks as he may select," and allowed " moneys so deposited " to "be withdrawn from such deposit for deposit with the regular authorized depositaries, or for the payment of public dues."[3]   Under this law the banks expected that the loan to the government would be managed in the same manner as a loan to a private person; they would credit the United States with a deposit of $50,000,000 upon their books, against which the secretary of the treasury could draw as he had occasion.   But Mr. Chase's instinctive distrust of bank issues permitted no modification of the subtreasury system.

---

[1] Acts of July 4, 1840, secs. 19 and 20, 5 *Statutes at Large*, p. 385; and of August 6, 1846, secs. 18, 19 and 20, 9 *Statutes at Large*, p. 59.

[2] See the letter of Mr. E. G. Spaulding, who drafted the section in question, *op. cit.*, Appendix, p. 51; and remarks of W. P. Fessenden, chairman of the senate finance committee, *Congressional Globe*, 37th Cong., 1st Sess., p. 396.

[3] Sec. 6, 12 *Statutes at Large*, p. 313.

He declined to make payments in bank checks on the ground that, though the eastern institutions were ready to pay such checks in coin, their western correspondents on whom they might draw would possibly ask creditors of the government to accept bank notes in satisfaction. He therefore insisted that the loan be paid in specie into the vaults of the sub-treasury. Much against their will, the banks complied.[1]

Nor was this the only point in which the banks found the policy of the treasury an obstacle to the success of the loans. Beside borrowing from the banks to secure funds, Mr. Chase took advantage of his discretionary power to issue non-interest-bearing treasury notes.[2] Though payable on demand in gold at the subtreasuries, and receivable for taxes and customs dues, these notes were accepted with reluctance. To facilitate their circulation, the secretary and other treasury officials signed a paper agreeing to take them in payment of their salaries, and General Scott issued a circular setting forth the superior convenience of paper money to soldiers desiring to send home a portion of their pay.[3] But the banks feared the government paper money would drive their own issues from circulation, and declined to receive the demand notes except on "special deposit." Should they receive the notes as current funds, bankers said, they would

[1] Secretary Chase's reasons for refusing to draw directly on the banks are given in a letter to Mr. Trowbridge,(WARDEN, *Life of Chase*, p. 387). The side of the banks is represented in G. S. Coe's letter to Spaulding (*History of the Legal Tender Paper Money*, 2d ed., Appendix, pp. 91, 92); J. E. Williams's letter to Chase of October 4, 1861 (*ibid.*, pp. 97–9), and his *War Loans of the Associated Banks to the Government in 1861*, (New York, 1876); JAMES GALLATIN, *The National Finances, Currency, Banking, etc.* (New York, 1864). Most writers have concurred in the opinion that Mr. Chase's refusal was an error. *Cf. Our National Finances, What Shall be Done?* [anon.] (Boston, 1862); SPAULDING, *op. cit.*, Introduction to 2d ed., pp. 1–4, and Appendix, pp. 51–3; F. A. CONKLING, *ibid.*, Appendix, p. 85; J. S. GIBBONS, *The Public Debt of the United States* (New York, 1867), pp. 135, 136; H. V. POOR, *Money and its Laws*, 2d ed. (New York, 1877), pp. 562–4; HORACE WHITE, *Money and Banking* (Boston, 1896), pp. 150–52.

[2] Acts of July 17, 1861, sec. 1, 12 *Statutes at Large*, p. 259, and of August 5, 1861, sec. 5 (*ibid.*, p. 313).

[3] Text in *American Annual Cyclopædia*, 1861, p. 299.

be under obligation to redeem them in coin on demand, and this would increase the burden which their reserves had to carry, and so endanger the maintenance of specie payments. Furthermore, the existence of a large amount of obligations, which the treasury might be called upon to redeem in coin at any moment of panic, was a standing menace to the solvency of the government, and in so far injured its credit, and made more difficult the rapid sale of the securities held by the banks to the public, on which the success of the loans depended. But it was in vain that the banks appealed to Mr. Chase to cease his issues. He replied: " If you can lend me all the coin required, or show me where I can borrow it elsewhere at fair rates, I will withdraw every note already issued, and pledge myself never to issue another; but if you cannot, you must let me stick to United States notes." [1] Unable to induce the secretary to alter this resolution, the banks again reluctantly yielded.[2]

But though the position of the banks was weakened by Mr. Chase's refusal to allow the proceeds of the loan to remain on deposit until paid out to the creditors of the government, and by his issue of paper money, all went well for a time. Mr. Chase appointed agents in over two hundred

---

[1] Letter to Trowbridge, WARDEN, *op. cit.*, p. 388.

[2] The banks were the more annoyed at Mr. Chase's refusal to make payments in checks drawn upon them and at his issue of treasury notes, because when the arrangement regarding the loan was made they had understood him to agree to conform his action in these respects to their wishes. See J. E. Williams's letter of October 4, 1861, to Chase and George S. Coe's letter of October 8, 1865, to Spaulding in SPAULDING, *op. cit.*, Appendix, pp. 97-9 and 92 respectively. Mr. Chase, however, said in his report of December, 1861, that " it was . . . . understood that the secretary of the treasury should issue a limited amount of United States notes, payable on demand" (p. 9).

On the inconvenience caused the banks by the issue of the demand notes, see "Objections to Government Demand Notes, by a New York Bank Officer," *Bankers' Magazine* (New York), Vol. XVI, pp. 353-7; GEORGE MARSLAND, "The Banks and the Greenbacks," *Bankers' Magazine* (New York), Vol. XXXI, pp. 173-81; BOLLES, *Financial History of the United States*, 1861-85, pp. 34 and 37; H. V. POOR, *Money and its Laws*, 2d ed. (New York, 1877), pp. 564 ff.; J. K. UPTON, *Money in Politics*, 2d ed. (Boston, 1895), pp. 72 ff.; R. M. BRECKENRIDGE, "The Demand Notes of 1861," in *Sound Currency*, (New York, October, 1898), Vol. V, pp. 336, 337.

towns to receive subscriptions for 7.30 treasury notes,[1] and
issued an urgent address, appealing to the people to assist in
making the "national loan" successful.[2] His efforts were
warmly seconded by the newspaper press, which explained
the advantages of the loan to investors, and represented subscription as an act of patriotism. On their side the New
York banks strengthened themselves by putting their coin
into a common fund, and reviving the organization entered
into to check the panic of the preceding November. The
"loan committee," then appointed under the chairmanship
of Moses Taylor, was entrusted with the superintendence of
the execution of the contract with the government. It was
part of the arrangement that the stock of specie should not
be allowed to fall below one-fourth of the net liabilities,
exclusive of circulation and the credit given the treasury. In
case any bank failed to maintain this proportion of reserve,
the loan committee was directed to charge interest on the
deficit, and to pay the interest received to the institutions
holding the highest percentage of specie.[3]

The associated banks agreed to divide the subscriptions
to the loan between themselves in proportion to their respective capitals. Each bank was to pay 10 per cent. of its subscription into the subtreasury at once, and to place the balance to the credit of the government upon its books.[4]
Against these credits Mr. Chase was to draw only as fast as

[1] See list in *Bankers' Magazine*, (New York), Vol. XVI, pp. 308-10. Aside from
treasury officials there were 148 agents.—*H. R. Executive Document No. 66*, p. 2,
38th Cong., 1st Sess.

[2] Text is to be found in *Bankers' Magazine*, Vol. XVI, pp. 290-2. The notes were
offered at par, and were to draw interest from August 19, but on taking the bonds
subscribers were required to pay interest from that date to day of subscription, so
that the interest received by the purchaser began with the date of his purchase.

[3] *Cf.* note 1, p. 32, below. The best authority for the banking operations is the
"Report of the New York Loan Committee," June 12, 1862, published in the *Bankers'
Magazine*, Vol. XVII, and in *H. R. Executive Document No. 25*, 37th Cong., 3d Sess.,
pp. 125-42.

[4] See text of agreement of banks with government, and proceedings of the meeting of bankers in reference to it.—*Bankers' Magazine*, Vol. XVI, pp. 161-70.

he needed funds for disbursement.   It was anticipated that his drafts would be about 10 per cent. of the loan a week.[1] Consequently, the effect of the transaction may be traced in the weekly bank returns of the three cities.   In New York the first instalment of the loan, $3,500,000, was paid into the subtreasury August 19, 1861.[2]   Comparing the reports of August 17 and August 24, one finds a decrease of $2,600,-000 in the specie holdings of the banks, and a like increase in the coin held by the subtreasury.[3]   At the same time the balance of the government loan was added to the line of discounts, increasing the loans reported by $29,000,000. Finally, the sum placed upon the books of the banks to the credit of the government to be drawn against produced a nominal increase of $26,500,000 in the deposits.[4]   Similar changes are seen on comparing the situation of the Boston and Philadelphia banks on August 17 and 31.   In Boston payments to the subtreasury diminished reserves less than $300,000, while discounts and deposits were increased $3,600,000 and $4,200,000, respectively, in consequence of the government loans.   The Philadelphia banks lost $600,-000 in specie during the two weeks, and increased their discounts $4,600,000 and their deposits $3,700,000.

But the situation immediately began to change.   The banks paid over the loan in instalments of about $5,000,000 at intervals of six days.[5]   Each payment thus made into the subtreasuries decreased the sum credited to the government as a deposit.   Loans also declined, for as fast as the 7.30

[1] *American Annual Cyclopœdia*, 1861, p. 64.   *Cf.* Chase's letter of October 2, 1861, to Larz Anderson, in SCHUCKERS, *Life of Chase*, pp. 430, 431.

[2] "Report of the New York Loan Committee," *Bankers' Magazine*, Vol. XVII, p. 139.

[3] For this and the similar subsequent comparisons see the table showing the condition of the banks of New York, Boston, and Philadelphia, p. 30, and the accompanying chart.

[4] *Cf.* "Report of the Bank Commissioners of Massachusetts, October, 1861," *H R. Executive Document No. 25*, p. 56, 37th Cong., 3d Sess.

[5] Letter of G. S. Coe, in SPAULDING, *op. cit.*, Appendix, p. 92.

TABLE I

CONDITION OF THE BANKS PARTICIPATING IN THE $150,000,000 LOAN OF 1861

Compiled from tables in *Ex. Doc.*, No. 25, p. 107, 37th Cong., 3d Sess.; Appleton's *American Annual Cyclopædia*, 1861, pp. 64, 65; *Hunt's Merchants' Magazine*, Vol. XLVI, p. 393.   00,000 omitted

	New York Banks						Boston Banks				Philadelphia Banks			
	Loans	Specie	Circulation	Deposits	W'kly cl'r'ngs	Specie in subt'ry	Loans	Specie	Circulation	Deposits	Loans	Specie	Circulation	Deposits
January 5, 1861	$129.6	$24.8	$8.7	$86.5	$96.0	$3.6	$62.0	$4.2	$7.0	$18.7	$26.9	$4.0	$2.7	$15.3
February 2	121.9	31.1	8.1	87.9	122.1	4.3	63.3	4.6	6.2	18.2	25.8	4.6	2.8	15.3
March 2	121.9	34.5	8.3	89.6	126.7	9.2	62.7	4.8	6.4	18.0	25.1	5.0	2.8	14.9
April 6	122.1	41.7	8.9	94.0	123.3	8.5	62.9	5.8	7.0	19.9	25.4	6.5	3.1	16.0
May 4	124.6	38.1	9.3	95.0	106.4	9.8	61.9	5.8	6.9	18.8	25.4	5.9	2.7	15.7
June 1	118.3	37.5	8.7	90.2	88.8	11.5	60.2	6.5	6.9	18.5	24.1	5.7	2.3	15.3
July 6	112.1	45.6	8.9	90.6	88.3	4.6	60.3	6.1	6.4	18.5	24.2	7.0	2.2	15.9
August 3	111.7	46.2	8.6	92.2	81.4	6.7	61.1	6.2	6.4	18.1	24.2	6.7	2.1	15.9
August 10	110.0	48.6	8.7	92.0	80.4	5.6	60.8	6.4	6.5	18.0	24.1	6.8	2.1	15.6
August 17	108.7	49.7	8.5	92.0	80.2	4.4	61.8	6.7	6.2	18.2	24.1	6.8	2.1	15.3
August 24	137.7	47.1	8.8	118.5	82.9	7.0	64.5	6.4	6.2	19.5	27.5	6.5	2.0	18.2
August 31	141.1	45.1	8.9	120.4	83.4	8.9	64.3	7.1	6.5	22.4	28.6	6.2	2.1	19.0
September 7	139.2	41.9	8.9	114.1	89.1	13.1	62.3	6.7	6.4	22.2	28.3	5.0	2.1	18.3
September 14	136.6	37.5	8.8	106.8	95.6	14.3	No data				27.9	4.7	2.2	17.0
September 21	130.2	33.8	8.7	99.3	97.1	14.5	63.7	5.7	6.3	20.0	27.5	5.2	2.2	16.5
September 28	126.1	38.1	8.6	96.6	85.7	13.1	63.7	6.4	6.7	23.2	26.7	5.4	2.2	16.3
October 5	149.3	39.8	8.9	121.4	110.7	10.1	65.6	7.2	6.7	25.5	30.5	5.9	2.2	20.3
October 12	156.3	41.1	8.7	129.2	114.0	10.8	65.1	7.0	6.6	25.5	30.3	5.4	2.3	20.9
October 19	151.8	42.3	8.6	126.4	112.8	9.5	64.4	7.2	6.3	25.1	29.7	6.5	2.2	21.1
October 26	147.3	42.3	8.4	121.7	111.2	7.3	67.5	7.0	6.2	24.8	28.8	6.5	2.3	20.3
November 2	144.0	41.3	8.6	117.9	113.8	9.1	63.3	7.3	6.6	24.4	28.4	6.9	2.3	20.4
November 9	140.6	41.2	8.9	116.7	116.7	7.8	65.2	7.5	6.4	25.3	27.9	6.9	2.2	20.0
November 16	137.3	41.5	8.8	113.4	117.5	7.4	66.3	7.6	6.1	26.7	27.6	7.1	2.2	19.6
November 23	158.5	41.6	8.6	111.2	121.6	7.9	66.3	7.7	6.0	27.9	29.5	7.4	2.2	22.3
November 30	162.8	41.5	8.5	133.4	104.7	7.0	66.9	7.7	6.3	27.8	30.0	7.3	2.2	23.0
December 7	159.8	42.3	8.8	133.6	120.0	6.7	66.2	8.5	6.3	27.8	31.3	7.3	2.2	23.0
December 14	157.6	39.4	8.8	129.4	114.7	7.8	66.0	9.7	6.1	28.1	31.2	7.4	2.2	22.9
December 21	155.8	36.8	8.6	124.9	125.3	2.8	65.6	10.1	6.1	27.6	31.0	6.2	2.1	22.7
December 28	154.8	29.4	8.4	116.5	91.1	4.0	65.6	9.0	6.5	27.1	30.9	5.5	2.0	21.0
January 4, 1862	154.4	24.0	8.6	111.8	100.6	.....	65.6	8.9	6.6	25.6	31.0	5.7	2.1	21.4
January 11	152.1	25.4	8.1	113.9	105.6	.....	64.4	8.6	6.5	25.4	31.1	5.7	2.1	21.3
January 18	149.1	25.1	7.4	113.3	107.7	.....	63.0	8.6	6.3	24.0	30.6	5.7	2.1	20.7
January 25	145.8	26.7	6.8	110.9	100.0	.....					30.4	5.8	2.1	20.1

CHART I

GRAPHIC ILLUSTRATION OF THE EFFECT UPON THE NEW YORK BANKS OF THE $150,000,000 LOAN

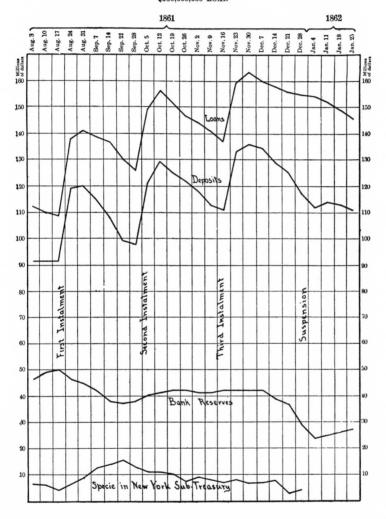

notes were sold to the public through the treasury agencies the proceeds were remitted to the banks and deducted by them from the loan to the government. From August 31 to September 28 the decline of bank loans was $15,000,000 in New York, $2,000,000 in Boston, and $2,000,000 in Philadelphia. The corresponding decline in deposits amounted to $23,800,000, $2,400,000, and $2,700,000 respectively.

The point of crucial importance for the success of the bank loan, however, was the change in the stocks of specie held. The payments into the subtreasuries drained the bank reserves of about $5,000,000 a week. This loss was offset in part by the re-deposit in the banks of money paid out by the government to army contractors and other creditors, and in part by sums received from the treasury on account of sales of 7.30 notes to the public through the subscription agencies—though it was not until September 3 that the banks received any reimbursement from this latter source.[1] For the first five weeks the withdrawal of specie from the banks so far exceeded receipts as to cause a rapid reduction of reserves. From August 17 to September 21 the New York banks lost $13,000,000 of specie. Whither the money had gone is shown by the contemporaneous gain of $11,000,000 in the coin held by the New York subtreasury. During the same time the Philadelphia banks lost $2,000,000, or over 30 per cent. of their specie. In Boston the reserves increased slightly for the first three weeks and the subsequent loss was less serious than in the other cities, a trifle less than 20 per cent. In New York the loan committee found that the loss of coin reduced the reserves of some of the associated banks below the stipulated proportion of 25 per cent. to net deposits, making necessary a

[1] "Report of the New York Loan Committee," *H. R. Executive Document No. 25*, 37th Cong., 3d Sess., p. 128.

reapportionment of the specie for the first time on September 2.[1]

After September 21, however, the tide turned. " The disbursements of the government for the war were so rapid," said Mr. Coe, a New York bank president, "and the consequent internal trade movement was so intense, that the coin paid out upon each instalment of the loan came back to the banks through the community in about one week."[2] Such fresh deposits, together with the reimbursements received through the treasurer from the public subscriptions to the loan, came to exceed the payments of specie into the subtreasury, and the reserves consequently rose again. By the middle of October the New York banks held $5,500,000 more specie than on September 21. Meanwhile government disburdsements had reduced the specie holdings of the subtreasury by $6,000,000. In about the same period the reserves of Boston banks gained $1,500,000 and those of the Philadelphia banks $1,700,000.

Encouraged by the gain in specie, the banks agreed to take a second $50,000,000 of the 7.30 three-year treasury notes October 1, fifteen days earlier than the time agreed upon in August, although they had not yet completed their

[1] The apportionment was at first managed by charging interest upon the deficiency of reserve; but on September 21 this account was closed, and "thereafter the specie apportionment was made by requiring the banks to exchange loan certificates for specie whenever their specie was less than 25 per cent. of their net deposits, exclusive of the amount to the credit of the government." From September 21 to December 30 a daily apportionment of specie was made in this fashion. The committee issued loan certificates drawing 7 per cent. interest to banks whose reserves had fallen below the limit, for 90 per cent. of the amount of 7.30 notes, or assistant treasurer's receipts for payments on the loan, deposited with them. An issue of $10,000,000 of such certificates had been authorized by the banks April 24, 1861. This was increased to $15,000,000 December 18, to $20,000,000 December 28, and to $25,000,000 January 20, 1862. The total issues were $22,585,000, and the largest amount outstanding was $21,960,000 from February 3 to February 7, 1862. The interest amounted to $396,436.32. Certificates were issued to thirty-nine of the fifty associated banks, thirty-one of which paid more interest than they received. All the certificates were redeemed by April 28, 1862.—*Ibid.*, pp. 126-33.

[2] Letter of October 8, 1875, in SPAULDING, *op. cit.*, Appendix, p. 93.

payments upon the first loan.[1]   There was but one ominous
sign—the popular subscription under the management of
the treasury department had not been an unqualified success.
In the hope of stimulating the lagging subscriptions, the
Boston banks had issued a card September 11, saying:

The banks are meeting their engagements and furnishing the
$50,000,000 with no practical inconvenience to themselves or the
mercantile community; and if no more money was required no
difficulty would be experienced. . . . . *But who is to furnish the
next $50,000,000?* Are the banks expected to do so? If they are,
the men of means, large and small, must take and pay for the first
$50,000,000 during the present month or early in October—other-
wise it cannot be accomplished.[2]

But, despite such appeals and the efforts of the secretary and the press, subscriptions became so slow, after about
$45,000,000 of the first loan had been sold to the public,
that the treasury agencies were closed and the banks undertook to dispose of the second $50,000,000 themselves without
the aid of the government.[3]

Changes in the accounts of the banks, similar to those
resulting from the first loan, followed the taking of the second.   On comparing the reports for September 28 and October 12, one sees an increase of loans amounting to $30,000,-
000 in New York, $3,300,000 in Boston, and $3,600,000 in
Philadelphia.   At the same time, the credit given the government upon the books of the banks created a corresponding
increase of deposits amounting to $32,600,000, $5,500,-

---

[1] *Cf. Bankers' Magazine* (New York), Vol. XVI, p. 397, and "Report of the New
York Loan Committee," *ibid.*, Vol. XVII, p. 140.

[2] *Bankers' Magazine* (New York), Vol. XVI, pp. 366, 367.

[3] Chase's letter to Trowbridge, WARDEN, *op. cit.*, p. 387. The banks continued,
however, to receive drafts from the treasury on account of the sales made to the
public by the treasury agencies on their account. The final cash reimbursement was
not received in New York until January 13, 1862.—*Executive Document No. 25*, p. 128,
37th Cong., 3d Sess. Of the $45,000,000 sold, $24,700,000 were disposed of by private
agents and the balance by department officials. It was by his success in obtaining
subscriptions for over $5,000,000 of 7.30s that Jay Cooke attracted Mr. Chase's atten-
tion.—See *H. R. Executive Document No. 66*, 38th Cong., 1st Sess.

000, and $4,600,000 respectively. But, instead of falling off as in August, the reserves of the banks increased, maintaining a high level throughout October, November, and the first half of December. Of course, as successive $5,000,-000 instalments were paid into the subtreasuries by the banks, their deposits declined again after October 12, as they had after August 31, and the loans were reduced by continued receipts from the proceeds of the popular subscription. By November 16 (the last report made before the taking of the third loan) the fall of deposits in New York was $18,000,000, and of loans $19,000,000. The corresponding figures for Philadelphia were $1,300,000 and $2,700,000; and for Boston (October 12 to November 9) $1,100,000 and $2,300,000.

All this time, while supplying the federal treasury with specie on so large a scale, the banks had also to furnish the usual accommodations to the mercantile community. But they were able to serve both the government and the public with comparative ease. For, as the Massachusetts bank commissioners reported in October, 1861, " the prostration of business robbed them of their usual customers, and the operations of the government, which have given rise to a new activity exerted in the public service, have caused the making of very little business paper, such as banks are in the habit of discounting. Public contractors are usually paid in cash at intervals shorter than the average length of bank accommodations, and they have little occasion to borrow money." [1]

The last instalment of the first $50,000,000 was paid into the subtreasuries by the banks October 24, and payment on the second loan was begun five days later. [2] The operation

[1] *Executive Document No. 25*, 37th Cong., 3d Sess., p. 56.

[2] " Report of the New York Loan Committee," *Bankers' Magazine* (New York), Vol. XVII, pp. 139, 140.

proceeded smoothly, the decline of the reserves being insignificant, and the banks determined to take a third $50,000,-000 of government securities November 16, a month before the date set in the agreement of August. But, because of the difficulty experienced in disposing of the three-year 7.30 treasury notes to the public, they declined to accept more of these securities, and received instead twenty-year 6 per cent. bonds at a rate equivalent to par for 7 per cent.,[1] in the expectation that such bonds could be sold at a profit in Europe.[2] At the same time, the banks were given the option of taking on January 1, 1862, a fourth loan of $50,000,000 upon the same terms as the first and second.[3] In pursuance of this arrangement, the government was given credit upon the books of the banks for $45,795,478.48—the proceeds of the $50,000,000 bonds at the given rate[4]—which increased once more the sum of loans and deposits.[5]

For several weeks after the third loan was taken everything went well. The banks continued to pay regular instalments on the second loan into the subtreasuries of New York, Boston, and Philadelphia, and did not make the first payment on the third until December 10.[6] Meanwhile the specie reserves increased slightly in each of the three cities, so that by December 7 New York banks held as much coin as at any time since August, and the Boston and Philadelphia

---

[1] This rate is 89.322463831—*Executive Document No. 25*, p. 129, 37th Cong., 3d Sess. This arrangement was made under authority of sec. 7 of the act of August 5, 1861, 12 *Statutes at Large*, p. 313.

[2] See the letter from a New York bank president published in the New York *Tribune*, December 25, 1861, p. 7.

[3] *Report of the Secretary of the Treasury*, December, 1861, p. 10.

[4] *Ibid., loc. cit. Cf. Executive Document No. 25*, p. 129, 37th Cong., 3d Sess.

[5] For New York the gain from November 16 to November 30 was $25,500,000 in loans and $25,100,000 in deposits. For Philadelphia the corresponding figures are $2,400,000 and $3,400,000. The Boston banks gained $3,600,000 in loans from the second to the fourth week in November and $3,500,000 in deposits.

[6] "Report of the New York Loan Committee," *Bankers' Magazine*, Vol. XVII, p. 140.

banks were actually stronger in specie than at the time when the first government loan was made.

About this time, however, two untoward events occurred. The first was the publication, December 10, of the annual report of the secretary of the treasury. In his report to the extra session of Congress in the preceding July, Mr. Chase had estimated that receipts from customs dues and sales of public land would yield during the current fiscal year (July 1, 1861, to June 30, 1862), a revenue of $60,-000,000, while the expenditures of the government would probably reach $318,519,582.[1] Enormous as this budget seemed, the succeeding months proved its inadequacy. The December report showed that the estimate of expenses should be increased $214,000,000, while the estimate of revenue from customs and land sales should be reduced $25,000,000.[2] But more than this, it had been generally felt that the plan of borrowing from banks could be only a temporary makeshift to serve until a permanent policy was matured. It was hoped that the report of December would present a definite plan of finance based upon adequate taxation. But Mr. Chase proposed taxes yielding only $50,000,000,[3] and put his main reliance upon a scheme for reorganizing the banks of the country in such a way as to compel them to buy a large amount of government bonds.[4] The disappointment caused by the report was keen.[5]

The second event was the Trent affair. November 8, 1861, Captain Wilkes, of the American warship San Jacinto, removed two commissioners of the Confederate States—

---

[1] *Senate Executive Document No. 2*, pp. 5 and 8, 37th Cong., 1st Sess.

[2] *Report of the Secretary of the Treasury*, December, 1861, pp. 11, 12.

[3] *Ibid.*, p. 15.

[4] *Ibid.*, pp. 17–20.

[5] *Cf.* "Federal Finances Examined" (anon.) *Hunt's Merchants' Magazine*, Vol. XLVII, December, 1862, p. 507; *Appleton's Annual Cyclopœdia*, 1861, p. 66; BLAINE, *Twenty Years of Congress*, (Norwich, Conn., 1884), Vol. I, p. 407.

Messrs. Mason and Slidell—by force from the British steamer Trent, plying between Havana and Southampton. In the United States lively satisfaction was felt in this capture, and Wilkes was dined by clubs and thanked by Congress. But when the news reached England, November 27, there was great indignation over what was felt to be a wanton insult to the British flag; and the government dispatched a queen's messenger to Washington to demand the surrender of the prisoners and an apology. If this demand were not complied with in seven days the English ambassador was instructed "to repair immediately to London." This was a plain threat of war. Intelligence of the action taken by the English cabinet was received in New York on December 16. As the report had gone out that the Confederates would not be released it seemed highly probable that the federal government would be involved in a second war.[1]

The receipt of the news on the 16th caused a panic in the New York markets. On the stock exchange government securities fell 2–2½ per cent. Shares of all kinds participated in the decline,[2] and sterling exchange rose two points.[3] Wall street was filled with rumors of an agreement among the banks to suspend specie payments, and men with balances in banks began to turn them into special deposits.[4] Next day a meeting of the associated banks was called to consider the situation. A motion was made to suspend specie payments at once, but the proposal failed of adoption. Instead, in the hope of quelling the panic, the banks unanimously adopted a series of vigorous resolutions, declaring that there was "nothing in the position of the loans to the government to

[1] *Cf.* J. F. RHODES, *History of the United States*, Vol. III (New York, 1895), pp. 520–43.

[2] *Bankers' Magazine* (New York), Vol. XVI, pp. 558 and 491; and stock quotations, *ibid.*, p. 559.

[3] *Ibid.*, Vol. XVI, p. 736.

[4] *Ibid.*, Vol. XVI, pp. 491 and 558.

cause uneasiness," and that they saw "no reason, justification, or necessity for a suspension of specie payments." [1]

But these resolutions availed little. While the banks continued to pay specie into the subtreasury at the usual rate, the money paid out by the goverment to contractors and others, owing to the alarmed state of the public mind and the fear of a suspension, did not flow back as before into their reserves.[2] This cut off the chief source from which the reserves had been recruited. Meanwhile the banks of Boston and the West began to draw heavily upon their balances in New York, so that the deposits fell off $17,000,000 in three weeks.[3] To meet this double drain—coming from the subtreasury and the interior banks—the New York institutions had no available resource. Over $50,000,000 of their resources seem to have been locked up in government securities,[4] which could not be sold to obtain specie ; for the fall in the price of stocks made it impossible to dispose of 7.30 treasury notes at home except at a heavy sacrifice,[5] and the danger of war with England cut off all hope of negotiating the 6 per cent. bonds in Europe.[6] The result of the situation was a rapid depletion of the reserves. The week that Mr. Chase's report on the finances was published the New York banks lost $2,900,000 of specie. The next report — made after the receipt of warlike news from England —

[1] See copy of the resolutions in *Hunt's Merchants' Magazine*, Vol. XLVI, p. 101. *Cf.* the comment in the New York *Tribune*, December 23, p. 8, and December 30, p. 8; New York *Herald*, December 19, p. 6; and New York *Times*, December 30, p. 4.

[2] *Cf.* letter from a New York bank president in New York *Tribune*, December 25, 1861, p. 7.

[3] *Cf.* New York *Tribune* of December 23, p. 8, and of December 30, p. 8. The table, p. 30, above, shows that the Boston banks increased their specie, while those of New York were losing rapidly.

[4] *Cf. Bankers' Magazine* (New York), Vol. XVI, p. 560.

[5] Most of the 7.30 notes sold by public subscription had been taken by "small investors, and they were already again offering them in the market to an extent which reduced the price to 96 for those that were indorsed and 98 for clean notes."— *American Annual Cyclopædia*, 1861, p. 299.

[6] Letter from bank president in New York *Tribune*, December 25, 1861, p. 7.

exhibited a further loss of $2,600,000. During the next seven days the rate of depletion was even more rapid, and the loss for the week amounted to $7,400,000.

Under such a drain the complete exhaustion of the reserves was evidently a question of only a short time. Saturday, December 28, the banks held another meeting to decide what measures should be taken. After a "rather stormy" session of six or seven hours, the resolution to suspend specie payments upon the following Monday, December 30, was carried by a vote of 25 of the institutions represented to 15.[1]

[1] *Cf.* "Remarks made by Mr. James Gallatin at the Meeting of Bank Officers, ... December 28, 1861," *Bankers' Magazine* (New York), Vol. XVI, pp. 625-31; H. W. DOMETT, *History of the Bank of New York*, 2d ed. (New York, 1884), p. 97, and accounts of the meeting in the New York daily papers of December 30, 1861.

It is to be noted that suspension was rather a measure of precaution to prevent further depletion of the reserves than one of necessity; for on the day when suspension was decided upon the New York banks held $4,600,000 more specie than they had at the commencement of the year. Their attitude was expressed in Mr. Gallatin's remarks: "The government must suspend specie payments or we must, and it is only a question of a few more days' time as to who suspends first and who shall hold the specie now in our vaults. If we hold it, the people and the government will be alike benefited. If government takes it, the whole will be expended and hoarded by a few people."—*Bankers' Magazine* (New York), Vol. XVI, p. 627.

At the time of suspension the account of the banks with the government stood as follows (*ibid.*, p. 560)

	Subscribed to Loan	Paid in	Received back from Government	Due to Government
Banks of New York - - -	$102,056,835	$81,056,835	$27,125,000	$21,000,000
Banks of Boston - - -	29,159,095	23,159,095	7,750,000	6,000,000
Banks of Philadelphia - -	14,579,548	11,579,548	3,875,000	3,000,000
	$145,795,478	$115,795,478	$38,750,000	$30,000,000

The government made its last cash payment to the banks January 13, 1862, and the banks paid the last instalment of money due upon the second loan January 15, and on the third loan February 4. January 24 the banks still owed the government $9,375,000. (*Cf.* "Report New York Loan Committee," *Bankers' Magazine*, Vol. XVII, pp. 139, 140, and comment on the money market, *ibid.*, Vol. XVI, pp. 560 and 655.)

There was a vexatious delay in the delivery to the banks of the securities they had purchased. The 7.30 treasury notes for the portion of the first loan which was not sold to the public ($5,625,000) were not received by the banks till January 24, 1862. The notes for the second loan were delivered in four instalments between January 22 and February 5; and the 6 per cent. bonds for the third loan in nine instalments between January 27 and March 5.—" Report of the New York Loan Committee," *loc. cit.*

"As fortunately as unexpectedly," reported the New York Loan Committee June 12, 1862, in regard to the operation, "it has resulted profitably for the associates, and has probably enabled them to employ their means to nearly as much

"The suspension of the banks [of New York] was received in commercial and monetary circles without surprise."[1] The banks of Philadelphia, which had lost nearly $2,000,000 of specie in a fortnight, followed suit; and so did those of Boston, although the latter had managed to increase their reserves $1,600,000 between December 7 and 21, and had then lost but $1,100,000 by the 28th, thus suspending with $2,300,000 more specie than on August 17, when the contract for the first government loan was taken.   With the exception of the banks of Ohio, Indiana, and Kentucky, and a few scattered institutions, the suspension of specie payments immediately became general.[2]

The suspension of the national treasury followed of necessity hard upon that of the banks.   As Mr. Chase said, after the banks had ceased paying in specie, it was "certain that the government could no longer obtain coin on loans in any adequate amounts."[3]   Consequently the treasury was obliged to cease redeeming in coin the demand treasury notes in circulation.[4]

The responsibility for the suspension of the banks and

advantage as would have been done but for the political disturbances of the country. Most of the government securities which have been sold by the associates have been sold by themselves at different times, and it is not possible for your committee to state the amount of interest for the capital invested which has been received thereon; but the associates still hold a large amount of them, the market value of which is much higher than the price at which they were taken."—*Loc. cit.*, p. 148.

Moreover, the banks drew interest at 7.3 per cent. upon the entire $50,000,000 of the first loan from August 19, upon the second from October 1, and upon the third from November 16. As they paid up these loans at the rate of about $5,000,000 per week, not completing the payments on the first loan till October 24, 1861, on the second till January 15, 1862, and on the third till February 4, 1862, they were for a considerable time paid interest on funds that had not left their possession. On that portion of the first loan sold to the public, the banks received interest from August 19, 1861, to the dates of sale, amounting altogether to $621,290.—" Report of the New York Loan Committee," *Bankers' Magazine*, pp. 139–42, and *Report of the Secretary of the Treasury*, 1861, p. 9.

[1] New York *Tribune*, December 31, 1861, p. 3.

[2] *Cf.* Part II, chap. ii, sec. ii, below.

[3] Letter to Trowbridge, WARDEN, *Life of Chase*. p. 388.

[4] On the subsequent history of these treasury notes see Part II, chap. ii, sec. iii, and chap. iii, sec. ii, below.

government has frequently been placed upon Mr. Chase for his issue of demand treasury notes and his refusal to draw directly upon the banks in making payments.[1] Examination of the condition of the banks, as shown in their weekly reports, however, hardly bears out this opinion. Doubtless the position of the banks would have been stronger had the secretary conformed his policy to their wishes. But, inasmuch as no serious trouble had been experienced up to the second week of December, despite Mr. Chase's refusal to do as the banks desired, it seems unreasonable to attribute the sudden loss of specie in the last three weeks of December, which caused suspension, to the policy pursued by him throughout — especially when the result is so adequately accounted for by the depression due to the unfavorable treasury report and to the fear of a war with England. These events made clear the weakness inherent in the plan of the bank loan. Suspension was inevitable whenever anything occurred to check the re-deposit in the banks of money paid out by the treasury, or to prevent the banks from replenishing their reserves by selling the securities received from the government. A severe blow to the national credit would inevitably produce such effects. It so happened that the publication of the disappointing treasury report and the Trent affair were the first occurrences of this nature momentous enough to arouse general uneasiness. Had there been no threat of war with England, and had the condition of the federal finances revealed in the report of December been less gloomy, the banks would probably have been able to carry out their program of taking a fourth $50,000,000 of treasury notes on January 1. Suspension would then have been postponed, but, in all probability, not prevented. To assume that the banks could have continued indefinitely to carry their double burden — supplying both government and

[1] For examples see the citations in note 1, p. 26, and note 2, p. 27, above.

public with loans — is to assume that no serious reverse would have befallen the national credit; for, as has been twice said, a disturbance of public confidence would have led to the withdrawal of deposits and the hoarding of specie; the government securities held by the banks would have become unsalable and suspension would have followed.

As it was, the specie standard was abandoned within six months after the Civil War had fairly begun. The country was left at the beginning of the new year, 1862, with a mixed circulation of paper money which neither the issuing banks nor the federal treasury were prepared to redeem in coin. How Congress met the situation thus created forms the subject of the following chapter.[1]

[1] General accounts of the $150,000,000 bank loan and the suspension of specie payments are to be found in *Report of the Secretary of the Treasury*, December, 1861, pp. 8-10; letter of Chase to Trowbridge, in WARDEN, *Life of Chase*, pp. 386-8; SCHUCKERS, *Life of Chase*, pp. 225-31; "Report of the Loan Committee of the New York Banks," *Executive Document No. 25*, 37th Cong., 3d Sess., pp. 125-42, and *Bankers' Magazine* (New York), Vol. XVII, pp. 136-49 (details of the management of the loan by the New York banks); GEORGE S. COE, letter of October 8, 1875, to E. G. Spaulding, in latter's *History of the Legal-Tender Paper Money*, 2d ed. (Buffalo, 1875), Appendix, pp. 89-96; republished under title, "Financial History of the War," in *Bankers' Magazine*, Vol. XXX, pp. 536-44 (written from point of view of the banks, as is the next also); J. E. WILLIAMS, *The War Loans of the Associated Banks to the Government in 1861* (New York, 1876); *American Annual Cyclopædia*, 1861, article "Finances of the United States," and pp. 61-6 (impartial); "Federal Finances Examined" (anon); *Hunt's Merchants' Magazine*, Vol. XLVII, pp. 506 ff. (criticism of Mr. Chase); VON HOCK, *Die Finanzen und die Finanzgeschichte der Vereinigten Staaten* (Stuttgart, 1867), pp. 442-6 (deficient in information); W. A. BERKEY, *The Money Question*, 4th ed., Grand Rapids (Mich.), 1878, pp. 154-8 (version of the "greenback" party); BOLLES, *Financial History of the United States*, 1860-85, pp. 20-42 (loosely written); W. G. SUMNER, *History of Banking in the United States*, (New York, 1896) [Vol. I of *History of Banking in all Nations*], pp. 458-61.

CHAPTER II

THE FIRST LEGAL-TENDER ACT

I. *The Legal-Tender Bills:*
Spaulding's Legal-Tender Bill — Discussion in Committee — The Bankers' Convention — Revision of Spaulding's Bill.

II. *Debate in Congress:*
Constitutional Argument — Argument from Experience — Economic, Moral, and Fiscal Objections — Argument from Necessity — Alternatives Proposed — A Temporary Measure.

III. *Attitude of Secretary Chase:*
Chase's Reluctant Assent to Legal-Tender Clause — Later Denial of Necessity for It — Opinions of Financial Critics.

IV. *Passage of the Act:*
Three Substitutes for Legal-Tender Bill — Vote in House — Senate Amendments — Votes in Senate — Conference Committee — Provisions of Law — Attitude of the Business Public and of the Press.

I.   THE LEGAL-TENDER BILLS

On the very day that the New York banks suspended specie payments, a proposal was made in Congress that the United States resort to the issue of an irredeemable paper currency of legal-tender notes. This bill, so promptly presented, originated in the following manner:

In his report of December 9 Mr. Chase had estimated the probable deficit for the coming six months at $214,000,000. To secure this sum he proposed an increase of only $50,000,000 in taxation and for the remainder reliance upon loans. With the purpose of making it easier to borrow he suggested a national reorganization of the state banking system requiring all banks to purchase United States stocks to hold as security for their circulating notes[1]—a proposal

---

[1] *Report of the Secretary of the Treasury*, December, 1861, pp. 11-20; *Notes Explanatory of Mr. Chase's Plan of National Finance* (Washington, 1861), p. 15.

out of which the national banking system developed some two years later.

According to the usual course of business this report was read in the House of Representatives and referred to the Committee of Ways and Means. The large amount of work which devolved upon this committee had made necessary a division of labor among its members. The chairman, Mr. Thaddeus Stevens, of Pennsylvania, whose radical anti-slavery opinions, imperious temper, and vigorous use of invective had made him the Republican leader of the House, devoted himself to pushing the appropriation bills. To the remaining eight members fell the task of preparing new measures. They organized in two subcommittees, one of which, presided over by the leading tariff advocate of the day, Justin S. Morrill, of Vermont, undertook to frame a program of war taxation, leaving the other subcommittee to consider the loan bills.[1]

It was to this second subcommittee that Mr. Chase's national currency scheme was submitted. The chairman was Elbridge G. Spaulding, a Buffalo banker who had been state treasurer of New York and had served two terms in Congress. His colleagues were a retired Boston merchant, Samuel Hooper, who had entered politics as a Republican after accumulating a fortune in business, and Erastus Corning, an Albany millionaire possessing executive ability but no talent for speech-making. These three gentlemen immediately adopted the secretary's plan and began to draft a bill for a national currency secured by a pledge of government bonds. But on Saturday, December 28, they learned that the New York banks had decided to suspend specie payments on the following Monday. Suspension would of course drive gold from circulation and leave the country

---

[1] E. G. SPAULDING, *History of the Legal-Tender Paper Money Issued During the Great Rebellion* (Buffalo, 1869), pp. 7, 8.

with no other currency than the $33,000,000 demand notes issued by the treasury, the notes of the suspended state banks, and small change of silver and minor coins. Even when redeemable in specie the bank notes, issued by some 1,600 different institutions according to no general plan and varying widely in value, made a very unsatisfactory currency. Moreover, bank notes could not legally be accepted and paid out by the federal treasury under the provisions of the subtreasury law. Mr. Chase's plan for reorganizing the banking system would perhaps furnish a sounder circulation, but the banking bill contained sixty sections and was certain to encounter opposition from the friends of state banks that would delay its enactment several months. "So long a delay," thought Mr. Spaulding, "would be fatal to the union cause." Accordingly, he "changed the legal tender section, intended originally to accompany the bank bill, into a separate bill, ... and on his own motion introduced it into the House by unanimous consent on the 30th of December."[1]

After being twice read in the House of Representatives, this bill was referred back to the Committee of Ways and Means. Upon its wisdom the members of the committee were equally divided. Of the subcommittee, Spaulding and Hooper favored the bill, while Corning opposed it. Thaddeus Stevens at first objected to the legal-tender clause as unconstitutional; but he soon overcame his scruples and decided to vote for the bill. Morrill, of Vermont, and Horton, of Ohio, joined Corning in opposition. Maynard, of Tennessee, and Stratton, of New York, took no part in the discussion; but the former was inclined to support the proposal, while Stratton was undecided. There was thus a deadlock in the committee — four members favored and four

---

[1] SPAULDING, op. cit., p. 14. This was H. R. bill No. 182. It authorized the issue of $50,000,000 of legal-tender treasury notes. For text see SPAULDING, pp. 14, 15.

opposed the bill. The ninth member, John S. Phelps, of Missouri, was not in Washington at the time. But finally the wavering member, Stratton, consented to vote for the bill in order that it might go before Congress for consideration.[1] Thus, after a narrow escape from defeat in the committee, the legal-tender bill was formally reported to the House by Mr. Spaulding, January 7, 1862.[2]

Mr. Spaulding's reasons for urging a legal-tender bill upon Congress at this juncture were given in a letter to a gentleman who ventured to suggest that heavy taxation was preferable to the issue of irredeemable paper as a method of securing revenue. Spaulding wrote:

> The treasury-note bill . . . . is a measure of *necessity* and not one of *choice*. . . . . We will be out of means to pay the daily expenses in *about thirty days*, and the committee do not see any other way to get along till we can get the tax bills ready, except to issue temporarily Treasury notes. . . . . We must have at least $100,000,000 during the next three months, or the Government must stop payment.

And the letter closed with an intimation that unless the gentleman could suggest some other plan for raising the said $100,000,000 it would best become him not to criticise the bill.[3]

By the publication of copies of the legal-tender bill in various newspapers, the country was quickly informed of the radical step which Congress was considering. When the bankers of New York, Boston, and Philadelphia who had been supplying the government with funds heard of the proposal, a number of the most prominent went to Washington to persuade Secretary Chase that the situation could be

---

[1] SPAULDING, *History*, p. 16.

[2] This second bill (H. R. bill No. 187) differed from the first in increasing the issue of legal-tender notes from $50,000,000 to $100,000,000 and in making the demand notes authorized in July, 1861, also a legal tender. For text see *ibid.*, pp. 16, 17.

[3] Letter of E. G. Spaulding to Isaac Sherman, January 8, 1862, SPAULDING, *History*, pp. 17, 18.

met with a remedy less heroic than the issue of an irredeemable paper currency. January 11, 1862, these gentlemen
had an informal conference with Mr. Chase, the members of
the House Committee of Ways and Means, and of the Senate
finance committee.[1]

As spokesman for the banks, Mr. James Gallatin, president of the Gallatin Bank of New York, pointed out the evil
consequences that would follow the emission of legal-tender
paper money, and submitted an alternative plan for relieving
the necessities of the treasury. The main features of his
proposal were: first, heavy taxation; second, the sale of
long-time bonds at their market value. Adequate taxation,
he argued, would give the long-needed assurance that the
treasury had ample revenue to pay interest on loans. Bonds
could then be sold on better terms, especially after the
futile attempt to fix a minimum value for them by legislation
forbidding sales below par should have been abandoned.[2]

Simple and efficient as this plan seems, it did not meet
with the approval of the secretary or the congressional
committees. Mr. Spaulding, who replied to Gallatin, stated
the grounds of their dissent as follows:

Mr. Spaulding objected to any and every form of "shinning" by
government through Wall or State streets to begin with; objected
to the knocking down of government stocks to 75 or 60 cents on the

---

[1] SPAULDING, op. cit., pp. 18-20.—The bankers who took part in this conference
seem to have had no official position as delegates of the association of banks. However,
they were men of such prominence that much weight was attached to the opinions they
expressed on financial topics. According to Spaulding, Coe, Vermilye, Martin, and
Gallatin came from New York; Haven, Walley, and Bates from Boston; and Rogers,
Mercer, and Patterson from Philadelphia (ibid., p. 19). But that the views of these
gentlemen were not shared by all their associates appears from the letters received
about this time by Mr. Spaulding from other bankers (ibid., p. 23-5). See also the
New York Herald financial column dated January 13, 1862.

[2] There were four other points in Mr. Gallatin's plan: (1) cessation of issue of
demand notes beyond the $50,000,000 already authorized; (2) the issue of $100,000,000
of two-year treasury notes receivable for government dues except customs; (3) suspension of the subtreasury act so as to allow banks to become government depositories; (4) authorization of temporary loans secured by pledges of government
stock.—Ibid., p. 20.

dollar, the inevitable result of throwing a new and large loan on the market, *without limitation as to price;* claimed for treasury notes as much virtue of par value as the notes of banks which have suspended specie payments, but which yet circulate in the trade of the North; and finished with firmly refusing to assent to any scheme which should permit a speculation by brokers, bankers, and others in government securities, and particularly any scheme which should double the public debt of the country, and double the expenses of the war by damaging the credit of the government to the extent of sending it to "shin" through the shaving shops of New York, Boston, and Philadelphia.[1]

This reply of Mr. Spaulding to Mr. Gallatin is interesting because it shows plainly the curious inconsistency in the position taken by the promoters of the legal-tender bill from beginning to end of the discussion. They professed to advocate the issue of paper money upon the ground of sheer necessity. By this means alone, said Mr. Spaulding, in the letter quoted above, could the immediate wants of the treasury be met. To substantiate this argument it was of course necessary to show that no other feasible method of obtaining funds existed. When, then, bankers declared that there was an alternative, that the government could secure means by adopting a policy of vigorous taxation and selling its bonds at their market value, the only logical answer for the friends of the legal-tender bill was to show that the bankers were mistaken. But such was not the answer that Mr. Spaulding made. He replied instead that selling bonds below par was more objectionable than issuing paper money. And in this view the committee of Congress apparently concurred. Thus, when the delegates of the banks called attention to the possibility of borrowing, the argument for the legal-tender bill was shifted from the ground of necessity to that of expediency. The choice lay not between irredeemable paper money and federal bankruptcy, but between irredeem-

[1] SPAULDING, p. 21.

able paper money and borrowing at high rates of interest. The financial leaders of the government deliberately preferred the former course. Whether their choice was wise or not, even from the strictly financial point of view; whether the increase of debt, which Mr. Spaulding saw would result from selling bonds below par, was avoided by the issue of paper money; whether "the knocking down of government stocks to 75 or 60 cents on the dollar" was prevented, are questions that must be left for the chapter on the effect of paper issues upon the cost of the war.[1]

As has been said, Mr. Spaulding's reply convinced the congressional committees that the legal-tender bill was a better method of relieving the embarrassment of the treasury than the bankers' proposal to sell bonds at their market value. Subsequently, however, the delegates of the banks succeeded in formulating a plan which received the indorsement of the secretary of the treasury. New loans of $250,-000,000 or $300,000,000 and the enactment of the national banking bill advocated in Mr. Chase's report were its chief points. The issue of demand notes in excess of the $50,-000,000 already authorized, and the making those already issued a legal tender, was to be avoided as unnecessary.[2] But this plan also was rejected by the committees of Congress as inadequate to the crisis. Plainly, it would be of small avail to authorize bonds at par when capitalists would buy them only at a discount, and to sales below par the committees would not agree. Consequently, the attempt of the representative bankers of New York, Boston, and Philadelphia to give the government the benefit of their advice came to nought. The plans suggested by them are of interest, however, because they show that in the opinion of experienced

---

[1] Part II, chap. x, below. *Cf.* HENRY ADAMS, *Historical Essays* (New York, 1891), pp. 289–93 and 63, 64 below.

[2] SPAULDING, pp. 21, 22.

men the legal-tender act was not the only escape from the difficulties into which the treasury had drifted.

After the convention of bankers had broken up, Mr. Spaulding added another section to the legal-tender bill, recast it in pursuance of suggestions from Secretary Chase,[1] and introduced it again into the House of Representatives, where it was made the special order for January 28, 1862. As it came before Congress the measure provided for the issue of $100,000,000 of United States notes to be "a legal tender in payment of all debts, public and private," and exchangeable for 6 per cent. twenty-year bonds of which the secretary was authorized to issue $500,000,000.[2] Upon the appointed day the House resolved itself into a committee of the whole upon the state of the Union, and Mr. Spaulding made an elaborate introductory speech, explaining and recommending the bill.[3] But opposition to the making of treasury notes a legal tender developed at once, and it was not until after four weeks of earnest discussion that the fate of the bill was decided. What motives actuated Congress in its final decision can best be learned by study of the debate.

II. DEBATE IN CONGRESS[4]

Logically, the first point in the case of the promoters of the treasury-note bill was the proof that Congress had power under the constitution to make paper money a legal tender in the payment of debts. Foreseeing that this power

[1] SPAULDING, pp. 26, 27.

[2] H. R. bill No. 240, *ibid.*, p. 27; full text in *Congressional Globe*, 37th Cong., 2d Sess., p. 522.

[3] *Congressional Globe, loc. cit.*, pp. 523-6; SPAULDING, pp. 28-42.

[4] In the following section I have attempted to give an analysis of the whole discussion in both houses of Congress, rather than to show the attitude of prominent individuals. Accounts of the debate from the latter point of view are numerous. See, *e. g.*: SPAULDING, pp. 28-152; J. G. BLAINE, *Twenty Years of Congress* (Norwich, Conn., 1884), Vol. I, chap. xix; J. J. KNOX, *United States Notes*, 2d ed. (London, 1885), pp. 119-37; A. S. BOLLES, *Financial History of the United States, 1861-1885* (New York, 1886), Book I, chap. iv; J. F. RHODES, *History of the United*

would be challenged, Mr. Spaulding read an unofficial opinion of the attorney-general, Edward Bates, which was interpreted, not quite fairly, to mean that Congress could make treasury notes a legal tender since it was not forbidden to do so by the constitution.[1] To this it was answered that under the tenth amendment Congress possessed no powers except those explicitly or implicitly granted it, and therefore that no authority for making paper money a legal tender could be inferred from the silence of the constitution on the point.[2]

So conclusive was this reply that the supporters of the bill found it necessary to seek other ground for their contention by deducing the right to make paper bills legal tender from some of the powers expressly delegated to Congress. Appeal was made to the clause authorizing Congress "to make all laws necessary and proper for carrying into execution" the powers specifically granted it. Mr. Spaulding coupled this clause with the authorization to levy war. "This bill," he argued, "is a *necessary means* of carrying into execution the powers granted in the constitution 'to raise and *support* armies' and 'to provide and *maintain* a navy.'"[3] Thaddeus Stevens added the necessary clincher by saying: "Whether such necessity exists is solely for the decision of Congress."[4] Two attempts were made to over-

States, from 1850 (New York, 1895), Vol. III, pp. 561–7; J. K. UPTON, *Money in Politics*, 2d ed. (Boston, 1895), pp. 75–89; J. L. LAUGHLIN, *Report of the Monetary Commission* (Chicago, 1898), pp. 408–10; F. A. WALKER, *Money* (New York, 1891), pp. 369–73; F. A. WALKER and HENRY ADAMS, "The Legal-Tender Act," *North American Review*, April, 1870; "The Greenbacks in Congress," *Sound Currency*, Vol. III, No. 4, January, 1896.

[1] *Congressional Globe*, 37th Cong., 2d Sess., Part I, p. 525; SPAULDING, pp. 15, 16. Bates's real meaning seems to be that Congress is no more prohibited from making bills of credit a legal tender than it is from issuing them, and the latter right no one contests.

[2] *Ibid.* See remarks of Messrs. Pendleton, p. 550; Cowan, p. 791; Sheffield, p. 640; Thomas, p. 681; Collamer, p. 768; Pearce, p. 803; Crisfield, Appendix, p. 48; Bayard, p. 795; Conkling, p. 635; Wright, p. 662.

[3] *Ibid.*, p. 524. Similar arguments were made by Messrs. Blake, p. 686; Howe, Appendix, p. 54; Stevens, p. 688.

[4] *Ibid.*

throw this position. Such an argument, said Mr. Crisfield, amounts to a claim of unlimited authority; for, if one granted it, by asserting that the act was necessary "to insure public safety," Congress could enact any law, no matter how injudicious, provided it were not expressly forbidden by the constitution.[1] Mr. Pendleton took different ground. Granted, he argued, that Congress could make treasury notes a legal tender if this were necessary to pay the army, it still remained to prove that this necessity existed. He himself was unable to see the necessity in the pending case. Therefore, to him the bill was unconstitutional.[2]

A second form of the "necessary means" argument was made by Mr. Bingham, of Ohio. Congress, he said, has power to regulate commerce, and the determination of what shall be lawful tender in discharge of debts is a necessary incident of this regulation.[3] But it was answered, first, that it was a mere subterfuge to pretend that regulation of commerce was the object of the bill;[4] second, that the power of Congress over commerce extended only to "commerce with foreign nations, and among the several states, and with the Indian tribes," while a legal-tender act affected only transactions between individuals;[5] and third, that the substitution of a paper for a metallic standard, so far from "regulating and promoting" commerce, tended rather to "disturb and destroy" it.[6]

Senators Howard and Sherman elaborated a third variation of the argument. Making treasury notes a legal tender they held was one of the necessary and proper means for borrowing money.[7] Senator Collamer anticipated this contention, and replied that where power was granted to do a

---

[1] *Congressional Globe*, 37th Cong., 2d Sess., Appendix, p. 48.   [2] *Ibid.*, p. 550.

[3] *Ibid.*, p. 637; *cf.* remarks of Mr. Kellogg, p. 679.

[4] Mr. Crisfield, Appendix, p. 49.   [5] Mr. Collamer, p. 769.

[6] Mr. Crisfield, Appendix, p. 49.   [7] Mr. Sherman, p. 790; Mr. Howard, p. 796.

certain thing in a certain way it was not permissible to seek
inferential authority to accomplish the same end in a different manner. Now Congress was empowered to raise money
first, by levying taxes, second, by negotiating loans. The
issue of legal-tender notes, being neither a tax nor a loan,
came under neither of these express grants; and not coming
under the express grants, no authority could be inferred for
it as a means of raising money.[1]

The last argument for the constitutionality of the bill —
the one that found no adequate answer — was Charles Sumner's. He called attention to the fact that Congress had
long been conceded the right to issue treasury notes. Reviewing the financial history of the American colonies, he showed
that ten of the thirteen had at different times issued paper
money, usually making it a legal tender. In America, he
argued, " the legal tender was a constant, though not insepa-
rable incident of the bill of credit." The conclusion was
that the unquestioned power of issuing treasury notes carried
with it the right to make the notes a legal tender.[2]

But, after spending much time and ingenuity in debating
the constitutional questions raised by the legal-tender clause,
the members of Congress apparently concluded that they had
multiplied words to little purpose. While a few declared
that constitutional scruples would prevent them from voting
for the bill,[3] the more general feeling was that it would be
unreasonable to decide a question of such importance upon a

---

[1] Congressional Globe, 37th Cong., 2d Sess., p. 767.

[2] Ibid., pp. 797, 798. An amusingly fantastic argument for the constitutionality
of the bill was made by Senator McDougall of California, who attempted to deduce
the right to issue legal-tender treasury notes from the power to coin money, by
showing that the word "coin" was etymologically equivalent to the word " stamp,"
and therefore that the right of coinage must include the right to stamp paper notes.
Unfortunately for the argument, the canon of interpretation which insists that
words are used in the constitution in strict accordance with their etymological
significance did not commend itself to the lawyers of the Senate.— Ibid., Appendix,
p. 60, for his argument; with which compare the remarks of Mr. Thomas, p. 681.

[3] E. g., Senators Collamer, ibid., pp. 767, 770; Powell, p. 804; Saulsbury, p. 804.

doubtful technicality which could be settled only by the courts. If the measure was expedient there need be little hesitation at such a crisis in construing liberally the powers of Congress.[1] The fate of the bill was affected, then, much less by the inconclusive constitutional argument than by the debate upon the merits of the issue of legal-tender notes as a financial policy.

Considering the bill thus upon its merits, the opposition called attention prominently to the lessons of experience. Could it be shown that the resort to an inconvertible paper currency had always been attended in the past with evil results, a strong presumption would be created against the wisdom of a repetition of the experiment. Consequently rhetoric was employed to picture in vivid colors the unhappy consequences that had followed the issue of paper money by France during the Revolution,[2] by England in the Napoleonic wars,[3] by Austria,[4] and Turkey,[5] by Rhode Island[6] in colonial days, by the Continental Congress in the War of Independence,[7] and finally by the Confederate States, then fairly launched upon the paper-money policy.[8]

To break the force of these historical parallels, which told so heavily against the bill, its supporters sought to show that causes, which under different conditions had led to depreciation, would not be operative in the case of the United States in 1862. Thus, it was said, the continental notes of the American Revolution depreciated because of the poverty of the country, which offered no security for their redemption; the vastly greater wealth of the nation in 1862 would prevent a repetition of the experience.[9] The depreciation of the issues

---

[1] Remarks of Fessenden, *Congressional Globe*, 37th Cong., 2d Sess., p. 767; Wilson, p. 788; Alley, p. 659; Sherman, p. 791; Pike, p. 658; Campbell, p. 686.

[2] Mr. Cowan, *ibid.*, p. 792; *cf.* Sumner, p. 798; Pike, p. 657.

[3] Mr. Morrill, p. 631; *cf.* Spaulding, p. 526; Stevens, p. 689.

[4] Mr. Morrill, p. 631.   [5] Mr. Simmons, p. 794.   [6] Mr. Sheffield, p. 164.

[7] Mr. Collamer, pp. 767-8; Sumner, p. 798; *cf.* Kellogg, p. 680; Pike, p. 656.

[8] Mr. Horton, p. 665.   [9] Mr. Kellogg, p. 680.

of Louis XIV was explained on the ground that France was then exhausted by heavy taxation to maintain a profligate court.[1] The cases of the French Revolution and the Confederate States were accounted for by the fact that these governments were revolutionary.[2] Some gentlemen even denied that depreciated currencies had proved evils. "It would be far from a blunder," said Senator Howe, "to say that the 'golden age' of England was during that long period when the only currency she knew was one of irredeemable paper;"[3] and Mr. Kellogg declared the paper issues of the Revolution had increased confidence, clothed the army, and revived commerce.[4] Another supporter of the bill tried to evade the historical argument by maintaining that the true lesson of experience was that of moderate issues.[5] But no one seems to have taken these ingenious pleas very seriously, for it was easy to show that one of the striking lessons of experiments with paper money is that such moderation, which the issuer at first intends to observe, has almost invariably been soon forgotten.[6]

If the argument from experience was strongly against the bill, the cognate economic argument was hardly less so. The opponents of paper issues assumed the offensive, declaring emphatically that the proposed legal-tender notes were certain to depreciate in value. Mr. Lovejoy said:

It is not in the power of this Congress . . . . to accomplish an impossibility in making something out of nothing. The piece of paper you stamp as five dollars is not five dollars, and it never will be, unless it is convertible into a five dollar gold piece ; and to profess that it is, is simply a delusion and a fallacy.[7]

[1] Mr. Howe, Appendix, p. 55, *Congressional Globe*, 37th Cong., 2d Sess.
[2] Mr. Kellogg, p. 680; Howe, Appendix, p. 55.
[3] Appendix, p. 55; *cf.* Spaulding, p. 526.
[4] *Ibid.*, p. 681.   [5] Mr. Pike, p. 657.
[6] Messrs. Thomas, p. 682; Cowan, p. 793; Morrill, pp. 631, 886; Pomeroy, p. 884; Collamer, p. 770; Lovejoy, 691.
[7] *Ibid.*, p. 691.

Various shifts were tried to meet this attack. Mr. Kellogg boldly asserted that the legal tender quality of the notes would prevent fluctuation of their value;[1] but more faith was put in the reply that the total wealth of the country was security for the notes, and this security being ample the value of the paper would not decline.[2] The rejoinder to this was first, that the security for the notes was not the total wealth of the people, but only such part of it as the government could obtain by taxation; and second, that though the security for ultimate redemption might be ample, the notes would nevertheless depreciate in value if the holders were unable to secure immediate payment.[3]

A different argument to show the improbability of depreciation was based by Thaddeus Stevens upon the quantity theory of money as expounded by McCulloch. "The value of legal tender notes," said he, "depends on the amount issued compared with the business of the country. If a less quantity were issued than the usual and needed circulation, they would be more valuable than gold."[4] The opponents of the bill replied, not by attacking the quantity theory, but by insisting that all experience showed that, after one issue of paper money had been made, other issues were sure to follow, until the currency became redundant and depreciated. "The experience of mankind," said Mr. Thomas, "shows the danger of entering upon this path; that boundaries are fixed only to be overrun; promises made only to be broken."[5] "The same necessity," added Mr. Pomeroy, "which now requires the amount of inconvertible paper now authorized, will require sixty days hence a similar issue, and then another, each one requiring a larger nominal amount to

---

[1] *Congressional Globe*, 37th Congress, 2d Sess., p. 681; *cf.* the answer of Senator Collamer, p. 767.

[2] Messrs. Spaulding, p. 524; Howe, Appendix, p. 55; Kellogg, pp. 680, 681.

[3] *Cf.* Mr. Morrill, p. 630, Thomas, p. 682.

[4] *Ibid.*, p. 668.   [5] *Ibid.*, p. 682.

represent the same intrinsic value." [1]   To such assertions,
backed by the weight of historical evidence, the supporters
of the bill could respond only that the case of the United
States would be an exception; the American government
would not yield, as other governments had done, to the
temptation to make further issues. [2]

Some of the more astute friends of the bill admitted the
probability of a redundant currency, and relied, not on limitation of issues, but on a funding scheme to prevent depreciation.   Section one of the bill provided that holders of
legal-tender notes could at any time exchange them at par
for 6 per cent. twenty-year bonds. [3]   Under this arrangement, it was supposed, the value of the notes could never be
less than that of the bonds, and, as bonds could by law not
be sold for less than par, it followed that the notes could not
greatly depreciate. [4]   Unfortunately for the argument, even
while Congress was debating the bill, bonds were selling in
New York at ninety cents upon the dollar in notes of the
suspended banks. [5]   Hence the force of Mr. Morrill's remark:
" By making our notes a legal tender we make them better
for a moment than we can make our bonds, and men might
be willing to exchange bonds for the notes; but notes for
bonds never." [6]

Having proved to their satisfaction that the legal-tender
notes would depreciate, the opponents of the bill pursued
their advantage by dwelling upon the evil consequences that
would result.   Coin would disappear from circulation, said
they, prices would rise suddenly, fixed incomes would decline,

---

[1] *Congressional Globe*, 37th Cong., 2d Sess., p. 884. Mr. Pomeroy, however, supported the bill when amended to provide for payment of interest in coin. *Cf.* also
Collamer, p. 770; Lovejoy, p. 691; Horton, p. 664; Cowan, p. 793; Morrill, p. 631.

[2] *Cf.* the remarks of Messrs. Pike, p. 657; Hooper, p. 617; Stevens, p. 688.

[3] See text of bill, *ibid.*, p. 522, and Mr. Stevens's explanation, p. 688. *Cf.*
Spaulding, p. 526.

[4] Mr. Hooper, *ibid.*, p. 617.   [5] Mr. Pendleton, p. 551.   [6] *Ibid.*, p. 630.

creditors be defrauded, and the widows and orphans would suffer.[1] Senator Collamer showed how depositors in savings banks would lose by depreciation,[2] and Senator Fessenden how labor would be injured by a rise of prices exceeding the rise of wages.[3] Finally, Mr. Crisfield represented forcibly the instability of a paper standard of value and the consequent danger to business.[4]

To all of this the promoters of the bill found it hard to reply. On the other hand they sought support in the contention that the country needed money,[5] and that the government should regulate the paper currency furnished by the banks.[6] Of course the rejoinder was, first, that, granted the existence of the doubtful need of more money, the issue of a depreciated paper currency was a very bad method of supplying it; and, second, that if the banknote currency required regulation the proper means was a reorganization of the banking system, not a legal-tender act.

Not content with showing the economic evils of a depreciated paper currency, the opponents of the bill denounced it roundly as immoral. To pay contractors and soldiers in depreciated money, they declared, was dishonorable. "The bill says to the world," asserted Mr. Horton, "that we are bankrupt, and we are not only weak, but we are not honest."[7] The injustice, however, extended not only to creditors of the government, but to all persons who would be compelled to accept in payment money of less value than that which they had contracted to receive.[8] And by thus encouraging the

---

[1] Cf. the remarks of Messrs. Pendleton, *Congressional Globe*, 37th Cong., 2d Sess., p. 551; Morrill, p. 630; Horton, p. 664; Sheffield, p. 641; Fessenden, p. 765.

[2] *Ibid.*, p. 770. Cf. the reply of Senator McDougall, Appendix, p. 60.

[3] *Ibid.*, p. 766. [4] *Ibid.*, Appendix, p. 50.

[5] Cf. the remarks of Messrs. Alley, p. 659; Hooper, p. 617; Kellogg, p. 681.

[6] Senator Doolittle, Appendix p. 57.

[7] *Ibid.*, p. 664; cf. also Sumner, p. 798; Fessenden, p. 765; Crisfield, Appendix, pp. 49, 50; Pearce, p. 804.

[8] Cf. Messrs. Pendleton, p. 549; Thomas, p. 682. See Sherman's attempted reply, p. 790.

debtor to defraud his creditor, urged Senator Fessenden, the
bill would lower the moral standards of the people.[1] To these
charges, also, the promoters of the bill had little to say.

Upon the fiscal aspect of the bill the case of the opposition
was hardly less clear. First, they declared, the resort to an
irredeemable paper currency was a practical confession of
bankruptcy, and would therefore injure the credit of the
government, and make less favorable the conditions on
which it could borrow. "We . . . . go out to the country,"
said Fessenden, " with the declaration that we are unable to
pay or borrow at the present time, and such a confession is
not likely to increase our credit."[2] Second, it was pointed
out that the depreciation of the currency would cause the
prices of everything which the government had to buy to rise,
and thus would vastly increase the cost of the war. As Senator
Cowan put it, the government "might as well lose 25 per cent.
on the sale of her [sic] bonds, as to be obliged, in avoiding
it, to pay 25 per cent. more for everything she buys."[3]

This discussion of the economic, moral, and fiscal consequences of issuing a legal-tender paper currency produced
in Congress the feeling that under ordinary circumstances
such a proposal would be indefensible. The vigor with
which the opposition had presented the case against the bill
made a deep impression. On the other hand, the reasoning
by which the supporters of the bill had sought to establish
the constitutional power of Congress to make treasury notes
a legal tender was felt to be inconclusive. The force of the
telling argument from experience had not been broken; the
probability of depreciation had not been disproved; no adequate reply had been found to the indictment of the bill on

[1] *Congressional Globe*, 37th Cong., 2d Sess., p. 765; *cf.* Messrs. Conkling, p. 635;
Horton, p. 664.

[2] *Ibid.*, p. 765. *Cf.* Messrs. Vallandingham, Appendix, p. 44; Sheffield, p. 641;
Collamer, p. 769; Horton, p. 664; Crisfield, Appendix, p. 49; Willey, p. 796; Sumner,
p. 798; Thomas, p. 682.

[3] *Ibid.*, p. 793; *cf.* the remarks of Sheffield, p. 641, and Morrill, p. 630.

moral grounds; and, finally, it had not been denied that resort to paper issues would injure the credit of the government and increase the cost of the war. So generally was the objectionable character of the measure realized that Senator Fessenden could say:

All the opinions that I have heard expressed agree in this: that only with extreme reluctance, only with fear and trembling as to the consequences, can we have recourse to a measure like this of making our paper a legal tender in payment of debts.[1]

And yet an argument was found that overcame the "extreme reluctance" of a majority of the members and induced them to vote for the bill. This argument was the plea of absolute necessity. As has been seen, it was to necessity that Mr. Spaulding had appealed in justification of his first draft of the legal-tender bill.[2] In opening the debate in Congress he repeated the argument with emphasis. "The bill before us," said he, "is a war measure, a measure of *necessity* and not of choice, presented . . . . to meet the most pressing demands upon the Treasury."[3] The cry of necessity was taken up by the other supporters of the bill, who relied upon it to meet all the objections urged by the opposition.[4] How effective a plea it was is shown by the influence it had upon those who appreciated the ills of a paper currency. "Beneficent as this measure is, as one of relief," said Mr. Alley, "nothing could induce me to give it sanction but uncontrollable necessity."[5] "I shall . . . . support the bill," said Mr. Doolittle, "as a measure of war necessity, with more misgivings as to its effect at home and abroad, than of any other measure for which I have given my vote in this body."[6]

1 *Congressional Globe*, 37th Cong., 2d Sess., p. 763.
2 Mr. Spaulding's letter quoted, p. 44, above.
3 *Congressional Globe*, 37th Cong., 2d Sess., p. 523.
4 *Cf.* the remarks of Messrs. Campbell, p. 686; Walton, p. 692; Edwards, p. 684; Stevens, p. 687; and of Senators Sherman, p. 789; Howe, Appendix, p. 55; McDougall, Appendix, p. 58.
5 *Ibid.*, p. 659.   6 *Ibid.*, Appendix, p. 58.

That the assertion of necessity might carry the added force of official sanction, Secretary Chase was induced to send a note to the chairman of the Committee of Ways and Means to be read to the House. He wrote:

I have felt, nor do I wish to conceal that I now feel, a great aversion to making anything but coin a legal tender in payment of debts. It has been my anxious wish to avoid the necessity of such legislation. It is, however, at present impossible, in consequence of the large expenditures entailed by the war, and the suspension of the banks, to procure sufficient coin for disbursements, and it has therefore become indispensably necessary that we should resort to the issue of United States notes.[1]

This letter made the bill an "administration measure," and so was an important factor in its success. Desire to support the government at all costs led members to whom an irredeemable currency was very repugnant to vote for the bill when the secretary of the treasury declared it to be necessary. "I have . . . . had great doubt as to the propriety of voting for this bill . . . ." said Mr. Hickman, "but, being assured . . . . that the Treasury, and perhaps the Administration, regard this as a governmental necessity, I am disposed to waive the question of propriety or expediency, and to vote for it as a necessity."[2]

[1] *Congressional Globe*, 37th Cong., 2d Sess., p. 618. *Cf.* Mr. Chase's letter to Spaulding, in the latter's *History*, p. 59; and McCULLOCH, *Men and Measures of Half a Century* (New York, 1889), pp. 170, 171.

[2] *Congressional Globe*, 37th Cong., 2d Sess., p. 690. *Cf.* Sumner's conclusion: "Surely we must all be against paper money — we must all insist upon maintaining the integrity of the Government — and we must all set our faces against any proposition like the present, except as a temporary expedient, rendered imperative by the exigency of the hour. If I vote for this proposition it will be only because I am unwilling to refuse to the Government, especially charged with this responsibility, that confidence which is hardly less important to the public interests than the money itself. Others may doubt if the exigency is sufficiently imperative, but the secretary of the treasury, whose duty it is to understand the occasion, does not doubt. In his opinion the war requires this sacrifice. . . . . Your soldiers in the field must be paid and fed. Here there can be no failure or postponement. A remedy which at another moment you would reject is now proposed. Whatever may be the national resources, they are not now within reach, except by summary process. Reluctantly, painfully, I consent that the process should issue" (pp. 799, 800). See also McDougall, Appendix, p. 58.

In replying to the plea of necessity, the opposition candidly admitted it would be better to issue a forced currency than to stop payment, provided there were no alternative. "If the necessity exists," said Senator Fessenden, "I have no hesitation upon the subject and shall have none. If there is nothing left for us to do but that, and that will effect the object, I am perfectly willing to do that."[1] But that such was the case was emphatically denied. "It has been asserted . . . . with the utmost apparent sincerity," said Mr. Horton, "that this is a measure not of choice, but of necessity. But Mr. Chairman, that assertion is only reiterated, not proved. Where is the proof that this is a matter of necessity? There may be proofs abundant, but they have not been produced."[2]

Not only did the opposition deny the necessity, but they were ready also with suggestions of other means of securing the needed funds. One suggestion was adequate war taxation. "Not a dollar of tax has been raised," said Mr. Thomas, "and yet we are talking of national bankruptcy, and launching upon a paper currency. I may be very dull, but I cannot see the necessity, or the wisdom, of such a course."[3] It was by this time generally acknowledged that the omission to impose heavy taxes at the extra session of July, 1861, was a serious blunder which Congress should repair as soon as possible.[4] But the supporters of the bill argued[5] that the pending situation could not be met by taxation, for the needs of the treasury were too pressing to wait until new taxes could be assessed and collected.

[1] *Congressional Globe*, 37th Cong., 2d Sess., p. 764.

[2] *Ibid.*, p. 663; *cf.* pp. 664, 665.

[3] *Ibid.*, p. 682; *cf.* the remarks of Roscoe Conkling, p. 633; Wright, p. 663; Collamer, pp. 770, 771; Bayard, p. 796.

[4] A joint resolution to raise $150,000,000 per annum by taxation had been adopted by a vote of 134 to 5 in the House, January 15, and 39 to 1 in the Senate on the 17th. —*Ibid.*, pp. 349, 376.

[5] *E. g.*, see remarks of Mr. Walton, *ibid.*, p. 692.

To this the rejoinder was made: If it will take too long to wait for the proceeds of taxes, let the government supply its immediate wants by selling bonds at their market value, and in the meantime frame a permanent system of taxation that will yield an adequate revenue.[1] This plan was the same that the delegation of bankers had urged upon the secretary and the committees of Congress,[2] and it encountered the same opposition. Senator Howe was unwilling, as Mr. Spaulding had been, that government bonds should be sold below par. "The experience of half a century," said he, "has demonstrated that the use of money is not worth more than six per cent.; that sum the Government ought to pay."[3] Senator Fessenden replied: " Money in the market is always worth what it will sell for. It is an article of merchandise like anything else, and the Government has no reason to suppose, unless it can offer much better security, that it should get money at a better rate than anybody else." [4]

But there were other men who, while apparently ready to admit that government need not always insist on receiving quite par for its bonds, still believed that under existing circumstances the discount demanded by lenders would be ruinously high. "I maintain," said Thaddeus Stevens, "that the highest sums you could sell your bonds at would be 75 per cent. payable in currency, itself at a discount. That would produce a loss which no nation . . . . could stand a year." [5]

Of course it was not possible without offering a loan to determine precisely at what rates the government could sell its bonds; but the opponents of the bill believed that Mr.

---

[1] See the speeches of Mr. Lovejoy, p. 691; and Senators Cowan, p. 793, and Bayard, p. 796.

[2] See p. 48, above.

[3] *Congressional Globe*, 37th Cong., 2d Sess., Appendix, p. 56.

[4] *Ibid.*, p. 763.

[5] *Ibid.*, p. 689; *cf.* the remarks of Messrs. Edwards, p. 683, and Pike, p. 656.

Stevens and Mr. Spaulding exaggerated when they predicted that the price realized would range between 50 and 80.[1] Should a plan of finance based upon taxation heavy enough to inspire confidence in the management of the treasury be adopted, they were convinced that the government could secure loans without serious sacrifice.[2]   And further, their fiscal argument showed that an increase in the cost of the war would not be avoided by the rival plan of issuing an inconvertible paper currency.[3]

Still a third alternative was proposed by the opposition— the issue of treasury notes without the legal-tender quality. This suggestion was embodied in the three rival plans introduced into the House as substitutes for the bill.[4]   The discussion of their merits naturally elicited debate upon the efficacy of the legal-tender clause.   The supporters of the bill were ready enough with assertions of the importance of the clause to the success of the measure;[5] but they found it difficult to explain precisely what its value was.   One said, "By making these notes a legal tender we prevent the money sharks from robbing our soldiers of their hard earnings."[6]   Another argued that unless the United States notes were made a legal tender, the banks would seek to depreciate them in order to retain the field of circulation for their own issues.[7]   A third declared, "If we make the government issues a legal tender, the demand for specie will be so limited that they will maintain their value."[8]   Finally, Senator Sherman argued that the banks would not receive the government notes unless compelled to do so by the legal-tender clause, and that if not received by the banks as current funds

[1] Cf. Mr. Spaulding, Congressional Globe, 37th Cong., 2d Sess., p. 524.
[2] Cf. the remarks of Roscoe Conkling, p. 634, and of Senator Cowan, p. 793.
[3] P. 60, above.   [4] P. 75, below.
[5] E. g., Mr. Pike, Congressional Globe, 37th Cong., 2d Sess., p. 657.
[6] Mr. Blake, p. 686; cf. the similar remarks of Messrs. Edwards, p. 683, and Shellabarger, p. 690; Campbell, p. 687; and of Senator Henry Wilson, p. 788.
[7] Mr. Kellogg, p. 681.   [8] Mr. Campbell, p. 687.

the notes would become hopelessly depreciated.[1] In response
Senator Fessenden pointed to the clause authorizing the subtreasuries to receive the notes on deposit at 5 per cent.
interest. This clause would make discrimination against the
notes impracticable, he argued; for should the banks refuse
to receive notes as deposits they would lose business, because
the holders would prefer to deposit with the subtreasuries,
which would pay 5 per cent. interest instead of with banks.[2]

If these attempts to prove the utility of the legal-tender
clause seem rather weak, so do the criticisms urged by the
opposition. The advocates of the rival bills proposing to
issue treasury notes without the legal-tender quality might
have been expected to dwell upon the fact that their plans
left the standard of value undisturbed, and so avoided a
depreciation that would unsettle business, lower real wages,
defraud creditors, and increase the cost of all supplies government had to buy. Instead, they attempted only to show
that the legal-tender clause would impair faith in the paper
currency. "The fair inference is in the mind of every man,
however stupid," said Senator Cowan, "that you yourselves
first doubted the validity of it, and that, therefore, you
attempted to give it this quality of paying debts perforce,
to compensate it for the lack of essential value."[3]

From this review it is clear that the position of those who
urged the argument of necessity for the legal-tender bill in
Congress betrayed the lack of consistency noticed in Mr.
Spaulding's reply to the bank delegates.[4] When the opposition suggested that the wants of the treasury could be met
either by borrowing or by issuing treasury notes not a legal
tender, it was incumbent on those who mantained the position that the bill was "a measure not of choice but of neces-

---

[1] *Congressional Globe*, 37th Cong., 2d Sess., pp. 790, 791.   [2] *Ibid.*, p. 766.

[3] *Ibid.*, p. 792; *cf.* the remarks of Messrs. Crisfield, Appendix, p. 50; and of Senators Fessenden, p. 766; and Simmons, p. 794.

[4] P. 49, above.

sity" to deny the possibility of securing funds by these methods. But such a denial was not attempted. Instead they tried to show that the issue of an irredeemable paper currency was a better method of securing means than borrowing at a discount or issuing treasury notes not a legal tender. It is curious to note the naïveté with which the most strenuous promoters of the legal-tender bill asserted in one breath that it was a measure of sheer necessity, and in the next breath admitted the existence of alternatives. Mr. Spaulding himself said after emphasizing the necessity: "We have this alternative, either to go into the market and sell our bonds for what they will command, or to pass this bill."[1] And Thaddeus Stevens, who began by asserting the necessity, shifted, before concluding, to this position: "Here, then, in a few words lies your choice. Throw bonds at 6 or 7 per cent. on the market, ... or issue United States notes."[2] Obvious as is the contradiction, the opposition failed to call attention prominently to it. By thus allowing the logic of the argument from necessity to pass unchallenged, they left room for the impression to arise that the paper issues of the Civil War can hardly be made the subject of serious criticism, because "necessity knows no law."

But while Mr. Spaulding and his fellows were strenuous in protesting the necessity of the legal-tender act as a measure of immediate relief, they were careful to state that it was intended to be temporary, and not to inaugurate a regular paper-money policy. "When peace is secured," said Mr. Spaulding, "I will be among the first to advocate a speedy return to specie payments."[3] Fessenden dwelt on the point at length. He said:

[1] *Congressional Globe*, 37th Cong., 2d Sess., p. 524.

[2] *Ibid.*, p. 689; *cf.* the remarks of Mr. Blake, p. 686, and the divergent views as to the nature of the alleged necessity expressed by Mr. Hooper, p. 617, and by Senator Sherman, p. 791.

[3] *Ibid.*, p. 526. This promise was well kept. See the prefaces of SPAULDING's *History*.

The . . . . secretary of the treasury . . . . has declared that in his judgment [the bill] is, and ought to be, but a temporary measure, not to be resorted to as a policy, but simply on this single occasion, because the country is driven to the necessity of resorting to it. I have not heard anybody express a contrary opinion, or, at least, any man who has spoken on the subject in Congress. The chairman of the committee of Ways and Means, in advocating the measure, declared that it was not contemplated, and he did not believe it would be necessary, to issue more than the $150,000,000 of treasury notes made a legal tender provided by this bill. All the gentlemen who have spoken on the subject, and all pretty much who have written on the subject, except some wild speculators in currency, have declared that as a policy, it would be ruinous to any people ; and it has been defended, as I have stated, simply and solely upon the ground that it is to be a single measure, standing by itself, and not to be repeated.[1]

Similar and hardly less emphatic statements were made by other members of Congress.[2] If any one possessed such ideas of the beneficence of an irredeemable paper currency as afterward animated members of the Greenback party, he kept them to himself.

III.   ATTITUDE OF SECRETARY CHASE

In discussions of the financial policy pursued by the federal government the impression soon gained currency that the legal-tender acts were unavoidable necessities. This impression was deepened by the fact that when the unhappy consequences of the laws began to make themselves felt, members and friends of the administration took the ground that, however deplorable in its effects, such legislation had been inevitable from the beginning of the war.[3] After peace

---

[1] *Congressional Globe*, 37th Cong., 2d Sess., p. 764.

[2] *Cf.* remarks of Morrill, *ibid.*, p. 631 ; Pomeroy, p. 884.

[3] *Cf.* Lincoln's message to Congress, December 1, 1862, *Complete Works*, ed. NICOLAY AND HAY, Vol. II, p. 264; letters of Seward and Stanton in SPAULDING'S *History*, introduction to 2d ed., pp. 27, 29. A number of letters of like tenor from other men of prominence are given in Spaulding's Introduction and Appendices.

was restored this became the common doctrine of the Republican party. It is a very notable fact, however, that Secretary Chase — the one man most conversant with the financial situation of the government in the winter of 1861–62 — came afterward to the conclusion that the passage of the legal-tender bill was a blunder. His attitude toward the measure is worthy of careful attention.

Apparently the sudden suspension of specie payments bewildered Mr. Chase for a time. It seemed to make necessary a recasting of his financial program,[1] and for the moment he was at a loss what to do. The only man in official circles who had a definite plan in mind was Spaulding, and while others hesitated, he pushed forward the simple though crude expedient of issuing legal-tender notes most vigorously. All Chase's traditions and all his official utterances committed him to opposition. But not knowing precisely how to avoid the measure, he promoted the meeting between the bankers from New York, Boston, and Philadelphia, and the financial committees of House and Senate, in the hope that some feasible plan for raising funds without resort to legal-tender notes might be agreed upon.[2] His hopes were destroyed by the unwillingness of the Congressmen to consent to the sale of bonds at their market price — an unwillingness shared in some measure by most of the opponents of the legal-tender bill in Congress.[3] After this disappointment the secretary of the treasury appears to have surrendered the lead to the Committee of Ways and Means. He could formulate no plan which commanded the

---

[1] *Cf. Report of the Secretary of the Treasury*, December, 1862, p. 7.

[2] See sec. i of the present chapter.

[3] All of the substitutes for the legal-tender bill proposed in the House provided that the bonds to be issued should not be sold below par. See p. 75 below. There were few men who sympathized with Senator Cowan's vigorous declaration that he preferred a " shave of forty per cent." upon bonds to an inconvertible paper currency.—*Congressional Globe*, 37th Cong., 2d Sess., p. 793.

confidence of others, and so acquiesced unwillingly in what the energetic Mr. Spaulding proposed.[1]

When Spaulding sent him the legal-tender bill for revision, Chase returned it with a letter, dated January 22, expressing his exceeding regret that it was found necessary to resort to a legal-tender act, but expressing also his hearty desire " to co-operate with the committee [of Ways and Means]."[2] This letter was regarded by a majority of the committee as "non-committal on the legal-tender clause." So they sought and " after considerable delay " obtained a more explicit approval of the bill as a measure of necessity, part of which was read to Congress.[3]

Chase's feeling at this time is best indicated by the frank letter which he sent to Spaulding February 3:

Mr. Seward said to me on yesterday that you observed to him that my hesitation in coming up to the legal-tender proposition embarrassed you, and I am very sorry to observe it, for my anxious wish is to support you in all respects.

It is true that I came with reluctance to the conclusion that the legal-tender clause is a necessity, but I came to it decidedly, and I support it earnestly. I do not hesitate when I have made up my mind, however much regret I may feel over the necessity of the conclusion to which I come.[4]

It is clear from these letters that Spaulding and not Chase was the real financial leader in the critical months of January and February, 1862.[5] Spaulding's position was recognized by a colleague in the House, who referred to him as " the able and distinguished Representative who has

[1] It should be noted that Chase was daily receiving letters from business men whose views he was bound to consider, urging him to agree to the treasury-note bill. But a small minority of his correspondents seem to have stood out against the legal-tender clause.—Cf. HART, S. P. Chase, pp. 250, 251.

[2] SPAULDING, p. 27.

[3] Ibid., p. 45 and p. 62 above.

[4] SPAULDING, History, p. 59. Cf. Chase's letter of similar tenor written the next day to Bryant.—WARDEN, Life of Chase, p. 409.

[5] Cf. Chase's report of December, 1862, pp. 8, 9.

originated this measure and carried it triumphantly over the Administration and through Congress."[1]

But while harried by the unaccustomed perplexities of his position, Chase yielded to Spaulding and gave an official sanction to the bill, it did not commend itself to his calmer judgment. His later views are stated at length in a dissenting opinion which he rendered, as Chief Justice, upon the "Legal Tender Cases," in December, 1870. Of his own course as secretary of the treasury, he said:

He thought it indispensably necessary that the authority to issue these notes should be granted by Congress. The passage of the bill was delayed, if not jeoparded, by the difference of opinion which prevailed on the question of making them a legal tender. It was under these circumstances that he expressed the opinion, when called upon by the Committee on Ways and Means, that it was necessary. . . . . Examination and reflection under more propitious circumstances have satisfied him that this opinion was erroneous, and he does not hesitate to declare it. . . . . Was the making of the notes a legal tender necessary to the carrying on the war? In other words, was it necessary to the execution of the power to borrow money? . . . . If the notes would circulate as well without as with this quality it is idle to urge the plea of such necessity. But the circulation of the notes was amply provided for by making them receivable for all national taxes, all dues to the government, and all loans. This was the provision relied upon for the purpose by the secretary when the bill was first prepared, and his reflections since have convinced him that it was sufficient. . . . . In their legitimate use the notes are hurt, not helped, by being made a legal tender. The legal-tender quality is only valuable for purposes of dishonesty. Every honest purpose is answered as well and better without it.

We have no hesitation, therefore, in declaring our conviction that the making of these notes a legal tender, was not a necessary or proper means to the carrying on war or to the exercise of any express power of the government.[2]

[1] Mr. Pomeroy.—*Congressional Globe*, 37th Cong., 2d Sess., p. 884.
[2] 12 WALLACE, 576-9.

Competent critics have usually been inclined to accept Chase's later in preference to his earlier opinion. They have held that the treasury crisis which rendered the argument of necessity plausible need not have occurred had Congress adopted a more vigorous policy of taxation at its extra session in July and August, 1861. Tax laws then enacted might not have added greatly to the revenue before the close of the year, but they would have strengthened the credit of the government and so enabled it to borrow more freely and on better terms.

But though this failure to tax adequately was unfortunate, it was not unnatural. The secretary of the treasury, with whom the initiative rested, was inexperienced and was devoting a large part of his attention to military matters.[1] Moreover, the Union leaders feared that the temper of the North was not firm enough to submit cheerfully to the onerous burden of a heavy federal income tax or high internal duties. Such taxation had been unknown for more than a generation; the Republican party was young, composed of heterogenous elements not yet completely fused, and led by men not sustained by consciousness of unhesitating popular support. Realizing their dependence upon public opinion for success, it is not strange that Mr. Lincoln's administration hesitated to take steps likely from all precedent to prove unpopular.[2]

Perhaps even more important in explaining the failure to tax heavily at the outset of the war was the confident expectation of its early end. Even in February, 1862, Justin Morrill, one of the firmest opponents of the legal-tender clause, could say in rhetorical strain:

The ice that now chokes up the Mississippi is not more sure to melt and disappear with the approaching vernal season, than are

[1] *Cf.* HART, *S. P. Chase*, pp. 211–14.

[2] *Cf.* M. B. FIELD, *Memories of Many Men and of Some Women*, 1874, pp. 255, 278; HART, *op. cit.*, p. 237.

the rebellious armies upon its banks when our western army shall
break from its moorings, and, rushing with the current to the Gulf,
baptize as it goes in blood the people to a fresher allegiance. . . . .
We can close this war by the 30th day of July next as well as in
thirty years.[1]

Had such optimistic expectations been realized, Chase's plan
of raising by taxation means sufficient only for ordinary
expenditures, interest, and a sinking fund need have caused
no serious disorder in the finances.[2]

But, granting that a mistake was made in not levying
heavier taxes at the extra session of Congress, the question
still remains: Was the issue of legal-tender treasury notes
necessary to relieve the treasury from the embarrassments
existing in January and February, 1862? Certainly there
was no such pressing necessity as Spaulding, for example,
asserted in the first panic. His letter of January 8, quoted
above, declares that the government "will be out of means
to pay the daily expenses in *about thirty days.*"[3] But it
was forty-eight days before the legal-tender act was passed,
and over thirty-four days more before the first notes were
issued. None of the legal-tender notes were paid out until
April,[4] three months after the treasury had suspended specie
payments. Whatever were the immediate needs of the
treasury, then, they were supplied from other sources.[5] Had
these three months been utilized energetically in passing a

---

[1] *Congressional Globe*, 37th Cong., 2d Sess., p. 630. *Cf.* the similar remarks of
Fessenden, *ibid.*, p. 765, Chandler, p. 774, and Simmons, p. 794. The most impressive
evidence of confidence in an early peace, however, is the issue of General Order No.
33 by the adjutant general, April 3, 1862, stopping the enlistment of fresh troops.—
See RHODES, *History of the United States*, Vol. III, p. 636.

[2] *Cf.* Chase's discussion of the question in his report of December, 1863, pp. 10–12.

[3] SPAULDING, p. 17; *cf.* his opening speech in the House, *Congressional Globe*,
37th Cong., 2d Sess., p. 524.

[4] The New York *Times* of April 7, 1862, reports that "the first instalment of
United States notes . . . . was received at the subtreasury in this city Saturday
morning (April 5)." *Cf.* R. A. BAYLEY, *National Loans of the United States* (Washington, 1881), p. 157.

[5] See chap. iii, sec. i, p. 88, below.

few simple sections of an internal revenue tax act, imposing duties on whiskey, beer, and tobacco, and in organizing machinery for the sale of bonds, there seems to be slight reason for believing that the government would have failed to obtain sufficient funds, particularly when account is taken of the improvement of credit caused by the military successes of the winter and spring.[1]

After all, discussion of the "necessity" of the legal-tender act is rather beside the point. For no one, not even Stevens and Spaulding, denied the possibility of borrowing, provided the government was ready to sell its bonds at their market price. The real question is, was the making of United States notes a legal tender preferable to selling bonds at a discount? Upon this question the following chapters will throw some light by showing what were the consequences of the course pursued, both for the people and for the government.[2]

IV.   PASSAGE OF THE ACT

The debate upon the legal-tender act, a logical analysis of which has been presented in a preceding section, began in the House of Representatives January 28, 1862. Mr. Stevens and Mr. Spaulding pushed the measure vigor-

[1] *Cf.* Part II, chap. iii, sec. iii, below.

[2] On the question of necessity see SIMON NEWCOMB, *Critical Examination of Our Financial Policy* (New York, 1865), chap. vii; J. K. UPTON, *Money in Politics*, 2d ed. (Boston, 1895), p. 103; W. G. SUMNER, *History of American Currency* (New York, 1875), pp. 197–209; S. T. SPEAR, *The Legal-Tender Acts* (New York, 1875), chap. xii; F. W. TAUSSIG, p. 537 of *The United States of America*, ed. N. S. Shaler, Vol. II (New York, 1894); C. F. DORÉ, *Die Papier-währungswirthschaft der Union*, Berlin, 1877; C. VON HOCK, *Die Finanzen und die Finanzgeschichte der Vereinigten Staaten* (Stuttgart, 1867), pp. 471, 472; CHARLES A. MANN, *Paper Money the Root of Evil* (New York, 1872), pp. 147, 148; NICOLAY AND HAY, *A. Lincoln: A History* (New York, 1890), Vol. VI, chap. xi; GEORGE B. BUTLER, *The Currency Question*, New York, 1864; J. F. RHODES, *History of the United States*, Vol. III, pp. 556, 557; HUGH McCULLOCH, *Men and Measures of Half a Century* (New York, 1888), p. 175; HART, *S. P. Chase*, 1899, pp. 248–51; HENRY C. ADAMS, *Public Debts* (New York, 1887), pp. 126–33; HENRY ADAMS, "The Legal Tender Act," *Historical Essays*, New York, 1891; and especially DON C. BARRETT, "The Supposed Necessity of the Legal Tender Paper," *Quarterly Journal of Economics*, Vol. XVI, pp. 323–54.

ously. Three bills were proposed as substitutes by the
opposition. One, introduced by Mr. Vallandingham, provided (1) for the issue of $150,000,000 of treasury notes,
receivable for government dues, bearing no interest,
exchangeable for bonds, but not a legal tender; (2) for the
sale of $200,000,000 of 6 per cent., twenty-year bonds—at
rates not less than par.[1] A second, offered by Roscoe
Conkling, proposed (1) to sell $500,000,000 of 6 per cent.
twenty-year bonds at rates not less than the equivalent of
par for 7 per cent. stocks; (2) to allow the secretary of the
treasury at his discretion to issue $200,000,000 of one-year
treasury notes, either bearing no interest or interest at $2\frac{1}{2}$
per cent., and not legal tender, in place of an equivalent
amount of bonds.[2] Finally, Mr. Horton's and Mr. Morrill's
substitute, favored by one-half of the Committee of Ways
and Means, authorized (1) the issue of $100,000,000 treasury
notes, bearing interest at 3.65 per cent., receivable for government dues except duties on imports, exchangeable at par
for all bonds issued, and not a legal tender; (2) the sale of
$200,000,000 of 7.3 per cent., ten-year bonds, and of
$300,000,000 of 6 per cent., twenty-four-year bonds at
prices not less than par; (3) the payment of interest on the
bonds in coin.[3]

Nine days after the debate began a vote was taken on the
substitution of the third of these measures for the legal-
tender bill. It resulted 55 yeas to 95 nays.[4] Then the
vote was taken on the legal-tender bill itself, and it was
passed by 93 to 59—a majority of 34.[5] An analysis of the
vote upon the legal-tender clause shows that it was not a
strict party division. Of the 95 votes for the legal-tender

[1] Congressional Globe, 37th Cong., 2d Sess., p. 614.

[2] Ibid., p. 615.   [3] Ibid., p. 693; SPAULDING, pp. 92-4.

[4] Congressional Globe, 37th Cong., 2d Sess., p. 695; SPAULDING, p. 94.

[5] Congressional Globe, loc. cit.; SPAULDING, pp. 95, 96.

clause 8 were cast by Democrats and 3 by "old line Whigs."
With the 25 Democrats who voted against the clause were 7
"old line Whigs" and 23 Republicans. Nor is a marked
sectional division of the vote apparent. Of the members
from New England States 16 voted for and 11 against the
legal-tender clause; of the delegations from the Middle
States the corresponding votes were 36 and 18; of the
Southern States 7 and 10; of the Central States 27 and 13;
and of the Western States 9 and 3. The most noticeable
feature of the vote was the number and standing of the regular
supporters of the administration who on this occasion sided
with the opposition. Among them were Roscoe Conkling,
Justin S. Morrill, Valentine B. Horton, Edward H. Rollins,
Benjamin F. Thomas, and Owen Lovejoy.

As the bill went to the Senate, it provided for the issue
of $150,000,000 of United States legal-tender notes; but
of this sum $50,000,000 were intended to take the place
of the like sum of "old demand notes" authorized at the
extra session of Congress in July, 1861.[1] A very important amendment was made by the Senate finance committee.
In order to "raise and support the credit of the government
obligations," they proposed to pay the interest on the public
debt in coin. The committee had considered the advisa-
bility of making customs duties payable in specie to
obtain the coin necessary for interest; but they finally preferred to set aside the proceeds of sales of public lands,
confiscations of rebel property and import duties as a fund
to be used for the purpose. To provide for the possible
case when this fund would be insufficient, the secretary of
the treasury was authorized to sell bonds at their market
price to get coin.[2]

---

[1] For the text of the bill as it passed the House see SPAULDING, pp. 96–8.

[2] See Senator Fessenden's speech explaining the House bill and the committee's
amendments, *Congressional Globe*, 37th Cong., 2d Sess., p. 763.

In this modified form the bill passed the Senate by a vote as devoid of partisan or of sectional character as had been the vote in the House. A motion to strike out the legal-tender clause failed by a majority of 5—17 yeas to 22 nays.[1] Of the yeas nine were Republicans—Senators Anthony of Rhode Island, Collamer and Foot of Vermont, Fessenden of Maine, King of New York, Cowan of Pennsylvania, Foster of Connecticut, and Willey of Virginia. On the other hand, three Democrats—Senators McDougall of California, Rice of Minnesota, and Wilson of Missouri—voted for the clause. But when it was seen that the bill would pass, legal-tender clause and all, the final vote was 30 for and 7 against it.[2] Of the seven, three were Republicans, three Democrats, and one an "old line Whig."

The House refused to concur in the Senate amendment for the payment of interest on the public debt in coin. Mr. Spaulding declared that such an arrangement would create intolerable discrimination between different classes of government creditors. To pay the army in depreciated paper money and the money lender in coin was unjust to the soldier risking his life on the field of battle.[3] "It makes," said Mr. Stevens, "two classes of money — one for the banks and brokers, and another for the people."[4] Further, argued Mr. Hooper, the refusal to use United States notes for interest would be an admission in advance of a difference in value between paper and coin, the effect of which would be to discredit the government's issues.[5] Mr. Pomeroy replied first, that so far from exaggerating the depreciation of paper currency, the amendment would diminish it ; for coin interest would tend to increase the value of bonds and so indirectly of the notes which were to be exchangeable for bonds

[1] *Ibid.*, p. 800.   [2] *Ibid.*, p. 804.
[3] *Ibid.*, pp. 881–3.   [4] *Ibid.*, p. 900.
[5] *Ibid.*, p. 899.

at par; and second, that only by paying interest in coin could the government borrow on favorable terms.[1]

To terminate the disagreement conference committees were appointed — for the Senate, Fessenden, Sherman, and Carlisle;[2] for the House, Stevens, Horton, and Sedgwick[3] — and a compromise was agreed upon. Interest was to be paid in coin, but the method of obtaining the coin was changed. Instead of pledging receipts from customs, sales of public lands and confiscations, with an ultimate resort to selling bonds at the market price, it was decided to make import duties payable in specie.[4] Both Senate and House concurred in this change,[5] and the bill received the approval of President Lincoln, February 25, 1862.[6]

In its final form the act authorized the issue of $150,000,-000 of United States notes in denominations not less than five dollars. Fifty millions of this sum was in place of the "old demand notes," which were to be withdrawn as rapidly as practicable. The notes were declared to be "lawful money and a legal tender in payment of all debts, public and pri-

---

[1] *Congressional Globe*, 37th Cong., 2d Sess., p. 884; *cf.* similar arguments of Messrs. Morrill, p. 886, and C. B. Calvert, p. 886.

[2] *Ibid.*, p. 899.   [3] *Ibid.*, p. 909.

[4] Text of report, *ibid.*, p. 938.   [5] *Ibid.*, pp. 929 and 939 respectively.

[6] 12 *Statutes at Large*, p. 345. In the version of the financial history of the war later current with the greenback party, this limitation of the legal-tender quality of United States notes, by using coin for interest on the public debt and for customs dues, was represented as a serious blunder, marring the otherwise perfectly symmetrical paper-money system. *E.g.*, see G. F. WILSON, *A Practical Consideration of the Currency of the United States*, 1874, p. 5; PLINY FREEMAN, *Correspondence on National Finance*, 1875; H. C. BAIRD, *Money and Its Substitutes*, 1876, p. 14; PETER COOPER, *Political and Financial Opinions*, 1877, p. 9. Indeed, the charge was often more serious. It was said that the "conspiracy" of bank delegates who visited Washington in January, 1862, "corruptly or not" used their influence to induce the secretary of the treasury and the Senate to "mutilate" the House bill by inserting the "exception clause" limiting the full legal-tender power of the United States notes. See, *e. g.*, J. G. DREW, *Our Money Muss*, 1874; W. A. BERKEY, *The Money Question*, 1876, pp. 176–9; NEVAH, *The "Legal-Tender" Acts*, [date ?], pp. 3–7; JESSE HARPER, *Thirty Years' Conflict*, 1881, p. 13; HENRY S. FITCH, *Speech in the State Convention of the National Currency Party of California*, 1877, pp. 9–21; MRS. S. E. V. EMERY, *Seven Financial Conspiracies*, 1887, chap. ii. Thaddeus Stevens in a measure countenanced such views. See his speech of June 23, 1864, *Congressional Globe*, 38th Cong., 1st Sess., pp. 3212 ff.

vate, within the United States, except duties on imports and interest on the public debt," which were expressly made payable in coin. Further, the notes were exchangeable at any time in sums of fifty dollars or multiples of fifty for 6 per cent. five-twenty bonds, $500,000,000 of which were authorized by the second section. Sec. 4 provided that holders of the notes might deposit them with any designated depository of the United States, and receive 5 per cent. interest. But such deposits could not be made for less than thirty days and ten days' notice was required for withdrawal. The sum of these temporary deposits was limited to $25,000,-000. By sec. 5 the coin received from duties on imports was set apart as a special fund to be applied, first, to the payment in specie of interest on the public debt; second, to the purchase of 1 per cent. of the entire debt yearly to be set aside as a sinking fund; third, to the general expenses of the government, if any residue remained.

The attitude of the general public toward the legal-tender act was divided between doubt and hesitation on the part of a few who appreciated clearly the evils of an irredeemable paper currency, and cheerful acceptance on the part of those who felt that scruples, justifiable under ordinary circumstances should not be allowed to interfere with decisive action in the face of such a crisis. Organized opposition to the bill by the business community ceased with the failure of the bankers' convention. The opinions expressed by practical financiers showed marked diversity — a fact that was not without influence upon the fate of the bill in Congress. Senator Sumner said of the advice given by business men : "Some tell us that the legal tender will be most beneficent; others insist that it will be dishonorable and pernicious. Which shall we follow?"[1] On the other hand,

[1] *Congressional Globe*, 37th Cong., 2d Sess., p. 798; *cf.* remarks of Senator Fessenden, *ibid.*, p. 766.

Senator Henry Wilson received a letter signed by several Massachusetts firms of high standing, saying they did "not know a merchant in the city of Boston engaged in active business" who was not in favor of the legal-tender clause.[1] Of greater weight was the resolution adopted by the New York Chamber of Commerce that "the present financial condition of the government and of the country requires the immediate passage of the [legal-tender] bill."[2]   Mr. Stevens and Mr. Spaulding said that similar encouragement was received by the promoters of the bill from the boards of trade in Boston, Philadelphia, Buffalo, Cincinnati, Louisville, St. Louis, Chicago, and Milwaukee.[3]   "I have never known any measure," said Mr. Spaulding, "receive a more hearty approval from the people."[4]

Newspapers showed similar differences of opinion.   When the proposal was made to issue legal-tender treasury notes, the New York *Tribune* said, "We ponder and hesitate."[5] Mr. Greeley believed that "heavy taxing, light stealing, and hard fighting," would remove the alleged necessity for the bill,[6] and advocated "a stirring appeal to the people for a Patriotic Loan of Two or Three Hundred Millions."[7]   But by the middle of February he concluded that, "there has been so much delay and hesitation and vacillation, that it is possible that no other means of giving immediate relief to the Treasury now remains."[8]   He finally acquiesced with an ill grace in the enactment of the bill, and supported very vigorously the amendments of the Senate making interest payable in coin.[9]   More decided opposition to the legal-

[1] *Ibid.*, p. 789; *cf.* Senator Simmons, p. 794.

[2] *Proceedings of the Chamber of Commerce of the State of New York for the Year Ending December 31, 1862*, p. 12.

[3] *Congressional Globe*, 37th Cong., 2d Sess., pp. 900 and 882.   [4] *Ibid.*, p. 882.

[5] New York *Tribune*, January 13, 1862.   [6] *Ibid.*, January 22, 1862.

[7] *Ibid.*, February 1, 1862.   [8] *Ibid.*, February 10, 1862.

[9] *Ibid.*, February 18, 1862; *cf.* the issues of February 19 and 26.

tender clause was made by the New York *World*[1] and *Journal of Commerce*,[2] the Springfield (Mass.) *Republican*,[3] and the Boston *Daily Advertiser*.[4] On the other hand the New York *Herald* espoused the cause of the bill. With heavy taxation and the provision for exchanging notes for bonds, it thought the greatest depreciation could "not exceed 10 per cent. and that not before a lapse of two years"—especially not after the interest had been made payable in coin.[5] Somewhat similar was the attitude of the New York *Times*, which thought the legal-tender clause was necessary to protect the notes from bank competition and hostility;[6] of the Philadelphia *Press*, which regarded the issue of irredeemable paper as an unavoidable evil which it was "not manly to bemoan;"[7] of the New York *Commercial Advertiser*, which acquiesced "in the measure, as the best on the whole that could be done under the existing circumstances;"[8] of the *National Intelligencer* of Washington, which thought the measure would be of great assistance to the government provided the notes were fundable in bonds bearing interest in coin;[9] of the Boston *Post*, which advocated "a national issue of paper, *legal-tender*, as the best thing to be done under the circumstances;"[10] and of the Boston *Journal*, which declared that people who feared the bill would be a step toward an irredeemable currency were "too timid for the times."[11]

[1] *E. g.*, see the issues of January 6 and 10.

[2] Extract from the New York *Journal of Commerce*, reprinted in the Baltimore *Sun*, January 16, 1862.

[3] See the issues of January 7, 8, 15, 18, 21, 29, and of February 5, 8, and 18, 1862.

[4] See the issues of January 24, 28, and 31, and of February 5, 6, 11, 13, 17, and 22, 1862.

[5] See the issues of January 11, 20, 21, 23, 30, 31, and of February 5, 10, 13, and 15, 1862.

[6] See the issues of January 13, 16, 18, 22, 23, 27, 29, and of February 3, 5, 7, 10, 12, and 14, 1862.

[7] See the issues of January 18, February 8, 14, and 21, 1862.

[8] See the issues of February 7 and January 29, 1862.

[9] See the issues of January 11, 25, and of February 1 and 10, 1862.

[10] See the issues of January 14, 21, 28, and of February 1, 1862.

[11] See the issues of January 8 and of February 3 and 7, 1862.

CHAPTER III

THE SECOND LEGAL-TENDER ACT

I. *Government Finances January to June, 1862:*
Deficit in the Revenues — Existing Authority to Borrow — Second
Issue of Old Demand Notes — Temporary Loan — Certificates of
Indebtedness — Receipts, January to March — Relief Afforded by
Issues of Greenbacks — Small Amount of "Conversions" — Receipts
April to June — Position of Treasury, June 30, 1862.

II. *The Second Legal-Tender Act:*
Chase's Request for Second Issue of Greenbacks — Chandler's
Attempt to Forestall its Consideration—Debate in House and
Senate — Provisions of the Act.

III. *The Postage-Currency Act:*
Embarrassment of Treasury from Disappearance of Small Change
— Remedies Proposed by Chase — Passage of Postage Currency Act.

I. GOVERNMENT FINANCES JANUARY TO JUNE, 1862

"WITHIN sixty days," Justin Morrill had prophesied in
discussing the first legal-tender act, " we must have at least
twice the amount of notes which is proposed now." [1] His
prophecy was fulfilled, but not until double the time set had
elapsed.

During this interval between the first and second legal-
tender acts, Secretary Chase perforce depended mainly upon
loans. At the time of suspension "expenditures had
already reached an average of nearly a million and a quarter of dollars each secular day; while the revenue from all
sources hardly exceeded one-tenth of that sum." [2] In the

---

[1] *Congressional Globe*, 37th Cong., 2d Sess., p. 886. *Cf.* the similar predictions
cited in note 1, p. 58, above.

[2] *Report of the Secretary of the Treasury*, December, 1862, p. 7. The advocates of
the legal-tender bill in their anxiety to prove the necessity of the measure seem to
have exaggerated the expenses of government. January 28 Spaulding set the amount
at "more than $1,600,000" per day (*Congressional Globe*, 37th Cong., 2d Sess., p. 524), and
by February 6 Stevens declared daily expenditures had reached "about $2,000,000"
(*ibid.*, p. 687). But on June 7 Chase still put the sum at $1,000,000, with the admis-

82

quarter January to March the ordinary income of the government from customs, sales of public lands, and miscellaneous sources was hardly $15,000,000. Though in the next quarter the income from these sources increased $4,000,000 and was supplemented by the first receipts from the direct tax imposed the summer preceding, the total came to but $21,000,000.[1] This made total receipts for the six months of $36,000,000 from ordinary sources, while expenditures were probably between $325,000,000 and $350,000,000.[2] Of course the difference between these sums had to be borrowed.

When the banks and the treasury ceased paying in specie Chase found that his authority to borrow was confined practically to the loan acts passed at the summer session of Congress. These acts, it will be remembered, permitted the secretary to borrow $250,000,000 and to issue a variety of bonds and treasury notes as security.[3] Under this authority Mr. Chase had already arranged with the associated banks for three loans amounting to $150,000,000. $30,000,000 of the bank subscriptions, however, had not yet been paid into the treasury.[4] This balance formed his first immediate resource. His second was found in the fact that of the $50,000,000 of demand notes authorized, but $33,-500,000 had been issued.[5] This left a sum of $16,500,000 which he could pay out at once. Finally, after the funds

sion, however, that this amount would probably be exceeded in the near future (*H. R. Miscellaneous Document No. 81*, p. 2, 37th Cong., 2d Sess.). In fact, the daily expenses did not reach quite two millions a day even for the fiscal year of 1862-3. (*Cf. Report of the Secretary of the Treasury*, December, 1863, p. 29.)

[1] *Report of the Secretary of the Treasury*, December, 1862, p. 37.

[2] Expenditures — unlike receipts — are not given by quarters in the reports of the secretary of the treasury, except for the three months, July to September. The above figures are the result of a rough estimate made after considering the expenditures from July to September, 1861, the total for the fiscal year 1862, and the ratio of increase from 1862 to 1863.

[3] See chap. i, p. 17, above.   [4] *Ibid.*, p. 40, note.

[5] *Report of the Secretary of the Treasury*, December, 1862, p. 9.

obtained from the $150,000,000 bank loan and the $50,000,-
000 of demand notes had been exhausted, there still
remained $50,000,000 of the $250,000,000 which the secretary had been authorized to borrow. But this $50,000,000
was not for the moment available. For, though it could be
borrowed on either 7.30 three-year notes at par, or on 6
per cent. bonds at 89.3+, the equivalent of par for 7 per
cent. stocks, the sixes already issued were selling in the
market at 89 and the seven-thirties at 98.[1]

Under these circumstances Mr. Chase continued to draw
upon the banks from week to week until their last instalment
upon the $150,000,000 loan was paid on February 4.[2] At
the same time he issued demand notes freely, and also
persuaded a few government creditors much in need of
funds to accept 7.30 notes at par in satisfaction of their
claims.[3] But these resources were not adequate for the
needs of the treasury, and on February 7, the day after
the legal-tender bill had passed the House of Representatives, Chase was obliged to request authority to issue
another $10,000,000 of the demand notes to tide over the
time until the Senate could act upon the pending measure.[4]
The short bill which he sent with his letter was passed at
once by the Senate without debate or even reference to
committee, and on the following Monday it was acted upon
by the House with similar dispatch.[5]

Ten millions, however, was a small sum compared with
the needs of the treasury, and Chase found it necessary to
resort to various new devices to obtain additional means.

[1] See the table of prices of government stocks in the *American Annual Cyclopædia*, 1862, p. 474.

[2] Chap. i, p. 40, note, above.

[3] Thaddeus Stevens said in the House on February 6 that such issues of seven-
thirties had then reached about $10,000,000.—*Congressional Globe*, 37th Cong., 2d Sess.,
p. 687.

[4] See his letter to Fessenden, *ibid.*, p. 705.

[5] *Ibid.*, p. 726; 12 *Statutes at Large*, p. 338.

One plan that ultimately had marked success was suggested by Mr. John J. Cisco, the chief of the New York sub-treasury.[1] February 8 he published a notice stating that he had been "authorized by the Secretary of the Treasury to receive on deposit United States notes as a temporary loan" at 5 per cent. interest, with the condition that sums deposited could be withdrawn at any time after ten days' notice.[2] About $2,000,000 were deposited in this fashion within a fortnight; but Secretary Chase seems to have entertained some doubts of his authority to make such an arrangement, and accordingly he requested the Senate finance committee to insert an amendment in the legal-tender bill then in their hands granting him power to accept such deposits to an amount not exceeding $25,000,-000.[3] Senator Sherman and others demurred on the ground that if men could draw 5 per cent. interest on notes deposited but temporarily with the subtreasuries they would be slow to lock up their capital by funding notes in 6 per cent. bonds.[4] But after Fessenden and Chandler had explained that the secretary believed that the plan would induce banks to accept the notes more freely and that whatever sums were deposited would constitute a loan to the government at 5 per cent., the measure was finally passed by a vote of 21 to 18.[5] No objection was raised to the plan in the House, and with some minor changes the amendment was incorporated into the legal-tender act as sec. 4.[6]

[1] SCHUCKERS, *Life of Chase*, p. 269.

[2] See financial columns of the New York papers and the *Annual American Cyclopædia*, 1862, p. 454, for text of the notice. The object of this plan was at first rather to secure a readier acceptance of the old demand notes by the banks than to raise a loan at 5 per cent. *Cf.* Part II, chap. ii, sec. iii, below.

[3] *Congressional Globe*, 37th Cong., 2d Sess., p. 772.

[4] See the discussion of the amendment, *ibid.*, pp. 772, 773, 802, 803.

[5] *Ibid.*, p. 803.

[6] 12 *Statutes at Large*, p. 346.

The opportunity afforded by this measure of obtaining 5 per cent. interest on current funds proved very attractive to the banks. March 7 a meeting of the New York Clearing House Association voted to employ such certificates of deposit in payment of balances at the clearing house, and their agents arranged with Mr. Cisco to issue for the purpose certificates payable to the order of any bank in the association.[1] As the New York banks wished to take out $20,000,000 of these certificates, Mr. Chase saw that the $25,000,000 limit imposed by the act of February 25 would not allow him sufficient margin for similar issues in other cities. Consequently he asked the finance committee of the Senate to add an amendment raising the limit to $50,000,000 to the bill that had just been sent up by the House providing for the purchase of coin for interest on the public debt. This request was acceded to, though not without further objections from Senator Sherman, and the new limit was provided for by sec. 3 of the act which was approved March 17.[2] By the end of the month the treasury had received over $20,000,000 on account of the "temporary loan," as it was called, and had redeemed less than $1,500,000.[3]

Another shift for obtaining means was the issue of "certificates of indebtedness." During the winter a floating debt had been gradually accumulating, variously estimated

[1] *Bankers' Magazine*, Vol. XVI, pp. 809–11.

[2] 12 *Statutes at Large*, p. 370; *Congressional Globe*, 37th Cong., 2d Sess., pp. 1156, 1162–4, 1235.

[3] BAYLEY, *National Loans of the United States*, p. 158. The table compiled by Professor D. C. Barrett from Senator Chandler's speech of June 17, 1862, and published in the *Quarterly Journal of Economics*, Vol. XVI, p. 327, does not agree with Bayley's figures. According to Bayley's table the amount of the temporary loan outstanding March 31 was $18,876,404.43; according to Barrett the amount on April 1 was $12,227,-185. Chandler's figures, on which Barrett relies, are inconsistent — the totals do not agree with the several items. Perhaps the reason is that he includes in the totals the deposits received under Cisco's notice of February 8, before congressional authorization had been given to the temporary loan. Moreover, if his figures are for the end of the day they would include the notes deposited April 1, but these deposits could not have been a large sum, for the net increase that week was, according to Barrett, only $746,691.

at from $80,000,000 to $180,000,000.[1] Mr. Chase did not have sufficient ready money to pay even those creditors whose claims had been audited. As a measure of relief he requested authority to issue to creditors who might desire to receive them, certificates of indebtedness bearing 6 per cent. interest and payable in one year or earlier at the option of the government.[2] This request was granted by the prompt passage of the act of March 1.[3] March 17 authority was granted to issue such certificates in payment of disbursing officers' checks as well as in payment of audited accounts.[4] Army contractors and similar creditors found great relief in these provisions, for the delay in obtaining payment for supplies had interfered with their operations seriously, the more so because banks showed a disinclination to lend on their claims even after the claims had been approved by the treasury. Under the new system contractors could at any time obtain 6 per cent. obligations of government which could be sold in the market at a slight discount, or used as first-class collateral in securing loans from a bank.[5]

By these various shifts Mr. Chase obtained means sufficient to tide the treasury over the trying quarter between suspension of specie payments and the time when the resources provided by the legal-tender act became available. The following brief recapitulation may give a clearer idea of the situation. Against expenses of perhaps $112,500,000 to $137,500,000 the ordinary receipts were:

[1] January 16 the financial column of the New York *Herald* gave $80,000,000 as the current estimate. January 28, Spaulding put the floating debt at $100,000,000 (*Congressional Globe*, 37th Cong., 2d Sess., p. 523); February 6 Stevens declared it to be $180,000,000 (*ibid.*, p. 687).

[2] *Congressional Globe*, 37th Cong., 2d Sess., pp. 945, 954, 955.

[3] 12 *Statutes at Large*, p. 352.

[4] *Ibid.*, p. 370.

[5] *Cf. Annual American Cyclopædia*, 1862, p. 456.

From customs - - - - - - -	$14,618,558.44
From sales of public lands - - - - -	27,019.74
From miscellaneous sources (estimated) - -	232,946.91

$14,878,525.09

Meanwhile the issues of government securities were:

Oregon war debt - - - - - -	$ 297,000.00
6 per cent. twenty-year bonds - - - -	20,374,753.43
7.30 three-year notes - - - - - -	11,170,598.24
Old demand notes - - - - - - -	25,900,000.00
Temporary loan (less withdrawals) - - -	18,876,404.43
Certificates of indebtedness - - - - -	5,629.000.00

[1]$81,247,756.10

The operations of the next three months, April to June, require less notice because no new measures were adopted. There was an increase of about one-half in ordinary receipts, but it was still necessary to borrow about nine-tenths of the funds required. In borrowing Secretary Chase made use of all the resources employed the quarter before except the issue of 6 per cent. twenty-year bonds. On the other hand he was able to employ also the means provided by the legal-tender act. He did this chiefly by paying out the new legal-tender notes which differed from the "old demand notes" in not being receivable for duties. Of these new notes — which were almost immediately christened the "greenbacks" — $99,500,000 were issued by the end of June.

The other grand resource provided by the legal-tender act proved for the time being a vain reliance. An issue of

[1] For the revenues of the quarter see *Report of the Secretary of the Treasury*, December, 1862, p. 37. The receipts from miscellaneous sources are taken as a quarter of the amount for the whole year. The issues of securities are compiled from BAYLEY, *National Loans of the United States*. The Oregon war issues were authorized by the act of March 2, 1861 (12 *Statutes at Large*, p. 198), for the payment of expenses incurred by Oregon and Washington during the Indian troubles of 1855 and 1856. All of the 6 per cent. bonds and about $2,500,000 of the seven-thirties were issued to the associated banks for the loans negotiated before suspension.

$500,000,000 of 6 per cent. bonds had been authorized —
called "five-twenties" from the fact that they were redeemable after five and payable after twenty years — and it
had been provided that the legal-tender notes might be
exchanged for these bonds at the desire of the holders.[1]
Much had been hoped from this "funding provision" by
the supporters of the bill. Thaddeus Stevens expressed
their theory most concisely:

My distinguished colleague from Vermont [referring to Justin
Morrill] fears that enormous issues [of legal-tender notes] would
follow to supply the expenses of the war. I do not think any more
would be needed than the $150,000,000. The notes bear no interest.
No one would seek them for investment. . . . . This money would
soon lodge in large quantities with the capitalists and banks. . . . .
Where could they invest it? In United States loans at 6 per cent.,
redeemable in gold in twenty years, the best and most valuable
permanent investment that could be desired. The Government
would thus again possess such notes in exchange for bonds, and
again re-issue them. I have no doubt that the $500,000,000 of
bonds authorized would be absorbed in less time than would be
needed by Government; and thus $150,000,000 would do the work
of $500,000,000 of bonds. When further loans are wanted you
need only authorize the sale of more bonds; the same $150,000,000
of notes will be ready to take them.[2]

Experience proved that such expectations as Mr. Stevens
indulged were far too sanguine. While the government was
in the midst of an enormously expensive war of which the
end could not be foreseen, its credit was not high enough to
make men desire its 6 per cent. coin interest bonds on the
conditions permitted by the first legal-tender act. Consequently conversions of greenbacks into bonds were slow —
less than $14,000,000 of the five-twenties were disposed of
in the first three months after they were ready for issue.[3]

[1] Sec. 2, 12 *Statutes at Large*, p. 345.
[2] *Congressional Globe*, 37th Cong., 2d Sess., p. 688. *Cf.* the remarks of Spaulding,
ibid., p. 526; Sherman, p. 791; and Pomeroy, p. 884.
[3] BAYLEY, *National Loans of the United States*, p. 156.

Instead of its being necessary, as Mr. Stevens forecast in February, to issue more bonds to take up the legal-tender notes constantly offered for conversion, it became necessary to issue more greenbacks to compensate for the small demand for bonds.[1]

The treasury operations for the quarter April to June may best be presented in a summary like the one given above for January to March.

RECEIPTS FROM ORDINARY SOURCES

From customs - - - - - - -	$18,930,170.16
From sales of public lands - - - - -	49,558.54
From miscellaneous sources (estimated) - -	232,946.91
From direct tax - - - - - - -	1,795,331.73
	$21,008,007.34

ISSUES OF GOVERNMENT SECURITIES

Oregon war debt - - - - - -	$ 198,850.00
6 per cent. twenty-year bonds - - - -	
7.30 three-year notes - - - - -	13,997,936.64
Old demand notes - - - - - -	30,000.00
Temporary loan (less withdrawals) - - -	39,049,712.14
Certificates of indebtedness - - - - -	44,252,979.73
	$97,529,478.51
Legal-tender notes (greenbacks) - - - -	98,620,000.00
Five-twenties of 1862 - - - - -	13,845,500.00
	[2] $209,994,978.51

The free issue of greenbacks put the treasury by the end of the quarter in a very much better position than it had been in at the beginning. The floating debt that had accumulated during the preceding three months was all cleared away and current expenses were paid promptly. On July 1, said Mr. Chase in his December report:

[1] For the subsequent history of the "conversion" scheme, see chap. iv, pp. 104, 107, 108, 115, 116, below.

[2] For authorities see above, p. 88, note.

Not a single requisition from any department upon the treasury remained unanswered. Every audited and settled claim on the government, and every quartermaster's check for supplies furnished, which had reached the treasury, had been met. And there remained in the treasury a balance of $13,043,546.81.[1]

II. THE SECOND LEGAL-TENDER ACT

While it is true, as has just been shown, that the treasury worked into comfortable condition during the quarter April to June, 1862, and possessed abundant funds to meet all current demands, Mr. Chase foresaw that this pleasant situation could not continue long without further grants from Congress. The credit was due in large measure to the rapid issues of greenbacks, and when the whole amount of these notes authorized by the act of February, 1865, had been put into circulation stringency would recur. This matter he called to the attention of Congress by a letter written June 7 to Thaddeus Stevens, chairman of the Committee of Ways and Means.[2]

According to the terms of the first legal-tender act, he reminded Congress, $150,000,000 of United States notes might be issued, but $60,000,000 of this sum must be used to replace the old demand notes authorized by the acts of July 17, 1861, and February 12, 1862. The new issues, therefore, were confined to $90,000,000. This limit, he said, had already been reached, and accordingly further issues could be made only as equal sums of the old notes were retired. Moreover, no more temporary deposits could be received, because the amount on hand had reached $50,000,-000 — the full sum authorized by Congress — despite a reduction in the rate of interest from 5 to 4 per cent. Thus the only available resources were receipts from customs, and

[1] *Report of the Secretary of the Treasury*, December, 1862, p. 10.

[2] *H. R. Miscellaneous Document No. 81*, 37th Cong., 2d Sess. The date of the letter as given by this document is April 7, but this is an error of the press. See the remarks of Mr. Stevens, *Congressional Globe*, 37th Cong., 2d Sess., p. 2768.

sales of five-twenty bonds for greenbacks, or "conversions." But these resources were far from adequate to meet the expenditures.

No safe reliance [said Mr. Chase] can be placed on conversions so far as experience has afforded any grounds of estimate, for more than $150,000 daily; and the daily average revenue from customs, during the past month, has been about $230,000.

The aggregate daily receipts from both these sources, therefore, cannot be estimated at more than $380,000, and may very possibly fall short of that sum; while the average daily expenditure cannot be estimated at less than $1,000,000, and will, probably, unless very considerable retrenchments are made, exceed that sum.

To meet the deficit the secretary proposed two measures: first, the "removal of the restriction upon temporary deposits;" second, the issue of another $150,000,000 of legal-tender notes. The first measure would enable him to take full advantage of the disposition of business men to lend their means to the government temporarily at a low rate of interest. Mr. Chase thought that not less than $30,000,000 would be added at 4 per cent. to the $50,000,000 of deposits already received. To provide for the prompt redemption of such of these deposits as were withdrawn, he proposed that a reserve of $33\frac{1}{3}$ per cent. be provided out of the new issues of greenbacks.

Another suggestion, indicative of the state into which the circulating medium of the country had already fallen, was that $25,000,000 of the new United States notes should be of denominations less than five dollars.

Payments to public creditors, and especially to soldiers [Mr. Chase said in explanation], now require large amounts of coin to satisfy fractional demands less than five dollars. Great inconveniences in payment of the troops are thus occasioned. With every effort on the part of the treasury to provide the necessary amount of coin, it is found impracticable always to satisfy the demand. When the amount required is furnished, the temptation to disbursing officers to exchange it for any small bank notes that the soldiers or the public creditors will take, is too great to be always resisted. And even when the coin reaches the creditors it is seldom held, but passes, in general, immediately into the hands of sutlers and others, and disappears at once from circulation.[1]

With this letter Mr. Chase sent a bill embodying his recommendations. "The condition of the treasury," he said, in conclusion, " renders prompt action highly desirable."

This communication was laid before the House June 11. The request for a second issue of legal-tender notes immediately alarmed the opponents of paper money. With the hope of preventing its consideration, Senator Chandler, of Michigan, introduced a resolution: "That the amount of legal tender treasury notes already authorized by law, shall never be increased." [2] Speaking in support of this resolution he said that the effect which the passage of a second legal-tender bill would have was shown by the fact that the mere publication of Secretary Chase's request, " without any action of Congress on the subject, has created such a panic, and has so convinced the money center of the world that we are to be flooded with this paper, that gold has risen in price from $2\frac{3}{4}$ to 7 per cent. premium." If full use were made of other resources, he continued, the disastrous consequences of fresh paper money emissions could be avoided. By paying 5 per cent. interest an indefinitely large sum could be obtained on temporary deposit and the lagging conversions of greenbacks into bonds could be stimulated by an appeal to the patriotism of the people.[3]

Senator Fessenden, chairman of the finance committee, replied in a moderate vein. Reliance upon temporary deposits, he pointed out, would be very hazardous, because if any severe shocks occurred to the credit of the government, large sums might be withdrawn within a few days,

[1] *Cf.* Part II, chap. ii, sec. iv, below.
[2] *Congressional Globe*, 37th Cong., 2d Sess., p. 2746.   [3] *Ibid.*, pp. 2774, 2775.

and Mr. Chase be left without funds. He regretted that
the secretary had found it necessary to request the issue of
more notes, and he was not convinced that such a course
would be wise. But until the secretary's reasons were fully
known he thought it would be wrong to resolve not to grant
his request. Therefore, he moved that the resolution be
referred to his committee for consideration. This was done,
and nothing more was heard of the matter by the Senate.[1]

Meanwhile Mr. Chase's bill was introduced into the
House.[2] As before, Mr. Spaulding fathered the measure.
The tone of the debate was quite different from that upon
the first legal-tender act. The advocates of paper money
spoke in a less apologetic tone, boldly assuming the
offensive. The first experiment, they held, had demonstrated the wisdom of their policy. Mr. Spaulding declared
that the act of February 25 had " worked well," and had
"exceeded the most sanguine expectations of its warmest
advocates."[3] Some members who had voted against the
first bill were won over by such claims to vote for the
second. Senator Simmons, for instance, said the first issue
" has given great practical relief to the country, and inasmuch as it has done so, I . . . . give my consent to authorize a further issue."[4] Other members agreed to the bill
because of the hopelessness of opposition. Owen Lovejoy,
who had spoken vigorously against the bill in February,
explained that he still thought the policy pernicious but that
he would not "persist in any factious opposition to what is
a foregone conclusion."[5] On the other hand, there were
members who had voted for the first bill as a measure of

---

[1] *Congressional Globe*, 37th Cong., 2d Sess., pp. 2774, 2775.

[2] *Ibid.*, p. 2665. The bill as reported from the Committee of Ways and Means
differed from the bill submitted by Chase in not authorizing the issue of notes less
than five dollars. See the text, p. 2766.

[3] *Ibid.*, p. 2766. *Cf.* on the other side Mr. Sheffield, p. 2888.

[4] *Ibid.*, p. 3077.   [5] *Ibid.*, p. 2885.

temporary necessity, but who opposed the second on the ground that it inaugurated a regular policy of depending on inconvertible paper.[1] Thus the character both of the support and of the opposition shifted somewhat.

In the debate one point especially received relatively more attention than in February. Mr. Hooper based his argument for the bill on the country's need of a currency of uniform value. It was a question, said he, between bank notes and government notes, and he preferred the latter.[2] "If anybody," said Mr. Lovejoy, "is to have the advantage of a depreciated currency—the advantage, in other words, of not paying interest on what they [sic] owe—I say let the government have that advantage; and let the bankers share with the rest of us."[3] In order to secure this advantage to the government, Senator Sherman proposed an amendment to the bill imposing a tax upon bank notes.[4]

But it was again the argument of necessity that did duty as the chief reason for the bill. In opening the debate Mr. Spaulding reiterated it explicitly. "The ground upon which the secretary of the treasury, and upon which the Committee of Ways and Means, rest this issue of notes," he said, "is the necessity of the case."[5] By the opposition the alleged necessity was once again emphatically denied. Mr. Pomeroy made an elaborate attempt to show that Secretary Chase had underestimated the probable receipts of the government, and that the daily deficit instead of being $620,-000 was only $166,166.[6] Mr. Pike, who had voted for the

---

[1] Cf. the remarks of Mr. Pike, ibid., p. 2798, and Senator Davis, p. 3078.

[2] Ibid., p. 2882.   [3] Ibid., p. 2885.

[4] Ibid., pp. 3071, 3072. This proposition was opposed by Senators Collamer, p. 3073; Simmons, pp. 3076, 3077; and Davis, p. 3078.

[5] Ibid., p. 2768. Cf. remarks of Messrs. Baily, ibid., Appendix, p. 298; and Edwards, ibid., p. 2888.

[6] Mr. Pomeroy estimated "conversions" at $275,000 instead of $150,000 daily, and further added $333,000 per day as the expected receipts from the internal revenue act then just enacted.—Ibid., p. 2797. As a matter of fact this act yielded about $103,000 instead of $333,000 daily in the fiscal year, 1863.—Report of the Secretary of the Treasury, 1863, p. 28.

first bill on the ground of necessity, refused to vote for
the pending measure, which could be advocated only upon
"the mere ground of convenience."[1]   And Mr. Morrill
declared that after the recent victories of the federal armies
and the passage of the tax bill there was not only no necessity, but no excuse, for the issue of more paper.[2]

Nor were these gentlemen who denied the necessity at a
loss for an alternative. "The true policy," said Mr. Morrill,
"is to put upon the market the small amount which will be
required . . . . in the bonds of the Government, at whatever they would bring."[3]   Mr. Sheffield concluded his
speech by saying : "I am persuaded that it would be far
better for the people of the country to sell bonds at a large
discount than to further disturb the relation between price
and value by a further issue of these notes."[4]   Mr. Horton
put these suggestions into formal shape by presenting, as a
substitute for the bill, a measure authorizing the secretary
of the treasury to borrow $100,000,000 on 6 per cent.,
twenty-five year bonds.[5]

As in the first debate, the supporters of the bill implicitly
gave away the argument of necessity in the answer made to
the proposal of borrowing.   Instead of showing that it was
impracticable to sell bonds, they responded that, as a method
of securing revenue, it was better to issue inconvertible paper
money than to borrow below par. "When money can be
obtained at par on six per cent. bonds," said Mr. Spaulding,
"I would prefer to have that done to the issuing a very
large amount of legal tender notes."[6]   Mr. Edwards followed suit, "I would gladly give my consent," said he, "to
. . . . the sale of bonds . . . . if I were assured those
bonds could be sold at par."[7]

[1] *Congressional Globe*, 37th Cong., 2d Sess., p. 2798.
[2] *Ibid.*, p. 2885.   See also Mr. Baker, *ibid.*, p. 2881.
[3] *Ibid.*, p. 2885.   [4] *Ibid.*, p. 2888.   [5] *Ibid.*, p. 2794.   [6] *Ibid.*, p. 2767.
[7] *Ibid.*, p. 2888.   *Cf.* on the other side Mr. Pomeroy, *ibid.*, p. 2796.

The legal-tender debate in June and July was by no means so exhaustive as had been the debate in January and February. Apparently members felt it would be a fruitless waste of time to discuss again the questions debated at such length five months before. An attempt was made, however, to learn whether this was the last issue that would be asked for. Mr. Stevens, the chairman of the Committee of Ways and Means, to whom the question was put, replied frankly that he did not know where the issues would stop.[1] To offset this damaging admission the supporters of the bill praised the paper currency,[2] and asserted that there was no reason why a new issue should increase depreciation.[3]

The measure came to a vote in the House June 24. It passed by 76 yeas to 47 nays. Of those who voted in the affirmative five had opposed the legal-tender clause in the first act. On the contrary, of the nays, seven had supported the legal-tender clause in February. The large majority of members, however, voted upon the second act as they had upon the first. The yeas included four Democrats and the nays fifteen Republicans, so that the division was not a party vote.[4]

In the Senate the vote was 22 to 13. Four senators voted for the bill who had opposed the legal-tender clause of the first act, and three senators — John Sherman among them — who had supported the first act opposed the second. Twenty-one Republicans voted in the affirmative and nine in the negative. Of the four democratic votes one was in favor of the bill. As in the case of the first act the vote was devoid of sectional and of party character.[5]

---

[1] *Ibid.*, p. 2886.

[2] Mr. Spaulding, *e. g.*, said the act of February 25, 1862, "had given the country a sound national currency, in which the people have had entire confidence."—*Ibid.*, p. 2767.

[3] Mr. Hooper said he had "no apprehension of any depreciation of the currency being produced by the passage of the bill."—*Ibid.*, p. 2883.

[4] *Ibid.*, p. 2903.   [5] *Ibid.*, p. 3079.

President Lincoln approved the second legal-tender act
July 11, 1862.   The law authorized the issue of $150,-
000,000 United States notes.   In addition the limit upon
the amount of temporary deposits that might be received
was raised from $50,000,000 to $100,000,000.   In order to
provide for the prompt payment of these deposits the
secretary was directed to retain as a reserve fund not less
than $50,000,000 of the newly authorized notes.[1]

<h3 style="text-align:center">III.   THE POSTAGE CURRENCY ACT</h3>

It has been seen that Secretary Chase's letter requesting
authority for a second issue of greenbacks referred to the
difficulty experienced by disbursing officers in making
change for sums of less than $5.   To relieve this difficulty
it was provided in the act of July 11 that $35,000,000 of
the new issues should be of lower denominations than $5,
but it was also provided that no note should "be issued for
the fractional part of a dollar."[2]

Hardly had this act been approved by President Lincoln
when Mr. Chase found it necessary to request authority to
use paper money, not only in payments of one and two dollars, but also in payments of 50, 25, and even 10 cents.
July 14 he wrote a letter to Thaddeus Stevens, saying:

> The depreciation of the currency, resulting, in great measure,
> from the unrestricted issues of non-specie-paying banks and
> unauthorized associations and persons, causes the rapid disappear-
> ance from circulation of small coins.   To supply the want of these
> coins, tokens and checks for sums less than one dollar are being
> issued by hotels, business houses, and dealers generally; and the
> most serious inconveniences and evils are apprehended unless
> these issues can be checked and the small coins of the Government
> kept in circulation, or a substitute provided.[3]

[1] 12 *Statutes at Large*, p. 532.   [2] *Ibid., loc. cit.*

[3] *Congressional Globe*, 37th Cong., 2d Sess., p. 3405.   On the disappearance of
subsidiary silver from circulation see Part II, chap. ii, sec. iv, below.

Chase proposed two methods of meeting this situation. One was to diminish the weight of the subsidiary coins to such a point that as bullion they would be worth less than their face value as money; the other was to authorize the use of postage and other stamps in payments of fractional parts of a dollar. For the convenience of the Committee of Ways and Means the secretary submitted two bills embodying these suggestions. The second expedient seemed preferable to the committee, and accordingly the bill providing for the use of stamps as currency was introduced by Mr. Hooper July 17 and passed at once by a vote of 62 to 40, with no debate aside from an objection raised on constitutional grounds against the clause forbidding the issue of small notes by state banks.[1] The Senate passed the bill the same day without debate or division,[2] and President Lincoln signed it before night.

The act directed the secretary of the treasury "to furnish to the Assistant Treasurers, and such designated depositaries of the United States as may be by him selected, in such sums as he may deem expedient, the postage and other stamps of the United States, to be exchanged by them, on application, for United States notes."

Such stamps were not made a legal tender between individuals, but their currency was assured by providing that they should be receivable in payment of all dues to the United States less than $5, and that they should be redeemed in greenbacks on demand by the treasury officials. The second section forbade any "private corporation, banking association, firm, or individual" to put in circulation notes or tokens of any character for sums less than a dollar.[3]

[1] *Congressional Globe*, 37th Cong., 2d Sess., pp. 3405, 3406.

[2] *Ibid.*, p. 3402.

[3] 12 *Statutes at Large*, p. 592. On the authorization of fractional currency to take the place of postage currency, see Part I, chap. iv, p. 118, below. On the circulation of both these forms of small change see Part II, chap. ii, sec. iv.

CHAPTER IV

THE THIRD LEGAL-TENDER ACT

I. THE FINANCES FROM JUNE TO DECEMBER, 1862

On July 1, 1862, the beginning of the new fiscal year, the treasury was in easy circumstances, as has been shown. All audited claims had been met, and there was a balance of $13,000,000 on hand.[1] But in the next quarter the treasury began to run behind again. The futile ending of McClellan's campaign in the Peninsula, from which so much had been hoped, showed that the end of the war was not at hand, and on July 1 President Lincoln issued a call for 300,000 additional troops.[2] Enlarging the army of course promised an increase of demands on the treasury. During the quarter July to September, however, the warrants drawn against the treasurer for other purposes than payment of the public debt were slightly less than the quarterly average for the fiscal year 1862 had been — viz., $111,000,000 as compared with $119,000,000.[3] But at the

[1] Pp. 90, 91, above.

[2] *Complete Works*, ed. NICOLAY AND HAY, Vol. II, pp. 194, 195.

[3] See the statements of expenditures in the *Report of the Secretary of the Treasury*, December, 1862, pp. 41, 43.

same time some $45,500,000 more had to be used in redeeming old demand notes, greenbacks, certificates of indebtedness and certificates of deposits.[1]

To help in meeting these total expenditures of $156,-500,000 there was a slight increase in the receipts from taxation and miscellaneous sources. This revenue rose from about $21,000,000 in the preceding quarter, to $24,000,-000.[2] For the rest Mr. Chase had to borrow. As conversions of greenbacks into five-twenty bonds amounted to but $2,500,000, he relied mainly on issues of greenbacks and various short-time obligations.[3] Altogether he succeeded in obtaining $114,500,000 from loans, but the necessity of paying $45,500,000 of the principal of the debt reduced the net increase of means from loans to $69,000,000. This sum, with the receipts from ordinary sources, gave the secretary $93,000,000 to meet warrants of $111,000,000.[4] The difference between these sums swallowed up the balance of $13,000,000 on hand July 1 and left an accumulation of unpaid warrants amounting to $5,000,000.

Unpromising as the situation of the treasury was at the end of September, it became worse during October and November. The increase of the army began to be felt by the treasury. The expenditures during these two months other than those for payment of debt were almost as great as the total for the three months preceding—viz., $109,000,000 as compared with $111,000,000.[5] Mr. Chase was not able to raise money fast enough to meet these expenses, and though he borrowed $85,500,000,[6] the accumulation of unpaid requisitions at the end of November reached $48,000,000.[7]

---

[1] *Ibid.*, p. 43.

[2] *Ibid.*, pp. 37, 43.

[3] $3,500,000 of seven-thirty notes, $72,500,000 of greenbacks, $12,000,000 of certificates of indebtedness and $23,000,000 of certificates of deposit were issued.—*Ibid.*, p. 43.

[4] Exclusive of payments of the principal of the debt.

[5] *Ibid.*, p. 10.   [6] *Ibid.*, p. 3.   [7] *Ibid.*, p. 10.

When the secretary prepared his annual report to Congress early in December, he estimated that the expenditures for the remainder of the fiscal year would be $485,000,000. The addition of the $48,000,000 of accumulated floating debt made the total to be provided $533,000,000. Against this sum Mr. Chase expected to receive $125,000,000 from taxes of all kinds and miscellaneous sources. This left $408,000,000 to be raised from loans. Under existing laws the secretary expected to secure $27,000,000 from issues of greenbacks, $36,000,000 from postage currency, $13,000,000 from certificates of indebtedness, and $20,000,000 from temporary deposits. These sums, with an estimated sale of five-twenty bonds amounting to $35,000,000, made a total of $131,000,000; which, subtracted from the $408,000,000 to be borrowed, left loans of $277,000,000 to be provided for by new legislation.[1]

In discussing how this sum should be procured Secretary Chase took emphatic ground against any considerable increase in the emission of greenbacks:

[1] *Report of the Secretary of the Treasury*, December, 1862, pp. 3-5, 11, 12. The figures in the report give estimated receipts and expenditures for the whole fiscal year, while the figures above are confined to the months December, 1862, to July, 1863. In obtaining the latter figures from the former it is necessary to cast out the expenses actually paid from July to November. This can be done with certainty for the months July to September because a full statement is given of the receipts and expenditures of that quarter. But for October and November the statements show only receipts from loans ($86,000,000), and expenditures for objects other than payment of the principal of the debt ($109,000,-000). It is, therefore, necessary to estimate the receipts from ordinary sources and the amount paid on the principal of the debt. Such an estimate is not difficult to make, because the figures actually given show that the latter sum exceeded the former by $20,000,000. The difference between the stated expenditures and receipts is $23,000,000. But it is also stated that the accumulation of unpaid requisitions rose from $5,000,000 at the end of September to $48,000,000 at the end of November. Since the treasury thus fell behind $43,000,000 on all expenditures and only $23,000,000 on stated expenditures it must have been because expenditures not stated exceeded receipts not stated by $20,000,000. With this guide and that afforded by the figures for the quarter July to September, I have estimated the receipts from customs, etc., during October and November at $18,000,000 and the payments on the principal of the debt at $38,000,000. The figures for the amounts to be borrowed given in the text, however, agree with those in the secretary's report and are not affected by any inaccuracy of these guesses, for, if the estimated receipts from taxation are too small they are compensated for by correspondingly deficient estimates of expenditure on the principal of the debt.

The easiest mode [of obtaining the $277,000,000] doubtless would be an issue of the required amount in United States notes; but such an issue, especially in the absence of proper restrictions on corporate circulation, would, in the judgment of the Secretary, be as injurious as it would be easy. The addition of so vast a volume to the existing circulation would convert a currency, of which the benefits have thus far greatly outweighed the inconveniences, into a positive calamity. Its consequences would be inflation of prices, increase of expenditures, augmentation of debt, and ultimately, disastrous defeat of the very purposes sought to be attained by it.[1]

While the secretary thus opposed further issues of greenbacks, he had no suggestions to make of increased taxation. Instead, he proposed to secure the additional $277,000,000 solely by borrowing. In order to facilitate the negotiation of loans as well as to provide a better currency, he urged again upon Congress the plan proposed in his report of the year before for reorganizing the banking system. Banks that desired to issue circulating notes were to be required to purchase United States bonds to be held as security. This plan, he thought, would make a market for not less than $250,000,000 of bonds "within a very few years."[2] Moreover, the steady sale of bonds to banks would strengthen the credit of the government and enable it to borrow from others on better terms.[3]

If reliance were to be placed upon loans, the question as to what form of security had best be offered became important. Mr. Chase opposed any increase beyond five years in the length of time that bonds should run before they became redeemable, and any increase in the rate of interest beyond 6 per cent. As an alternative he preferred the issue of 7.30 three-year notes, "convertible into five-twenty sixes at or before maturity, and of smaller notes bearing an interest of 3.65 per cent."[4]

[1] Ibid., p. 12. [2] Ibid., p.18.
[3] Ibid., pp. 18, 24, 26. [4] Ibid., p. 25.

No prudent legislator [said he] at a time when the gold in the world is increasing by a hundred millions a year, and interest must necessarily and soon decline, will consent to impose on the labor and business of the people a fixed interest of 6 per cent. on a great debt, for twenty years, unless the necessity is far more urgent than is now believed to exist.[1]

Accordingly, he recommended no change in the law providing for the issue of bonds beyond the necessary increase in amount and the repeal of two clauses which in his view limited the sale of the five-twenties already authorized.[2] These clauses, however, or rather Mr. Chase's interpretation of them, require some attention.

The first legal-tender act of February 25, 1862, as will be remembered, had authorized the issue of $500,000,000 6 per cent. five-twenty bonds, which the secretary was permitted to sell "at the market value thereof." The law also provided that holders of greenbacks might exchange them in sums of $50 or multiples of $50 for these bonds at par.[3] Under this authorization the secretary had been able to dispose of but relatively few of the five-twenty bonds. Up to the first of December "conversions" amounted to less than $24,000,000.[4] Mr. Chase now declared that these small sales were due to the clauses restricting sales to the "market value" of the bonds and permitting "conversions" of greenbacks into five-twenties at par.

Considerable amounts [he explained] are seldom taken, except with a view to resales at a profit, and resales at any profit are impossible under the law. Negotiations below market value are not allowed, and if not allowed the taker of the bonds can expect no advance, unless a market value considerably below par shall become established. The act makes advance above par impossible, by authorizing conversion of United States notes into bonds at that rate.[5]

---

[1] *Report of the Secretary of the Treasury*, December, 1862, p. 25.
[2] *Ibid.*, p. 26.   [3] 12 *Statutes at Large*, pp. 345, 346.
[4] *Report of the Secretary of the Treasury*, December, 1862, p. 12.   [5] *Ibid.*, p. 52.

What this peculiar explanation meant Congress did not understand, and, as will soon appear, the secretary was asked to interpret it.

II. THE JOINT RESOLUTION OF JANUARY 17, 1863

This report was laid before the House of Representatives December 5 and referred to the Committee of Ways and Means, which at once set about drafting finance bills along the general lines indicated by the secretary.[1] But this was a task that necessarily required some time. It was not until the 8th of January that Mr. Stevens was able to report the loan bill and the bill for reorganizing the banks of issue.[2]

Meanwhile the treasury continued to run behind as it had done in October and November, and the accumulation of requisitions which could not be paid for lack of funds became larger. This state of affairs attracted much attention in Congress because the pay of the army fell into arrears. Members began to receive letters from constituents who were serving in the field, complaining that their families at home were suffering from lack of the money which the government owed but did not pay them.[3] Such complaints found a ready response. December 11 the House adopted a resolution asking the secretary of war to report "what regiments remain unpaid and how long have the soldiers of such regiments remained without pay."[4] As Mr. Stanton did not reply promptly,[5] the House adopted another resolution December 15, directed to the secretary of the treasury:

[1] *Congressional Globe*, 37th Cong., 3d Sess., p. 15.

[2] *Ibid.*, pp. 235–7. It was the Senate banking bill introduced by Sherman January 26, "a little different from the bill introduced in the House of Representatives" (p. 505), that was finally passed. *Cf.* SPAULDING, *op. cit.*, p. 186.

[3] See, *e. g.*, the remarks of Mr. Gurley, *Congressional Globe*, 37th Cong., 3d Sess., p. 344.

[4] *Ibid.*. pp. 75, 76.   [5] No answer had been received up to January 12.—*Ibid.*, p. 283.

Whereas grievous delays happen in the payment of money due soldiers: Therefore, in order to ascertain if any and what legislation may be necessary to remedy such delays,

Resolved, That the Secretary of the Treasury be requested to furnish to this House the reasons why requisitions of paymasters in the Army are not promptly filled.[1]

Mr. Chase answered that the unpaid army requisitions then in the treasury amounted to $28,700,000. Payments of requisitions designated by the war and navy departments as most urgent were being made at the rate of about $1,000,000 daily from the proceeds of customs, internal revenue taxes, conversions, temporary deposit loans, and new issues of greenbacks. These resources, he concluded were insufficient, but he could not obtain more funds until Congress should adopt the measures recommended in his report.[2]

The House replied to this communication the day before adjourning for the holidays by passing a joint resolution declaring that in the opinion of Congress "immediate steps ought to be taken by the Treasury Department to pay the sums due the soldiers . . . . and that to this end a preference be given to this class of Government creditors over every other."[3] After the recess Henry Wilson, of the Committee on Military Affairs, reported this resolution to the Senate with an amendment which authorized the issue of an additional $50,000,000 of greenbacks to enable the secretary to carry out its directions. Senator Fessenden, however, pointed out that before such a measure was adopted Mr. Chase ought to be consulted, and for this purpose he requested and the Senate consented that the matter be referred to the Committee on Finance.[4]

---

[1] *Congressional Globe,* 37th Cong., 3d Sess., p. 93.

[2] *H. R. Executive Document No 16,* 37th Cong., 3d Sess.,Dated December 18, 1862.

[3] Adopted December 22, 1862.—*Congressional Globe,* 37th Cong., 3d Sess., p. 167. For the text see p. 199.

[4] *Ibid.,* pp. 199, 200.

When the resolution was sent to Chase he declared that the means provided by it would be insufficient. The existing resources of $1,000,000 a day did not cover current expenditures, and the addition of $50,000,000 of greenbacks would not suffice for the arrears in the pay of the army and navy, which probably approached $60,000,000. Therefore, as a substitute for the joint resolution, he sent in a bill providing for the sale at the best rates obtainable of $100,-000,000 of 6 per cent. ten-year bonds, the issue of $50,000,-000 of United States notes, and of a like sum of two-year 4 per cent. treasury notes.[1] On recommendation of the Committee on Finance the Senate postponed indefinitely the resolution adopted by the House and passed in its place the bill prepared by Chase.[2]

While the joint resolution was pending in the Senate, the House followed up its inquiry into the non-payment of the soldiers by requiring Secretary Chase to explain why he had not availed himself of the authority conferred upon him by the act of February 25, 1862, to sell $500,000,000 of 6 per cent. five-twenty bonds.[3] In replying, Chase laid the blame for the failure to use this authority, as he had done in his annual report, upon the clause specifying that the bonds should be sold at "the market value thereof." "The market value," he said, "can only be ascertained by the daily quotations of sales in New York." But he could not sell large amounts of securities at these market quotations, for heavy purchasers as a rule bought to sell again, and resales at a profit were impossible unless bonds could be bought from the government at prices less than those ruling in the market.[4]

The question whether Chase or Congress was respon-

[1] The text of his letter is published *ibid.*, p. 270.

[2] *Ibid.*, p. 270; January 12.

[3] Resolution adopted January 8.—*Ibid.*, p. 237.

[4] *H. R. Executive Document No. 29*, 37th Cong., 3d Sess.

sible for the emptiness of the treasury thus turned upon
the meaning of the phrase "market value" of bonds. Chase,
who construed it to mean the quotations of the New
York stock market, was no doubt right in saying that sales
of large amounts at these quotations were impossible. His
critics in Congress, however, regarded his interpretation as
a legal quibble which ought not to stand in the way of
supplying the pressing needs of soldiers. "Everybody
knows," said Mr. Gurley, impatiently, that the market
value of bonds "is the price they will bring when placed upon
the market; . . . . no far fetched construction of this sort
should prevent their sale."[1]

Though the majority of congressmen probably shared
Mr. Gurley's feeling that in his fear of exceeding the powers
conferred upon him the secretary had been over-nice, the
needs of the hour were too urgent to permit of further fen-
cing. The great Ways and Means bill which had been
reported from the committee while this dispute about the
pay of soldiers was going on, contained a section which
authorized the issue of $300,000,000 additional greenbacks
"if required by the exigencies of the public service, for the
payment of the army and navy and other creditors of the
Government."[2] Debate upon it began January 12 with an
elaborate speech by Mr. Spaulding.[3] The same day the
joint resolution giving soldiers preference over all other
government creditors which the House had passed December
22 was rejected by the Senate in favor of Chase's substitute.[4]
Just before adjournment, still on this same day, the latter
bill was referred to the Committee of Ways and Means in
the House.[5] Though this committee felt that steps should
be taken at once for the relief of the soldiers, they did not
approve of Secretary Chase's proposals. The Ways and

[1] *Congressional Globe*, 37th Cong., 3d Sess. p. 343.   *Cf.* pp. 389, 390, 927.
[2] *Ibid.*, p. 284.   [3] *Ibid.*, p. 284-9.   [4] Pp. 106, 107, above.
[5] *Congressional Globe*, 37th Cong., 3d Sess., p. 291.

Means bill which they had framed would grant abundant power to borrow money, but they knew that it could not be passed much before the end of the session. Consequently they determined to put the simplest of the proposals of the Ways and Means bill into a separate measure and ask for immediate action. With this view, on the 14th of January, Thaddeus Stevens introduced a " Joint Resolution to provide for the immediate payment of the Army and Navy of the United States." It was very brief, merely authorizing the issue of $50,000,000 additional greenbacks to be included in the issue provided for by the pending bill. On Lovejoy's motion the amount was doubled. Then without any discussion the resolution was passed.[1] The next day the Senate acted upon it with similar expedition,[2] and President Lincoln signed it on the 17th.[3] In notifying the House of his approval of the measure the president expressed his "sincere regret that it has been found necessary to authorize so large an additional issue of United States notes," and urged prompt enactment of Chase's plan for a national banking system.[4]

A third issue of greenbacks was thus determined upon with much less discussion than had been bestowed upon the first and second issues. The opening for it was made by Secretary Chase's peculiar interpretation of the loan sections of the first legal-tender act. Had he taken the "market value" of bonds to mean what Congress seems to have intended — the price which they would bring when sold on the market — it is probable that he could have negotiated a much larger amount of the five-twenties in the summer and autumn of 1862. Then the pay of the army would not have fallen into arrears and the occasion for the joint resolution of January 17 would not have presented itself.

1 *Congressional Globe*, 37th Cong., 3d Sess., p. 314.

2 *Ibid.*, p. 323.   3 12 *Statutes at Large*, p. 822.

4 *Congressional Globe*, 37th Cong., 3d Sess., pp. 392, 393.

III.   THE THIRD LEGAL-TENDER ACT

The greenbacks authorized by the joint resolution, however, formed but a third of the issues proposed by the Ways and Means bill reported by the committee. This bill authorized the secretary of the treasury to borrow $900,000,000, intended partly to supply the wants of the current fiscal year and partly of the year that would begin July 1, 1863. To secure this sum the secretary might sell "upon the best terms he can obtain, not less than par," twenty-year bonds, bearing interest at 6 per cent., in coin. He might also issue $300,000,000 of three-year treasury notes bearing coin interest at $5.47\frac{1}{2}$ per cent.; *i. e.*, a cent and a half per day on $100. Further, "if required by the exigencies of the public service," he might issue $300,000,000 of greenbacks. To prevent the avenues of circulation from being closed against government paper money by enlarged issues of bank notes, a tax of 2 per cent. per annum was proposed on the circulation of banks beyond certain limits, which varied from 25 per cent. of the capital in the case of institutions with a capital of over $2,000,000 to 90 per cent. of the capital of banks with capitals of $100,000 or less.[1]

Rather curiously, the discussion of this sweeping measure centered not in the question how best to borrow the $900,000,000 needed, nor in the policy of issuing more legal-tender notes, but in the proposed tax on bank notes. Congressmen acquiesced with little dispute in the recommendations concerning the loans;[2] but they discussed at much length and with much warmth the alleged attack upon the banks. Of strenuous opposition to the increase of the irredeemable currency there was none. It was clearly enough seen that

[1] The text of the bill is given *Congressional Globe*, 37th Cong., 3d Sess., pp. 283, 284.

[2] See, *e. g.*, the speeches of Messrs. Spaulding, *ibid.*, p. 287; Morrill, p. 296; Sheffield, p. 367; Hooper, p. 384; Riddle, p. 383; Lovejoy, p. 345; Gurley, p. 342; Walker, p. 339.

the bill would cause further depreciation,[1] injure the government's credit,[2] increase the cost of the war, work injury to recipients of fixed wages—particularly soldiers—to savings bank depositors and all creditors, and that it would still further excite the "spirit of speculation."[3] But this recital of the ill effects which would follow the bill apparently had little influence. Even Amasa Walker—then serving his short term in the House—who saw these evils most clearly, could lightly waive them aside. "One thing is certain," said he, " we are in such an emergency at the present time that it is not worth while for us to be very particular."[4] He frankly admitted that he could see no alternative.[5] Similarly Justin S. Morrill, who had opposed the first and second legal-tender acts, felt constrained to vote for the bill because he knew of no better way of securing funds. "The patient has got accustomed to opiates," said he, "and the dose cannot now be withheld without peril."[6] Mr. Horton took the same stand. He had opposed the whole paper-money system, but now that the country was "launched . . . . on this current of paper money," there seemed to him to be no turning back.[7] While even these staunch opponents of irredeemable currency admitted the necessity of the bill, Mr. Spaulding and his associates proclaimed it as they had done in the case of the first and second issues. "I have an aversion," said Mr. Spaulding, "to any considerable further issue of legal tender notes, and can only consent to it as an imperative necessity. I think too large an issue will tend to inflate prices; but I do not see how it can be avoided."[8]

In the recognition of the ill effects of an irredeemable paper currency and the assertion of necessity the discussion

[1] Senator Sherman, *ibid.*, p. 841.
[2] Amasa Walker, *ibid.*, p. 339.
[3] See remarks of Messrs. Walker, *loc. cit.;* Ward, *ibid.*, p. 337; and Pike, p. 347.
[4] *Ibid.*, p. 392.   [5] *Ibid.*, p. 339.   [6] *Ibid.*, p. 294.
[7] *Congressional Globe*, 37th Cong., 3d Sess., p. 387.   [8] *Ibid.*, p. 289.

of the third legal-tender act was but a repetition of the two former debates. One new topic, however—whether or no the currency was "inflated"—attracted much attention. The apologists of the legal-tender system were anxious to minimize the evils incident to it, and especially to show that the government notes were not redundant and had not depreciated. Mr. Chase had set the example by attributing the premium on gold to the anxiety of timid investors, foreign and native, to sell American securities even at heavy sacrifice for coin which could be exported or hoarded. Speculators, he said, had made the most of this situation to effect a great rise of gold. That the high premium was "not due wholly, or even in greatest part, to the increase of the currency," he sought to show by estimates of the monetary circulation before and after suspension. According to his figures the circulation of the loyal states had increased between November 1, 1861, and November 1, 1862, but from $355,000,000 to $377,000,000. Nearly or quite all of this moderate gain of $22,000,000 he thought was required by the greater activity of business and the greater government transactions. That this was the case seemed to him sufficiently well attested by the fact that the prices of various staple products such as wheat, mess pork, corn, hay, beef, etc., had risen little if at all. Moreover, he showed that the fluctuations in the premium had not coincided with changes in the volume of the circulation. Finally, he argued, "if there be a considerable real depreciation of the circulation — which is by no means admitted —" it is due not to redundancy of greenbacks, but to the needless increase in the note and deposit currency of banks.[1]

Mr. Chase's arguments reappeared during the debate in a number of variations. One gentleman declared that a

[1] *Report of the Secretary of the Treasury*, December, 1862, pp. 12–15. *Cf.* Part II, chaps. ii, iii and iv, below, on the circulating medium, the premium on gold and the prices of commodities.

bushel of wheat sold for a gold dollar in Europe and a paper dollar in America, and that as the wheat had everywhere the same intrinsic value there could be in reality no such difference between the value of paper money and coin as the premium on gold indicated.[1] Another member propounded the doctrine that the rate of interest is an infallible test of the adequacy of the money supply. Since the rate of interest in the money market was high he refused to believe that the currency was unduly expanded.[2] Mr. Edwards declared that "a more fallacious idea was never put forth" than that "the difference between gold and the currency issued by the Government is the measure of depreciation." In his opinion the difference was due to the fact that gold was and greenbacks were not receivable at the customs houses. Gold had become "an article of merchandise." The supply of it was not equal to the demand, and in the scramble it had become "a monopoly in the hands of a few who hoard it because they know they can get a good price for it from the customer who is obliged to buy it."[3]

To refute such proofs that the currency was not redundant, Amasa Walker declared, on the authority of Calhoun, that the amount of currency required by the community was just one dollar for every twenty-five dollars of property. He estimated the property of the loyal states at $12,500,000,000. The proper amount of currency was therefore one-twenty-fifth of this sum, or $500,000,000. But there was in circulation some $850,000,000 of currency. That is, by his estimate, there was a redundancy of $350,000,000.[4]

---

[1] Mr. Shellabarger, *Congressional Globe*, 37th Cong., 3d Sess., p. 407.

[2] Mr. Watts, *ibid.*, p. 391.   [3] *Ibid.*, p. 409.

[4] *Ibid.*, p. 339. Mr. Walker included bank deposits in his estimate of the volume of the currency. Calhoun's statement of the theory is not quite so bold and dogmatic as Mr. Walker represented it. See *Works of John C. Calhoun* (New York, 1853), Vol. II, p. 347.

Replying to Walker, Mr. Riddle raised no objection to the method of his argument, but declared that an important element had been omitted in the calculation—the government required much more currency in time of war than in time of peace. "So far from there being a redundancy of the currency," he concluded, "I believe there is a deficiency."[1] The commonest rejoinder to the statement of redundancy, however, was the assertion that prices of commodities had not risen materially.[2]

But the matter was carried farther. Not satisfied with denying the depreciation of the paper currency, some members asserted that further inflation was necessary to facilitate borrowing. This argument, too, seems to have been derived from a passage in Mr. Chase's report:

> The government can resort to borrowing only when the issue [of United States notes] has become sufficiently large to warrant a just expectation that loans of the notes can be had from those who hold or can obtain them at rates not less advantageous than those of coin loans before suspension.[3]

This language can hardly mean anything else than that the government should continue to issue its notes until their value had been so depressed that holders would be ready to exchange $100 of currency for an annual gold payment of $6. Congressmen at least took this view. Mr. Horton declared a further issue of currency necessary "in order to fund a large amount of debt."[4] Similarly Mr. Hooper opposed selling bonds below par and preferred to adhere to the policy of previous legislation, which, according to him, had been "to issue legal-tender notes in sufficient amount . . . . to float . . . . bonds and keep them at par."[5]   Mr. Spaulding

[1] *Congressional Globe*, 37th Cong., 3d Sess., p. 383.

[2] *Cf. ibid.*, remarks of Messrs. Hooper, p. 386, Watts, p. 391, Riddle, p. 383, and Walker's rather feeble reply, p. 407.

[3] *Report of the Secretary of the Treasury*, December, 1862, p. 14.

[4] *Congressional Globe*, 37th Cong., 3d Sess., p. 387.   [5] *Ibid.*, p. 412.

urged the same argument. The treasury found difficulty, said he, in borrowing currency to pay for the necessary loans; consequently more currency should be issued.[1] Finally, Mr. Watts declared that he would issue legal-tender notes, "until the rate of interest should come down to such a reasonable notch that the government could afford to go with some prospect of ultimately paying the amount of its indebtedness and interest."[2]

Such talk marks the extreme length to which the idea that government should not sell bonds below par was carried. When the treasury was unable to get funds by selling bonds at par there were three possible courses: (1) to make the securities offered more attractive to investors by raising the rate of interest or lengthening the time for which they would run; (2) to make no change in the terms of the bonds but to accept the market price for them; (3) to decrease the value of the currency to a point where $100 in greenbacks was worth less in the minds of the public than the promise of a gold income of $6 for a term of years and final repayment in coin. The third course necessarily involved all the disorders caused by a depreciation of the money that served the community in its economic relations as a standard of value. But the demand for fresh issues to facilitate borrowing was virtually a recommendation of this third course.

One amendment to the bill, destined in later years to be the subject of much criticism was made during the discussion in committee of the whole. Despite Secretary Chase's urgent recommendation, the "conversion" clause permitting holders of greenbacks to exchange them at par for 6 per cent. bonds was retained in the bill as reported by the Committee of Ways and Means.[3] Near the end of the debate, however, Mr. Horton moved to strike out this clause. "It simply leaves the option in the hands of the secretary of the

[1] *Ibid.*, p. 287.   [2] *Ibid.*, p. 391.   [3] Sec. 3, *Ibid.*, p. 284.

treasury," he said in explaining the proposed amendment, "instead of the holders of the currency."[1] Very little attention was paid to the change. Shellabarger and Stevens showed a disposition to question its wisdom, but it was accepted in committee of the whole without a division,[2] and when Shellabarger called for the yeas and nays upon it in the House they were not ordered.[3]

Three substitutes were proposed for the bill brought in by the Committee of Ways and Means. Thaddeus Stevens proposed one, of which the characteristic features were the issue of $300,000,000 in United States notes, payment of interest on bonds in "lawful money" instead of in coin, and repeal of the legislation authorizing the acceptance of deposit loans.[4] When this substitute was rejected by a vote of 39 to 66,[5] Mr. Stevens imperturbably proposed a second.[6] As the House was disposed to insist upon payment of interest in coin—a measure which seemed to Mr. Stevens to destroy "the simplicity and harmony" of the paper-money system[7]— he accepted this principle and proposed that any part of $900,000,000 might be borrowed on treasury notes bearing 3.65 per cent. interest in coin, a legal tender to the same extent as greenbacks and redeemable at the pleasure of the government.[8] This proposition was defeated by a yea and nay vote of 37 to 91.[9] The third substitute, introduced by Mr. Hooper, reproduced with a few modifications of wording a bill submitted by Secretary Chase at their request to the Committee of Ways and Means, but not accepted by them.[10] As Chase observed in his letter to the committee, "the provision in respect to loans is very general."[11] In order to secure $900,000,000 the bill authorized the secretary of the treasury to issue 6 per cent. bonds running twenty years or

[1] Congressional Globe, 37th Cong., 3d Sess., p. 455.   [2] Ibid., loc. cit.
[3] Ibid., p. 522.   [4] For text see ibid., p. 284.   [5] Ibid., p. 487.
[6] Ibid., p. 490.   [7] Ibid., p. 145.   [8] For text see ibid., p. 520.
[9] Ibid., p. 522.   [10] See Hooper's explanations, ibid., p. 485.   [11] Ibid., loc. cit.

less, or 6 per cent. treasury notes running not more than
three years, or United States notes, without specifying any
limit to the amount of these various securities to be issued
beyond the provision that the aggregate of bonds, treasury
notes, and United States notes should not exceed $900,000,-
000.[1] This bill met a fate similar to Stevens's by an equally
emphatic majority — 32 to 67.[2] After these substitutes had
been rejected the bill of the committee was passed without a
division and sent to the Senate.[3]

In the Senate the finance committee proposed several
amendments, of which the most important was the reduction
of the issue of greenbacks from $300,000,000 to $150,000,-
000.[4] Why the House Committee of Ways and Means had
set the issue at $300,000,000 is not clear. Mr. Hooper,
after a conference with Chase, told the House that the secretary seemed not to consider so large an issue necessary.[5] Yet
the amount was not reduced, nor was there any discussion of
the subject. However, no objection was raised to the Senate's amendment reducing the issue by one-half. Apparently, the House was proceeding on Amasa Walker's maxim
that in such an emergency it was "not worth while . . . .
to be very particular."[6] Had it not been for the action of
Senator Fessenden's committee the amount of greenbacks
authorized during the war would have been $600,000,000
instead of $450,000,000.

The debate in the Senate was brief, and even more largely
devoted to the clause taxing bank notes than had been the
case in the House. The final vote was yeas 32, nays 4.[7]
March 3, 1863, the bill received President Lincoln's
approval.

This law authorized the secretary of the treasury to bor-

1 For the text see ibid., p. 484.
2 Ibid., p. 487.   3 Ibid., p. 522.   4 Ibid., p. 927.
5 Ibid., p. 366.   6 Ibid., p. 392.   7 Ibid., p. 945.

row on the credit of the United States $900,000,000. He could sell 6 per cent. coin-interest, ten-forty bonds on such terms as he might "deem most advisable." Of this sum $400,000,000 might be in three-year treasury notes bearing not more than 6 per cent. interest payable in "lawful money." These notes were to be a legal tender for their face value, excluding interest, of denominations not less than ten dollars and could be sold " on the best terms that can be obtained," or paid to creditors willing to accept them at par. Further, the secretary was empowered "if required by the exigencies of the public service, for the payment of the army and navy, and other creditors of the government, to issue . . . . the sum of $150,000,000 of United States notes, including the amount of such notes [$100,000,000] heretofore authorized by the joint resolution approved January 17, 1863." The clauses in the first and second legal-tender acts restricting "the negotiation of bonds to market value" were repealed; and holders of United States notes who desired to "convert" them into five-twenty bonds were required to present their notes for this purpose on or before July 1, 1863, after which date the right to exchange should "cease and determine." Finally, to take the place of the unsatisfactory postal currency, the secretary was authorized to issue notes for fractional parts of a dollar to an amount not exceeding $50,000,000, and a tax of 5 per cent. each half-year was imposed on fractional notes issued by any bank, corporation or individual.[1]

[1] 12 *Statutes at Large*, p. 709.

CHAPTER V

HOW FURTHER ISSUES OF GREENBACKS WERE AVOIDED
IN 1864 AND 1865

I. *The Congressional Pledge to Issue no More U. S. Notes:*
Avoidance of Greenback Issues in Latter Part of War — Due Chiefly to Increase of Taxation — Success of 5-20 Loan in 1863 — Finance Report of 1863 — Greenbacks in First Session of Thirty-eighth Congress.

II. *The Financial Difficulties of 1864:*
Chase's Difficulties from January to June — Change of Secretaries — Financial Straits During the Summer — Fessenden's Report in December — Improvement in the Situation.

III. *Secretary McCulloch and the Alley Resolution :*
7-30 Loan of 1865 — Finance Report — The Alley Resolution.

IV. *Recapitulation:*
Government Receipts of 1861-66 — Decreasing Relative Importance of Loans — Financial Rôle of the Greenbacks.

I. THE CONGRESSIONAL PLEDGE TO ISSUE NO MORE
U. S. NOTES

SINCE no further issues of greenbacks were authorized after March 3, 1863, it may seem that discussion of the war legislation regarding them should end with the last chapter. But in passing upon the paper-money policy it is quite as necessary to understand how the issue of more greenbacks was avoided in the latter half of the war as it is to discover why such issues were made in 1862 and 1863. For this purpose a brief review of the treasury policy in 1864 and 1865 must be added.

Of course, the demands made upon the treasury in these later years were much heavier than they had been during the first half of the war. The expenditures other than payments of principal of the debt rose from $470,000,000 in 1862 and $719,000,000 in 1863 to $865,000,000 in 1864 and

$1,297,000,000 in 1865.[1] If recourse to United States notes was avoided in the second half of the struggle despite these enormously increased disbursements, the chief reason must be found in the more efficient revenue system. The slowness of the secretary to recommend and of Congress to enact heavy taxes in the earlier stages of the war has been commented upon.[2] There was no great hesitation in raising the customs dues on imported articles, but the results from the fiscal point of view were not of great moment, because Congress seemed more inclined to strengthen the protective than the revenue features of the tariff. The direct tax imposed by the summer session in 1861 was of slight avail. In no year during the war did the receipts from this source reach $2,000,000. Internal taxes were not levied until July 1, 1862, when a very elaborate system was created, according to which almost everything that seemed to Congress susceptible of yielding a revenue was subjected to a duty.[3] This system was amended and extended by the acts of June 30, 1864, and March 3, 1865.[4] At first the results of this system did not meet expectations. Chase estimated for the first year of its operation that the receipts would be $85,500,000, and they proved to be but $37,500,000 — less than half the anticipated sum.[5] But as the tax officials became more familiar with their duties and the imperfections shown by experience to exist in the first legislation were remedied, receipts increased very rapidly. In 1864 they were $110,000,000, in 1865 $209,-000,000, and in 1866 $309,000,000.

Such large receipts from taxation not only provided an increasing proportion of the sums needed to meet expenditures, but also improved the credit of the government as a

---

[1] For these and similar figures given below see the table of receipts and expenditures for past years published in every *Report of the Secretary of the Treasury*.

[2] *Cf.* Part I, chap. i, p. 18, and chap. ii, p. 72, above.

[3] 12 *Statutes at Large*, p. 432.   [4] 13 *Statutes at Large*, pp. 223, 469.

[5] *Report of the Secretary of the Treasury*, December, 1863, p. 3.

borrower. At the same time more efficient methods of negotiating loans were devised. The happiest of Mr. Chase's financial expedients was the arrangement into which he entered with Jay Cooke in October, 1862, for selling the five-twenties authorized by the first legal-tender act. The system of agencies which Mr. Cooke organized was so successful in obtaining subscriptions that the fiscal year, 1863, which had opened badly, ended most fortunately, despite the untoward military events of May and June, when Grant seemed to the public to be making little advance against Vicksburg, and Lee and Bragg were invading the North. The accumulation of unpaid requisitions that was already a cause of solicitude when Chase sent his report to Congress in December, 1862, had mounted by the close of the session to $72,000,000. But when the third legal-tender act, with its ample provision for loans and repeal of the funding clause, had become a law, the lagging sale of bonds became so rapid that "within two months after the adjournment of Congress the whole mass of suspended requisitions had been satisfied, all current demands promptly met, and full provision made for the pay of the army and navy." At the end of the fiscal year there was a balance of over $5,000,000 in the treasury.[1]

Encouraged by Cooke's continued success, Mr. Chase in his report of 1863 took ground against further issues of greenbacks. " The limit prescribed by law to the issue of United States notes," said he, "has been reached, and the Secretary thinks it clearly inexpedient to increase the amount." [2] Instead, he recommended such modifications of the internal revenue system as should increase the receipts to $150,000,000.[3] If this recommendation should be followed he entertained "little doubt of being able to obtain

[1] *Report of the Secretary of the Treasury*, December, 1863, p. 2. On the arrangement with Jay Cooke see *H. R. Executive Document No. 66*, 37th Cong., 1st Sess.

[2] *Report of the Secretary of the Treasury*, December, 1863, p. 17.   [3] *Ibid.*, p. 10.

whatever funds will be needed, through loans, at reasonable rates of interest, for bonds or treasury notes."[1]

Apparently Congress concurred in the secretary's belief that further issues of United States notes would be detrimental. Justin S. Morrill seems to have expressed the general feeling:

> To force the Treasury to issue legal tender notes in any way beyond the present limits — though the wages of labor, though the pay of salaried men and of the soldier, should be increased — would result in disappointment and disaster. . . . . Let us have taxes; let us have loans; something, at all events, which will reduce the amount of legal tenders now outstanding.[2]

Not only did the thirty-eighth Congress decline to increase the issues of United States notes, but it inserted in the "act to provide ways and means for the support of the Government," approved June 30, 1864, the following proviso:

> . . . . nor shall the total amount of United States notes, issued or to be issued, ever exceed four hundred millions of dollars, and such additional sum, not exceeding fifty millions of dollars, as may be temporarily required for the redemption of temporary loan [sic].[3]

This important clause, pledging that no more United States notes would be issued, attracted slight attention. But one feature of the debate is of interest. Thaddeus Stevens, consistent to the last, made "one more effort to save the national credit," as he put it, by proposing to pay the interest on the new loans in paper money instead of in coin.[4] Again he failed.

II. FINANCIAL DIFFICULTIES OF 1864

The pledge thus given by the first session of the thirty-eighth Congress was kept despite the financial embarrassments of the summer of 1864, and the enormous expen-

[1] *Report of the Secretary of the Treasury*, December, 1863, p. 18.
[2] *Congressional Globe*, 38th Cong., 1st Sess., p. 1716.
[3] Sec. 2, 13 *Statutes at Large*, p. 219.
[4] *Congressional Globe*, 38th Cong., 1st Sess., pp. 3212 ff.

ditures of 1865. During the year ending June 30, 1864, the expenditures exceeded Mr. Chase's anticipations by $116,-000,000.[1] Though there was a similar excess of the actual over the estimated receipts from taxation and miscellaneous sources of $104,000,000,[2] it was still necessary to borrow immense sums. Over $320,000,000 of the five-twenties were sold by Mr. Cooke and the treasury agencies, but the sub-scription books closed January 21. In arranging for a new loan Mr. Chase made three changes. He offered bonds that would run twice the time of the five-twenties, but he reduced the rate of interest from 6 to 5 per cent., and instead of employing Jay Cooke again as general agent he tried to sell the bonds through national banks and other agencies under supervision of the treasury department.[3] In consequence of these changes and the slow progress of the northern armies in the winter and spring of 1864 the "ten-forty loan," as it was called, was as marked a failure as the five-twenty loan had been a success. By the end of the fiscal year only $73,-000,000 had been sold.[4]

This failure left a deficit which Mr. Chase could find no better way of filling than by issuing more legal-tender notes. The new issues, however, were of a type different from the greenbacks in that they ran for definite terms and bore interest which it was hoped would lead holders to retain them as an investment instead of putting them into circula-tion as money. During the half year January to June, 1864, issues of such interest-bearing legal-tender notes in

[1] Compare *Reports of the Secretary of the Treasury*, December, 1863, p. 5, and 1864, p. 6.

[2] *Ibid.*, 1864, *loc. cit.*

[3] See Chase's letter to Fessenden, SCHUCKERS, *op. cit.*, p. 416. In explaining this change of plan Chase wrote: "I have not forgotten the calumnies for which my employment of a general agent was made the occasion, and I confess it was princi-pally with a view of avoiding these calumnies that I abandoned the general agency system."

[4] BAYLEY, *op. cit.*, p. 164.

excess of redemptions were made to the amount of $163,-
000,000.[1] Despite all Chase's efforts to obtain funds, however, demands upon the treasury piled up more rapidly than
they could be met. Though on the 1st of July there was a
nominal balance of $19,000,000 on hand, there were also
unpaid requisitions that on the 5th amounted to $72,000,000.[2]

At this uneasy juncture a change of secretaries occurred.
In May, John J. Cisco, the experienced chief of the New
York subtreasury, had sent in his resignation to take effect
June 30. Chase and Senator Morgan, of New York, came
into conflict over the appointment of his successor. Though
the cause of disagreement was finally removed by Cisco's
consenting to remain in office, Chase could not resist the
temptation to impress upon the president the necessity of
deferring to the wishes of his secretary of the treasury by
sending him a note of resignation. Three or four times
before when Mr. Chase had tried ·similar tactics to carry a
point, Mr. Lincoln had begged him to reconsider the step.
Consequently, Chase was disagreeably surprised when, on
June 30, he received a note from the president accepting his
resignation.[3] After the vacant position had been refused by
Governor David Tod, of Ohio, W. P. Fessenden, of Maine,
chairman of the Senate finance committee, reluctantly consented to assume its responsibilities.

The new secretary found himself in a very difficult position. Beside the $72,000,000 of unpaid requisitions, there
were outstanding $162,000,000 of certificates of indebted-
ness. Receipts from customs were hardly more than enough
to pay interest on the debt, and from internal revenue duties

[1] There were three varieties of these issues: the one-year and the two-year notes
of 1863, and the compound interest notes. See BAYLEY, op. cit., pp. 161-3; Report of
the Secretary of the Treasury, December, 1864, p. 3. On their circulation as money
see Part II, chap. ii, sec. vi, below.

[2] Report of the Secretary of the Treasury, December, 1864, p. 19.

[3] See the letters published in WARDEN, op. cit., p. 614; cf. SCHUCKERS, op. cit.,
chap. xlv, and pp. 505-10; HART, op. cit., pp. 315-18.

not more than $750,000 a day was expected. Meanwhile the
daily expenses were estimated at not less than $2,250,000.[1]
Nor was the prospect bright for securing funds by borrowing. Three days before Fessenden came into office a loan
on seventeen year 6 per cent. bonds offered by Chase at
104 or above was withdrawn from lack of takers.[2] A promising attempt to secure $50,000,000 from the banks of New
York, Boston, and Philadelphia, was blocked by the subtreasury law which was held to prevent the secretary from
drawing upon any but national banks.[3] Fessenden then
decided upon a popular subscription for seven-thirty notes
authorized by the act of June 30, 1864. Although he
incurred considerable expense in advertising this loan the
sums realized were not large.[4] The unpaid requisitions
now amounted to more than $130,000,000, and the secretary
" resolved to use all the means at his command to pay so
much, at least, as was due to . . . . soldiers, who were suffering from the long delay in satisfying their just claims."
For this purpose he was compelled, much against his will,
to issue over $80,000,000 of legal-tender compound-interest
notes. He also used over $20,000,000 of seven-thirties in
paying the army, and raised $33,000,000 more on the sev-
enteen-year bonds which Mr. Chase had been unable to sell.[5]
But all these shifts did not bring in sufficient means, and
the quarter ending with September showed a deficit of
$130,000,000.[6]

Still, when Secretary Fessenden prepared his report to
Congress he did not recommend an increase in the issues of
greenbacks. To push the circulation of government notes

---

[1] *Report of the Secretary of the Treasury*, December, 1864, pp. 19, 20.

[2] See Chase's letter to Fessenden, Schuckers, *op. cit.*, p. 415; *cf. Hunt's Merchants' Magazine*, Vol. LI, pp. 42 and 129.

[3] *Report of the Secretary of the Treasury*, December, 1864, p. 20; *Hunt's Merchants'
Magazine*, Vol. LI, pp. 129, 130.

[4] *Report* cited in preceding note, p. 20.   [5] *Ibid.*, p. 21.   [6] *Ibid.*, p. 39.

"far, if at all, beyond its present limit," he said, "could only be justified by absolute necessity."[1] The operations of the treasury during his brief incumbency had satisfied him "not only of the ability of the people to furnish, at a short notice, such sums as may be required, but [also] of the entire confidence felt in the national securities."[2] What sort of loans should be offered he left for Congress to decide, but he felt that as an aid in negotiations the secretary should be granted a discretionary power to increase the currency.[3] For the rest, he recommended that the internal revenue duties be increased and extended to a point where they would yield $300,000,000 a year.[4]

Even before this report was sent to Congress the financial situation seems to have improved. This improvement was doubtless due in large measure to the successes of the Union armies that began to hold out an increasingly definite promise of peace. Under such circumstances borrowing became easier. During the quarter October to December Fessenden secured $20,000,000 from compound interest notes, $36,000,000 from ten-forties, $54,000,000 from seven-thirties, and $77,-000,000 from five-twenties. In the next three months he raised $56,000,000 on ten-forties and $185,000,000 on seven-thirties. Meanwhile the redemptions of greenbacks were slightly, and of certificates of indebtedness largely, in excess of issues, and while considerable amounts of compound interest notes were paid out they were more than offset by redemptions of one and two-year notes of 1863.[5]

III.   SECRETARY McCULLOCH AND THE ALLEY RESOLUTION

When President Lincoln entered upon his second term Fessenden was allowed to lay down his uncongenial burden. His successor, Hugh McCulloch, was strongly recommended

---

[1] *Report of the Secretary of the Treasury*, December, 1864, p. 17.
[2] *Ibid.*, p. 21.   [3] *Ibid.*, p. 22.
[4] *Ibid.*, p. 14.   [5] *Cf.* Bayley, *op. cit.*, pp. 157-63.

by his success as president of the Bank of the State of Indiana and his services as the first comptroller of the treasury in organizing the national banking system.

Though the war was obviously nearing its end, the task of the new secretary was by no means easy. The armies could not well be disbanded until the government was provided with funds sufficient to meet all arrears of pay, including bounties and cost of transportation. To secure means, Mr. McCulloch arranged for a popular subscription for seven-thirty notes, and employed Jay Cooke as general agent. As before, Cooke was eminently successful. By the end of July $530,000,000 of seven-thirties had been sold, and McCulloch had, in his own words, "the unexpected satisfaction of being able, with the receipts from customs and internal revenue and a small inerease of the temporary loan, to meet all the requisitions upon the treasury."[1]

The war over, McCulloch set himself to reducing the government finances to more manageable shape. In his annual report for 1865 he estimated that at the close of the current fiscal year the national debt would amount to about $3,000,000,000.[2] To reduce this sum, the secretary proposed that $200,000,000 be spent each year in payment of interest and principal.[3] Such payments, he showed, would extinguish the debt, if funded at $5\frac{1}{2}$ per cent., in thirty-two years.[4] But he laid chief stress upon the desirability of reducing the volume of currency as a preliminary to resuming specie payments at an early date.

The present legal-tender acts [he said] were war measures, and while the repeal of those provisions which made the United States notes lawful money is not now recommended, the Secretary is of the opinion that they ought not to remain in force one day longer than shall be necessary to enable the people to prepare for a return to the constitutional currency.[5]

[1] *Report of the Secretary of the Treasury*, December, 1865, pp. 36, 37.

[2] *Ibid.*, p. 22.   [3] *Ibid.*, p. 25.   [4] *Ibid.*, p. 23.   [5] *Ibid.*, p. 4.

He therefore recommended that he be empowered to sell bonds "for the purpose of retiring not only compound interest notes, but [also] the United States notes."[1]

That Congress shared the secretary's desire to resume specie payments speedily seemed to be sufficiently shown by the prompt action of the House of Representatives upon a resolution introduced by John B. Alley, of Massachusetts. It ran as follows:

Resolved, That this House cordially concurs in the views of the Secretary of the Treasury in relation to the necessity of a contraction of the currency with a view to as early a resumption of specie payments as the business interests of the country will permit; and we hereby pledge co-operative action to this end as speedily as practicable.

This resolution was adopted without debate on December 18, by a vote of 144 to 6.[2] The story of how the fulfilment of the promise of resumption was delayed for thirteen years does not belong to the war history of the greenbacks.

IV.   RECAPITULATION

The rôle played by the greenbacks as a financial resource at different stages of the Civil War can best be shown by a tabular recapitulation of the receipts of the treasury from different sources during the fiscal years 1861–66.

The "net ordinary receipts" shown in this table are taken from the reports of the secretary of the treasury. They include, besides import duties and internal-revenue taxes, proceeds of sales of public lands and all miscellaneous items. The notable fact concerning them is the rapid increase from year to year—an increase for which the internal-revenue system deserves the lion's share of credit. From a tenth in 1862, the proportion of ordinary to total receipts rose

---

[1] *Report of the Secretary of the Treasury,* December, 1865, p. 14.

[2] Thirty-two members did not vote.— *Congressional Globe,* 39th Cong., 1st Sess., p. 75.

TABLE II

RECEIPTS OF THE FEDERAL GOVERNMENT FOR THE FISCAL YEARS 1861-66

	1861		1862		1863		1864		1865		1866	
	Mil-lions of Doll'rs	Per cent.	Mil-lions of Doll'rs	Per cent.	Mil-lions of Doll'rs	Per cent.	Mil-lions of Doll'rs	Per cent.	Mil-lions of Doll'rs	Per cent.	Mil-lions of Doll'rs	Per cent.
Total net receipts	64.5	100.0	484.4	100.0	708.2	100.0	941.1	100.0	1,197.0	100.0	626.1	100.0
Net ordinary receipts	41.5	64.3	51.9	10.7	112.1	15.8	243.4	25.9	322.0	26.9	519.9	83.0
Customs	39.6	61.4	49.1	10.1	69.1	9.8	102.3	10.9	84.9	7.1	179.0	28.6
Internal revenue	......	......	......	......	37.6	5.3	109.7	11.7	209.5	17.5	309.2	49.4
Net receipts from loans	23.0	35.7	432.5	89.3	596.1	84.2	697.7	74.1	875.0	73.1	106.2	17.0
Bonds	23.3	36.2	59.6	12.3	172.5	24.4	468.2	49.7	344.2	28.8	127.3	20.4
Short-time interest-bearing obligations	-.3	-.5	214.4	44.3	170.4	24.1	185.9	19.8	528.1	44.1	7.7	1.2
Non-interest-bearing obligations	......	......	158.5	32.7	253.2	35.7	43.6	4.6	2.7	.2	-28.8	-4.6
[United States notes]	......	......	[98.6]	[20.4]	[289.2]	[40.8]	[43.9]	[4.7]	[-.2]	[-.2]	[-30.4]	[-4.9]

to a quarter in 1864, and it would have been considerably instead of slightly larger in 1865 had not customs duties fallen off so largely in consequence of the tariff act of June 30, 1864, which discouraged legal importations and stimulated smuggling.[1]

By "net receipts from loans" is meant the receipts minus sums employed in paying principal of the public debt. These receipts are divided into three classes, according to the kind of security upon which money was borrowed. Each class is charged with all redemptions of securities falling within it and credited with all new issues, including premiums realized on sales.[2] When the redemptions exceed the issues the fact is indicated by placing a minus sign before the figures.

Two matters of interest are brought out by the exhibit. The first is the correlative of the point already noticed; as the revenue system became more efficient, a smaller proportion of the means necessary to carry on the war had to be borrowed. From nine-tenths in 1862 the proportion fell to three-quarters in 1864 and 1865. The second matter concerns the method of borrowing. At first reliance was placed rather on issues of circulating currency than on sales of bonds; but with increasing experience the secretaries used bonds and interest-bearing treasury notes more and greenbacks less. To make this clearer a supplementary table is added giving the proportions of the net receipts from loans obtained from the three classes of securities.

From this table it appears that the greenbacks were not an important financial resource after June, 1863. In the fiscal year, 1862, more than a fifth, and in 1863 nearly half of the

---

[1] *Cf. Report of the Secretary of the Treasury*, December, 1864, pp. 13, 26.

[2] Issues and redemptions of the principal of the debt are compiled from BAYLEY, *op. cit.* Premiums are as given by DE KNIGHT, *History of the Currency of the Country and of the Loans of the United States, Treasury Department Document No. 1943*, pp. 121, 122.

TABLE III

PROPORTION OF THE NET RECEIPTS FROM LOANS DERIVED FROM BONDS, SHORT-
TIME INTEREST-BEARING OBLIGATIONS, AND FROM NON-INTEREST BEAR-
ING OBLIGATIONS FOR THE FISCAL YEARS 1861-66

	1861	1862	1863	1864	1865	1866
Net receipts from loans	100%	100%	100%	100%	100%	100%
Bonds.......................	101.3	13.8	28.9	67.1	39.3	119.9
Short-time interest-bearing obligations.........	−1.3	49.6	28.6	26.7	60.4	7.2
Non-interest-bearing obligations................	......	36.6	42.5	6.2	.3	−27.1
[United States notes]....	[....]	[22.8]	[48.5]	[6.3]	[−.2]	[−28.6]

loans were represented by issues of United States notes, but
in 1864 the proportion fell to a sixteenth, and thereafter the
redemptions were greater than the issues. This statement,
however, does not by any means show the real financial
effect of the greenback policy. More important than the
nominal amount of the issues was the influence of the paper
money upon the price of supplies bought by the government.
But this is a large subject that must be reserved for a future
chapter.[1]

[1] See Part II, chap. x, below.

PART II

Economic Consequences of the Legal-Tender Acts

CHAPTER I

PRELIMINARY SKETCH

THE preceding chapters have shown that the policy of issuing irredeemable paper money was adopted because of the financial embarrassments of the federal government. But the policy thus adopted for purely fiscal reasons had serious consequences of quite other than a fiscal nature. It caused a grave disturbance of established economic relations and affected for good or ill the economic circumstances of almost every person in the country. The purpose of the present part is to trace out these consequences in as clear a fashion as the available materials permit. Of necessity the analysis must be intricate and tedious, because to be faithful it must deal with a bewildering complexity of conditions and must attempt to distinguish between the effects of a multiplicity of economic causes. Perhaps the best way to give a degree of coherence to the details will be to preface the analysis with a sketch of the general nature of the economic disturbances that characterized the period.

In the first place, then, suspension of specie payments threw the monetary circulation of the loyal states into disorder by causing the withdrawal of gold and silver coin from common use as money. The inconveniences that attended this withdrawal and the various substitutes that were employed to take the place of specie as media of exchange form the subject of the next chapter.

But, though the inconveniences caused by these changes in the medium of exchange were not slight, they were less serious than were the results produced by the change in the standard of value. For about nine years before suspension

the money unit of the United States in which all prices
were reckoned and debts discharged, had been, in fact, if
not in legal theory, the gold dollar.[1] The legal-tender
acts substituted the greenback for the gold dollar as this
unit. Now the gold dollar had contained 23.2 grains of
pure metal, but the greenback dollar that took its place was
at no time during the war worth so much as this. A year
after the passage of the first legal-tender act a greenback
dollar would purchase but 14.5 grains of gold. Though
from this point its value advanced until in August, 1863, it
was worth 18.4 grains, the rally was followed by a serious
relapse that culminated in July, 1864, when the paper
dollar was worth but 9.0 grains. Another advance carried
the value to 17.1 grains in May, 1865, and another relapse
reduced it to 15.9 grains at the end of the year. The course
and causes of these fluctuations in the gold value of the
standard money are dealt with in chap. iii.

It was this depreciation of the money unit that gave rise
to the most complicated and interesting economic develop-
ments of the war period. Of course, in exchanging commodities for money men were unwilling to give as much for
a dollar worth 9 grains of gold as they had given for the dollar worth 23.2 grains. What is tantamount to giving less
goods for the dollar, they demanded more dollars for the
goods. The decline in the specie value of the greenbacks,
therefore, produced an extraordinary rise of prices, which is
investigated in chap. iv.

From the very organization of a modern industrial
society, such a rise of prices must produce far-reaching disturbances. The complex process of producing and distributing wealth is carried on by a succession of money payments.
Business-men buy materials for money prices, lease land for
money rents, borrow capital expressed in money for the pay-

---

[1] Cf. LAUGHLIN, History of Bimetallism in the United States (4th ed., 1897), p. 86.

ment of money interest, hire labor for money wages, sell their products for money, and in money reckon their profits. At bottom, of course, this highly developed system of money payments is only a mechanism for distributing among the members of society the economic satisfactions which are the real goal of effort. But under the present régime the economic satisfactions which any individual can obtain — what may be called his "real income"—depend proximately on the purchasing power of his money income. The rise of prices that resulted from depreciation decreased, of course, the purchasing power of a given money income. As a result the economic satisfactions received by all those whose money incomes did not rise as quickly and in as great degree as prices, were diminished.

But the matter could not rest there. Men did not long remain content with the same money return, when the economic satisfactions it enabled them to command had declined so considerably. As prices rose, then, all classes in the community which contributed of their property or their services to the process of production insistently demanded a larger sum of money for their co-operation. The economic situation apparently favored their success. For depreciation of the currency of itself did not decrease the amount of commodities produced and services offered — the source from which the real income of all classes in the community is drawn — nor did it affect directly the relative supply of and demand for the various factors of production; it altered only the division of these commodities and services among the various classes that shared in them. Those persons whose money incomes had not advanced *pari passu* with prices received a less proportion than before, and those whose money incomes had increased more rapidly than prices commanded a larger proportion. But it was the former distribution of wealth that was the outcome of the existing economic conditions. The change in the distribution, caused by depreciation of the standard of values, was from the standpoint of the situation before suspension an artificial disturbance. Under the operation of free competition, a readjustment of the nominal amounts of money payments — the mechanism by which real income is distributed — was therefore to be expected, in the direction of restoring the relative distribution of wealth between different classes prevailing before the disturbance had occurred.

A further consequence of depreciation, therefore, was to start a readjustment of money incomes, whether derived from rents, interest, or wages. But this process of readjusting the whole system of money payments so as to restore real incomes was certain to encounter serious obstacles.

1. At any given time business men are bound to a considerable extent by legal contracts calling for the payment or receipt of specified sums for specified goods or services. They are under engagement to pay set amounts for rent and interest; they owe others and others owe them accounts payable in legal money; they have agreed to buy materials at fixed prices, or to supply others with their own products; they have borrowed and lent money; when due the loans are to be paid in the standard currency; they have contracted with others to give or receive their services at certain salaries, etc. Whether the purchasing power of dollars rises or falls, such contracts are fulfilled by the payment of the specified number of dollars. Until the termination of the contracts there is no alteration in the nominal amount of the money to be paid. In this way the scale of money payments existing before depreciation is legally petrified and enforced for a while in the new situation where the same sum of money means less economic satisfactions.

2. Rapid readjustment is further hindered by the fact that the nominal amount of many money payments is a conventional sum, not subject as a rule to bargaining between

the parties. The fee of the bootblack, the barber, the notary, the physician; the price of a newspaper, a cigar, a ride in the street-car, in some places the monthly wage of a farm hand—these and many other payments are not easily changed in amount.

3. Even where legal contracts are not in the way, and the prices paid are mostly the subject of bargaining, the change in the amount of payments produces friction. The complex system of money payments, by which the distribution of wealth is effected, is an organic whole, and a change in one part encounters serious opposition unless all the other parts are similarly altered. A change in the scale of money payments that affects all simultaneously and in the same proportion would proceed smoothly and work hardship to no one. But changes do not occur in this manner. They always start somewhere, and extend spasmodically over the rest of the field. Persons whose products or services do not at once rise in price, oppose, so far as they can, changes which increase their money expenditures. Laborers may demand an increase of wages because the price of food has risen. But the employer cannot accede to the request, without injuring himself, until the price of his products has advanced. If he sell to other dealers, they object strenuously to paying higher prices unless sure the increase can be shifted onto others. And consumers exceedingly dislike paying more for their goods especially if their own money incomes have not risen. So at every step the advance in the scale of money payments is impeded.

4. The readjustment in the scale of money payments, then, that is necessitated by an alteration in the standard money works itself out in a period of economic stress and strain. During the Civil War the tenseness of the situation was increased by the constantly varying degrees of depreciation. There was not a single shift from a higher to a lower level; the standard of value was fluctuating *all* the time.

Before a readjustment of money payments to a scale that, at the existing value of a dollar, would restore real incomes approximately to what they had been could be worked out, the value of the dollar had changed again and a new adjustment on a new basis began.[1] The price level was constantly changing, and each new change unsettled real incomes afresh and precipitated a new struggle for a readjustment of money payments. While the war continued no adjustment could be even tolerably stable, for the next week's war news might raise or lower the value of the government's notes which served as the community's money several per cent., and so produce new confusion.

A study of the economic consequences of the issue of legal-tender paper currency as a measure of "war necessity" becomes, then, primarily an examination of the intricate effects of the changes in the purchasing power of the standard money upon the distribution of what Marshall calls the "national dividend." The most important problem is to discover how the real incomes of laborers, landlords, capitalists, and active business managers were affected. Beyond this problem lies the question what effect these changes in real income had upon the consumption and production of wealth. Such in brief are the subjects discussed in chaps. v–ix.

[1] The rapidity and violence of these fluctuations may best be seen from the following tabular statement of the percentage of alternating depreciation and appreciation in the specie value of the greenback dollar:

Month	Average Gold Value of $1 in Paper Money	Rise (+), or Fall (−)	Per Cent. of Appreciation or Depreciation in Gold Value of the Currency
December, 1861..........	$1.00		
February, 1862..........	.966	−0.034	Fall of 3.40 per cent. in 2 months
April, 1862..........	.985	+ .019	Rise of 1.97 per cent. in 2 months
February, 1863..........	.623	− .362	Fall of 36.75 per cent. in 10 months
August, 1863..........	.795	+ .172	Rise of 27.61 per cent. in 6 months
July, 1864..........	.387	− .408	Fall of 51.32 per cent. in 11 months
May, 1865..........	.737	+ .350	Rise of 90.44 per cent. in 10 months
December, 1865..........	.684	− .053	Fall of 7.19 per cent. in 7 months

CHAPTER II

THE CIRCULATING MEDIUM

I. *Gold and Silver Coin:*
Money in Use Before Suspension—Disappearance of Gold After Suspension in East—Continued Use in California.

II. *Bank Notes:*
Exceptions to Rule of Suspension—Obstacles to Free Circulation of Bank Notes—Redemption in Greenbacks—Increase of Note Issues.

III. *Old Demand Notes:*
Attitude of Banks—Demand Notes at a Discount—Temporary Loan Scheme—Effect of Legal-Tender Act.

IV. *"Shinplasters" and Fractional Currency:*
Disappearance of Silver Coin—Issues of "Shinplasters"—Postage Currency—Fractional Currency.

V. *Minor Coins:*
The Premium on Nickel Cents—Its Cause—New Bronze Cents—Other Minor Coins.

VI. *Treasury Notes:*
Greenbacks—One and Two Year Notes of 1863—Compound Interest Notes—Use of Certificates of Indebtedness and Seven-thirties as Currency.

VII. *Recapitulation:*
Chaotic Condition of Circulating Medium—Uncertainty Regarding Volume.

I.   GOLD AND SILVER COIN

BEFORE the banks and the treasury suspended specie payments, December 30, 1861,[1] the monetary circulation of the United States consisted of (1) gold coin, (2) subsidiary silver coins for fractional parts of a dollar, (3) one-cent pieces of a copper and nickel alloy, (4) treasury notes of the government payable on demand, and (5) circulating notes issued

[1] See Part I, chap. i, pp. 40, 41.

by banks chartered under state laws.[1] The specie in circulation was estimated by the director of the mint in October, 1861, at from $275,000,000 to $300,000,000, of which he thought not more than $20,000,000 was at the South;[2] the demand notes outstanding were $33,500,000,[3] and the bank notes reported as issued by the 1,289 institutions in the loyal states amounted to about $129,000,000.[4]

Suspension threw this whole system into disorder. Gold coin, the only full legal-tender money in use, was withdrawn from general circulation as soon as the banks and the treasury ceased paying it out, and the country was left dependent upon a currency of paper money which the issuers were not prepared to redeem in specie.

It is not quite accurate to say that gold coin ceased to circulate. The banks continued to hold large amounts of specie in their reserves,[5] while the government paid interest on a large portion of its debt in gold and required the use of gold by importers in payment at the customs houses. More than this, there was a section of the country where the greenbacks did not succeed in displacing coin even in common business transactions.

In 1862 there were but very few banks in states west of Kansas and Nebraska.[6] Indeed, in California, the wealthiest and most populous of the far western states, the existence of banks of issue was expressly prohibited by the state

[1] Silver dollars had not been in common use for many years, because they were worth more as bullion than as money. See the table showing the average value of an American silver dollar each year from 1834 to 1862 in H. R. LINDERMAN's *Money and Legal Tender in the United States* (New York, 1879), p. 161, and compare LAUGHLIN, *History of Bimetallism in the United States*, chaps. iv, v.

[2] *Finance Report*, 1861, p. 62.   [3] *Ibid.*, 1862, p. 9.

[4] Compiled from the "Synopsis of the Returns of the Banks in the Different States," published in the *Finance Report* for 1862, pp. 189 ff.

[5] According to the "Annual Reports on the Condition of the Banks," the amount of specie held by institutions in the loyal states increased from $76,400,000 at the beginning of 1862 to $81,500,000 at the beginning of 1863.— *H. R. Executive Document No. 25*, 37th Cong., 3d Sess., p. 209; and *No. 20*, 38th Cong., 1st Sess., p. 211.

[6] See the bank reports cited in preceding notes.

constitution.[1] "Suspension" was, therefore, a much less momentous occurrence for these communities than for those of the East, where business centered around highly developed banking systems. West of the Rocky Mountains men continued to buy and sell for coin, giving little thought to the fact that bank notes in circulation elsewhere were no longer redeemed in specie.

But when Congress, by the act of February 25, 1862, provided for the issue of $150,000,000 of United States notes and made them a legal tender between individuals, the currency troubles of the rest of the country were brought home even to Californians. Under this law it was technically possible for a person who had bought goods from a San Francisco jobbing merchant to compel his creditor to accept in payment greenbacks worth considerably less than the expected gold. Elsewhere this situation had been prepared for by the use of notes of suspended banks for three months before the first United States notes were issued, and men adjusted their business transactions to suit the currency. But on the Pacific coast people had been accustomed to a circulation of specie only and were very loath to surrender it. Business men consequently cast around for some means by which they could maintain the circulation of gold and prevent debtors from forcing them to accept greenbacks. One means to this end was the formation among the merchants of San Francisco in November of an agreement "not to receive or pay out legal-tender notes at any but the market value, gold being adhered to as the standard." Firms that refused to enter into this agreement, or to abide by it, were to be listed in a black book and required in future dealings to pay cash gold for goods which they purchased.

Loyal observance of such a voluntary agreement, however, was difficult to maintain, and vigorous efforts were

[1] Article IV, secs. 34, 35. There were, however, a few deposit banks. See J. J. KNOX, *A History of Banking in the United States* (New York, 1900), pp. 843-5.

accordingly made to secure such action from the state legislature as would secure the same end by legal means. After several other proposals had been rejected, a "specific contract act" was finally passed and approved April 27, 1863. It provided in substance that contracts for the payment of specific kinds of money should be enforceable by legal process. After the constitutionality of this law had been affirmed by the state courts, business-men were able to protect themselves against tenders of greenbacks effectively by inserting in all their contracts clauses specifying that payment should be made in gold coin. This became the general practice, and consequently the people of California maintained a large circulation of specie during all the seventeen years that the rest of the United States were using paper money. Greenbacks were not prevented from circulating, but when they were passed it was usually at their gold, not at their nominal, value.[1]

II. BANK NOTES

As has been said, the withdrawal of gold from circulation in other parts of the United States left the notes of the state banks and the federal treasury the only monetary circulation, aside from "deposit currency," available for use in large transactions. But neither the bank nor the treasury notes were at that time a legal tender, and consequently the circulation of both was for a time beset with difficulties that require discussion in some detail.

Though all the banks, with the exception of the banks of the states of Ohio, Kentucky, and Indiana, and a few scattering institutions elsewhere like the Chemical Bank of New York, had followed the example of the New York banks very

[1] BERNARD MOSES, "Legal tender Notes in California," *Quarterly Journal of Economics*, Vol. VII, pp. 1-25; J. A. FERRIS, *The Financial Economy of the United States Illustrated* (San Francisco, 1867), Nos. V, XV.

promptly in suspending specie payments,[1] the suspension was perhaps nowhere complete. Banks very generally continued for some time to supply coin to their customers who required it for the payment of duties or any other necessary purpose.[2] Indeed, in those states where the banking laws imposed penalties for refusal to pay notes in coin the banks were obliged to redeem their notes whenever the holder insisted upon their so doing. Such was the case in New York. The state superintendent of banking was required by law to close any institution that failed to redeem its notes in coin within fifteen days after the notes had been protested.[3] As the superintendent had no discretion in the matter, the banks were at the mercy of any note holder who chose to insist upon redemption in gold. Certain speculators in currency took advantage of the situation to collect bank notes systematically and send them in to the issuing institutions for payment in coin, which they then sold at a premium.[4] Fear of such operations made the banks unwilling to pay out their notes freely. Instead of notes they issued many certified checks, which for a time formed a prominent part of the circulating medium.[5]

For such reasons there was a marked contraction in the bank-note circulation in the first months of 1862. January 4, the New York city banks had outstanding $8,600,000 of notes; by March 1 this circulation had fallen to $5,400,000. The hesitation of the banks ceased, however, when the treasury notes in circulation were made legal tender, for this measure provided funds other than coin which note holders

---

[1] *Bankers' Magazine* (New York), Vol. XVI, p. 650.

[2] *Ibid.*, Vol. XVI, p. 648 (Rhode Island); p. 649 (Philadelphia); Vol. XVII, p. 760 (Boston); *H.R. Executive Document No. 25*, 37th Cong., 3d Sess., p. 80 (Connecticut); p. 28 (New Hampshire); New York *Herald*, January 5, 1862. This and the subsequent references to newspapers give the date of the "financial column."

[3] See text of the law, *Bankers' Magazine*, Vol. XVI, p. 811.

[4] New York *Herald*, January 20, 1862.

[5] *Hunt's Merchants' Magazine*, Vol. XLVI, p. 309.

pressing for redemption could be compelled to accept. Accordingly, the banks began to pay out their notes again, and by May 3 their circulation was practically as large as it had been January 4.[1]

The situation in Ohio, Kentucky, and Indiana where the state banks did not suspend specie payments immediately, did not long maintain its peculiarity. These banks were deterred from following the example of eastern institutions by clauses in their charters which forbade the redemption of their notes in anything but coin. In Ohio, however, the legislature enacted a law January 16, which granted immunity from the penalties for suspension to such banks as should advance coin to be used in paying the interest on the state's foreign debt.[2] Similarly in Kentucky, "the banks of issue having consented to loan to the citizens of the state $1,000,000 . . . . the legislature passed an act on March 8, 1862, relieving the banks from the penalties for suspension of specie payments and authorizing them to pay out United States legal-tender notes."[3]

The Bank of the State of Indiana and its branches, under the presidency of Hugh McCulloch, held out somewhat longer. December 31 McCulloch issued a statement that under no circumstances would the bank fail to redeem the pledge it had given to pay its notes in coin.[4] In pursuance of this policy the managers of the branches were instructed. "to redeem promptly in coin all notes that might be presented; to anticipate and prevent their return, as far as might be practicable, by taking them up at commercial points with other cash means; [and] to make arrangements with depositors by which deposits of gold should be paid in gold,

---

[1] See the New York city bank statements, *ibid.*, p. 559; compare *Report of the Secretary of the Treasury*, December, 1862, p. 15.

[2] *Bankers' Magazine*, Vol. XVII, pp. 163, and 793, 794.

[3] KNOX, *History of Banking in the United States* (New York, 1900), p. 642.

[4] *Bankers' Magazine*, Vol. XVI, p. 650.

deposits of bank notes . . . . in bank notes."[1] By this course "in a few weeks the larger part of the circulating notes of the branches were at rest in their vaults, and the business of the branches was reduced to what could be safely done upon their capitals and deposits." When, however, the legal-tender act had been passed the question arose whether the bank might not legally use United States notes in discharge of its notes. After ascertaining that the courts would give prompt trial to a case involving this important question, Mr. McCulloch, in order to make a test case, directed that greenbacks .be tendered in payment of a note. The supreme court of Indiana decided that the legal-tender act was constitutional, and that the bank might redeem its notes in notes of the government. When this decision was rendered, the bank at once commenced paying out its notes again.[2]

The same question regarding the availability of greenbacks for redemption of bank notes that under state laws were payable only in coin, had to be faced in other states. In New York the question was peculiarly pressing because the legislature was powerless under the constitution to pass such measures of relief as were enacted in Ohio and Kentucky.[3] To determine whether banks could avail themselves of the act of Congress making treasury notes a legal tender, test cases were arranged by the superintendent of the banking department and a decision obtained in June, 1863, from the court of appeals maintaining the constitutionality of the law.[4] This and similar decisions rendered in other states

---

[1] H. McCulloch, Men and Measures of Half a Century, p. 136.   [2] Ibid., pp. 136–8.

[3] Article VIII, sec. 5 of the constitution provided that "the legislature shall have no power to pass any law sanctioning in any manner . . . . the suspension of specie payments by any person, association, or corporation issuing bank notes of any description."—Bankers' Magazine, Vol. XVIII, p. 811.

[4] See Annual Report of the Superintendent of the Banking Department of the State of New York, January 7, 1864; Bankers' Magazine, Vol. XVIII, pp. 811–13. The full text of the court's opinion is published ibid., pp. 345 ff.

removed the last doubt about the right of banks to use the greenbacks instead of gold coin as reserves and put them in a position to issue their own notes freely.

The increase in the circulation of the state banks after the passage of the legal-tender act was very general. Secretary Chase estimated that the notes issued by banks in the loyal states amounted to $167,000,000, November 1, 1862, as compared with $130,000,000 a year before.[1] The *Annual Report on the Banks in the United States* for 1863, though not without omissions, made the circulation in the same states about the first of the year nearly $181,000,000.[2] Bank deposits increased with like rapidity. According to the bank reports, the deposits in the loyal states were $257,000,000 in January, 1862, and $367,000,000 in January, 1863.[3] After April 1, 1863, however, the increase of circulation seems to have been checked by the tax imposed of 1 per cent. a year on certain proportions of the notes outstanding and 2 per cent. on amounts in excess of the specified proportions.[4]

Shortly thereafter the organization of new national banks and the conversion of state into national banks introduced a new element into the circulating medium. As the issue of national bank notes proceeded for several years more rapidly than the withdrawal of the state-bank issues, there was again an increase in the total bank circulation.[5] But aside from this increase the change was merely the substitution of a more uniform and better-secured kind of notes for the diverse issues of the state banks.

---

[1] *Report of the Secretary of the Treasury*, December, 1862, p. 14.

[2] *H. R. Executive Document No. 20*, 38th Cong., 1st Sess., p. 210.

[3] *Ibid., loc. cit.*, for 1863, and *H. R. Executive Document No. 25*, 37th Cong., 3d Sess., p. 208, for 1862.

[4] Act of March 3, 1863, sec. 7; 12 *Statutes at Large*, p. 712.

[5] See the statement of bank notes outstanding in the *Statistical Abstract of the United States*, 1878, p. 14.

III. OLD DEMAND NOTES

The circulation of the demand treasury notes was for a time beset by more difficulties even than was the circulation of bank notes. The first issues of these notes by Secretary Chase in the late summer and autumn of 1861 was opposed by the banks which subscribed to the $150,000,000 loan. When the secretary insisted on making the issues, however, they yielded, and with few exceptions made no difficulty about receiving such of the notes as were brought to them by depositors.[1] The situation changed, however, when the treasury, by suspending specie payments, gave notice that these notes would not be redeemed in coin.[2] At this time there were $33,460,000 in circulation.[3] Early in January the New York banks held a meeting to discuss what policy should be pursued with regard to them. Opinion was divided, and the meeting ended with the adoption of a vague resolution:

That before we consent to receive such notes, we must require that such legal provision be made by Congress as shall insure their speedy redemption, and that a committee of this association be appointed to consider that subject and report to an adjourned meeting.[4]

[1] *Cf.* Part I, chap. i, pp. 26, 27, above.

[2] It has been stated in an official document that "the demand notes were paid in gold when presented for redemption," and that such payment with their receivability for all public dues, "prevented their depreciation."—*Information Respecting United States Bonds, Paper Currency, Coin*, etc., revised ed., *United States Treasury Department Circular No. 123*, July 1, 1896, p. 7. This has been the common view and is found, *e. g.*, even in the work of so recent a writer as Professor A. B. HART (*Life of Chase*, p. 242). But none the less it is certainly an error. Mr. Chase himself said: "The banks of New York suspended on the 30th of December, 1861. . . . . and the government yielded to the same necessity in respect to the United States notes then in circulation." —*Report of the Secretary of the Treasury*, 1862, p. 7: *cf. American Annual Cyclopædia*, 1861, p. 300, and *Hunt's Merchants' Magazine*, Vol. XLVII, p. 509. More than this, the "old demand notes," as the issue came to be called, did depreciate in value, which could hardly have happened had they been "paid in gold when presented for redemption;" *cf.* Part II, chap. iii, sec. ii, below.

[3] *Report of the Secretary of the Treasury*, December, 1862, p. 9.

[4] *Bankers' Magazine*, Vol. XVI, p. 647.

Of course, this resolution procured no action by Congress, and the committee was unable to frame a policy acceptable to all the banks. Some institutions took the notes without question as current funds, while others did not.[1] The American Exchange Bank, for example, issued a circular dated January 1, 1862, informing its dealers and correspondents that it would not accept treasury notes from them, unless they would sign a contract to accept payment in the same notes at par.[2]

But so long as a portion of the subscriptions to the $150,000,000 loan remained unpaid, almost all of the banks were ready to receive demand notes at least in small quantities, because they could be used in making payments into the subtreasury.[3]

After the last instalment of the loan had been paid on the morning of February 4, the disinclination to receive the notes as current funds became much stronger. Banks could no longer find an outlet for them at the subtreasury, and they could not be certain that depositors would accept such notes in payment of checks, since the notes were not yet legal-tender. The metropolitan banks seem to have been rather more liberal than those of Boston, Philadelphia, and other cities.[4] But even in New York there was apparently a considerable number of large institutions that discriminated against the treasury notes and accepted them only as

[1] New York *Herald*, January 2, 5, and 6, 1862.

[2] *Bankers' Magazine*, Vol. XVI, p. 647. Compare the similar circulars received by Chicago banks from their New York correspondents, *Hunt's Merchants' Magazine*, Vol. XLVI, p. 293.

[3] New York *Herald*, February 4, 1862, and *Hunt's Merchants' Magazine*, Vol. XLVI, p. 309. The banks of Boston acted in similar fashion. Though these banks were forbidden by their charters to pay out any notes except their own, a resolution was adopted, January 10, that banks concerned in the government loan should accept treasury notes " receivable for government dues to the extent of 25 per cent. of their subscriptions to said loan, including such notes as they may have on hand."—*Bankers' Magazine*, Vol. XVI, p. 648.

[4] New York *Herald*, January 24 and 29, 1862.

"special deposits," repayable in kind.[1] Refusal to take the notes on the part of even a few banks in the clearing-house association made serious trouble for the other institutions that desired to receive them without question. For, if one of the more liberal banks accepted demand notes on deposit as current funds, it had to make provision for meeting checks drawn against this deposit and presented at the clearing-house by other institutions. At the clearing-house, however, the demand notes would not be accepted in payment of a balance, and the bank that had taken such notes from its customers had therefore to provide other funds for meeting the checks, or, if it did not have sufficient currency of other kinds, to take out loan certificates on which 7 per cent. interest was charged.[2]

This situation seems to have given much concern to the treasury authorities. Though the treasury notes were commonly accepted in business transactions between individuals without question,[3] men could not use them freely at the banks, and consequently persons who received large quantities were compelled to sell them at a slight discount.[4] It was the desire to prevent such discrimination against the treasury notes that Mr. Chase gave as his reason for urging the retention of the legal-tender clause in the bill introduced by Mr. Spaulding.[5]

While the bill was still pending, another scheme for the same purpose was devised. Mr. Cisco, the head of the New

[1] *Ibid.*, February 4 and 5, 1862. *Hunt's Merchants' Magazine* states that this course was pursued by a majority of the banks.—Vol, XLVI, p. 309.

[2] *Hunt's Merchants' Magazine*, Vol. XLVI, p. 309. *Cf.* the remarks of Senator Simmons in the *Congressional Globe*, 37th Cong., 2d sess., p. 794.

[3] New York *Herald*, February 9; *Shipping and Commercial List*, February 19, 1862.

[4] According to the New York *Tribune*, February 13, 1862, the selling price was one-fifth of one per cent. below par, while notes could be bought of the street brokers at half this discount.

[5] Letter of January 29, 1862, to Thaddeus Stevens.—*Congressional Globe*, 37th Cong., 3d Sess., p. 618; *cf.* remarks of Mr. Bingham, *ibid.*, p. 639.

York subtreasury, suggested, and Chase authorized, the acceptance of the treasury notes on deposit at the sub-treasuries at 5 per cent. interest.[1] It was apparently their expectation that the banks would now accept the notes with the intention of depositing them at the subtreasury and so drawing interest upon a part of their current funds.[2] But the plan was received less kindly than had been hoped. On February 8 about half a million was deposited with Mr. Cisco, and by the 11th another million had been added.[3] But these deposits seem to have come mainly from savings banks and out-of-town institutions.[4] Most of the city banks looked upon the plan as a bid to induce the public to deposit with the subtreasury instead of with themselves.[5]

For the time, therefore, this plan accomplished little, and the demand notes continued to rule at a slight discount until the passage of the legal-tender act.[6] The first reports of the law that reached New York indicated that the treasury notes already in circulation, as well as the new issues, had been made a legal tender.[7] An amendment to this effect had, indeed, been made by the Senate on motion of John Sherman;[8] but it had not been agreed to by the House of Representatives,[9] and at the recommendation of the committee of conference the Senate receded from it.[10] Though the report was false, it changed the attitude of the hesitating banks toward the notes. The new law provided that customs should be paid, not in paper money, but in coin. From this

[1] Cf. SCHUCKERS, Life of Chase, p. 269.

[2] Cf. Hunt's Merchants' Magazine, Vol. XLVI, p. 310; New York Herald, February 9, 1862.

[3] New York Herald, February 8 and 11, 1862.   [4] Ibid., February 14.

[5] Hunt's Merchants' Magazine. Vol. XLVI, p. 310.

[6] New York Tribune, February 13, and Shipping and Commercial List, February 19, 1862.

[7] New York Times, February 26; Herald, March 3.

[8] Congressional Globe, 37th Cong., 2d Sess., p. 771.

[9] Ibid., p. 888.   [10] Ibid., p. 929.

rule, however, an exception was made in favor of the old demand notes, because the act under which they were issued declared them " receivable in payment of public dues."[1] If made legal tender, then, the old notes would differ from the new only in possessing a virtue lacked by the latter — availability for use at the customs house in place of coin. As but $60,000,000 of the demand notes had been authorized, and as they were to be replaced as rapidly as feasible by the new issues, it seemed likely that there would be a strong demand for them from importers who had duties to pay. Consequently even the banks that had hitherto refused to receive the notes as current funds now refused to pay them out, and instead of being at a discount of $\frac{1}{10}$ to $\frac{1}{8}$ they rose to a premium of $\frac{1}{8}$ to $\frac{1}{4}$.[2] This advance to a premium, however, proved premature. When after three or four days it was found that the retirement of the old notes could not commence until the new notes were printed, that printing would require at least a month, and that in the meantime the treasury must continue to pay out the old notes, they fell again to par.[3] And when on the 4th of March the full text of the legal-tender act was received, and it was found that the legal-tender clause included only the new issues, some of the banks reverted to their former policy and began again to discriminate against the government notes. Accordingly the notes fell once more to a discount.[4]

The discovery that the old demand notes had not been made legal tender seems to have been as much of a surprise to many members of Congress as it was to business men in New York. Steps were taken at once to remedy the omis-

[1] Act of August 5, 1861, Sec. 5, 12 *Statutes at Large*, p. 313.
[2] New York *Times*, February 26 and 27, 1862; *Herald*, February 27 and 28; *Commercial Advertiser*, February 26, 27, 28, and March 1; *Shipping and Commercial List*, March 1.
[3] New York *Herald*, March 1 and 3; *Times*, March 3.
[4] New York *Herald*, March 4; *Commercial Advertiser* and *Shipping and Commercial List*, March 5.

sion.   A clause making the treasury notes already in circulation a legal tender was inserted in the bill to authorize the purchase of coin for the payment of interest on the public debt, which Thaddeus Stevens introduced into the House March 6.[1]   When this bill received President Lincoln's signature, March 17,[2] there was no longer any reason for discriminating against the demand notes, and they returned for a short time to par.[3]

Meanwhile the New York banks had taken action that put an end to all opposition on their part to the use of the treasury notes.   At a meeting held March 7, 1862, they determined to make their clearings in certificates issued by the assistant treasurer for deposit of the demand notes with him at 5 per cent. interest.[4]   This arrangement, which went into effect March 10, made treasury notes the standard for all banking operations in current funds.[5]   Foreseeing that when the new notes were ready for issue the old notes receivable for customs would be more valuable, Mr. Cisco published a notice March 14, that all certificates of deposit issued in the future would be paid in any notes that were legal tender.[6]   The new respect in which the old demand notes were coming to be held was shown by the fact that this notice caused a falling off in the daily deposits.   The check was only temporary, however, for the new notes became themselves available for deposit early in April.

From the 7th of March, then, the old demand notes were current funds in New York and passed without question at par.   But soon after the appearance of the greenbacks their

---

[1] *Congressional Globe*, 37th Cong., 2d Sess., pp. 1103 and 1116.

[2] 12 *Statutes at Large*, p. 370.

[3] In fact, the notes returned to par as soon as it was known that the clause had been introduced, because it was a foregone conclusion that the measure would become a law.— New York *Commercial Advertiser*, March 8.

[4] *Bankers' Magazine*, Vol. XVI, pp. 809–11.

[5] *Cf.* New York *Times*, March 10.

[6] See the text in *Annual American Cyclopædia*, 1862, p. 456.

position changed again.   The first greenbacks in New York came in a remittance of $4,000,000 received by the assistant treasurer April 5.[1] A large sum was paid out the same day, and from this time on issues were so rapid that $90,000,000 was outstanding before the 7th of June.[2] All through April the old demand notes circulated side by side with the new notes at par.[3] But, as the supplies of the latter currency became sufficient for the wants of business, a difference became apparent between the treatment of the two issues. Owing to their receivability for customs, the old demand notes were preferred, and as early as the second week in May they began to be quoted regularly at a premium which, slight at first, gradually rose as the volume in circulation became smaller and the premium on gold for which they served as a substitute at the customs-house became higher. The possibility of obtaining this premium caused holders of old demand notes to hoard them just as they had hoarded gold in January.   When Mr. Chase wrote his letter of June 7 requesting authority for a second issue of greenbacks, he said that the $56,500,000 of the old demand notes then outstanding were "held by banks and capitalists, and not used as circulation."[4] They were sold from time to time to importers and used in the payment of duties. As they came into the treasury through the customs-houses, the old demand notes were canceled and replaced by greenbacks. By this process the amount outstanding had been reduced to $3,300,000 by June 30, 1863.[5] This withdrawal from circulation in May, 1862, closed the brief but eventful history of the old demand notes as a part of the circulating medium.

[1] See the financial columns of the New York papers under this date.
[2] H.R. Miscellaneous Document No. 81, 37th Cong., 2d Sess., p. 1.
[3] Hunt's Merchants' Magazine, Vol. XLVII, p. 33.
[4] H.R. Miscellaneous Document No. 81, 37th Cong., 2d Sess., p. 1.
[5] Report of the Secretary of the Treasury, December, 1863, p. 45.

From what has been said it is clear that the business public must have suffered considerable inconvenience from the uncertainty regarding the currency between the time of suspension and of abundant issues of the greenbacks. Gold had ceased to be used in ordinary transactions; notes of state banks, always inconvenient, were in many cases not issued freely for prudential reasons and had to be replaced in considerable measure by certified checks, and the treasury notes were most of the time discriminated against by many banks. The appearance of the greenbacks in large amounts afforded relief from such difficulties, though the wide and rapid fluctuations in their value gave rise to other embarrassments of a more serious character.

IV.   "SHINPLASTERS" AND FRACTIONAL CURRENCY

One difficulty with the currency, however, the greenbacks could not meet. While they served as a convenient medium of exchange in large transactions, they did not supply the want of small change, for the first legal-tender act had forbidden the issue of notes of less than five dollars.[1]   Hardly had the perplexities of business men who handled currency in large amounts been relieved by the free issues of the greenbacks, when yet greater inconveniences began to be felt by everyone from the lack of fractional coins.

When specie payments were suspended the subsidiary silver coins did not disappear from circulation at once, as did gold, for reasons found in existing coinage laws.   While a dollar contained 371.25 grains of pure silver, only 345.6 grains were put into two half-dollars, four quarters, or ten dimes.[2]   In January, 1862, one grain of gold was selling for 15.35 grains of silver.[3]   At this ratio a silver dollar was worth

[1] Sec. 1, 12 *Statutes at Large*, p. 345.

[2] Act of February 21, 1853, 10 *Statutes at Large*, p. 160; *cf.* LAUGHLIN, *History of Bimetallism in the United States*, chap. v, sec. 4.

[3] See the table in LAUGHLIN, *op. cit.*, Appendix II, F.

$1.04 in gold, while two halves, four quarters, or ten dimes were worth but 97.05 cents. While, therefore, there was a profit in treating gold coin as bullion instead of as money, the moment a fractional premium appeared upon it in paper, there was no profit in exporting or in melting subsidiary silver coins until the premium on gold had risen sufficiently above 3.1 per cent. to give brokers compensation for collecting the coins and shipping them to Canada. For, when gold stood at $103\frac{1}{10}$, a paper dollar was worth 97 cents in gold — just as much as ten dimes. It was therefore a matter of indifference to the possessor of subsidiary silver coins whether he paid it over as current funds in purchasing commodities or sold it for paper money. But when gold rose above $103\frac{1}{10}$, a paper dollar became worth less than ten dimes, and a person who had the latter could make them go farther in the payment of debts by selling them for paper money and giving it to his creditor than by handing him the silver itself. Since, however, some trouble and expense were involved in melting or exporting coins of small denominations, it was a nice question how high the premium on gold must rise above $3\frac{1}{10}$ before the silver would disappear from circulation.

For the first week after payments in specie had been stopped the premium on gold varied from 1 to 3 per cent.[1] But on the 8th of January it rose to $3\frac{1}{2}$ and on the 9th to $4\frac{1}{4}$. At the latter premium a paper dollar was worth 95.92 cents in gold, or 1.13 cents less than ten dimes. According to the money column of the New York *Herald*, this slight difference sufficed to induce brokers to begin the purchase of silver coins. "An inquiry has sprung up for silver," reports the financial writer on the 9th, "which has been held at 1 per cent. premium." It is not improbable, how-

---

[1] For this and subsequent references to premium on gold see tables in Appendix A, below.

ever, that purchases of silver on so slight a margin were prompted rather by anticipations of the profit that could be made if the premium on gold continued to advance, than by the opportunity for immediate profit. If so, the buyers of silver were disappointed, for after rising to 5 on the 10th of January, the premium fell again below 4. During February the average premium was 3.5, during March 1.8, during April 1.5, and during May 3.3. At such low prices for gold, or, more accurately, at such high prices for paper money, there was no profit in buying subsidiary silver coins for export or melting, and consequently they continued to circulate as money. But in June, when the hopes of a speedy end of the war were being dispelled, the paper money fell in value, that is, the premium took an upward turn. From $3\frac{9}{16}$ on the first Monday of the month, the premium rose to $4\frac{5}{16}$ on the second Monday, $6\frac{5}{8}$ on the third, $7\frac{3}{8}$ on the fourth, and $9\frac{1}{16}$ on the fifth.[1] With gold at the last-named premium, a paper dollar was worth 91.69 cents in gold — a price which afforded an ample margin of profit for the purchase for export of silver coins worth 97.05 cents.

Accordingly, the newspapers late in June and early in July began to remark a rapid disappearance of small change from circulation. For example, the Springfield *Republican* of July 2, 1862, said: "The ruling premium of 5 to 6 per cent. on silver coin, as compared with the paper currency in use, is fast driving it out of circulation. Laboring people and those of small means are constantly to be seen at brokers' offices selling $10 to $50 of silver change at $2\frac{1}{2}$ per cent. premium, which the brokers ship to Europe where they can realize 6 or 7 per cent. in comparison with our irredeemable paper currency." Similarly, the New York *Times*

---

[1] These figures are averages of the highest and lowest prices of gold recorded each day.

of July 18 declared that "the annoyances suffered in this city and throughout the country during the last two or three weeks, on account of the scarcity of specie, have been unspeakable, and in many lines of business the loss of custom and profit has been heavy."[1] Though over $45,-000,000 of subsidiary coins had been struck under the act of 1853,[2] of which perhaps three-fifths circulated in the loyal states,[3] nearly the whole amount seems to have been withdrawn from use as currency between the middle of June and the middle of July. Apparently, the brokers who purchased the coin exported a large portion of it. Over $3,750,000 were carried to Canada in 1862 by a single express company.[4] American coin became a drug in the Canadian market and was accepted only at a discount.[5] Considerable amounts were shipped also to South America and a sum large in the aggregate was no doubt kept for a long time in small hoards.[6]

Of course, the disappearance of the silver coins from circulation caused serious inconvenience in retail trade. Various shifts were tried to supply their place. In Philadelphia, and perhaps elsewhere, old Spanish quarter-dollars were brought again into use. These coins had formed a considerable portion of the small change before an abundant supply of American silver was furnished under the act of 1853. From long wear they had become light in weight. The act of February 21, 1857, provided that they should be accepted by the government offices for 20 instead of 25 cents.[7]

[1] Compare New York *Tribune*, July 9 and 16; *Commercial Advertiser*, July 10 and 16; Chicago *Post*, July 15; and other references in the following notes.

[2] *Report of the Director of the Mint*, October, 1862, p. 49.

[3] *Cf. Hunt's Merchants' Magazine*, Vol. XLVII, p. 155.

[4] *Annual American Cyclopædia*, 1862, p. 468.

[5] *Cf. Bankers' Magazine*, Vol. XVIII, pp. 83, 482; Vol. XIX, p. 699.

[6] KNOX, *United States Notes*, p. 100.

[7] 11 *Statutes at Large*, p. 163, and LINDERMAN, *Money and Legal Tender*, p. 32.

When the American silver was withdrawn a few of these old coins, because of the less amount of silver left in them, came out of retirement and passed current again as quarters of a dollar.[1]

Another method of meeting the situation was to decline to make change for paper bills at all, or else to charge a premium for the silver returned. This plan is said to have been adopted for a time by transportation companies and many retail shops in New York city.[2] A third device was to cut dollar bank bills into halves or quarters and pass these pieces for 50 and 25 cents. In Hartford, Conn., it was said that some $20,000 of the bills of the Ætna Bank were floating about cut in two.[3] A more ingenious scheme was hit upon by the Farmers' Bank of Mount Holly, N. J., which paid out notes for $1.25, $1.50, and $1.75 to enable people to make change within 25 cents by returning a dollar bill.[4] Much commoner, however, was the issue of notes for fractional parts of a dollar, colloquially called "shinplasters." Though the laws of many states forbade any bank to put into circulation notes less than one dollar, a few institutions adopted this plan, relying on the obvious need of fractional currency to secure immunity from prosecution.[5] But most of the "shinplasters" seem to have been issued by individuals or firms not engaged in banking. In Chicago, for instance, the city railway company supplied 25-cent tickets which the conductors gave in exchange for paper bills and accepted for fares.[6] In Boston, Young's Hotel started a system of checks for 15, 25, and 50 cents

[1] Springfield *Republican*, July 15, 1862.

[2] New York *Tribune*, July 9 and 16.

[3] *Bankers' Magazine*, Vol. XVII, p. 404. On similar practices elsewhere see *ibid.*, p. 821.

[4] *Ibid.*, p. 316.

[5] For example of such illegal issues by a banker of Reading, Pa., see *ibid.*, p. 475.

[6] Chicago *Post*, July 15, 1862.

with the proprietor's signature attached — an example that
saloons, restaurants, and retail shops were quick to follow.[1]
Many of these issues were made by irresponsible persons
and consequently resulted in loss to those who accepted
them.[2] Partly to protect the public from such losses and
partly to obtain a "loan without interest," several towns and
cities provided for municipal issues of small notes. The
city council of Newark, N. J., for instance, voted July 11,
"to issue promissory notes to the amount of $50,000 in
denominations ranging from ten cents to fifty cents" and
redeemable by the city in sums of $10 or more.[3] This
example was followed by Jersey City, Wilmington, and
Albany, and a proposition of similar character was dropped
in Philadelphia only because it was found to be contrary to
state law.[4]

These various substitutes for the silver coins furnished a
fractional currency that, although unsatisfactory, had to be
tolerated for a time as a makeshift. Secretary Chase,
however, took steps promptly to relieve the general
embarrassment. He called the attention of Congress to the
matter in a letter written July 14, and Congress responded
by authorizing the use of "the postage and other stamps of
the United States" as currency.[5]

Though this act was approved by the president only
three days after Chase's letter was written, some time
elapsed before it afforded substantial relief. The chief
immediate effect was to cause the use of ordinary letter
postage stamps for small change. In New York where as a
rule about $3,000 of stamps were sold daily, the sales ran up

[1] Springfield *Republican*, July 15, 1862.

[2] *Cf.* quotations from the Philadelphia *Ledger* in the *Bankers' Magazine*, Vol.
XVII, p. 823.

[3] New York *Times*, July 13, 1862.

[4] See *Bankers' Magazine*, Vol. XVII, pp. 823, 566, 316, and 161 respectively.

[5] Act of July 17, 1862, 12 *Statutes at Large*, p. 592. See Part I, chap. iii, sec. iii.

to $10,000 on the day after the bill was approved, and next day to $16,000.[1] Such stamps, however, were exceedingly inconvenient for use as currency because of their small size and their propensity for sticking together and getting crumpled. To take their place Secretary Chase caused a series of special stamps in denominations of 5, 10, 25, and 50 cents to be prepared.[2] They were about $2\frac{3}{4}$ by $3\frac{3}{8}$ inches in size, printed on both sides and not gummed.[3] The first issues were made late in August.[4]

In order to force the withdrawal of the "shinplasters," attorneys of the national and local governments in some districts published notices warning the public that the penalties imposed by federal and state laws upon the issue of small notes by unauthorized persons would be vigorously enforced by prosecutions.[5] Municipal "shinplasters," however, were not affected by the Postage Currency Act, which forbade such issues only to "private corporations," firms, and individuals.[6] Town and city notes continued therefore to circulate unhindered for a considerable time.

The difficulties with the fractional currency do not seem to have come to an end even by the close of 1862. The various substitutes for coin could not be dispensed with until the "postage currency" became abundant enough to supply the demand for small change, and at first the issues were rather slow. By the end of September but $787,700 had been placed in circulation, and in the next two months the total

---

[1] *Bankers' Magazine*, Vol. XVII, p. 159.

[2] *Report of the Secretary of the Treasury*, December 1862, p. 28.

[3] Representations of this " postage currency " are given by KNOX, *United States Notes*, pp 105–8.

[4] KNOX, *ibid.*, p. 104; *Bankers' Magazine*, Vol. XVII, p. 239.

[5] For example, see the notice given in New York city, *Bankers' Magazine*, Vol. XVII, p. 256, and compare the action taken by the bank commissioners of Illinois, *ibid.*, p. 567.

[6] Sec. 2, 12 *Statutes at Large*, p. 592. See also the correspondence between the chairman of the finance committee of Wilmington and the commissioner of internal revenue.—*Bankers' Magazine*, Vol. XVII, p. 566.

reached less than $4,000,000.[1] In December Mr. Chase reported that it had been "found impossible to keep pace with the public demand for this currency," and that, although the daily issue had "been rapidly increased to $100,000," and was then being "extended as fast as practicable to twice that amount," the supply was still " largely deficient." [2]

In the West the St. Louis *Republican* of December 10 stated that " there is still much complaint of the scarcity of small change," [3] and in the East the Springfield *Republican* of the same date reported that "shinplasters " were still in circulation. In the same month the city council of New York passed an ordinance providing for the issue of 5, 10, 25, and 50-cent notes, which the *Bankers' Magazine* declared to be " a necessity growing out of the scarcity of change in this city." [4] Ordinary postage stamps also continued in use side by side with the deficient "postage currency" despite the efforts of the post-office department to prevent it. The post-master-general in his report dated December 1, 1862, said :

Postmasters were specially instructed to discontinue sales of stamps to persons evidently designing them for use as currency; but, notwithstanding the precaution taken and the checks adopted, ... the demand has until quite recently been largely in advance of the daily manufacture . . . . the majority of applications . . . . from postmasters were only partially filled, generally but one-half the number asked for having been sent. . . . . The aggregate value of the postage stamps and stamped envelopes sold at 29 of the larger post-offices during the third quarter of 1862 was $1,400,937.48, and during the corresponding quarter of 1861 was $606,597.40, showing an excess in favor of 1862 of $794,340.08. . . . . Nearly the entire excess . . . . has been or is now in use as currency.[5]

[1] *Report of the Secretary of the Treasury*, December, 1862, pp. 43 and 12.

[2] *Ibid.*, pp. 28, 29.

[3] Quoted in *Bankers' Magazine*, Vol. XVII, p. 568.

[4] Vol. XVII, p. 562. Mayor Opdyke, however, did not agree with this view, and vetoed the measure.—New York *Tribune*, December 22, 1862.

[5] *H. R. Executive Document No. 1*, 37th Cong., 3d Sess., Vol. IV, pp. 131, 132.

In the winter months, however, the supply of "postage currency" became more adequate to the needs of retail trade. Nearly $7,000,000 had been issued by the end of December, 1862, and $12,000,000 more were added in the next three months.[1]   When people could obtain this federal currency, they manifested a strong disposition to reject postage stamps and "shinplasters" — even those issued by the towns.   The Springfield *Republican* of January 29 said :

There is a general agreement throughout the country to banish all private and corporate shinplasters and use only the government postage currency for change after the first of February. In Boston, already, none but those of the Parker House remain in circulation, and these are refused at many stores, and are being fast retired. . . . . A few choice shinplasters may be temporarily retained in special localities, till sufficient of the postal currency works in to accommodate public wants. . . . . There are large amounts of the postal currency in circulation, and much is hoarded that will come out as soon as the other sort is banished.[2]

As late as March the Philadelphia *Ledger* said :

Now Philadelphia is tolerably well supplied with small currency authorized by the government, while at New York and other eastern points they are suffering great inconvenience and much loss by an immense circulation of all sorts of trash. . . . . So intolerable has the nuisance become, everybody is denying them, causing quite a panic among the poorer classes — those least able to bear the loss. . . . . Nobody but the brokers will deal in them now. . . . . The corporation issues of Newark and Jersey City . . . . more popular than others . . . . are included in the general decree of banishment. . . . . The people will take nothing but government postage currency for small change. There appears to be no lack of it now.[3]

To protect holders of postage stamps that had been used as currency from losses similar to those suffered by holders

[1] BAYLEY, *National Loans of the United States*, p. 159.

[2] Compare the notice published by the same newspaper at the head of its editorial section January 23, that "no shinplasters or postage stamps except in the sheet" would be received in remittances after that date. See also notice of January 27.

[3] Quoted in *Bankers' Magazine*, Vol. XVII, p. 823.

of shinplasters the postmaster-general was obliged to order the redemption of such stamps as were evidently uncanceled.[1]

May 27, 1863, issues of the postage currency ceased, after $20,000,000 had been placed in circulation.   Its place was taken by the "fractional currency" authorized by the act of March 3, 1863.[2]   The new notes were made of thinner but stronger paper, could not be counterfeited easily, and were not injured by wetting.[3]   But aside from the technical superiority of the new issues as currency, the change was one only in name.   The title "postage currency" had been a misnomer, for the notes were not like ordinary postage stamps.   Issues of the new notes commenced October 10, 1863.   By the 30th of June, 1864, about $7,750,000 of the fractional currency had been put in circulation, while $5,000,-000 of the postage currency had been withdrawn, so that the whole amount outstanding was not quite $23,000,000.[4]   The same process of withdrawal of the old and substitution of the new notes was continued during the next year.   The amount of postage currency decreased from $15,000,000 to $10,000,000, while the amount of the fractional currency increased from $7,750,000 to $15,000,000.   Thus at the end of the war the aggregate fractional currency of both kinds in use was $25,000,000.[5]

V. MINOR COINS

The difficulties with the circulating medium did not stop with the subsidiary coins of silver, but extended even to the minor coins of base metals.   The act of February 21, 1857, had provided for replacing the old copper cents of 168 grains by coins weighing 72 grains and composed of 88

---

[1] *Report of the Postmaster-General*, cited above, p. 133, and *Annual American Cyclopædia*, 1862, p. 463.

[2] 12 *Statutes at Large*, p. 711.   [3] *Bankers' Magazine*, Vol. XVIII, p. 364.

[4] *Report of the Secretary of the Treasury*, December, 1864, p. 45.

[5] *Report of the Secretary of the Treasury*, December, 1865, p. 53.

parts copper and 12 parts nickel.[1]   Of these new cents there had been issued 116,066,000 by June 30, 1862.[2]   The work of exchanging the new for the old coins was still going on, but the director of the mint reported in October, 1862, that the number of old cents was rapidly diminishing and that they would soon disappear altogether from circulation.[3]   The new cents, together with such of the old as still remained in use, were the only minor coins, for the making of half-cents had been stopped by the act of 1857, and two, three, and five-cent pieces were not authorized until 1864, 1865, and 1866, respectively.[4]

The withdrawal of the silver coins from circulation in June and July caused a marked extension in the use of the nickel cents as substitutes.   To make them serve more conveniently in the place of silver, cents were sometimes done up in rolls of twenty-five and passed from hand to hand, frequently without opening.[5]   The demand for these coins at the mint suddenly became very great.   As many as 3,600,000 pieces were struck at Philadelphia in July, and there was a great rush to procure them.[6]   " Large amounts," said the director of the mint in October, " have been sent to every part of the country, and orders beyond our ability to fill are constantly forwarded to the mint."[7]   The number of cents coined increased from 10,000,000 in the fiscal year 1861 and 12,000,000 in 1862, to 48,000,000 in 1863.[8]

It is a curious but well-attested fact that the nickel cents went to a premium almost as soon as the subsidiary silver coins.   The New York *Commercial Advertiser* of July 10

[1] Sec. 4, 11 *Statutes at Large*, p. 163.

[2] *Reports of the Director of the Mint*, October, 1857 and 1862, pp. 49 and 75 respectively.   Here and in other citations of the *Reports of the Director of the Mint* the pages refer to the finance reports.

[3] *Ibid.*, p. 46.   [4] *Coinage Laws of the United States, 1792 to 1894*, 4th ed., p. 89.

[5] Springfield *Republican*, July 15, 1862.

[6] *Bankers' Magazine*, Vol. XVII, p. 390.

[7] *Report*, p. 46.   [8] *Report of the Director of the Mint*, October, 1865, p. 237.

reported that while gold was at 17 per cent. premium in paper, silver was at 10 and nickel at 4 per cent. A similar condition was noted by the Springfield *Republican* July 15, and the director of the mint in his annual report for 1863 said that "for the past two years" cents had "commanded a premium" and were then "scarcely to be had." [1]

The cause for this premium on cents in 1862 must have been different from the cause for the premium on gold and silver coins. The latter were at a premium because the bullion in them was of more value than the corresponding sums of paper money. According to the director of the mint, however, the cent in 1862 cost "the government scarcely half a cent," [2] and again in 1863 he reported that nickel cents contained a "half cent's worth of metal, more or less, according to market fluctuations." [3] These statements of cost to the government, however, do not necessarily show the market value of cents as bullion, because a large part of the metal used in their manufacture was imported, [4] and the duties which private men would have to pay were remitted to the mint. But these duties were not heavy enough to make a very great difference. Under the tariff act of July 14, 1862, imported nickel paid a tax of but 10 per cent. *ad valorem*, and under the act of June 30, 1864, this rate was increased to but 15 per cent. [5] Meanwhile copper in pigs, bars, or ingots paid two cents a pound according to the act of March 2, 1861, and $2\frac{1}{2}$ cents according to the act of June 30, 1864. [6]

Consequently, even if the director's estimates of cost be taken to mean cost on a specie basis and 10 per cent. be added for the duties, 100 of the 1-cent coins would have had

[1] P. 189.   [2] *Report*, p. 49.   [3] *Report*, p. 188.

[4] *Ibid.*, p. 189, and letter of the director of the mint to Chase, March 16, 1864, in *Congressional Globe*, 38th Cong., 1st sess., p. 1228.

[5] 12 *Statutes at Large*, p. 550, and 13 *Statutes*, p. 211.

[6] 12 *Statutes at Large*, p. 182, and 13 *Statutes*, p. 206.

a market value as bullion of not more than 55 cents in gold. On this estimate cents would not have gone to a premium in paper currency for the same reason that gold and silver did, until the specie value of a paper dollar was less than 55 cents — that is, until gold was at a premium of almost 82 per cent. But so high a premium was not reached until April, 1864. In July, 1862, when a premium is said to have been paid for cents, the average value of paper dollars was 86.6 cents in gold, and the metal in 100 nickel cents was worth at most about 63½ cents in paper. If men were ready to pay a premium for cents, then, it must have been because of their anxiety to procure a part of the insufficient supply for use as small change — not because they could make a profit by melting or exporting the coins.

This need for 1-cent pieces continued to be felt even after the issue of the postage and fractional currency, for the lowest denominations of the latter were 5 and 3 cents respectively.[1] That the supply of cents was not sufficient to meet the demand is clear. Before suspension they were "considered redundant in quantity," according to the director of the mint, and it "was part of the hourly finesse of buyers and sellers to get rid of them."[2] Although 116,-000,000 of the nickel coins had been issued by June 30, 1862, and 48,000,000 more were added during the next year, the supply was still so short in comparison with the demand that not less than three hundred varieties of illegal cent tokens of the same size, but less weight than the mint cent, and containing no nickel, were issued by private parties in direct violation of the law and "until suppressed were freely used as coin by the public."[3] Since the supply was thus deficient, it is perhaps not surprising that business houses were willing to pay a slight premium for their small change.

[1] KNOX, *United States Notes*, pp. 103 and 104.
[2] *Report of 1863*, p. 189.   [3] *Ibid.*

As the amount of cents called for continued to be so great, and as nickel was a costly ingredient, the director of the mint proposed in October, 1863, to substitute bronze for the alloy of nickel and copper.[1] No action was taken upon this recommendation at the time, and on March 2, 1864, the director wrote a letter to Secretary Chase, calling attention again to the subject:

This change in the material of the cent . . . . has become a necessity from the advance[d] price of nickel (for a supply of which we are at present entirely dependent upon the foreign market, paying for it in gold or its equivalent), and the great uncertainty of procuring an adequate supply for the future from any source at a price within the legal limit, ... if nickel is retained it will be impossible to meet the enormous demand for cents, and the increasing cost of production may compel a cessation of that coinage. The demand for cents is now far beyond our ability to supply it.[2]

Chase sent this letter with one of his own, supporting the director's recommendations, to Fessenden.[3] When the proposal to drop nickel as an ingredient in the coinage became known, it encountered serious opposition from the friends of Mr. Joseph Wharton, from whose works in Pennsylvania and New Jersey came the entire domestic supply.[4] To remove their objections Mr. Pollock, the director, wrote a second letter March 16, recommending as a compromise that the old alloy of 88 per cent. copper and 12 per cent. nickel be retained, but that the weight of the cent be reduced from 72 to 48 grains.[5] Mr. Clark, from the Senate finance committee,

[1] *Ibid.*

[2] *Congressional Globe*, 38th Cong., 1st Sess., p. 1228.   [3] *Ibid.*, p. 1227.

[4] Mr. Wharton himself prepared a little pamphlet, *Project for Reorganizing the Small Coinage of the United States of America*, in which he offered to provide all the nickel that would be necessary for making not only one- and two-cent pieces, but also other coins less than twenty-five cents at $2.50 per pound. At this price he estimated that one- and two-cent pieces could be made at a profit of 33⅓ per cent. to the government. The pamphlet bears the date April 15, 1864.

[5] *Congressional Globe*, 38th Cong., 1st Sess., p. 1228.

however, brought in a bill for a bronze cent of 48 grains and a 2-cent piece of the same composition, but twice the weight.[1] This measure was at once passed by the Senate[2] and a month later by the House after very brief discussion.[3]

In October the director of the mint reported that the new coinage law had been "highly successful." "The demand for the one and two-cent pieces," he added, "has been unprecedented, and every effort has been made to meet it." In explaining why the demand continued greater than the supply, despite daily issues largely in excess of any former period, he said:

Large quantities are hoarded and thus kept from circulation. They have also been bought and sold by small brokers at a premium. This has induced individuals to collect them for the purpose of sale, thus producing a scarcity and inconvenience to the public that ought not to exist.[4]

The letters of Mr. Pollock to Secretary Chase and these remarks in the October report indicate that the time had at last come when the bullion value of nickel cents was approximating their nominal value as currency. Indeed, as early as March, 1864, Lyman Trumbull, of Illinois, remarked in the Senate:

The cent as a general thing does not circulate in the country now, I think. We see some few of them here, but in my travels I very seldom see a cent. I do not know how it may be in other portions of the country.[5]

At this time, March 21, gold was at 162 and paper was accordingly worth 61.7 in specie. If cents were being hoarded, it must have been because the advance in the price of nickel, of which Mr. Pollock complained, had carried the bullion value of 100 coins above 62 cents in gold. But

---

1 *Congressional Globe*, 38th Cong., 1st Sess., p. 1227.   2 *Ibid.*, p. 1228.

3 *Ibid.*, p. 1763; act of April 22, 1864; 13 *Statutes at Large*, p. 54.

4 *Report*, October, 1864, p. 213.

5 *Congressional Globe*, 38th Cong., 1st Sess., p. 1227.

whether there was a profit in melting or exporting the minor coins in March, 1864, there apparently was one in June and the following months. The monthly average price of gold was above 200 from June until February of the next year, inclusive. During this period the average specie value of paper dollars varied from 38.7 cents in July to 48.7 cents in February. Even had there been no advance in the gold price of nickel, there would have been a margin of profit in collecting coins which would pass current as money at a gold equivalent of considerably less than 50 cents, but could be sold as bullion for perhaps 55 or more. Consequently, it is not improbable that some of the brokers who bought nickel cents at a premium in the summer of 1864 purchased them to melt or export, not to sell again for change. On the other hand, it should be pointed out that the expense of collecting and handling one-cent pieces would be much greater in proportion to their bullion value than in the case of silver coins.

The situation was, of course, somewhat different with the cents struck under the new coinage law. These coins contained no nickel and weighed but two-thirds as much as the previous issues. During the fiscal year 1865 the government made a profit of about $400,000 from their manufacture.[1] If any premium was paid for them, it must consequently have been from the desire to obtain change. As the nickel cents appear, from what Senator Trumbull and the director say, to have gone out of circulation in large measure, the scarcity of change less than three cents — the smallest fractional note — must have been severe. Of the bronze cents 5,874,000 were struck before July 1 and of the two-cent pieces 1,822,500.[2]

[1] *Report of the Director of the Mint*, September, 1865, p. 232.

[2] No separate statement is made by the director of the mint of the coinage of nickel and bronze cents in the fiscal year of 1864, but the above figures are obtained by subtracting from the total coinage of cents up to June 30, 1864, the total number of copper and nickel cents struck as given in *Coinage Laws of the United States, 1792 –1894*, 4th ed., p. 89.

Though the coinage during the fiscal year 1865 was very rapid—an average of 2,250,000 two-cent pieces and 4,500,-000 cents each month[1]—the supply could not have been sufficient to meet the demand.

One more change was made in the circulation of minor coins before the end of the war. From a price of 226 the last day of 1864 gold fell to 200 by the 1st of March, and the rapid progress of the northern armies then promised a still further fall, which was realized in April and May, when the average price was 148.5 and 135.6 respectively. This fall in gold or rise of paper money seemed to show that the day was close at hand when minor coins would remain in circulation without difficulty.[2] Accordingly a bill was passed without discussion by Congress,[3] authorizing the issue of a three-cent piece, made of copper and nickel, in the proportion of 75 parts of the first and 25 parts of the second. This coin was to be legal tender in payments of sixty cents, and the one and two-cent pieces in payments of four cents. At the same time it was provided that thereafter no fractional notes should be issued of denominations less than five cents, and that any such notes outstanding should be destroyed when paid into the treasury.[4]

When the director of the mint prepared his report at the end of September, 1865, he made no further complaints about the premium on minor coins. Paper dollars had then a value of more than sixty-nine cents in gold, and even the three-cent pieces, containing 25 per cent. of nickel, seemed to have been worth more as currency than as bullion. "The coinage of the cent and the two-cent piece from the bronze alloy," the director said, "has been very large, but not in

[1] Report of the Director of the Mint, 1865, p. 235.

[2] Hunt's Merchants' Magazine for May, 1865, includes "coppers" in its statement of "the active circulation of the country," Vol. LII, p. 381.

[3] Congressional Globe, 38th Cong., 2d Sess., pp. 1391 and 1403.

[4] Act of March 3, 1865; 13 Statutes at Large, p. 517.

excess of the demand.   They have been distributed to almost
every part of the United States, and many into states, west
and south, that heretofore refused to use such coin as currency."[1]   He closed by suggesting that the policy pursued
in issuing a three-cent piece be followed further by making
five-cent coins also of 25 per cent. nickel, and that, to make
room for their circulation, all fractional notes below ten cents
be withdrawn.

VI. TREASURY NOTES

As was said above, the first greenbacks were issued early
in April, 1862.   From this time on until specie payments
were resumed, January 1, 1879, they served as the standard
of value in all business transactions and also as an important part of the circulating medium.   United States notes to
the amount of $98,600,000 were issued before July 1, 1862.
From this time on for two years the treasury was paying out
large sums in these notes, but was also redeeming those paid
in to it and then reissuing them.   During the next fiscal year
the issues were $291,300,000 as compared with the redemp-
tions of $2,100,000; during 1864, $86,400,000, as compared
with $42,600,000, and during 1865, $4,200,000, as compared
with $4,300,000.   Thus $431,000,000 were left outstanding
at the close of the war.[2]   The greenbacks served as a
medium of exchange, not only in large, but also in small
transactions, for while the first act provided that $5 should
be the lowest denomination, the second and third acts permitted any denomination not less than a dollar.   The amount
of the several denominations in use is indicated by the following table:

[1] P. 232.

[2] BAYLEY, *National Loans of the United States*, p. 157.   These statements differ
slightly from those given year by year in the contemporaneous reports of the secretary of the treasury.

TABLE IV

UNITED STATES NOTES OF THE SEVERAL DENOMINATIONS OUTSTANDING AT THE CLOSE
OF EACH FISCAL YEAR FROM 1862 TO 1866 [1]

(In millions of dollars)

	1862	1863	1864	1865	1866
One dollar............	....	16.0	16.8	17.8	17.2
Two dollars..........	....	17.0	17.7	19.6	18.8
Five dollars..........	17.1	79.9	95.5	96.0	95.4
Ten dollars..........	15.4	90.0	108.7	109.5	109.0
Twenty dollars.......	15.0	74.9	86.6	86.1	85.1
Fifty dollars.........	13.0	23.0	29.9	29.7	29.3
One hundred dollars.	13.0	30.8	34.2	33.8	33.3
Five hundred dollars.	13.0	26.5	25.4	24.8	35.4
One thousand dollars.	10.0	29.5	37.1	35.8	57.1
Total	96.6	387.6	451.9	453.1	480.7
Denomination un-known, in reserve...	....	....	4.6	22.0	79.9
Net..............	96.6	387.6	447.3	431.1	400.8

But the greenbacks were by no means the only form of government obligations employed as currency. Three other sorts of treasury notes were made a legal tender to the same extent as United States notes, but differed from the latter in that they bore interest. The third legal-tender act, approved March 3, 1863, authorized the issue of $400,000,-000 treasury notes, bearing not more than 6 per cent. interest, redeemable in not more than three years, and a legal tender for their face value, excluding interest.[2] Under this act Mr. Chase issued $166,500,000 of two-year 5 per cent. notes between July 1, 1863, and June 30, 1864, and $44,500,000 of one-year 5 per cent. notes between January 1 and June 30, 1864.[3]

How far these notes were employed as currency is altogether uncertain. It was apparently the expectation of the

[1] *Report of the Secretary of the Treasury*, December, 1896, p. 62.
[2] 12 *Statutes at Large*, sec. 2, p. 710.
[3] BAYLEY, *op. cit.*, p 161.

treasury that banks and capitalists into whose hands they came would retain the notes to secure the interest. This would probably have happened very generally had the interest been paid only at maturity. But when, in the autumn of 1863, Mr. Chase borrowed money for paying the troops from the banks, to be repaid in 5 per cent. notes, the banks stipulated that the notes given them should bear half-yearly interest coupons.[1] One hundred and fifty millions of the $166,500,000 of two-year notes issued were of this form.[2] They were found in practice to be a most unsatisfactory form of currency. After Secretary Chase had ruled that the interest coupons must be detached in the presence of an officer of the treasury or of a national bank,[3] the notes were usually paid out with no regard to the interest until the date on which the next coupon was payable approached, then hoarded for a time, and as soon as the interest had been collected, once more thrown into circulation.[4] This tended, of course, to cause periodical expansions and contractions of the currency embarrassing alike to the business public and to the treasury. The circulation was also rendered irregular by fluctuations in the current rates of interest on short-time loans in the New York market. When money was at 5 per cent. or less, men found it advantageous to retain the government notes in their own hands; but when the rates rose to 7 or 8, few would choose to keep their funds in a short-time 5 per cent. security.[5]

Appreciating these evils, Mr. Chase and Mr. Fessenden, who succeeded him as secretary of the treasury on July 5, 1864, determined to withdraw the coupon notes as rapidly

1 *Hunt's Merchants' Magazine*, Vol. L, p. 455.

2 *Report of the Treasurer*, November, 1864, p. 75.

3 *Hunt's Merchants' Magazine*, Vol. L, p. 455.

4 *Report of the Secretary of the Treasury*, 1864, p. 18; *Hunt's Merchants' Magazine*, Vol. L, pp. 215, 216, and Vol. LI, p. 447.

5 *Hunt's Merchants' Magazine*, Vol. L, pp. 215 and 455.

as possible. Before December, Secretary Fessenden reported, about $90,000,000 of the $150,000,000 issued had
been retired.[1] Their place was occupied by another form
of interest-bearing, legal-tender treasury notes issued under
the authority of the acts of March 3, 1863, and June 30,
1864.[2] The new notes ran three years and bore interest
at 6 per cent., compounded half-yearly but payable only at
maturity. Some $17,000,000 were issued before the close of
the fiscal year 1864, and $180,000,000 during the next year.[3]
These issues were called compound-interest notes. They were
commonly regarded as the least injurious form of treasury
notes devised during the war because of the inducement which
the compound interest gave for keeping them as an investment.[4] Of course, this inducement became stronger the longer
the note had been issued. Thus a $10 note—the smallest de-
nomination—was worth $10.60 at the end of the first year,
$11.25 at the end of the second, and $11.94 at the end of
the third. Anyone who paid the note away at the end of
the first year would therefore lose 60 cents, at the end of the
second $1.25, and at the end of the third $1.94.

Nevertheless the compound-interest notes served to increase the currency inflation to an uncertain extent, both
directly and indirectly. The comptroller of the currency
thought that in October, 1865, perhaps $10,000,000 of these
notes were in actual circulation as money,[5] and in December
the secretary of the treasury thought it was "safe to estimate" that $30,000,000 of the one- and two-year notes of
1863 and the compound-interest notes together were so
used.[6] Perhaps the indirect use was really more important.

[1] *Report*, p. 18. *Cf.* Chase's letter of April 17, 1865, to Colonel J. D. Van Buren
in Schuckers's *Life*, p. 413.

[2] 12 *Statutes at Large*, p. 710, and 13 *Statutes*, p. 218; *cf.* Bayley, p. 84.

[3] Bayley, p. 163. The form of these notes is given by Knox, p. 111.

[4] *Report of the Secretary of the Treasury*, 1864, p. 18.

[5] *H. R. Executive Document No. 4*, 39th Cong., 1st. Sess., p. 5.   [6] *Report*, p. 9.

This was found in practice of banks of holding compound-interest notes as reserves in place of greenbacks that bore no interest. The comptroller of the currency stated that the amount held by national banks October 2, 1865, was $74,-250,000.[1] Similar use was made of the one- and two-year 5 per cent. notes left outstanding.[2] In so far as interest-bearing, legal-tender notes were kept in this fashion, they set free greenbacks for circulation among individuals.

The list of government obligations employed as currency is not yet complete. Two other forms, although not a legal tender, were used as a circulating medium. The issue of certificates of indebtedness, bearing interest at 6 per cent. and payable in one year, had been authorized without limitation of amount by the act of March 1, 1862.[3] This method of postponing claims which they had not the funds to meet at once was availed of on a large scale by the secretaries of the treasury during the entire war. Fifty millions of such certificates were issued in the fiscal year of 1862, $157,000,000 in 1863, $169,000,000 in 1864, and $131,-000,000 in 1865.[4] Most of these notes were paid out to contractors and by them used either as collateral for procuring bank loans or directly as currency. Much of the time certificates of indebtedness were at a small discount, but despite this they passed freely from hand to hand as current funds.[5]

Similar use was made of the "seven-thirties." This was the name given to the three-year treasury notes bearing 7.3 per cent. interest issued under the acts of July 17, 1861, June 30, 1864, and March 3, 1865.[6] Interest on notes

---

[1] See reference in note 5 on preceding page. They were not, however, a legal tender in payment of bank notes.—13 *Statutes at Large*, p. 219.

[2] *Bankers' Magazine*, Vol. XVIII, p. 827; *Hunt's Merchants' Magazine*, Vol. XLIX, p. 384.

[3] 12 *Statutes at Large*, p. 352. [4] BAYLEY, p. 159.

[5] *Cf. Hunt's Merchants' Magazine*, Vol. LII, p. 382.

[6] 12 *Statutes at Large*, p. 259; 13 *Statutes*, pp. 218 and 468.

issued under the first of these laws was paid in gold, but the second and third issues were payable, principal and interest, in lawful money. In the summer and autumn of 1864 Secretary Fessenden offered 7.30 notes of the second issue in small denominations to army officers and soldiers in payment of their wages. Over $20,000,000 were thus paid out in place of greenbacks.[1] In December, 1865, Secretary McCulloch reported that many seven-thirties of these small denominations were in circulation as money.[2]

VII.   RECAPITULATION

Perhaps the clearest view of the confused state of the monetary circulation of the United States during the Civil War can be obtained from a summary statement of the various coins, government obligations used as currency, and bank notes outstanding at the close of the several fiscal years, so far as the amounts can be ascertained. Such a statement is presented on the following page, with a few explanatory notes.

This table is intended rather as an indication of the various kinds of currency in use than as a quantitative statement of the circulating medium. Few of the items can be regarded as showing with any degree of definiteness amounts in use as money. The specie circulation, for example, is computed on the basis of the statistics of coinage and the director of the mint's estimate that in 1861 there were from $275,000,-000 to $300,000,000 of specie in the country and that in 1862 there were $45,000,000 of silver coinage.[3]   A different

---

[1] *Report of the Secretary of the Treasury*, 1864, p. 21.

[2] *Report*, 1865, p. 9.   Under the act of June 30, 1864, it was provided that such of the notes as should be made payable principal and interest at maturity should be a legal tender (13 *Statutes at Large*, p. 218).   As, however, the secretary preferred to attach interest coupons of which only the last was payable with the note at maturity, they did not possess this property.   *Cf.* W. F. DE KNIGHT, *History of the Currency of the Country and of the Loans of the United States* (Treasury Department Doc. No. 1943), 1897, p. 96, and form of the 7-30's as given on the following pages.

[3] *Report* of 1861, p. 62; *Report*, 1862, p. 49.

TABLE V

CURRENCY OF THE LOYAL STATES AT THE CLOSE OF EACH FISCAL YEAR FROM 1860
TO 1866

(In millions of dollars)

	1860	1861	1862	1863	1864	1865	1866
I. *Specie :*[1]							
1. Gold coins......	184.6	245.3	22.0	22.0	22.0	22.0	22.0
2. Silver dollars...	.....	.....	.....	.....	.....	.....	.....
3. Subsidiary silver	39.6	42.2	3.0	3.0	3.0	3.0	3.0
4. Minor coins.....	.9	1.0	1.2	1.6	2.1	3.3	3.9
II. *Postage and fractional currency :*[2]							
1. Postage currency	.....	.....	.....	20.2	15.2	9.9	7.0
2. Fractional curr.	.....	.....	.....	.....	7.7	15.1	20.0
III. *Non-interest bearing, legal-tender, treasury notes:*							
1. Old demand notes[2]..........	.....	.....	53.0	3.4	.8	.5	.3
2. Greenbacks[3]....	.....	.....	96.6	387.6	447.3	431.1	400.8
IV. *Bank notes:*[4]							
1. Notes, state b'ks	207.1	202.0	183.8	238.7	179.2	142.9	20.0
2. Notes, nat'l b'ks	.....	.....	.....	.....	31.2	146.1	281.5
V. *Interest-bearing, legal-tender, treasury notes :*[2]							
1. One-year, 5 per cent., treasury notes of 1863....	.....	.....	.....	.....	44.5	42.3	3.5
2. Two-year, 5 per cent., treasury notes of 1863....	.....	.....	.....	.....	109.0		
3. Compound interest notes........	.....	.....	.....	.....	15.0	193.8	159.0
VI. *Government obligations not a legal tender :*[2]							
1. Certificates of indebtedness......	.....	.....	49.9	156.8	160.7	115.8	26.4
2. 7-30 treasury notes of 1864....	.....	.....	.....	.....	.....	234.4	806.3
3. 7-30 treasury notes of 1865....	.....	.....	.....	.....	.....	437.2	
VII. *Coin, bullion, and paper money in the Treasury*[5]...	6.7	3.6	23.8	79.5	35.9	55.4	80.8

[1] See explanations in text below.

[2] Compiled from the annual *Reports of the Secretary of the Treasury.*

[3] See Table IV above.

[4] *Statistical Abstract of the United States*, 1878, p. 14.

[5] "Information Respecting U. S. Bonds, Paper Currency, Coin," etc. (revised ed., *Treasury Department Circular No. 123*, July 1, 1896), p. 52.

result would have been reached had Mr. Chase's guess at the amount of coin been taken in place of the director's.[1] Of course, the coins put down as circulating after 1862 were used only on the Pacific coast. The common guess is that about $25,000,000 were employed there, and this sum has been divided between gold and subsidiary silver again by guesswork.[2] The figures for the minor coins show the amounts struck under the acts of 1857 and the laws of 1864, 1865, and 1866, as given in the current reports of the director of the mint. But, as has been shown, it is probable that a considerable part of these coins were withdrawn from circulation at least during the summer, autumn, and winter of 1864. On the other hand, some of the old copper cents made before 1857 remained still in circulation in 1862 and large amounts of cent tokens were privately issued in 1863.

The figures for the postage and fractional currency are drawn from the public debt statements of the annual reports of the secretary of the treasury. They are subject to a considerable but indefinite error, particularly in the later years, on account of the large number of these little notes lost and destroyed. It must also be remembered that the place in the currency which they were intended to fill was largely occupied from July, 1862, to perhaps February or March, 1863, by shinplasters and postage stamps.

The next four items in the table are less uncertain. It is well ascertained that the old demand notes were not commonly used as currency after May, 1862. From that time on they were seldom paid out except as a substitute for gold at the customs-houses. The circulation of greenbacks during the war is subject to small doubt, although different official

---

[1] Chase made the coin of the loyal states November 1, 1861, not less than $210,000,-000 (*Report*, 1862, p. 13). The director of the mint made this same sum somewhere between $255,000,000 and $280,000,000. See note 3, p. 178, above.

[2] *Cf.* "Information Respecting United States Bonds, Paper Currency, Coins, etc." (revised ed., *Treasury Department Circular No. 123*, July 1, 1896), p. 52, note 1.

documents do not give precisely identical figures, and the same is true regarding the notes of state and national banks.

In the next two divisions — interest-bearing government obligations which were and which were not a legal tender — the amount outstanding is stated with accuracy by the register of the treasury, but no reliable estimate can be made of the amount that was in actual use as currency at the different dates.

Statements of the volume of the monetary circulation of the United States during the Civil War have been published from time to time in official documents[1] and frequently accepted uncritically as the basis of argument in currency discussions. The preceding review of the situation, indefinite and tedious as it is, has at least the negative merit of showing that such statements are subject to a much wider margin of error than is commonly the case — and few would be found to claim a high degree of accuracy for statements of this sort under the most favorable circumstances. To cast up the totals of the above table would be not only useless, but positively misleading, because several of the items are mere guesses, and in the case of others where the amounts are reasonably certain, not all of the sums set down were in use at any time as currency. Nor could any estimate be made on the basis of the totals that would command confidence. But, while the amount of currency in circulation is not and cannot be known, it is evident from the discussion that not least among the unhappy consequences of the legal-tender acts was the disorder into which the circulating medium was thrown — a disorder that caused much inconvenience to the business public. The more serious effects produced by the disturbance of the standard of value remain to be discussed in other chapters.

---

[1] See for example the *Statistical Abstract* for 1878, p. 14, and the circular of the Treasury Department referred to above.

CHAPTER III

THE SPECIE VALUE OF THE PAPER CURRENCY

I. *The Markets for Gold:*
First Dealings in Gold—The Stock Exchange—The Gold Exchange—The "Open Board"—The Evening Exchange—Nature of the Business in Gold—Tables of the Premium.

II. *Factors which Affected the Gold Price of the Currency:*
Various Theories of the Premium—The Supply of and Demand for Gold—Effect of Receivability for Taxes, Convertibility into Bonds and of the Legal-Tender Clause on the Value of Greenbacks—Effect of Additional Issues—Of Finance Reports—Of "War News"—Of Political Events—Of Foreign Affairs—The Premium and the Quantity Theory—Speculation.

III. *The Course of Depreciation, January, 1862, to December, 1865:*
1. January to April, 1862—2. The Fall from May, 1862, to February, 1863—3. The Rise from March to August, 1863—4. The Fall from September, 1863, to July, 1864—Chase's Campaign against the Gold Speculators—5. The Rise from August, 1864, to May, 1865—6. The Decline from June to December, 1865.

THE MARKETS FOR GOLD[1]

A PREMIUM appeared upon gold as soon as it became known that the treasury and the New York banks had determined to suspend specie payments. This premium represented the difference between the community's valuation of gold coin, on the one hand, and of the paper currency, on the other. In January, 1862, the latter consisted of bank and treasury notes that had been put into circulation as tacit or explicit promises to pay gold coin. Of course, men did not esteem such promises as equivalent to gold itself after the promisors had given public notice that they were unable to redeem

[1] See K. CORNWALLIS, *The Gold Room and the New York Stock Exchange and Clearing House* ("Atlas Series," No. 8), New York, 1879; JAMES K. MEDBERRY, *Men and Mysteries of Wall Street* (Boston, 1870), chapters xii, xiii; HORACE WHITE, *Money and Banking* (Boston, 1896), pp. 174–90; and further references in footnotes below.

their promises for the present, and when no one knew how long such redemption would be postponed. Hence, when men who required gold coin for any purpose sought to procure it in exchange for paper money, they had to pay more than $100 of paper for $100 of gold. Whatever excess they paid was, of course, a premium on gold.

For about a fortnight after suspension there was no organized market for gold in New York. People desiring to buy gold naturally went to the dealers in foreign coin who displayed the precious metals in their shop windows, and people who had specie to sell took it to the same places. But very soon the business became too large to be conducted in this fashion. The small offices of the money brokers were overcrowded, and traders blocked the sidewalks of narrow Wall street to such an extent that the police were given special orders to keep the crowds moving. This state of affairs led to an organization of the traffic and the formation of gold exchanges.

From the published tables of the premium it appears that regular dealing in gold began on the New York stock exchange January 13, 1862. Here it was regarded as the gentlemanly and patriotic thing to sell gold, and the majority of members of the exchange who engaged in the traffic at all were on the "bear" side of the market. A second and less decorous market was formed in a dingy cellar in William street, dubbed the "coal hole." A number of men who were devoting themselves exclusively to dealing in gold took refuge in this place when their business grew too large to be conducted in their private offices or in the street. As the number of brokers increased, the "coal hole" was found too small and the company moved to more commodious quarters, first in Gilpin's News Room at the corner of William street and Exchange place; later in the rooms of the old stock board at No. 24 Beaver street; and finally in New street, next door to the stock exchange. For some time the members of this exchange, that came to be known as the "Gold Room," contented themselves with a very loose organization. It was not until October, 1864, that a constitution and by-laws were adopted and regular officers elected.

Besides the stock exchange and the "Gold Room," there were two other markets for gold in New York — the "open board" and Gallagher's evening exchange. The "open board" of stock brokers was a more popular organization, running as a rival of the "regular board"—*i. e.*, the stock exchange—with which it was amalgamated in 1869. The "evening exchange" was a characteristic excrescence of the times. Speculation was carried to an unprecedented extent in New York during the winter and spring of 1864. Though the regular exchange was kept open long hours, crowds of men thronged the corridors of the Fifth Avenue hotel speculating at night. A certain Mr. Gallagher seized upon the opportunity in March, 1864, to open a luxuriously appointed room opposite the hotel, where gold and railway and petroleum stocks could be bought and sold till midnight. So injurious was this continual round of feverish business deemed that after the disclosure of the Ketchum gold-certificate forgeries[1] in August, 1865, the city banks, the stock exchange, the "open board," and the gold exchange united in an effort to suppress the evening exchange by forbidding their members to frequent it. As a result Gallagher was forced to close his rooms.[2]

The volume of transactions in these markets became very great. Importers came to buy gold, not only for payment of customs dues and for making payments to foreigners, but also for protection against fluctuations in the value of the currency between the time goods were bought and sold.

[1] See, *e. g.*, *Hunt's Merchants' Magazine*, Vol. LIII, p. 226.

[2] *Cf.* New York *Herald* of August 20, and the money article of August 24, 1865; *Tribune*, news columns of March 22, 1864.

Bankers doing business in foreign exchange had to purchase gold for remittances.   Exporters and apparently many men engaged in domestic trade or manufactures bought or sold like importers to guard against changes in the value of the currency.   But the volume of speculative dealings probably far exceeded these transactions growing out of the needs of business.   Indeed, gold became as favorite an article to speculate in as petroleum stocks or railway shares.   Many persons whose occupations presented no need for such operations bought and sold gold — clergymen, physicians, lawyers, small merchants, anyone who had sufficient funds to provide the necessary 10 per cent. margins.   Members of Congress, clerks in the government departments, and newspaper reporters frequently tried to obtain pecuniary advantage from their positions by operating through gold brokers on the information that came to them before it was given to the public.   Most large operators in gold had correspondents in Washington, Baltimore, or Louisville — the centers of war news — charged with sending them early dispatches concerning any event that could affect the credit of the government.   In the "gold room" itself the struggle between opposite parties of speculators partook largely of the sectional feeling of the time ; and when the air was full of exciting war news, the "bulls" would often sing "Dixie," and the "bears" try to drown their voices by chanting "John Brown" in chorus.[1]

The price of gold in currency, as determined by transactions in these New York markets, was regularly reported by telegraph in all considerable towns of the United States, and everywhere accepted as authoritative.   There is no necessity for taking account of the premium on gold in other places, because local markets were dominated by the New York quotations.   The money columns of the daily newspapers

[1] See CORNWALLIS, op. cit., pp. 4–7.

and the weekly or monthly issues of the financial journals gave full reports of current fluctuations, and more permanent records were made by the compilation of a number of tables showing the highest and lowest prices each day for a series of years. Such tables may be found in *Hunt's Merchants' Magazine*, the *Commercial and Financial Chronicle*, the *Bankers' Magazine*, and the annual *Reports of the Chamber of Commerce of the State of New York*.[1]

All of these tables appear to be constructed in the same general manner from the recorded transactions of the most important of the New York markets. From January 13, 1862, to June 20, 1864, they are based upon sales at the stock exchange. On June 21 the "gold bill" went into effect and stopped all dealing in gold outside the private offices of brokers.[2] From this time until the repeal of the "gold bill" by the act of July 2, there was no organized market, and the quotations are those ruling on the street. After the repeal, transactions in gold on the stock exchange were infrequent, and most of the business was done in the "gold room." From July, 1864, on, therefore, the tables are based upon the latter market.[3]

In studying the fluctuations in the gold value of the paper currency it is necessary to go back to these records of the daily premium. As the differences between the tables mentioned are slight, it matters little which set is accepted as a basis for the investigation. I have decided to use the tables published in the chamber of commerce reports, not only because of the official character of the source from which they are taken, but also because they contain fewer obvious errors of the press than some of the others. To adapt them better to the

---

[1] Schuckers, *op. cit.*, pp. 631-4, publishes similar tables for the years 1862-65 prepared by Messrs. B. K. Jamison & Co., bankers, of Philadelphia.

[2] See p. 231, below.

[3] Compare the explanations made regarding the *Commercial and Financial Chronicle* tables; *e. g.*, Vol. I, p. 168.

purposes of the present chapter I have altered their form. As published, the tables show the highest and lowest price paid each day in currency for $100 in gold. This form of statement gives the impression that the fluctuations were due to extraordinary changes in the valuation at which gold was held by the community, whereas in fact they were due mainly to changes in the community's valuation of the notes of the government. When the market quotation was 200 the explanation, of course, was not that men esteemed gold twice as highly as they had done in 1861, but rather that they esteemed the paper currency but half as highly as they had when it was redeemable in specie. A much juster impression of the significance of the change in the relative values of gold and paper money is therefore given by quoting currency at a discount in gold than by quoting gold at a premium in paper; by saying, to use a numerical example, that $100 in greenbacks was worth $50 in gold, than by saying that $100 in gold was worth $200 in greenbacks. For this reason the chamber of commerce tables for the years 1862 to 1865 have been converted into tables showing the highest and lowest daily prices of currency in gold. These tables, given in full in the Appendix,[1] furnish a basis for studying the remarkable changes in the gold value of the currency during the Civil War.

II.   FACTORS WHICH AFFECTED THE GOLD PRICE OF THE CURRENCY

So rapid and so violent were the fluctuations in the gold markets that, despite the absorbing interest of military events, they attracted much attention from the treasury officials and the general public. Various attempts were made to account for the changes. Perhaps the simplest theory was that a nominal advance of gold had been produced by

Pp. 425-8, below.

the nefarious acts of disloyal speculators, who took advantage of the fact that "gold had become a mere commodity" to monopolize the supply and raise the price. This theory logically involved the conclusion that the currency had not depreciated, but that gold had risen in value—a conclusion that was commonly accepted and defended by instancing the case of various commodities that had not advanced in price.[1] One buoyant adherent of this view went so far as to congratulate the country upon the increase in its wealth produced by the advance of gold.[2]

The plausibility of such views diminished in proportion as the rise in the price of commodities progressed, and after the winter of 1862–63 few were found to deny that the paper money had depreciated. It then became common to ascribe depreciation to inflation of the currency, which some charged on the banks, some on the treasury, and some on both. In view of the dominance of the quantity theory of the value of money among economists of the time, inflation was the most natural explanation of the rise of prices. But the fluctuations in the premium on gold were so much more rapid and violent than the changes in the volume of the circulating medium that not even academic economists could regard the quantity theory as an adequate explanation of all the phenomena.[3] Sometimes they charged the fluctuations that did not accompany changes in the quantity of money to mere speculation, sometimes to a variety of other causes. Indeed, in discussing the question, it was common to begin by demonstrating that the premium and the volume of the

[1] Compare the congressional speeches cited above, pp. 113, 114; and *Report of the Secretary of the Treasury*, December, 1862, pp. 12–15.

[2] S. P. TOWNSEND, *The Great Speech of the Late Political Campaign, etc.* (New York: J. A. Houston, 1862), p. 10.

[3] PRESIDENT J. T. CHAMPLIN of Colby University, for example, who enunciated a stiff form of the quantity theory in his little text-book, *Lessons on Political Economy*, 1868, admitted that the value of a paper dollar depends "partly upon the prospect of its being ultimately redeemed in real values" (p. 125).

currency did not vary concomitantly, as they legitimately
should have done, and then to launch into a tirade against
the unpatriotic gold gamblers.[1]

Men who observed the transactions of the gold markets
with care and did not allow their conclusions to be controlled
by preconceived theories, as a rule gave less simple explanations of the changes. The momentary credit of the government, the course of military events, the policy of the banks,
the export of specie, the demand for gold from importers,
the probability of fresh issues of legal-tender paper, treasury
sales of gold, speculative manipulation of the markets, the
chance of resumption of specie payments—these and similar
matters were declared to affect the premium. Some writers
jumbled such matters together indiscriminately and implied
that the price of gold depended in the same manner on all;
others attempted to show the logical connection between
one set of factors and another; but perhaps no one who
studied the situation with care failed to see that the oscilla-
tions of the indicator in the gold room generally followed
the news dispatches from Washington and the front.[2]

Anyone who undertakes nowadays to investigate the
grounds for these divergent opinions regarding the premium
on gold must make a patient study of the transactions in
the gold market from day to day in order to discover what
considerations influenced those who bought and sold.   For

[1] *Cf.*, *e. g.*, FESSENDEN and McCULLOCH in the *Finance Report* of 1864, pp. 22, 23
and 52, 53, respectively. Perhaps as near an approach as any to a strict quantity
theory of the premium is found in *Hunt's Merchants' Magazine*, Vol. L, p. 299.

[2] See as examples A. B. JOHNSON, *The Advanced Value of Gold, Suspended Specie
Payments, etc.* (Utica, N. Y., 1862); ALEXANDER DELMAR, *Gold Money and
Paper Money* (New York, 1863); HENRY C. CAREY, *The Way to Outdo England
without Fighting Her*, 1865, Letters XII–XVI, and other of Carey's pamphlets on the
currency; CARL VON HOCK, *Die Finanzen und die Finanzgeschichte der Vereinigten
Staaten* (Stuttgart, 1867), pp. 585-90; H. M. FITZHUGH, *Cash and Credit* (Baltimore,
1868); CHARLES A. MANN, *Paper Money the Root of Evil* (New York, 1872), pp.
166–79; CHARLES MORAN, *Money, Currencies and Banking* (New York, 1875), p. 21;
R. E. THOMPSON, *Social Science and National Economy* (Philadelphia, 1875), p. 205;
CARL SCHURZ, *Honest Money and Labor: An Address* (New York, 1879), p. 35; GEORGE
M. WESTON, *Money* (New York, 1882), pp. 77-80.

this purpose it is necessary to have recourse to the financial columns of the newspapers, in which the fluctuations of the premium were reported and attempts made to account for them. Such reading, however, merely supplies a mass of material of uneven value and contradictory meaning that requires careful analysis before much can be made of it. And at best the investigator is forced to admit that his conclusions regarding many of the fluctuations are open to doubt, either because some of the factors affecting the situation are unknown to him, or because it is difficult to assign their relative importance to the different factors that were active at the same time. The difficulties arise mainly in explaining the quantitative effects of given causes; one often feels that for aught one knows a certain event might have produced equally well half or double the actual effect. But, as in the case of most economic questions, the qualitative analysis is less uncertain; one can see why the known factors should have produced a certain sort of consequences, though one would be puzzled to say why these consequences were of the given magnitude.

In analyzing the influences that made themselves felt on the stock exchange and in the gold room, after this fashion, one naturally begins by distinguishing two broad classes. Since the price quoted showed the ratio between gold and paper currency, and changed whenever anything occurred to alter the supply of, or the demand for, either, the factors to be taken account of may be ranged under these heads: (1) factors affecting the valuation of gold, (2) factors affecting the valuation of greenbacks.

But brief attention need be given to the first category. The common assertion that the high premium was due, not to depreciation of the currency, but to an advance in the valuation of gold produced by speculation, commands scant respect in face of the evidence borne by exports of precious

metals and by the price tables.   Gold has a world-market perhaps more truly than any other commodity, and the fact is
well ascertained that in the early sixties its value in European markets was declining.   If, then, the value of gold
had been notably augmented in the United States by
"speculation " or any other cause, the export of the precious
metals would inevitably have declined and imports might
have begun.   But such was by no means the case.   In the
fiscal year 1861 imports of gold exceeded exports by $14,900,-
000, but after specie payments had been suspended in 1862
exports exceeded imports by $21,500,000, in 1863 by
$56,600,000, in 1864 by $89,500,000, in 1865 by $51,900,-
000, and in 1866 by $63,000,000.[1]   As was remarked at the
time, gold really became redundant in the United States
when it had been withdrawn from current circulation as
money, and when bankers were asked for exchange they
could "find no commodity so cheap as gold to ship and
draw against." [2]

Equally decisive is the testimony of the price tables.   If
the "gold-room gambling " actually caused a rise of gold,
prices of commodities reckoned in gold must have fallen.
But, as will be shown at length in the next chapter, this did
not happen.   On the contrary, the price of gold in currency,
momentary fluctuations apart, rose less than the currency
prices of most commodities.   This evidence of the price-
tables accords perfectly with the evidence of the gold-export
tables and effectually disproves the theory which explains
the premium as a consequence of an advance of gold engin-
eered by mercenary speculators.

The demonstration, however, that gold did not appreciate
in value in the United States during the war, does not exclude
the possibility of temporary fluctuations in the premium

[1] *Statistical Abstract of the United States*, 1901, p. 73.
[2] *Hunt's Merchants' Magazine*, Vol. XLVIII, p. 224.

caused by changes in the supply and demand for gold in the local market. Indeed, it is certain that such changes exercised a perceptible influence upon the gold quotations, especially in quiet times. New York's supply of gold came mainly from inland towns and from California. Receipts reported from the latter source, it is true, fell from $32,600,000 in 1861 to $10,400,000 in 1863, because of danger of capture by Confederate cruisers that haunted the track of the Aspinwall steamers. But this simply meant that gold destined for export was shipped directly from California under a foreign flag, instead of being brought through New York as heretofore. While the shipments from California to New York declined $22,200,000 between 1861 and 1863, the shipments to England increased $24,400,000.[1]

Demand for gold in New York was mainly either for payment of customs duties or for export. According to the official tables, the monthly customs receipts varied during the war from $2,500,000 in December, 1862, to nearly $14,000,000 in April, 1864, while the exports of specie and bullion varied from less than $500,000 in March, 1865, to nearly $10,000,000 in June, 1862.[2] If the fluctuations in the amount of gold used for these two purposes each month from January, 1862, to December, 1865, be compared with the corresponding changes in the average value of the premium each month, only twenty-two of the forty-seven cases are found to present concomitant variations. But while this comparison shows that the demand for gold for such purposes was not the dominant factor in the market, it does not show that this demand had no effect. On the contrary, there can be little doubt that when the market was free

---

[1] See tables of exports of specie from San Francisco in *Commercial and Financial Chronicle*, Vol. II, p. 135; and compare *Hunt's Merchants' Magazine*, Vol. LIV, p. 96.

[2] See the tables published in the *Commercial and Financial Chronicle*, Vol. II, pp. 230, 231.

from more powerful influences, purchases of gold for the payment of duties sometimes caused relatively slight increases of the premium; and that the export demand had similar effects is sufficiently shown by the fact that news that the Bank of England had raised its discount rate could send up the premium because it made probable larger exports to London.[1]

It was a fact noted at the time that what influence this market demand and supply had upon the premium was often in the direction of moderating instead of increasing the fluctuations. When the premium rose sharply, gold that had been hoarded would be sent to be sold on the stock exchange in order to benefit by the high price. At this high price, however, importers would find it unprofitable to buy the gold they required to pay customs duties or remit abroad. Thus, demand would decrease while the supply increased. Precisely the opposite results were noticed when the price fell rapidly. To an extent, therefore, the supply and demand for gold, instead of controlling, were themselves controlled by the fluctuations of the premium.[2]

Aside from fluctuations caused by changes in the actual supply of and demand for gold, it was possible for a strong clique of dealers to produce fluctuations by "cornering" the local supply at a time when many men had entered into contracts that required the purchase of gold in large amounts within a limited time. Such attempts at "manipulating" the market appear to have been frequent, but their effect was necessarily temporary. Unless the clique could persuade the public that there was some real reason for a low valuation of the government's notes in comparison with gold, they could not long maintain an

---

[1] See, e. g., money articles of New York *Times*, February 3, 1864; May 17, 1864.

[2] See *Hunt's Merchants' Magazine*, Vol. LIV, pp. 96, 97; money articles of New York *Times* for June 16, 17, and July 24, 1862.

artificial rise.   Black Friday itself — the culmination of the greatest of these raids upon the market — was followed by a fall more rapid than the rise had been.   While, then, speculative manipulation of the gold supply was at times the dominant influence in the market, the abiding forces that governed the premium are to be looked for elsewhere.   They are found in the second-mentioned category of influences, viz., the considerations which entered into the community's valuation of the paper currency.

What, then, were these considerations?   Obviously, the utility of the material of which the currency was made was not one of them; for the bits of engraved paper were themselves nearly worthless.   Congress, however, attempted by inserting certain provisions in the legal-tender acts to give these bits of paper a high value in exchange.   United States notes were made receivable for all taxes except duties on imports; they were exchangeable at par for bonds bearing an interest of 6 per cent. in gold; and they were declared a legal tender in the payment of debts.[1]

Had the issues of greenbacks not exceeded the sums required for the payment of internal revenue taxes, etc., the first of these provisions might have been efficacious, at least in some measure.   But the volume of paper money available for such uses was many times too great to be absorbed by them.[2] After the war, writers of the greenback party fell into the habit of declaring that the failure of the clause making greenbacks receivable for taxes to prevent their depreciation, was due to the exception of customs dues, which continued to be payable in gold.[3]   This contention was supported by referring   to   the   case   of   the   old   demand   notes   that

[1] Act of February 25, 1862, sec. 1; 12 Statutes at Large, p. 345.

[2] It has already been shown that several other forms of paper issues were made legal tender to the same extent as the greenbacks.   See Part II, chap. ii, sec. vi, above.

[3] This exception was made, it will be remembered, in order to obtain coin for the payment of interest on the debt.   See Part I, chap. ii, sec. iv, p. 76, above.

commanded a premium in greenbacks from early in May, 1862, because they were receivable for all dues to the government without exception.[1] Had the greenbacks been unlimited legal tender like the old demand notes, ran the argument, they would have maintained as high a value.[2] It is not true, however, as was so frequently asserted, that the old demand notes did not depreciate after suspension. Their availability for customs, in conjunction with their relatively small amount, caused them to be preferred above greenbacks, but the premium which they bore was not equal to the premium upon gold, until practically all had been withdrawn from circulation. The degree of their depreciation as compared with that of greenbacks is shown by the following table, based upon the weekly quotations given in *Hunt's Merchants' Magazine.*

While this table shows that receivability for customs limited the maximum depreciation of the old demand notes to less than 10 per cent. in gold, it does not at all follow that the greenbacks would have remained as near par had they been endowed with the same property. Indeed, this property had so powerful an effect in buoying up the demand notes precisely because it was not shared with other forms of paper money. Only $60,000,000 of the demand notes were issued, and the first legal-tender act provided that they should be canceled and replaced by United States notes as rapidly as feasible. In contrast, more than seven times this amount of greenbacks were issued and they were paid out again about as rapidly as they were paid in.

The second congressional provision for sustaining the value of the greenbacks—the privilege of exchanging them at par for bonds bearing 6 per cent. interest in coin, redeem-

---

[1] See Part II, chap. ii, sec. iii, above.

[2] See citations from greenback literature given by R. M. BRECKENRIDGE, "The Demand Notes of 1861," *Sound Currency*, Vol. V, p. 331.

TABLE VI

RELATIVE DEPRECIATION OF UNITED STATES NOTES AND OF OLD DEMAND NOTES
AT VARIOUS DATES IN 1862 AND 1863 [1]

DATE	CURRENCY VALUE OF		GOLD VALUE OF		DATE	CURRENCY VALUE OF		GOLD VALUE OF	
	Gold	Old Demand Notes	Currency	Old Demand Notes		Gold	Old Demand Notes	Currency	Old Demand Notes
1862					**1862**				
Apr. 12	$101\frac{7}{8}$	100	98.1	98.1	Oct. 4	$122\frac{3}{4}$	$119\frac{1}{2}$	81.5	97.3
19	$101\frac{9}{16}$	100	98.4	98.4	11	$128\frac{1}{8}$	$123\frac{3}{4}$	78.1	96.6
26	$101\frac{9}{16}$	100	98.4	98.4	18	$130\frac{1}{8}$	129	76.8	99.1
May 3	$102\frac{5}{8}$	100	97.4	97.4	25	$130\frac{5}{8}$	127	76.6	97.2
10	$103\frac{5}{16}$	$100\frac{1}{4}$	96.8	97.0	Nov. 1	$130\frac{7}{16}$	$126\frac{1}{2}$	76.7	97.0
17	$103\frac{1}{16}$	$100\frac{5}{8}$	97.0	97.6	8	$132\frac{1}{4}$	126	75.6	95.3
24	$103\frac{1}{2}$	$100\frac{5}{8}$	96.6	97.2	15	$131\frac{7}{8}$	$126\frac{1}{2}$	75.8	95.9
31	$103\frac{9}{16}$	$100\frac{5}{8}$	96.6	97.2	22	$130\frac{5}{8}$	$124\frac{1}{2}$	76.6	95.1
June 7	$104\frac{1}{16}$	101	96.1	97.1	29	$129\frac{1}{8}$	$124\frac{1}{4}$	77.5	96.4
14	$105\frac{11}{16}$	103	94.6	97.5	Dec. 6	$131\frac{1}{4}$	125	76.2	95.2
23	$107\frac{3}{8}$	103	93.1	95.9	13	$131\frac{9}{16}$	$126\frac{1}{2}$	76.0	96.2
26	$109\frac{1}{4}$	$104\frac{1}{2}$	91.7	95.8	20	$132\frac{7}{16}$	$127\frac{1}{2}$	75.5	96.3
July 5	$109\frac{11}{16}$	$105\frac{1}{4}$	91.2	96.0	27	$132\frac{1}{4}$	129	75.6	97.5
12	$114\frac{3}{16}$	$107\frac{1}{4}$	87.6	93.9	**1863**	....	....	....	....
19	$118\frac{3}{8}$	108	84.5	91.2	Jan. 3	$134\frac{1}{4}$	129	74.6	96.2
26	$117\frac{1}{4}$	$106\frac{1}{2}$	85.3	90.8	10	$137\frac{15}{16}$	135	72.6	98.0
Aug. 2	$115\frac{1}{8}$	$105\frac{1}{4}$	86.9	91.4	17	$147\frac{1}{4}$	143	67.9	97.1
9	$112\frac{11}{16}$	$105\frac{1}{4}$	88.7	93.6	24	$149\frac{3}{16}$	$144\frac{3}{4}$	67.0	97.0
16	$114\frac{9}{16}$	$107\frac{1}{2}$	87.3	93.8	31	$159\frac{3}{4}$	153	62.5	95.7
23	$115\frac{1}{2}$	108	86.6	93.5	Feb. 7	$157\frac{1}{4}$	155	63.6	98.6
30	$115\frac{11}{16}$	$108\frac{1}{4}$	86.4	93.6	14	$155\frac{5}{8}$	151	64.3	97.0
Sept. 6	119	108	84.0	90.8	21	$162\frac{3}{4}$	162	61.5	99.5
13	$118\frac{1}{8}$	$108\frac{3}{4}$	84.7	92.1	28	172	171	58.1	99.4
20	$116\frac{15}{16}$	$112\frac{1}{4}$	85.5	96.2	Mar. 7	$155\frac{1}{8}$	153	64.5	98.6
26	$120\frac{3}{8}$	$116\frac{1}{2}$	83.1	96.8	14	$158\frac{1}{4}$	153	63.2	96.7

able in five and payable in twenty years—was never very effective and was repealed after a year and a half's trial. There has already been occasion to remark that the right of conversion was little exercised in 1862, and that, in the hope

[1] Quotations of gold are from the New York *Chamber of Commerce Reports* referred to above; quotations of old demand notes from *Hunt's Merchants' Magazine*, Vol. XLVII, pp. 33, 338; Vol. XLVIII, pp. 69, 305. The statements of the premium on gold in the latter source differ slightly from those used; they are not taken because of inconsistencies and obvious misprints.— See, *e. g.*, last reference. Quotations of old demand notes cease in *Hunt's Merchants' Magazine* after March 14, when all but about $5,375,000 had been retired. The daily papers, however, continued to quote them for a few weeks longer.

of getting better terms for bonds, discretionary power was granted Secretary Chase to abrogate the right after July 1, 1863.[1] During the continuance of the war, however, this repeal of the funding provision made little difference in the value of the currency, because holders of greenbacks who desired to invest them in government securities could still get five-twenty bonds at rates not far from par. Up to the close of subscriptions for the five-twenties of 1862 under the agency of Jay Cooke these bonds could be bought at par from the government. After this date, January 21, 1864, they could be bought in the New York stock market at the following rates:

TABLE VII

MONTHLY HIGHEST AND LOWEST PRICES OF FIVE-TWENTY COUPON BONDS IN THE
NEW YORK STOCK MARKET IN 1864 AND 1865 [2]

Month	1864		1865	
	Lowest	Highest	Lowest	Highest
January	$101\frac{1}{2}$	$104\frac{7}{8}$	$106\frac{3}{8}$	110
February	$103\frac{3}{4}$	107	$108\frac{7}{8}$	112
March	107	$110\frac{1}{2}$	$104\frac{3}{4}$	$111\frac{3}{4}$
April	105	114	$105\frac{1}{8}$	$109\frac{1}{4}$
May	$105\frac{1}{2}$	$107\frac{1}{4}$	$102\frac{1}{4}$	107
June	101	$106\frac{3}{4}$	102	$104\frac{1}{4}$
July	$101\frac{1}{2}$	109	$103\frac{7}{8}$	106
August	$106\frac{1}{2}$	113	$105\frac{1}{2}$	$106\frac{7}{8}$
September	105	$111\frac{3}{8}$	$105\frac{7}{8}$	$108\frac{1}{8}$
October	$106\frac{1}{2}$	$108\frac{1}{2}$	$101\frac{3}{4}$	$105\frac{1}{4}$
November	$100\frac{1}{2}$	$107\frac{1}{4}$	$99\frac{1}{4}$	103
December	$106\frac{1}{8}$	110	100	$105\frac{1}{8}$

This table shows that, after allowance is made for accumulated interest, the five-twenties at no time in 1864 or 1865 rose more than a few per cent. above par in the paper currency. This few per cent. marks the maximum difference which continuation of the right of exchanging United States

[1] See Part I, chap. iv, pp. 104, 107, 115, above.

[2] From the *Financial Review*, 1873, p. 17 (supplement of the *Commerical and Financial Chronicle*).

notes at par for five-twenties could possibly have added to the value of the former. Of course, the reason why the conversion scheme was not more effective, while it lasted, in preventing depreciation of the currency is found in the fact, that while the government was waging a war of enormous cost and uncertain issue, investors did not put a high value upon its bonds. To attempt to maintain the credit of one set of promises to pay by means of a second set could avail little when the ability of the promisor to keep either set was regarded as doubtful.[1]

As for the legal-tender clause — the third provision against depreciation — it could compel a creditor to receive paper money as the equivalent of gold only for debts already contracted. It could not control contracts to be made in the future. Sellers were free to charge higher prices for their goods when they knew the payment would be in greenbacks; and they did so. Not only did the legal-tender clause fail to prevent depreciation, but, had it been the only support of the value of the greenbacks, the depreciation might have been as great as was the depreciation, for example, of the Russian legal-tender paper money in the first quarter of last century.

But, though these artificial provisions proved futile, one important consideration remained. Greenbacks were notes of the government of the United States, and as such their value — like the value of the notes of a private person — depended upon the credit of the issuer. If confidence in the government's ability ultimately to redeem its notes had been entirely destroyed, the paper money would have depreciated to the level finally reached by the Confederate currency. On the other hand, if the credit of the government had suffered no diminution, its notes would have depreciated

---

[1] Whether the abrogation of the right of funding greenbacks in bonds delayed resumption of specie payments after the war is a further question, discussion of which is not in place here.

little, if at all.   Fluctuations between these two limits — par and zero — followed the varying estimates which the community was all the time making of the government's present and prospective ability to meet its obligations.   It is therefore necessary to analyze the elements that entered into these varying estimates.

First, it is plain that an increase in the amount of the demand debt made speedy repayment more doubtful. Hence the effect of every suggestion of an increase in the amount of the paper currency was to decrease the value of the greenbacks already in circulation.   This is clearly shown by the influence of the second and third legal-tender acts.

June 11, 1862, the gold value of $100 in paper currency was $96.22.[1]   The next day it was officially announced that the secretary of the treasury had requested Congress to authorize a second issue of United States notes.[2]   Immediately the value of the currency declined to $94.96.   As the probability increased that the request would be complied with, the fall continued, until, on the day when the final vote was taken on the second legal-tender act, July 8, the currency price was $89.79.[3]

Even more striking was the fall caused by the third legal-tender act.   December 1, 1862, just before Congress convened, currency was worth $76.94.   Three days later a fall to $74.63 was caused by a rumor that the annual finance report would recommend another issue of United States notes.[4]   A denial produced a reaction to $76.63.   But on the 8th Thaddeus Stevens introduced a bill providing for

---

[1] See the tables of daily prices in the Appendix, pp. 425–8. The figures in the text for certain days are sometimes the highest or lowest prices, sometimes (as here) the average of the two.

[2] See the New York *Times*, June 12, 1862.

[3] *Congressional Globe*, 37th Cong., 2d Sess., p. 3182.

[4] *Bankers' Magazine*, New York, Vol. XVII, p. 560.

an issue of $200,000,000,[1] which brought about a relapse the next day to $75.19. When he admitted, a few days later, that there was no chance of his measure passing, a slight rise followed.[2] But January 8 the Committee of Ways and Means submitted a measure authorizing the issue of $300,000,000 of United States notes,[3] The currency fell to $72.99. Six days later the House of Representatives passed a joint resolution for the issue of $100,000,000 to secure the immediate payment of the army and navy.[4] The fall reached $67.57. The acquiescence of the Senate caused a slight further decline.

Meanwhile the Ways and Means bill was under discussion in the House. When it was passed and sent to the Senate, the notes were depressed to $65.90.[5] Three weeks later the measure came back with the Senate amendments, one of which reduced the new issue of legal-tender notes from $300,000,000 to $150,000,000. A drop of $1.46 followed the House's refusal to agree to the change. During the next two days it was thought in New York that the Senate would yield, and the decline of the currency continued to $60.98. When this idea was dissipated there was another reaction. But February 26 the House yielded and passed the bill.[6] This action made the increase of notes certain, and their value fell to $57.97. After this extreme depression came a slight reaction to $58.48 on the day the bill became a law.[7]

<hr>

[1] *Congressional Globe*, 37th Cong., 3d Sess., pp. 23, 145; New York *Times*, December 9, 1862. The references to the daily papers are, unless otherwise specified, to the date of the money articles.

[2] *Congressional Globe*, loc. cit., p. 146.

[3] *Ibid.*, p. 235. See sec. 3 of the bill, p. 284.

[4] *Ibid.*, p. 314.   [5] January 26.—*Ibid.*, p. 522.

[6] For Senate amendments see *ibid.*, pp. 926, 927; for action of the House, pp. 1039, 1312.

[7] March 3, 1863. The probability of further issues of greenbacks was, however, by no means the only depressing influence affecting the value of the currency while either the second or third legal-tender bills was pending in Congress. See pp. 213, 216, below.

Not only the amount of notes which the government issued, but also the condition of the resources at its disposal for meeting obligations, affected the probability of a speedy redemption of the paper currency. This explains why almost every important public event was reflected in the fluctuations of the gold market. Few things could happen to the government that would not directly or indirectly influence its credit, and therefore the value of its notes. Consequently notice must be taken of the effect of financial, military, political, and diplomatic events upon the course of the depreciation.

Since the first condition of redeeming the paper currency was financial strength, the condition of the treasury was narrowly watched by the gold market. For example, the annual reports of the secretary of the treasury were anxiously awaited each December and their appearance caused a rise or fall of the currency according as the condition of the finances presented seemed hopeful or gloomy. In December, 1862, the day before the report was published, a rumor was circulated in New York that another issue of greenbacks would be proposed. The currency fell from $76.34 to $74.63, but rose again to $76.63, when the report appeared recommending a national bank currency as preferable to government notes. Next year the report was responsible for a slight decline; for, though Secretary Chase declared specifically against an increase of the greenbacks, the estimated expenditures so far exceeded receipts that he was obliged to ask for a loan of $900,000,000. Again in 1864 the report caused a fall, for even the New York *Tribune* admitted that it was disappointing.[1] By December, 1865, the gold market had become much steadier, but Secretary McCulloch's report recommending a speedy resumption of

---

[1] See the editorial article in the issue of December 8, 1864, and the money article for December 7.

specie payments was warmly received and caused a rise of the currency from $67.34 on the 5th to $68.14 on the 6th.[1]

Ability of the government to borrow also influenced the value of the currency; for the fate of a loan indicated public confidence or distrust, and success provided means for continuing the war without the issue of more legal-tender notes. Thus, in the spring of 1863, Mr. Jay Cooke's success as agent of the government in obtaining subscriptions for five-twenty bonds at the rate of $2,000,000 a day caused the currency to rise from a level of about $65, prior to March 23, to $71.68 on the 25th, when the favorable result of his operations seemed assured.[2]   In October, 1863, the report that a foreign loan had been obtained caused a rise from $68.49 on the 21st to $70.05 on the 22d.   Next day the report was discredited, and the currency fell back to $68.26.[3]   Again, in September, 1864, a loan of some $32,-500,000 was subscribed twice over and the sum advertised awarded at a premium of 4 per cent. and upwards.   This news caused a rise from $42.37 on the 9th to $45.87 on the 10th.[4]

Changes in the officials of the Treasury Department constituted another important factor.   The resignation of the assistant treasurer in New York caused a fall June 2, 1864, from $53.05 to $52.63.   July 1, of the same year, Secretary Chase's resignation depressed the currency to $40.   A few hours later, upon the receipt of a dispatch announcing Senator Fessenden's appointment to the vacant post, there was a reaction to $45.05.   Mr. McCulloch's nomination the following March occasioned an advance from $50.25 on the 7th to $51.05 on the 8th.

[1] See comments of New York papers of December 6; and *Hunt's Merchants' Magazine*, Vol. LIV, p. 77.

[2] New York *Times*, money article for March 24, 1863.

[3] New York *Times*, money articles for October 22 and 23, 1863.

[4] *Hunt's Merchants' Magazine*, Vol. L I, p. 292; *Report of the Secretary of the Treasury*, December, 1864, p. 21.

Even more striking than the influence of financial events upon the currency was the effect of the "war news." While the war continued there could be no thought of redeeming the government's notes. Hence every victory that made the end of hostilities seem nearer raised the value of the currency, and every defeat depressed it. The failures and successes of the Union armies were recorded by the indicator in the gold room more rapidly than by the daily press. A few instances may be cited.

Chancellorsville, fought May 3, 1863, was one of the most disastrous battles of the war. But the first reports that reached New York were favorable, and caused a rise of the currency to $67.45. Next day, however, adverse rumors began to arrive, and the quotations were lower. On the 6th a partial confirmation of the bad news continued the fall. When all uncertainty about the disaster was removed on the 7th, the currency dropped to $64.62.[1]

Following up the advantage gained at Chancellorsville, General Lee crossed the Potomac and invaded the North. With the progress of his movement the currency fell from $71.17 on the 10th of June, 1863, to $67.40 on the 16th.

Similarly the battle of Chickamauga caused a decline from $74.77 on the 19th of September, 1863, to $71.81 on the 21st; in April, 1864, the currency fell from $57.43 on the 23d to $54.79 on the 25th, because of the report that the Confederates had captured Plymouth, N. C.; General Butler's failure to take Fort Fisher was the occasion of a drop from $46.24 to $44.64, December 28, 1864: the knowledge of the ill success of the Yazoo river expedition brought a fall of over $4, from $67.34 March 31 to $63.34 April 1, 1863.[2]

The power of victories to raise the value of the currency

[1] See conflicting reports from the battles in the New York papers of May 4 to 8, 1863.

[2] See the news columns of the papers of April 2, 1863.

was most strikingly illustrated by the series of triumphs in July, 1863. On the first three days of that month the battle of Gettysburg was being fought. The 4th was the national holiday; the 5th Sunday. When the gold market opened on the 6th, currency, which on the 1st had been at $68.97, rose to $72.46. Next day news came of the capture of Vicksburg; currency reached $75.47. Despite the draft riots in New York city, the reaction was small, and when the capture of Port Hudson was announced, July 15, there was a further advance to $77.59. With the increase of confidence the currency continued to appreciate, until upon the 20th it was worth $81.14. Thus the gain was $12.17 in twenty days, due to favorable war news.

Grant's series of victories at Chattanooga caused a rise of $4.99 in four days. The victory of Sheridan over Early at Opequan Creek and two days later at Fisher's Hill led to an advance from $44.10 to $46.30. Sherman's capture of Atlanta, announced in New York September 3, 1864, occasioned a rise from $39.29 on the preceding day to $42.37. Later, after Sherman had started north from Georgia, no news came from his army for some time, and fears were entertained for his safety until March 14, 1865, when a dispatch was received stating that he had reached Laurel Hill, N. C., and that all was well. This news caused the currency to appreciate from $52.22 to $56.26. More examples might readily be given.

Many of the fluctuations of the currency were due to mistaken reports of military events. Thus, September 3, 1862, an absurd story that Stonewall Jackson was marching on Baltimore with 40,000 men caused a fall from $85.84 — the price of the previous day — to $84.75.[1] A rumor that Atlanta had been evacuated by the Confederates produced a rise from $38.80 to $39.92 on July 22, 1864.[2] Another false report of

---

[1] New York *Times*, money article, September, 3, 1862.
[2] *Ibid.*, money article for July 22, 1864.

the fall of Petersburg led to an advance from $48.78 to $51.28.[1] A similar story of the evacuation of Richmond was the occasion of the change from $56.54 to $58.74 on the 16th of March, 1865.[2] Peace rumors were especially frequent. The "peace mission" of the two Blairs was followed with much anxiety. A report that the elder Blair was in Richmond caused a rise from $46.54 to $48.08 January 19, 1865.[3] On the last day of the month news came that three Confederate commissioners were within the Union lines.[4] Currency rose from $47.39 to $49.50; but fell back again to $46.62 on the announcement, a few days later, that the conference would accomplish nothing.

Being of less frequent occurrence, political changes played a less prominent rôle in the gold market than financial and military affairs. The best example of their influence is shown by the events attending the presidential election of 1864. Mr. Lincoln was the Republican nominee. The Democratic party, which did not hold its convention until August 31, finally nominated General McClellan. News of this choice caused the currency to fall from $42.73 to $41.15. The canvass that followed was spirited, and for a time the result seemed doubtful to many. The Pennsylvania state election in October was looked to for an indication of the probable outcome. For a day or two after the votes had been cast it was uncertain which party had won. October 11 the New York *World* claimed that the Democrats had made large gains and would carry the state. Because of this report the currency fell from $50.41 to $49.17. Curiously, the Republican triumph in November had the same effect upon the currency as this promise of Democratic success had exercised. It seems to have been argued that

---

1 September 28, 1864; see New York *Herald*, money article.

2 New York *Herald*, money article, March 16, 1865.

3 *Ibid.*, January 19, 1865.   4 *Ibid.*, January 31, 1865.

President Lincoln's re-election meant an indefinite prolonga-
tion of the war, and hence destroyed any chance of a speedy
redemption of the paper money.[1] On the strength of this
view there was a fall on the 9th from $40.65 to $38.46.
However, a reaction quickly followed.

President Lincoln's assassination occurred after the regular gold market had closed on the evening of April 14, 1865.
Currency had ranged between $67.97 and $68.49.   The
news was received, however, at the "evening exchange."   At
the first shock there was a fall to $60.61.   This fall was
followed by a quick reaction, so that the market closed about
$63.90.[2] Next day the gold exchanges remained closed, and
the following day was Sunday.   The intermission gave an
opportunity for the panic to subside.   On Monday the
opening price was $65.36, but it soon rose to $67.51, and the
next day the currency nearly regained the level which it had
held before the assassination.

Though the country's foreign relations were overshadowed
during the war by domestic affairs, they exercised some influence upon the value of the paper money.   There were two
important matters of diplomatic concern: the chance of foreign intervention between the federal and confederate
governments and the French occupation of Mexico.   Fears on
the former score were in a measure put to rest on July 30,
1862, by the arrival of a steamer from England bringing
reports of a speech of the prime minister, Lord Palmerston,
which was interpreted to mean that the British government had no intention of interfering in the American
war.[3] Currency rose from $85.84—the lowest price on the
29th—to $87.43.   On the 10th of the following February
a report that the French emperor was attempting to bring

[1] See editorial article in New York *Express*, November 9, 1864.

[2] New York *Herald*, money article dated April 16, 1865.

[3] See the dispatches to the New York papers of July 31, 1862, and editorial comments.

about a conference between the North and South caused the paper money to appreciate from $63.90 to $65.57.[1] The news of the withdrawal by England of the recognition which it had accorded the Confederacy as a belligerent occasioned a rise from $68.91 to $71.43 on the 19th of June, 1865.[2]

May 3, 1864, the publication in *Le Moniteur* of the convention assuring the stay of French troops in Mexico caused the currency to depreciate from $56.50 to $55.63.[3] At the close of the war the administration attacked the Mexican question with vigor. June 5, 1865, word came that Napoleon had been urged to withdraw his troops. This news showed the possibility of trouble with France, and caused a slight decline —from $73.94 to $73.13.[4] During the summer many conflicting reports were circulated concerning complications on the Rio Grande, causing considerable fluctuations in the gold market.[5] But the beginning of the end came November 7, with the report that the cabinet had decided to notify the French government that the sending of further troops to Mexico would meet with the disapprobation of the United States. That little fear of a serious complication was entertained is shown by the slight extent of the fall caused by this news—$68.03 on the 6th to $67.91 on the 7th.[6]

Perhaps some explanation should be given why two matters of which much was made by contemporary commentators on the premium have been passed over so lightly in the preceding analysis, viz., the quantity of money in circulation and speculation. Statistical attempts to demonstrate or disprove the validity of the quantity theory of the value of money must always be inconclusive so long as there are no

---

[1] New York *Times*, money article, February 10, 1863.

[2] New York *Herald*, money article, June 19, 1865.

[3] New York *Times*, money article, May 3, 1864.

[4] New York *Herald*, money article, June 5, 1865.

[5] *Hunt's Merchants' Magazine*, Vol. LIII, p. 133.

[6] New York *Herald*, money article, November 7, 1865.

accurate data regarding the volume of exchanges to be performed by the use of money and the rapidity of circulation.[1] Of course, no such data are to be had for the years of the Civil War, and besides there is the added embarrassment that the quantity of money in use is involved in even more obscurity than common.[2] A rigorous comparison between the quantity and the gold value of the currency or between quantity and prices is therefore out of the question. But at least this much may be said with confidence : the fluctuations of the gold premium cannot be accounted for by actual issues and redemptions of government notes. As the above remarks upon the second and third legal-tender acts show, additional issues of United States notes affected the value of the notes already in circulation as soon as their probability was known and long before they were actually made or even authorized. Indeed, in the six months following the passage of the third legal-tender act, when notes were being issued in accordance with its provisions, the value of the currency appreciated in a marked degree.[3] That is, the quantity of the greenbacks influenced their specie value rather by affecting the credit of the government than by altering the volume of the circulating medium.

Nor is the case of the quantity theorist improved by taking account of all forms of money in circulation instead of the greenbacks alone. Most discussions of the value of an inconvertible paper currency proceed on the assumption that its quantity is arbitrarily determined by government, and that the business community must adapt itself to the situation. But such an assumption is hardly more true of the North during the war than of the whole country before suspension. In both periods free use was made of bank

---

[1] I feel none the less convinced of the soundness of this proposition because I once made such an attempt.—*Journal of Political Economy*, Vol. IV, pp. 159–65.

[2] See Part II, chap. ii, sec. vii, above.   [3] See pp. 217–20, below.

notes and bank deposits as currency, and of course the volume of these elements in the circulating medium followed the needs of the public. More than this, the amount of government currency in use as money was in neither case determined solely by treasury policy. Before suspension, free coinage and free export provided for an automatic regulation of the supply of specie; after suspension a somewhat similar element of elasticity was found in the presence of legal-tender, interest-bearing treasury notes which could be treated as an investment or used as money at the convenience of the holder.[1] It would be difficult, indeed, to show that the volume of a currency comprising elements so elastic as these interest-bearing legal tenders and the notes and deposits of banks was the ultimate fact that regulated the value of the whole circulating medium.

As for speculation, there seems to be more danger of exaggerating than of minimizing its importance as an independent factor in the gold market. No doubt, as has been suggested, the formation of highly organized markets, where engagements were entered into to receive or deliver large amounts of gold within stipulated times, gave opportunity for artificial manipulation. No doubt, also, many of the false rumors so industriously circulated were concocted by operators with special intent to affect the premium.[2] But it must be remembered that there were two parties in the market, and the arts of "bulls" were set off against the arts of

[1] See Part II, chap. ii, sec. vi, above.

[2] The most notable instance of this character was the fraudulent proclamation of President Lincoln, taken by unknown persons to the offices of all the New York papers except the *Tribune* about 3:30 o'clock on the morning of May 18, 1864. It stated that Grant's campaign was virtually at an end; that the Red River expedition was a failure, that 400,000 additional men would be raised by draft if the state quotas were not filled by June 15, and that May 26 would be observed as a day of fasting and prayer. Though the *World* and *Journal of Commerce* alone were duped into publishing the document, it caused a rapid rise in the premium before the opening of the exchanges. As the *World* at once denounced the forgery on its bulletin board, the fright subsided quickly and the transactions on the stock exchange were at a very slight advance over the preceding day. See the newspapers of May 18 and 19.

"bears." Which party carried the day depended in the long run on matters over which neither had control — primarily the condition of the finances and the war news. Viewed in a broad way, it is therefore a serious mistake to look on the gold market as a place where a few gamblers were tossing the premium about to suit their selfish schemes; a much saner view is that it was the place where the community's estimate of the government's credit was visibly recorded. Here, as in other markets, those operators succeeded who forecast the future correctly, and men who tried to advance the price of gold when public confidence was increasing, or to depress it when confidence was on the wane, learned to their cost that they were not masters of the situation.

III.　THE COURSE OF DEPRECIATION, JANUARY, 1862, TO DECEMBER, 1865

In order to facilitate study of the progress of depreciation during the war, the highest, average and lowest gold value of the currency for each month from 1862 to 1865 is shown upon the accompanying chart. From this graphic representation it is readily seen that there were six strongly marked periods in the general course of the fluctuations: (1) January to April, 1862, the depreciation was slight and almost constant. (2) After April there occurred an almost unbroken fall until February, 1863, when the average value of the currency for the month was but $62.30. (3) This fall was succeeded by an appreciation, which culminated in the following August, when the average price reached to $79.50. (4) A second and more serious decline followed, until, in July, 1864, the lowest value of the war was reached—$38.70 for the month. (5) August, 1864, to May, 1865, an upward movement, interrupted by a reaction in November, carried the currency to $73.70. (6) After May there was a slow decline till the end of the year.

CHART II

FLUCTUATIONS IN THE GOLD VALUE OF $100 IN AMERICAN PAPER MONEY FROM
JANUARY, 1862, TO DECEMBER, 1865

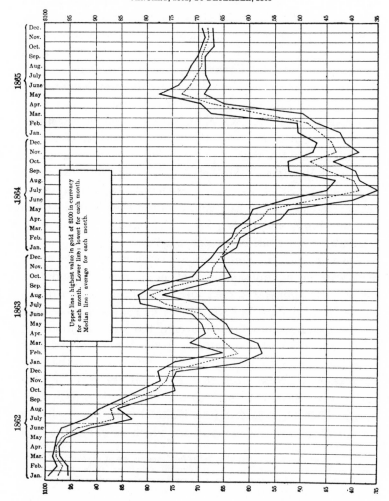

1. *January to April, 1862.*—From a gold value of $99.50 on the 1st of January the currency fell as low as $95.24 on the 10th, but from this point there was a rally, so that the average value for the month was $97.60. The perplexities of the financial situation, particularly the slowness of Congress in framing tax bills, exercised a depressing influence in the first half of February, that was counteracted in the latter half by Grant's capture of Fort Donelson and the provision made for the treasury by the first legal-tender act. Despite this rally, the average for the month was $1 less than in January. March, however, more than restored this loss. Curtis defeated the Confederates decisively at Pea Ridge, the "Monitor" proved itself more than a match for the "Merrimac," McClellan advanced into Western Virginia, and Shields defeated Stonewall Jackson at Winchester on the 23rd.[1] Confidence in the speedy end of the war was high, and consequently the value of the currency was but 1.8 per cent. below par in gold.

During April the depreciation was even less. So confident was the administration that peace was at hand that the adjutant-general issued an order stopping recruiting. While Grant suffered a severe check at Pittsburgh Landing on the 6th, he more than recovered the lost ground on the 7th. Island No. 10 surrendered, Halleck telegraphed that Pope had captured 6,000 prisoners in Missouri; on the 15th news came to New York that Fort Pulaski, guarding the entrance to Savannah, had been taken; and to crown the month, New Orleans fell into Union hands, in its closing week. Moreover, the greenbacks, which now, for the first

[1] As most of the events referred to in the following review of the course of depreciation are very well known, I have not considered it necessary to insert references to war histories. The newspapers have been my main reliance, because the premium was affected rather by what was reported concerning battles, etc., than by what really happened; but I have also used the diaries in *Harper's Monthly Magazine*, and MOORE's *Record of the Rebellion*, besides DRAPER's *Civil War in America*, and J. F. RHODES's *History of the United States*.

time, began to come into general circulation, were most favorably received, for it was considered highly patriotic to accept the government's notes as nearly the equivalent of gold. Thus, under the stimulus of victories and universal confidence, the paper money reached the highest value of the war —$98.50, a depreciation of but $1.50.

2. *The fall from May, 1862, to February, 1863.*—In May military operations turned against the North. The Confederates quietly slipped out of Yorktown after McClellan had made elaborate preparations for a siege, and McClellan followed so slowly as to lose his advantage. Farragut took Natchez on the 13th, but all the successes of the month were overshadowed by Jackson's brilliant operations iu the Shenandoah valley, where he defeated the Union forces at Front Royal, drove Banks across the Potomac, eluded the attempts of McDowell and Fremont to cut off his retreat, repulsed their attacks at Cross Keys and Port Republic, and finally effected a junction with Lee. So great was the consternation at Washington that the governors were called upon by Stanton to forward all their militia and volunteers for the defense of the capital. From $97.92 on the 1st of the month the currency declined to $96.04 on the 27th, when the fright in Washington was at its height and the average for the month was $1.70 less than it had been in April.

A further fall of $2.90 came in June. Hanover Court-House, Seven Pines, and Fair Oaks caused a slight rise in the last days of May and the first days of June; Fort Pillow was taken on the 4th and Memphis two days later. But on the 12th Chase's request for a second issue of greenbacks was announced. Meanwhile McClellan lay inactive while Stuart's cavalry rode around his army, capturing prisoners and burning supplies.

July brought yet greater disasters. McClellan's peninsu-

lar campaign, which was to have ended with the capture of
Richmond, ended instead with the desperate retreat to Harri-
son's Landing, where he remained quiescent for the rest of the
month. The dream of a prompt close of hostilities was
rudely dispelled, and the president issued a call for 300,000
volunteers. Meanwhile Morgan was raiding in Kentucky, and
Congress passed the second legal-tender act. Under such
depressing influences the currency fell rapidly, and the
average for the month was $7.30 less than in June.

After the 22d of July there was a rally from the extreme
depression that lasted during the first part of August. Halleck's appointment as general-in-chief had a good effect.
Reports were received of a debate in the House of Commons
that was interpreted to mean that the English government
had no intention of intervening in favor of the South.
Such news more than offset the draft of 300,000 nine-
months' militia ordered on the 4th. But after the 11th of
August the current set in the opposite direction. Lee forced
Pope into the defenses before Washington, and opened the
way into Maryland, while Bragg was executing a similar
northward movement in Kentucky. About the same time
the Sioux Indians suddenly commenced their outrages in
Minnesota.

During September the depreciation continued. Lee's
advance caused grave fears for the safety of Baltimore, Har-
risburg, and Philadelphia. The public archives of Pennsylvania were sent to New York for safekeeping, and Governor
Curtin called for 50,000 men to repel the invasion. Similar
fears were entertained for Louisville and Cincinnati, which
Bragg and Kirby Smith were threatening. The fall was
stopped for a week in the middle of the month by the battles
of South Mountain on the 14th and Antietam on the 17th,
but the latter was too dearly bought a victory to compensate
for Jackson's capture of Harper's Ferry with its immense

stores and garrison of over 11,000 men. When it was found that McClellan had failed to follow up his advantage and that Lee had recrossed the Potomac in safety, the disappointment was keen, and despite Rosecrans's victory at Iuka the fall of the currency recommenced, and the lowest price was that of the last day of the month.

In October McClellan remained inactive, despite the urging of the president and the impatience of the public. Lee had time to recover in a measure from the losses of his sortie into the free states, and he caused great exasperation by sending Stuart on another raid entirely around McClellan's idle army. In the West military operations favored the North. The desperate attempt to recapture Corinth was foiled by Rosecrans; and Bragg, after his failure to capture Louisville, retreated from Kentucky, suffering rather greater loss than he inflicted at the battle of Perryville on the way. While these successes tended to offset Stuart's raid and McClellan's inactivity, the autumn elections had a very depressing influence. Almost everywhere the administration lost ground. In Maine and Michigan the Republican majorities were greatly reduced; Wisconsin, Illinois, Ohio, Indiana, Pennsylvania, and New York went Democratic. A majority for the opposition was predicted in the House of Representatives.[1] The net effect of these various influences was an average price of the currency $6.60 below that of September.

November was a quieter month, with a much narrower range of fluctuations, although the average value of the currency was somewhat less. Military events were not of great consequence, and the market was dull awaiting the convening of Congress in December. The lowest quotation of the month occurred on the 10th, when the order relieving General McClellan was published.[2]

[1] Cf. BLAINE, Twenty Years of Congress, Vol. I, pp. 441-3.
[2] Cf. money article in New York Times, November 10, 1862.

When Congress assembled Chase's report showed that unpaid requisitions were accumulating at a rapid rate, and that the secretary had no suggestions for increased taxation, but laid great stress upon his widely distrusted banking scheme. Presently, inquiry in Congress called public attention to the fact that the pay of the army was in arrears, and a third issue of United States notes was foreshadowed. The administration was also sharply attacked for the suspension of the writ of *habeas corpus* and for the monitory proclamation of emancipation. Meanwhile there was a quarrel in the Republican ranks. The caucus of the Senate advised the president to reconstruct his cabinet, and in consequence the secretaries of state and of the treasury both resigned, but were prevailed upon by Mr. Lincoln to remain in office. The great military event of the month was Burnside's bloody repulse at Fredericksburg with a loss of nearly 14,000 men. Under this combination of depressing influences the first year of the paper standard closed with a depreciation of 25 per cent.

In January and February the fall of the currency was accelerated in the manner shown above by the framing of the third legal-tender act. On the Potomac Hooker, who succeeded Burnside, was quietly engaged in reorganizing the army and preparing for a spring campaign. Meanwhile it became known that Grant's first campaign against Vicksburg had been frustrated by the destruction of his depot at Holly Springs, and by Sherman's repulse at Chickasaw Bayou on the 29th of December. The next day the "Monitor" foundered off Cape Hatteras, Forrest's Confederate cavalry were beaten at Parker's Cross Roads, and the great battle of Murfreesboro began. On the first of the new year Magruder recaptured Galveston, but ten days later Sherman, on his return from the Yazoo river, captured Arkansas Post with 5,000 prisoners. Early in February a Federal attack on Fort McAllister in Georgia and a Confederate attack on Fort

Donelson in Tennessee were repulsed. The rest of the month was rather quiet and the dominating influence in the gold market was the progress of the third legal-tender act.

This period, May, 1862, to February, 1863, commenced with a depreciation of but 2 per cent., and ended with one of 42 per cent. From May to November the dominating causes of the decline were military disasters and the second issue of greenbacks. McClellan's peninsular campaign was a melancholy failure. Richmond was not taken; instead, Lee invaded the North. Though his sortie was checked at Antietam, full advantage was not taken of the situation. When the offensive was at last resumed with vigor, the defeat of Fredericksburg resulted. What slight advantages had been gained in the West could not counterbalance such disasters. To this ill fortune in war was added the political defeat of the administration in the autumn elections, the dissensions among Republican leaders in Congress and the cabinet, and the gloomy financial prospect. In January and February the depreciation was accelerated, but now because of the legislation pending in Congress rather than because of military events.

3. *The rise from March to August, 1863.*—February closed with the currency at about $58. In March a reaction began. There were no decisive military operations; for Grant was vainly trying to get at Vicksburg from the North, Farragut bombarded Port Hudson without result, and in Tennessee and Virginia the fighting was mainly confined to the cavalry. But Congress had passed the supplementary internal revenue act, the national banking act, and the $900,-000,000 loan act; and the enactment of these laws was followed, as Secretary Chase said, "by an immediate revival of public credit."[1]

The same favorable causes continued to operate in April.

[1] *Report of the Secretary of the Treasury,* December 1863, p. 2.

Jay Cooke now had his system of agencies for the five-twenty loan well organized, and subscriptions began to come in. An unsuccessful bombardment of the forts in Charleston harbor checked the rise for a time; but Banks was successful in his operations along the Bayou Teche in Louisiana, and Grant shifted his forces to the west of the Mississippi, marched them south of Vicksburg, ran his gunboats and transports past the batteries with slight loss, and prepared to cross again and attack the city from the south.   Meanwhile Hooker executed a well-planned movement across the Rappahannock and seemed to have Lee at a disadvantage. For these reasons the average value of the currency was a little higher in April than in March.

During the first week in May there was a fall caused by the disastrous battle of Chancellorsville.   But Grant's cavalry reached Baton Rouge after cutting the communications of Vicksburg with the East, and his main army effected its landing on the eastern bank of the Mississippi and won the series of victories that forced Pemberton back into the city and completed its investment.   A trifle later in the month Banks closed in on Port Hudson farther down the river. These events with increasing subscriptions to the loan[1] caused another advance in the value of the currency, so that the average for the month was slightly higher than for April.

June presents a striking example of an appreciation of the currency — small, to be sure — despite military reverses. After Chancellorsville, the Army of Virginia was reinforced by conscriptions and fitted out better than ever before.   On the 3d of June Lee set forward on a second grand invasion of the North. At Winchester he captured nearly 4,000 prisoners, with many guns and large supplies, and proceeded through the Shenandoah valley to Chambersburg in Pennsylvania.

1 *Cf. Bankers' Magazine*, Vol. XVII, p. 817.

On the 15th President Lincoln issued a call for 100,000 militia from Maryland, Pennsylvania, Ohio, and West Virginia, to aid in repelling the invasion. In the West nothing decisive was accomplished. Grant was pressing Vicksburg closely and Banks Port Hudson, but their attacks upon the works were repulsed without substantial gains. Meanwhile the political opponents of the administration seized the moment to push their agitation against the conduct of the war. Mr. C. L. Vallandingham, who had been arrested for treasonable utterances, was nominated for governor of Ohio. At New York a great "peace meeting" was held. All this made the latter half of June a very dark period for the Union cause. But the machinery of the national loan was now thoroughly organized, and, while Lee was advancing, the treasury was receiving $1,500,000 to $2,500,000 daily for government bonds.[1] The fact that the government was able to borrow on so large a scale, even at this crisis, had a great effect in maintaining its credit, and hence the value of its notes. So, while Lee's invasion caused a heavy fall in the middle of the month, there was a reaction after the first scare subsided, and for the month the average value of the currency was $2 higher than in May.

If June had shown the possibility of a rise in the face of military reverses, July showed how powerful a stimulant was military success. It was a month of victories — Gettysburg, Vicksburg, and Port Hudson. These great successes, with Sherman's expulsion of Johnson from Jackson, the repulse of the Confederates at Helena, and the capture of Morgan and his raiders in Ohio, completely overshadowed the draft riot in New York and a few Union reverses. On the 15th President Lincoln appointed a day of thanksgiving, and on the 25th President Davis a day of fasting and prayer. The advance of the currency over June was $7.40.

[1] *Bankers' Magazine*, Vol. XVIII, p. 607.

August continued the good times.   In a military way the
month lacked dramatic features, for Grant, Meade, and Lee
were allowing their troops a rest, essential after the furious
campaigning of July.   Rosecrans, however, began his
advance against Bragg at Chattanooga, and Burnside moved
on Knoxville.   Much encouragement was received from the
vigorous pushing of the siege of Charleston.[1]   The draft in
New York, which had been interrupted by riots, was resumed
and completed.   Elections in Kentucky, Vermont, and California resulted most favorably for the administration candi-
dates.   Under these circumstances the currency reached
$79.50 — a higher level than was again attained during the
war.

4. *The fall from September, 1863, to July, 1864.*—Many
had expected after the great victories of July that the end
of the rebellion was at hand.   But much to the chagrin of
the president and the public, Lee, instead of being annihi-
lated was suffered to withdraw unmolested across the Potomac, and was soon confronting Meade in the old positions
along the Rappahannock.   Early in September news of
positive disaster was added to this disappointment.   At
Chickamauga Rosecrans lost 16,000 men and narrowly
escaped the destruction of his whole army.   The news
caused a fall of nearly $3 in a single day.   So the currency
declined from $78.82 on the opening day of September to
$69.87 on the 29th.

From the last of September to the close of the year there
was a slow but tolerably steady depreciation.   The lowest
point of the period was $63.80, October 15, caused by rumors
of another forward movement by Lee.   After Longstreet had
been sent west to reinforce Bragg, Hooker was also dispatched
with two corps to help Rosecrans.   Lee then threatened to
turn Meade's flank and compelled him to fall back on Bull

[1] New York *Times*, money articles, July 15, 17, and August 25, 1863.

Run. The operations in Virginia, however, were less important than those in Tennessee, where Grant relieved Rosecrans, who had allowed himself to be cooped up in Chattanooga by Bragg. In November the lowest prices, those of the 21st and 23d, were due to the investment by Longstreet of Knoxville, where Burnside's forces lay; the highest, on the 27th, to Grant's spectacular victories at Chattanooga. December was a very quiet month with a slight range of variation. Sherman averted disaster to Burnside by hurrying from Chattanooga to Knoxville and forcing Longstreet to raise the siege. In the East Meade recrossed the Rapidan and went into winter quarters. Congress assembled and received a treasury report of rather cheerful tenor, despite the fact that Chase found it necessary to ask authority for borrowing $900,000,000.

During the first three months of 1864 the slow decline continued. In January the armies lay nearly still both east and west. On the 1st of February a draft was ordered for half a million men to serve three years or for the war. Butler's sally from Fortress Monroe, made in the hope of taking Richmond by surprise and freeing the prisoners of war, was frustrated by a deserter who alarmed the Confederates, and Kilpatrick's cavalry on a similar mission succeeded in penetrating the first and second line of defenses about the city, but were repulsed from the third. Late in the month the Florida expedition received a serious check at Olustree. In Mississippi Sherman succeeded in destroying Meridian and effectually cutting the line of railway that supplied Mobile from the North, but the hoped-for destruction of Pope's army was not accomplished because the co-operating cavalry failed to do its expected part in the campaign. In March the ill-fated Red River expedition set out, and the Confederate general Forrest defeated W. S. Smith at Okalona, re-captured Jackson, the capital of Mississippi, but late in the month was repulsed at Paducah with a loss of 1,500 men. More important in its effect upon the gold market was the slowness of Congress in passing the finance bills. Even the New York *Tribune* became impatient. "A Congress fit to exist," it said, "would have matured and perfected *some* sort of finance system before the close of its fourth month."[1]

In April Congress still passed no revenue laws, and the war news was unfavorable. The massacre of Fort Pillow, the failure of the Red River expedition, Steel's forced evacuation of his position in Arkansas, the Confederate capture of Fort Williams, and later of Plymouth, in North Carolina, all combined to make a gloomy commencement of the spring campaign.[2] Slight successes in Texas, Grant's preparations for a vigorous advance, and Union gains in the elections in Connecticut, Rhode Island, Missouri, and New Jersey could not counterbalance these disasters and the inactivity of Congress. Consequently the currency fell $3.50 below the average of March.

In the first half of May there was a rise. Sherman setting out from Chattanooga succeeded by skilful maneuvers in forcing Johnson back from Dalton, then from Resaca and then from Allatoona Pass. At the same time Grant crossed the Rapidan and fought the desperate battles of the Wilderness and Spottsylvania Court House. Every rumor from the field caused a rise or fall of the currency,[3] but despite Grant's enormous losses, he was believed to have the advantage, so that the general trend of the fluctuations was upward until near the middle of the month. But on the 10th Ave-

[1] Editorial article, March 29, 1864.

[2] The feeling of depression is shown by the New York *Tribune's* remark: "With perhaps a single exception, the important military events which we have been called upon to record since the early opening of the campaign have been disasters to the national cause" (April 29, 1864).

[3] *E. g.*, see New York *Times*, money article, May 12, 1864.

rill's cavalry was defeated by Stuart, on the 15th Siegel was routed at Newmarket, and on the 16th Beauregard forced Butler back upon Bermuda Hundred and intrenched along his front so strongly as to prevent his co-operating with Grant. Meantime Lee forestalled Grant in his movement to the North Anna, and Congress still failed to pass the tax bills. Consequently after the 10th currency fell again; by the 17th it was back to the opening value of the month, and as the depreciation continued the average value was $1.20 less than in April.

During these first five months of 1864 there had been a depreciation of less than $2 a month, due to lack of progress in subduing the rebellion and the dilatoriness of Congress in voting taxes. In the next two months this rate of depreciation was greatly accelerated, in part at least because of the appearance of a new factor in the market — the "gold bill." This measure, however, was only the last of a series of governmental attempts to control the price of gold. As was shown in the preceding section, the treasury officials believed that the premium was in very large measure due to a rise in the value of gold effected by the nefarious arts of speculators. Could this speculation be broken up, they thought that the premium would fall back to a moderate figure and the credit of the government be greatly enhanced. Acting on this principle, Congress, on March 3, 1863, laid a stamp tax upon time sales of gold, amounting to one-half of 1 per cent. of the amount plus interest at 6 per cent. per annum, and at the same time forbade loans on the pledge of coin in excess of its par value.[1] News of the passing of this law was followed by an advance of the currency from $58.22

---

[1] 12 *Statutes at Large*, secs. 4, 5, p. 719. At the same time a bill was pending in the New York legislature to prohibit banks from selling specie above par and from loaning upon specie so long as specie payments were suspended. It had some effect upon the market, although it finally failed of becoming law. See money articles of New York *Tribune*, February 6, 7, and March 5, 1863; *Times*, March 4, and April 17, 1863.

on the 3d of March to $66.67 on the 6th; but the gold market quickly rallied, and by the 10th the currency had fallen again to $61.35.[1]

Though this measure produced but little effect, for other reasons, the average gold value of the currency advanced slowly from March to June, 1863, and much more rapidly in July and August. During this period, therefore, the public concerned itself little with the iniquity of gold speculation. But when the current turned and the premium began to advance again, denunciation of the speculators recommenced. As a specimen of the way in which they and their works were regarded by a large section of the most earnest northern people, one of the numerous editorial articles on the subject may be quoted from the New York *Tribune*:

For years past, the partisans of the Rebellion quartered in our city have systematically and by concert striven and employed their means to increase the premium on gold. Their intercepted letters prove that they did this in behalf of their master, Jeff. Davis, and in the conviction that they were aiding the Rebellion as truly and palpably as though they were wielding muskets in the front ranks of Lee's army.[2]

When Congress assembled in December the prevalence of the feeling that the premium was largely due to speculation, and speculation to treason, manifested itself in proposals to enact restrictive legislation. But it was some time before these proposals were given serious attention. In the Senate Mr. Lane, of Kansas, introduced a bill December 15, 1863, to prohibit speculative transactions in gold, and another January 13, prohibiting the sale of gold at a price higher than that of 6 per cent. federal bonds. Both these measures

---

[1] See money articles of this period.

[2] June 15, 1864. More or less similar outbursts can be found in most of the New York papers at any time that the premium was advancing rapidly. *Cf.*, *e. g.*, New York *Times*, money article, February 3, 1864.

were referred to the Committee on Finance and were no more heard of.[1] A third bill of the same character met a similar fate, though introduced by so influential a senator as John Sherman.[2] In the House Mr. Clay's "bill to regulate contracts for gold" was killed by the Committee on Judiciary, to which it had been referred.[3] But while Congress was not yet ready to attack the business of dealing in gold directly, it assented to a measure of which the object was the reduction of the premium.

Just at this time the government was receiving more gold from customs duties than was required for meeting the interest on the public debt. The excess was accumulating in the New York subtreasury. It was thought that, if this large supply could be suddenly thrown on the market, it would break the "corner" in gold and cause the premium to fall. With this intent, the secretary of the treasury was authorized to dispose of any surplus gold not required for interest.[4] The passage of this measure, like that of the tax provision of March, 1863, was followed by a temporary appreciation of the currency from $59.61 on the 9th of March, when its defeat was expected, to $62.06 on the 17th, when it was approved by the president.[5]

Mr. Chase, however, was loath to use the power thus

---

[1] *Congressional Globe*, 38th Cong., 1st Sess., pp. 24, 173. When the committee was asked what it had done with the bills, Fessenden replied that it still had the matter under consideration.—*Ibid.*, p. 360.

[2] *Ibid.*, p. 539.　　　　　　　　　　　　　　[3] *Ibid.*, pp. 730, 2773.

[4] Joint resolution of March 17, 1864, 13 *Statutes at Large*, p. 404. For the grounds on which the bill was urged see Sherman, *Congressional Globe*, 38th Cong., 1st Sess., p. 1023; Hooper, *ibid.*, p. 731; Kasson, pp. 707, 737, 738; Garfield, p. 734. On the other side see Pendleton, pp. 731, 732; Brooks, p. 733; Hendricks, pp. 1045, 1046; Reverdy Johnson, pp. 1050, 1051. As the bill passed the House, it merely authorized the secretary to anticipate the payment of interest in gold, but the Senate Committee on Finance reported an amendment permitting the secretary to sell any gold in the treasury not needed for the payment of interest (p. 1023). This resolution as amended was adopted by the Senate after a yea and nay vote of 30 to 8 on March 11 (p. 1052), and after much discussion was accepted by the House March 16, by 84 votes to 57 (p. 1147).

[5] New York *Times*, money articles, March 9, 11, 12, 15, 1864.

given him to sell gold, except as a last resort. He had another plan. Importers with customs duties to pay had to buy the necessary coin in the gold room or on the stock exchange. Chase thought the premium might fall if this demand were taken out of the market. Consequently he announced that importers would be allowed to deposit paper currency with the subtreasury, receive in return certificates of deposit of gold at a rate a trifle below the current premium, and use these certificates in payment of customs.[1]

The announcement of this plan caused a fall of gold from $169\frac{3}{4}$ on the 26th to $165\frac{3}{4}$ on the 29th of March. This day certificates were sold at $165\frac{1}{2}$, and for the 30th the price was set at 164. The market quotation followed, and for the next day the price of certificates was $163\frac{1}{2}$. But this time the market did not yield, and in consequence the rate for certificates had to be raised to 165 on April 1, and to 166 on the 2d. This advance meant the defeat of the plan. Instead of the treasury being able to dictate to the market what the price of gold should be each day, it was obliged itself to accept the dictation of the market. However, the plan was kept in operation two weeks longer. The rate for certificates was set permanently at 165; but the market quotation regardless of this rose to 175 on the 12th. The next day Mr. Chase issued an order stopping the sale of certificates after the 16th.[2]

Balked in his first scheme, Mr. Chase went to New York on the night of April 13 and ordered the surplus gold in the subtreasury to be sold.[3] On the 14th the gold quotation reached $177\frac{1}{4}$. By selling about $11,000,000 of gold in five days Chase forced the premium down to $66\frac{7}{8}$ on the 21st. In comparison with the effort made, the result was trifling.

1 See official announcement in the New York papers of March 29, 1864.
2 Published in New York *Tribune*, money article, April 16, 1864. These operations can all be followed best in the current money articles.
3 SCHUCKERS, *op. cit.*, p. 358.

The policy could not be continued indefinitely, because sufficient gold had to be kept in the treasury to meet interest. When the pressure was removed, the advance recommenced, and by the 25th of April the premium was higher than ever.[1] At the outset of this campaign in the gold market Mr. Chase seems to have been influenced by outside pressure rather than by any conviction of his own that the expedients adopted would produce a permanently beneficial result. Many business men as well as many politicians, who had become alarmed by the rapid leaps upward of the premium in the spring of 1864, were urging him to suppress the gambling in gold by any means in his power.[2] But even when he was beginning the sales of gold Chase wrote to President Lincoln: "The sales which have been made—yesterday and today—*seem* to have reduced the price, but the reduction is only temporary, unless most decisive measures for reducing the amount of circulation and arresting the rapid increase of debt, be adopted."[3] And after the sales were over he wrote to Mr. S. D. Bloodgood, of New York: "I see that gold is again going up. This is not unexpected. Military success is indispensable to its permanent decline, or, in the absence of military success, taxation sufficient upon state bank issues and state bank credits to secure . . . . an exclusive national currency; and sufficient, also, to defray so large a proportion of current expenditures as to reduce the necessity for borrowing to the minimum."[4]

But neither this clear insight into the situation, nor his

[1] Though these operations had but a fleeting effect upon the price of gold, they produced a severe panic in the stock market. Money became exceedingly "close," and speculators holding stocks for an advance were obliged to sell at heavy sacrifices. *Cf.* CORNWALLIS, *The Gold Room*, p. 8; MEDBERRY, *Men and Mysteries of Wall Street*, pp. 248, 249.

[2] *Cf.* SCHUCKERS, *op. cit.*, pp. 357, 358. Schuckers says that the plan of selling customs-house certificates was adopted at the recommendation of the New York chamber of commerce (p. 361).

[3] Letter of April 15, *ibid.*, pp. 358, 359.

[4] Letter of April 26, 1864, WARDEN, *Life of Chase*, p. 582.

former failures, deterred Chase from trying a third plan —
that of satisfying the export demand for gold by selling
exchange upon London at a rate below that prevailing in
the market.[1]   This plan had still less effect than its predecessors.   It caused a fall of gold from $181\frac{5}{8}$ on May 19 to
181 on the 20th.   But the next day gold began to rise
again, and on the 24th the treasury was forced to raise its
price for exchange,[2] thus acknowledging another defeat.

Why all the attempts to reduce the premium on gold had
failed is not difficult to see.   They were based on the
assumption that speculators had increased the value of gold
— while the fact was rather that the government's notes had
fallen in common esteem.   Neither increasing the market
supply of gold by selling the coin in the treasury, nor diminishing the market demand for gold by selling customs-house
certificates or foreign exchange, could better the government's credit, and therefore such measures could have nothing more than a temporary effect upon the premium.   What
was needed was, as Mr. Chase himself wrote, victories and
heavier taxes.

By this time, however, the secretary's temper had become
ruffled by defeat, and he was ready to try extreme measures.   "The price of gold must and shall come down," he
wrote to Horace Greeley, June 16, "or I'll quit and let
somebody else try."[3]   One resort was left: the government
had failed to control the gold market; it remained to try
abolishing the market altogether.

A bill with this purpose had been sent by Chase to the
Senate Committee on Finance and reported by Sherman
April 14.[4]   This measure prohibited under heavy penalties
all contracts for the sale of gold for future delivery and also

1 New York *Times*, money article, May 20, 1864.
2 *Ibid.*, May 24.   3 WARDEN, *op. cit.*, p. 603.
4 *Congressional Globe*, 38th Cong., 1st Sess., p. 1618.   Compare Fessenden's explanations of the source of the bill, p. 1669.

forbade the sale of gold by a broker outside his own office.[1] Of course the bill, if it became law, would make dealing in "futures" illegal, break up the gold room, and prevent sales at the stock exchange.

It was with much misgiving that the Committee on Finance brought the bill before the Senate and few advocates were found who would say more than that they hoped it might accomplish some good. Fessenden spoke for the majority of his colleagues when he said:

Although we may not believe . . . . that a bill of this kind will necessarily produce the effect . . . . it is nevertheless a duty in the present condition of things in this country to leave nothing untried which offers even a reasonable ground of hope ; and it is upon that supposition . . . . that the committee recommend the measure . . . . a bill of this kind may produce an effect in two ways; first by operating upon public opinion, and second by high penalties . . . . it may . . . . have an effect to check in some, perhaps not any inconsiderable, degree, the rampant and heartless and wicked spirit which is actuating men with reference to this subject.[2]

If those who voted for the bill spoke doubtfully of it, those who voted against it were more certain of their ground. With one accord they declared that such legislation could not accomplish what the secretary expected. Mr. Henderson, for example, reminded the Senate that the act authorizing sales of gold had been " a total failure " and added: " It is utterly futile for us, unless we can keep up the character of the currency of the United States, to undertake to interfere with the price of gold." [3]

Senator Collamer took similar ground: " Gold does not fluctuate in price," he said, " . . . . because they gamble

1 See text, *ibid.*, p. 1640.

2 *Ibid.*, p. 1640; compare similar remarks of Chandler, p. 1644; Hale, p. 1671; Sherman, pp. 1640, 1646.

3 *Ibid.*, p. 1670. *Cf.* remarks of Clark, p. 1643; Powell, p. 1671; Reverdy Johnson, p. 1645.

in it; but they gamble in it because it fluctuates. . . . . But the fluctuation is not in the gold; the fluctuation is in the currency, and it is a fluctuation utterly beyond the control of individuals." [1]

The true way to restore national credit, said Cowan, was not to pass futile enactments against gold speculation, but to prosecute the war vigorously and to raise large sums by taxation. "If we do that," he concluded, "if in the first place we satisfy the money lender that we are going to put down the rebellion, and in the second place that we are going to pay the expenses . . . . then the public credit at once will appreciate and public securities will rise, or, if you choose the other phrase, gold will apparently go down." [2]

Perhaps the only senator who heartily approved of the bill was Lane, of Kansas: "It is my opinion," he said, "and the opinion of loyal and sagacious business men of the city of New York, that the Confederate government is to day, and has been since last December, through its foreign agents, engaged in the effort to depreciate our currency by gambling." His only objection was that Secretary Chase was being credited with the authorship of the bill, when he himself had introduced a very similar measure several months before. [3]

Though the bill was passed by the Senate April 16, [4] its consideration in the House was delayed while Mr. Chase was trying his other experiments in the gold market. When they had all failed he wrote a note to Samuel Hooper urging that the bill be acted on. "Its passage," he said, "will probably check the advance and give a little time for further measures." [5] Accordingly the bill was taken up June 7, but so closely was opinion divided that the speaker's casting

[1] *Ibid.*, pp. 1666, 1667.   [2] *Ibid.*, p. 1641.   [3] *Ibid.*, p. 1669.
[4] The final vote was 23 to 17.—*Ibid.*, p. 1673.
[5] Letter of June 2, WARDEN, *op. cit.*, p. 599.

vote was required to secure consideration for the subject.[1] A week later the bill was passed after very little discussion in the House by a vote of 76 yeas to 62 nays.[2] It received the president's signature June 17.[3]

Gold opened in June at 190 and rose at the prospect that the gold bill would be passed.   On the 14th, when the House agreed to the bill, the price touched 197½.   When the law was put in operation on the 21st of June, the gold room was closed, and at the stock exchange the precious metals were dropped from the call list; for it was now unlawful for brokers to buy and sell gold outside of their offices.   Persons who needed gold to pay customs or to send abroad were forced to go from one office to another inquiring the price.[4]   There being no organized market, there was no regular quotation, and the prices demanded by different brokers varied so widely that June 27 there was a difference of 19 points between the lowest and highest selling rates reported.   Business was so greatly inconvenienced that a meeting of bankers and merchants convened on the 22d and appointed a committee to recommend necessary alterations in the law.[5]   Two days later the committee called upon Mr. Chase in Washington to urge the repeal of the act.[6]   At a loss what to do, Chase had already authorized the assistant treasurer at New York and Mr. Jay Cooke to take such measures as would arrest the rise of the premium.[7]   But they could do nothing, and the rise went on.   Mr. Chase was very loath to recommend the repeal of the bill, and yet he saw no other way

[1] *Congressional Globe*, 38th Cong., 1st Sess., pp. 2793, 2794.

[2] Forty-three members did not vote.—*Ibid.*, p. 2937. The Senate concurred in the House amendments. which did not affect the substance of the bill, on the same day.—P. 2930.

[3] 13 *Statutes at Large*, p. 132.

[4] New York *Herald*, editorial article, June 24, 1864.

[5] See account of the meeting in New York papers of June 23, 1864.

[6] Extract from Chase's diary, WARDEN, *Life of Chase*, p. 607.

[7] Letter to J. Cooke, June 21, WARDEN, p. 606.

to remedy the situation.[1] Before this dilemma was settled he
sent his resignation to President Lincoln, June 29, and next
day it was accepted. The vacant position was offered to
Governor David Tod of Ohio. When he declined it, Senator
Fessenden was prevailed upon to assume its duties.[2]

Meanwhile the gold bill had been repealed. Unanimous
consent to introduce a bill for this purpose was granted to
Senator Reverdy Johnson on the 22d of June.[3] July 1,
this bill was called up and passed with no debate except
Johnson's brief explanation:

> The universal impression, so far as I have been able to collect
> it, in Congress and out of Congress, now is that . . . . the gold
> bill is doing nothing but mischief ; and I have communications, and
> other Senators have received them, from New York especially, beg-
> ging that that bill shall be repealed. I do not know any member
> of the Senate who formerly was willing to give that bill his sanction
> who is not now just as willing to repeal it. It has had its trial and
> has failed to produce anything but mischief.[4]

Later in the same day the bill for repeal was passed by
the House without any discussion.[5] It was signed by President Lincoln July 2;[6] the 3d was Sunday, and the 4th Independence Day, but on the 5th the gold room was reopened
and the business of dealing in gold resumed its wonted
course.[7]

The great fall of the currency, shown by the spectacular
advance of the premium in June and July, was by no
means due solely to the gold-bill blunder. Military news
was unfavorable. After his frightful losses in the Wilder-

[1] See his own account of what he said to Fessenden in regard to the matter,
WARDEN, p. 619.

[2] Compare Part I, chap. v, sec. ii, p. 124, above.

[3] *Congressional Globe*, 38th Cong., 1st Sess., p. 3160.   [4] *Ibid.*, p. 3446.

[5] *Ibid.*, p. 3468. The vote was: yeas, 87; nays, 29; not voting, 66.

[6] 13 *Statutes at Large*, p. 344.

[7] At the stock exchange, however, transactions in gold were never regularly
resumed after June 20. *Cf. Commercial and Financial Chronicle*, Vol. I, p. 168.

ness and at Spottsylvania, Grant had been compelled to give up his plan of taking Richmond by assaults on Lee's lines. The bloody repulse at Cold Harbor, June 3, was followed by ten days of inaction. When Grant crossed the James in the middle of the month, Lee merely fell back on Richmond and seemed as safe as before. The attempt to secure the Weldon railway south of Petersburg by swinging infantry corps to the left was foiled by Ewell's fierce attacks, and though Wilson's cavalry succeeded in cutting the railway, they were afterward defeated and the damage repaired. On the last day of June the mine was exploded at Petersburg, but the assault through the breach failed miserably. Meantime Hunter, advancing on Lynchburg, was compelled to retreat into West Virginia by the sudden appearance of Early on his front with a superior force. This move opened the way for Early's dash on Washington in the first fortnight of July, which was almost successful. Though missing this prize, the Confederates operated in the Shenandoah for the rest of the month and on the 30th burned Chambersburg in Pennsylvania. Grant in the meanwhile was reduced to acting on the defensive ; for he had been compelled to send an army corps and two divisions of cavalry to confront Early. In the South Sherman seemed to be making slow progress against the wary Johnston in his campaign about Atlanta, and all attempts to capture Forrest's cavalry in Mississippi proved futile. It seemed, indeed, in June and July that almost no progress was being made toward subduing the Confederacy, despite the prodigious expenditure of money and blood.

The financial outlook was no better. In contrast with the five-twenty loan which had closed in January, the ten-forty loan was a dismal failure. Another loan on seventeen-year bonds advertised June 25 met with so unflattering a reception that it had to be withdrawn on the 2d of July.

The outstanding certificates of indebtedness had mounted to $162,000,000 and there were unpaid requisitions on the treasurer of $72,000,000. The expenditures were $2,250,000 a day, while the income from customs was hardly more than sufficient to pay the coin interest on the debt, and even the secretary's overestimate made the daily receipts from internal taxes but $750,000.[1]   Add to this the fact that there was little chance of quick improvement because Congress had delayed passing the revenue bills until the last day of June, and the unhappy state of the finances becomes apparent.[2]

Under the combination of unfavorable circumstances it is not strange that the value of the currency fell rapidly. News of Mr. Chase's resignation came to New York July 1, and was declared by the *World* to mean that the treasury was practically bankrupt.[3] This seems to have been the construction generally put on the resignation at first, and it was not until July 7 that the *Tribune* denied this story and declared that Chase withdrew simply because he and the president could not agree on a successor to Mr. Cisco.   Senator Fessenden's appointment produced a temporary reaction, but Early's raid was creating too much consternation to allow of much improvement.   Sunday, July 10, he was within ten miles of Washington, where there was no force that seemed capable of withstanding his veterans. Next day the price of gold touched 285 — the highest value of the war — that is, the currency fell to a specie value of $35.09.[4]   Though the crisis was passed, the market yielded stubbornly. Fessen-

[1] *Cf. Report of the Secretary of the Treasury*, December, 1864, pp. 19, 20, and Part I, chap. v, sec. ii, above.

[2] The tariff act, the ways and means act, and the internal revenue act were all approved June 30.—13 *Statutes at Large*, pp. 202, 218, 223.

[3] See the reply of the *Tribune*, July 7.

[4] After the regular market had closed for the day, transactions in gold at a still higher price are said to have taken place. MEDBERRY tells a circumstantial story of a frightened Missouri banker who bought $100,000 of gold at 310, in *Men and Mysteries of Wall Street,* p. 250.

den's attempt to relieve the treasury by securing a loan
from the banks failed on account of the limitations imposed
by the subtreasury law, and the seven-thirty loan which he
advertised on the 25th of July was not very well received.[1]
Consequently while the currency reached $40.98 on the 15th,
it fell back again and closed for the month at about $39.

Contemporary observers were wont to declare that this
extraordinary rise of the premium after the gold room had
been reopened was due solely to a well-concerted corner
which had been arranged while the gold bill was still in
force.[2] When one examines the military and financial
situation, however, one finds little ground for surprise that
the credit of the federal treasury was at a low ebb in the
first half of July. No doubt the "bulls" in the gold room
were doing their utmost to raise the price, but their signal
triumph over the "bears" would have been impossible had
July, 1864, been like July, 1863, a month of great subscriptions to national loans and decisive victories in the
field.

5. *The rise from August, 1864, to May, 1865.*—In August there was a slow but tolerably steady appreciation in
the value of the currency, due to the improving military
prospect. Sheridan took command in the Shenandoah, and
while he accomplished nothing decisive against Early until
September, all fear of the capture of Washington was
removed. Grant was able at last to resume the offensive
against Lee, and by feinting with his right wing succeeded
in seizing the Weldon railway with his left and holding it
against fierce assaults. In the South Sherman continued
his flanking movements against Atlanta, and Farragut captured the Confederate vessels in Mobile bay and reduced

---

[1] Part I, chap. v, sec. ii, p. 125, above.

[2] *Cf.* MEDBERRY, *op. cit.*, p. 250; CORNWALLIS, *op. cit.*, p. 10; Chase's letter of
June 21, to Jay Cooke, WARDEN, *op. cit.*, p. 606; editorial articles of New York
Tribune, July 8 and 15.

the forts. The rate of advance, however, was checked by the condition of the finances. At one time the unpaid requisitions reached $130,000,000,[1] and the secretary's attempts to sell bonds were but moderately successful.

Early in September news came of the capture of Atlanta, and later in the month Sheridan defeated Early at Opequan and Fisher's Hill. The meeting of the Democratic convention in Chicago at the very end of August had caused a reaction, but this was overcome by the good news from the front, and the average value of the currency for the month was $5.50 above that for the previous month.

During October the appreciation continued, for though Kautz's cavalry was defeated on the 7th and lost its guns, Hood in his advance into Tennessee was repulsed at Allatoona Pass and Resaca, Sheridan destroyed Early's army at Cedar Creek, Lieutenant Cushing sank the "Albemarle" with a torpedo, and the cruiser "Florida" was captured. In November there was a curious reaction, due mainly to the presidential election. Mr. Lincoln's triumph was taken to mean an indefinite continuation of the war, and so depressed the value of the government's notes. In a military way the most important event was that Sherman cut connections with the North and started from Atlanta on his march to the sea. Hood meanwhile was still pressing north, while the imperturbable Thomas continued quiet preparations for his reception at Nashville. Schofield's withdrawal from the field after the battle of Franklin was construed as a defeat.

The interrupted rise recommenced in December when word was received from Sherman that he had reached the sea in perfect safety and taken Savannah. A little later Thomas destroyed Hood's army at the battle of Nashville. The favorable effect of these great successes was partially neutralized by the disappointment felt over Secretary Fes-

[1] *Report of the Secretary of the Treasury*, December, 1864, p. 21.

senden's finance report, by a curious bill introduced into the House of Representatives by Thaddeus Stevens imposing penalties upon anyone who should pay more than its face value for gold coin, or less than its full value for paper money,[1] and by Butler's failure to take Fort Fisher.

In January Terry did what Butler had failed to do by capturing Fort Fisher, and Sherman got ready for his march north from Savannah. On the 23d an attempt to destroy Grant's shipping in the James failed. These events, with the prevalence of peace rumors, sufficed to continue the gradual advance of the currency. In February Grant's attempt to turn the Confederate lines at Hatcher's Run was unsuccessful, but Charleston and Wilmington fell in consequence of Sherman's advance. The failure of the "peace conference" at Hampton Roads was depressing. Still, the rise continued until the currency regained the level which it had held in October before the relapse caused by the election.

In March the very slow rate of appreciation suddenly became very rapid, because of the opening of the spring campaign. Word came March 14 from Sherman, who had not been heard from since early in February, that his army had safely reached Laurel Hill, in North Carolina ; and later came reports of his victories at Averysboro and Bentonville. Meantime Sheridan joined Grant before Petersburg. Lee's position becoming desperate, he made a last assault upon the encompassing lines, but was driven back. Then Grant began the advance that was to end the war. In Washington President Lincoln's second inauguration occurred, and Senator Fessenden was replaced by Hugh McCulloch as secretary of the treasury. All this was favorable, and the average value of currency for the month was $8.80 higher than it had been in February.

---

[1] The full text of this bill may be found in the New York *Tribune*, December 10, 1864. For its effect upon the gold market see *ibid.*, money articles, December 6 and 7.

In the first two weeks of April matters culminated with the victory of Five Forks, the capture of Petersburg and Richmond, Lee's retreat and surrender. A little later Sherman took Raleigh, and Johnston's army capitulated. President Lincoln's death was the one untoward event. Notwithstanding it, the currency gained $9.80 over March.

During May there was a further advance of $6.40 above the average for April. Armed resistance ceased, President Davis was captured, and the war was over. Moreover, Jay Cooke was meeting with great success in selling seven-thirty notes to obtain funds for paying the army. In these last three months of the war there was an appreciation above February of $25.

6. *Decline from June to December, 1865.*— After the war was over, the gold market became calm, indeed, compared with what it had been. Great fluctuations gave place to slight variations from day to day. A reaction naturally followed on the first joy caused by the cessation of hostilities. May 11 marked the high-water point— $77.82. After that there was a slow decline. Although the seven-thirty loan was readily subscribed, it led to a great increase of the debt. Moreover, there was some danger of war with France because of Napoleon's maintenance of Maximilian in Mexico. By November the currency had depreciated $5.70 below the level for May.

In December there was a slight reaction, due to McCulloch's finance report recommending a speedy resumption of specie payments and the warm indorsement of this policy by the House of Representatives. [1]

[1] See Part I, chap. v, sec. iii, above.

CHAPTER IV

PRICES

I. FALKNER'S TABLE OF RELATIVE PRICES

FOR the study of prices during the Civil War the most copious and trustworthy source of material is the report upon *Wholesale Prices, Wages, and Transportation* made by Mr. Aldrich from the Senate Committee on Finance in 1893.[1] In Part I of this document there is an elaborate table, com-

---

[1] *Senate Report No. 1394,* 52d Cong., 2d Sess. (four parts), pp. 658, 1956. For the sake of brevity this document is hereafter cited simply as the *Aldrich Report.*

239

piled under the direction of Professor Roland P. Falkner, the statistician of the committee, showing the relative prices at wholesale of some 230 commodities each year from 1860 to 1891. As the base from which variations in price are measured in this table is 1860, a proper starting-point for investigating the effect of the legal-tender acts upon prices, it may seem that the present chapter can be confined to an analysis of Professor Falkner's carefully elaborated results. Slight examination of the table, however, suffices to show that it cannot be accepted as a satisfactory index of the course of prices during the war.

In the first place, Falkner's table gives but a single index number for each year, and therefore does not enable one to investigate in any detail the point of primary interest—the relation between the fluctuations of prices and the constantly changing premium on coin. Second, the prices of the single commodities used in computing the average relative price for each year do not all refer to the same month. In collecting material, Professor Falkner explains, an attempt was made to get four quotations each year for every article. In a few cases, however, this was not possible, and it was necessary to take instead average prices for the year. Where the prices were obtained by quarters the analysis proceeded on the basis of the quotations for January. "An exception to this rule is made, of course," he continues, "for articles for which the January price is not the distinctive price for the year, as for fresh vegetables and the like. Thus, in the cost of potatoes, October is taken as the typical month, but the exceptions to the rule that January is the basis of the comparison are very few."[1]

It is probable that in years of less violent price fluctuations this use of some quotations for July, for example, in place of quotations for January would make little, if any,

[1] *Aldrich Report*, Part I, p. 29.

difference in the general average for all commodities. But in the years of the Civil War the case is different. The tables of the last chapter show that the specie value of the currency in which all prices were reckoned, fell 40 per cent. between January and July, 1864, and rose 52 per cent. between January and July, 1865. When one is trying to ascertain what effect changes in the specie value of the currency had upon prices, it is clearly inadmissible to include in the index numbers for years marked by such extraordinary perturbations relative prices for both January and July.

Nor is this point one of merely theoretical significance. To determine how frequent is the use of quotations for other months than January, I have recomputed from the original data in Part II of the *Aldrich Report* all the relative prices given in Table I for 1865. The result indicates that the cases of divergence from the general rule of using the January price are much more numerous than Professor Falkner's language would lead one to infer. Of the 222 relative prices for that year only 99 are based on quotations for January. Of the remainder, 74 refer to unstated months or to averages for the year, 26 to July, 6 to March, 6 to the average of January and July, 4 to February, and 7 to various other months.[1]

---

[1] As these statements seem in some measure inconsistent with the impression given by the language of the report, I append a list of the relative prices for 1865 that are not based on January quotations:

1. Time within year not specified: fish, mackerel, No. 1, No. 2, No. 3; lard, pure leaf; meat, bacon clear and ham; salt, coarse solar, and fine boiled; blankets, cotton warp, all wool filling; broadcloths, first and second quality; cassimeres, Nos. 1, 2, and 3; checks; hides; horse blankets; shawls; sole leather; wool, medium and fine; anvils; bar-iron; door knobs; iron rails; iron rods; lead, pig, No. 2; locks, mortise and rim; meat cutters; nails; pig iron; pocketknives, Nos. 1 to 25; saws, Nos. 1 to 4; scythes; carbonate of lead; maple boards; oak boards; shingles, Nos. 3 and 4; calomel; glycerine; glassware, Nos. 1 to 5.

2. July: starch, corn, No. 2; calico; print cloths, Nos. 1 and 2; iron wire; brick; cement; chestnut logs; hemlock logs; lime; oxide of zinc; pine boards, Nos. 1, 3, 5, and 6; pine logs; putty; shingles, No. 1; spruce boards; tar; turpentine; window glass, Nos. 1 to 4; starch, ordinary laundry.

3. Average of January and July: doors; hemlock boards; pine boards, Nos. 2, 4, and 7; pine shingles, No. 2.

Precisely how great an effect these very frequent deviations from the rule have upon Falkner's index number for 1865 it is impossible to tell. In eleven of the above cases of deviation the price for the other month is identical with that for January, but in the majority of instances where a January quotation is available for comparison the difference is considerable. Perhaps the best way to get a quantitative expression of this difference is to examine the case of the twenty-three commodities for which both January and July prices are given in the exhibits, but where the relative prices for 1865 are based on the latter quotation. The average relative price of these articles for **January is 268,** for **July 202**—a difference of 66 points.

It is evident that Professor **Falkner's** average which includes relative prices based upon these twenty-three July quotations, to say nothing of the much larger number of relative prices based upon quotations for other months besides January, cannot show the true average relative price of the 222 articles for January, or for any single month, or for the year as a whole, and therefore cannot with propriety be compared with the premium on gold for any single month or for the year.[1] Clearly, then, all thought of using the table of relative prices in the form in which it is published in the report for investigating the relation between the rise of prices and the depreciation of the currency in relation to specie must be given up.[2]

4. March: plate glass, Nos. 1 to 6.
5. February: fish, cod; meat, beef loins, beef ribs, and mutton.
6. April: carpets, Wilton; starch, Ontario.
7. October: coal, anthracite, pea; potatoes, No. 2.
8. May: powder, rifle, No. 2.
9. August: meat, lamb.
10. November: potatoes, No. 1.

[1] Professor Falkner, overlooking the nature of his average, divides the average relative price for each year from 1862 to 1878 by the premium on gold in January, and thus obtains a table which he calls " Relative Prices in Gold."—*Ibid.,* p. 99.

[2] Other objections might be urged against Falkner's table, such as the inclusion of many different series for slightly different forms of the same article, etc. But what has been said is sufficient to show the reason for compiling a new table.

Fortunately, while the table of relative prices published in Part I of the *Aldrich Report* is thus unsuitable for the present purpose, all of the material from which that table was constructed is published at length in the "Exhibits" of Part II. As this collection of data was made from authentic sources with scrupulous care, the student who finds that he cannot employ Professor Falkner's averages is able in many cases to go back to the original material and compile from it new tables specially adapted to his needs. This is the task attempted in the next section.

II.   A NEW TABLE OF RELATIVE PRICES BY QUARTERS

The preceding criticism of Falkner's table of relative prices indicates what should be the distinctive features of the new table.   First, in order that the comparison between the fluctuations of prices and of gold may be as full as possible, it is desirable that several index numbers should be obtained for each year — the more the better.   The attainment of this desideratum in partial measure is made possible by the fact that for a large number of articles prices are given four times a year — for January, April, July, and October, and in a very few cases for February, May, August, and November.   Second, in order that the meaning of the averages shall be clear when they are obtained, all articles that are not quoted in this manner must be excluded.   By observing these two rules, a table can be made that will show the relative prices of a considerable number of commodities at four dates in each year for the period of the Civil War.

Two points remain to be settled — What prices shall be used as the basis upon which to compute variations, and, How shall the average of the price variations of the single commodities be struck?   On the first point it seems well to follow the precedent set by Professor Falkner and take the quotations for January, 1860, as the basis, except in cases where the quotation for some other month or for the year as a whole is clearly more representative.[1] As prices remained nearly stationary during this whole year and the first quarter of 1861, the general results obtained in this fashion will not vary appreciably from those that might be obtained from the use of the average for the year 1860, or for the fifteen months from January, 1860, to April, 1861. The advantage of the course chosen is that it facilitates comparison with Falkner's table.

The same reason may be given for taking a simple arithmetic mean of the several relative prices each quarter as the first average. Afterward other methods of averaging will be tried. Weights, however, will not be in place in any of the averages that may be employed in this chapter. When one is concerned simply with ascertaining what effect monetary conditions have had upon prices, the importance of a commodity for purposes of consumption is a wholly irrelevant fact. To take a concrete illustration, the fluctuations in the price of cotton, while more significant than the fluctuations of, say, wood-screws, when a computation is being made of the increase in cost of living, are much less significant when the effect of the greenback issues upon prices is the subject of investigation. In the following tables, therefore, all commodities will be treated precisely alike, so far as the quantities produced or consumed are concerned.

Examination of Table XI of Part II of the *Aldrich Report*, from which Falkner's table of relative prices was made, shows that there are tolerably complete series of quarterly quotations for 120 commodities. In Part IV there is a supplementary table (XXI) that furnishes two more series. Further, as there is no reason for excluding from the investigation any class of commodities for which the requisite data are obtainable, thirteen more series may be added for the

[1] In dealing with agricultural products, for example, it is best to use the average of the quarterly quotations for 1860.

farm products grouped by themselves in Table X of Part II. This makes a total of 135 nominally distinct articles—a number considerably smaller than that included in Falkner's table, but larger than the number included in some of the currently received foreign tables. The relative prices of these commodities have been computed in the usual fashion as percentages of the quotations for 1860. All of the resulting series are published at length in the Appendix.

Anyone who looks over these individual series will find that, while there was a very general and violent advance of prices from 1860 to 1865, this advance was far from uniform. A few of the most extreme examples of dissimilar fluctuations may be presented, side by side to show how great the differences were:

TABLE VIII

EXAMPLES OF DISSIMILAR PRICE FLUCTUATIONS

	Silk: Raw Italian	Cotton: Upland Middling	Matches	Mercury	Wood Screws	Gold
1860, January	100	100	100	100	100	100
April	100	101	100	100	100	100
July	106	98	100	100	81	100
October	100	98	100	100	117	100
1861, January	100	109	100	100	117	100
April	83	117	100	100	117	100
July	78	134	100	100	117	100
October	72	196	100	82	117	100
1862, January	72	327	100	82	117	103
April	72	250	100	82	117	102
July	83	336	100	82	117	116
October	81	509	100	109	117	129
1863, January	75	614	100	127	135	145
April	72	664	100	127	158	152
July	67	627	100	127	158	131
October	67	768	100	142	119	148
1864, January	69	736	100	151	158	156
April	75	691	100	200	158	173
July	89	1400	208	282	216	258
October	94	1091	208	346	216	207
1865, January	89	1091	208	251	216	216
April	100	318	396	182	216	149
July	111	455	396	96	216	142
October	100	400	396	96	216	146

A less spectacular, but more comprehensive, view of the range of price fluctuations may be had from Table IX, which shows the 135 commodities classified each quarter according to the degree of their rise or fall in price.

The chief value of such an exhibit is that it emphasizes a fact that one interested in tracing the effect upon prices of the monetary changes of the war is prone to slur over — namely, that, however powerful a factor in determining the ratios of exchange between dollars and commodities, the shift from a specie to an irredeemable paper standard may have been, it was by no means solely responsible for the changes that took place.   Every article bought and sold continued to feel in undiminished force the effect of all changes in the conditions affecting its own particular demand and supply, as well as of changes in the specie value of the currency. But from the present point of view all matters that caused price fluctuations, except those connected with the currency, are disturbing factors to be eliminated so far as possible.   To attain this end it is customary to strike an average of the relative prices at stated intervals, on the theory that in such an average the effect of the conditions peculiar to each article that cause some to rise while others fall will neutralize each other and thus leave evident only those changes connected with the currency or some other common cause. Accordingly, in Table X are shown the arithmetic means of the relative prices of the 135 quarterly series, side by side with Falkner's corresponding figures for 230 commodities.

In examining this table and the material from which it is made, one finds two matters that shake confidence in the representative character of the results.   The more obvious is the not inconsiderable discrepancy between the figures of the quarterly table and of Falkner's annual table.   This discrepancy, however, is more apparent than real, and need cause little uneasiness.   From what was said in the preceding section of

TABLE IX

COMMODITIES DISTRIBUTED ACCORDING TO DEGREE OF RISE OR FALL IN PRICE, BY QUARTERS, 1860–65

Relative Prices as Compared with 1860	1860 Jan.	1860 Apr.	1860 July	1860 Oct.	1861 Jan.	1861 Apr.	1861 July	1861 Oct.	1862 Jan.	1862 Apr.	1862 July	1862 Oct.	1863 Jan.	1863 Apr.	1863 July	1863 Oct.	1864 Jan.	1864 Apr.	1864 July	1864 Oct.	1865 Jan.	1865 Apr.	1865 July	1865 Oct.
Below 100		34	51	45	64	72	81	68	57	55	53	32	18	6	9	6	1	2	1	1	1	0	4	1
100–124		95	81	83	63	54	44	52	47	40	46	54	42	29	31	33	18	9	3	0	3	8	16	9
125–149		3	3	6	6	6	8	9	18	26	14	23	34	35	39	43	33	21	11	13	4	15	23	20
150–174				1	1	2		1	7	8	11	10	18	27	22	20	31	29	8	21	12	19	35	26
175–199						1		2	2	3	5	6	5	6	10	13	18	23	20	19	23	33	19	13
200–224							1			1	1	3	7	11	9	5	12	17	20	23	19	23	12	25
225–249								1	1	1	1	1	1	5	1	4	7	7	9	11	18	9	4	7
250–274										1		2	4	3	5	1	4	7	11	16	20	6	4	9
275–299												2	2	4		2	1	4	10	2	9	3	3	5
300–349									1		3		1	1	2	1	4	4	6	13	8	5	6	5
350–399								1	1				1	1			1	2	6	2	3	3	3	4
400–449														1	1	2	2	1	4	1	3	2	1	3
450–499																		2	1	2	3	1	4	4
500–749												2	2	2	1	1	2	1	5	9	6	2		
750–999															1	1	1	1	2		2	1	1	1
1000+																			1	1	1			
Relative prices lacking		3	0	0	1	0	1	1	1	0	1	0	0	4	4	3	0	5	0	1	0	5	0	3

TABLE X

ARITHMETIC MEAN OF THE RELATIVE PRICES AT WHOLESALE OF 135 COMMODITIES
BY QUARTERS, 1860-65 [1]

Date	135 Commodities	Falkner's General Average	Date	135 Commodities	Falkner's General Average
1860, January..	101 [2]	100	1863, January..	147	149
April	102		April.....	165	
July......	100		July	159	
October..	102		October..	160	
1861, January..	98	101	1864, January..	185	191
April	98		April.....	201	
July	94		July	254	
October..	101		October..	254	
1862, January..	111	118	1865, January..	262	217
April	111		April.....	211	
July	115		July	193	
October..	130		October..	213	

the elements from which Falkner's average is constructed, it follows that the two averages would not agree, even were the list of articles included in both identical. The use of so many quotations for other months than January necessarily makes Falkner's figure higher than that in the other table for January in years when prices were rising, and lower in years when prices were falling. As the observed discrepancies are

[1] A table somewhat like the above was made in 1895 by MISS S. McLEAN HARDY and published in the *Journal of Political Economy*, Vol. III, p. 158. Her table, however, covered only the quarters from January, 1861, to January, 1865, inclusive, and contained 114 instead of 135 commodities. She omitted the thirteen farm products, raw silk, and tin plates from Table XXI of the *Aldrich Report*, and calico, denims, tickings, shovels, castor oil, and jute from Table XI. The omission of the last two articles of this list alone is explained, but the reasons given — that the price of jute is expressed part of the time in gold and that there is a change in the unit of measure applied to castor oil — do not apply to the period covered by either table. I have not been able to use Miss Hardy's figures even for the articles and quarters common to both tables, because of the discovery of numerous errors in her computations. Most of these, however, are minute, and the only case in which they seem appreciably to affect the general result is in October, 1861, when her table, apparently because of a mistake in addition, shows a very sudden advance from 95 to 125, followed by a fall to 113. In no other quarter is the difference between Miss Hardy's results for 114 commodities and mine for 135 greater than four points.

[2] The reason why the arithmetic mean in January, 1860, is not 100 is that the relative prices of agricultural products is based upon the average prices for four quarters, and, of course, the January price is in most cases above this average.

of this character, they are cause for confidence rather than for distrust.

The second reason for doubting the fairness of the quarterly table as an index of price movements, though less obtrusive, is more serious. On looking over the 135 series that enter into the quarterly table one finds a considerable number of cases where two or more series of relative prices are given for more or less similar varieties of the same commodities. These cases are as follows: bread—Boston crackers, three series; beeves — beef loins, beef ribs, salt mess beef; sheep, mutton; hogs and pork — pork, salt mess; molasses—New Orleans and Porto Rico; salt—Ashton's, Ashton's Liverpool fine, Turk's Island; sugar — fair refining, Havana brown, refined; vegetables—fresh potatoes, two series; carpets—Brussels, ingrain, Wilton; print cloths— metacomet, standard; sugar of lead—brown, white; furniture—chairs, bedroom, kitchen; pails—wooden, two-hoops (two series), three-hoops, tubs (four series); starch—Ontario, pearl, pure, refined, silver gloss; coal, anthracite—chestnut, egg, grate, stove; copper—ingot, sheet; lead—drop shot, pig, pipe; rope — Manila, tarred American; pine — boards, lumber in log; window-glass—American firsts and thirds, French firsts and thirds.

Now, according to the logic of the average when used for such a purpose as the present, it is not admissible to include more than one series of relative prices for any single article. For, as has been said, the average is employed here as a device for eliminating price changes due to conditions affecting the supply and demand of the individual commodities. This elimination is believed to take place because, when a large number of commodities are selected at random, it is probable that the cases where these changes in supply and demand are in the direction of higher prices will be about as numerous as the cases where they are in the direction of lower prices. But if one commodity is counted two or more times, and others but once, the factors affecting that one commodity are given undue prominence, and the chance is diminished of their being offset by changes of an opposite character in the case of other commodities.[1]

The inclusion of several series for different varieties of the same article is not quite so objectionable as the counting of a single series several times over, because the chances are small that these different varieties will all be subject to precisely the same changes of supply and demand. To take the instance of starch, for which the greatest number of series are given in the quarterly table it appears from the table on the following page that no two of the five series showed the same variations.

But while the fluctuations in the relative prices of the several kinds of any commodity may not be identical — there is a difference of 56 points between the highest and lowest relative prices of starch in January, 1865 — they usually resemble each other enough to substantiate the belief that there are certain broad conditions of supply and demand that affect all the varieties in somewhat the same fashion. By including series for the different varieties these broad conditions are given more prominence than similar conditions affecting other commodities. Therefore the chance of obtaining an average in which the effect of price changes due to fluctuations in the supply and demand for the various commodities is substantially eliminated, seems to be improved by taking but one series for each distinct commodity. But the question what shall be deemed distinct commodities is not easy to answer. The general rule must be that com-

[1] Of course, these remarks have no application to index-numbers when used for purposes that make weighted averages desirable. Frequently in such cases the weighting can best be performed by using several series for articles of great importance and but one for the majority of other articles. But, as has been explained, weights are to be avoided when one is investigating the effect of monetary changes upon the general trend of prices.

TABLE XI

RELATIVE PRICES OF FIVE VARIETIES OF STARCH

Date	Ontario	Pearl	Pure	Refined	Silv'r Gloss	Average
1860, Jan...	...	100	100	100	100	100
Apr...	100	100	100	100	100	100
July..	100	100	100	100	100	100
Oct...	100	100	100	100	100	100
1861, Jan...	100	100	100	100	100	100
Apr...	100	100	100	100	100	100
July..	100	100	100	100	100	100
Oct...	100	92	92	93	94	94
1862, Jan...	100	92	92	93	94	94
Apr...	100	92	92	93	94	94
July..	100	92	92	93	94	94
Oct...	110	100	100	100	100	102
1863, Jan...	130	117	115	114	113	118
Apr...	140	125	123	121	119	126
July..	130	117	115	114	113	118
Oct...	130	117	115	114	113	118
1864, Jan...	160	142	139	136	132	142
Apr...	180	158	154	150	145	158
July..	200	175	169	164	158	173
Oct...	244	192	185	179	171	194
1865, Jan...	240	208	200	193	184	205
Apr...	240	208	200	193	184	205
July..	200	175	169	164	158	173
Oct...	200	175	169	164	158	173

modities are distinct for the present purpose when the conditions affecting their production and consumption, their supply and demand, are distinct. This line, however, is difficult to draw because of the many degrees of relationship between different goods. While everyone may admit that the difference between wooden pails with two hoops and with three hoops is not sufficient to entitle the articles to be treated as distinct commodities, there is room for difference of opinion regarding such articles as brown and refined sugar, Brussels, ingrain and Wilton carpets, etc. In the present case, I have thought it best to err rather on the side of drawing the line too strictly than too loosely. With this purpose I have taken the average relative prices of all the above enumerated groups of related articles, and recomputed the arithmetic mean for each quarter, using these averages in place of the original series. This procedure reduces the number of series that enter into the average from 135 to 97. It will be noticed that the new series of averages is somewhat higher than the former one from Table X, which is introduced into the new table to facilitate comparison.

TABLE XII

ARITHMETIC MEAN OF RELATIVE PRICES OF 135 COMMODITIES BEFORE AND AFTER
AVERAGING SERIES FOR DIFFERENT VARIETIES OF THE SAME COMMODITY

Date	Before Averaging Series for Different Varieties of Same Commodity	After Averaging Series for Different Varieties of Same Commodity	Date	Before Averaging Series for Different Varieties of Same Commodity	After Averaging Series for Different Varieties of Same Commodity
1860, January..	101	102	1863, January..	147	154
April	102	102	April....	165	173
July.....	100	100	July.....	159	165
October..	102	104	October..	160	166
1861, January..	98	98	1864, January..	185	193
April	98	98	April....	201	208
July.....	94	94	July.....	254	264
October..	101	101	October..	254	262
1862, January..	111	114	1865, January..	262	272
April	111	113	April....	211	216
July.....	115	117	July.....	193	197
October..	130	134	October..	213	214

One objection against the average, even after the correction has been made for different varieties of the same commodities, remains to be dealt with. On looking over the amended list of series one finds a number of articles that show extraordinary fluctuations which are clearly due to other causes than the currency—especially the staple southern products, cotton, molasses, sugar, turpentine, and finished products made of these materials, like cotton fabrics. It may seem at first sight that there can be no question about the propriety of excluding all such articles from the list on the ground that their price perturbations are assignable in large measure to known causes other than the changes in the currency. But, after all, the matter is not so simple. Every series in the table has a value .not only as an indication of the effect of the currency on the price of the specific commodity which it represents, but also as bearing within it a corrective for the effect upon the average of changes in the supply and demand of other commodities. If, then, one commodity is thrown out because the investigator happens to know something of the conditions affecting its demand and supply, there is danger that the effect of opposite conditions affecting some other commodity about which he happens to know less will not be offset.

In other words, use of the average to ascertain the effect upon prices of any general cause like the issue of an irredeemable paper currency, implies reliance upon the laws of chance, and the operation of these laws should not be lightly interfered with by limiting the number of cases submitted to them. Of course, this reliance upon chance is not and should not be blind. The investigator properly uses his discretion in determining whether the material which he subjects to the process of averaging is of a representative character. Under this head comes, for example, his liberty to combine series that represent the effects of the same set of particular conditions. But the mere fact that he happens to know something of the reasons why one article advanced or fell in price much more than the majority gives him no logical right to throw it out. If he were to commence upon the process of excluding all articles for the deviation of which from the mode he could account, consistency would demand that he make a careful study of the conditions affecting the supply of and demand for all articles in his list and try to distinguish in each and every case between the effects upon price of the monetary conditions and of other factors. But it is precisely because such discrimination of the part played by different causes in producing the given result is admitted to be impossible that he has recourse to the device of the average. When he employs that device at all, he should employ it consistently, and not allow his accidental knowledge of the market conditions affecting certain commodities, and his inevitable ignorance of the market conditions affecting other commodities, to interfere with the operations of the laws of chance.

But, while it would be inconsistent to exclude the whole list of southern products because the cause of their remarkable advance in price is known, there is the same reason for cutting down the representation of one group of them as for using but a single series for the five different kinds of starch. The extreme advance in the price of cotton caused by the practical cessation of exports from the South, communicated itself in large measure to all goods made of cotton—print cloths, drillings, shirtings, sheetings, calico, denims, and tickings. To include all of these separate series would give an undue prominence to the changes in the supply of and demand for cotton, precisely like the undue prominence given to the corresponding particular conditions affecting starch by the use of the five series for it. Therefore it seems probable that the representative character of the average will be improved by treating cotton and cotton fabrics like the other groups of closely related commodities, i. e., by substituting for the original eight series their average relative price. When this change has been made the new average given in the next table side by side with the preceding two is obtained.

The preceding discussion points to the conclusion that the third of these columns has a better claim upon acceptance as an index of the general trend of price fluctuations

TABLE XIII

ARITHMETIC MEAN OF 135 SERIES OF RELATIVE PRICES ACCORDING TO THREE METH-
ODS OF GROUPING

Date	Before Averaging Series for Different Varieties of Same Commodity	After Averaging Series for Different Varieties of Same Commodity	Same, after Averaging Also Series for Cotton and Cotton Textiles	Date	Before Averaging Series for Different Varieties of Same Commodity	After Averaging Series for Different Varieties of Same Commodity	Same, after Averaging Also Series for Cotton and Cotton Textiles
1860, January.	101	102	102	1863, January..	147	154	142
April....	102	102	102	April.....	165	173	162
July.....	100	100	100	July......	159	165	156
October.	102	104	104	October..	160	166	154
1861, January.	98	98	97	1864, January..	185	193	176
April....	98	98	98	April.....	201	208	194
July.....	94	94	93	July......	254	264	233
October.	101	101	100	October..	254	262	234
1862, January.	111	114	111	1865, January..	262	272	247
April....	111	113	110	April.....	211	216	207
July.....	115	117	113	July......	193	197	184
October.	130	134	124	October..	213	214	199

than either of the others. But, granting that this series
rests upon the best arrangement of the available data, the
question may well be asked whether the arithmetic mean is
the best method of averaging to employ. It has been
pointed out frequently since the days of Jevons that in an
arithmetic mean a few cases of extraordinary advance in
price will offset many cases of decline. As such cases of
unusual advance are not wanting in the series even as finally
amended, it seems wise to try some method of striking an
average not open to this criticism. For this purpose the
median may be used — that is, the point which divides the
whole number of relative prices each quarter into two equal
groups, one showing advances in price greater than the
median, and the other less. In ascertaining the median, the
final grouping of price series used in making Table XIII has

been used as the basis, and the results are presented side by side with the final set of arithmetic means from the same table.

TABLE XIV

MEDIAN AND ARITHMETIC MEAN OF THE 135 SERIES OF RELATIVE PRICES AFTER AVER-
AGING ALL CLOSELY RELATED SERIES

Date	Median	Arithmetic Mean	Date	Median	Arithmetic Mean
1860, January..	100	102	1863, January..	130	142
April.....	100	102	April.....	142	162
July......	100	100	July	139	156
October ..	100	104	October ..	140	154
1861, January..	100	97	1864, January..	161	176
April.....	97	98	April.....	175	194
July......	95	93	July	200	233
October ..	100	100	October ..	208	234
1862, January..	100	111	1865, January..	228	247
April.....	100	110	April.....	184	207
July......	103	113	July	160	184
October ..	117	124	October ..	180	199

On the whole, I incline to believe that the column show-ing the median is the most trustworthy indication of the general character and degree of price fluctuations that can be obtained from the data for wholesale prices given in the *Aldrich Report*. It is interesting, however, to see whether the results thus obtained agree with corresponding figures from other sources. Such material as is available for the purpose of comparison is analyzed in the next two sections.

III.   RELATIVE PRICES PAID BY THE FEDERAL GOVERNMENT
FOR SUPPLIES

In Part IV of the *Aldrich Report* there is a series of tables showing the prices paid by various bureaus of the federal government for a large variety of articles. From these tables it is possible to obtain fifty series representing the sums paid contractors for various kinds of food, clothing, and drugs for the years 1860 to 1865, and twenty-nine additional series of similar character for 1861 to 1865. In the majority of cases it is stated that the prices are averages for the year, or else the prices are given by months so that an average can be struck; but in the case of twenty-three of the series the time of the year to which they refer is not explicitly indicated. For this reason, because there were probably changes in the quality of the supplies furnished by army contractors from time to time, and because nearly half of the series are for a single class of articles—drugs— these data have not so high a character as the data dealt with in sec. ii. However, any credible price data deserve a brief analysis, if only for the purpose of comparison with the preceding tables. With this end in view the arithmetic means of the series have been computed, first before, and second after, grouping the intimately related articles, and then the medians of the series as they stand after grouping have been ascertained. These three sets of results are presented in the next table side by side with the annual averages of the quarterly index-numbers obtained by similar methods from the data for wholesale prices:

TABLE XV

RELATIVE PRICES PAID BY THE FEDERAL GOVERNMENT FOR SUPPLIES COMPARED WITH
RELATIVE PRICES IN WHOLESALE MARKETS

DATE	ARITHMETIC MEAN OF ALL SERIES BEFORE GROUPING OF RELATED COMMODITIES		ARITHMETIC MEAN AFTER GROUPING OF RELATED COMMODITIES		MEDIAN AFTER GROUPING OF RELATED COMMODITIES	
	Government Supplies	Wholesale Market Prices	Government Supplies	Wholesale Market Prices	Government Supplies	Wholesale Market Prices
1860........	100	101	100	102	100	100
1861........	101	98	101	97	100	98
1862........	110	117	109	115	100	105
1863........	126	158	123	154	113	138
1864........	179	224	176	209	173	186
1865........	206	220	202	209	187	188

It will be noticed that the grouping of the related series reduces the average relative prices of government supplies somewhat less than it reduces the average relative wholesale prices, and the same is true of the substitution of the median for the arithmetic mean as an average. Whatever method of grouping and averaging is employed, however, the table indicates that the advance in the price of the commodities purchased by the government for which data are available was less than the advance in the price of a somewhat larger list of commodities dealt in upon the wholesale markets. Whether this result is due to the imperfections of the materials on which the table is based, or whether it is fairly representative of the relative advance in the prices paid by the government and by private persons, it is difficult to say. The common opinion has been that the demand for war supplies was a very important factor in causing the advance of prices and that those articles purchased by the government on a large scale advanced much more in price than the majority of other things. No doubt this opinion is well founded when expressed with reference to the first year of the war, when there was a sudden as well as a large increase in the quantities of goods ordered by the war and navy departments. To fill such large orders at once was difficult, and accordingly competing contractors found it possible and necessary to advance prices. This condition of affairs is reflected by the table, which indicates that, while there was a general decline in the prices paid in wholesale markets in 1861, the prices of government supplies did not fall but rose slightly. But one need not be surprised to find that after sufficient time had been given to readjust the machinery of production to meet the government demand and to organize the intricate business of furnishing supplies, the very increase in the quantities ordered enabled contractors to supply the majority of articles at an advance in price some.

what less than purchasers in the open market were asked to pay. While, however, there is no inherent improbability in the results of the comparison between the advance in prices paid by government and by private persons, the statistical material on which that comparison is based is not of sufficient scope or of sufficiently uniform character to make one comfortably sure of its reliability.

IV.   RELATIVE PRICES OF VARIOUS NECESSITIES AT RETAIL

Another interesting body of price data is found in the twentieth volume of the Tenth Census, which contains a "Report on the Average Retail Prices of Necessaries of Life in the United States," by Joseph D. Weeks. The material for this report was collected by sending a large number of schedules to retail merchants in various sections of the country, with the request that they report the prices of specified staple articles in which they dealt. Some 409 returns were received giving the retail prices of about sixty different commodities for longer or shorter periods of time. As Mr. Weeks says, it is not probable that the articles quoted by different dealers under the same caption — as, *e.g.*, rice, cheese, starch, beans, etc.—are all of precisely the same quality. But this fact did not seriously diminish the value of the material for the calculation of *relative* prices in Mr. Weeks's opinion, because he thought it "fair to presume that in a given tabulation the price of the same quality or grade of each article, as near as is possible, is quoted for the different years, as the report is made by the same person and of the prices at the same shop." [1]

While the material thus collected was tabulated with care and published at length in Mr. Weeks's report, no attempt was made to analyze or combine the different series for the same or different articles in such a manner as to show the

[1] P. 2 of the "Report."

general trend of price movements. Consequently, little, if any, use has ever been made of this source by students of prices. In the hope of getting some light upon the very interesting question of the relation between the fluctuations of prices at wholesale and at retail, however, it seems well worth while to see what can be made of Weeks's data for the years of the Civil War by applying to them the methods used in dealing with the material of the *Aldrich Report.*

A collation of the list of articles for which this Census report gives retail prices with the wholesale price lists of the *Aldrich Report* shows that there are twenty-three commodities included in both sources that seem to be identical, or very similar. .This fact makes possible a comparison between the relative prices of these articles at wholesale and at retail. There is, however, one obstacle. The census series used purport to show average prices for the year, while the Aldrich series give returns as a rule for four months only — in most cases January, April, July, and October. It is accordingly necessary to take the average prices of these four months as representing the average for the year — a procedure that seems from comparison of other tables to be legitimate. The full detail of the comparison is given in the Appendix and a summary of the results is presented in Table XVI.

This table indicates that prices at retail continued to correspond roughly with the fluctuations in wholesale prices, despite the disturbances caused by the paper currency, but that their movements were more sluggish. From the figures it seems that the fall in wholesale prices in the spring and summer of 1861 caused by the cessation of remittances from the South that embarrassed so many large jobbing houses[1] was not reflected in retail prices — probably because it was followed by the sharp upward turn in the last quarter of the

[1] Compare Part I, chap. i, p. 21, above.

PRICES 261

TABLE XVI
RELATIVE PRICES OF TWENTY-THREE COMMODI-
TIES AT WHOLESALE AND AT RETAIL [1]

DATE	AVERAGE PRICES PER YEAR	
	Whole-sale	Retail
1860	100	100
1861	88	107
1862	105	129
1863	138	165
1864	221	211
1865	222	214
1866	206	202

year.[2] On the other hand, the advance of wholesale prices from 1863 to 1864 under the stimulus of the paper issues was more prompt and more considerable than the advance of prices at retail. Finally wholesale prices fell rather more rapidly when the war ended and the paper money began to appreciate in value.

The uses of the census data, however, are not exhausted by this comparison of the relative prices of the articles which appear both in the Weeks and the *Aldrich Report*. Similar materials are given for the retail prices of thirty-seven other commodities, and it will be well to employ all the data available in the computation of a new set of index-numbers. While the whole number of commodities included by Mr. Weeks's investigation (sixty) is less than half as great as the number in the preceding quarterly tables and is only one-quarter as great as that in Falkner's table, it is still considerable enough to afford a fair average. In transcribing the actual prices as given in the census volume, all series

[1] While the number of articles included in this table is not large, the changes in the relative retail prices are almost identical with those of the fifty-eight articles for which prices are given below from the same source. On the average there are more than ten series from different towns for each of the twenty-three articles.

[2] See Table XIV above.

were rejected except those which were explicitly said to give average prices for the several years. This course was necessary to secure uniform material, and while it reduces considerably the number of series for some articles, 556 are left —an average of more than nine series for each of the sixty articles. In constructing the table all of the series of relative prices for each article were averaged to form a single series, and then these average series were treated as the representatives of the articles to which they referred. The whole material may be found in the Appendix and a notion of its general character and scope formed from the next table:

TABLE XVII

RELATIVE RETAIL PRICES OF SIXTY COMMODITIES

Groups of Articles	Number of Articles in Group	Number of Price-Series	1860	1861	1862	1863	1864	1865	1866
Dry goods..............	9	108	100	126	199	290	402	364	296
Boots	1	27	100	102	119	138	196	165	154
Groceries	11	84	100	104	128	162	205	212	211
Flour and meal.........	4	33	100	107	114	150	185	198	202
Rice, beans, and potatoes	3	26	100	107	137	158	182	182	193
Beef	4	35	100	108	112	129	158	167	167
Veal	3	20	100	108	109	126	157	160	161
Mutton	3	17	100	109	111	122	135	158	158
Pork and hog products.	7	50	100	111	117	131	165	187	186
Fish, dried or pickled...	2	14	100	98	112	127	150	155	159
Eggs and dairy products	4	34	100	99	107	130	162	183	182
Fuel	5	41	100	104	118	154	173	176	171
House rent.............	2	38	100	99	107	116	131	136	139
Board	2	29	100	109	119	136	154	160	156
Total...............	60	556							
Average relative price of all articles (except board)			100	109	130	165	208	211	201

In this table the average relative price is not the average of the index numbers of the groups, but the average of the relative prices of the fifty-eight commodities. Board is excluded from the average because of the probability that the character of the food furnished at most boarding-houses changed very much as the result of the advance in prices.

As in the case of the wholesale-price tables, a considerable variety is to be observed in the price movements of the different groups. For example, in 1865 dry goods, which here consist entirely of cotton fabrics, show an advance of 264 per cent. over the prices prevailing before the war, while fish show an increase of 55 and house rent of but 36 per cent. A study of the 556 series given in the Appendix from which the averages for the several groups have been made will discover still greater divergencies. Even in the case of the same articles the relative change in the retail price in different towns is by no means uniform, for the equalizing effect of competition is much less felt in the case of prices at retail than at wholesale. But the number of quotations used is considerable enough to give some ground for accepting the general average as fairly representative of the fluctuations in the retail prices of some of the most important articles of daily consumption.

In order to make possible comparisons with what have been regarded as the better forms of the preceding tables, a new series of arithmetic means and one of medians have been computed from the above data after grouping the closely related commodities. The results of these computations with the corresponding figures for wholesale prices and for government supplies are shown in Table XVIII. In order to make the character of the material more uniform, ordinary commodities alone are included—that is, the series for board and house rent are not used.

TABLE XVIII

ARITHMETIC MEAN AND MEDIAN OF RELATIVE RETAIL, WHOLESALE AND GOVERN-
MENT PRICES, AFTER AVERAGING SERIES FOR RELATED ARTICLES

DATE	ARITHMETIC MEAN OF			MEDIAN OF		
	Relative Retail Prices	Relative Wholesale Prices	Relative Prices of Governm't Supplies	Relative Retail Prices	Relative Wholesale Prices	Relative Prices of Governm't Supplies
1860........	100	102	100	100	100	100
1861........	105	97	101	103	98	100
1862........	121	115	109	115	105	100
1863........	150	154	123	144	138	113
1864........	184	209	176	172	186	173
1865........	191	209	202	181	188	187

When the differences between the sources from which
the data for these three sets of averages are drawn, the
lists of articles which enter into them, and the character
of the material, are taken account of, the correspondence
between them must be regarded as fairly close. Confidence
in the representative character of each series is materially
increased by the confirmation borne by the other two. The
greatest advance is shown by the largest and most fully
authenticated set of series—that for wholesale prices. Retail prices, on the contrary, show the steadiest movement—
a fact that may be due in part to the less complete organization of retail markets and in part perhaps to the fact that
the series used for each commodity in making up the table
is itself an average of several series from different towns.

V. GENERAL CAUSES OF THE PRICE FLUCTUATIONS OTHER
THAN THE CURRENCY

The tables in the three preceding sections present the
facts concerning the price changes of the Civil War as fully
as they can be ascertained from the available data by the
common methods of analysis. But, while a price table may

show with approximate fairness the general trend of price movements, it does not show to what causes these movements are due. The only help a table gives in solving this problem is by eliminating the effect of fluctuations in the particular supply of and demand for single commodities or small groups of commodities. But if changes of a tolerably uniform character have taken place in the supply of and demand for a large number of the commodities included in the table, their effect will not be eliminated by the process of averaging. Before concluding that the results shown by the price tables were produced by the issue of the greenbacks, it is therefore necessary to consider what other general causes of price perturbations were active during the Civil War. Such a study is the more imperative because contemporary observers were in many cases inclined to ascribe the price disturbances mainly to other factors than the currency.

Two of these other factors on which much stress has been laid have already been noticed briefly — government purchases and the interruption in the supply of southern products. On the whole, there seems to be much more danger of over-than of underestimating the importance of both these causes. The government demand for many articles was not at all an increase in the whole amount required by the community, but amounted merely to a change in the channel through which the commodities reached their consumers. For example, the War Department purchased each year thousands of uniforms and vast quantities of rations; but had the volunteers remained at home, they would doubtless have bought nearly as much clothing and eaten an equal amount of food. While the demand for certain kinds of food and clothing was increased, the demand for other kinds fell off in nearly the same degree. Indeed it is not unlikely that the increase of price from the former cause was less considerable than the decrease from the latter, because a given quantity can be furnished at lower prices when there is but little variety in quantity and style, as in the case of army uniforms and rations, than when there is a great diversity in these respects as is the case with food and clothing used by the general public. Finally, if the war increased the total demand for certain articles, like lead, it indirectly decreased the total demand for others, like brick.[1] Such opposite changes in the demand for different articles may be expected to neutralize each other in the averages of a large price table. But speculative analysis is not the only resort in dealing with this question. It has already been shown that there is available a considerable body of statistical data regarding the prices paid by government bureaus for war supplies, and that these data indicate an average increase rather less than that indicated by other data for ordinary wholesale markets. If one accepts the evidence, therefore, one must conclude that this factor is responsible in very slight degree, if at all, for the great advance in prices shown by the tables.

Much the same must be said of the interruption in the supply of the staple products of the Confederate states. The diminished supply of cotton, tar, turpentine, etc., caused a spectacular advance in their prices; but it is also true that the cessation of southern demand for northern products tended to lower the prices of the latter articles. The latter effect was much less noticeable than the former, because less extreme, but it was probably felt by a larger number of commodities. In the preceding price tables, as they stand after the grouping of cotton and cotton fabrics under a single series, there seems little reason to fear that the peculiar conditions affecting the few southern products included in the list exercise undue influence upon the general averages —

[1] Relatively few new buildings seem to have been constructed during the war.

especially when the median is substituted for the arithmetic mean.[1]

A third much-emphasized factor in causing the advance of prices was the war taxation. In its need of revenue the federal government subjected almost all imported articles to heavy customs duties, and levied internal taxes upon almost all articles produced within the country. These taxes, it has been held, were equivalent to a general increase in cost of production and as such were added to the selling prices of products.[2]

This contention raises a most complex question which it is obviously impossible to discuss fully in this place — namely, the incidence of the war taxes. But a little consideration serves to show that the danger again lies in unduly exaggerating rather than in unduly minimizing the importance of the factor. For, in the first place, not all of the internal taxes at least were of a nature to be shifted — e, g., the tax upon incomes was not. And, second, the shifting of the taxes upon manufactures, sales, etc., was seriously impeded by the very universality of the levies. A tax upon a few competitive products is usually transferred to the consumers, because, unless they will submit to the addition of the tax to the price, the producers out of whose pockets the money is taken in the first instance have the alternative of gradually turning their attention at least in part to untaxed branches of industry. But when nearly all branches of industry are taxed at a tolerably uniform rate, as was the case during the Civil War, there is no such alternative open to the producer. He must pay the tax out of his profits and sell at the old rates, or add all or a part

[1] For, as stated above, an advance in relative price very much in excess of the average, has no more effect upon the median than an advance very little in excess of the average.

[2] See, e. g., J. S. GIBBONS, The Public Debt of the United States (New York, 1867), pp. 219–32.

of the tax to his price and submit to a diminished volume of sales in consequence. Which policy will be pursued will depend upon a number of circumstances, such as the elasticity of the demand for the products taxed, the closeness of competition among producers, etc. If this statement be true, it is clearly inadmissible to assume that in the case of all articles the full amount of tax was added to the price, though some addition must have been made in many cases on this account. It is accordingly impossible to determine, by reasoning upon the incidence of the internal taxes, how much importance should be attached to taxation in advancing prices.

Unfortunately no satisfactory statistical test can be applied to supplement this indeterminate analysis. The most promising test case turns out on examination to have little significance. The 5 per cent. tax on sales, of which most has been said as a factor in raising prices, imposed by the act of June 30, 1864, and increased to 6 per cent. in March, 1865, applied to most domestic products except lumber, breadstuffs and a few less important articles.[1] Accordingly one might hope to gauge the effect of this levy roughly by seeing whether by 1865 these excepted articles had risen in price less than the average.[2] Examination shows that the average relative price of the eight grains and the five

[1] *H. R. Executive Document No. 34*, p. 13, 39th Cong., 1st Sess.

[2] The average relative prices of the thirteen commodities referred to compare as follows with the general index numbers for 1862 and 1865:

Month	1862		1865	
	Thirteen Commodities	All Commodities	Thirteen Commodities	All Commodities
January......	101	111	212	247
April..........	107	110	179	207
July	106	113	157	184
October	113	124	168	199

kinds of lumber included in the quarterly table of sec. ii was indeed less than the average for all articles in 1865, but also that it was less before this tax was thought of. Accordingly, quite aside from the objection that might hold against this comparison on the score of the scanty number of commodities included, it throws no new light on the problem.

There are two facts, however, of some significance, to which attention may be called: first, prices had reached almost their highest point before the 5 per cent. tax on sales was imposed; second, the repeal of the internal revenue duties after the war did not cause any considerable decline of prices. David A. Wells, special commissioner of the revenue, who had maintained in his report of December, 1866, that "the burden of national taxation" was "perhaps the most influential" of the causes to which the "inflation of prices may be attributed," admitted in his report of January, 1869, that he was "constrained to confess, that thus far the abatement of prices consequent upon the large annual reduction of taxes has not been what was anticipated."[1]

A somewhat more definite conclusion can be reached regarding the effect of duties on imports. Successive tariff acts advanced these duties to a much higher point than had ever been reached before in the United States, and as the legal tender acts forbade the acceptance of greenbacks at the customs house, the real increase of taxation was greater than in the case of excises which were paid in paper money. Importers had consequently to buy goods abroad for specie, pay duties upon them in gold, and finally sell them for paper money. New duties would therefore increase directly the prices charged to American consumers of imported

[1] *Senate Executive Document No. 2*, p. 26, 39th Cong., 2d Sess., and *H. R. Executive Document No. 16*, p. 23, 40th Cong., 3d Sess.

goods without compelling the foreign producer to accept a lower price — except perhaps indirectly if there were a considerable falling off in sales which the producer hoped to remedy by making concessions. One expects to find, therefore, that imported commodities on the average advanced somewhat more rapidly in price than domestic products, and an examination of the price series in the Appendix will show that this expectation is justified, so far as materials for making the comparison exist. It seems altogether probable, therefore, that the war tariffs and perhaps the internal taxes also are responsible for some portion of the advance in prices as shown in the preceding tables.

Three other matters that have played rôles in the discussions of war prices may be dismissed more briefly. Withdrawal of men from their ordinary occupations to fill the armies, it has been frequently argued, made labor scarce; consequently wages rose, expenses of production increased in proportion, and this increase made it necessary to advance prices.[1] But, as will be shown in the next chapter, the rise of wages was subsequent, not prior, to the rise of prices. Wages did not advance first and increase prices by augmenting cost; but quite the contrary, prices rose so sharply as to decrease real wages in a marked degree, and this decrease led, though not immediately, to an increase in money wages. That the rise of money wages when once secured was an obstacle in the way of reducing prices is true, but it can hardly be that the advance of wages caused the preceding rise of prices. In fact, depreciation actually decreased the cost of labor to the employer and so worked in the direction of a fall, not a rise, of prices.

Contemporary observers were apt to hold speculation responsible for the advance of prices as for the advance of

[1] E. g., see C. A. MANN, Paper Money (New York, 1872), p. 239; JOHN EADIE, Panics in the Money Market (New York, 1873), p. 24.

the premium on gold.[1] But it would probably be more true
to say that the marked speculation of the war time was the
effect than that it was the cause of the price movements—
although neither statement is true without qualification.
So universal and long-continued a rise of prices cannot have
been due to artificial cornering of the supply of nearly all
articles. The really important part, with reference to prices,
that speculators played then as at other times, was in foreseeing the advances that were coming from the general
conditions of the market—monetary and other—and purchasing commodities at a lower range of prices in the
hope of selling at a higher. Such operations had the
effect of accelerating the advance, but also of tempering
its excesses, for the stocks of speculators, sold after prices
had risen in order to realize profits, tended to depress the
market.

Finally a word may be said about the relation between
prices and the quantity of money in circulation—a subject
that was much debated by the pamphleteers of the greenback
agitation.[2] It is altogether impossible to determine whether
there was a close correspondence between the course of
prices and the volume of the currency, as was affirmed by
some writers and denied by others, because, as has been
shown at length,[3] the quantity of money in use cannot be
ascertained. And more than this, the circumspect quantity-
theorist would hardly expect to find a close correspondence
at a time when "other things" were so far from "being
equal." To add one important, but unobstrusive, point to
the list of these inconstant "other things" that readily
come to mind—there was a very decided contraction of

[1] E. g., see Commercial and Financial Chronicle, Vol. II, p. 2.

[2] See, e. g., H. C. CAREY, Contraction or Expansion? (Philadelphia, 1866), Letters
III and IV; J. S. GIBBONS, Public Debt of the United States (New York, 1867), pp.
219–32.

[3] Part II, chap. ii, sec. vii.

credit during the war, arising from the unstable volume of the paper currency, and consequently, a considerably larger proportion of exchanges than usual was performed by the use of cash.[1]

While the importance of all the foregoing considerations in the study of the war prices has been frequently observed and exaggerated, there remains another factor that has attracted little, if any, attention. The notion that prices in any country which has important commercial relations with other nations are necessarily influenced by the course of prices elsewhere has long been familiar, but it was probably not until the compilation of elaborate tables of relative prices for different countries that the degree of correspondence between the direction of price movements was duly appreciated. After examining such tables, a careful student would hardly think of discussing the fluctuations in the price level of the United States, without taking account of the trend of prices in England and Europe. But the abandonment of the specie for the greenback standard in 1862 seemed to sever the connection between prices in America and elsewhere. The fluctuations of prices in the United States were so exceedingly violent that they appeared to have no relation to the gentle undulations of the foreign price level. How great the differences were is best seen by comparing Sauerbeck's index-numbers for England and Soetbeer's for Germany, as recomputed by Falkner upon the basis of prices in 1860, with averages of the quarterly arithmetic means for each year from the preceding tables.

But this emancipation of American prices from the influence of the international markets for goods and gold was more apparent than real. Even the barriers of a war tariff did not greatly diminish the extent of exports and imports, and so long as such commercial relations continued,

[1] See Part II, chap. vii, sec iii.

TABLE XIX

COMPARISON OF RELATIVE PRICES IN THE UNITED STATES, ENGLAND, AND GERMANY[1]

Date	United States	England	Germany
1860	102	100	100
1861	97	99.6	97.6
1862	115	105.5	101.4
1863	154	109.3	103.7
1864	209	112.3	106.9
1865	209	105.8	101.4

the conditions of supply and demand in one market necessarily exercised a very considerable influence over the corresponding conditions in all related markets. During the paper-money period the influence of these commercial relations was towards making the advance of prices in the United States conform to the decline in the specie value of American currency, in the same manner that before suspension it had been toward making the movements of gold prices in the United States correspond in a general way with similar movements abroad. For, had the prices of exportable commodities in the United States not risen above their specie prices elsewhere in proportion as the price of gold in paper money advanced, there would have been a large profit in sending gold from London to New York, selling it for greenbacks, investing the latter in American products, and shipping them abroad to sell again for gold with which to repeat the operation. Of course, the influence of such operations would be to depress the price of gold and raise the prices of commodities until the divergence between their relative advances in price had been reduced to compara-

[1] For the English and German prices see *Aldrich Report*, Part I, pp. 255, 295. Sauerbeck's figures for England are distinctly superior to those of the *London Economist* at this period, because the inclusion in the latter of so many articles affected by the price of cotton gives altogether too much weight to the diminished supply of that article as a price factor. As recomputed on the basis of 1860, the *Economist* figures are, 1861, 102; 1862, 109; 1863, 135.9; 1864, 144.8; 1865, 135.5.—*Ibid.*, p. 226.

tively narrow limits. On the other hand, had the prices of commodities in the United States risen above their prices elsewhere much in excess of the advance in the premium on gold, a large profit would have been realized by shipping European products to the United States, selling them at the high currency prices, converting the paper money received into specie by buying gold in the gold room, and taking the coin back to Europe to invest anew in articles for export. Here again the effect would be in the direction of bringing the currency price of gold and commodities in the United States into tolerable harmony with the trend of the European equation between money and wares — but this time the means would be reduction of prices from the increased supply of imported articles, and a rise in the premium from the increased demand for gold.

Such a line of reasoning, however, must not be pushed too far. (1) While the purchase of American products for shipment abroad in case the premium was much above prices would not have been hindered by law, the converse operation when prices had ·outstripped the premium would have encountered an obstacle in the high duties upon importation of foreign commodities. Of course, the American prices for such articles might remain above the European level by the amount of the duties and the cost of transportation; but once given this difference in the general level, a divergence from it would be checked by the process indicated. (2) It is also true that such complicated operations would have been more than commonly hazardous during the war because of the rapid fluctuations both of the premium and of prices. A state of affairs that promised a large margin of profit one week might so far change before the series of transactions could be completed as to substitute loss for gain. The existence, then, of brief divergencies between the courses of the premium and of prices is quite compatible with the logic of the argument; but if the argument is valid, one would not expect to find a wide divergence long-continued. (3) The trend of the commercial forces was not in the direction of making the movement of commodity prices and of the gold premium in the United States parallel, but in the direction of making the movements harmonize with the relative value of commodities and gold abroad. At the time of the Civil War the purchasing power of gold was everywhere slowly declining in consequence of the immense production from the Californian and Australian mines. Consequently one would expect to find in the United States a corresponding advance of relative prices of commodities slightly greater than the advance of the premium on gold.

One must not be betrayed, then, by the very great difference between the course of specie prices in England and Germany and of greenback prices in the United States, into treating the latter as entirely independent of the former. In fact, barring the influence of increased taxation in this country, the connection between the markets of the great commercial nations was quite as real during the paper-money period as at other times, and the common influences upon prices were as truly felt, despite the fact that their effect in the United States was effectually concealed from superficial observation. Had there been no war and no paper standard, doubtless prices would have advanced here in somewhat the same degree as they advanced in England and Germany, and we seem bound to believe that some part—though, of course, a small part—of the violent rise actually experienced was due to the decline in the exchange value of gold.

VI. THE CURRENCY AS A CAUSE OF THE PRICE FLUCTUATIONS

The argument has at last reached a stage where the problem of chief interest may be attacked : How far were the fluctuations of prices due to the disorders of the greenback currency? By process of exclusion the conclusion has been reached that these fluctuations cannot be accounted for, except in small measure, on any other ground than has been suggested; but it remains to be seen whether any positive evidence can be adduced for the opinion that the monetary conditions preponderated over all other factors as a price determinant. The most effective method of dealing with this problem is to apply the test of concomitant variations by comparing the specie value of the currency with its relative purchasing power over commodities. To put the data in convenient form for making this test, the average monthly value of gold in currency, and the average relative prices of commodities at wholesale by quarters are platted on the accompanying diagram. Most value seems to attach to the median of the relative prices, but a line representing the arithmetic mean is added for purposes of comparison.

Examination of this chart shows that there is a general correspondence between the relative prices of specie and of commodities in greenbacks. Agreement in detail is precluded by the nature of the data; for prices are given but once a quarter, and the intermediate monthly fluctuations answering to those of gold can only be surmised. But in general direction and to a less extent in degree of movement the gold and commodity lines harmonize well. There are, however, two noticeable differences. First, the fluctuations of prices are more sluggish than those of gold, partly, no doubt, because the lines for commodity prices represent averages, and partly because the market for gold was more highly organized, and therefore more immediately sensitive to all changes in conditions of supply and demand, than even wholesale markets for commodities. Second, the advance of commodities does not halt at any time until it has considerably outstripped the advance of gold. In this excess of prices above the premium we see the effect of various

CHART III

RELATIVE PRICES AT WHOLESALE AND THE VALUE OF GOLD COIN IN CURRENCY,
1860–65

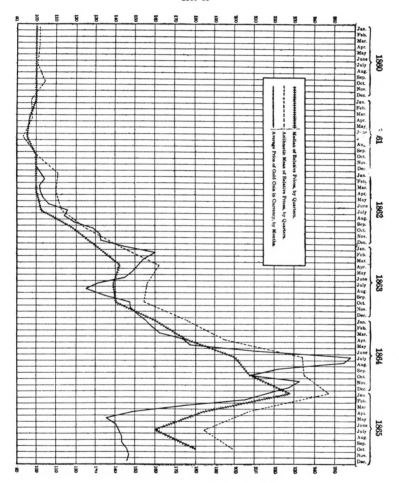

general causes other than the currency — particularly war
taxation and the world-wide decline in the exchange value
of gold. But to appreciate fully the facts as shown by the
chart it is necessary to follow the course of prices and of
gold quarter by quarter. In so doing attention will be
directed to the median, rather than the arithmetic mean.

Throughout 1860, then, prices remained practically constant, but in the summer of 1861 the general business depression caused a rather general but moderate decline. In the
autumn, however, business improved somewhat and immense
government purchases caused a sharp stiffening in the price
of supplies. The class of articles affected, however, was not
large, and consequently the median shows merely a return to
the price level of 1860. Suspension of specie payments and
the appearance of a small premium upon gold had no appre-
ciable effect upon prices for the first six months; but when
the premium began to rise rapidly after the failure of
McClellan's campaign against Richmond, prices followed.
The rise of gold, however, was considerably faster, so that
by January, 1863, its average value was 145 against a median
relative price of 130. But after the advance of gold had
culminated in February and the current turned sharply in
the other direction, prices still continued to rise for three
months and then reacted very little, so that by July prices
were higher than the premium.

Very similar maneuvers were executed from the middle of
1863 to the end of 1865. There was a rapid rush upward
of gold in which prices were left behind; then gold fell,
while prices continued to climb until they had outstripped
the premium once more. The chief difference between the
two periods, aside from the greater scale of the fluctuations,
is that in the beginning the advance of the premium was not
so fast, but that prices could keep fairly even pace with it.
But in June and July of 1864 the premium advanced at a

pace that made the progress of prices seem slow, and it was not until October, when the premium had been falling rapidly for three months, while prices continued to rise at a scarcely diminished rate, that the two were on even terms again. Another sudden advance of gold in November gave it a momentary advantage, but after its great fall began prices passed it once more, and, declining with less precipitance after January, remained for the rest of the year considerably higher.

In all these movements from 1862 to 1865 the lines representing the premium and the median of relative prices correspond so well that one cannot resist the conclusion that these changes are mainly due to a common cause, which can hardly be other than the varying esteem in which the notes of the government that constituted the standard money of the country were held. If this conclusion be accepted, it follows that the suspension of specie payments and the legal-tender acts must be held almost entirely responsible for all the far-reaching economic disturbances following from the price upheaval which it is the task of the following chapters to trace in detail.

CHAPTER V

WAGES

I. FALKNER'S TABLE OF RELATIVE WAGES

FOR the study of money wages, as for the study of prices, the most important source of material is the *Aldrich Report*. Part I contains a table — No. 37 — prepared under the direction of Professor Falkner, showing the relative wages of working people in twenty-one industries from 1860 to 1891. But this table, like the corresponding table of prices, is found on close examination to be constructed in such a manner as to be unfit for the purposes of the present investigation. From the point of view of statistical method, its chief defects are as follows:

1. Only one index-number is given for each year. This index-number is usually computed from the wages paid in January; but in some cases—what cases is not specifically stated—from the wages paid in July or October. For the present purpose more than one index-number per year is highly desirable, and the indiscriminate use of returns for different months is to be deprecated. An average into which enter figures for several different months cannot be taken to represent the condition of affairs at any specific time, and therefore is of little value for comparisons with the data regarding prices.

2. No attempt is made to distinguish between the wages of men and women, or between the wages of groups of workers possessing different degrees of skill and receiving unlike remuneration. As will be shown later, the paper standard did not produce the same effect upon the wages of the different sexes or the different groups, and a table must be had which will permit an investigation of these divergences.

3. The 543 wage series included in this table are classified by industries, but not by occupations. It is as important, e. g., to know the variations in the wages of carpenters, machinists, etc., wherever employed, as it is to know the variations in wages paid in the building and metallic industries as a whole.

4. In computing the average variations of wages in each industry Professor Falkner treated all wage series as if they

possessed precisely the same importance, quite irrespective
of whether they represented the pay of a single man or that
of several hundreds.   But if the table is to be employed as
an index of the probable average variation in the wages of
the great mass of workers, a return which shows the pay of
many men is of much greater importance than one which
shows the pay of but few.   Every series, that is, should be
given a weight in the computations, proportioned to the number of persons whose pay it represents.

Recognition of these defects has the unhappy consequence that Professor Falkner's table of relative wages must
be discarded altogether and a fresh table of relative wages,
like the fresh table of relative prices, laboriously compiled
from the data published in the "exhibits" of the *Aldrich
Report.*[1]

---

[1] More extended criticisms of the wage-tables of the *Aldrich Report* may be
found in several places.   In 1894 F. C. WAITE published in Washington a pamphlet
entitled *Prices and Wages: A Dissection of the Senate Finance Committee's Great
Report.*   This was a rather acrid criticism of the methods employed by Falkner in
analyzing the wage-data and of the conclusions drawn from his results.   In 1895 an
article by A. L. BOWLEY appeared in the *Economic Journal* (Vol. V, pp 369-83) under
the title "Comparison of the Rates of Increase of Wages in the United States and in
Great Britain, 1860-91."   Bowley took exception to Falkner's methods.   His chief
objections were (1) that there was no guarantee that the establishments from which
returns were obtained were typical of the industries to which they belonged;
(2) that no account was taken of the number of men represented by the different
series; (3) that the relative importance of the series was unwarrantedly assumed to
have remained constant throughout the whole period; and (4) that the tables showed,
not the change in average wages, but the average change in wages.   Bowley, however,
like Waite, put a high value upon the material published in the "exhibits" of the
Report.   Again, C. B. SPAHR, in his *Essay on the Present Distribution of Wealth in
the United States* (New York, 1896), declared that it is "necessary to throw away
the work done by the committee's experts."   He did not hesitate to charge that the
Aldrich Report was "prepared by men who wished to show the highest possible
level of wages," and that the statisticians "employed to summarize the returns were
to a hurtful extent in sympathy with the political aim of the investigation" (pp.
103, 106).   Finally PROFESSOR C. J. BULLOCK in his "Contributions to the Study of
Wage Statistics" (*Publications of the American Economic Association,* Vol. VI, pp.
187-218) subjected Falkner's tables once more to a searching criticism, which, however, added little to the points developed by his predecessors.   It seems to have been
this systematic critique of Bullock's that led FALKNER to publish his article upon
"Wage Statistics, in Theory and Practice" (*Publications of the American Statistical
Association,* Vol. VI, pp. 275-89).   To the detailed criticisms of the methods which he
had followed, however, he found no effective answer.

II. SCOPE OF THE DATA CONCERNING WAGES IN TABLE XII
OF THE ALDRICH REPORT

These data, which are all brought together in Table XII, were collected by the Department of Labor from actual payrolls and show the daily wages paid in January and July—or, in a few cases, October—of each year to the different classes of employees in twenty-one industries, together with the number and sex of the employees and the length of the working-day. Some 1,268 pages are covered by this exhibit.

Though the material thus supplied is much more comprehensive than that from which most wage tables have been constructed, it suffers from serious limitations.

1. The data are confined almost entirely to manual laborers engaged in manufactures or transportation. Professional earnings are represented only by a scant supplementary report upon the salaries of school-teachers. Clerical work is omitted entirely, while three wage series from two New Hampshire stores give the only data for the large body of sales-people. No account is taken of domestic servants, nor of fishermen, while miners again are treated in a supplementary report for which the data were collected in a different fashion.[1] Last and most important, agricultural laborers —the most numerous group of workingmen in the United States of the Civil War—are entirely unrepresented.

2. The exhibit is incomplete even for manufactures and transportation. Nominally there are returns for eighteen manufacturing industries; but of these industries three are of slight importance, viz., sidewalks, spice, and white lead. On the other hand, certain very important branches are represented only in the supplementary reports—as is the case with the iron, glass, and pottery industries; or else are not represented at all—as is the case with the boot and shoe, the milling and baking, dressmaking and millinery, tailoring,

[1] *Aldrich Report*, Part I, p. 180, and Part IV, Table XIII.

ship-building, tobacco, and brick industries.   Furthermore,
the data for some of the important industries included are
very meager.   This may best be seen from the following
table, which shows for each of the twenty-one industries the
number of establishments from which returns were obtained
covering the war period, the number of wage series, and the
number of employees whose pay is reported.

TABLE XX

CONSPECTUS OF WAGE DATA FOR THE YEARS 1860 TO 1866 GIVEN IN TABLE XII OF
THE ALDRICH REPORT

Industries	Number of Establishments	Number of Wage Series	Number of Employees Jan., 1860
Agricultural implements.......	1	5	9
Ale, beer, and porter............	1	5	40
Books and newspapers.........	3	17	76
Building trades................	21	42	216
Carriages and wagons..........	1	4	14
City public works.............	4	22	1,955
Cotton goods..................	3	105	639
Dry goods.....................	1	3	10
Ginghams	1	30	568
Groceries	1	2	3
Illuminating gas	4	22	460
Leather	2	16	46
Lumber	2	5	35
Metals and metallic goods......	19	138	803
Paper.........................	1	7	41
Railways......................	1	11	263
Sidewalks	1	4	31
Spice.........................	1	4	8
Stone.........................	6	19	227
White lead....................	1	4	20
Woolen goods.................	3	62	177
Total...................	78	527	5,641

If it be thought that returns for 100 employees is as narrow a basis as can well be accepted in computing the probable
wage fluctuations in any industry, ten of the eighteen
branches of manufacture would have to be excluded.

3. Of the seventy-eight establishments included in the
above table, all but five were situated in the North Atlantic

states, and of these five four were in Maryland and one — a
gas plant — was in Ohio.[1] Thus the material shows the
course of wages in but one section of the country.

4. While the material of Table XII seems to have been
collected and published with scrupulous care, it nevertheless
suffers from a defect characteristic of wage statistics in
general. It frequently occurs that when several men are
employed in an establishment to do substantially similar
work they are paid different rates of wages, which vary as
their efficiency, the length of time they have been connected
with the firm, etc. In this case, when the several men are
not distinguished in the reports, it is necessary to take the
average wage as the basis of calculation. But at any time
some of these hands may be discharged. If the ones sent
away are the recipients of the lower wages, the average pay
rises; on the other hand, if the better-paid men are dismissed, the average falls. A similar change is effected by
taking on new men at wages differing from the pay of the
old employees. Thus the table may show a fluctuation in
wages, though no change whatever has taken place in the
pay of the men who have had steady employment.[2] Of
course, a fall in average wages caused by the employment of
more men is not an injury to wage-earners, and a rise caused
by the discharge of the lower-paid portion of a force is a
purely fictitious gain. But while the effect of such adventi-
tious changes cannot be wholly eliminated by any manipulation of the material, it may be expected that in a large
number of cases the depressing influence of some such
changes upon the general average will be counterbalanced
more or less completely by the opposite influence of others.

It may seem that the imperfections of the material to

[1] The distribution of the establishments by states was as follows: New Hampshire, 4; Massachusetts, 21; Rhode Island, 1; Connecticut, 9; New York, 25; New
Jersey, 2 ; Pennsylvania, 11 ; Maryland, 4 ; Ohio, 1.

[2] For examples see the "Exhibits," pp. 947, 973, 982, 1318, and 1510.

which attention has been called are so serious as to invalidate any conclusions regarding the general trend of wages that may be based upon it. But, after all has been said, the fact remains that Table XII of the *Aldrich Report* shows the actual wages paid to more than 5,000 men and women throughout the war period. Of course, the whole number of wage-earners, even in the North Atlantic States alone, was many times 5,000 ; but if there be any considerable degree of truth in the common assumption regarding the effect of competition upon the price paid for similar services there seems to be sufficient reason for believing that a range of observation so considerable as the table affords may be accepted as fairly typical. The assumption involved in the use of such material as the basis for generalizations is that a common cause — the rise of prices — which is shown to have had a certain average effect upon the remuneration of 5,000 persons had a substantially similar effect upon the remuneration of the thousands doing similar work whose pay is not recorded.

III.   NEW TABLES OF RELATIVE MONEY WAGES BASED UPON THE DATA IN TABLE XII OF THE ALDRICH REPORT

In order to get the material of these elaborate "exhibits" into usable shape the series of actual wages were reduced to series of relative wages on the "index-number plan." Every series in Table XII that gave tolerably complete returns twice a year from 1860 to 1866 was transcribed upon a card. The industry, number, and location of the establishment, and the number and sex of the workers were recorded as well as the rates of pay. Then the relative wages in January and July of each year were computed as percentages of the wage in January, 1860. Next, in order to secure to the most important occupations a weight proportionate to their numbers, the series of relative wages were multiplied by the number of persons whose pay they represented. Finally, these products were added together, and the resulting sums divided by the whole number of persons employed. Thus the results show in all cases the arithmetical average change in the pay of all the persons included in any group. By arranging the cards in different ways it was possible to classify the wage-earners by industries, occupations, sex, establishments, *per diem* wages, etc., and to compute the average changes in pay for the varying groups thus formed.

In carrying out this general plan the most serious problem that presented itself was in what manner the weighting of the several series according to number of employees should be performed. The choice lay between multiplying the relative wage shown by each series for each successive January and July by the average number of persons employed during the whole period under investigation, and multiplying by the number actually employed at different dates. In the many cases of series which show no change in number of employees the results of the two methods— which for convenience may be called the methods of " constant " and of " variable weights " — are identical. But there are many and important series that show considerable variations in number of employees, and it is accordingly necessary to canvass the relative merits of the rival methods.

The distinctive advantage of the method of variable weights is that it shows the average change in the money wages of a division of the industrial army as it was actually constituted. Changes in number of employees are a constant and important feature of the industrial situation and one of peculiar significance for the wage-earning classes, whose interests are at present the subject of investigation. To adopt a scheme of weighting which takes no account of such changes would be to eliminate this important element in the situation. If an increase in the numbers employed in

certain kinds of work as compared with the numbers employed
in other kinds causes a change in the average relative wage
for the whole body of working men that change is as real
in its effect upon the well-being of laborers as if it had been
due to some other cause.   Accordingly, it may be argued, no
scheme of analysis can be trusted that will exclude the effect
of changes in number of employees.

On the other hand, one who examines the wage-series
and notes how frequent and how considerable are the fluctuations in numbers employed, is not unlikely to distrust an
average made up of such shifting elements.   The total number of employees represented by the series included in the
following tables as working in January, 1860, is 5,641.   In
July the number rose to 6,444.   Then followed a gradual
decline to 4,009 in January, 1863, and afterward a rise to
5,576 in July, 1866.   If these changes in aggregate numbers were produced by uniform changes of corresponding
degree in all the series, variable weights would make no
difference in the results, because, while the number of men
represented by any series would vary absolutely, it would
bear a constant proportion to the numbers in all other series.
But, of course, the variations of numbers in the different
series are not thus uniform, and the weights therefore fluctuate relatively as well as absolutely.   To take the most
extreme example — common laborers employed by some city
in the state of New York — the number of employees varies
from 1,500 in July, 1860, to 420 in January, 1866, and the
proportion of these numbers to the aggregate number of all
employees varies from 23 per cent. at the first date to 8 per
cent. at the second.   Now, it may be argued, if the object is
to ascertain the effect of the paper currency upon money
wages, it would be improper to compute the average of
changes in a fashion that would expose the results to the
influence of such fluctuations in the constitution of the
wage-earning class as those represented by the Aldrich data.

In deciding, on the basis of the preceding arguments, what course to pursue in regard to weighting, the question seems to turn upon the character of the changes in numbers. If these changes are largely due to particular causes — such for example, as the completion of an elaborate plan for paving streets that would reduce the number of men employed by a city, or the sale of a factory followed by a new policy of rapid expansion that would increase the working force — they cannot properly be allowed consideration. In this case the method of constant weights is to be preferred. But if the changes in numbers are not mainly due to causes that may from the present point of view be regarded as accidental; if, on the contrary, they should prove to be largely an indirect consequence of the monetary situation itself, then careful account should be taken of them and variable weights used for this purpose. Inasmuch as it is difficult, if not impossible, to determine in advance whether the changes are of the one kind or the other, the best course to pursue is to employ both methods of weighting, see what differences exist between the two sets of results, and try to form some conclusion regarding the significance of these differences.

All of the series used in the following computations are published in the Appendix, where they are arranged according to industries, establishments, sex, and occupation. To save space, the initial wage, number of employees, and relative wages alone are given, but to show more clearly how the computations have been made, a specimen of the card actually used in making the tables is placed here.

It will be noticed that on this specimen card the series is extended through 1866. This last year is included in all the following wage-tables in order to supply data for determining whether or not the withdrawal of wage-earners from the labor market into the army was a chief cause of the

SPECIMEN CARD

METALS				BLACKSMITHS	
ESTABLISHMENT 57			MALES	MARYLAND	

Date	Wages	Num-ber	Relative Wages	Products	
				Variable Weights	Constant Weights
1860, January........	$1.565	8	100	800	590.0
July	1.605	8	103	824	607.7
1861, January........	1.555	3	99	297	584.1
July	1.50	2	96	192	566.4
1862, January........	1.48	4	95	380	560.5
July	1.48	4	95	380	560.5
1863, January........	1.705	6	109	654	643.1
July	1.83	6	117	702	690.3
1864, January........	2.105	7	135	945	796.5
July	2.655	8	170	1,360	1,003.0
1865, January........	2.75	7	176	1,232	1,038.4
July	2.71	6	173	1,038	1,020.7
1866, January........	2.875	6	184	1,104	1,085.6
July	2.78	8	178	1,424	1,050.2
		5.9			

advance in money wages. If it appears that when the volunteers were disbanded and returned to their usual occupations wages did not fall, there will be a strong presumption that some other cause than enlistments was a more powerful factor in determining wages.

A study of the individual series of relative wages, as given in the Appendix, shows that during the war the range of fluctuations was considerably narrower in the price of labor than in the price of commodities. For a comparison it is best to take the changes between January, 1860, and January, 1865 — the culminating point of prices. The greatest relative advance in price shown by the quarterly table between these dates was 991 per cent. (cotton), and the greatest fall 11 points (raw Italian silk). On the other hand, the greatest advance in wages was 220 per cent. (slate and metal roofers), and the greatest fall 37 per cent. (steam-

and gas-fitters' helpers). Thus while the prices of the commodities included in the table covered a range of 1,002 points, the prices of labor covered but 257. Of the 135 articles for which relative prices are given in 1865 some 67 per cent. had doubled or more than doubled in price ; but this was true of only 3 per cent. of the wage-series and of an even smaller proportion of the wage-earners.

Within this comparatively restricted range, however, no great degree of uniformity is observable in the fluctuations of wages. This may best be seen from the subjoined table, in which the wage-earners for whom reports are given in January, 1865, are classified according to the degree in which their wages had changed since 1860:

TABLE XXI

WAGE-EARNERS IN JANUARY, 1865, CLASSIFIED ACCORDING TO RELATIVE CHANGE IN WAGES SINCE 1860

RATIO OF WAGES IN JANUARY, 1865, TO WAGES IN 1860	NUMBER OF EMPLOYEES IN THE RESPECTIVE GROUPS		PERCENTAGE OF WHOLE NUMBER OF EMPLOYEES IN THE RESPECTIVE GROUPS	
	Males	Females	Males	Females
60– 69%............	4	...	0.10%	.....
70– 79	3	...	0.07	.....
80– 89	16	6	0.39	0.96%
90– 99	30	12	0.73	1.91
100–109	72	52	1.74	8.28
110–119	183	144	4.44	22.94
120–129	444	54	10.77	8.60
130–139	414	206	10.04	32.80
140–149	459	130	11.13	20.70
150–159	787	10	19.09	1.59
160–169	370	1	8.97	0.16
170–179	385	2	9.34	0.32
180–189	379	5	9.19	0.79
190–199	539	5	13.07	0.79
200–224	30	1	0.73	0.16
225–249	2	...	0.05	.....
250–299	4	...	0.10	.....
300 and over.......	2	...	0.05	.....
Totals.........	4,123	628	100.00%	100.00%

This table shows that over nine-tenths of the men had received an increase of between 20 and 100 per cent., and nearly nine-tenths of the women an increase of between 10 and 50 per cent. But there is no very striking concentration on any one point in the scale of increase, except that nearly one-third of the women had gained about one-third, and nearly one-fifth of the men had gained between 50 and 59 per cent. in pay.

The absence of cases of extreme variation in the wage-series makes it unnecessary to work out averages in two ways, as was done in the chapter on prices. The reason given for using the median there was that the few commodities which showed an extraordinary advance in price affected the arithmetic mean much more powerfully than the few commodities which were just as extraordinary in not rising at all. Accordingly, the median which is not affected by the degree of divergence from the average shown by any series gave results considerably lower than the arithmetic mean. With the wage data, however, the two methods of averaging give almost the same results. In the above table the median point is found in the group 50–54 per cent. for males and 30–34 per cent. for females. The corresponding arithmetic means are 55 and 28 per cent. Such differences are hardly sufficient to justify the laborious computation of two sets of results.[1]

More concrete ideas regarding the change in wages are given by study of the actual amounts of money received per day in 1860 and 1865. An average wage computed for such diverse kinds of labor as those included in the material would mean little, and consequently a "classified" table has been arranged for the purpose of the comparison.

The significant fact brought out by this exhibit is the

[1] It may be added that arithmetic means of both wages and prices were computed before the superiority of the median in averaging the price series was fully appreciated.

TABLE XXII

EMPLOYEES IN JANUARY OF 1860 AND OF 1865 CLASSIFIED ACCORDING TO AMOUNT
OF DAILY WAGES [1]

WAGE CLASSES	MALES				FEMALES			
	Number of Employees		Percentage of Whole Number		Number of Employees		Percentage of Whole Number	
	1860	1865	1860	1865	1860	1865	1860	1865
$0.25–0.49	118	51	2.31%	1.24%	139	16	21.99%	2.71%
0.50–0.74	123	86	2.41	2.09	469	250	74.21	42.30
0.75–0.99	599	57	11.72	1.39	14	313	2.22	52.96
1.00–1.24	2,186	276	42.77	6.72	10	1	1.58	.17
1.25–1.49	542	567	10.61	13.81	....	11	....	1.86
1.50 1.74	609	381	11.92	9.28	....	....	....	....
1.75–1.99	184	897	3.60	21.85	....	....	....	....
2.00–2.24	628	614	12.29	14.96	....	....	....	....
2.25–2.49	66	332	1.29	80.9	....	....	....	....
2.50–2.74	23	319	.45	7.77	....	....	....	....
2.75–2.99	1	181	.01	4.41	....	....	....	....
3.00–3.24	28	259	.55	6.31	....	....	....	....
3.25–3.49	1	31	.01	.76	....	....	....	....
3.50+	3	54	.06	1.32	....	....	....	....
	5,111	4,105	100.00%	100.00%	632	591	100.00%	100.00%

decrease in the number of persons of both sexes in the
lower wage classes and the increase in the higher. Among
males the largest group of wage earners in 1860 was the
$1–$1.24 class, and in 1865 the $1.75–$1.99 class ; among
females, the $0.50–$0.74 class in 1860, and the $0.75–$0.99
class in 1865. The median wage for males was $1.05½ in
1860 and $1.90 in 1865. For females it was $0.56 in 1860
and $0.80 in 1865.

Greater significance attaches to the results obtained
when the numerous wage-series are classified according to

[1] The totals of Tables XXI and XXII do not agree, because in a few cases the
Aldrich Report gives piece-rate wages instead of time wages, and in a few other
cases gives wages with board furnished. As these series show changes in relative
pay, they are included in Table XXI, but as they do not show net earnings, they are
excluded from Table XXII and all subsequent computations in which actual, instead
of relative, wages is regarded.

the various economic groups to which the wage-earners
belonged. One such classification—that according to
industries—is made in the next table. No industry is
included in which returns are not given for an average of at
least 200 employees. The results are presented according
to both the systems of weighting described above.

Comparison of these industries shows that the slightest
advance of relative wages occurred in the textile trades
which employ numerous women and children. At the
other extreme, with the greatest advance are city public
works and the manufacture of gas in which the employees
represented by the data are all men and mostly men who
rank as unskilled laborers.

It will be noticed that the two systems of weighting produce results that vary but little. What difference exists,
however, is, on the whole, on the side of higher figures for
the constant weights. If one compares the two sets of
index-numbers for each of the nine industries from January,
1864, when the full effects of the paper currency began to
be felt, to July, 1866, one finds that in ten cases the constant weights give the same figure as the variable weights,
in twelve cases a lower figure, and in thirty-two cases a
higher figure. Observation of these differences raises again
the problem that was mentioned in discussing the two systems of weighting: What is the cause of the differences—
are they accidental results due to the imperfections of the
data, or are they indicative of some general feature of the
wage situation which has so far been overlooked?

In answer to these questions a hypothetical explanation
may be suggested. In organizing the labor force of a factory, a railway, or a commercial house, it is often possible to
secure substantially similar results at about the same cost
from several different combinations of laborers belonging to
different trades or possessing different degrees of skill. For

TABLE XXIII

RELATIVE WAGES IN NINE INDUSTRIES

	City Public Works		Illuminating Gas		Stone[1]		Building Trades		Metals and Met. Goods		Railways		Cotton Textiles		Ginghams		Woolen Textiles	
	Variable Weights	Constant Weights	Variable Weights	Constant Weights	Variable Weights	Constant Weights	Variable Weights	Constant Weights	Variable Weights	Constant Weights	Variable Weights	Constant Weights	Variable Weights	Constant Weights	Variable Weights	Constant Weights	Variable Weights	Constant Weights
Average Number of Employees	1,180		407		330		315		1,090		208		555		505		219	
1860, January	100	100	100	100	100	100	100	100	100	100	100	100	100	100	100	100	100	100
July	100	100	99	99	100	100	102	101	101	101	103	104	101	101	100	100	103	103
1861, January	100	100	100	99	128	122	101	101	102	103	105	106	97	98	103	102	106	107
July	91	92	99	99	91	91	102	100	103	103	105	106	97	97	109	109	107	107
1862, January	99	99	99	99	96	97	103	104	105	105	105	105	98	98	105	105	108	109
July	99	98	103	103	90	90	107	107	108	107	103	100	98	99	110	111	111	110
1863, January	122	119	125	125	100	103	118	116	114	114	106	105	107	106	109	109	120	118
July	123	122	142	143	113	112	118	119	120	119	109	110	109	109	107	108	114	115
1864, January	144	144	157	155	143	141	128	126	126	129	114	116	123	124	118	108	122	124
July	169	170	162	156	135	135	143	144	139	140	112	114	130	131	118	119	128	129
1865, January	175	180	176	175	155	155	145	148	149	149	144	143	138	141	131	131	142	143
July	178	180	175	176	151	152	158	160	150	150	146	146	141	144	148	147	142	143
1866, January	181	182	183	182	172	173	162	166	155	154	138	140	163	163	160	160	149	151
July	182	183	181	178	158	158	171	173	157	156	148	146	163	165	169	169	153	154

[1] Because of the regular difference between the summer and winter wages of quarrymen, it was necessary to compute their relative wages for January of each year as percentages of their wages in January, 1860, and for July as percentages of their wages in July, 1860. This course produces a somewhat irregular series for the industry, but one less irregular than would the use of the wage in January, 1860, as the base for relative wages in July.

example, in different factories producing the same products one is likely to find more foremen employed by one manager, more skilled mechanics by another, more unskilled laborers by a third. Now, any change in the relative rates of pay given to these various classes of workingmen may make it profitable to alter the constitution of a given force by hiring relatively fewer of those persons whose wages have risen most and more of those whose wages have risen least. Of course, the use of constant weights conceals any effect that such substitutions of one kind of labor for other kinds may have upon the results, for in multiplying the relative wages of each series always by the same number one introduces the arbitrary assumption that no changes take place in the proportional numbers of workingmen of different sorts employed. The variable weights, on the contrary, representing the actual number of men of various trades employed at each successive period, allow any changes of the sort described to have their due influence upon the averages.

To test whether the observed differences may be explained in the manner indicated, it is necessary to make a new classification of the wage-series according to ratio of increase in relative wages, and then to ascertain whether there was in fact a change in the constitution of the labor force in the direction of relatively larger employment of men whose wages had increased little, and relatively smaller employment of men whose wages had increased much. With this object in view, the wage-series belonging to each of the nine industries included in the last table were divided into two equal groups, one containing all series that show an increase in relative wages between January, 1860, and January, 1865, less than the median increase, and the other all series that show an increase greater than the median. Then the proportionate number of the total employees belonging to these two groups at the two dates was computed for each

of the industries, generally with the result of finding that
the group of series showing an increase less than the median
had a larger percentage of the whole number of employees
in 1865 than in 1860. The figures for the several industries
are as follows:

TABLE XXIV

PROPORTION OF TOTAL NUMBER OF EMPLOYEES IN NINE INDUSTRIES IN JANUARY OF
1860 AND 1865, BELONGING TO WAGE-SERIES SHOWING AN INCREASE IN RELA-
TIVE WAGES

Industry	Less than the Median for All Series in the Industry		Greater than the Median for All Series in the Industry	
	1860	1865	1860	1865
City public works..............	7%	22%	93%	78%
Illuminating gas...............	9	8	91	92
Stone	8	11	92	89
Building trades................	41	52	59	48
Metals and metallic goods......	48	46	52	54
Railways	43	42	57	58
Cotton textiles................	39	47	61	53
Ginghams	16	18	84	82
Woolen textiles...............	39	39	61	61

Of course, it cannot be assumed that desire to substitute
men whose wages had risen less for men whose wages had
risen more for the performance of the same work, wherever
feasible, was the sole cause of changes in the constitution of
working forces.   Numerous other causes in individual instances no doubt led to similar changes.   In the case of
city public works, for example, the change shown by the
above figures is probably due in large part to some alteration in the kind of tasks that were being performed—a
change that happened to create a much greater proportionate demand for men belonging to those groups whose
pay had increased less.[1]   But such changes as are due to

[1] As an industry city public works is rather unsatisfactory because of the inter-
mittent character of the work and the change in its nature from time to time. During the war there seems to have been a decrease in the attention devoted to civic
undertakings — at least the figures from the *Aldrich Report* show a marked falling

accidental causes may be expected to counterbalance each other over a field of observation so wide as the present; and as the cases of increased relative employment of men whose pay had increased less than the median for all kinds preponderate decidedly over the cases of an opposite character, one is forced to the conclusion that the figures reflect the results of the obvious economic motive to reconstitute forces of workingmen in such a fashion as to secure given results most cheaply. And, to return to the starting-point, it is clear that such substitutions of men whose labor had become relatively cheaper for others must produce differences of the kind observed between the averages of Table XXIII obtained by the use of constant and of variable weights.

A similar conspectus of changes in relative wages, but one based on a classification of wage-earners according to occupations instead of industries, is presented in the next table.

This table, though including a much larger number of groups, shows but a slightly greater range of fluctuations than Table XXIII. The maximum and minimum relative wages in January, 1865, of the twenty-seven occupations included are 173 (laborers) and 122 (machinists' helpers), as compared with 176 (illuminating gas) and 131 (ginghams)

off in the number of employees. As this falling off is particularly great in the case of the largest series — "Laborers, Establishment 35" — one which shows an uncommonly rapid increase in pay, the difference in the constitution of the working force in 1860 and 1865 shown by the above table may be thought to be exaggerated unduly. But if this series be omitted, the proportionate change is found to be even greater, as the following figures show:

EMPLOYEES REPRESENTED BY SERIES SHOWING AN INCREASE IN RELATIVE WAGES

	Less than the Median		Greater than the Median	
	1860	1865	1860	1865
City public works after exclusion of "Laborers, Establishment No. 35"..	18%	58%	82%	42%

TABLE XXV

RELATIVE WAGES IN VARIOUS OCCUPATIONS, 1860 TO 1866

	Laborers	Watchmen	Teamsters	Quarrymen	Masons	M's'ns' Helpers	Stone-cutters	Painters	Carpenters	Pattern Makers	Molders	Molders' Helpers	Blacksmiths	Blacksmiths' Helpers	Boiler-M'k'rs	Boil'r-M'k'rs' Helpers	Machinists	Machinists' Helpers	Engineers	Firemen	Printers	S'c'nd-Hands (Textiles)	Spinners (Female)	Weav'rs Males	Weav'rs F'm'l's	Overseers and Foremen	Apprentices
No. of wage-series	32	13	12	3	12	7	7	13	21	13	9	4	17	12	4	3	25	6	13	6	5	6	2	3	6	63	13
Av. No. employees	1300	35	25	341	123	63	91	69	215	49	108	33	67	62	45	35	440	69	68	224	34	35	43	96	188	106	49
Av. wages per day in 1860	$1.01	$1.04	$1.18	$1.11	$1.98	$1.08	$2.00	$1.53	$1.57	$1.65	$1.64	$0.99	$1.81	$1.09	$1.60	$0.96	$1.62	$1.16	$2.17	$1.25	$1.70	$1.33	$0.51	$0.93	$0.65	$2.13	$0.65
Relative wages — 1860, January	100	100	100	100	100	100	100	100	100	100	100	100	100	100	100	100	100	100	100	100	100	100	100	100	100	100	100
July	100	100	104	100	99	109	101	101	99	102	102	106	100	102	94	95	100	99	100	102	100	101	98	99	99	101	98
1861, January	100	97	103	114	101	103	100	103	99	102	104	99	98	98	106	109	103	104	100	103	100	92	99	103	103	102	96
July	93	99	100	91	95	108	91	103	101	103	104	106	98	98	114	108	104	100	100	102	100	90	98	106	109	103	98
1862, January	100	97	103	98	99	105	95	106	103	103	105	105	103	106	111	111	107	103	100	102	100	91	103	101	104	101	104
July	101	99	104	90	103	110	103	100	103	105	106	112	106	107	110	112	110	102	100	109	100	89	103	108	112	102	103
1863, January	123	100	107	102	110	133	103	109	104	108	110	115	111	114	113	111	120	107	103	120	100	103	99	119	111	108	101
July	125	103	115	113	111	127	111	110	110	118	116	125	120	126	126	119	123	104	105	140	104	102	101	113	110	112	107
1864, January	143	116	117	148	123	138	121	110	125	127	122	124	131	134	135	117	128	108	106	162	115	112	115	112	109	122	113
July	167	134	129	137	131	156	146	142	139	143	136	127	149	157	157	137	142	117	109	158	143	114	123	119	116	134	111
1865, January	173	138	134	163	144	150	156	144	152	152	148	135	160	163	165	142	152	122	127	170	154	125	128	144	134	140	119
July	176	140	141	154	147	158	159	165	157	156	150	133	159	164	163	146	152	126	131	170	154	131	149	138	147	141	124
1866, January	178	157	143	176	149	167	163	157	153	164	152	131	164	167	165	145	158	128	131	177	153	139	182	163	158	146	135
July	177	156	144	157	160	176	167	170	164	167	156	139	163	167	163	147	161	133	132	178	155	145	181	176	166	152	130

1 Compare the note upon the stone industry appended to Table XXIII. In computing the "average wages per day in 1860" both the January and July wages were taken account of.

among the nine industries. Since these groups are much more homogeneous than those of Table XXIII, which are composed of persons belonging to dissimilar trades but employed in the same industry, the question of the relative weights attached to different series is of less consequence, and I have not thought it necessary to work out new averages by the use of constant weights. The only occupation in which inspection of the data makes it certain that different results would be obtained is the first — laborers. Here a somewhat greater advance would be shown by the application of constant weights.

Because of the large number of occupations represented in Table XXV the detail is rather confusing. A simpler and clearer result may be obtained from the same data by grouping the occupations according to the degree of skill and responsibility which they require. For this purpose four groups may be constituted: (1) superintendents, (2) skilled handicraftsmen, (3) assistants of artisans, (4) unskilled laborers. The results of this grouping are presented in Table XXVI.

This table shows clearly that men in the lower ranks of the industrial army received a relatively greater increase in pay during the war than men in the higher ranks.[1]

The two series in Table XXV representing wages of women are not included in the groups of Table XXVI. A glance at them shows that they indicate a relatively smaller increase in wages than was received by men in the majority of the occupations for which figures are given. The computation of median wages based on Table XXI, and also the relatively small advance found from Table XXIII to characterize the textile industries, point to a similar conclusion — that women on the whole succeeded less well than men in

[1] The reason for this difference, and the question whether the greater relative increase in wages meant also a greater absolute addition to the pay received, will be discussed presently.

TABLE XXVI

RELATIVE WAGES OF FOUR GRADES OF WAGE-EARNERS, 1860–66 [1]

	Unskilled Laborers	Assistants of Handi-craftsmen	Skilled Handi-craftsmen	Superin-tendents
Number of series...............	60	51	142	69
Average number of employees..	1,701	535	1,404	140
Average wages per day in 1860 .	$1.00	$1.10	$1.66	$1.95
1860, January.................	100	100	100	100
July....................	100	102	100	102
1861, January.................	103	101	101	099
July	093	103	101	101
1862, January.................	100	103	104	099
July	099	108	106	099
1863, January.................	121	116	112	107
July	121	127	116	111
1864, January.................	143	137	125	119
July	157	144	139	131
1865, January.................	169	151	151	137
July	167	155	153	140
1866, January.................	176	161	156	144
July	169	163	162	152

the struggle to readjust money wages to the increased cost of living. But all these indications are less accurate than a comparison that can readily be made by computing the relative wages of men and women in all industries in which the material shows the employment of persons of both sexes. Figures for this purpose are given in Table XXVII. To save space only one set of results is given under each industry — that obtained by the application of variable weights — but the totals for all the industries are presented in both forms. It will be noticed that the differences between the results produced by the two systems of weighting are slight.

[1] The occupations included in the several groups are as follows: (1) unskilled laborers — laborers, watchmen, teamsters, quarrymen; (2) assistants of handicrafts-men — helpers of machinists, boilermakers, molders, masons, and blacksmiths, fire-men, and apprentices; (3) skilled handicraftsmen — stonecutters, masons, painters, carpenters, machinists, engineers, blacksmiths, patternmakers, printers, weavers (males), molders, and boilermakers; (4) superintendents — foremen and overseers and second-hands.

TABLE XXVII

RELATIVE WAGES OF MALE AND FEMALE EMPLOYEES IN INDUSTRIES IN WHICH BOTH SEXES WERE EMPLOYED, 1860-66 [1]

	COTTON		GING-HAMS		WOOL-ENS		PAPER		BOOKS, NEWS-PAPERS		SPICE		DRY GOODS		ALL INDUSTRIES			
															Var. Wts.		Con. Wts.	
	M.[2]	F.	M.	F.	M.	F.	M.	F.	M.	F.	M.	F.	M.	F.	M.	F.	M.	F.
No. of series. Av.No.	83	23	21	9	51	11	5	2	14	3	3	1	2	1	179	50	179	50
of em-ploy's.	354	201	182	323	171	48	21	16	58	27	8	9	5	5	799	628	799	628
'60,Jan.	100	100	100	100	100	100	100	100	100	100	100	100	100	100	100	100	100	100
July	100	101	100	101	103	103	100	100	100	101	100	100	...	...	100	101	100	101
'61,Jan.	96	98	100	104	106	108	100	100	96	93	101	100	...	...	99	102	99	101
July	97	98	102	113	107	106	100	100	92	96	102	100	100	100	100	106	101	106
'62,Jan.	98	97	99	109	107	112	86	80	99	97	101	100	100	100	100	104	100	105
July	99	96	101	116	110	115	88	80	97	103	104	100	100	100	102	107	101	109
'63,Jan.	107	106	101	113	121	117	105	100	100	106	109	100	150	100	110	109	108	110
July	109	108	101	110	113	116	105	100	100	[152]	111	100	150	100	109	109	109	110
64,Jan.	127	115	104	109	122	120	106	100	114	[152]	113	100	150	100	120	112	121	112
July	136	121	117	118	128	127	137	117	135	127	144	100	150	100	130	120	130	121
65,Jan.	144	125	128	133	146	130	152	117	146	118	145	100	167	104	142	128	142	130
July	148	130	143	151	144	136	163	122	147	128	154	100	167	104	146	142	147	142
66,Jan.	159	159	158	161	152	143	156	120	145	132	150	100	167	104	156	156	156	159
July	162	163	167	171	155	148	157	134	145	145	150	100	167	104	161	163	159	167

From this table it appears that in all the industries except the manufacture of ginghams the wages of women advanced less rapidly than the wages of men, while prices continued to rise, but that after prices had begun to recede the relative wages of women caught up and at the end of the period covered by the figures were on the whole slightly in the lead. It is also noticeable that in these industries in which many of the male employees were exposed to the competition of women their wages increased rather less rapidly than in

[1] The sudden rise from 106 in January, 1863, to 152 in July, followed by a drop to 127 in the relative wages of females employed in the manufacture of books and newspapers, is an aggravated instance of a defect of wage statistics mentioned in sec. ii, above. It is due to the fact that of the twenty-one employees at work in January, 1863, twenty were discharged before July, while forty new women had been taken on again by July, 1864. The one woman who remained at work steadily received wages considerably greater than most of her companions.

[2] M.= Male; F.= Female.

other industries. It is true, however, that the number of returns for spice and dry goods are too slender to possess much significance, and the same remark applies in a less degree to paper and to books. Of the series in the table, those for the three textile industries alone are based upon fairly comprehensive material.

Table XXV, in which wage-earners are classified according to occupations, and still more clearly Table XXVI, in which these occupations are grouped according to degree of skill and responsibility, suggest that there may have been some connection between actual earnings before prices rose and the degree of advance in relative wages during the war. If the increased cost of living was the primary factor in producing the rise of money wages, the existence of some such relation between actual income and degree of increase seems not improbable. For increased cost of living would necessarily press more severely upon families barely able to make both ends meet before the war than upon families which had a comfortable margin above subsistence, and would therefore force the breadwinners of families in the first class to be particularly strenuous in demanding higher pay. To discover whether such a connection actually existed, all of the wage-series have been reclassified according to the *per diem* wage received in 1860, and the relative increase of pay has been computed for the groups thus formed. The results obtained by the use of variable weights are presented in Table XXVIII A.

These figures indicate that there was an important nexus between the advance of wages and earnings before the suspension of specie payments. In the case both of men and of women the higher grades of employees received a relatively less increase in pay than the lower grades. It will be observed, however, that among males the group that fared relatively best was not the lowest paid, but the fourth in

TABLE XXVIII A

RELATIVE WAGES OF EMPLOYEES CLASSIFIED ACCORDING TO DAILY WAGES
RECEIVED IN 1860. (25-CENT GROUPS)

Per diem Wages Received in 1860	No. of Wage-Series	Av. Number of Employees [1]	1860		1861		1862		1863		1864		1865		1866	
			Jan.	July	Jan.	July	Jan.	July	Jan.	July	Jan.	July	Jan.	July	Jan.	July
Males:																
$0.25–0.49..	13	103	100	105	101	105	106	113	123	127	135	138	152	156	171	180
0.50–0.74..	23	98	100	101	99	101	103	106	115	118	124	122	143	145	155	156
0.75–0.99..	58	414	100	101	100	102	101	104	112	116	126	141	148	150	161	166
1.00–1.24..	108	1,979	100	100	103	94	101	101	121	122	144	155	165	165	173	169
1.25–1.49..	69	551	100	100	100	100	102	101	113	119	125	137	149	153	153	159
1.50–1.74..	80	661	100	101	103	103	107	109	118	121	127	140	152	155	160	164
1.75–1.99..	41	212	100	99	101	100	100	105	107	115	123	132	142	144	147	154
2.00–2.24..	43	319	100	100	100	97	98	99	103	108	120	140	146	154	155	162
2.25–2.49..	9	58	100	100	100	101	100	100	105	105	106	113	128	131	132	138
2.50–2.99..	13	27	100	100	101	103	101	97	95	101	108	115	122	123	127	132
3.00–3.49..	13	27	100	100	97	97	97	97	101	101	104	108	121	121	124	124
3.50+.....	3	3	100	100	100	100	117	117	125	125	138	134	159	128	138	137
Females:																
$0.25–0.49..	16	144	100	101	100	100	105	105	106	113	123	130	126	134	163	170
0.50–0.74..	26	426	100	101	102	108	104	109	111	109	109	117	132	148	159	167
0.75–0.99..	3	14	100	110	118	114	115	114	120	108	118	117	131	122	126	147
1.00–1.24..	2	8	100	105	106	105	74	76	67	67	105	105	93	99	116	134

rank — persons receiving from $1 to $1.24 per day. And it will also be noticed that the decline in relative increase does not hold perfectly of each successive group. For instance, in January, 1865, the group $1.50—$1.74 shows a slightly greater gain than the group $1.25—$1.49, and the very small highest group, that includes but three one-man series, shows among its irregularities some very considerable increases. To facilitate the study of the connection in a broader way by reducing the detail, and to get series that are more significant and regular because larger, it is convenient to regroup the male employees in the manner suggested by the braces on the margin. The results of such a regrouping are presented in Table XXVIII B.

This summary exhibits a higher degree of regularity than Table XXVIII A. It shows that from the time when the increased cost of living began to be an important factor

[1] July, 1860, to July, 1866, inclusive.

TABLE XXVIII B

RELATIVE WAGES OF MALE EMPLOYEES CLASSIFIED ACCORDING TO PER DIEM WAGES RECEIVED IN 1860. (50-CENT GROUPS)

Per diem Wages Received in 1860	No. of Wage Series	Av. Number of Employees[1]	1860		1861		1862		1863		1864		1865		1866	
			Jan.	July	Jan.	July	Jan.	July	Jan.	July	Jan.	July	Jan.	July	Jan.	July
$0.25–0.99[2]....	94	615	100	102	100	102	102	106	115	118	127	137	148	150	162	166
1.00–1.49.....	177	2,530	100	100	102	95	101	101	119	121	140	151	161	162	168	166
1.50–1.99.....	121	873	100	100	102	102	105	108	116	119	127	138	150	152	157	160
2.00–2.49.....	52	377	100	100	100	98	99	100	103	108	117	136	142	149	150	158
2.50+	29	57	100	100	99	100	100	98	98	101	106	113	123	122	126	128
	473	4,451														

—about the close of 1862—to the end of the period covered by the figures, the increase in relative wages varied in a rough way inversely as *per diem* wages in 1860, with the important exception that men earning less than $1 per day received a less proportional increase in pay than men in the second class. It also shows that when the rapid fall of prices began early in 1865 these differences between the relative rates of increase in money wages became less. If we take men paid less than $2.50 per day in 1860—over 98 per cent. of the whole number—we find that the difference between the increase in the relative wages of the various groups declined from 23 points in January, 1864, to 19 points in January, 1865, and to 8 points in July, 1866.

As already suggested, the general fact of a connection between the relative increase of wages and the amount

[1] July, 1860, to July, 1866, inclusive.

[2] Were female employees included with male, the first two series in the above table would be as follows:

Per diem Wages in 1860	Av. Number of Employees	1860		1861		1862		1863		1864		1865		1866	
		Jan.	July	Jan.	July	Jan.	July	Jan.	July	Jan.	July	Jan.	Jnly	Jan.	July
$0.25–0.99	1,199	100	101	101	104	103	107	113	114	120	128	138	146	160	167
1.00–1.49	2,538	100	100	102	96	101	101	119	121	139	150	161	161	167	166

earned before the sudden advance in cost of living is readily explainable on the hypothesis that the rise of prices rather than the withdrawal of men into the army or any other cause was the chief reason for the higher pay. Though it may not seem so clear at first, both the exception to this general rule in the case of men earning less than $1 per day before the war, and the decreasing divergence between the series after prices had begun to fall, can be accounted for on similar grounds. It is probable that most of the men represented in the table who received less than $1 a day before the war were unmarried, or at least that a considerably larger proportion of them than of men earning from $1 to $1.49 were without family responsibilities. On the average, a single man is better off, from the material point of view, on a wage of, say, 75 cents a day than a man with a family on a wage of, say, $1.25 a day. If this be so, there is the same reason why men in the first of our groups should receive a less average increase in money wages because of the increased cost of living that there is why men in the third group should receive a less average advance than men in the second, men in the fourth less than men in the third, and men in the fifth group less than men in the fourth.

As for the decreasing divergencies between the series of relative wages, a study of the table shows its cause to be that after prices began to fall in January, 1865, the rate of increase in wages became distinctly smaller in the case of the group that had been most affected by the increased cost of living, but not in the case of the other groups. As the changes in the pay of men earning from $1–$1.49 per day conformed more closely to the changes in cost of living when the cost was advancing than did the changes in the pay of other men earning either more or less, so also, when the cost of living declined, this group was the first to show the effect of the change.

Similar considerations explain why on the whole the wages of women increased less than the wages of men. One of the reasons commonly given for the fact that female employees are paid less than men for similar work is that they have smaller family responsibilities.[1] If such is the case, an increase in the cost of living would press on the average less severely upon working women than upon working men, just as it would press less severely on men receiving high, than upon men receiving low, wages.

It would be an error, however, not to note that this connection between earnings and change in relative wages holds true only in a broad and general way. The contrast between the first and second forms of Table XXVIII shows that the rule does not hold uniformly in the smaller wage-groups. Similarly, reference to Table XXV will show that, while the better-paid occupations on the whole exhibit a less considerable increase in relative wages than the poorer-paid occupations, this is not true in every individual case. For example, the average increase in the pay of 440 machinists who received an average wage of $1.62 per day in 1860 was 52 per cent. by January, 1865, as compared with 22 per cent. in the case of 69 of their helpers, who got but $1.16 a day in 1860. This qualification means nothing more, however, than that the general law of statistics applies to these figures—uniformities are discovered only when large groups are taken.

Another misapprehension may be guarded against by call-

---

[1] A rough illustration of this fact is furnished by the following classification of male and female breadwinners in the United States in 1890 according to conjugal condition—computed from *Eleventh Census*, "Population," Part II, p. cxxvi.

	Total	Single	Married	Widowed	Divorced
Males	100%	39.2%	57.1%	3.4%	0.3%
Females	100%	69.8%	13.2%	16.1%	0.9%

ing attention to the fact that the above discussion refers only to the relative—not to the absolute—increase in money wages. The fact that men earning from $1 to $1.49 per day in 1860 received a relatively greater advance in pay than any other class does not mean that the extra sums given them were as large as the sums added to the pay of employees of higher grade. As a matter of fact, the actual increase was greater in the pay of men receiving higher wages at the outset. To bring out this fact, Table XXIX has been prepared by computing the average *actual* increase of pay represented by the average *relative* increase for each of the groups of Table XXVIII B. A wage midway between the greatest and the least included in each group has been taken as the basis for the computations.

TABLE XXIX

AVERAGE ACTUAL INCREASE IN DAILY WAGES OF MALE EMPLOYEES, COMPUTED FROM TABLE XXVIII B

Per diem Wage Assumed for 1860	1860		1861		1862		1863		1864		1865		1866	
	January	July	January	July	January	July	January	July	January	July	January	July	January	July
$0.62	$.00	$.01	$.00	$.01	$.01	$.04	$.09	$.11	$.17	$.23	$.30	$.31	$.38	$.41
1.25	.00	.00	.03	.06	.01	.01	.24	.26	.50	.64	.76	.78	.85	.83
1.75	.00	.00	.04	.04	.09	.14	.28	.33	.47	.67	.88	.91	1.00	1.05
2.25	.00	.00	.00	.05	.02	.00	.07	.18	.38	.81	.95	1.10	1.13	1.31
3.00	.00	.00	.03	.00	.00	.06	.06	.03	.18	.39	.69	.66	.78	.84

According to this table the most considerable average increase in actual wages was that of men earning from $2 to $2.49 per day in 1860; but the relative increase was greater in the case of men earning less, because the smaller actual additions bore a higher proportion to the lower initial wages. Of the two forms of presentation—relative and actual increase—the former seems to possess more significance when one is concerned with the economic well being of wage-earners, for the reason that the importance of a given sum added to an income depends upon the amount of that income before the addition is made. An increase of 75 cents to the daily wage of an unskilled laborer who formerly received $1.25 means more to him than an increase of $1 to the daily wage of a carpenter who had been paid $2.25. Consequently a better idea of the alteration in the circumstances of the two men is afforded by saying that the day-laborer's pay had been increased 60 per cent. and the carpenter's 44 per cent., than by saying that the former's pay had been increased 75 cents and the latter's $1.

As has been said, an average wage computed from the returns of employees of such diverse character as the persons for whom the *Aldrich Report* gives returns means comparatively little; but there is no valid objection to a computation of the average *variation* in the pay of men in unlike occupations. While a series of such averages does not present the facts concerning the changes in the wages of any specific individuals or groups, it is nevertheless the only means by which a general notion regarding the circumstances of the whole class of workingmen can be arrived at. Consequently it seems worth while to present a summary of the average relative wages of all employees for whom we have data and to compare it with the results obtained by Professor Falkner from practically the same material. This is the purpose of Table XXX.

Between the two forms of the semiannual table it is found again that the differences are slight, but that the constant weights give slightly higher figures. In order to test once again the explanation given above for this difference, all of the wage-series have been divided into two nearly equal groups, one containing the 255 series that show an advance by January, 1865, of 42 per cent. or less, and the other the 257 series that show an advance of 43 per cent. or more. The

TABLE XXX

AVERAGE RELATIVE WAGES OF ALL EMPLOYEES FOR WHOM DATA ARE GIVEN IN TABLE
XII OF THE ALDRICH REPORT

| | | Semiannual Table | | | Falkner's Table[1] | |
		Variable Weights	Constant Weights		Simple Average	Weighted Average
1860, January	-	100	100 ⎱	-	100.0	100.0
July	- -	100	99 ⎰			
1861, January	-	102	102 ⎱	- -	100.8	100.7
July	- -	99	99 ⎰			
1862, January	-	102	102 ⎱	-	102.9	103.7
July	- -	104	103 ⎰			
1863, January	-	116	114 ⎱	- -	110.5	118.8
July	- -	119	119 ⎰			
1864, January	-	131	132 ⎱	-	125.6	134.0
July	- -	142	144 ⎰			
1865, January	-	152	156 ⎱	- -	143.1	148.6
July	- -	155	159 ⎰			
1866, January	-	161	165 ⎱	-	152.4	155.6
July	- -	164	166 ⎰			

former group includes 27 per cent. of the whole number of
employees in 1860 and 38 per cent. in 1865; conversely, the
latter group includes 73 per cent. of the whole number in
1860 and 62 per cent. in 1865.   Lest it be thought that this
difference is due to the prominence of the one very large
series—laborers employed by establishment 35—the figures
have been recomputed after excluding it.   Then the result is
that the group of series showing an increase less than the
median include 35 per cent. of the employees in 1860 and 42
per cent. of the employees in 1865, while the corresponding
figures for the other group are 65 and 58 per cent.   The
data thus show unmistakably the tendency to substitute
employees whose pay had increased relatively less for
employees whose pay had increased relatively more, wherever such a change was feasible.

[1] *Aldrich Report*, Part I, pp. 174, 176.

The discrepancies between both the columns of the semi-annual table and the two sets of results obtained by Falkner are much greater than the differences produced by variable and constant weights. These discrepancies deserve careful attention, because they show clearly the effects produced by dissimilar methods of analyzing substantially the same data.

The first of the Falkner summaries was obtained by striking a simple arithmetic average of the 500 or more wage-series, all of which were treated as having precisely the same importance. In the semiannual table, on the contrary, each series was weighted by the number of persons whose pay it represented. That this difference in the method of striking the averages must produce somewhat divergent results may be seen from Table XXVIII A or B. Not only are the wage-groups in this table that show the greatest increase in pay represented by a larger number of series than the groups that show a smaller increase, but, more than this, their series include on the average a larger number of employees. Falkner's method of preparing a general average of variations would allow to each of these groups an influence upon the result in proportion to the number of series included in it; but the method adopted in constructing the semiannual table would give each group an importance in proportion to the number of employees. For example, in computing the index number for January, 1865, the group $1–$1.49, which shows the greatest advance in money wages, would have a weight of 35 per cent., according to Professor Falkner's method, because 179 of the 505 series fall within it, and a weight of 50 per cent. according to the second method, because 2,325 of the 4,696 employees fall within it. It is further true that the average index number for this group is higher when calculated according to the second method, because the large series as a rule show a somewhat greater increase than the small series. This last fact may perhaps mean that establishments requiring the services of many hands found it necessary in order to secure full quotas to offer wages rather higher than a small employer was compelled to pay to secure two or three men.

The second of the Falkner series in Table XXX, like the semiannual series, is a "weighted" average. But the methods of weighting adopted in the two cases are very different. Instead of multiplying each relative wage by the number of employees whose pay it represented, Professor Falkner struck a simple average of the relative wages in each industry and then multiplied the series for each industry by the number of persons engaged in it according to the federal census reports. As several of his critics have pointed out, there are grave objections to this procedure. First, the census does not purport to show the number of persons engaged in industries—like the manufacture of agricultural implements, for example; but the number of persons engaged in various occupations—like painting, bricklaying, tailoring, carpentering, and the like. Nor is it possible to ascertain from these returns for occupations the numbers employed in industries. To take one example, the first of Falkner's industries — "Agricultural Implements" — is weighted for the years 1880–91 by the number of persons reported in the occupation tables of the Tenth Census under the caption "Agricultural Implement Makers"—viz., 4,891.[1] But that this number does not include by any means all the persons engaged in this industry is indicated by the following footnote appended to the caption in the census table: "Generally reported as 'iron founders,' 'carpenters,' 'machinists,' 'painters and varnishers,' etc."

Second, if the weights used are erratic, some of the series for the industries to which they are applied are not less so.

[1] *Tenth Census*, Vol. I, "Population," p. 746; *cf. Aldrich Report*, Part I, p. 175.

It has been pointed out above that the number of wage-
series in several of the "industries" of the *Aldrich Report*
is altogether insufficient to give a reliable indication of the
general trend of wages.[1]   To take the most extreme cases,
there are but two series for "Groceries" and three for
"Dry Goods."[2]   Of course this is an altogether inadequate
basis for conclusions about the wages of salesmen, yet "Dry
Goods" receives, in Professor Falkner's table, a weight second only to that of "Building Trades."

   In considering which of the four series of relative wages
in Table XXX has the best claim to acceptance, therefore,
Falkner's weighted series must be discarded.   Curiously
enough it approaches the results of the semiannual tables
more closely than its companion series of simple averages.
But in view of the faulty method by which the weights
were obtained and the recklessness with which they were
applied, this closer approach must be regarded as an accidental virtue.

   Of the three remaining series, Professor Falkner's simple
average will be preferred only by those, if any such there
be, who believe that in computing average variations in
wages no attention should be paid to the number of persons
employed at different rates of pay.   On the other hand,
the semiannual table will be preferred by those in whose
eyes the numbers are important.   Perhaps the difference
between the two tables can best be expressed by saying that
Falkner's simple average shows the average change in the
price paid for various *kinds of work*, allowing to each kind
an importance in proportion to the number of reporting
establishments in which it is performed, while the semiannual table shows the average change in the pay of all the
wage-earners for whom returns are given.

[1] See sec. ii, above.
[2] See Table XX, above.

IV. RELATIVE MONEY WAGES IN THE COAL, IRON, GLASS, AND
POTTERY INDUSTRIES

The preceding discussion has been confined to the material afforded by Table XII of the *Aldrich Report*. Before combining the figures for money wages with the tables of prices it is in order to seek what additional wage-data may be found in other sources.

The task of collecting material for the Aldrich committee regarding wages in the coal, iron, glass, and pottery industries was intrusted to Mr. Joseph D. Weeks. His report presented the data in such a different form that they cannot readily be compared with the uniform returns for other industries secured by the Department of Labor. Not only do Mr. Weeks's tables fail to report number and sex of the workers, but they also do not give wages for the same

TABLE XXXI

RELATIVE WAGES OF COAL MINERS [1]

ANTHRACITE COAL		BITUMINOUS COAL	ANTHRACITE COAL		BITUMINOUS COAL	
Date	Relative Wages	Relative Wages	Date	Date	Relative Wages	Relative Wages	Date
1859, Nov.	93	100	1859	1865, May..	208	250	1865
1860, March ..	107	100	1860	July..	162	...	....
Dec.	93	...	....	Sep	185	...	....
1861, May.. ..	107	50	1861	Oct........	208	...	....
Aug.....	93	75	1861	1866, Jan	169	200	1866
1862, May.. ..	100	88	1861	Feb	181	...	....
July.. ..	107	88	1862	April.....	166	...	....
Nov.. ..	123	100	1862	June.	185	...	....
1863, July.. ..	154	150	1863	Aug......	208	...	....
Sep......	185	200	1863	Dec..	166	...	....
1864, May.. ..	208	250	1864				
July.. ..	239	...	....				

[1] In computing the relative wages in the first of these series the average of the wage paid in November, 1859 ($6 per week), and March, 1860 ($6.96), was taken as the basis. In the case of the second series the months of the year in which the specified wages were paid are not stated.

months in the year. As a glance at any of the previous tables will show, this second lack of uniformity is particularly serious when one is studying the effects of the greenback issues, because wages changed so rapidly during the war. It is, therefore, necessary to take up Mr. Weeks's reports for the several industries separately.

For the coal industry he gives two series, one presenting the weekly wages of a miner of anthracite coal doing "company work" in Luzerne county, Pa., and the other showing the price paid per bushel for mining bituminous coal near Pittsburg. These series are shown in the preceding table.

Both these series show a somewhat greater relative

TABLE XXXII

RELATIVE WAGES OF IRON-ORE MINERS

NEW JERSEY		OXFORD , N. J.		CORNWALL, PA.			PORT HENRY DISTRICT, N. Y.
Blasters and Drillers		Miners		Un-skilled Laborers	Skilled Laborers		Miners
Per diem wage, 1860	$1.00	Per diem wage, 1860	$1.00	Per diem wage, 1860	$0.75	$0.95	$1.25
1860.....	100	1860.....	100	1860.....	100	100	100
Oct.	113	....	...				
1861.....	100	1861, Oct.	90	1861.....	107	105	100
1862.....	100	1862, July	100	1862.....	120	116	108
1863.....	144	1863, July	125	1863.....	133	126	112
1864, Jan.	144	....	...	....	...	...	...
Feb.	163						
Apr.	200	....	...	1864.....	207	179	200
July	250	1864, July	175	....	...	...	...
1865, Jan.	250	....	...	....			
Apr.	200			1865.....	187	179	120
July	150	1865, July	188	....	...	...	...
1866, Jan.	165	1866, Jan.	138	1866.....	193	184	132
		1866, July	150				

increase of pay than any of the occupations included in Table XXV, but not greater than some of the individual series, as may be seen by referring to Table XXI. The anthracite miners belong in the $1.00–$1.24 wage group, for their pay per day before the war averaged $1.08. In which group the bituminous miners belong it is difficult to say. During the nine years, 1852 to 1860, they had been paid two cents a bushel, and according to Mr. Weeks men in good mines working full time could mine about 100 bushels a day. What average earnings per day had been, however, we do not know.

Among men engaged in mining iron ore Mr. Weeks's figures also show not only a large increase in money wages, but also violent fluctuations from time to time. An attempt to compare the five series relating to this industry is made in Table XXXII.

Men employed in making pig iron, on the contrary, received an advance in pay below the average, if the two series given by Mr. Weeks and represented in Table XXXIII give a correct impression.

TABLE XXXIII

RELATIVE WAGES IN THE PIG IRON INDUSTRY

CATASAUQUA, PA.

Year	Fillers at Blast Furnace	Keepers at Blast Furnace
Per diem wage, 1860.	$1.37	$1.85
1860................	100	100
1861................	105	103
1862................	91	91
1863................	101	103
1864................	153	146
1865................	141	135
1866................	142	130

TABLE XXXIV

RELATIVE EARNINGS IN THE BAR IRON INDUSTRY

Date	Puddling Iron Etna, Pa.			Puddling Iron Duncannon, Pa.			Rolling Iron Duncannon, Pa.	
	Tonnage Rates	Puddlers	Puddlers' Helpers	Tonnage Rates	Puddlers	Puddlers' Helpers	Tonnage Rates	Bar Rollers
Per diem wage,'60	.....	$2.67	$1.33	.....	$2.01	$1.01	.....	$3.20
1860	100	100	100	100	100	100	...	...
September 8	...	...	...	...	...	...	100	100
1861	100	100	100	100	100	100	100	100
1862,April 12	...	...	...	...	...	...	113	113
July 12	...	...	...	114	114	114	...	...
August 23	...	...	...	129	129	129	...	...
September 1	113	112	113	...	...	...	...	...
September22	...	...	...	...	...	...	125	125
October	125	125	126	...	...	...	...	...
October 18	...	...	...	136	136	136	...	...
November 35	...	...	...	143	143	143	...	...
1863,April	138	137	138	...	...	...	...	...
April25	...	...	...	157	158	156	...	...
May 2	...	...	...	...	...	...	138	138
June	150	150	150	...	...	...	...	...
July	...	...	...	...	189	188	...	...
December	163	162	163	...	...	...	...	...
1864,January 30	...	...	...	171	206	205	150	150
April 9	...	...	...	186	223	222	...	...
May	175	175	175	...	...	...	...	...
May 17	...	...	...	...	...	...	163	163
June	188	187	188	...	...	...	...	...
June 4	...	...	...	214	257	256	...	...
July	200	200	201	...	...	...	...	...
August 27	...	...	...	...	...	...	175	175
October 1	...	...	...	229	275	273	...	...
December	225	225	226	...	...	...	...	...
1865,February 4	...	...	...	200	240	240	165	165
March	200	200	201	...	...	...	...	...
April	150	150	150	...	...	...	...	...
May 13	...	...	...	171	206	205	150	150
July	144	143	144	...	...	...	...	...
September	200	200	201	...	...	...	...	...
September 9	...	...	...	157	189	188	138	138
September23	...	...	...	171	205	205	150	150
October 21	...	...	...	200	240	240	165	165
1866	...	...	...	200	240	240	...	...
January 6	...	...	...	...	...	...	158	158
January 27	...	...	...	...	...	...	165	165
March 31	200	201	202	...	...	...	...	...
December 22	225	226	227	...	...	...	...	...

For the bar iron industry Mr. Weeks's reports are not quite so restricted. They indicate a large increase in the pay of puddlers and their helpers, checked by a brief reaction in 1865, and for the better paid bar-rollers an increase not greatly in advance of that of pig-iron workers.

The two series given by Mr. Weeks as representative of the pottery industry are both for men making very high wages. The net earnings of the hollow-ware pressers from 1859 to 1863 are reported as $10 a day, and of the handlers as $9. The dollar a day added to their earnings in 1864 accordingly represented a relatively slight increase.

TABLE XXXV

RELATIVE EARNINGS OF POTTERS

Year	Hollow-Ware Pressers	Handlers
Average net earnings in 1860.	$10.00	$9.00
1860.	100	100
1861.	100	100
1862.	100	100
1863.	100	100
1864.	110	111
1865.	110	111
1866.	110	111

Finally, Mr. Weeks gives six series representing the average daily earnings of glass-blowers engaged in making window glass and green-glass bottles of various sizes. These figures are for years beginning in September and ending in May or June, for glass-blowing is generally suspended during the summer months. Table XXXVI shows that until May, 1866, the average earnings of blowers had increased slightly less than wages in the industries represented in Table XXX.

TABLE XXXVI

RELATIVE EARNINGS OF GLASS BLOWERS

YEAR	Blowers of Window-Glass	BLOWERS OF GREEN GLASS BOTTLES				
		2 oz.	4 oz.	8 oz.	Pint	Quart
Av. earnings a day in 1859-60............	$3.32	$2.25	$2.25	$2.40	$2.97	$3.08
1859-60..............	100	100	100	100	100	100
1860-61..............	100	93	98	96	91	94
1861-62..............	100	100	107	110	121	125
1862-63..............	100	100	107	110	121	125
1863-64..............	100	100	107	110	121	125
1864-65..............	136	149	156	156	148	155
1865-66..............	151	149	156	156	148	155
1866-67..............	213	233	231	225	167	159

V. RELATIVE SALARIES OF SCHOOL TEACHERS

The Aldrich committee found it impractical to collect data regarding the earnings of professional men, such as lawyers, physicians, or even clergymen; but as in a measure representative of this whole class their statistician used a few carefully selected returns of the salaries of teachers in the public schools of four cities—Boston, Baltimore, Cincinnati, and St. Louis—and of two rural counties in Massachusetts—Franklin and Barnstable. These returns are presented in Table XXXVII.

On the whole, these results accord well with those of the preceding sections. The average increase in the salaries of male teachers is less than that shown by any of the twenty-seven occupations represented in Table XXV with two exceptions. The discussion based on Table XXVIII suggests that the reason for this slight increase is found in the high initial earnings. On the other hand, a seeming contradiction of the rule is found in the fact that the advance in the salaries of women teachers is greater than in the case of men. But this exception is one in seeming only. In gathering

TABLE XXXVII

RELATIVE SALARIES OF SCHOOL TEACHERS, 1860-66

	BOSTON		BALTIMORE		CINCIN'ATI		ST. LOUIS		COUNTRY SCHOOLS IN MASS.		AVERAGE OF ALL SERIES		
	M.	Fem.	M.	Fem.	M.	Fem.	M.	Fem.	M.	Fem.	M.	Fem	Both
No. of series	3	2	3	6	3	3	2	2	2	2	13	15	28
Av'r'ge sal'ries	$2,267	$400	$1,167	$292	$1,423	$390	$1,225	$400	$34.09	$17.52			
	pr yr.	pr yr.	pr yr.	pr yr.	pr yr.	pr yr.	pr yr.	pr yr.	pr mo	pr mo			
Year.													
1860....	100	100	100	100	100	100	100	100	100	100	100	100	100
1861....	100	100	100	100	87	91	66	78	102	95	92	95	93
1862....	100	100	100	100	87	91	82	91	100	99	94	97	96
1863....	100	100	100	100	100	100	...	...	101	97	100	100	100
1864....	109	127	130	178	120	100	123	131	106	101	118	139	129
1865....	125	145	130	178	120	100	123	131	128	115	125	143	135
1866....	125	145	159	249	138	117	139	143	137	126	140	183	164

their data the agents of the Aldrich committee found it possible to include only the highest and the lowest grades of teachers; because the intermediate grades are so many and show such variations in pay that no satisfactory data could be obtained regarding them.[1] Since the highest grades of teachers in American schools are men and the lowest women, the figures of the report for women relate to teachers with very low salaries and the figures for men to well-paid teachers. The salaries of the women range from $100 to $500 a year and those of the men from $900 to $2,800. Now, while it has been shown that in most industries in which both sexes participate the average increase in the pay of men was greater, it does not follow that the increase in the wages of the best-paid men was greater than that in the wages of the worst-paid women. Indeed, a comparison of the two parts of Table XXVIII A will show that the men belonging in the wage-groups $2.25–$2.49 and above received on the whole a smaller average advance than the 628 females for whom we have returns. Of course, in Table XXXVII we are com-

[1] Aldrich Report, Part I, p. 184.

paring with women men receiving on the average considerably more than $2.25 a day.

A less definite, but nevertheless an important contribution to knowledge of the economic situation of professional men during the war, is supplied by an inquiry made in 1869 by David A. Wells, then special commissioner of the revenue. "The answers," he says in his fourth report, "to a large number of circulars sent out by the commissioner during the past year to clergymen, teachers and other professional men, lead to the conclusion that, while their salaries or incomes have, as a general rule, been advanced since 1861, the advance has not been equal, by any means, in extent, to the advance in the price of commodities."[1]

Since prices fell after January, 1865, while money earnings of such persons apparently continued to increase, it follows that the case of these correspondents was probably worse during the war than when their troubles were laid before Mr. Wells in 1869.

VI. RELATIVE WAGES OF FARM LABORERS

It is especially regretable that wages of farm laborers are not included in the exhibits of the *Aldrich Report*, because they formed in the United States of the Civil War the largest single class of wage-earners.[2] Nor can this gap be satisfactorily closed with material drawn from other sources. The Department of Agriculture has made several investigations into the wages of farm laborers, but the earliest of these was not undertaken until 1866, and no systematic

---

[1] *H. R. Executive Document No. 27*, p. xlii, 41st Cong., 2d Sess.

[2] In the occupations table of the Census of 1860 the number of "farm laborers" in the nine states represented in the material of the *Aldrich Report* (see sec. 2) is reported as 335,246, while the number of "laborers" given is 512,481. But the preponderance of the latter class is probably due to the fact that in rural districts a farm hand is often reported simply as a "laborer" on the schedules filled in by the enumerator and tabulated as such in the Census Office, when he should have been reported as an "agricultural laborer."

attempt was made then to ascertain what wages had been paid in former years. Mr. Dodge, the statistician of the department, however, gave it as his opinion that there had been an increase of about 50 per cent. between 1861 and 1866.[1] But when the ninth of these investigations was made, in 1892, the department requested its correspondents to send it copies of any accessible wage-records relating to years before 1866. A considerable number of replies was received from different sections of the country and published by Mr. Dodge in his report.[2] Fragmentary as is this material, one can glean from it a few series that may give some notion of the changes in the pay of farm hands during the war. The results of such an attempt are presented in Table XXXVIII.

TABLE XXXVIII

RELATIVE WAGES OF FARM LABORERS

Terms	1860	1861	1862	1863	1864	1865
MALES						
Per month, without board, Mass	100	92	120	...	133	147
Per month, with board, Mass., Southampton....	100	89	84	126	137	132
Per month, with board, Mass....................	100	99	127	129	135	154
Per month, with board, Mass., Groton..........	100	90	137	167	167	173
Per month, with board, N.J., for summer only..	100	108	108	138	154	154
Per month, with board, N.J., for whole year....	100	109	109	136	145	145
Per month, with board, Pa......	100	108	108	117	133	167
Per month, with board [?], Ohio, Butler Co.....	100	100	89	104	125	154
Per month, with board, Ohio, Lake Co..........	100	100	100	138	154	...
Per month, with board, Ill., Champaign Co.....	100	88	100	106	129	147
Per day, with board, common labor, N.J........	100	100	117	133	167	167
Per day, with board, common labor, Pa.........	100	104	104	125	167	167
Per day, with board, harvest, Pa...............	100	100	100	120	160	160
Per day, with board [?], Ohio, Butler Co........	100	100	100	117	150	183
Per day, without bd. [?], harvest, O., Butler Co.	100	100	100	93	133	167
FEMALES						
Per week, with board [?] Ohio, Butler Co.......	100	100	100	136	136	155
Average relative wages of the sixteen series....	100	99	107	126	145	158

Scanty as is this material, it seems to be the most authentic upon the subject, and some interest attaches,

[1] *Annual Report, Department of Agriculture*, 1866, p. 81.

[2] *Wages of Farm Labor in the United States* (Department of Agriculture, Division of Statistics, Misc. Series, Report No. 4, 1892), pp. 54–69.

therefore, to a comparison with the fuller returns for other occupations. To facilitate such comparison the series for "farm laborers," "all employees," "laborers," and "unskilled laborers" are placed side by side in Table XXXIX.

TABLE XXXIX

COMPARISON OF RELATIVE WAGES OF FARM LABORERS AND OTHER WAGE-EARNERS

Date	Farm Laborers Tab. XXXVIII	All Employees Table XXX	Laborers Table XXV	Unskilled Laborers Table XXVI
1860, January	...	100	100	100
July	100	100	100	100
1861, January	...	102	100	103
July	99	99	93	93
1862, January	...	102	100	100
July	107	104	101	99
1863, January	...	116	123	121
July	126	119	125	121
1864, January	...	131	143	143
July	145	142	167	157
1865, January	...	152	173	169
July	158	155	176	167

From this comparison it appears that farm laborers received an advance in money wages slightly greater than the average for the 5,000 employees for whom the *Aldrich Report* gives returns, but considerably less than the advance in the pay of the groups with which they have most in common. This result is what the previous analysis would lead one to anticipate. As the rise of wages seems to have been due primarily to an increase in living expenses, one would expect to find that when part of this increased expense was assumed by the employer in furnishing board, the advance in money wages would be less than when the person had to find himself. Table XXXVIII shows that in the case of but one of the sixteen series is it positively stated that the pay was "without board." Second, there seems reason to believe that, as a rule, farm hands have smaller family responsibilities than unskilled laborers in towns.

The occupation returns of the census of 1860 are not classified by conjugal condition, but it is improbable that there
was a change in this respect in the next generation sufficient
to invalidate the application of the ratios shown by the
census of 1890. According to the latter census, in the nine
states covered by the Aldrich returns, slightly more than
one-half of the "unspecified laborers" were married as compared with but three-tenths of the "agricultural laborers."
As many who belong in the latter class are probably classified erroneously in the former, the real difference would
appear greater, could it be ascertained accurately.[1] As has
been suggested, a single man is less affected by a sudden
increase in the cost of living than one with a family, and the
previous discussions seem to show that wage-earners received
an increase in money wages roughly proportioned to the distress caused them by the rise of prices.

VII.   TABLES OF RELATIVE MONEY WAGES BASED UPON THE
MATERIAL IN VOL. XX OF THE TENTH CENSUS

The second of the great collections of data regarding
wages in the United States covering the period of the Civil
War is found in Vol. XX of the *Tenth Census* (1880).
Beginning in 1820, the Census Office had made attempts to
ascertain the rates of wages paid in the census year; but in
1880 this investigation was extended to cover a long series
of years. Blank schedules were sent to the proprietors of a
large number of carefully selected manufacturing establishments representing over fifty measurably distinct industries
and located in different sections of the country, with the

[1] The figures compiled from Table CXVI of the second volume on *Population* are
as follows:

	Agricultural Laborers	Laborers, Unspecified
Whole number - - - - -	470,105	782,844
Single, number - - - -	312,603	353,124
Single, per cent. - - - . -	67	45
Married, number - - - -	141,341	398,359
Married, per cent. - - - -	30	51

request that they report the wages paid to certain important
classes of their employees for as many years as their records
allowed. When these schedules were received by the Census
Office they were examined, and when necessary sent back to
the manufacturers for correction, completion, or explanation.
"Not infrequently," it is stated in the report, "schedules
were passed backward and forward several times before a
final adjustment was reached."[1]

Owing to the care exercised in their compilation, the
figures as finally published have borne a good reputation;[2]
but very little use has been made of them because of the
inconvenient form of publication. Mr. Joseph D. Weeks,
the special agent in charge of the investigation, made no
attempt to analyze or combine the data obtained, or to
discuss their significance. He confined his efforts to
collecting and verifying materials from many sources, and
published the reports made to him by some 600 factories
substantially as received. Consequently anyone who
desired to make use of the material was under the hard
necessity of working it into intelligible form for himself.

An examination of the figures as published, however,
shows sufficient promise in them to warrant an attempt to
discover how far they bear out the inferences drawn from
the materials already dealt with. In particular, the Census
figures have the great merit of being more comprehensive
than the data of the *Aldrich Report.* Nearly three times
as many wage-series available for the present investigation
can be collected from the former source as from the latter,
and these series represent a larger number of branches of
manufacture and a larger geographical area. A conspectus

---

[1] *Tenth Census*, Vol. XX, p. **xv.**

[2] See, for example, the opinion expressed by C. J. BULLOCK in his paper upon
"Wage Statistics and the Federal Census," in *The Federal Census* (" Publications
American Economic Association," New Series, No. 2), pp. 351, 352, and the prefatory
note by General F. A. WALKER in the report itself, p. x.

of the material derived from the census is afforded by Table XL.

In this exhibit twelve industries are marked by a star (*) to indicate that they are not represented in the wage-

TABLE XL

CLASSIFICATION OF WAGE-SERIES FROM THE TENTH CENSUS

I. ACCORDING TO INDUSTRIES	Number of Establishments	Number of Wage-Series	II. ACCORDING TO LOCATION	Number of Establishments	Number of Wage-Series
Agricultural implements	1	5	East:		
Boots and shoes*........	3	17	Maine..........	3	51
Breweries..............	1	4	New Hampshire.	8	114
Brick*.................	3	32	Massachusetts..	16	208
Carriages	9	73	Connecticut....	8	116
Carpets*...............	1	18	New York......	26	265
Clothing*..............	3	17	New Jersey.....	7	52
Cotton................	14	258	Pennsylvania...	12	134
Flint glass†............	4	62	Delaware.......	2	4
Flour mills*............	5	28	Maryland...... ..	2	13
Furniture*.	13	117	District of Columbia.	1	1
Gas and coke..........	2	4	West Virginia..	1	11
Hardware..	7	47		—	—–
Ice*..................	1	9		86	969
Iron blast furnaces†.....	8	76			
Iron mining†...........	2	3			
Machinery.............	11	98	West:		
Marble................	2	11	Ohio.......... ...	13	128
Paper.................	7	103	Indiana.........	13	100
Pianos*...............	3	26	Illinois.........	7	63
Pins*.................	1	3	Kentucky.......	6	51
Pottery†..............	4	38	Michigan	3	23
Rolling mills†..........	1	6	Wisconsin......	6	45
Saw mills.............	7	61	Iowa.........	2	9
Ship carpentry*.........	2	8	Missouri.	6	41
Stove foundries†..	4	46		—	—–
Tanneries.............	8	63		56	460
Tin*..................	1	7			
Tobacco*..............	4	16	Total East and		
Woolen......	10	173	West.......	142	1429
Total.............	142	1429			

tables of the *Aldrich Report*, and six more by a dagger (†)
to indicate that they are included only in the supplementary returns discussed in sec. iv above.[1]   Quite as
important as the larger number of industries is the greater
geographical range of the material.   As was pointed out in
sec. ii, all the establishments for which returns are inserted
in the main wage-table of the *Aldrich Report* were situated
in states east of Ohio, with the exception of a single gas plant.
But of the series obtained from the Tenth Census nearly
one-third are from the middle West.   This makes it possible to compare the fluctuations of money wages in different
sections of the country.

On the other hand, the character of the Census series is in
several respects distinctly inferior to that of the Aldrich series.
(1) But one wage is reported for the different kinds of labor
in each year, and it is not stated whether this quotation represents the average wages for the whole year, or the wages
paid in some one month.   This must be regarded as a decided
blemish, particularly unfortunate for the study of money
wages during the war; for the preceding summaries show
distinctly that from 1863 to 1865 wages were fluctuating so
violently that there was on the average a considerable
difference between the rates paid at the beginning, middle,
and end of the year, and that the average for twelve months
might differ from the wage at any specified date within the
year.   (2) The sex of the employees is not uniformly
reported, so that it is impossible to separate the female from
the male series.   (3) The number of persons whose pay is
represented by the series is not stated.   Thus it becomes
necessary in making up summaries from these series to treat
them in the way that Professor Falkner treated the Aldrich
material — that is, to disregard the number of wage-earners

[1] This division cannot be made with entire confidence in every case, because no
precise statement is made of the nature of the establishments included in the
twenty-one " industries " of the *Aldrich Report*.

belonging to the different groups altogether. (4) The material is even more strictly confined to manufacturing industries than that of the *Aldrich Report*.

Because of these limitations of the Census wage material —particularly the absence of information regarding the numbers employed at different wages—it seems advisable to confine the comparison between it and the series from the *Aldrich Report* to a few of the most general forms of presentation. We may begin by comparing the average variation in relative wages as computed from all the series derived from both sources.

TABLE XLI

COMPARISON OF RELATIVE WAGES COMPUTED FROM THE TENTH CENSUS AND THE ALDRICH REPORT

	CENSUS OF 1880			Falkner's Table	Semi-annual Table
	Total	East	West		
Number of series.....	1,429	969	460	543	520
1860.............	100	100	100	100	100
					102
1861....	102	101	103	101	99
					102
1862.....	106	104	112	103	104
					116
1863.............	117	112	127	111	119
					131
1864.....	133	127	144	126	142
					152
1865.............	145	141	153	143	155
					161
1866.....	152	150	155	152	164

It will be observed that there is a remarkably close correspondence between the average variation in wages computed from the Census material for the eastern states and Professor Falkner's average for all industries. This correspondence enhances confidence in the approximate accuracy of both sets of data. These are the two columns that ought logically to agree, because they refer to practically the same district and the averages are obtained in the same way. On the other hand, the lack of correspondence between the results of the Census series and the semiannual table does not disturb faith in the latter, because of the unavoidable difference in the methods employed. As has just been explained, in the latter case each relative wage was weighted by the number of persons whose pay it represented, while in the case of the Census series this could not be done for lack of data. Substantial agreement is here shown by differences nearly identical with those between the two series obtained from the Aldrich material by the two methods of computation.

But while the general average variation in wages appears practically the same in the Census and the Falkner tables, the fluctuations of the individual series from the two sources are somewhat different. This is best shown by Table XLII:

TABLE XLII

WAGE-SERIES FROM THE TENTH CENSUS AND THE ALDRICH REPORT CLASSIFIED
ACCORDING TO RELATIVE CHANGE IN WAGES BETWEEN 1860 AND 1865

RATIO OF WAGES IN 1865 TO WAGES IN 1860	NO. OF SERIES IN EACH GROUP				PERCENTAGE OF SERIES IN EACH GROUP			
	Census of 1880			Aldr'ch Report Series	Census of 1880			Aldr'ch Report Series
	Total	East	West		Total	East	West	
60-99 %	21	19	2	19	1.5%	1.9%	0.4%	3.7%
No change.......	182	111	71	13	12.7	11.5	15.4	2.5
101-119 %	164	128	36	71	11.5	13.2	7.8	13.9
120-139..........	349	273	76	132	24.4	28.2	16.6	25.8
140-159..........	268	185	83	148	18.8	19.1	18.1	29.0
160-179..........	208	144	64	80	14.6	14.9	13.9	15.7
180-199..........	75	35	40	33	5.2	3.6	8.7	6.5
200-219..........	112	50	62	10	7.8	5.2	13.5	1.9
220-259..........	41	19	22	3	2.9	1.9	4.8	0.6
260-299..........	7	5	2	1	0.5	0.5	0.4	0.2
300 and over.....	2	...	2	1	0.1	.....	0.4	0.2
	1429	969	460	511	100.0	100.0	100.0	100.0

As shown here, the grouping of the series from the Census is somewhat less symmetrical. A relatively larger number show no variation or a very considerable increase. Of the series used in the semiannual table 71 per cent. show an increase of from 20 to 79 per cent. in wages, as compared with 62 per cent. of the eastern and 49 per cent. of the western Census series.

A second fact brought out by Table XLI is that the increase in relative wages seems to have been greater in the Mississippi valley than on the Atlantic slope. This difference is due, in part at least, to the fact that the textile industries that furnish over 30 per cent. of the Census series (Table XL) had their chief seats in the East, and in them the relative increase of wages has been shown to have been least among the industries represented in Table XII of the *Aldrich Report*.[1] But this fact cannot account for the whole difference, because among persons belonging to the same economic groups the average increase in pay was generally greater in the West. The following table has been arranged to bring out this relation. It shows the relative wages paid in the eastern and western states to men following the eight trades most fully represented in the Tenth Census returns.

It will be noticed that in six of these eight cases western workingmen received a larger average increase in pay than their fellows in the East. Why this should have been so is a question that can best be discussed after the course of prices in the two sections of the country has been investigated.[2]

There is one feature of this table that seems to contradict certain of the conclusions drawn from the *Aldrich Report* data. In Table XXV it appears that the poorest-paid occupations as a rule show the greatest relative gain in wages, but the same is not true of Table XLIII. This

[1] See Table XXIII, above.   [2] See pp. 346, 347, below.

TABLE XLIII

RELATIVE WAGES IN THE EAST AND WEST IN EIGHT OCCUPATIONS

	Engineers		Machinists		Blacksmiths		Blacksmiths' Helpers		Carpenters		Painters		Teamsters		Laborers	
	East	West	East	West	East	West	East	West	East	West	East	West	East	West	East	West
No. of Wage ser.	26	27	32	7	14	15	5	7	23	8	10	8	23	19	55	44
Av. wages in 1860	$1.53	$1.94	$1.63	$1.63	$1.53	$1.71	$1.01	$1.07	$1.45	$1.76	$1.48	$1.57	$1.13	$1.07	$1.05	$1.01
1860	100	100	100	100	100	100	100	100	100	100	100	100	100	100	100	100
1861	104	102	101	103	101	102	101	102	98	110	99	102	99	105	100	103
1862	112	105	103	115	103	112	109	114	100	124	97	114	104	113	103	108
1863	123	112	113	131	121	131	118	121	107	131	103	128	109	135	114	131
1864	137	131	128	153	141	155	156	133	116	162	120	148	117	158	129	153
1865	153	138	146	167	148	170	155	147	141	161	128	147	132	161	140	162
1866	153	149	156	175	155	174	165	147	152	166	140	151	134	160	147	161

observation suggests that the connection between ratio of increase and earnings per day, of which so much has been made, may not be shown by the Census material. When, however, these series are all classified according to daily wages received in 1860 and the average rates of increase computed for the several groups, this inference is found to be mistaken. The figures for the comparison are given in Table XLIV, A and B, which corresponds to Table XXVIII, A and B.

TABLE XLIV

WAGE-SERIES FROM THE TENTH CENSUS CLASSIFIED ACCORDING TO DAILY WAGES RECEIVED IN 1860

A

Per Diem Wages Received in 1860	No. of Series	1860	1861	1862	1863	1864	1865	1866
$0.15-0.49.......	63	100	101	103	116	126	146	162
0.50-0.74.......	126	100	103	108	114	128	144	158
0.75-0.99.......	169	100	101	107	119	140	158	167
1.00-1.24.......	262	100	101	106	118	138	149	156
1.25-1.49.......	191	100	103	109	123	138	149	156
1.50-1.74.......	254	100	101	106	116	134	143	149
1.75-1.99.......	108	100	102	107	118	132	143	145
2.00-2.24.......	120	100	101	106	114	126	136	140
2.25-2.49.......	28	100	99	101	105	117	120	124
2.50-3.99.......	89	100	101	106	113	120	127	131
4.00-6.99.......	19	100	102	102	105	112	126	127

B

Per Diem Wages Received in 1860	No. of Series	1860	1861	1862	1863	1864	1865	1866
Under $1.00.....	358	100	102	107	117	133	151	163
$1.00-1.49.......	453	100	102	107	120	138	149	156
1.50-1.99.......	362	100	101	106	117	133	143	148
2.00-2.49.......	148	100	101	105	112	124	133	137
2.50+	108	100	101	106	112	119	126	131

While the general rule that there is a regular connection between the advance in pay under the stimulus of the price disturbances and the amount of wages earned before the war is fully confirmed by this exhibit, it is noticeable that the most considerable gain is found, not among persons earning $1–$1.24 a day, but in the next lower group. When, however, the fifty-cent groups are taken instead of the twenty-five, the second group — $1–$1.24 — shows the greatest gain in both tables in the years 1863 and 1864, while by the end of the period the first group takes the lead. It is also true of both sets of data that, while employees in the lower groups received a greater relative increase in pay, the actual sums added to their wages were less than in the higher groups. The application of the method of Table XXIX to the figures for 1865 in Table XLIV B shows the average actual increase in the daily wages of the five groups to be 32, 61, 75, 74, and 78 cents, respectively.

VIII. PAY OF GOVERNMENT EMPLOYEES

An interesting side light is thrown upon the advance of wages during the war by the position of government employees as represented in the reports of officials. Of course, the war caused a vast increase in the amount of business to be transacted by most of the departments, and the clerical force employed in Washington was increased accordingly. The salaries paid for clerks were generally regarded as fairly liberal before the war, but as the cost of living rose after the issue of the greenbacks many employees, especially men with families, began to find themselves pinched for funds. Congressional action was required to increase the rates of pay allowed, and in the face of the enormous expenditures for the military and naval service Congress was unwilling to pass any general act that would involve an increased outlay for clerks. Consequently many men resigned their positions in Washington to accept places with private employers. So general did this movement become that the heads of several bureaus found themselves seriously embarrassed by the difficulty of securing and retaining sufficient skilled assistants. The reports of 1864 and 1865 are full of such complaints. General F. E. Spinner, for example, the treasurer of the United States, declared in his report for 1864 that "But for the employment of females, whose compensation is low, and in most cases too low, it would have been impossible to have carried on the business of the office with the compensation allowed. During the year many clerks who were employed in this office have been obliged, in justice to themselves, to resign their positions, in order to enter into business for themselves, or to take places with moneyed and other corporations, or in business houses, where their talents and services were better appreciated and rewarded."[1] Similar remarks can readily be found in the reports of General Spinner's colleagues.[2]

The rank and file of the army fared somewhat better than the clerks in Washington. At the outbreak of the war the pay of privates was $11 per month.[3] One of the first of the war measures passed in August, 1861, increased this pay to $13.[4] As the rise of prices proceeded, much was heard in Congress of the distress caused to the soldiers by the decline in the purchasing power of their pay. True, the soldier himself was supplied with food and clothing, so that his position was less serious than that of a clerk who had to pay board and tailor bills; but the soldier's family, if dependent on his earnings, was no better off than the clerk's. At last in June, 1864, when the specie value of $13 in greenbacks had fallen to $6.18, Congress undertook to

[1] *Finance Report*, 1864, p. 76.

[2] For examples see reports of the secretary of the navy, 1864, p. xlii, and 1866, p. 37; secretary of the treasury, 1865, p. 42; comptroller of the currency, 1864, p. 55 of *Finance Report;* treasurer, *ibid.*, 1865, p. 98; second auditor of the treasury, *ibid.*, 1864, p. 99, and 1865, p. 127; fourth auditor, *ibid.*, 1864, p. 110; commissioner of internal revenue, *ibid.*, 1865, p. 92.

[3] Act of August 4, 1854, 10 *Statutes at Large*, p. 575.

[4] Act of August 6, 1861, 12 *Statutes at Large*, p. 326.

relieve the army. Rejecting a proposition to pay the $13 a month in gold, or an amount of paper equivalent at the market rate to $13 in gold,[1] Congress added $3 to the monthly pay.[2] This act raised the stipend to $16 per month, at which figure it remained for the rest of the war. The advance was but 23 per cent. on the old rate — an increase in relative wages less, according to all our tables, than that received by the majority of workingmen. It must be remembered, however, that both the local and federal governments were paying lavish bounties for volunteers. Of course these extra sums mitigated somewhat the hardships suffered by soldiers' families.

IX. INCREASE IN LIVING EXPENSES

Statistics of relative money wages, no matter how elaborate, throw no light upon the relative well-being of the working classes until they have been compared with figures that show the changes in cost of living. In the present case satisfactory figures of the latter sort are extremely difficult to obtain. Of course, the tables of relative prices in the preceding chapter may be made to serve as a general guide of increased expenditure, but it will be remembered that in making up these tables, all commodities were treated as having the same importance. From the point of view of statistical theory this procedure was correct in the last chapter, for there the object was simply to ascertain how far the changes in the specie value of the paper currency were reflected in the prices of commodities. But here, when an index of variation in the living expenses of workingmen's families is the desideratum, another form of computation would be preferable. Theoretically, each commodity should

---

[1] This proposition was made by Senator Powell, of Kentucky.— *Congressional Globe*, 38th Cong., 1st Sess., p. 2306.

[2] Act approved June 20, 1864 (13 *Statutes at Large*, p. 144). This act took effect from May 1, 1864. Privates in the cavalry, artillery and infantry were all included.

now be weighted according to its importance as an item of expenditure to wage earners. Professor Falkner has performed this process upon his table of wholesale prices by using weights for groups of expenditure obtained from an elaborate collection of American workingmen's budgets. The results of the weighting are lower index numbers for all the years of the war except 1865.[1] Reasons have been given in the preceding chapter, however, for distrusting Falkner's table of prices, and it therefore seems unwise to accept the weighted series, which is but a modification of the unweighted, and open to all criticisms urged against the latter.

If Falkner's figures are not to be used, the question becomes serious whether it is not possible to weight the tables that have been preferred to his in such fashion as to take account of the relative importance of various items of expenditure. The obstacle in the way is that the tables do not contain price series for many of the commodities that figure most prominently in family outlay. In the quarterly table of wholesale prices, there are no series for men's clothing, tea, or house rent, and in many other cases it would be necessary to infer changes in the price of consumption goods from changes in the price of materials — e. g., shoes from harness leather. The same obstacle is even more serious in the case of the table of retail prices, for it contains even fewer series than the quarterly table. Of course, an elaborate scheme of weights is of no advantage unless one has corresponding price series to which to apply the weights. Without such data the attempt at improving the character of the table by weighting is futile.

The fact that a satisfactory plan of allowing for the importance of the various price series is not attainable with the budgetary and price data at our disposal ought not, how-

[1] *Aldrich Report*, Part I, pp. 93, 94.

ever, to prejudice us in advance against the results that can be obtained from our unweighted tables. Statistical experience has shown abundantly that where there is no biased error in the figures, the application of weights to a large number of series makes little change in the final averages. Even in a time of such remarkable fluctuations as that of the Civil War, Falkner's simple and weighted series are very similar, and there is no reason for assuming that an application of weights to the tables of the last chapter, were such an application possible, would seriously modify the character of the results.[1] As has been said frequently before, the margin of error in all such computations as the present is wide, and the differences introduced by weighting would not be great in comparison with differences that might be made by the possession of a wider range of data for prices or money wages.

If we are to content ourselves with the tables of the last chapter from a conviction that with the data at hand we cannot weight them satisfactorily, it remains only to decide what series shall be used as the index of increase in living expenses. Both the wholesale and retail series have characteristic advantages. The former contains a larger number of articles and, moreover, gives index numbers for January and July that can readily be applied to the figures for relative wages obtained from the *Aldrich Report*. On the other hand, the latter table is better because based on retail-price returns. But a glance back at Table XVIII, where the two series are presented side by side, shows that it does

---

[1] It may be pointed out that the problem of weighting as affecting the wage tables is quite different from the problem as affecting the price tables. The reason for this difference is that there is a biased error in the wage statistics — that is, the wage-series representing the lower and most numerous grades of laborers show rather uniformly a more considerable advance in pay than the series representing the higher and less numerous grades. Therefore, weighting the series according to number of employees represented gives higher figures. But there is no reason for assuming that the articles of much importance as items of expenditure would show a uniformly higher or lower range of prices than the articles of slight importance.

not matter greatly which series is used. The chief difference is that prices at retail show a somewhat more sluggish movement than prices at wholesale — not exhibiting a
fall in 1861, rising less rapidly from 1862 to 1864, and falling less promptly in 1865. Consequently it seems fair to
use in any case the series that applies most conveniently to
the wage statistics in hand, but with the constant remem-
brance that the wholesale figures probably show somewhat
too large a purchasing power of wages in 1861 and again in
1865, and too small a purchasing power in the earlier years
of the war.

One other question remains: Shall the arithmetic mean
or the median of the price tables be employed ? In the last
chapter it was argued that the latter is a more significant
form of average for the years of the war, but in the present
chapter the arithmetic mean alone has been used in making
the wage tables. The median was not used in the latter case,
however, simply because the absence from among the wage-
series in Tables XXI and XLII of such cases of extreme
advance as are found among the price-series, shows that
the fluctuations of relative wages were much more uniform
than the fluctuations of relative prices as exhibited in Table
IX. Therefore, there can be no such divergence between
the two forms of average for relative wages as for relative
prices. A trial of the semiannual wage-table for the single
date, January, 1865, has shown that the median is a trifle
lower than the arithmetic mean for males and a trifle higher
for females.[1] Since the results of the two methods of averaging are so nearly identical, there is no valid objection against
using the arithmetic mean of relative wages in the same way
that the median would be used had two sets of averages been
computed. In the tables of the following section, therefore,
the median of the price-series will be employed, for the rea-

[1] Sec. iii, p. 292, above.

son that it was preferred in chap. iv. Computations based
on the arithmetic mean would show a lower range of real
wages.

X. RELATIVE REAL WAGES

It is now possible to combine the results of the investigations into money wages and into prices with the purpose of obtaining an idea of the manner in which the
issue of greenbacks affected the material well-being of
families dependent on wages. Despite all that has been
said, it may not be superfluous to enter once again a
caution that the results obtained can be nothing more
than rough approximations. The limitations of the wage
data have been dwelt upon at length, and the tables have
shown that the money incomes of some workingmen's
families increased much more than those of others. No
columns of "average variations" can give an adequate
notion of these differences. If one set of figures shows
fairly the changes in the pay of any one man or class of
men, it must from that very fact be inaccurate as applied to
others. Limitations not less serious exist in the price-
series that are to be used as indicative of changes in the
cost of living. Families living side by side in the same
town have different scales of expenditure, and therefore will
be affected in different degrees by price fluctuations. And
an examination of the retail-price series, as given in the
Appendix, will show that the living expenses of men receiving similar incomes did not vary in the same degree in different towns. To bring this fact out more clearly a table
has been compiled showing the average variations in the
retail prices of thirty-six articles in the four towns for which
the fullest reports are found in the Census volume.

If it is well to enter this caution, it is equally well to
guard against an undervaluation of the results. Though
the data both of wages and of prices leave much to be

TABLE XLV

RELATIVE RETAIL PRICES OF THIRTY-SIX COMMODITIES IN FOUR TOWNS (AVERAGE
PRICES FOR EACH YEAR)

Year	New Cumber-land, W. Va.	Canton, O.	Zanesville, O.	Lawrence-burg, Ind.
1860	100	100	100	100
1861	155	93	115	99
1862	203	141	135	128
1863	236	210	176	165
1864	264	283	248	218
1865	265	246	221	183
1866	222	207	209	170

desired in fulness, they have been carefully collected from reliable sources and show the actual wages paid to thousands of employees for work of a diverse character performed in many different places, and the actual prices paid at wholesale and at retail for many articles of great importance. So far as the material extends, there is little reason to doubt its substantial accuracy. Confidence in its representative character is strongly supported by the uniformity in the results obtained regarding both wages and prices from the figures drawn from different sources. Finally, though there are many deviations from the general averages, the trend of fluctuations is the same in almost all cases. It seems, then, that we may proceed to combine the two sets of tables with a considerable degree of confidence in the significance of their results.

This combination may begin with Tables XXI and XIV. In Table XXI the wage-earners included in the series drawn from the main exhibits of the *Aldrich Report* are classified according to the relative change in wages between 1860 and January, 1865. The more conservative price-series of Table XIV indicates that prices had more than doubled within this period. But of the 4,751 employees accounted for in Table XXI the pay of but thirty-nine

had increased as much as 100 per cent.—less than one
in a hundred. The remaining ninety-nine wage-earners
in every hundred must have suffered in no inconsiderable degree from the paper standard of value, because
their money incomes had risen less rapidly than the
cost of commodities. Of the men, half had received an
increase of less than 54 per cent. in pay, and of the women
half less than 34 per cent. If money income increases but
one-half, while living expenses double, real income is
reduced a quarter; this, or worse than this, appears to have
been the case with half the men and much more than half
the women. It seems clear, then, that practically all wage-
earners found themselves in more straightened circumstances
in 1865 than in 1860, and that in the majority of cases the
inconvenience suffered was not slight.

This combination refers to a single year. Some notion
of the rapidity of the changes that took place in the circumstances of working-people may be gained by turning to the
tables that represent the fluctuations of money wages year
by year. Table XXX gives the average relative wages of
over 5,000 persons from 1860 to 1866. A series showing
average changes in real wages to July, 1865, may be readily
computed from these figures and the price index numbers of
Table XIV. In making the computation both columns for
relative wages and the lower column for relative prices—
the median — have been employed.

According to these figures, the average relative purchasing power of money wages over the commodities included in
our largest price table was at its lowest ebb from the middle
of 1864 to the beginning of 1865 — although money wages
at this time were nearly half again as great as they had
been before the war. From this low point there was an
extraordinary recovery owing to the very rapid fall of prices
between January and July, 1865. It must not be forgotten,

TABLE XLVI

AVERAGE CHANGE IN REAL WAGES OF OVER 5,000 WAGE-EARNERS, COMPUTED
FROM TABLES XIV AND XXX

Date	Variable Weights	Constant Weights	Date	Variable Weights	Constant Weights
1860, January..	100	100	1863, January..	89	88
July.	100	99	July	86	86
1861, January..	102	102	1864, January..	81	82
July.	104	104	July.. ...	71	72
1862, January..	102	102	1865, January..	67	68
July.. ..	101	100	July.. ...	97	99

however, that this fall was much more sudden in wholesale than in retail markets, and therefore the figures give an altogether too favorable picture of the situation of the workingman's family in the middle of 1865. Even according to the wholesale price table there was a sharp reaction of prices in the latter part of the year that would make the real wage-index number for October considerably less than that for July, had we data for computing it.

It would be interesting to apply the retail-price table to these same figures for relative wages and see how different the results would be. But such an application is scarcely legitimate, because the retail prices are averages for the year and the wages are the rates prevailing in but two months. On the whole, therefore, it seems best to rest content with the rather vague modification of the preceding series suggested by the relation between wholesale and retail prices brought out in the last chapter.

With these results may be compared similar figures computed from the tables of the *Aldrich Report.* The re-working of the price data in the last chapter and of the wage data in the present chapter has led to the conclusion that Falkner's methods of analysis show too slight an advance in both cases. The question remains whether the failure to gauge the full extent of the rise in prices is offset by the failure to gauge the full extent of the rise of money wages. To answer this question two series of relative real wages have been computed from Falkner's tables by using his weighted and his simple averages for both wages and prices.

TABLE XLVII

COMPARISON OF RELATIVE REAL WAGES AS SHOWN IN TABLE XLVI, WITH RELATIVE
REAL WAGES COMPUTED FROM FALKNER'S TABLES

	Table XLVI		Falkner's Tables Simple Averages	Weighted Averages
1860, January	100 }		100	100
July	100 }			
1861, January	102 }		100	107
July	104 }			
1862, January	102 }		87	100
July	101 }			
1863, January	89 }		74	90
July	86 }			
1864, January	81 }		66	78
July	71 }			
1865, January	67 }		66	64
July	97 }			

On the whole, there is less difference between these results for real wages than between the results of the tables of prices or of money wages. The extreme depression of real wages in all three series is about the same, and except in 1865 the impression left by Falkner's weighted average agrees very closely with that left by the series from Table XLVI. The chief difference is that the semiannual figures show the recovery of real wages in the middle of the last year—a recovery that certainly took place, although its completeness is exaggerated by the enforced reliance upon wholesale instead of retail price data.

This examination of the decline in the real wages of all employees represented in Table XII of the *Aldrich Report* might be elaborated by making similar computations of real wages in the several industries, occupations, and wage-groups of the preceding tables. The reader who will compare the figures for money wages in these tables with the figures for prices will find that in no case did the wage-earners escape a considerable loss in real income. By way of illustration, three tables based upon the most significant groupings of the wage-series are presented below. In examining them, one must remember that, like the preceding tables, they overstate real wages in July, 1865.

TABLE XLVIII

AVERAGE CHANGE IN REAL WAGES IN NINE INDUSTRIES, COMPUTED FROM TABLES XIV AND XXIII [1]

Date	City Public Works	Illuminating Gas	Stone	Building Trades	Metals and Metallic Goods	Railways	Cotton Goods	Ginghams	Wo'len Goods
1860, Jan..	100	100	100	100	100	100	100	100	100
July.	100	99	100	102	101	103	101	100	103
1861, Jan..	100	100	128	101	102	105	97	103	106
July.	96	104	96	107	108	111	102	115	113
1862, Jan..	99	100	96	103	105	105	98	105	108
July.	96	100	87	104	105	100	95	107	108
1863, Jan..	94	96	77	91	88	82	82	84	92
July.	88	102	81	85	86	78	78	77	82
1864, Jan..	89	98	89	80	78	71	76	66	76
July.	85	81	68	72	70	56	65	59	64
1865, Jan..	77	77	68	64	65	63	61	57	62
July.	111	109	94	99	94	91	88	93	89

Extended comment upon these tables is superfluous. While the fluctuations of real wages are seen to have been by no means uniform in all cases, there is no industry or occupation in which the advance in money wages kept pace with the advance in prices. The differences represent merely greater or less degrees of inconvenience, not to say suffering. Perhaps the most interesting of the tables is the third, for it brings out once more the rule that the incomes of those families nearest the minimum of subsistence before

[1] The variable-weight wage-series are used here.

TABLE XLIX

AVERAGE CHANGE IN REAL WAGES, IN NINE OCCUPATIONS, COMPUTED FROM TABLES
XIV AND XXV

Date	Labor-ers	Quar-rymen	Masons	Stone-cutters	Car-penters	Mold-ers	Machi-nists	Fire-men	Weav-ers, Female
1860, Jan..	100	100	100	100	100	100	100	100	100
July.	100	100	99	101	100	102	100	102	99
1861, Jan..	100	114	101	100	99	104	103	103	103
July.	98	96	100	108	106	108	109	107	115
1862, Jan..	100	100	99	91	103	105	107	102	104
July.	98	87	100	92	100	103	107	106	109
1863, Jan..	95	78	85	79	80	85	92	92	85
July.	90	81	80	80	79	83	89	101	79
1864, Jan..	89	92	76	75	78	76	80	101	68
July.	84	69	66	73	70	68	71	79	58
1865, Jan..	76	71	63	68	67	65	67	75	59
July.	110	96	92	99	98	94	95	106	92

the war were reduced relatively less than the incomes of families in easier circumstances.

It does not seem worth while to multiply examples of decline in the purchasing power of the money incomes of wage-earners by computations based on the wage-series

TABLE L

AVERAGE CHANGE IN REAL WAGES IN FIVE WAGE-GROUPS COMPUTED FROM TABLES
XIV AND XXVIII B

Date	Males Earnings in 1860, Daily Wages of				
	$0.25—$0.99	$1.00—$1.49	$1.50—$1.99	$2.00—$2.49	$2.50+
1860, January........	100	100	100	100	100
July............	102	100	100	100	100
1861, January........	100	102	102	100	99
July............	107	100	107	103	105
1862, January........	102	101	105	99	100
July............	103	98	105	97	95
1863, January........	88	92	89	79	75
July............	85	87	86	78	73
1864, January........	79	87	79	73	66
July............	69	76	69	68	57
1865, January........	65	71	66	62	54
July............	94	101	95	93	76

drawn from the Tenth Census. Were this done, a somewhat harsher state of affairs would be shown, for the
absence of data regarding numbers employed produces a
general average advance in wages less than that computed
from the completer data of the *Aldrich Report*.[1] But there
is one point brought out by Table XLI that deserves
further notice — viz., the difference between the rise of
wages in the East and West. It was found that even if the
comparison be confined to members of the same trade, the
average increase in wages seems to have been somewhat
greater in the north central than in the north Atlantic states.
It is interesting to see whether this difference can be
accounted for on our general hypothesis, that the rise of
wages was due chiefly to the increased cost of living. If
so, prices must have advanced more rapidly in the West
than in the East. The Census statistics of retail prices
make it possible to discover whether or not this was the
case, for there are 239 series from the East and 287 from
the West. An exhibit of the relative prices of the fifty-

TABLE LI

RELATIVE RETAIL PRICES OF FIFTY-EIGHT ARTICLES IN THE EAST AND WEST
BY GROUPS

	Dry Goods		Men's Heavy Boots		Groceries		Flour and Meal		Rice, Beans, Potat's		Meat and Fish		Eggs, Dairy Prdcts.		Fuel		House Rent	
	E	W	E	W	E	W	E	W	E	W	E	W	E	W	E	W	E	W
No. of Articl's	9	9	1	1	11	11	4	4	3	3	19	19	4	4	5	5	2	2
No. of Pr. Ser.	42	66	8	19	33	51	17	16	12	14	79	57	14	20	22	18	12	26
1860...	100	100	100	100	100	100	100	100	100	100	100	100	100	100	100	100	100	100
1861....	132	122	105	101	116	98	103	111	111	103	113	103	112	92	118	105	100	99
1862....	219	186	116	121	143	119	111	117	145	130	117	110	116	109	128	126	106	109
1863....	299	285	129	142	166	159	124	179	156	160	125	135	128	131	162	161	105	120
1864....	386	414	151	216	207	201	160	212	178	185	145	168	149	174	185	168	123	136
1865....	365	365	157	168	209	211	166	235	183	183	164	175	172	196	188	164	132	139
1866....	287	301	156	153	205	215	167	243	184	203	172	174	168	195	183	162	138	141

[1] See sec. vii, p. 328, above.

eight articles arranged in nine groups is presented in
Table LI.

This table indicates that boots, flour and meal, meat and
fish, and eggs and dairy products increased more in price in
the West, while the opposite is true of fuel, and the remaining groups—dry goods, groceries, rice, beans, and potatoes,
and house rent—varied in about the same degree in both
sections. If the arithmetic mean be struck of the relative
prices of all the fifty-eight articles in the Census list, the
advance is found to be greater in the West, as the next table
shows :

TABLE LII

AVERAGE RELATIVE PRICES AT RETAIL OF FIFTY-EIGHT COMMODITIES IN THE
EAST AND WEST

Date	East	West
1860......	100	100
1861......	116	105
1862......	139	126
1863......	164	169
1864......	200	216
1865......	206	215
1866......	196	207

These figures lend strong support to the view that the
difference between the advance of relative wages in the two
sections of the North was in large measure due to the unlike
changes in relative cost of living.

XI.   CONCLUSION

All of the statistical evidence that has been presented in
the preceding pages supports unequivocally the common
theory that persons whose incomes are derived from wages
suffer seriously from a depreciation of the currency. The
confirmation seems particularly striking when the conditions
other than monetary affecting the labor market are taken
into consideration. American workingmen are intelligent

and keenly alive to their interests. There are probably few districts where custom plays a smaller and competition a larger rôle in determining wages than in the northern states. While labor organizations had not yet attained their present power, manual laborers did not fail to avail themselves of the help of concerted action in the attempt to secure more pay. Strikes were frequent.[1] All these facts favored a speedy readjustment of money wages to correspond with changed prices. But more than all else, a very considerable part of the labor supply was withdrawn from the market into the army and navy. In 1864 and 1865 about one million of men seem to have been enrolled.[2] What proportion this number forms of the wage-earners can be very roughly estimated from the Census statistics of occupations. According to the Eighth Census, there were 6,791,844 persons engaged in gainful occupations in the loyal states in 1860.[3] If we assume that as large a proportion of wage-earners went to the war as of those who were working on their own account, it follows that about one-seventh of the labor supply withdrew from the market. But despite all these favoring circumstances, the men who stayed at home did not succeed in obtaining an advance in pay at all commensurate with the increase in living expenses.

It is sometimes argued that the withdrawal of laborers

[1] The *Springfield Republican* of March 26, 1863, said: ". . . . the workmen of almost every branch of trade have had their strike within the last few months. No less than six strikes are reported by the New York papers this week, of laborers on the Erie, Hudson River, and Camden and Amboy railroads, the journeymen tailors of the city, and the employees of two large manufacturing companies . . . . in almost every instance . . . . the demands of the employed have been acceded to. These strikes, which have all been conducted very quietly, ... have led to the formation of numerous trade leagues or unions."

[2] The *Report of the Secretary of War* for 1865 states the number of men enrolled as 970,710, May 1, 1864; 965,591, March 1, 1865; and 1,000,516, May 1, 1865.—Pp. 1, 5, and 13. The *Report of the Secretary of the Navy* for the same year states that the number of men in service in the navy increased from 7,600 at the commencement of the war to 51,500 at its close. The number of men employed in the navy yards increased in the same period from 3,844 to 16,880.—P. xiii.

[3] Compiled from the table on p. 680 of the volume on *Population*.

from industrial life was the chief cause of the price disturbances of the war period. This withdrawal, it is said,
caused the advance of wages, and greater cost of labor led to
the rise of prices. The baselessness of this view is shown
by two facts, established by the preceding tables — first, that
the advance of wages was later than the advance of prices,
and second, that wages continued to rise in 1866 after the
volunteer armies had been disbanded and the men gone
back to work.

Though the figures developed in the foregoing analysis
show a slightly smaller decline in real wages than those
heretofore accepted on the authority of the *Aldrich Report*,
it is probable that even the new figures overstate rather
than understate the actual injury suffered by wage-earners.
The tables used as an index of the change in cost of living
really show what would have been the relative cost of the
articles included in the price lists had people continued to
purchase them in the same proportions as before the war.
But, of course, the character of the consumption of most
families did not remain unchanged. In many cases it was
possible to substitute some other article for one which had
risen more than common in price. Thus woolen, linen, and
other fabrics were largely made to take the place of cotton
goods, and cheaper beverages took the place of tea and
coffee. In so far as the substitutes were less agreeable as
articles of consumption, the change represents a loss of economic satisfaction. But the degree of this loss of satisfaction is exaggerated somewhat by a table that shows the
increase in cost of the less-used article ; for the motive for
buying other things is found precisely in the possibility of
thus avoiding a portion of the inconvenience caused by the
high prices.

As the price tables probably exaggerate the increase in
relative living expenses, so the wage tables probably under-

estimate the increase in the income of working-people. The reason for thinking thus is that wage-earners seem to have been more fully employed during the war than in common times of prosperity. Of course, the enlistment of so many thousands of the most efficient workers made places for many who might otherwise have found it difficult to secure work. Moreover, the paper currency itself tended to obtain full employment for the laborer, for the very reason that it diminished his real income. In the distribution of what Marshall has termed the "national dividend" a diminution of the proportion received by the laborer must have been accompanied by an increase in the share of someone else. Nor is it difficult to determine who this person was. The beneficiary was the active employer, who found that the money wages, interest, and rent he had to pay increased less rapidly than the money prices of his products. The difference between the increase of receipts and the increase of expenses swelled his profits. Of course, the possibility of making high profits provided an incentive for employing as many hands as possible. But here we are trenching upon the subject of a later chapter.

The importance of these factors—the changes in the character of consumption and the fuller employment—as affecting the material well-being of wage-earners is incapable of statistical measurement with the materials at hand. But while they must be recognized as modifying in considerable measure the inferences to be drawn from the series of "changes in real wages" given above, it can hardly be that they sufficed to compensate many families for the increased money cost of living. Most families were doubtless forced to practice economies of a very uncomfortable character to make both ends meet.

After such an examination of the change in the condition of the great mass of wage-earners, it may seem surprising that few complaints were heard from them of unusual privations.[1] This silence may be due in part to the fact that a con.iderable increase of money income produces in the minds of many a fatuous feeling of prosperity, even though it be more than offset by an increase of prices. But doubtless the chief reason is to be found in the absorption of public interest in the events of the war. The people both of the South and North were so vitally concerned with the struggle that they bore without murmuring the hardships it entailed of whatever kind. Government taxation that under other circumstances might have been felt to be intolerable was submitted to with cheerfulness. The paper currency imposed upon wage-earners a heavier tax—amounting to confiscation of perhaps a fifth or a sixth of real incomes. But the workingmen of the North were receiving considerably more than a bare subsistence minimum before the war, and reduction of consumption was possible without producing serious want. Accordingly the currency tax, like the tariff and the internal revenue duties, was accepted as a necessary sacrifice to the common cause and paid without protest by severe retrenchment.

[1] Compare D. A. WELLS, *Recent Financial, Industrial, and Commercial Experiences of the United States* (New York, 1872), p. 22.

CHAPTER VI

RENT

I. *Urban Rents:*
Use of Term "Rent"—Long and Short Leases—Wells's Investigations into House Rents — Statistical Data from the *Tenth Census*—Rents in Eastern and Western States — In Cities and Towns — Narrow Range of the Data.

II. *Farm Rents:*
Farms Let for Money Rents — Farms Let "on Shares."

I. URBAN RENTS

In studying the influence of depreciation upon rent, it is necessary to use that term in its popular rather than in its scientific sense. The distinction, so dear to the economist, between payment for situation and return on capital invested in improvements, cannot be maintained in a discussion based on figures which show simply the sums paid for the use of real property. This fact is less to be lamented, because the theorist himself admits that the distinction becomes sadly blurred when he attempts to deal with short intervals of time. Capital once invested in improvements can seldom be withdrawn rapidly. In "the short run," therefore, it is practically a part of the land, and the return to it follows the analogy of rent rather than of interest.[1]

Like the lending capitalist, the renting landlord found that the degree in which he was affected by the fluctuations in the value of the paper money depended largely upon the terms of the contract into which he had entered. It is clear from the preceding chapters that the landlord who before suspension had leased his property for a considerable period without opportunity for revaluation must have suffered

[1] Compare MARSHALL, *Principles of Economics*, Book V, chaps. viii, ix.

352

severely if paid in greenbacks. The number of "dollars" received as rental might be the same in 1865 as in 1860, but their purchasing power was less than one-half as great. Somewhat less hard was the situation of the landlord who had let his property for but one or two years. At the expiration of the leases he had opportunities to make new contracts with the tenants. To ascertain accurately how far he succeeded in recouping himself for the rise of prices by increasing rentals, elaborate statistics of the sums paid for the use of different classes of real estate would be necessary. Unfortunately, such figures are scanty, and such as are available refer entirely to urban property.

In his capacity as special commissioner of the revenue, Mr. David A. Wells devoted some attention to the rise of rent. His report for December, 1866, says:

The average advance in the rents of houses occupied by mechanics and laborers in the great manufacturing centers of the country is estimated to have been about 90 per cent.; in some sections, however, a much greater advance has been experienced, as, for example, at Pittsburg, where 200 per cent. and upward is reported. In many of the rural districts, on the other hand, the advance has been much less.[1]

In his third annual report, dated January, 1869, Mr. Wells modified this estimate somewhat. Edward Young had prepared for him "tables showing the comparative cost of provisions, groceries, domestic dry goods, house rent, etc., in the manufacturing towns of the United States in the respective years 1860–61 and 1867–68." These tables made out an average increase of about 65 per cent. in rents. Mr. Wells remarked, however, that

this . . . . average is . . . . largely affected by the circumstance that in New England, where manufacturing companies . . . . very generally own the tenements occupied by the operatives, rents have

[1] *Senate Executive Document No. 2*, 39th Cong., 2d Sess., p. 14.

not been advanced to any considerable extent. Excluding New England from the calculation, the average advance in rents for 1867, as compared with 1860–61, must be estimated at a much higher figure. Thus in the smaller manufacturing towns of Pennsylvania the average increase in the rents of houses occupied by operatives is believed to have been about 81 per cent., and in New Jersey 111 per cent. In the cities of New York, Philadelphia, Newark, and Pittsburg the increase has been from 90 to 100 per cent.[1]

Young's figures, on which these conclusions were based, are as follows:

TABLE LIII

HOUSE RENT IN MANUFACTURING TOWNS 1860–61 AND 1867–68 [2]

STATE	FOUR-ROOM TENEMENTS			SIX-ROOM TENEMENTS		
	1860–61	1867–68	Per cent. of In- crease	1860–61	1867–68	Per cent. of In- crease
Maine............	$3.25	$5.67	74	$4.67	$8.17	75
N. Hamp., Vermont	2.42	3.68	52	3.17	5.75	81
Massachusetts....	5.86	10.28	75	6.54	10.14	55
Rhode Island.....	5.93	9.63	62	9.11	11.69	28
Connecticut......	4.04	5.77	43	4.56	6.81	49
New York	4.20	6.85	51	5.78	9.37	62
Pennsylvania	5.60	9.60	71	8.00	15.20	90
New Jersey.......	4.67	10.00	114	7.17	15.00	109
Delaware.........	4.00	5.00	25	5.17	6.33	22
General average ..	$4.44	$7.39	66	$6.02	$9.83	63

These figures become more significant for the present purpose when interpreted in the light of the similar data already presented in part in the chapter on prices.[3] The latter figures are taken from Mr. Weeks's report in the *Tenth Census* and show the relative rents paid for four- and six-

[1] *H. R. Executive Document No. 16*, 40th Cong., 3d Sess., p. 14.
[2] *Ibid.*, Appendix D, pp. 118–21.
[3] See Part II, chap. iv, sec. iv, Table XVII.

or seven-room houses in twenty towns scattered over eleven states from Massachusetts to Missouri. Comparison with Young's figures, however, should be confined to eastern towns, and of these returns are given but for five.[1] In these five towns the average increase in rents between 1860 and 1868 was somewhat less than Young makes out for four-room tenements—viz., 56 instead of 66 per cent.—and slightly greater in the case of six-room tenements—viz., 68 as compared with 63 per cent.

But though it be inferred, as both these sets of data indicate, that rents of workingmen's houses in eastern towns were on the average some 60 or 65 per cent. higher in 1868 than they had been before the war, it does not at all follow that rents had advanced so much as this in 1864 and 1865. In fact, the Census figures that cover the intervening years indicate that in most towns rents rose during the war more slowly than prices, but that, like wages, they continued to rise for some time after prices had fallen. Table LIV com-

TABLE LIV

RELATIVE RENTS IN FIVE EASTERN TOWNS AND RELATIVE PRICES [2]

(Arithmetic means)

YEAR	RENTS	PRICES	
		Retail	Wholesale
1860........................	100	100	100
1861........................	100	116	101
1862........................	101	139	118
1863........................	101	164	149
1864........................	120	200	191
1865........................	132	206	217
1866........................	138	196	191
1867........................	141		172
1868........................	163		161

[1] Boston; Jewett City, Conn.; Camden, N. J.; Philadelphia and Hokendauqua, Pa. New Cumberland, W. Va., which is included in the East in the table of the preceding chapter, is excluded here because Young gives no figures for West Virginia.

[2] The figures for rent are simple averages of the ten series for the five towns; the retail prices are from Table LII of chap. v, and the wholesale prices are from the *Aldrich Report*, Part I, p. 91.

pares the fluctuations of rent in the five eastern towns with the index numbers for retail prices in the East, as far as they extend, and with Falkner's unweighted average of the relative prices of all articles.

According to this table, though owners of small houses in these towns may have found themselves approximately as well off in 1868 as before the war, they had not escaped severe injury from the depreciation of the currency during the interim. Elsewhere landlords seem to have been in a rather worse plight. In the fifteen western towns for which the *Tenth Census* gave returns the increase in rents of similar property seems to have been somewhat less, as Table LV shows:

TABLE LV

RELATIVE RENTS IN FIFTEEN WESTERN TOWNS [1]

1860	-	-	-	-	100	1865	-	-	-	-	138
1861	-	-	-	-	99	1866	-	-	-	-	139
1862	-	-	-	-	108	1867	-	-	-	-	137
1863	-	-	-	-	121	1868	-	-	-	-	135
1864	-	-	-	-	135						

This contrast between rents in the East and West is vitiated to a certain extent by the fact that a much larger proportion of the western towns were small places. More significant is the comparison between rents in the five cities for which figures are given—Boston, Philadelphia, Cincinnati, Louisville, and St. Louis—and the fifteen lesser towns.[2] Table LVI presents the data in succinct form.

The conclusion, supported by these figures, that the advance in rents was greater in cities than in minor towns, is not difficult to accept. In two of the cities—Cincinnati and Louisville—owners of workingmen's tenements appear

[1] The figures are simple arithmetic means of the twenty-eight series. New Cumberland, W. Va., is included.

[2] Louisville, with 68,033 inhabitants in 1860, is the smallest of the cities, and Indianapolis, with 18,611 inhabitants, the largest of the towns.

TABLE LVI

RELATIVE RENTS IN CITIES AND TOWNS

Year	Boston	Phila-del-phia	Cincin-nati	Louis-ville	St. Louis	Average for Preceding Cities	Average for Fifteen Lesser Towns
1860	100	100	100	100	100	100	100
1861	100	100	84	129	90	101	99
1862	100	100	84	129	90	101	110
1863	100	100	117	167	131	123	115
1864	138	133	207	221	131	166	120
1865	138	167	207	221	131	173	124
1866	138	200	207	221	157	185	122
1867	138	200	167	167	157	166	128
1868	196	200	167	167	157	177	128

to have been able to increase their money incomes rather more rapidly than prices advanced, but in Boston, Philadelphia, St. Louis, and in all the smaller towns on the list, with the possible exception of Terre Haute, their money incomes appear to have increased more slowly than living expenses.[1]

It must be remembered that these conclusions rest on a narrow statistical basis. No figures for house rent can be altogether satisfactory because of the change in the character of accommodation from time to time. What figures are available refer to one class of property alone — such tenements as are occupied by working people in manufacturing towns. For houses of other classes and for business property of all kinds no reliable data are known to me. And even for the workingmen's tenements the *Tenth Census* gives but two or three series for each town. But though all this be true, the fact remains that the figures seem to be worthy of credence for one class of urban property at least, and, in the absence of evidence to the contrary, establish a presumption that relatively few owners of urban real estate of other descriptions escaped injury from the greenback issues.

[1] The figures for all the towns are given in detail in the Appendix,

Even in those cases where rents advanced more rapidly than commodity prices it is probable that the greenbacks deprived the landlords of a portion of the gains that they would otherwise have made.

II. FARM RENTS

All the foregoing refers to the rent of urban property. For agricultural rents Wells and Weeks give no data. Inasmuch, however, as custom seems to play a larger rôle in determining the price paid per acre for farms than the price paid per month for city houses, it is probable that much the same difference existed between the advance of rents in the country and in the small towns that Table LVI indicates as having existed between the advance in towns and in cities. If this conjecture be just, it follows that the rural landowner suffered serious injury from the paper currency when he let his land for a money rent.

But renting farms for a fixed sum of money has always been less common in the United States than renting for a definite share of the products. Prior to 1880 the Census Office made no attempt to ascertain the tenure on which farms were held. In that year, however, 30 per cent. of the farms not occupied by their owners are reported as "rented for a fixed money value" in the northern and western states, and 70 per cent. as "rented for a share of the products." Since the enumeration of 1890 showed that the practice of accepting money rent was increasing, so that the above percentages had become 35 and 65 respectively,[1] it is probable that at the time of the Civil War more than three-quarters of the rented farms were let "on shares." Inasmuch as no money payments entered into such arrangements, the pecuniary relations of landlord and tenant were not directly affected

[1] Percentages computed from Table 3 of the *Report on the Statistics of Agriculture at the Eleventh Census*, pp. 116, 117.

by the change in the monetary standard. Farm owners who had let their places on these conditions escaped the direct losses that weighed so heavily on the recipients of money rents. But even they did not avoid all loss. For, as will be shown at length in chap. viii, the price of agricultural products for the greater part of the war period lagged considerably behind the price of other goods. This difference, of course, meant loss to men whose incomes were paid in bushels of grain.

CHAPTER VII

INTEREST AND LOAN CAPITAL

I. THE PROBLEM OF LENDERS AND BORROWERS OF CAPITAL

THE task of ascertaining the effect of the greenback issues upon the situation of lenders and borrowers of capital is in one respect more simple and in another respect more complex than the task of dealing with wage-earners. It is simpler in that there are not different grades of capital to be considered like the different grades of labor. But it is more complex in that the capitalist must be considered not only as the recipient of a money income, as is the laborer, but also as the possessor of certain property that may be affected by changes in the standard money.

The problem is further complicated by the fact that the relative importance of these two items — rate of interest and value of principal—is not the same in all cases. Whether a lender is affected more by the one item or the other depends upon what he intends to do with his property at the expiration of existing contracts. A widow left in 1860 with an estate of say $10,000, who expected to keep this sum constantly at interest and to find new borrowers as soon as the old loans were paid, could neglect everything but the net rate of interest received. On the other hand, if this estate had been left to a youth of twenty who intended to invest his property in some business after a few years, the rate of interest would be of relatively less importance to him than the purchasing power of the principal when the time came to set up for himself.

Of course, the same difference exists, *mutatis mutandis*, in the case of different borrowers. Those borrowers who expected to renew old loans on maturity would have to consider little beyond the interest demanded by lenders, while borrowers who expected to pay off the loans out of the proceeds of their ventures would be interested primarily in the amount of goods that would sell for sufficient money to make up the principal.

Although these two classes of cases are by no means independent of each other, the following discussion will be rendered clearer by observing the broad difference between them. Accordingly, attention will first be directed to the effect of the price fluctuations upon the purchasing power of the principal of loans, and afterward to changes in the rate of interest.

II. PURCHASING POWER OF THE PRINCIPAL OF LOANS

It follows directly from the chapter upon prices that most persons who made loans in the earlier part of the Civil War and were repaid in greenbacks must have suffered heavy losses from the smaller purchasing power of the

principal when it was returned to them. But while this
general fact is clear, it is difficult to make a quantitative
statement of the degree of the loss that will be even tolerably
satisfactory. Indeed, no single series of percentages can
represent the loss of all lenders, any more than any single
series can represent the decline in the real wages of all
laborers, for the reason that the loss depends both upon
the time of lending and repayment, and upon the particular
commodities which the capitalist wishes to purchase. Probably the best course to pursue is to take the median of
relative prices at wholesale as the most reliable index of
general price movements, and work out a table based upon
it which shall show the relative rise or fall in the purchasing
power of money from quarter to quarter. Such a table is
given on the next page.

The first line of figures across the top of this table,
showing the relative purchasing power of money, is
obtained by computing the reciprocals of the corresponding
index numbers for prices as given in Table XIV. To see
how the variations shown by this series of figures affected
the interests of lenders, a number of loans is supposed
to be made each quarter, one of which matures and is repaid
each subsequent quarter. The second to the twenty-fourth
lines of figures across the table show what was the percentage of loss or gain in the purchasing power of the principal in the months of repayment as compared with the
months when the loans were made. To obtain these series,
the figure representing the relative purchasing power
of money each quarter is taken as the starting-point, and
the corresponding figures for each subsequent quarter are
treated as percentages of the first. For example, the loss
on a loan made in January, 1863, and repaid in January,
1865, is stated as 43 per cent., because 44, which represents
the relative power of money at the later date, is only 57

TABLE LVII

PERCENTAGE OF LOSS (−) OR GAIN (+) TO CREDITOR IN PURCHASING POWER OF PRINCIPAL OF LOANS MADE AND REPAID AT DATES INDICATED [1]

Date of repayment indicated by index at top; date of making of loan indicated by index at side.

Date of making of loan	Jan. 1860	April 1860	July 1860	Oct. 1860	Jan. 1861	April 1861	July 1861	Oct. 1861	Jan. 1862	April 1862	July 1862	Oct. 1862	Jan. 1863	April 1863	July 1863	Oct. 1863	Jan. 1864	April 1864	July 1864	Oct. 1864	Jan. 1865	April 1865	July 1865	Oct. 1865
Average relative purchasing power of money over commodities at wholesale	100	100	100	100	100	103	105	100	100	100	97	85	77	70	72	71	62	57	50	48	44	54	63	56
Jan., 1860	0	0	0	0	0	+3	+5	0	0	0	−3	−15	−23	−30	−28	−29	−38	−43	−50	−52	−56	−46	−37	−44
April, 1860		0	0	0	0	+3	+5	0	0	0	−3	−15	−23	−30	−28	−29	−38	−43	−50	−52	−56	−46	−37	−44
July, 1860			0	0	0	+3	+5	0	0	0	−3	−15	−23	−30	−28	−29	−38	−43	−50	−52	−56	−46	−37	−44
Oct., 1860				0	0	+3	+5	0	0	0	−3	−15	−23	−30	−28	−29	−38	−43	−50	−52	−56	−46	−37	−44
Jan., 1861					0	+3	+5	0	0	0	−3	−15	−23	−30	−28	−29	−38	−43	−50	−52	−56	−46	−37	−44
April, 1861						0	+2	−3	−3	−3	−6	−17	−25	−32	−30	−31	−40	−45	−51	−53	−57	−48	−39	−46
July, 1861							0	−5	−5	−5	−8	−19	−27	−33	−31	−32	−41	−46	−52	−54	−58	−49	−40	−47
Oct., 1861								0	0	0	−3	−15	−23	−30	−28	−29	−38	−43	−50	−52	−56	−46	−37	−44
Jan., 1862									0	0	−3	−15	−23	−30	−28	−29	−38	−43	−50	−52	−56	−46	−37	−44
April, 1862										0	−3	−15	−23	−30	−28	−29	−38	−43	−50	−52	−56	−46	−37	−44
July, 1862											0	−12	−21	−28	−26	−27	−36	−41	−48	−52	−55	−44	−35	−42
Oct., 1862												0	−9	−18	−15	−16	−27	−33	−41	−44	−48	−36	−28	−34
Jan., 1863													0	−9	−6	−8	−19	−26	−35	−38	−43	−30	−18	−27
April, 1863														0	+3	+1	−11	−19	−29	−31	−37	−23	−10	−20
July, 1863															0	−1	−14	−21	−31	−33	−39	−25	−13	−22
Oct., 1863																0	−13	−20	−30	−32	−38	−24	−11	−21
Jan., 1864																	0	−8	−19	−23	−29	−13	+2	−10
April, 1864																		0	−12	−16	−23	−5	+11	−2
July, 1864																			0	−4	−12	+8	+26	+12
Oct., 1864																				0	−8	+13	+31	+17
Jan., 1865																					0	+23	+43	+27
April, 1865																						0	+17	+4
July, 1865																							0	−11

[1] Date of making of loans indicated by index at side; date of repayment by index at top.

per cent. of 77, which represents its purchasing power at the earlier date.[1]

The conclusion to be drawn from the table is so clear as hardly to require formal statement. In the case of almost all loans made before the middle of 1864 and repaid at any subsequent time embraced by the table, the creditor found that the sum returned to him had a purchasing power much less than the purchasing power that had been transferred to the borrower when the loan was made. According to the figures, this decline varied from 1 to more than 50 per cent. On loans made in the middle of 1864 or later, on the contrary, the creditor gained as a rule. In the case of loans made in January, 1865, and repaid six months later, the increase in purchasing power was over 40 per cent. It may not be unwise, however, to enter once again a caution against taking such figures too literally.[2]

III.   THE RATE OF INTEREST

In turning to study the fortunes of men who have no thought of employing their capital for themselves, but expect to seek new borrowers as rapidly as old loans are repaid, one finds it necessary to distinguish between

[1] A more strictly accurate method of estimating the relative loss or gain would be to compute the average relative prices of all the series anew on the basis of the actual prices at each successive period. But this would be a heavy task, and it is thought that the inaccuracy of the simple method employed is not greater than the inaccuracy of the material upon which the whole computation rests. To pretend to great refinement in the method of analysis for the purposes of so rough a statement as the present would be pedantic.

[2] Loans made before the passage of the first legal-tender act, February 25, 1862, are treated in the table as if they were all repaid in greenbacks. Some debtors, however, are said to have repaid such obligations in gold. (See letter of Judge Hoar to E. J. James in *Publications of the American Economic Association*, Vol. III, p. 51.) But so nice a sense of business honor was not universal, and the courts were called upon to adjudicate the question involved. In Hepburn *vs.* Griswold (8 *Wallace*, p. 603; 1869) the federal Supreme Court held that United States notes were not a legal tender for debts contracted before February 25, 1862; but within a year the court reversed this decision ("The Legal Tender Cases," 12 *Wallace*, p. 457). But the table indicates that losses on loans made in April, 1862, were not less heavy than on loans made in 1860.

cases where loans have been made for short and for long terms ; between the cases, that is, where there is and where there is not an opportunity to make a new contract regarding the rate of interest. The latter cases may be dismissed with a word. The capitalist who lent $10,000 for five years in April, 1862, at 6 per cent. interest would be in relatively the same position as the workingman who received no advance in money wages; while his money income remained the same, the rise of prices would decrease his real income in 1864 and 1865 by about one-half. Of course, this loss to the creditor is a gain to the debtor; for to the business man using borrowed capital the advance of prices means that he can raise his interest money by selling a smaller proportion of his output.

More interesting is the case of loans maturing and made afresh during the period under examination. The important question is : How far did the lender secure compensation for the diminished purchasing power of the money in which he was paid by contracting for a higher rate of interest? To answer this question adequately abundant statistics of the rate of interest received on loans of different kinds during the war are necessary. Unfortunately, however, it is extremely difficult to find such figures. To my knowledge there are no systematic records of rates of interest on long-time business loans, and the data for short-time loans are unusually meager and doubtful. In 1860 *Hunt's Merchants' Magazine* and the *Bankers' Magazine* — the most prominent business periodicals of the day— were publishing each month tables showing the rates of interest paid in New York for loans of several different kinds. But during the war they ceased these systematic reports and one can glean from them but occasional scattering statements. Professor Irving Fisher, however, in his *Appreciation and Interest* gives a table which purports to show the rate on "call" loans, "60 day" loans and "prime, two name, 60 day" loans for a period of years including 1860 to 1865. The third of these series was obtained, he states, from a diagram prepared by one of his students showing "the highest and lowest monthly rates"—though from what source the data were taken he does not say. The other two series were obtained from a table compiled by Mr. E. B. Elliott. Elliott made this table for a paper upon "The Periodicity of Rates of Interest," read before the American Association for the Advancement of Science in 1874. The paper was not published in the proceedings of the association, and the only record which I have been able to find of it is a brief abstract published in the *Bankers' Magazine*.[1] It is here said regarding the source of information upon which Elliott drew: "Being asked whence the data were obtained, Professor Elliott replied that they were collated from *The Bankers' Magazine, The Financial Chronicle* and *Hunt's Merchants' Magazine*." I have no doubt that this statement is correct for most of the years included in the table (1849 to 1874), but since the *Commercial and Financial Chronicle* was not established until July, 1865, and the other journals mentioned did not maintain these tables of interest regularly, it follows that Mr. Elliott must have had irregular data for the years of the war, or else that he went to some unknown source for his figures.

Under these circumstances it seems justifiable to attempt constructing a new table from the reports of the daily newspapers. On examination, however, one finds that this course also is open to objection. In the first place, regular statements can be found only for one kind of transactions — loans on call. In the second place, whenever the rates for call loans rise above 7 per cent. the reporter is apt to say

[1] Vol. XXIX, p. 220.

merely that the ruling rate is "the legal maximum plus a small commission." In the third place, one is justified in feeling some suspicions of the accuracy of newspaper reports. However, I have compiled a table from the financial columns of the newspapers of the rate for call loans every Saturday from 1862 to 1865. In doing so I have been compelled to supplement one paper by another, for no one gives the reports with perfect regularity for the whole period.[1]

Since none of these series have an unquestioned title to acceptance, they are all presented in the next table. The

TABLE LVIII

INTEREST RATES IN THE NEW YORK MONEY MARKET 1860 TO 1865

I. AVERAGE RATES PER YEAR

YEAR	CALL		SIXTY DAYS	PRIME TWO NAME 60 DAYS
	Elliott	Newspapers	Elliott	Fisher
1860.............	6.1%	...	8.4%	7.7%
1861.............	5.4	...	9.0	6.6
1862.............	5.6	5.2%	6.8	5.4
1863.............	5.0	6.2	6.7	5.8
1864.............	7.2	6.6	9.3	8.0
1865.............	6.1	6.2	10.2	8.2

II. AVERAGE RATES PER MONTH FOR CALL LOANS

	1862	1863	1864	1865
January...........	6.5%	6.1%	7.0%	7.0%
February..........	6.0	6.3	6.1	6.1
March.............	5.5	6.1	5.9	7.0
April.............	5.5	5.2	6.8	5.6
May..............	4.6	5.3	5.6	5.4
June.............	4.1	6.1	6.7	4.9
July.............	5.4	6.1	6.8	5.5
August...........	4.0	6.0	6.9	5.9
September.........	4.3	6.6	7.0	6.0
October...........	4.6	6.5	6.8	7.0
November.........	6.3	7.0	6.9	6.8
December.........	6.0	7.0	6.6	6.8

[1] The *Herald*, *Tribune*, *Evening Express*, and *World* have all been drawn upon.

exhibit of average annual rates is followed by a statement of the average rate each month based upon the newspaper reports.

While the different series showing annual average rates of interest do not agree with each other perfectly, they all indicate that the advance in the rate of interest was comparatively small — much too small to compensate persons whose income was derived from such sources for the increased cost of living. To bring this fact out clearly the next table shows the relative increase in the rates of interest side by side with the relative increase in prices and in money wages:

TABLE LIX

RELATIVE INCREASE IN INTEREST, PRICES, AND WAGES

YEAR	RATES OF INTEREST				PRICES		WAGES	
	CALL		60 DAYS	PRIME TWO NAME 60 DAYS	Wholesale	Retail	Variable Weights	Constant Weights
	Elliott	Newspapers	Elliott	Fisher				
1860............	100	...	100	100	100	100	100	100
1861............	89	...	107	86	98	103	101	101
1862............	92	100	81	70	105	115	103	103
1863............	82	119	80	75	138	144	118	117
1864............	118	127	111	104	186	172	137	138
1865............	100	100	121	106	188	181	154	158

The conclusion from these figures is not only that persons who derived their income from capital lent at interest for short terms were injured by the issues of the greenbacks, but also that their injuries were more serious than those suffered by wage-earners.

To explain this state of affairs is not easy. The first reason that suggests itself to the mind considering the problem is that both lenders and borrowers failed to foresee the changes that would take place in the purchasing power of money between the dates when loans were made and repaid. No doubt there is much force in this explanation. If, for instance, men arranging for loans in April, 1862, to be repaid a year later, had known that in the meantime the purchasing power of money would decline 30 per cent., they would have agreed upon a very high rate of interest. On the assumption that, monetary conditions aside, the rate would have been 6 per cent., the lender gifted with second sight would have demanded 50.52 per cent.; *i. e.*, 6 per cent. plus 42 per cent. of both capital and interest to offset the decline of 30 per cent. in the purchasing power of the dollars received in repayment as compared with that of the dollars lent. According to the table of relative prices, any interest rate less than this would have deprived capitalists of a portion of their ordinary returns; and, on the other hand, since the prices of products increased on the average 42 per cent. between April, 1862, and April, 1863, borrowers could afford to pay on the average 50.52 per cent. for loans quite as well as they could afford to pay 6 per cent. in years of stable prices. Men able to discern the future course of prices would not have lent money at the ordinary rates, and if, as the table indicates, the rates prevailing in the New York market throughout all 1862 and 1863 were less than 7 per cent., it must have been because the extraordinary rise of prices was not foreseen by borrowers and lenders.

Nor, if the arguments of the preceding chapters are valid, is it surprising that business men failed to see what was coming; for the course of prices depended chiefly upon the valuation set upon the greenbacks, and this valuation in turn depended chiefly upon the state of the finances and the fortunes of war — matters that no one could foresee with certainty. Indeed, there was much of the time a very general disposition to take an unwarrantedly optimistic view of the military situation and the chances of an early peace. Many members of the business community seem to have felt that the premium on gold was artificial and must soon drop, that prices were inflated and must collapse. To the extent that such views prevailed borrowers would be cautious about making engagements to repay money in a future that might well present a lower range of prices, and lenders would expect a gain instead of a loss from the changes in the purchasing power of money.

But the full explanation of the slight advance in interest cannot be found in this inability to foresee the future—at least not without further analysis of what consequences such inability entailed. Workingmen are commonly credited with less foresight than capitalists, and nevertheless they seem, according to the figures, to have succeeded better in making bargains with employers of labor than did lenders with employers of capital. The explanation of this less success seems to be found in the difference between the way in which depreciation affected what the capitalist and the laborer had to offer in return for interest and wages. There is no reason for assuming that an artisan who changed employers during the war would render less efficient service in his new than in his old position, or that a landlord who changed tenants had less advantages to put at the disposal of the incoming lessee. In both these cases the good offered to the active business man remained substantially the same, and it may safely be assumed that, other things being equal, this business man could afford to give quite as much for the labor and the land after as before suspension. From the business man's point of view, therefore, there seems to have been room for a doubling of money wages and rent when the purchasing power of money had fallen one-half. But in the case of the borrower of capital the like was not true. The thousand dollars which Mr. A. offered him in 1865 was not, like the labor of John Smith or the farm of Mr. B., as efficient for his purposes as it would have been five years before. For, with the thousand dollars he could not purchase anything like the same amount of machinery, material, or labor. And since the same nominal amount of capital was of less efficiency in the hands of the borrower, he could not without loss to himself increase the interest which he paid for new loans in proportion to the decline in the purchasing power of money, as he could increase the wages of laborers or the rent for land.

From the point of view of the lender this remark means simply that the expiration of old contracts and the making of fresh ones gave him no opportunity to remedy the mistakes of judgment once committed. If a farm hand in April, 1862, contracting to work a year, failed to foresee the advance of prices that would occur, and agreed to accept his usual wage of $15 a month and board, he would suffer during the year from having to pay more for clothing, etc.; but when he came to renew his bargain in April, 1863, he would be in a strong position to demand an increase of wages sufficient to offset the depreciation in the purchasing power of money. But if a capitalist with no more power of divination than the farm hand lent $1,000 in April, 1862, for a year at 6 per cent. interest, he would not only suffer during this time from the rise of prices, but he would also have no ground for asking from a new borrower compensation, in the form of higher interest, for the advance that had already taken place in prices. If both lender and borrower in April, 1863, anticipated that the rise of prices would continue during the next year, they might attempt to adjust the rate of interest so as to counterbalance the expected changes, but the borrower could give no compensation for the changes that had already taken place, inasmuch as these changes diminished the efficiency of the thousand dollars which the lender transferred to his control.

Thus ground once lost by a lender through monetary depreciation could not be recovered so long as prices continued to advance; the utmost that the lender could hope to accomplish was to keep from falling farther behind by obtaining a rate of interest sufficiently high to offset the further advances of the future. As has been shown, the capitalist who lent $1,000 in April, 1862, for a year should have charged 50.52 per cent. for interest. After deducting his income of 6 per cent. plus 42 per cent. of itself, he would have had left at the end of the year a nominal principal of $1,420, which in April, 1863, had the same purchasing power as $1,000 in April, 1862. With this number of paper dollars to put at the disposal of borrowers, the capitalist could prevent a decline in his real income if he were able to foresee that the purchasing power of money would depreciate 19 per cent. more during the next year and to persuade borrowers of the same fact. The rate charged should be 30.9 per cent.—i. e., 6 per cent. plus 23.4 per cent. of capital and interest to offset the diminution of 19 per cent. in purchasing power. This rate would give the usual real income to the capitalist and leave him in April, 1864, a nominal capital of $1,752, or the equivalent in purchasing power of $1,000 in April, 1862. For the next year the rate should be 11.61 per cent., which on $1,750 would give the usual real income and a principal of $1,841 in April, 1865, which again is equal to $1,000 in April, 1862. Failure to obtain these exceedingly high rates of interest in making the loan for any year would subject the lender to a heavy loss of real income not only for that year, but also for the years to come, beause it would not provide for an increase in the nominal amount of the principal sufficient to sustain its purchasing power undiminished.

The failure of the rate of interest to attain anything like the extraordinary rates which alone could have saved lenders from loss seems at first sight more remarkable when the government demand for loans and the high profits made by business men are taken into account. But neither of these factors had quite so much influence as one at first imagines. Just as the government's demand for food and clothing was not a new demand superadded to that formerly existing, but rather a part of the old demand making itself felt through a new channel, so in a measure the government demand for capital was a substitute for private demands rather than an increase in the whole sum required by the community. The government had become the employer of a considerable fraction of the working population, and it needed large sums of money to provide for these employees, in the same way that a corporation that increased the number of its hands would need a larger working capital to pay wages and purchase supplies. But after all there is a radical difference between the effect of war loans and industrial loans upon the rate of interest. The corporation would hope to direct the labor in such fashion that it would more than replace the capital consumed in providing for it; while the majority of the men employed by the federal government during the Civil War were not engaged in productive operations. Since the soldiers enlisted in 1862 did not produce an equivalent in commodities for the food they ate and the clothes they wore, the government had to borrow new sums of capital to maintain them in 1863, and new sums again in 1864 and 1865. Through the war loans the community was voluntarily devoting a not inconsiderable proportion of its labor and capital each year to employments that from the strictly economic point of view must be called unproductive, and so far as this was the case the process of accumulation was retarded. It seems therefore safe to say that though the government demand for loans was in considerable degree a substitute for private demands, the difference in the use made of the borrowed funds tended to raise the rate of interest for future years.

The modification required by the proposition that the high profits of trade were a factor of great importance in the loan market is more serious. That profits were uncommonly large during the war is not doubted; indeed, the next chapter will be devoted primarily to showing that such was the fact. Nor is it doubted that under ordinary circumstances high profits will tend powerfully to produce high rates of interest; both by making business men anxious to borrow capital with which to extend the scope of their existing operations or to undertake new ventures, and by making capitalists who have the choice between employing their means themselves and lending them to others prefer the former course. But during the Civil War this usual consequence of high profits conflicted with another consequence of the monetary situation—namely, the uncertainty about the future course of prices. Men were at any given time "making money," but they recognized that their unusual profits were in a large measure the product of monetary depreciation. If the premium on gold should drop suddenly, as it might at almost any time in consequence of a favorable change in the military situation, prices would probably follow, and the trend of affairs might set as strongly against the realization of high profits as it had set formerly in its favor. Under such circumstances prudence forbade men to enter into contracts that would call for the repayment of large sums of money in a future that might bring a low level of prices and make it necessary for the debtor to sell an unexpectedly large part of his product to obtain sufficient money to meet his obligations. A man would be in a safer position if he kept free of debt and confined his operations as closely as possible to business that he could manage with his own capital. In other words, men realized their inability to foresee the future and, knowing that it might bring great price fluctuations in either direction, sought protection against these changes by limiting their future pecuniary obligations as narrowly as possible.

That considerations of this character were carefully weighed by business men is clearly shown by the remarkable contraction of credit operations that took place during the war. When no one could foresee with confidence what would be the relative purchasing power of a dollar three months in advance, it was obviously risky for a merchant to accept a note due in ninety days for goods sold, or to give such a note for goods bought. Consequently, cash business increased in importance and credit operations diminished—a condition of affairs that was remarked in mercantile circles as early as August, 1862.[1] In proportion as the fluctuations of prices became more marked, credits were more strictly curtailed. "Even the West," said the New York *Times* of November 28, 1863, "which has long been wont to strain credit to its utmost, is now buying and selling for cash to an unprecedented degree." The circular published in 1864 by Dun's Mercantile Agency ascribed the small number of bankruptcies in large part " to that rigid caution which has obtained in our business community in dispensing credits."[2] Mr. McCulloch in his report as secretary of the treasury, December, 1865, said that " it is undoubtedly true that trade is carried on much more largely for cash than was ever the case previous to 1861." [3] In the autumn of the same year the *Commercial and Financial Chronicle* made a careful inquiry into the credits being granted to the South and West, and reached the following conclusions: "The great bulk of jobbing sales now being made are on short time, say from sixty days to four months. . . . . Half of the buyers

[1] Compare *Hunt's Merchants' Magazine*, Vol. XLVII, p. 333, and the " Commercial Chronicle and Review " of later issues.

[2] *Ibid.*, Vol. LII, p. 146.   [3] P. 11.

pay in cash, and a large portion of the remainder average less than three months in their credits, while but a very few obtain six or eight months." [1]

Of course, the increase in cash business meant that the demand for commercial loans was less, and this diminution in the quantity of commercial paper on the market may not improbably have offset the great increase in public securities offered to investors. It must be noticed, however, that in explaining the cause of the contraction of credit one finds himself brought back again to men's conscious inability to foresee the future course of prices as the controlling factor in the loan market. Ordinarily men treat the value of money as a constant and arrange their transactions with little conscious reference to its fluctuations. A paper standard, however, the value of which depends upon the varying credit of a government passing through a serious crisis, forces upon everyone a realization of the fact that the purchasing power of money is subject to great variations. But the realization of this fact is of little practical use in arranging business affairs unless men can foresee the character of the impending changes. During the Civil War the uncertainty was so great that such foresight was hardly possible. As a consequence it seems probable from what information is available that men made their bargains for borrowing and lending money upon terms not very unlike the terms prevailing in less unquiet times. The chief difference appears to have been that, so far as possible, everyone refrained from assuming obligations to receive or to pay money at future dates, because everyone realized that the sum which he would be called upon to give or take might well possess much less purchasing power than the sum which he had received or given — particularly when the time that would elapse between the making and repayment of the loan would be considerable.

[1] Vol. I, p. 325.

Lest too strong an impression be given of the losses of creditors during the war, it is well to call attention to the fact that against the losses during the period of rising prices, extending broadly from 1862 to January, 1865, were set similar gains during the period of falling prices, extending broadly from January, 1865, to the resumption of specie payments in 1879. If Falkner's index number of 100 for the latter year can be accepted, it follows that a man who had kept a sum of money at interest for the whole period from suspension to resumption would find its purchasing power at the end of the paper-money régime substantially the same as it had been at the beginning. In the meantime, however, he would have suffered a heavy loss of real income from 1862 to 1865, and on the other hand would have enjoyed an increase of real income from the latter date to 1879.

It should also be pointed out that on one important class of loans capitalists suffered comparatively little even during the war. Interest on many forms of government bonds was paid in gold. Capitalists who invested their means in these securities consequently received an income of unvarying specie value. But even these investors did not escape all the evil consequences of the paper-money system; because, as has been shown, prices rose in the end to a greater height than the premium upon gold. To illustrate the situation of such investors, suppose the case of a man who in 1860 had $10,000 of the fifteen-year 5 per cent. federal bonds of the loan of 1858. The following table shows what would be his income in gold and paper money, and how its purchasing power would fluctuate in consequence of the advance in prices.

While persons who had purchased bonds as an investment before the war suffered no great loss of income, persons who had sufficient faith in the stability of the federal government

TABLE LX

MONEY AND REAL INCOME YIELDED BY $10,000 OF BONDS OF LOAN OF 1858

Year	Income in Gold Coin	Average Value of $100 of Gold Coin in Currency	Equivalent of Gold Income in Currency	Relative Prices at Retail	Purchasing Power of Money Income	Relative Real Income
1860........	$500	$100.0	$500.0	100	500	100
1861........	500	100.0	500.0	103	485	97
1862........	500	113.3	566.5	115	493	99
1863........	500	145.2	726.0	144	504	101
1864........	500	203.3	1,016.5	172	591	118
1865........	500	157.3	786.5	181	435	87

to purchase its securities at the low prices that prevailed during the war realized a very high rate of interest. By way of rough illustration, consider the case of a foreigner who sent $1,000 in gold to New York every January and directed his broker to purchase 6 per cent. twenty-year bonds of the loan of 1861. The following table shows the amount of bonds which this sum would buy and the interest which the investment would yield:

TABLE LXI

INTEREST YIELDED BY AN INVESTMENT OF $1,000 IN GOLD IN UNITED STATES SIXES OF 1881, MADE IN JANUARY OF EACH YEAR FROM 1862 TO 1865

Date	Average Value in Currency of $1,000 in Gold	Average Price of U.S. 6's of 1881	Amount of Bonds Which $1,000 in Gold Would Buy	Gold Interest at 6 per cent. on Bonds Bought	Rate of Interest Realized
1862, January........	$1,025	89.6	$1,143	$68.58	6.9%
1863, January........	1,451	95.4	1,521	91.26	9.1
1864, January........	1,555	105.5	1,474	88.44	8.8
1865, January........	2,162	110.9	1,950	117.00	11.7

If the person who made these investments were an American, he would be able to sell his gold-interest money at a high premium, but he would also have to pay correspondingly high prices for commodities, so that upon the whole his position would not be greatly different from that of the foreign investor. That such opportunities for investment as these securities offered should exist when men were most of the time loaning money for short terms at 7 per cent. or less, is perhaps the most emphatic proof that could be offered of the inability of the public to foresee what the future had in store. Had men been able to make clearer forecasts, the rate of interest would have risen much more than it did, and had they not feared for the solvency of the federal government, its bonds would not have fallen so low. But, for that matter, this same distrust of the government's solvency, arising from the darkness of the future, may be said to have been fundamentally responsible for all the economic disturbances of the war times, because to it was due the varying depreciation of the greenbacks.

CHAPTER VIII

PROFITS

I. *Profits as a Share in the Distribution of the Product:*
Use of the Terms "Profits" and "Residual Claimants"—Gains of Residual Claimants at the Expense of Laborers, Landlords, and Lending Capitalists—Other Things being equal, Profits Varied Inversely as Average Wages Paid to Employees and Directly as the Complexity of Business Organization.

II. *Profits in Different Industries:*
Dependence of Profits on Relative Advance in Prices of Different Products — Profits of Farmers as an Illustration.

III. *Statistical Evidence Regarding Profits:*
Meagerness of the Evidence — Statistics of Failures.

I. PROFITS AS A SHARE IN THE DISTRIBUTION OF THE PRODUCT

In the three preceding chapters an attempt has been made to show in what manner the depreciation of the paper standard affected the real incomes of laborers, landlords, and lending capitalists. These classes are all alike in that the amount of the remuneration received by them for the aid which they render to production is commonly fixed in advance by agreement, and is not immediately affected by the profitableness or unprofitableness of the undertaking. It remains to examine the economic fortunes of those men whose money incomes are made up by the sums left over in any business after all the stipulated expenses have been met.

For the purposes of the discussion it is convenient to call these men "residual claimants," and to use the term "profits" to denote the sums which they receive. It will be observed that neither of these terms is used in the sense frequently assigned it in economic treatises. When one is investigating the consequences of monetary depreciation or appreciation, particularly within a limited period of time, one finds that the economic functions that men perform in the process of production are facts of less significance than the legal positions in which they stand with reference to the payment of their incomes. The residual claimant of the present chapter is likely to be that man in any business organization whom Marshall would call the undertaker; but the factor of importance in determining whether the rise of prices injures or benefits him is not the work that he performs in initiating and superintending operations, but the fact that, instead of having entered into a contract to accept a certain sum for his services, he has as his share whatever funds are left after paying all fixed charges and operating expenses. The residual claimant in this sense may be either manager, capitalist, landlord, or laborer, or any two or three, or all of these persons in one. Which man in any establishment of those who contribute services or property to aid the process of production is in the legal position of residual claimant depends upon the organization of the business. Many cases can be differentiated, varying in complexity from that of the farmer who works his own land without assistance of hired labor or borrowed capital, to that of the great corporation which leases its land, borrows most of its capital, hires its laborers, and pays fixed salaries to its officials. In the last case the residual claimants are the shareholders among whom the profits are divided in the form of dividends, and these shareholders may include among their number persons who are officials, or laborers, or bondholders, or landlords of the corporation, or who have no other connection with it than that of owning stock. But widely different as these residual claimants may be from other points of view, they are all alike in that the amount of their incomes depends upon the difference between the total receipts of the business and the sums paid to all the other co-operators in production who have commuted their claims to share in the product for a stipulated payment. The problem of the present chapter is: How did the depreciation of the greenbacks affect these differences between total receipts and the total of payments to other co-operators?

When the problem of profits is conceived of in this fashion, it becomes clear that a very important part of the solution has already been contributed by the preceding studies of wages, rent, and interest. The evidence has been found to support the conclusion that in almost all cases the sums of money wages, rent, and interest received by laborers, landlords and capitalists increased much less rapidly than did the general price level. If the wording of this conclusion be reversed — the prices of products rose more rapidly than wages, rent, or interest — we come at once to the proposition that as a rule profits must have increased more rapidly than prices. For, if the sums paid to all the other co-operating parties were increased in just the same ratio as the prices of the articles sold, it would follow that other things remaining the same, money profits also would increase in the same ratio. But if, while prices doubled, the payments to laborers, landlords, and capitalists increased in any ratio less than 100 per cent., the sums of money left for the residual claimants must have more than doubled. In other words, the effect of the depreciation of the paper currency upon the distribution of wealth may be summed up in the proposition: The shares of wage-earners, landowners, and lenders in the national dividend were diminished and the share of residual claimants was increased.

Real profits were unusually large during the Civil War, therefore, but large because real wages, rent, and interest were low. It must not be assumed, however, that the residual claimant necessarily gained as much as the other parties in distribution lost. In the chapter upon wages, for example, it was suggested that the efficiency of labor probably decreased somewhat during the Civil War, because a large number of the most efficient laborers had enlisted in the armies and their places had to be filled with less skilful hands. So far as this was the case, the volume of output must have diminished, and, of course, such diminution would decrease the difference between total income and total outgo that figures with us as profits. But if this was an important consideration, it was one due, not to the paper standard, but to the fact that the country was involved in a great war.

With regard to the relations between residual claimant and lending capitalist it must be said that the capital borrowed during the war decreased very much more in efficiency than the labor hired. When prices had doubled, $1,000 of capital was the equivalent of only $500 on the old level of prices, and if the borrower had to pay 8 instead of 6 per cent. interest, he seems to have been worse instead of better off in consequence of the depreciation of money. And, of course, the residual claimant is, in fact, worse off because of even a slight increase in the rate of interest which he has to pay—unless further depreciation takes place between the time that he invests the funds lent him and repays them to the lender. But if such depreciation does take place, he is likely to make a larger gain at the expense of the lender than he makes at the expense of the laborer, because the contract which he makes with the former is likely to run for a longer time than the contract with the latter, and consequently the person who finds himself injured by the course of events cannot seek relief so promptly by insisting upon making new terms. Moreover, the borrower gains not only by continuing to pay the same money income to the lender for a considerable period, as he may perhaps do with the laborer, but also by returning the principal sum lent in dollars of much less purchasing power than the dollars received. On the other hand, the borrower of capital feels the effect of a downward turn of prices much more quickly than the employer of labor. The wage-tables indicate that, though money wages continued to rise for some time after prices had begun to fall, they had nevertheless not caught up with prices by the end of the war. Therefore, while employers were making less extra gain at the expense of their hands at the close of 1865 than they had been making in 1863 and 1864, they were nevertheless receiving an extra profit as compared with the situation before the suspension of specie payments. The extra gain of the borrower, however, was turned into a positive loss as soon as the purchasing power of the dollars in which his obligations were repaid became greater than the purchasing power of dollars which had been lent to him.

As for the relations between the tenant and landlord, they were like those between employer and employee in that the efficiency of the good transferred was not affected by monetary conditions, and like those between borrower and lender in that the contract was likely to run for a considerable term. From the tables of chap. vi which indicate that money rents increased less rapidly than money wages, it follows that the gain of the residual claimant at the expense of his landlord was probably greater in degree than the gain at the expense of laborers.

Two other general propositions respecting profits are suggested by the results of preceding investigations. First, other things being equal, profits varied inversely as the average wage per day paid to employees. This conclusion follows directly from the demonstration in chap. v that the money wages of men earning \$1–\$1.49 per day before the perturbation of prices increased in higher ratio than those of men earning $1.50–$1.99; that the wages of the latter class increased more than the wages of men in the next higher wage class, etc. Second, other things being equal, profits varied directly as the complexity of the business organization. By this proposition is meant, for example, that a farmer who paid money rent, used borrowed capital, and employed hired laborers, made a higher percentage of profits than a farmer of whom any one of these suppositions did not hold true. If, as has been argued, the increase of profits was made at the expense of laborers, landlords, and capitalists, it follows that that residual claimant fared best whose contracts enabled him to exploit the largest number of these other persons.

II. PROFITS IN DIFFERENT INDUSTRIES

The effect of monetary depreciation upon profits resulting from the increase in the share of the residual claimant in the product at the expense of the shares of laborers, landlords, and capitalists, was felt more or less alike in all industries. Of course, the average advance of money wages was not uniform in all branches of production: there were probably similar differences in the increase of the sums paid as rent for locations of various sorts, and there may have been differences in the fluctuation of rates of interest charged to borrowers in dissimilar lines of business. But, despite these differences in degree of diminution in the shares of these three classes of participants in distribution, as compared with the share of residual claimants, the general character of this effect of depreciation was substantially the same in all industries.

There was another and hardly less important effect of depreciation upon profits, however, that was by no means uniform. In chap. iv emphasis was put upon the dissimilarity in the price fluctuations of different commodities.

These dissimilarities produced corresponding variations in the profits realized by producers. The residual claimant whose profits came from the production of commodities that advanced in price more rapidly than the majority of other commodities derived a second gain in addition to the gain made at the expense of his laborers, landlord, and creditors. Not only did such a residual claimant have a relatively larger share in the product, but the money value of that product was relatively larger as compared with the money value of other things that he might wish to buy. When the advance of the product in price was nearly the same as the advance of the articles which the residual claimant purchased, he enjoyed no such second gain — the only way in which he was benefited by the depreciation was through his ability to satisfy contracts with the proceeds of a smaller portion of the output. Finally, in the case of products that advanced in value less than the average the residual claimant not only made no second gain, but he even suffered a loss through the diminshed relative purchasing power of his product — a loss that might or might not be offset by the gains made at the expense of the other participants in distribution.

The statistical material is not complete enough to make possible an elaborate investigation of these differences in the profitableness of industries due to the dissimilar price fluctuations. But there is one case that merits attention, not only because of the relative fulness of the statistical record, but also because of the great importance of the industry. It will be remembered that thirteen agricultural products are included in the tables of relative prices at wholesale. Since this list comprises all the most important farm products of the northern states, it affords a fair basis for estimating how the farmer's money income was affected by price changes in comparison with that of other producers. Table LXII presents the data regarding the prices of farm products in two

TABLE LXII

RELATIVE WHOLESALE PRICES OF FARM PRODUCTS AND OF OTHER COMMODITIES

DATE	ARITHMETIC MEAN			MEDIAN		
	Thirteen Farm Products— Simple Average	Seven Farm Products— Weighted Average	All Articles Included in Table XIV	Thirteen Farm Products— Simple Average	Seven Farm Products— Weighted Average	All Articles Included in Table XIV
1860, Jan ...	103	108	102	101	102	100
April..	105	103	102	105	105	100
July ..	98	94	100	96	92	100
Oct ...	95	95	104	94	97	100
1861, Jan ...	92	91	97	94	90	100
April..	94	87	98	90	92	97
July ..	74	66	93	66	66	95
Oct ...	76	71	100	71	72	100
1862, Jan ...	83	78	111	84	79	100
April..	92	81	110	87	85	100
July ..	87	77	113	86	74	103
Oct ...	97	85	124	96	82	117
1863, Jan ...	119	100	142	100	94	130
April..	144	129	162	130	120	142
July ..	129	110	156	115	103	139
Oct ...	133	125	154	127	122	140
1864, Jan ...	159	157	176	152	153	161
April..	171	171	194	161	160	175
July ..	189	192	233	185	206	200
Oct ...	194	194	234	194	174	208
1865, Jan ...	223	216	247	224	212	228
April..	186	177	207	179	169	184
July ..	143	129	184	139	117	160
Oct ...	166	154	199	149	149	180

ways. The first column gives the simple arithmetic means of the relative prices of the thirteen agricultural products included in the general price tables; the second column gives a similar average of the relative prices of barley, corn, meats, oats, rye, tobacco, and wheat weighted according to the estimated money value of these products in the northern and western states in 1860;[1] the third column gives the arith-

[1] These weights are as follows in percentages: Corn, 39.4; meats, 32.2; wheat, 17.4; oats, 6.9; rye, 1.7; barley, 1.6; tobacco, 0.8. They are derived from the table of quantities and values prepared by the statistician of the Department of Agriculture for Senator Aldrich's committee and published in its report, Part I, p. 108. In order to exclude the south Atlantic and south central states, recourse was had to the census reports of farm yields in 1860, as given in the *Eleventh Census,* "Report upon Agriculture," Table 2.

metic mean of the relative prices of all articles included in the wholesale price-tables of chap. iv. A second set of averages is added in which the median is substituted for the arithmetic mean.

It seems safe to conclude from these figures that the farmers of the loyal states were among the unfortunate producers whose products rose in price less than the majority of other articles, and that from this standpoint they were losers rather than gainers by the paper currency. Of course, it is possible that the farmer's loss from this inequality of price fluctuations might be more than offset by his gains at the expense of laborers, landlord, and lending capitalist. But there is good reason for believing that the increase of the residual claimant's profits in the latter fashion was less in farming than in any other important industry. This conclusion seems to follow from the proposition that, other things being equal, profits varied directly as the complexity of business organization. The American farmers of the Civil War were in a large proportion of cases their own landlords, capitalists, and laborers. So far as this was true, they had few important pecuniary contracts with other persons of which they could take advantage by paying in depreciated dollars. Of those farmers who hired labor very many paid wages partly in board and lodging—an arrangement which threw a considerable part of the increased cost of living upon them instead of upon their employees. Finally, the renting farmer probably gained less on the average from the contract with his landlord than tenants of any other class, because in a majority of cases the rent was not a sum of money, but a share of the produce. While, then, the general effect of the paper standard was in the direction of increasing profits, it seems very doubtful whether farmers as a whole did not lose more than they gained because of the price disturbances.

III. STATISTICAL EVIDENCE REGARDING PROFITS

So far the conclusion that profits were on the whole much increased during the Civil War has been based mainly on the results of preceding chapters. It would be highly desirable to test these conclusions by means of direct information regarding profits made in various branches of trade, but the data available for such a purpose are more meager even than the data concerning rent or interest. What scraps of information are available, however, support the view that profits were uncommonly large. Mr. David A. Wells, for example, in his reports as special commissioner of the revenue, has stories of " most anomalous and extraordinary" profits that were realized in the paper, woolen, pig-iron, and salt industries.[1] A more general indication of the profitableness of business is afforded by the remark in the annual circular of Dun's Mercantile Agency for 1864, that "it is generally conceded that the average profits on trade range from 12 to 15 per cent."[2]

But the most important piece of evidence is found in the statistics of failures compiled by the same agency. The following table shows Dun's report of the number of bankruptcies and the amount of liabilities in the loyal states from the panic year 1857 to the end of the war:

TABLE LXIII

STATISTICS OF FAILURES IN THE LOYAL STATES FROM 1857 TO 1865 ACCORDING TO DUN'S MERCANTILE AGENCY[3]

Year	Number	Liabilities	Year	Number	Liabilities
1857.....	4,257	$265,500,000	1861....	5,935	$178,600,000
1858.....	3,113	73,600,000	1862....	1,652	23,000,000
1859.....	2,959	51,300,000	1863....	495	7,900,000
1860.....	2,733	61,700,000	1864....	510	8,600,000
			1865....	500	17,600,000

[1] *Executive Document No. 27*, 41st Cong., 2d Sess., pp. lxxxi, xciii, cvi; *Executive Document No. 16*, 40th Cong., 3d Sess., pp. 42, 46; *House of Representatives Report No. 72*, 41st Cong., 2d Sess., pp. 73, 74. *Cf.* also *Commercial and Financial Chronicle*, Vol. II, p. 227; C. B. CONANT in *Hunt's Merchants' Magazine*, Vol. LII, p. 359.

[2] *Hunt's Merchants' Magazine*, Vol. LII, p. 146.

[3] *Commercial and Financial Chronicle*, Vol. II, p. 34.

The very great decrease both in the number and the liabilities of firms that failed is the best proof that almost all business enterprises were "making money."

From one point of view the small number of failures is surprising. An unstable currency is generally held to make business unsafe, and seldom has the standard money of a mercantile community proven so unstable, undergone such violent fluctuations in so short a time, as in the United States of the Civil War. Yet, instead of being extremely hazardous, business seems from the statistics of failures to have been more than usually safe.

The explanation of the anomaly seems to be that the very extremity of the danger proved a safeguard. Business men realized that the inflation of prices was due to the depreciation of the currency, and that when the war was over gold would fall and prices follow. They realized very clearly the necessity of taking precautions against being caught in a position where a sudden decline of prices would ruin them. How they did this by curtailing credits has been shown in the preceding chapter. So long as prices continued to rise such precautions were really not needed by the man in active business except, in so far as he was a creditor of other men; but when prices commenced to fall prudence had its reward. Such a sudden and violent drop of prices as occurred between January and July, 1865, would have brought a financial revulsion of a most serious character upon a business community under ordinary circumstances. But so well had the change been prepared for, that the number of failures was actually less than it had been in the preceding year of rapidly rising prices.

The whole situation can hardly be explained better than it was by a New York business man writing in *Harper's Monthly Magazine:* "When the war ended," he said, " we all knew we should have a panic. Some of us, like Mr. Hoar, expected that greenbacks and volunteers would be disbanded together.   Others expected gold to fall to 101 or 102 in a few days.   Others saw a collapse of manufacturing industry, owing to the cessation of government purchases.   But we all knew a 'crisis' was coming, and having set our houses in order accordingly, the 'crisis' of course never came."[1]

[1] Vol. XL, p. 747.

CHAPTER IX

THE PRODUCTION AND CONSUMPTION OF WEALTH

I. *Production:*
Attempt of Publicists to Demonstrate Prosperity of the North
During the War — Contemporary Criticisms — Effect of the Paper
Currency on Production — Influence of High Profits on Industrial
Enterprises Counterbalanced by Uncertainty of the Future — And
by Attractiveness of Speculative Lines of Trade.

II. *Consumption:*
Contemporary Complaints of Extravagance — Increased Consumption of Articles of Luxury — Decreased Consumption of Necessities
and Comforts.

I. PRODUCTION

DURING the Civil War the question whether or not the
loyal states were really "prosperous" was debated with much
zeal. Supporters of the Greenback policy, like Spaulding
and Hooper, were in the habit of claiming that the paper
currency "operated very beneficially upon the business of
the country" and promoted the general well-being of the
people.[1] "It is an indisputable fact," said Hooper in January, 1863, "that the material interests of the North were
never more prosperous than at present."[2]

From Congress such assertions passed on to newspapers
and pamphleteers. Publicists of the prominence of Dr. William Elder, D. A. Wells, and Lorin Blodget employed their
pens in drawing most cheerful pictures of the condition and
prospects of the country. A brief citation from the first
writer will suffice to indicate the general character of the
conclusions at which these optimistic patriots arrived: "The
knowledge of an immensely enhanced activity in all branches

[1] Spaulding, *Congressional Globe*, 37th Cong., 3d Sess., p. 288.
[2] *Ibid.*, p. 386.

of industry," said Dr. Elder, "is brought home to everybody in the free states by the almost perfect distribution of its benefits. One class, and one class only, of the people, and that a class which the general prosperity always injures, suffers something—the class of annuitants, salaried officers, and people living upon accumulated capital."[1]

The general tone of all these pamphlets suggests that the primary object of the writers who prepared them was to encourage the public to accept heavy taxation without grumbling, and to invest their savings in government bonds without hesitation. Laudable as such a design may have been, it was not conducive to impartial selection of data or to successful analysis, and sober-minded critics had no difficulty in showing to such as would listen that the boasted prosperity was not so real as it seemed. The little pamphlet, "Are We Prosperous?" by "A Boston Merchant" is a good example of the protests against accepting the specious appearances of activity in business as sufficient evidence of actual increase in well-being. The booklet begins by admitting that "labor is fully employed, ... trade is active, ... money plenty," and that everywhere "are heard rejoicings over our prosperity." But, runs the argument, if true prosperity consists "in the productive employment of labor," there is no great ground for congratulation. For nearly a million of men are engaged in the service of the government and nearly a million more are making materials of war. So far as the work of supplying the wants of the community is concerned, all these persons are "not only non-producers, but are destroyers and consumers of the capital of the country." The "enhanced activity" of trade and

---

[1] *Debt and Resources of the United States* (Philadelphia, June, 1863), pp. 21, 23, 24; *cf.* WELLS, *Our Burden and Our Strength*, Troy, N. Y., 1864; BLODGET, *The Commercial and Financial Strength of the United States*, Philadelphia, 1864. Also see the series of letters published in London by ROBERT J. WALKER, under the title *American Finances and Resources*, 1863 and 1864.

the full employment of labor mean only that the people left at home are working more than usually hard in the effort to supply these non-producers as well as themselves with the requisites of life. The producers who sell to the government are receiving in exchange not products that are wealth, but evidences of debt., This unproductive employment of labor, consumption of capital without replacement, and rapid accumulation of debt, may quicken the pace of business, but it does not make true prosperity.[1]

From the present point of view it would be improper to enter at length upon the question in what degree the production and accumulation of wealth were retarded in the years from 1861 to 1865. Such a discussion would involve an attempt to gauge the relative importance of several indeterminate elements, such as the degree in which the labor force of the North was weakened by enlistments, how far the withdrawal of laborers into the army was compensated by the increased exertions of those who stayed at home, how far the introduction of labor-saving machinery in agriculture and other industries was promoted by the lack of hands, whether industry suffered from lack of capital because of the huge sums lent the government, etc. All these problems lie beyond the scope of the present inquiry. But it is pertinent to ask here: what influence did the greenback currency have as one of the many factors that affected the production of wealth? On this problem the preceding investigations throw some light.

In the first place, the paper standard was responsible in large measure for the feeling of "prosperity" that seems from all the evidence to have characterized the public's frame of mind. Almost every owner of property found that the price of his possessions had increased, and almost every

[1] *Is Our Prosperity a Delusion? Our National Debt and Currency,* by a Boston Merchant (A. W. STETSON ?), Boston, 1864. The title on the cover is *The Age of Greenbacks.*

wage-earner found that his pay was advanced. Strive as people may to emancipate themselves from the feeling that a dollar represents a fixed quantity of desirable things, it is very difficult for them to resist a pleasurable sensation when the money value of their property rises or their incomes increase. They are almost certain to feel cheerful over the larger sums that they can spend, even though the amount of commodities the larger sums will buy is decreased. Habit is too strong for arithmetic.

But, more than this, "business" in the common meaning of the word was unusually profitable during the war. The "residual claimant" of the last chapter is in most enterprises the active business man, and, as has been shown, his money income did as a rule rise more rapidly than the cost of living. Only in those cases where the advance of the product with which the given individual was concerned lagged so far behind the advance of those things that he wished to buy as to neutralize the gain which he made at the expense of his employees and creditors, was the business man actually worse off. In other words, "business" was, in reality as well as in appearance, rendered more profitable by the greenbacks. There is therefore no error in saying that the business of the country enjoyed unwonted prosperity during the war. And it may be added that the active business man is probably a more potent factor in determining the community's feeling about "good times" and "bad times" than is the working-man, the landlord, or the lending capitalist.

The effect of high profits, however, is not limited to producing a cheerful frame of mind among business men. Under ordinary circumstances one would say that when the great majority of men already in business are "making money" with more than usual rapidity they will be inclined to enlarge their operations, that others will be inclined to enter the field, and that thus the production of wealth will be stimulated. But the circumstances of the war period were not ordinary and this conclusion cannot be accepted without serious modifications.

1. It has been shown that business men realized the precariousness of all operations that depended for their success upon the future course of prices — and nearly all operations that involved any considerable time for their consummation were thus dependent. So far did this disposition prevail that it produced a marked curtailment in the use of credit. The prudent man might be willing to push his business as far as possible with the means at his own disposal, but he showed a disinclination to borrow for the purpose. Thus the uncertainty which all men felt about the future in a large measure counteracted the influence of high profits in increasing production.

2. The foregoing consideration of course weighed most heavily in the minds of cautious men. But not all business men are cautious. Among many the chance of winning large profits in case of success is sufficient to induce them to undertake heavy risks of loss. On the whole, Americans seem to display a decided propensity toward speculative ventures and are not easily deterred by having to take chances. To men of this type it seems that the business opportunities offered by the fluctuating currency would make a strong appeal. But, while the force of this observation may be admitted, it does not necessitate a reconsideration of the conclusion that the instability of prices tended to diminish the production of wealth. For in a time of great price fluctuations the possibilities of making fortunes rapidly are much greater in trade than in agriculture, mining, or manufactures. Every rise and fall in quotations holds out an alluring promise of quick gain to the man who believes in his shrewdness and good fortune, and who does not hesitate to take chances. The probable profits of productive industry

in the narrower sense might be larger than common, but this would not attract investors in large numbers if the probable profits of trading were larger yet; and such seems clearly to have been the case during the war when the paper currency offered such brilliant possibilities to fortunate speculators in gold, in stocks, or in commodities. Instead, then, of the greenbacks being credited with stimulating the production of wealth, they must be charged with offering inducements to abandon agriculture and manufactures for the more speculative forms of trade.

This tendency of the times did not escape observation. On the contrary, it was often remarked and lamented in terms that seem exaggerated. Hugh McCulloch, for instance, in his report as secretary of the treasury for 1865, said:

> There are no indications of real and permanent prosperity . . . . in the splendid fortunes reported to be made by skilful manipulations at the gold room or the stock board; no evidences of increasing wealth in the facts that railroads and steamboats are crowded with passengers, and hotels with guests; that cities are full to overflowing, and rents and the necessities of life, as well as luxuries, are daily advancing. All these things prove rather . . . . that the number of non-producers is increasing, and that productive industry is being diminished. There is no fact more manifest than that the plethora of paper money is not only undermining the morals of the people by encouraging waste and extravagance, but is striking at the root of our material prosperity by diminishing labor.[1]

More explicit was Mr. Wells's statement of the movement away from industry and toward speculative trading. In one of his reports as special commissioner of the revenue he said:

> During the last few years large numbers of our population, under the influence and example of high profits realized in trading during the period of monetary expansion, have abandoned employments directly productive of national wealth, and sought employments connected with commerce, trading, or speculation. As a

[1] P. 9.

consequence we everywhere find large additions to the population of our commercial cities, an increase in the number and cost of the buildings devoted to banking, brokerage, insurance, commission business, and agencies of all kinds, the spirit of trading and speculating pervading the whole community, as distinguished from the spirit of production.[1]

Within the period under review, then, it seems very doubtful whether the high profits had their usual effect of leading to a larger production of raw materials or to an increase in manufactures. The prudent man hesitated to expand his undertakings because of the instability of the inflated level of prices; the man with a turn for speculative ventures found more alluring opportunities in trade.

II.   CONSUMPTION

No one can read contemporary comments on American social life of the later years of the war without being impressed by the charges of extravagance made against the people of the North. Newspapers and pulpits were at one in denouncing the sinful waste that, they declared, was increasing at a most alarming rate. The "shoddy aristocracy" with its ostentatious display of wealth became a stock subject for cartoonists at home, and earned a well-merited reputation for vulgarity abroad. So common are the comments on this subject that no specific references need be given; one has only to examine the files of newspapers and magazines, or to read published sermons or letters, to find how universally observers were impressed by the prevalence of extravagant expenditure.

[1] *Executive Document No. 27*, 41st Cong., 2d Sess., p. xxxi. *Cf.* CHARLES A. MANN, *Paper Money*, pp. 187-94. The opponents of the greenback party were fond of pointing to the less rapid increase of national wealth between 1860 and 1870 than between 1850 and 1860, shown by the figures of the federal census, as an indication of the influence of the paper currency in discouraging production. *Cf.* AMASA WALKER, *The National Currency* (New York, 1876), p. 44; *The Nation* (New York), Vol. XII, p. 286; WELLS'S fourth report, cited at the beginning of this note, p. xxxi. The imperfections of the Census of 1870, however, to say nothing of the unreliability of statistics of national wealth in all American censuses, make these data of slight value.

In trying to account for this unpleasant phase of social development, men usually laid the blame upon the paper standard. High prices were said to make everyone feel suddenly richer and so to tempt everyone to adopt a more lavish style of living than his former wont. Thus the view gained general credence that the greenbacks were ultimately responsible for a great increase in the consumption of wealth.

If the conclusions reached in the preceding chapters regarding the changes in the distribution of wealth caused by the paper money are sound, however, such a view regarding the consumption of wealth can be but partially true. The enormous profits of "residual claimants" made possible the rapid accumulation of an unusual number of fortunes, and the families thus lifted into sudden affluence enjoyed spending their money in the ostentatious fashion characteristic of the newly rich. It is therefore true that the monetary situation was largely responsible for the appearance of a considerable class of persons— of whom the fortunate speculator and the army contractor are typical— who plunged into the recklessly extravagant habits that called down upon their heads the condemnation of the popular moralist.

But if the greenbacks were in the last resort a chief cause of the increased consumption of articles of luxury by families whom they had aided in enriching, they were not less truly a cause of restricted consumption by a much larger class of humbler folk. The laboring man whose money wages increased but one-half, while the cost of living doubled, could not continue to provide for his family's wants so fully as before. He was forced to practice economies — to wear his old clothing longer, to use less coffee and less sugar, to substitute cheaper for better qualities in every line of expenditure where possible. Similar retrenchment of living expenses must have been practiced by the families of many owners of land and lenders of capital. In other words, the war-time fortunes resulted in a very large measure from the mere transfer of wealth from a wide circle of persons to the relatively small number of residual claimants to the proceeds of business enterprises. The enlarged consumption of wealth which the paper currency made possible for the fortunate few was therefore contrasted with a diminished consumption on the part of the unfortunate many on whose slender means the greenbacks levied contributions for the benefit of their employers.

That the diminished consumption of wealth by large numbers of poor people escaped general notice, while the extravagance of the newly rich attracted so much attention, need not shake one's confidence in the validity of these conclusions. The purchase of a fast trotting-horse by a government contractor, and the elaborateness of his wife's gowns and jewelry, are much more conspicuous facts than the petty economies practiced by his employees. The same trait that leads fortunate people to flaunt their material prosperity in the eyes of the world leads the unfortunate to conceal their small privations. Even an attentive observer may fail to notice that the wives of workingmen are still wearing their last year's dresses and that the children are running barefoot longer than usual.

But though the newspapers were not full of comments on the enforced economies of the mass of the population, wholesale dealers in staple articles of food and clothing noticed a decrease in sales. In reviewing the trade situation in September, 1864, when real wages were near their lowest ebb, *Hunt's Merchants' Magazine* remarked that "the rise in the prices of commodities has . . . . outrun the power of consumption and the fall trade has been almost at a stand. Those articles such as coffee, sugar, low grade goods, which [form] the staple products of the great mass of the people in moderate circumstances, has [sic] reached such high rates that the decline in consumption is very marked, amounting almost to a stagnation of the fall trade." [1]

It would be of exceeding interest to trace the temporary change in the character of the consumption of the people that resulted from the artificial alteration of the distribution of wealth by the greenback currency — to see, for example, how the consumption of tobacco and liquors was affected as compared with the consumption of sugar, coffee, flour, and woolen fabrics. But unfortunately there are no reliable data to serve as the basis of such an investigation. The Revenue Commission of 1865–66 made an attempt to estimate the decline in the consumption of cotton, tea, coffee, sugar, and molasses, but its figures are too largely the results of guesswork to possess much significance. [2] All that can be said with assurance is that the consumption of many articles of luxury increased very greatly, while the consumption of many staple articles declined. It is probable that in the first year or two of the war a spirit of economy pervaded nearly all classes of the people. [3] As the characteristic effects of the greenback standard began to make themselves felt, still more careful supervision of expenditures was forced upon wage-earners and small owners of land and lenders of capital, while residual claimants began to find their profits uncommonly great. The great fall of prices in the first half of 1865, combined with the continued advance of money wages, alleviated the situation of the first class of persons, though it did not quite restore them to the situation that existed before the war. To residual claimants it brought a reduction in profits that was in part merely nominal — the expression of their fortunes in fewer figures,

[1] Vol. LI, p. 243; cf. also pp. 370, 447.

[2] H. R. Executive Document No. 34, 39th Cong., 1st Sess., Special Reports Nos.1-4.

[3] Cf., e. g., remarks of T. M. Parker, Congressional Globe, 37th Cong., 2d Sess., p. 885; "Report of the Bank Commissioners of the State of Maine," December, 1862, in Executive Document No. 20, 38th Cong., 1st Sess., p. 3.

but with a denominator of enhanced value — and in part real — the relative increase in the shares of the product that went to other co-operators in production and the increased value of the dollars in which whatever pecuniary obligations they had contracted must be paid. But, on the other hand, the fact that they had survived the sharp fall of prices that they had foreseen would come with the end of the war relieved their minds of a great source of anxiety, and put them in a position to enjoy the gains that they had saved. Consequently in 1865, consumption of goods of all kinds probably increased over that of 1864; of staple articles, because money wages had risen, while prices had fallen; of luxuries, because, though profits were less enormous, fortunes were felt to be less precarious.

CHAPTER X

THE GREENBACKS AND THE COST OF THE CIVIL WAR

I. *The Problem and the Method of Solution:*
Financial *vs.* Economic Consequences of the Legal-Tender Acts —
Various Estimates of Increase in Debt Caused by Greenbacks —
Method by which Estimate Should Proceed.

II. *The Greenbacks and Expenditures:*
Difference Between Increase of Expenditures for Commodities and
for Services — Difficulty of Distinguishing Between the two Classes
in Government Accounts — Estimate of Increase in Ordinary
Expenditures.

III. *The Greenbacks and Receipts:*
Effect of Depreciation on Various Items of Revenue — Indirect
Financial Consequences of the Legal-tender Acts.

IV. *The Greenbacks and the Public Debt:*
Danger of Double Computation of Loss by Greenbacks — Terms
on Which Bonds were Sold — Saving and Loss of Interest.

V. *Conclusion:*
Net Effect of Greenbacks on Amount of Debt Incurred During
War — Financial Consequences after Return of Peace.

I. THE PROBLEM AND THE METHOD OF SOLUTION

DISCUSSION of the consequences of the legal-tender acts
has so far been confined to the economic relations between
individuals. There is, however, another phase of the subject to be considered. The reader who turns back to the
account of the debates upon the legal-tender bills will find
that most of the unfortunate consequences that followed
their enactment were foretold in Congress — the decline of
real wages, the injury done creditors, the uncertainty of
prices that hampered legitimate business and fostered speculation. But a majority of this Congress were ready to subject the community to such ills because they believed that

403

the relief of the treasury from its embarrassments was of more importance than the maintenance of a relatively stable monetary standard. There was little of that confusion between economic and fiscal considerations that has frequently been held responsible for the attempts of government to use its power over the currency as a financial resource. Rather, there was a conscious subordination of the interest of the community in a stable monetary standard to the interest of the government in obtaining funds to carry on the war. It is therefore incumbent upon one who would judge the policy from the standpoint of its sponsors to inquire into the financial effects which to them seemed most important as well as into the effects on the distribution of wealth.

This topic has two aspects—one of which has already been discussed. Power to issue greenbacks formed a quickly available financial resource from which the treasury was able to meet large amounts of indebtedness already accumulated when the legal-tender acts were passed. But while such issues relieved immediate needs, their ultimate effect was to increase the future demands on the treasury. The first of these consequences has been dealt with in the historical chapters of Part I, where an attempt was made to show how much immediate help the greenbacks afforded Mr. Chase. It remains for the present chapter to treat the larger question: What effect had the greenbacks upon the amount of expenditures incurred?

Few questions raised by the legal-tender acts have attracted more attention than this last. Even while the first legal-tender bill was being considered its critics declared that if made a law it would increase the cost of waging the war by causing an advance in the prices of articles that the government had to buy.[1] As the war went

[1] See Part I, chap. ii, p. 57.

on the soundness of this view became apparent. Simon
Newcomb, writing early in 1865, estimated that by the end of
1864 the greenbacks had increased the amount of indebtedness incurred by the federal government $180,000,000
beyond the amount that would have been incurred had the
specie standard been maintained.   Even if the war should
end in 1865, he prophesied, $300,000,000 more would be
added to this needless augmentation of the debt.[1]

When the war was over and the divers reasons that had
deterred many men from criticising the financial policy of
the government were removed, competent writers began to
express similar views with freedom.   For example, Mr. H.
R. Hulburd, comptroller of the currency, said in his report
for 1867: "Probably not less than 33 per cent. of the
present indebtedness of the United States is owing to the
high prices paid by the government while its disbursements
were heaviest."[2]   Mr. C. P. Williams put the increase of
debt at one-third to two-fifths; C. A. Mann, at one-fourth;
S. T. Spear, at a billion dollars; L. H. Courtney, an English
critic, at nearly $900,000,000.[3]   Of later discussions that of
Professor H. C. Adams has attracted the most attention.
He estimated that of the gross receipts from debts created
between January 1, 1862, and September 30, 1865, amounting to $2,565,000,000 the gold value was but $1,695,-
000,000 — a difference of $870,000,000 between value received
and obligations incurred.[4]

All of these estimates seem to rest either upon guesses or
upon reduction of sums borrowed in currency to specie value.
The former method of arriving at the result inspires little

---

[1] *Critical Examination of our Financial Policy* (New York, 1865), pp. 171, 172.

[2] *Finance Report*, 1867, p. 15.

[3] See *A Review of the Financial Situation of Our Country* (Albany, 1868), p. 7;
Paper Money (New York, 1873), p. 184; *The Legal-Tender Acts* (New York, 1875), p. 78;
Journal of the Royal Statistical Society, Vol. XXXI, p. 204.

[4] *Public Debts*, p. 131.

confidence even when the guesses are made by men intimately familiar with the federal finances, and the latter method assumes that all government expenditures rose in proportion to the decline in the specie value of the greenback dollar, and that all revenues remained what they would have been on a special basis—assumptions subject to important exceptions.[1] The problem of ascertaining the financial consequences of the greenback issues is much too complex to be solved by methods so crude. Some branches of expenditure were much affected by the depreciation of the currency, other branches but little. The effect of the paper currency on the receipts of the government is quite as important a part of the problem as the effect on expenditures, and examination shows that here as there different items were affected in very different degrees. Finally, the greenbacks were themselves a "loan without interest" though, on the other hand, they increased the volume of the interest-bearing debt by augmenting expenditures. These three topics, then—the influence of the paper-money standard on ordinary expenditures and receipts, and on interest— must all be examined by anyone who hopes to frame an adequate estimate of the net effect of the greenbacks on the cost of the war. As will appear, however, examination of these topics is beset by serious difficulties.

II.   Greenbacks and Expenditures

It is a familiar remark of writers on public finance that all things required by government fall into one of two categories—commodities and services. If the conclusions of the preceding chapters on prices and wages are well founded, it follows that this elementary distinction regard-

---

[1] Professor Adams is free from this reproach, for he is careful not to say that his figures represent the difference made by the greenback policy in the cost of the war. This latter interpretation, however, has been commonly put upon the passage. *E. g.*, see H. White, *Money and Banking*, 1st ed., p. 162.

ing the objects of government expenditure is of very great importance for the present problem. For, since prices advanced in much greater ratio than wages, it is clear that the greenback issues must have increased the sums paid for commodities more than the sums paid for labor. Indeed, this difference between increase in cost of commodities and of labor seems to have been much wider in the case of the government than in the case of private persons; for, as was shown in sec. viii of chap. v, the wages of federal employees were advanced on the average considerably less than the wages of other persons. Clearly, then, the first step in any estimate of the effect of the legal-tender act upon the expenditures incurred by government during the war should be a careful separation of expenditures for commodities from expenditures for services.

Accordingly, it is a very serious obstacle that one encounters in finding that such a separation cannot readily be made. A statement of the expenditures of the preceding fiscal year is published in each annual report of the secretary of the treasury. But in these statements the items are arranged rather according to the department of government through or for which the specified sums were spent, than according to the object of expenditure. For example, the first general division of expenditures is placed under the caption "Civil," and under this caption the first three items are "For Congress, including books," "For executive," "For judiciary." It is obvious that each of these items must include payments for both commodities and services; but there is no way of separating the two classes of payments.

A more detailed statement is given in the annual *Account of the Receipts and Expenditures of the United States* rendered by the register of the treasury. But even these bulky documents do not make possible such a division of expenditures as is desired. A careful examination of the register's accounts for the fiscal years 1863–65 shows that about one-third of the total expenditures each year consists of items which appear to include payments for both labor and commodities in unknown proportions. Such, for example, are expenditures upon fortifications, armories, and hospitals, repairs of ships, construction of buildings, incidental expenses of various bureaus, and the like. The best that can be done with these accounts is to divide the items into three classes: (1) expenditures for salaries and the like, most of which appear to have been little affected by the paper currency; (2) expenditures for commodities; (3) expenditures that include payments for both commodities and labor. Even with such a scheme of classification it is sometimes difficult to decide where certain items should be placed.

If this division of expenditures be accepted, the next step is to determine in what ratio the expenditures falling within each of the three classes shall be assumed to have been increased. In the first class the largest items are the pay of the regular and volunteer armies. As was shown in sec. viii of chap. v the wages of private soldiers was increased from $13 to $16 per month after May 1, 1864. Since this increase was made with the avowed object of compensating soldiers in some measure for the decline in the purchasing power of the paper money, one must consider three-sixteenths of the pay of the army after that time as an addition to the money cost of the war. It is not improbable also that, had the specie standard been maintained, it would have been unnecessary to grant such lavish bounties to stimulate enlistments. If so, a part at least of the large sums reported as paid in bounties should be added to the increase in the cost of the war. To be on the safe side, however, this item will be neglected. As for other employees of the government besides the soldiers, it appears that in few cases were the money salaries increased beyond the scale prevailing before suspension. No doubt it was largely from motives of patriotism that so many men in humble as well as in conspicuous positions remained in the service of the government at wages they would have accepted from no private employer. Their self-sacrifice lessened the effect of the greenbacks upon the cost of the war in dollars and cents. But from any other than the narrowest fiscal point of view it was one of the most unfortunate consequences of the paper-money régime that the men who were serving the country faithfully were compelled to submit to a great decrease in their real incomes.

With respect to the second of the above described classes of expenditures, the question of interest is whether the depreciation of the currency affected the prices paid by the government for commodities as much as it did prices paid by private purchasers at wholesale. Reference to the tables in sec. iii of chap. iv will show that the statistical material gleaned from the *Aldrich Report* indicates that public contractors did not advance their prices quite as rapidly as other dealers. But it must be remembered that the two series there brought into comparison are not constructed in the same fashion—one series gives the averages of four relative prices each year; the other gives the relative average prices of twelve months in some cases and of prices for unstated dates in others. Moreover, many of the government series are based on prices for 1861 instead of for 1860, and in the former year the government seems to have been paying rather higher prices than in the latter. Still further the whole number of articles included in the government list is not great, and about half belong to a single and financially unimportant group — drugs and chemicals. Finally, it is not improbable that there were changes in the qualities of some articles accepted from contractors that account for a relatively slight increase in price. For these various reasons the divergence between the two series possesses little significance.

Much greater weight should be attached to the general conclusion drawn in chap. iv—that the dominant factor in determining prices during the war was the fluctuating valuation of the currency. There is no reason why knowledge that he would be paid in greenbacks should affect in different degrees the prices that a dealer would ask from the government and from private men. Since, then, the fairly satisfactory wholesale-price data show a rather close parallelism between prices of commodities and of gold, it seems fair to infer that the sums asked of the government for identical goods also rose and fell in rough agreement with the premium. True, prices seem not to have advanced so quickly as did the gold quotation, but neither did they fall so quickly. Everything considered, then, the most trustworthy index of the increase in the sums expended by the government upon commodities is probably found in the average premium upon gold in the several fiscal years.

An even larger element of conjecture enters into the estimate of the increase in the expenditures of the third class, which includes payments for both commodities and labor. So far as commodities are concerned it is as fair here as in Class II to apply the average premium upon gold as an index of the increase. But with reference to labor a new problem arises. The salaries of most persons in the regular service of the government, aside from soldiers, were not increased at all. But the titles of the items grouped in Class III as they appear in the register's accounts seem to indicate that the great mass of the labor was not that of officials, but that of workmen employed on a strictly commercial basis. In constructing fortifications, erecting and repairing public buildings, etc., it is probable that the government or its contractors paid as much for the labor hired as a private employer would have done. If so, it follows that the best index of the increased expenditure on the labor included in this class is found in the tables of chap. v, particularly Table XXX, which shows the averave relative wages for all em-

TABLE LXIV

ESTIMATED INCREASE IN THE ORDINARY EXPENDITURES OF THE FEDERAL GOVERN-
MENT CAUSED BY THE GREENBACKS

(In millions of dollars)

	FISCAL YEARS				
	1862 Six Months	1863	1864	1865	1866 Two Months
Expenditures:[1]					
Class I, salaries, etc........	92	242	259	408	45
Class II, commodities	82	214	258	402	43
Class III, both labor and commodities	89	238	294	405	44
Assumed ratio of increase:					
Class II[2].................	3%	37%	56%	102%	43%
Class III[3]	3%	27%	44%	77%	49%
Estimated actual increase:					
Class I, increase in pay of soldiers[4]	..	..	6	62	20
Class II..................	2	58	93	203	13
Class III	3	51	90	176	14
Total estimated increase each year	5	109	189	441	47

[1] The figures for the fiscal years 1863-65 are obtained from the annual reports on "Receipts and Expenditures." For the second half of the fiscal year 1862 the ordinary expenditures were estimated on the basis of the "Treasurer's Accounts" (*H. R. Ex. Doc. No. 4,* 38th Cong., 1st Sess.), and these expenditures were divided among the three classes according to the proportions given by the computations for 1863. Similarly, the expenditures for the months July and August, 1865, are assumed to be two-thirds of the total for the quarter July to September and are divided among the three classes in the same ratio as the expenditures for the fiscal year 1865.

[2] Average premium upon gold as given in Appendix A below.

[3] Average of premium on gold and increase in money wages according to system of variable weights, as shown by Table XXX above. For wages in each fiscal year I have taken the index number for January of the corresponding calendar year.

[4] Three-sixteenths of pay of army (except bounties) after May 1, 1864, as the pay is reported in "Receipts and Expenditures." For the months July and August, 1865, the increase is computed on one-half the sum stated by the paymaster-general as paid to the army between June 30 and October 31. (*Ex. Doc. No. 1,* Part II, p. 898, 39th Cong., 1st Sess.)

ployees for whom data are given in Table XII of the *Aldrich Report*. Assuming so much, we have two ratios of increase in expenditure for this class—one applicable to the prices of commodities, the other to the wages of labor. Since there is no way of distinguishing between expenditure for goods and labor it is necessary to make some purely arbitrary assumption regarding their relative amounts. The simplest assumption is that the increase in the total expenditures of Class III was midway between the average premium upon gold and the average increase in money wages. Perhaps this assumption may be accepted as well as any other, for, if no definite reason can be assigned for it, neither can any reason be assigned in favor of any rival assumption.

In accordance with the preceding plan, Table LXIV has been constructed to show the probable increase in the expenditure of the government caused by the issues of paper money between the date of suspension and August 31, 1865, when the public debt reached its maximum amount.[1] The total increase for the whole period is $791,000,000. After all that has been said of the elements that enter into the problem it is hardly necessary to insist strenuously that this total is but a very rough estimate.

III.   THE GREENBACKS AND RECEIPTS

Almost all the writers who have discussed the financial consequences of the legal-tender acts have confined their attention to the increase of expenditures. This procedure is perhaps natural for ardent critics of the paper-money policy, but a little consideration shows that it is unfair. The reports of the secretary of the treasury give the government revenue under five heads—customs, sales of public lands, direct tax, miscellaneous sources, and internal revenue. Of these receipts some were and some were not affected by

[1] *Report of the Secretary of the Treasury*, 1866, p. 6.

the greenback issues.   In accordance with the provisions of the first legal-tender act customs duties were paid in gold, and the *ad valorem* duties were assessed on the foreign specie valuation of goods.   The receipts from this source therefore remained on substantially the same footing as if specie payments had been maintained.   During the war receipts from the sales of public lands were an item of little importance—less than $1,000,000 per year—despite the decline in the value of the currency that might be paid by the purchaser of lands.   The receipts from direct taxes were all collected under one law passed six months before suspension.   This law fixed the total amount of the tax at $20,000,000 and determined the precise amount to be raised by each state.[1]   Accordingly the legal-tender acts had no effect upon this item—except that the states were enabled to pay their quotas in greenbacks instead of in gold.   The revenue derived from miscellaneous sources includes a considerable number of small items.   Of these, some were doubtless increased by depreciation, *e. g.*, proceeds of sales of captured and abandoned property.   Other items were unaffected, *e. g.*, receipts of fees by American consuls abroad.   Premiums on sales of gold coin among these miscellaneous receipts may be set down from the present point of view as clear gain.

The last of the enumerated government receipts remains, the internal-revenue duties.   This system of taxation was inaugurated by an elaborate law passed July 1, 1862, which imposed certain duties, partly *ad valorem*, partly specific, upon a great variety of manufactured articles; imposed a tax upon the gross receipts of canals, railroads, theaters, etc.; taxed auction and brokers' sales; required licenses for practicing professions; levied an income and a legacy tax, and placed certain taxes upon articles of luxury, such as carriages,

[1] Act of August 6, 1861; 12 *Statutes at Large*, p. 294.

pianos and plate.[1]   This law was superseded two years later
by another internal-revenue act which raised the rates of
taxation, and increased the number of articles made to pay
dnties.[2]

At the time the first law was passed the depreciation of
the currency was not great, and probably the rates of taxation imposed do not differ much from what they would have
been upon a specie basis.   But without any modification
of the terms of the law, the progressive rise of prices must
have caused an increase of the revenue from *ad valorem*
duties, and from taxes on gross receipts and upon incomes.
Receipts from specific duties, licenses, etc., however, probably did not increase except as changes were made in the
law or in its administration.   While, then, the yield of this
most important of the sources of federal revenue was materially affected by the legal-tender acts, it would be too much
to argue, as was done with reference to expenditures for
commodities, that it was increased in the ratio indicated by
the premium on gold.   Some arbitrary assumption, however,
must be made regarding the ratio of increase if any estimate
is to be had.   Again, it is perhaps best to adopt the simplest
expedient, and count the increase of receipts from internal
taxes at the full amount indicated by the premium, but, on
the other hand, take no account of the increase of receipts
from miscellaneous sources.   Since the latter sums are
relatively small, it is probable that an estimate thus made
will err rather on the side of over, than of understating the
increase of revenue.

The total increase of receipts shown by this method as
applied in Table LXV is $174,000,000.   Again the caution

[1] 12 *Statutes at Large*, pp. 432-89. The amendments to this act were not such as to
increase the total revenue derived from it. See acts of July 17, 1862 (12 *Statutes*, p.
627) ; March 3, 1863 (*ibid.*, pp. 713-31), and March 7, 1864 (13 *Statutes*, p. 14).

[2] Act of June 30, 1864, 13 *Statutes at Large*, pp. 223-306; amended by act of March
3, 1865, (*ibid.*, pp. 469-87).

TABLE LXV

ESTIMATED INCREASE IN THE ORDINARY RECEIPTS OF THE FEDERAL GOVERNMENT
CAUSED BY THE GREENBACKS

(In millions of dollars)

	Fiscal Year 1862 (Six Months)	Fiscal Year 1863	Fiscal Year 1864	Fiscal Year 1865	Fiscal Year 1866 (Two Months)
Current receipts:[1]					
From customs	33.5	69.1	102.3	84.9	31.3
From sales of public lands.	.1	.2	.6	1.0	.1
From direct tax...........	1.8	1.5	.5	1.2	.0
From miscellaneous sources	.5	3.0	47.5	33.0	12.3
From internal revenue	.....	37.6	109.7	209.5	64.4
	35.9	111.4	260.6	329.6	108.1
Assumed ratio of increase ...	3%	37%	56%	102%	43%
Estimated actual increase ...	0	10	39	106	19

is hardly necessary that the result is to be accepted subject to a wide margin of error.

So far the discussion of the increase both of expenditures and of revenues has proceeded as if the paper currency had exerted none but simple and direct effects.   There were other financial consequences of the shift from the specie to the paper standard, however, that were not unimportant, though they were indirect and difficult to gauge.   Three of the most prominent must be indicated.

1. It is probable that not a little of the lavishness with which public funds were appropriated by Congress during the war can be traced to the paper-money policy.   At least such was the opinion of a man so well placed to observe the operations of the treasury as Hugh McCulloch.   In his report of 1867 he said: "As long as notes could be issued and bonds could be sold at a premium or at par, for what the

[1] As given by the annual statements of the register of the treasury (see *Finance Reports*, 1862, p. 37; 1863, pp. 34, 35; 1864, p. 33; 1865, pp. 44, 45, 48).   For 1862 the receipts of the last two quarters of the year are given; for 1866 two-thirds of the receipts for the first quarter.

statute made money, there was a constant temptation to liberal, if not unnecessary, expenditures. Had the specie standard been maintained and bonds been sold at a discount for real money, there would have been an economy in all branches of the public service which unfortunately was not witnessed." [1]

2. If the paper currency tempted the government to reckless expenditures, it also predisposed the people to submit more willingly to heavy taxation. It has been remarked several times that the advance of money wages and of money prices made most people feel wealthier, and, feeling wealthier, they were less inclined to grumble over the taxes.

3. But while the feeling of prosperity may have been instrumental in procuring a cheerful acceptance of war taxes, it is very doubtful whether the net effect of the paper-money system was favorable to revenue. It was pointed out in the last chapter that the lagging of money wages behind money prices necessarily diminished the consumption of wealth among wage-earners. In so far as this diminution affected the consumption of articles that paid either an import or an excise duty—and there were but few articles exempt from taxation by one of these methods—the fall of real wages must have lessened the tax receipts. Much the same must have been true, although in less degree, of the indirect taxes collected from the consumption of the great agricultural class, if the conclusion of chap. viii is true, that farmers were injured rather than benefited by the price fluctuations. On the other hand, the extravagance of the fortunate families enriched by the receipt of high profits tended to increase the revenue for the time being; but it is improbable that the increase of receipts from the enlarged consumption of this limited class offset the decrease of receipts from the enforced economies of wage-earners and farmers.

[1] *Report of the Secretary of the Treasury*, November 30, 1867, p. xi.

While, then, these indirect effects of the paper currency on expenditures and receipts could not by any system of bookkeeping be brought to definite quantitative statement, it is probable that their net result was unfavorable to the treasury.

IV. THE GREENBACKS AND THE PUBLIC DEBT

It may seem that in a discussion of the financial consequences of the legal-tender acts account should be taken of the effect of the desertion of the specie standard upon the terms on which the government could borrow. The resort to a legal-tender paper currency, one may argue, is a confession of acute financial distress and as such must depress the market for bonds. Therefore, to the financial loss caused by the increase of expenditures should be added a second loss from the unfavorable terms to which the government had to submit in selling its securities.

Of course, it is true that the secretaries of the treasury in their efforts to borrow money were obliged to agree to some very hard bargains. There was little ground for exultation over the sale at par of bonds bearing interest at 5 or 6 per cent. in gold when the currency received from purchasers was worth in specie but 50 per cent. of its face value. But this loss arising from the difference in value between the paper dollars received by the treasury for bonds and the specie dollars which the treasury contracted to pay bond-holders after a term of years is not a further loss in addition to the losses discussed in the preceding sections, but rather these same losses looked at from another point of view. For, the estimate of the increase of expenditures above receipts, and therefore of debt contracted, rests precisely upon the decline in the value of the paper dollar from the specie standard. One may arrive at an estimate of the loss either by computing the increase in the number of dollars that had to be borrowed in paper money to be repaid in gold, or by estimating the decline in the specie value of the paper money raised by the sale of bonds; but to make estimates by both of these methods would be to include two guesses at the same item.

It is, of course, true that, had gold bonds been sold largely at less than par for paper money, a second loss would have been incurred from the discount in addition to the loss from the smaller purchasing power of the currency received. But, as a matter of fact, the deviations from par in the subscription prices for bonds were not of great importance. The prices of government securities did not fluctuate very widely during the war, for the very good reason that these prices showed merely the value of one set of government promises to pay, viz., bonds—in terms of another set—viz., greenbacks. Most factors that affected the credit of the government would affect the specie value of all its promises in much the same manner, and therefore would not alter materially the ratio of one to another.

It remains only to say a word about the effect of the legal-tender acts upon the interest charge borne by the government. The great financial argument in favor of the greenbacks has always been that they constitute a "loan without interest." However many millions the depreciation of this currency added to the principal of the public debt, the greenbacks should be credited with whatever sum was really saved in this fashion. But against the saving of interest effected by issuing greenbacks instead of selling bonds should be put down the loss of interest on the increase of debt arising from the augmentation of expenditures. If the rate of interest be taken at 6 per cent., a simple calculation shows that the interest saved by the greenbacks up to August 31, 1865, was but $28,000,000 greater than the interest lost through the excess of increase of expenditures over the increase of receipts as shown by Tables LXIV and LXV. By the end of this period the augmentation of debt caused by the greenbacks had apparently become greater than the volume of greenbacks in circulation, so that from this time forward the annual loss of interest probably exceeded the gain.

V. CONCLUSION

The public debt reached its maximum amount August 31, 1865, when it stood at $2,846,000,000.[1] Of this immense debt the preceding estimates indicate that some $589,000,000, or rather more than a fifth of the whole amount, was due to the substitution of United States notes for metallic money. Little as these estimates can pretend to accuracy, it seems safe at least to accept the conclusion that the greenbacks increased the debt incurred during the war by a sum running into the hundreds of millions. If so, it follows that, even from the narrowly financial point of view of their sponsors, the legal-tender acts had singularly unfortunate consequences.

The present chapter, to agree with its predecessors, must end with the Civil War. But it may be pointed out that the financial effects of the legal-tender acts, like the economic effects, did not cease with the return of peace. No additional discussion is required to show that the varying depreciation of the currency continued to affect the volume of both receipts and expenditures until resumption of specie payments in January, 1879, restored the greenbacks to equality with gold. It is equally clear that the United States notes continued to be a "loan without interest," and that, on the other hand, the government continued to pay interest on the unnecessary debt created during the war. But there is another phase of the subject that deserves spe-

---

[1] *Report of the Secretary of the Treasury*, 1866, p. 6.

cial remark, because it is frequently overlooked. A considerable portion of the immense public debt in existence
August 31, 1865, consisted of obligations expressly payable
in " lawful money." In so far as the government was able
to pay these debts out of revenue before the greenbacks had
appreciated to par, it effected a saving.[1] But all such topics — the continued effect of depreciation on government
expenditures and revenue, the annual loss or gain of interest, the cost at which the " lawful money" debt was paid,
the expense at which specie payments were resumed, and
the difficulties encountered in maintaining the convertibility
of the paper money into specie — belong to a later period in
the history of the greenbacks. It is probable, however, that
were a careful study made of these topics the indictment
brought against the greenbacks on financial grounds would
be rendered yet more serious.

[1] Of course, when the lawful money debt was paid by refunding operations —
that is, out of the proceeds of new loans themselves payable in gold — no such savings
resulted, unless the new bonds were sold at a premium. An estimate of the saving
actually effected may be found in the *Journal of Political Economy*, Vol. V, pp. 146-9.
The total arrived at is $72,000,000. If this sum be deducted from the above estimate
of the increase in debt, the net loss to the government caused by the greenbacks
during the war will still appear to have been over half a billion in gold.

STATISTICAL APPENDICES

APPENDIX A

GOLD VALUE OF THE PAPER CURRENCY, 1862–65

EXPLANATORY NOTE.—There are two well-authenticated tables that show the average monthly and yearly value of currency in gold during the Civil War: (1) a table published by the *American Almanac* (see, *e. g.*, issue of 1889, p. 341); (2) a table prepared by the Bureau of Statistics (*Finance, Commerce and Immigration of the United States*, Series of 1895–96, No. 4, p. 518). For the years 1862–65 these tables are identical; the figures given below are taken from the second. This table was prepared by Mr. E. B. Elliott, actuary of the treasury, in the following manner: four daily quotations of the rates of gold at New York, viz., the opening, highest, lowest, and closing prices, were recorded; from them a daily average was made, and from these average daily prices was prepared the average rate for each month.

The table of daily highest and lowest prices is based, for the reasons assigned in the text (Part II, chap. iii, sec. i), upon the table given in the *Report of the Chamber of Commerce of the State of New York* for 1865–66, Part II, pp. 130–33. The figures for the first eleven days of January, 1862, however, are supplied from the daily reports of the premium on gold in the New York *Commercial Advertiser*.

TABLE 1

MONTHLY HIGHEST, AVERAGE, AND LOWEST GOLD PRICE OF $100 OF PAPER MONEY
IN THE NEW YORK MARKET

1862

Month	Date of Highest Price	Highest [1]	Average	Lowest [1]	Date of Lowest Pr.
January.....	1	$99.50	$97.60	$95.24	10
February ...	27, 28	97.92	96.60	95.47	15
March	25	98.77	98.20	97.56	1
April........	8, 18, 19, 24, 25, 26	98.52	98.50	97.68	2
May........	1	97.92	96.80	96.04	27
June	11	96.74	93.90	91.32	27
July........	1	91.95	86.60	83.25	22
August	9, 11	88.89	87.30	86.02	29
September..	1, 2, 16, 17, 18	85.84	84.40	80.65	30
October.....	1	81.97	77.80	74.91	22
November...	29	77.52	76.30	75.05	10
December...	1	77.82	75.60	74.63	4

[1] The highest and lowest prices are taken from the following tables of daily prices.

423

TABLE 1 — *Continued*

MONTHLY HIGHEST, AVERAGE, AND LOWEST GOLD PRICE OF $100 OF PAPER MONEY
IN THE NEW YORK MARKET

1863

Month	Date of Highest Price	Highest [1]	Average	Lowest [1]	Date of Lowest Pr.
January.....	2	$74.84	$68.90	$62.21	31
February ...	10, 11	65.57	62.30	57.97	26, 28
March......	26	71.94	64.70	58.22	1, 2
April.......	8	68.73	66.00	63.34	1
May........	26, 28	69.69	67.20	64.62	7
June........	10	71.17	69.20	67.40	16
July........	20	81.14	76.60	68.97	1
August.....	25	81.88	79.50	77.07	1
September..	1	78.82	74.50	69.87	29
October.....	1	71.24	67.70	63.80	15
November...	27	69.93	67.60	64.94	21, 23
December...	1	67.51	66.20	65.47	4, 29

1864

Month	Date of Highest Price	Highest [1]	Average	Lowest [1]	Date of Lowest Pr.
January.....	6	$66.01	$64.30	$62.75	19
February ...	27	63.64	63.10	62.11	16
March.:....	1	62.89	61.40	58.91	26
April.......	4	60.15	57.90	54.13	26
May........	10	59.52	56.70	52.63	31
June........	2	53.05	47.50	40.00	29, 30
July........	1	45.05	38.70	35.09	11
August.....	30	43.20	39.40	38.20	6
September..	30	52.36	44.90	39.29	2
October.....	3	52.91	48.30	43.91	31
November...	18	47.62	42.80	38.46	9
December...	19	47.00	44.00	41.15	7

1865

Month	Date of Highest Price	Highest [1]	Average	Lowest [1]	Date of Lowest Pr.
January.....	21	$50.70	$46.30	$42.67	4
February ...	21	50.92	48.70	46.14	7
March......	24	67.51	57.50	49.75	1
April........	10	69.69	67.30	64.73	5
May........	11	77.82	73.70	68.91	1
June........	5	73.94	71.40	67.74	15
July........	3	72.14	70.40	68.43	28
August.....	11, 15	71.30	69.70	68.73	2
September..	15	70.11	69.50	68.97	1
October	2, 3	69.38	68.70	67.11	6
November ..	1	68.73	68.00	67.23	29
December ..	9	69.20	68.40	67.34	1, 4, 5

[1] The highest and lowest prices are taken from the following tables of daily prices.

TABLE 2

DAILY HIGHEST AND LOWEST VALUE IN GOLD OF $100 IN CURRENCY

1862

	January	February	March	April	May	June
1	$99.50–98.52	$96.62–96.62	$97.68–97.56	$98.16–98.04	$97.92–97.80	S.
2	99.01–98.77	S.	S.	98.04–97.68	97.80–97.56	$96.62–96.50
3	99.01–98.77	96.74–96.62	98.04–97.68	98.28–98.16	97.56–97.32	96.62–96.62
4	98.28–98.04	96.62–96.50	98.16–98.04	98.28–98.16	S.	96.62–96.50
5	S.	96.74–96.62	98.04–98.04	98.16–98.04	96.97–96.39	96.50–96.15
6	97.80–97.56	96.74–96.62	98.04–97.92	S.	97.44–96.73	96.15–95.92
7	97.32–97.09	96.74–96.50	98.04–97.92	97.92–97.80	97.68–97.32	96.15–95.04
8	96.62	96.62–96.50	98.28–98.16	98.52–97.92	97.32–97.09	S.
9	95.92	S.	S.	98.28–98.16	96.97–96.85	95.92–95.81
10	95.69–95.24	96.50–96.27	98.04–98.04	98.28–98.16	96.85–96.74	95.92–95.81
11	96.62–96.15	96.27–96.15	98.40–98.28	98.16–98.04	S.	96.74–95.69
12	S.	96.15–96.04	98.40–98.40	98.28–98.04	96.74–96.50	95.47–95.01
13	97.09–97.09	95.92–95.81	98.52–98.52	S.	96.85–96.74	95.01–94.90
14	97.32–96.85	95.81–95.58	98.52–98.40	98.28–98.16	96.85–96.85	94.67–94.56
15	97.56–97.33	95.58–95.47	98.52–98.52	98.28–98.16	96.85–96.50	S.
16	97.80–97.56	S.	S.	98.40–98.40	97.09–96.62	93.90–93.68
17	98.16–98.04	96.39–96.27	98.52–98.40	98.52–98.40	97.09–96.97	94.34–93.90
18	98.28–98.04	96.74–96.39	98.64–98.52	98.52–98.52	S.	94.90–94.45
19	S.	97.09–96.85	98.52–98.40	98.52–98.40	96.85–96.85	94.34–93.79
20	97.80–97.56	96.85–96.74	98.77–98.64	S.	96.85–96.74	94.01–93.79
21	97.80–97.56	96.97–96.97	98.77–98.52	98.40–98.40	96.85–96.62	94.01–93.90
22	97.44–97.21	97.09–97.09	98.77–98.64	98.40–98.40	96.62–96.50	S.
23	96.74–96.39	S.	S.	98.40–98.28	96.74–96.62	93.68–92.59
24	96.74–96.62	97.09–96.85	98.77–98.64	98.52–98.40	96.74–96.50	92.38–91.95
25	97.09–96.85	97.09–96.97	98.89–98.77	98.52–98.52	S.	92.38–91.95
26	S.	97.21–96.97	98.77–98.64	98.52–98.40	96.15–96.15	91.85–91.53
27	97.09–96.85	97.92–97.80	98.77–98.28	S.	96.15–96.04	91.43–91.32
28	96.74–96.74	97.92–97.80	98.77–98.64	98.40–98.28	96.27–96.15	91.74–91.64
29	96.85–96.74	....	98.52–98.52	98.28–98.28	96.39–96.27	S.
30	96.85–96.62	....	S.	98.04–98.04	96.50–96.50	91.85–91.53
31	96.62–96.50	....	98.64–98.28	....	96.62–96.50	....

	July	August	September	October	November	December
1	$91.95–91.53	$86.86–86.39	$85.84–85.47	$81.97–80.81	$77.15–76.19	$77.82–76.05
2	91.85–91.43	86.96–86.77	85.84–85.65	81.47–81.30	S.	76.34–76.05
3	91.32–91.32	S.	84.93–84.75	81.72–81.55	76.63–76.05	76.34–75.76
4	Holiday	87.24–86.96	84.93–84.84	81.63–81.30	77.22–76.63	75.19–74.63
5	91.32–91.01	87.34–87.15	84.57–83.95	S.	76.05–75.61	76.05–75.47
6	S.	87.24–87.15	84.21–83.88	81.38–80.56	76.05–75.76	76.63–75.76
7	90.91–90.70	87.72–87.05		81.30–80.72	76.05–75.76	S.
8	89.89–89.69	88.79–87.72	84.21–83.68	80.48–80.08	75.76–75.47	76.12–67.05
9	88.11–85.84	88.89–88.59	84.30–84.12	79.84–79.05	S.	75.40–75.19
10	86.49–85.11	S.	84.30–84.21	78.59–77.52	75.61–75.05	75.69–75.47
11	87.15–86.21	88.89–88.20	84.21–84.12	78.12–77.97	76.34–75.33	75.69–75.61
12	87.82–87.34	88.11–87.53	84.39–84.21	S.	76.05–75.76	76.05–75.90
13	S.	87.43–87.34	84.75–84.57	77.52–77.37	76.05–75.76	76.26–75.76
14	86.58–85.93	86.77–86.30		76.34–75.19	76.34–75.76	76.34–75.76
15	85.65–85.47	87.15–86.58	85.11–84.93	75.76–75.33	75.90–75.76	75.83–75.61
16	85.65–75.29	87.34–87.24	85.84–84.93	75.76–75.47	S.	75.76–75.26
17	84.93–84.12	S.	85.84–85.11	75.76–75.47	75.76–75.61	75.61–75.19
18	84.03–83.88	86.86–86.77	85.84–85.56	76.92–76.78	76.12–75.76	75.69–75.33
19	84.57–84.39	87.15–86.86	85.56–85.47	S.	76.92–76.34	75.61–75.33
20	S.	86.96–86.77	85.65–85.38	77.75–77.22	76.78–76.63	75.76–75.26
21	83.51–83.33	86.77–86.30		77.97–77.07	76.78–76.56	S.
22	83.59–83.25	86.58–86.02	85.38–85.11	75.19–74.91	76.63–76.48	75.61–75.40
23	84.03–83.88	86.86–86.30	84.93–84.21	75.47–75.19	S.	75.69–75.61
24	85.47–84.39	S.	84.30–84.03	76.34–75.76	76.85–76.48	75.76–75.69
25	87.53–85.84	86.77–86.39	83.33–82.81	76.92–76.19	77.00–76.92	Xmas Day
26	85.47–85.11	86.77–86.67	83.16–82.99	S.	77.37–77.22	75.83–75.76
27	S.	86.77–86.58	82.39–82.39	76.92–76.19	Thanks. Day	75.83–75.40
28	85.74–85.02	86.58–86.49		75.97–75.61	77.37–77.22	75.37–77.22
29	86.39–85.84	86.21–86.02	82.14–80.97	76.19–75.90	77.52–77.37	75.83–75.33
30	87.43–86.67	86.49–86.39	82.30–80.65	76.78–76.48	S.	75.40–75.19
31	87.34–86.67	S.	....	77.22–76.92	....	75.05–74.84

TABLE 2 — *Continued*

DAILY HIGHEST AND LOWEST VALUE IN GOLD OF $100 IN CURRENCY

1863

	January	February	March	April	May	June
1	N. Year's Day	S.	S.	$64.10–63.34	$66.34–66.01	$68.49–67.80
2	$74.84–74.70	$63.80–62.89	$58.31–58.22	66.25–63.69	66.72–66.45	68.14–67.91
3	74.77–74.35	64.73–64.46	58.48–58.22	65.36–65.15	S.	68.14–68.08
4	S.	63.69–63.09	60.61–59.52	64.62–64.41	67.45–66.67	68.49–68.26
5	74.28–73.94	63.85–63.29	63.69–63.29	S.	67.34–66.01	68.49–68.38
6	74.63–74.28	63.59–63.09	66.67–64.94	66.23–65.41	65.68–64.94	68.91–68.79
7	74.63–74.07	63.85–63.34	64.62–64.31	66.67–65.41	64.83–64.62	S.
8	73.60–72.99	S.	S.	68.73–68.03	64.83–64.73	69.93–69.93
9	72.46–72.20	64 73–63.90	64.21–63.59	68.38–67.57	67.11–66.56	70.36–70.24
10	73.06–72.07	65.57–64.99	62.50–61.35	68.26–67.11	S.	71.17–70.98
11	S.	65.57–65.04	63.34–63.09	66.45–65.57	67.34–67.11	70.54–70.42
12	71.11–70.30	64.88–64.73	63.09–62.45	S.	67.34–67.00	70.80–70.73
13	70.42–69.44	64.46–64.10	62.89–62.02	63.69–63.49	66.78–66.72	70.30–70.18
14	68.14–67.57	64.41–64.10	63.39–62.99	64.52–64.26	66.78–66.67	S.
15	67.51–67.23	S.	S.	65.79–64.94	66.78–66.67	69.20–68.49
16	68.73–68.61	64.15–63.49	64.73–64.31	65.79–65.04	66.78–66.56	67.68–67.40
17	68.08–67.74	63.19–62.79	64.67–64.41	65.25–64.21	S.	68.73–68.61
18	S.	62.31–61.73	65.20–64.52	66.12–65.52	66.78–66.67	69.87–69.14
19	67.68–67.23	61.92–60.98	64.57–64.15	S.	67.51–67.06	69.93–69.57
20	67.68–67.23	61.54–61.07	64.73–64.52	67.23–66.34	67.28–67.11	69.69–69.69
21	67.68–67.34	61.73–61.16	64.99–64.57	68.49–68.03	67.23–66.67	S.
22	67.91–67.34	S.	S.	68.61–68.03	67.34–66.78	69.75–69.50
23	68.03–67.57	61.16–60.65	66.23–65.15	67.40–66.67	67.34–66.89	69.75–69.69
24	67.40–66.67	59.61–58.31	68.73–62.89	66.01–65.79	S.	69.87–69.44
25	S.	58.31–58.01	71.68–70.55	65.79–64.94	68.61–68.26	69.08–68.61
26	67.17–65.90	59.00–57.97	71.94–71.30	S.	69.69–68.97	69.08–68.97
27	65.25–64.62	58.87–58.48	71.43–70.98	66.67–64.99	69.63–69.08	68.97–68.85
28	65.57–64.94	58.31–57.97	70.30–69.87	66.83–66.39	69.69–69.50	S.
29	65.36–64.41	....	S.	66.67–66.39	69.20–68.91	68.26–67.97
30	65.36–63.19	....	69.32–67.91	National Fast	69.03–68.85	68.43–68.14
31	62.89–62.21	....	67.34–66.67	....	S.	....

	July	August	September	October	November	December
1	$69.08–68.97	$77.29–77.07	$78.82–78.51	$71.24–71.24	S.	$67.51–67.40
2	69.50–69.32	S.	78.43–78.12	70.18–69.81	$68.55–68.26	67.34–67.28
3	69.44–69.32	78.43–78.28	77.37–74.49	70.11–69.87	68.43–68.38	66.01–65.57
4	Holiday	77.97–77.67	74.91–74.35	S.	68.49–68.43	65.57–65.47
5	S.	78.28–78.20	76.05–75.90	69.44–69.08	68.38–67.91	65.90–65.79
6	72.46–71.81	Nat'l Thanks.	S.	68.49–67.91	67.57–67.23	S.
7	75.47–72.20	78.74–78.28	75.19–75.05	68.38–68.26	68.38–67.85	66.23–65.74
8	76.12–75.90	79.21–79.13	75.76–75.69	68.55–68.49	S.	67.23–66.89
9	76.19–76.05	S.	75.54–75.40	68.14–68.03	68.38–68.20	67.34–67.28
10	75.61–75.47	79.29–78.90	76.26–76.12	67.40–67.34	68.97–68.73	67.23–66.83
11	75.69–75.47	79.21–79.05	77.29–77.07	S.	68.79–68.61	66.23–66.01
12	S.	79.29–79.13	77.59–77.52	66.89–66.56	68.20–68.03	66.56–66.50
13	76.19–75.97	78.97–78.74	S.	65.04–64.52	68.03–67.85	S.
14	76.19–76 05	79.84–79.05	76.41–75.97	65.57–65.04	68.20–68.03	66.78–66.50
15	77.59–77.37	79 76–79.68	76.34–75.69	64.10–63.80	S.	66.34–66.34
16	79 37–79.29	S.	76.12–75.61	64.88–64.83	68.03–67.97	67.00–66.78
17	79.52–79.37	79.60–79.52	75.61–75.47	67.00–66.67	67.62–67.34	66.56–66.45
18	79.84–79 84	79.60–79 60	75.19–75.05	S.	66.89–66.67	65.95–65.74
19	S.	80.32–79.92	74.77–74.63	66.28–64.31	66.23–65.47	66.01–65.79
20	81.14–79.76	80.08–80.08	S.	66.83–66.78	65.57–65.25	S.
21	79.37–78.51	79.84–79.76	71.94–71.81	69.57–68.49	65.15–64.94	65.74–65.57
22	80.32–79.52	80.16–80.08	72.86–72.20	70.05–69.32	S.	65.74–65.68
23	79.52–79.29	S.	72.73–72.33	68.61–68.26	65.36–64–94	65.79–65.57
24	79.29–79.21	80.65–80.65	73.13–72.99	68.14–68.03	66.45–65.79	65.95–65.90
25	79.52–79.44	81.88–80.97	72.46–72.40	S.	67.23–67.11	Xmas D'y
26	S.	81.63–81.14	71.94–71.81	66.89–66.78	Thanks. Day	66.01–66.01
27	78.43–78.12	80 32–80.08	S.	68.49–67.91	69.93–68.73	S.
28	78.43–78.28	80.65–80.40	71.81–71.75	68.61–68.26	69.20–69.14	65.90–65.52
29	78.43–78.28	80.16–80.08	70.18–69.87	68.03–67.57	S.	65.52–65.47
30	78.35–78.28	S.	70.80–70.42	68.49–68.32	67.57–67.23	65.90–65.57
31	78.05–77.52	78.74–77.97	....	68.79–68.73	....	65.84–65.84

TABLE 2— *Continued*

DAILY HIGHEST AND LOWEST VALUE IN GOLD OF $100 IN CURRENCY

1864

	January	February	March	April	May	June
1	N. Year's Day	$63.49-63.39	$62.89-62.50	$60.06-59.44	S.	$52.63-52.63
2	$65.95-65.79	63.59-63.54	62.65-62.65	60.06-59.97	$56.82-56.38	53.05-52.63
3	S.	63.39-63.29	62.31-62.11	S.	56.50-55.63	52.67-52.32
4	....	63.29-63.29	62.45-61.92	60.15 60.02	55.71-55.71	52.56-52.19
5	65.95-65.95	63.39-63.19	61.87-61.78	59.66-59.61	56.42-56.30	S.
6	66.01-66.01	63.39-63.19	S.	59.26-58.61	57.47-56.58	51.55-51.55
7	65.84-65.68	S.	61.82-61.82	58.61-58.48	57.89-57.85	51.81-51.35
8	65.90-65.68	62.99-62.79	61.49-61.26	59.00-59.00	S.	51.81-51.75
9	....	62.65-62.60	59.88-59.61	59.00-59.00	58.91-58.48	....
10	S.	62.79-62.79	60.70-60.70	S.	59.52-59.35	50.38-50.31
11	65.63-65.57	62.75-62.70	60.74-60.70	59.00-59.00	57.39-56.74	50.44-50.38
12	65.04-64.83	62.89-62.79	62.31-61.73	57.55-57.14	57.80-57.39	S.
13	65.04-64.99	62.70-62.65	S.	56.94-56.90	58.82-57.51	51.09-51.09
14	64.73-64.57	S.	62.31-62.21	56.82-56.42	58.14-58.06	51.15-50.63
15	64.41-64.31	62.55-62.35	61.63-61.44	57.64-57.55	S.	50.57-50.57
16	64.21-63.90	62.40-62.11	61.87-61.73	58.48-58.39	57.64-57.55	50.70-50.70
17	S.	62.55-62.50	62.06-61.92	S.	56.50-56.18	50.86-50.79
18	62.79-62.79	62.55-62.55	61.35-61.35	58.65-58.65	55.25-55.17	51.22 51.15
19	62.79-62.75	63.29-63.04	61.73-61.73	59.88-59.52	55.10-55.06	S.
20	63.19-62.94	62.84-62.79	S.	59.88-59.70	55.25-55.25	50.51-50.44
21	64.00-63.69	S.	61.73-61.73	59.93-59.70	55.10-55.10	50.25-48.08
22	63.80-63.44	62.89-62.89	....	57.64-57.22	S.	47.62-43.48
23	64.10-63.85	63.59-63.39	60.88-60.42	57.43-56.34	54.91-54.91	48.78-44.84
24	S.	63.59-63.49	60.06-60.06	S.	54.83-54.83	46.95-46.08
25	63.44-63.34	63.19-63.14	Good Friday	55.87-54.79	54.13-54.09	46.73-45.45
26	63.29-63.24	63.49-63 14	59.00-58.91	55.17-54.13	54.64-54.50	S.
27	63.69-63.69	63.64-63.49	S.	55.25-55.17	53.76-53.69	45.25-41.67
28	63.64-63.59	S.	....	56.22-55.48	53.76-53.76	42.73-41.67
29	63.80-63.44	62.89-62.79	60.33-60.29	56.30-55.48	S.	42.55-40.00
30	63.80-63.64	....	61.12-60.88	55.71-55.56	53.76-53.76	40.82-40.00.
31	S.	....	60.88-60.88	....	52.63-52.63	....

	July	August	September	October	November	December
1	$45.05-40.00	$39.84-38.61	$41.15-40.24	$52.63-51.61	$43.48-41.41	$44.10-43.67
2	43.48-40.00	39.06-38.68	40.24-39.29	S.	43.57-40.65	43.43-42.78
3	S.	39.06-38:68	42.37-41.07	52.91-52.15	44.00-42.24	43.81-43.29
4	Holiday	....	S.	52.63-52.02	43.17-41.91	S.
5	42.55-40.16	38.83-38.28	42.55-41.07	52.84-52.29	42.46-40.86	44.05-43.53
6	40.32-38.24	38.57-38.20	41.58-41.32	52.92-50.76	S.	43.48-42.60
7	38.17-36.63	S.	41.52-41.19	50.51-49.02	41.93-40.67	41.93-41.15
8	37.49-36.17	38.95-38.54	42.42-41.49	50.83-49.20	40.73-40.08	41.84-41.19
9	38.46-36.36	39.60-39.14	42.71-42.37	S.	40.65-38.46	41.75-41.26
10	J.	39.29-39.14	45.87-43.76	51.02-50.25	41.15-39.53	42.64-41.80
11	36.23-35.09	39.39-38.95	S.	50.41-49.17	42.22-40 90	S.
12	36.90-35.46	39.20-38.83	46.84-44.44	49.94-48.84	41.24-40.82	43.01-42.11
13	37.21-36.63	39.35-39.02	45.98-43.86	49.05-47.68	S.	42.87-42.46
14	38.76-37.31	S.	44.74-43.86	48.08-46.03	41.15-40.55	42.85-42.46
15	40.98-39.06	39.10-38.93	43.81-43.57	46.89-45.45	41.91-40.98	42.64-42.06
16	40.24-38.28	39.12-38.95	44.62-43.86	S.	43.76-41.67	42.78-42.60
17	S.	39.10-38.91	45.27-44.72	45.82-44.94	45.82-44.10	44.42-43 22
18	39.33-38.24	38.91-38.76	S.	48.48-46.51	47.62-45.66	S.
19	38.68-37.21	38.91-38.78	44.67-44.10	48.19-47.28	46.30-44.35	47.00-46.03
20	38.31-37.91	38.99-38.89	44.84-44.10	48.48-47.34	S.	45.35-44.05
21	38.99-38.46	S.	45.45-45.05	48.22-47.85	45.98-45.15	44.99-44 25
22	39.92-38.80	38.93-38.87	46.30-45.20	47.73-46.84	44.64-43.67	45.25-44.54
23	39.41-39.06	38.89-38.72	47.39-46.08	S.	44.35-44.74	45.35-44.89
24	S	39.35-38.91	50.00-47.17	47.11-46.11	Thanks. D'y	45.38-45.05
25	39.16-38.65	39.29-39.10	S.	46.57-45.71	46.14-45.20	S.
26	38.80-38.54	39.47-39.06	51.27-50.47	47.09-46.08	45.56-44.51	Holiday
27	39.37-38.87	40.82-39.53	52.02-51.27	46.54-46.16	S.	46.30-45.87
28	40.98-39.68	S.	51.28-48.78	46.48-45.92	44.20-42.78	46.24-44.64
29	40.00-39.45	42.53-40.82	51.48-49.50	45.92-45.20	43.10-42.35	45.05-44.42
30	39.53-38.76	43.20-42.37	52.36-51.51	S.	44.00-42.92	44.25-43.57
31	S.	42.73-41.15	....	45.15-43.91	....	44.59-43.88

TABLE 2—*Continued*

DAILY HIGHEST AND LOWEST VALUE IN GOLD OF $100 IN CURRENCY

1865

	January	February	March	April	May	June
1	S.	$49.38–48.63	$50.12–49.75	$66.23–65.79	$70.11–68.91	Fast day
2	Holiday	49.08–48.54	50.99–50.51	S.	71.05–70.18	$72.73–72.27
3	$44.25–43.57	48.72–47.68	50.47–50.25	68.73–67.57	70.86–70.48	73.26–72.99
4	43.29–42.67	47.93–46.62	50.25–50.00	68.32–67.23	70.42–69.75	S.
5	44.17–43.57	S.	S.	67.57–64.73	70.18–69.50	73.94–73.13
6	44.05–43.81	47.17–46.62	50.51–50.22	66.56–65.57	70.05–69.63	73.39–72.93
7	44.17–43.96	47.06–46.14	50.73–50.25	67.91–66.45	S.	72.99–72.66
8	S.	47.51–46.92	51.05–50.57	67.34–66.34	72.33–69.93	72.60–72.46
9	44.22–44.05	47.34–46.73	51.71–50.92	S.	73.66–72.86	72.93–72.46
10	44.94–43.69	47.51–47.20	53.58–52.32	69.69–68.67	76.26–73.66	72.93–72.60
11	45.45–44.69	48.87–47.85	53.12–52.22	68.49–68.03	77.82–75.90	S.
12	46.19–45.51	S.	S.	68.91–68.49	76.56–75.05	72.33–70.92
13	45.77–45.05	48.75–48.31	53.98–52.22	68.49–67.97	77.37–76.78	71.11–69.93
14	45.92–45.25	48.28–47.90	56.26–54.05	Pres. assass.	S.	70.61–69.93
15	S.	48.84–48.43	57.39–55.90	Exch. closed	77.07–76.63	69.69–67.74
16	45.85–45.22	49.26–48.78	58.74–56.54	S.	76.70–76.48	69.69–68.85
17	46.62–46.08	49.14–48.87	62.50–59.17	67.51–65.36	77.15–75.97	69.57–68.91
18	46.51–46.08	49.02–48.66	61.26–60.15	68.38–67.68	77.15–76.34	S.
19	48.08–46.54	S.	S.	Holiday	76.56–76.05	71.43–69.75
20	49.57–48.13	50.44–49.94	62.40–59.57	Holiday	76.78–76.34	72.60–71.62
21	50.70–48.54	50.92–50.06	64.73–62.79	67.91–66.83	S.	71.68–70.48
22	S.	Holiday	64.10–62.89	67.06–66.45	76.56–76.19	71.17–70.55
23	50.54–49.32	50.28–49.94	66.34–63.69	S.	76.26–75.54	70.61–70.30
24	50.54–49.08	50.28–49.94	67.51–65.57	Holiday	74.07–73.80	70.61–70.18
25	48.96–48.19	50.51–50.03	65.15–63.49	Holiday	73.53–72.14	S.
26	49.50–48.31	S.	S.	66.39–65.79	73.66–72.46	71.43–70.61
27	47.90–46.51	50.12–49.57	65.36–64.31	67.80–67.00	73.60–73.06	70.80–70.42
28	46.95–45.45	49.81–49.14	65.04–64.67	68.14–67.57	S.	71.81–70.80
29	S.	....	66.23–65.63	68.49–68.26	73.53–72.99	72.40–71.81
30	47.39–46.57	....	66.83–65.84	S.	72.86–72.07	71.94–70.80
31	49.50–47.39	....	66.12–65.84	....	73.26–72.73	....

	July	August	September	October	November	December
1	$71.75–70.92	$69.50–68.91	$69.26–68.97	S.	$68.73–68.55	$67.57–67.34
2	S.	69.03–68.73	69.32–69.14	$69.38–69.32	68.49–68.20	67.80–67.45
3	72.14–71.17	69.38–69.14	S.	69.38–69.08	68.20–68.03	S.
4	Holiday	69.75–69.32	69.50–69.26	69.08–68.14	68.14–67.97	67.62–67.34
5	71.68–71.24	69.87–69.57	69.38–69.14	68.26–67.91	S.	67.51–67.34
6	71.94–71.49	S.	69.20–68.97	68.43–67.11	68.03–67.85	68.14–67.57
7	71.68–71.56	69.69–69.44	69.14–69.03	68.49–68.08	68.08–67.91	Thanks. Day
8	71.56–71.36	69.32–69.08	69.20–69.08	S.	68.26–67.74	68.61–68.26
9	S.	69.57–69.20	69.14–69.08	68.61–68.14	68.43–68.14	69.20–68.91
10	71.88–71.30	70.30–69.63	S.	69.03–68.79	68.26–68.20	S.
11	71.75–71.43	71.30–70.48	69.20–69.14	69.08–68.91	68–26–68.08	69.08–68.85
12	71.05–70.42	70.98–70.42	69.57–69.20	68.97–68.79	S.	69.14–68.91
13	70.48–70.42	S.	69.81–69.57	69.14–69.03	68.14–67.97	68.97–68.73
14	70.18–69.63	70.30–69.99	69.87–69.57	69.14–69.03	68.03–67.91	68.85–68.43
15	70.42–70.18	71.30–70.73	70.11–69.81	S.	67.91–67.85	68.38–68.14
16	S.	70.86–70.39	70.05–69.81	69.67–68.32	67.97–67.91	68.49–68.26
17	70.42–69.93	70.55–70.11	S.	69.67–68.32	68.14–68.03	S.
18	69.93–69.75	70.18–69.57	69.75–69.57	68.49–68.38	68.08–68.03	68.43–68.20
19	70.30–69.57	69.63–69.32	69.63–69.44	68.26–68.03	S.	68.26–68.20
20	70.24–70.05	69.38–69.08	69.63–69.44	68.49–68.38	68.20–68.03	68.49–68.14
21	70.36–70.05	69 81–69.44	69.81–69.50	68.61–68.32	68.20–68.08	68.55–68.38
22	70 18–70.05	69 69–69.50	69.81–69.50	S.	68.08–68.03	68.55–68.43
23	S.	69 63–69.50	69.81–69.57	68.03–68.03	68.08–68.03	68.79–68.61
24	70.11–69.81	69 63–69.50	S.	68.49–68.38	68.14–68.08	S.
25	69.93–69 69	69.69–69.44	69.93–69.50	68.73–68.38	68.08–67.97	Xmas D'y
26	69.99–69.69	69.44–69.26	69.57–69.50	69.03–68.67	S.	68.85–68.73
27	69.81–68.85	S	69.50–69.32	68.73–68.55	67.97–67.74	68.85–68.79
28	69.14–68.43	69.50–69.38	69.57–69.38	68.85–68.67	67.85–67.40	68.79–68.67
29	70 05–68.73	69.38–69.26	69.50–69.38	S.	67.57–67 23	68.91–68.67
30	S.	69.44–69.03	69.44–69.32	68.67–68.62	67 91–67.40	69.03–68.97
31	69.87–69 38	69.20–68.97	....	68.55–68 38	....	S.

APPENDIX B

RELATIVE PRICES OF COMMODITIES

TABLE 1

RELATIVE PRICES OF FARM PRODUCTS

A. INDIVIDUAL SERIES

DATE	BARLEY			CLOVER SEED		CORN	
	New York	Chi-cago	Cin-cinnati	New York	Chi-cago	New York	Cin-cinnati
1860, January	103	101	84	103	99	122	107
April	100	117	109	94	88	97	95
July	...	93	98	...	99	87	97
October	96	89	109	103	114	94	101
1861, January	90	64	92	103	102	97	71
April	88	71	78	91	89	88	67
July	94	34	57	91	89	65	57
October	81	59	52	...	92	75	57
1862, January	94	59	57	84	85	89	57
April	113	80	80	98	105	79	69
July	...	101	80	89	83	75	73
October	75	131	115	89	102	82	81
1863, January	166	161	155	126	124	109	91
April	191	186	184	117	107	126	133
July	...	195	...	...	120	103	115
October	163	181	172	149	120	119	182
1864, January	178	205	190	161	143	178	208
April	165	233	155	183	139	178	212
July	...	233	...	...	161	217	218
October	232	248	224	251	193	217	242
1865, January	257	220	184	326	309	257	212
April	202	165	149	294	298	196	141
July	163	101	86	343	161	102	131
October	160	129	...	274	163	125	127
1866, January	135	110	161	160	158	127	107
April	153	89	132	123	114	106	97
July	135	76	172	...	137	120	125
October	175	140	184	183	137	130	166

TABLE 1 — *Continued*

RELATIVE PRICES OF FARM PRODUCTS

Date	Flax Seed		Hides			Meat: Beeves		
	New York	Cin-cinnati	Cin-cinnati	Chi-cago	New York	Cin-cinnati	New York	Chi-cago
1860, January ...	98	100	100	91	100	103	103	97
April	102	100	107	100	103	117	108	113
July	101	100	107	106	103	90	92	105
October....	99	100	85	103	94	90	97	85
1861, January ...	101	100	93	69	68	97	103	105
April	91	100	93	82	75	110	90	105
July	...	91	63	58	61	76	90	110
October....	98	91	85	69	86	90	90	77
1862, January ..	116	114	78	72	83	83	103	73
April	140	136	100	86	75	90	97	97
July	129	...	100	79	83	97	87	90
October....	125	114	100	103	94	76	87	85
1863, January ...	193	182	126	106	99	90	97	92
April	182	295	130	120	94	131	118	145
July	165	...	137	113	94	124	110	110
October....	165	182	137	141	103	97	103	101
1864, January ...	207	227	148	132	125	131	118	105
April	223	236	141	156	139	179	144	141
July	231	255	174	161	161	166	162	177
October....	200	255	159	120	133	193	178	153
1865, January ...	233	259	156	139	153	221	164	169
April	176	182	156	100	104	262	215	242
July	142	136	96	91	83	193	159	145
October....	190	245	119	122	128	166	190	222
1866, January ...	187	227	133	93	139	172	174	179
April	160	205	141	76	133	193	159	155
July	203	264	133	93	125	207	172	210
October....	209	255	133	120	139	193	169	185

Date	Meat: Sheep		Meat: Pork			Oats		Rye	
	New York	Cin-cinnati	Chi-cago	Cin-cinnati	New York	New York	Cin-cinnati	Cin-cinnati	New York
1860, Jan..	101	110	91	121	90	111	119	113	107
Apr..	110	138	100	101	97	103	106	119	100
July.	92	83	101	62	107	95	101	87	99
Oct..	97	69	108	116	106	92	74	81	94
1861, Jan..	101	138	87	115	86	90	64	70	..
Apr..	99	124	87	98	82	80	64	63	77
July.	78	55	53	63	68	72	57	52	..
Oct..	87	55	51	61	63	83	59	41	82

TABLE 1—*Continued*

RELATIVE PRICES OF FARM PRODUCTS

DATE	MEAT: SHEEP		MEAT: PORK			OATS		RYE	
	New York	Cincinnati	Chicago	Cincinnati	New York	New York	Cincinnati	Cincinnati	New York
1862, Jan..	106	90	48	65	60	99	69	49	101
April	110	110	52	65	74	93	72	63	94
July.	97	72	45	47	57	103	84	56	87
Oct..	101	103	57	63	67	138	99	66	75
1863, Jan..	110	83	69	94	75	166	128	69	107
April	138	179	84	76	88	200	173	113	126
July.	87	114	76	74	88	178	156	85	121
Oct..	97	121	79	57	79	168	173	113	130
1864, Jan..	136	145	92	141	113	224	205	153	152
April	179	200	144	151	139	214	195	149	151
July.	117	110	184	151	176	238	200	175	236
Oct..	147	166	142	237	179	208	185	158	173
1865, Jan..	175	207	227	314	219	261	212	164	203
April	211	276	197	227	191	212	148	113	145
July.	101	117	147	174	169	177	153	70	101
Oct..	124	152	235	257	229	144	111	88	119
1866, Jan..	161	166	176	244	165	122	96	85	121
April	140	179	175	189	171	115	101	73	101
July.	113	138	176	188	165	147	111	107	143
Oct..	108	131	183	196	173	137	111	127	149

DATE	TIMOTHY SEED			TOBACCO					
				Leaf Aver'ge	Leaf Fine	Wrap's Ohio	Wrap's Penn.	Wrap's Conn.	Leaf Ky.
	Cincinnati	Chicago	New York	Cincinnati	Cincinnati	New York	New York	New York	New York
1860, Jan..	87	83	94	100	100	100	100	126	112
April	121	113	110	100	100	100	100	91	98
July.	...	116	...	...	...	100	100	91	89
Oct..	92	87	96	...	...	100	100	91	101
1861, Jan..	...	89	98	...	...	100	100	91	104
April	107	85	120	...	...	100	100	91	98
July.	...	...	101	...	...	88	88	74	110
Oct..	58	57	72	84	118	88	88	74	125
1862, Jan..	58	64	77	145	123	88	88	74	146
April	66	65	82	116	105	104	104	94	152
July.	...	...	67	148	127	104	104	94	153
Oct.	64	60	74	222	182	131	131	118	223

TABLE 1—*Continued*

RELATIVE PRICES OF FARM PRODUCTS

DATE	TIMOTHY SEED			TOBACCO					
				Leaf Aver'ge	Leaf Fine	Wrap's Ohio	Wrap's Penn.	Wrap's Conn.	Leaf Ky.
	Cincinnati	Chicago	New York	Cincinnati	Cincinnati	New York	New York	New York	New York
1863, Jan..	68	72	110	241	218	131	131	118	259
April.	78	59	82	284	236	173	173	191	312
July.	...	...	94	284	236	173	173	191	238
Oct..	99	91	94	220	205	173	173	191	213
1864, Jan..	120	110	104	255	218	173	173	191	262
April.	110	101	106	253	218	231	231	235	262
July.	...	...	120	220	218	269	269	265	253
Oct..	229	162	192	216	205	269	269	265	318
1865, Jan..	227	218	226	261	295	269	269	265	333
April.	174	152	211	247	318	135	135	176	387
July.	...	181	134	273	341	96	96	135	226
Oct..	155	144	182	240	341	115	115	162	297
1866, Jan..	140	129	163	237	250	115	115	169	297
April.	136	147	163	216	205	115	115	169	297
July.	178	...	259	216	205	115	115	169	297
Oct..	128	114	127	212	205	115	115	169	232

DATE	WHEAT				
	Winter	Spring	Prime	No. 2 Winter	No. 2 Spring
	New York	New York	Cincinnati	Chicago	Chicago
1860, January	102	105	103	99	99
April	105	98	110	105	105
July	102	103	93	105	108
October	91	94	95	91	88
1861, January	98	97	84	...	82
April	99	102	83	96	81
July	78	65	63	...	57
October	95	94	66	76	74
1862, January	103	103	72	71	70
April	97	102	78	73	74
July	86	85	69	76	75
October	93	92	72	85	83
1863, January	107	103	83	93	86
April	125	99	108	112	110
July	108	102	89	100	97
October	98	103	93	95	104

TABLE 1—*Continued*

RELATIVE PRICES OF FARM PRODUCTS

DATE	WHEAT				
	Winter	Spring	Prime	No. 2 Winter	No. 2 Spring
	New York	New York	Cincinnati	Chicago	Chicago
1864, January..................	116	118	110	108	115
April......................	126	131	110	123	114
July......................	190	193	169	176	199
October..................	143	149	143	129	149
1865, January	185	184	173	144	160
April......................	134	137	127	...	101
July......................	107	103	105	111	92
October..................	166	141	181	132	126
1866, January..................	148	139	165	...	98
April	141	112	198	...	93
July......................	177	155	228	...	119
October..................	199	177	236	191	195

B. AVERAGES FOR THE SEVERAL PRODUCTS

Date	Barley	Clover Seed	Corn	Flax Seed	Hides	Meat: Beeves
1860, January.................	96	101	115	99	97	101
April...................	109	91	96	101	103	113
July...................	96	99	92	101	105	96
October	98	109	98	100	94	91
1861, January.................	82	103	84	101	77	102
April...................	79	90	78	96	83	102
July...................	62	90	61	91	61	92
October	64	92	66	95	80	86
1862, January.................	70	85	73	115	78	86
April...................	91	102	74	138	87	95
July	91	86	74	129	87	91
October	107	96	82	120	99	83
1863, January.................	161	125	100	188	110	93
April...................	187	112	130	239	115	131
July...................	195	120	109	165	115	115
October	172	135	151	174	127	100
1864, January.................	191	152	193	217	135	118
April...................	184	161	195	230	145	155
July	233	161	218	243	165	168
October	235	222	230	228	137	175

TABLE 1—*Continued*

RELATIVE PRICES OF FARM PRODUCTS

Date	Barley	Clover Seed	Corn	Flax Seed	Hides	Meat: Beeves
1865, January	220	318	235	246	149	185
April	172	296	169	179	120	240
July	117	252	117	139	90	166
October	145	219	126	218	123	193
1866, January	135	159	117	207	122	175
April	125	119	102	183	117	169
July	128	137	123	234	117	196
October	166	160	148	232	121	182

Date	Meat: Sheep	Meat: Pork	Oats	Rye	Tim. Seed	Tobacco	Wheat
1860, January	106	101	115	110	88	106	102
April	124	99	105	110	115	98	105
July	88	90	98	93	116	95	102
October	83	113	83	88	92	98	92
1861, January	120	96	77	70	94	99	90
April	112	89	72	70	156	97	92
July	67	61	65	52	101	90	66
October	71	58	71	62	62	96	81
1862, January	98	58	84	75	66	111	84
April	110	64	83	79	71	113	85
July	85	50	94	72	67	122	78
October	102	62	119	71	66	168	85
1863, January	97	76	147	88	83	183	94
April	159	83	187	120	73	228	111
July	101	79	167	103	94	216	99
October	109	72	171	122	95	196	99
1864, January	141	115	215	153	111	212	113
April	190	145	205	150	106	238	121
July	114	170	219	206	120	249	185
October	157	186	197	166	194	257	143
1865, January	191	253	237	184	224	282	169
April	194	205	180	129	179	233	125
July	109	163	165	86	158	195	104
October	138	240	128	104	160	212	149
1866, January	164	195	109	103	144	197	138
April	160	178	108	87	149	186	136
July	126	176	129	125	146	186	170
October	120	184	124	138	123	175	200

TABLE 2

RELATIVE PRICES OF VARIOUS COMMODITIES AT WHOLESALE

DATE	BEANS	BREAD			BUTTER	CHEESE
		Boston Crackers: 1	Boston Crackers: 2	Boston Crackers: Ex. Grade		
1860, Jan....	100.0	100.0	100.0	100.0	100.0	100.0
April..	93.3	100.0	100.0	100.0	81.0	110.0
July ..	93.3	100.0	100.0	100.0	81.0	75.0
Oct ...	120.0	100.0	100.0	100.0	95.2	100.0
1861, Jan....	100.0	107.1	117.6	116.7	81.0	100.0
April..	103.2	107 1	123.5	116.7	85.7	90.0
July ..	120.0	100.0	129.4	116.7	61.9	60.0
Oct ...	120.0	100 0	129.5	116.7	64.3	60.0
1862, Jan....	136.5	107.1	135.3	116.7	90.5	70.0
April..	116.6	107.1	141.2	120.8	97.6	75.0
July ..	173.3	100.0	147.1	120.8	73.8	65.0
Oct ...	153.3	100.0	147.1	120.8	90.5	80.0
1863, Jan ...	145.9	107.1	164.7	141.7	116.7	110.0
April..	153.3	107.1	152.9	133.3	119.1	145.0
July ..	180.0	107.1	147.1	133.3	92.9	105.0
Oct.. .	129.9	107.1	147.1	129.2	114.3	120.0
1864, Jan ...	160.5	185.7	152.9	133.3	145.2	140.0
April..	146.7	185.7	158.8	137.5	230.9	170.0
July ..	146.7	185.7	158.8	137.5	157.1	150.0
Oct ...	146.7	185.7	158.8	137.5	202.4	205.0
1865, Jan ...	173.3	185.7	117.6	116.7	250.0	225.0
April..	142.7	185.7	129.4	116.7	150.0	210.0
July ..	106.7	157.1	129.4	116.7	142.9	125.0
Oct ...	120.0	157.1	117.6	116.7	204.8	150.0

DATE	COFFEE: Rio, Fair	EGGS	FLOUR: Rye	FRUIT		FISH: Cod
				Apples: Dried	Currants: Zante	
1860, Jan ...	100.0	149.1	100.0	100.0	100.0	Feb. 100.0
April..	115.2	88.9	100.0	90.3	104.2	May 100.0
July ..	117.4	78.8	95.0	87.1	91.7	Aug. 112.5
Oct.. .	121.7	83.2	100.0	77.4	79.2	Nov. 125.0
1861, Jan ...	100.0	103.2	92.5	77.4	75.0	Feb. 125.0
April..	104.3	88.9	95.0	51.6	75.0	May 125.0
July ..	104.3	64.5	75.0	103.2	66.7	Aug. 125.0
Oct....	134.8	74.5	87.5	77.4	158.3	Nov. 125.0
1862, Jan ...	156.5	134.8	100.0	96.8	150.0	Feb. 125.0
April..	178.2	74.5	100.0	90.3	158.3	May 125.0
July ..	182.6	68.8	87.5	71.0	166.7	Aug. 300.0
Oct....	195.7	83.2	106.3	71.0	179.2	Nov. 125.0

TABLE 2—*Continued*

RELATIVE PRICES OF VARIOUS COMMODITIES AT WHOLESALE

Date	Coffee: Rio, Fair	Eggs	Flour: Rye	Fruit		Fish: Cod
				Apples: Dried	Currants: Zante	
1863, Jan ...	243.5	114.7	118.8	83.9	175.0	Feb. 150.0
April..	269.6	134.8	112.5	87.1	233.3	May 125.0
July ..	252.2	111.8	106.3	90.3	250.0	Aug. 150.0
Oct....	265.2	114.7	125.0	83.9	241.7	Nov. 150.0
1864, Jan ...	293.5	166.3	137.5	122.6	239.6	Feb. 200.0
April..	339.1	120.9	137.5	125.8	275.0	May 175.0
July ..	373.9	146.2	181.3	148.4	308.3	Aug. 200.0
Oct ...	317.4	166.3	187.5	167.7	283.3	Nov. ......
1865, Jan ...	378.3	252.3	212.5	200.0	341.7	Feb. 387.5
April..	279.6	106.1	143.8	177.4	216.7	May 225.0
July ..	243.7	152.0	127.5	132.3	208.3	Aug. 450.0
Oct ...	243.1	163.4	168.8	167.7	233.3	Nov. 200.0

Date	Fruit: Raisins	Lard	Meal: Corn, Yellow, Kiln-Dried	Meat		
				Beef: Salt Mess	Beef: Loins	Beef: Ribs
1860, Jan ...	100.0	100.0	100.0	100.0	Feb. 100.0	100.0
April..	103.3	97.6	96.4	91.3	May 100.0	93.3
July ..	106.5	114.3	89.2	87.0	Aug. 100.0	93.3
Oct ...	123.9	116.7	92.8	82.6	Nov. 94.4	93.3
1861, Jan ...	89.1	95.2	84.3	91.3	Feb. 88.9	93.3
April..	68.5	85.7	90.4	91.3	May 88.9	100.0
July ..	50.0	76.2	72.5	82.6	Aug. 83.3	93.3
Oct....	102.2	76.2	73.5	95.7	Nov. 83.3	86.7
1862, Jan ...	139.1	76.2	78.3	104.3	Feb. 83.3	86.7
April..	139.1	73.8	75.9	100.0	May 83.3	86.7
July ..	135.9	73.8	71.1	104.3	Aug. 83.3	86.7
Oct ..	154.3	73.8	94.0	113.0	Nov. 83.3	86.7
1863, Jan ...	152.2	88.1	108.4	108.7	Feb. 94.4	93.3
April..	173.9	100.0	112.0	113.0	May 100.0	100.0
July ..	184.8	89.3	106.0	100.0	Aug. 100.0	100.0
Oct....	180.4	102.4	115.7	104.3	Nov. 100.0	100.0
1864, Jan ...	173.9	114.3	144.6	106.5	Feb. 105.6	106.7
April..	178.3	126.2	148.2	95.7	May 138.9	146.7
July ..	184.8	157.1	192.8	217.4	Aug. 155.6	153.3
Oct ...	173.9	185.7	189.2	130.4	Nov. 150.0	146.7
1865, Jan ...	254.3	195.2	212.0	165.2	Feb. 194.4	186.7
April..	215.2	147.6	156.6	191.3	May 194.4	213.3
July ..	250.0	152.4	124.1	113.0	Aug. 177.8	186.7
Oct ...	204.3	233.3	122.9	139.1	Nov. 166.7	166.7

TABLE 2—*Continued*

RELATIVE PRICES OF VARIOUS COMMODITIES AT WHOLESALE

DATE	MOLASSES		SALT		MEAT	
	P'rto Rico: Best	N.Orleans: Prime	Ashton's	Ashton's Liv., fine	Pork: Salt Mess	Mutton
1860, Jan ...	100.0	100.0	100.0	100.0	100.0	Feb. 100.0
April..	107.9	90.6	76.9	77.9	109.1	May 120.0
July ..	100.0	90.6	89.7	90.9	109.8	Aug. 100.0
Oct ...	105.3	94.3	82.1	83.1	116.7	Nov. 100.0
1861, Jan ...	92.1	69.8	82.1	83.1	101.5	Feb. 110.0
April..	86.8	70.8	82.1	83.1	109.1	May 110.0
July ..	71.2	67.9	82.1	83.1	97.0	Aug. 100.0
Oct ..	118.4	103.8	84.6	85.7	90.9	Nov. 90.0
1862, Jan ...	105.3	103.8	87.2	88.3	75.0	Feb. 100.0
April..	100.0	84.9	92.3	93.5	76.5	May 100.0
July ..	97.4	.....	92.3	93.5	65.2	Aug. 90.0
Oct ...	131.6	90.6	105.1	106.5	71.2	Nov. 100.0
1863, Jan ...	126.3	105.7	110.3	111.7	86.4	Feb. 100.0
April..	118.4	105.7	143.6	145.5	98.5	May 125.0
July ..	139.5	94.3	138.5	140.2	84.8	Aug. 120.0
Oct ...	164.5	113.2	130.8	132.5	86.4	Nov. 125.0
1864, Jan ...	171.1	132.1	143.6	145.5	118.2	Feb. 120.0
April..	223.7	160.4	174.0	176.6	145.5	May 140.0
July ..	289.5	217.0	230.8	233.8	275.8	Aug. 160.0
Oct ...	223.7	311.3	256.4	259.7	254.5	Nov. 150.0
1865, Jan ...	289.5	283.0	243.6	246.8	212.1	Feb. 190.0
April..	184.2	207.5	161.5	163.6	162.1	May 190.0
July ..	184.2	217.0	166.7	168.8	163.6	Aug. 170.0
Oct ...	250.0	.....	212.8	223.1	213.6	Nov. 170.0

DATE	SALT: Turk's Island	SHIP BISCUIT	SPICES		STARCH: Corn	SUGAR: Fair, Refining
			Nutmegs	Pepper: Whole, Sumatra		
1860, Jan...	100.0	100.0	100.0	100.0	100.0	100.0
April..	90.0	100.0	102.4	98.5	100.0	93.1
July ..	97.5	100.0	101.2	98.5	100.0	91.4
Oct ...	100.0	100.0	100.0	101.5	100.0	86.2
1861, Jan...	85.0	112.5	90.5	95.5	100.0	74.1
April..	95.0	112.5	95.2	101.5	100.0	65.5
July ..	100.0	100.0	97.6	98.5	100.0	63.8
Oct ...	120.0	100.0	113.1	134.3	94.1	106.9
1862, Jan...	100.0	100.0	142.9	185.1	94.1	106.9
April..	120.0	100.0	160.7	191.0	94.1	101.7
July ..	150.0	100.0	154.8	209.0	94.1	101.7
Oct ...	155.0	100.0	161.7	238.8	100.0	120.7

TABLE 2 — *Continued*

RELATIVE PRICES OF VARIOUS COMMODITIES AT WHOLESALE

DATE	SALT: Turk's Island	SHIP BISCUIT	SPICES		STARCH: Corn	SUGAR: Fair, Refining
			Nutmegs	Pepper: Whole, Sumatra		
1863, Jan...	150.0	125.0	190.5	274.6	111.8	131.0
April..	185.0	125.0	208.3	322.4	117.6	134.5
July ..	210.0	125.0	190.5	316.4	111.8	141.4
Oct ...	220.0	125.0	184.5	304.5	111.8	158.6
1864, Jan...	240.0	193.8	214.3	346.3	129.4	165.5
April..	250.0	193.8	327.4	489.6	141.2	206.9
July ..	300.0	193.8	428.6	549.3	152.9	269.0
Oct ...	500.0	193.8	381 0	417.9	164.7	220.7
1865, Jan...	330.0	187.5	428.6	537.3	176.5	244.8
April..	250.0	187.5	297.6	358.2	176.5	141.4
July ..	255.0	137.5	273.8	346.3	152.9	158.6
Oct ...	275.0	137.5	342.7	395.2	152.9	189.6

DATE	SUGAR		TALLOW: Prime, City in hhds.	VEGETABLES		CALICO
	Havana: Brown	Refined, Crushed, and Granulat'd		Fresh Potatoes: White (1)	Fresh Potatoes: White (2)	
1860, Jan ...	100.0	100.0	100.0	Feb. 100.0	Jan. 143.8	100.0
April..	96.9	97.5	102.4	May 100.0	April 137.5	105.3
July ..	93.0	100.0	97.6	Aug. 128.6	July 112.5	100.0
Oct ...	91.4	93.8	97.6	Nov. 100.0	Oct. 100.0	100.0
1861, Jan ...	72.7	83.8	82.9	Feb. 100.0	Jan. 112.5	100.0
April..	67.2	80.0	95.1	May 128.6	April 118.8	94.7
July ..	64.1	77.5	78.0	Aug. 114.3	July 143.8	94.7
Oct ...	100.0	108.8	82.9	Nov. 114.3	Oct. 106.3	105.3
1862, Jan ...	97.7	110.0	92.7	Feb. 128.6	Jan. 112.5	131.6
April..	96.9	102.5	87.8	May 128.6	April 125.0	126.3
July ..	96.9	105.0	92.7	Aug. 100.0	July 106.3	131.6
Oct ...	118.8	128.8	109.8	Nov. 128.6	Oct. 106.3	179.0
1863, Jan ...	121.1	132.5	101.2	Feb. 121.4	Jan. 112.5	210.5
April..	126.6	145.0	112.2	May 107.1	April 131.3	.....
July ..	134.4	147.5	109.8	Aug. 128.6	July 131.3	.....
Oct ...	145.3	146.3	109.8	Nov. 142.9	Oct. 125.0	.....
1864, Jan ...	160.9	168.8	125.6	Feb. 128.6	Jan. 156.3	252.6
April..	195.3	178.8	124.4	May 214.3	April 231.3	263.2
July ..	271.9	300.0	165.8	Aug. 342.8	July 287.5	421.1
Oct ..	231.3	255.0	143.2	Nov. 171.4	Oct. 200.0	357.9
1865, Jan ...	239.1	285.0	175.6	Feb. 242.8	Jan. 237.5	389.5
April..	150.0	180.0	107.3	May 142.9	April 212.5	210.5
July ..	154.7	195.0	102.4	Aug. 142.9	July 112.5	289.5
Oct ...	176.6	202.5	141.4	Nov. 157.1	Oct. 193.8	315.8

TABLE 2—*Continued*

RELATIVE PRICES OF VARIOUS COMMODITIES AT WHOLESALE

DATE	CARPETS			COTTON: Upland Middling	DENIMS	DRILLINGS: 30-inch Pepperell
	Brussels	Ingrain	Wilton			
1860, Jan ...	100.0	100.0	.....	100.0	100.0	100.0
April..	96.2	100.3	100.0	101.1	103.5	97.2
July ..	92.3	99.3	97.3	97.7	103.5	100.0
Oct ...	92.3	98.0	97.3	97.7	103.5	100.0
1861, Jan ...	92.3	101.4	97.3	109.1	103.5	97.2
April .	96.2	95.0	100.0	117.0	103.5	97.2
July ..	96.2	95.1	100.0	134.1	103.5	97.2
Oct ...	96.2	92.6	100.0	195.5	105.2	116.8
1862, Jan ...	100.0	106.6	105.4	327.3	124.1	146 0
April..	100.0	109.1	105.4	250.0	136.2	146.0
July ..	107.7	119.3	108.1	336.4	137.9	157.2
Oct ...	115.4	123.4	116.2	509.1	210.3	292.0
1863, Jan ...	134.6	149.5	132.4	613.6	258.6	308.8
April..	165.4	174.5	151.4	663.6	.....	393.0
July ..	153.8	166.0	151.4	627.3	.....	308.8
Oct ...	146.2	154.9	143.2	768.2	.....	404.3
1864, Jan ...	165.4	179.4	162.2	736.4	379.3	449.2
April..	173.1	196.7	173.0	690.9	396.6	449.2
July ..	269.2	299.3	270.3	1400.0	425.8	701.8
Oct ...	269.2	250.9	270.3	1090.9	606.9	729.9
1865, Jan ...	269.2	260.6	270.3	1090.9	463.8	673.8
April..	192.3	208.2	202.7	318.2	412.1	336.9
July ..	192.3	219.9	202.7	454.6	424.1	336.9
Oct ...	211.5	241.2	216.2	400.0	455.2	404.3

DATE	LEATHER: Harness	PRINT CLOTHS		SHEETINGS: Brown, 4–4, Atlantic A	SHIRTINGS: Bleached, 4–4, N. Y. Mills	SILK : Raw Italian
		28-inch, 7 yds. to lb. Standard	28-inch, 64 × 64. Metacomet			
1860, Jan ...	100.0	100.0	100.0	100.0	100.0	100.0
April..	100.0	97.8	100.0	102.9	100.0	100.0
July ..	102.9	100.0	100.0	102.9	100.0	105.6
Oct ...	100.0	97.8	100.0	102.9	100.0	100.0
1861, Jan ...	94.3	84.4	86.0	102.9	96.8	100.0
April..	88.6	77.8	79.1	102.9	96.8	83.3
July ..	85.7	80.0	76.7	105.8	96.8	77.8
Oct ...	100.0	106.7	104.7	135.1	103.2	72.2
1862, Jan ...	94.3	160.0	107.0	164.5	109.7	72.2
April..	94.3	128.9	125.6	164.5	116.1	72.2
July ..	91.4	153.3	155.8	188.0	129.0	83.3
Oct ...	102.9	220.0	251.1	296.9	167.5	80.6

TABLE 2—*Continued*

RELATIVE PRICES OF VARIOUS COMMODITIES AT WHOLESALE

DATE	LEATHER: Harness	PRINT CLOTHS		SHEET-INGS: Brown, 4–4, Atlantic A	SHIRT-INGS: Bleached, 4–4, N. Y. Mills	SILK: Raw Italian
		28 inch, 7 yds. to lb., Standard.	28 inch, 64 × 64, Metacomet			
1863, Jan. . .	108.6	253.3	279.1	356.3	209.7	75.0
April..	128.6	257.8	297.7	445.4	209.7	72.2
July..	128.6	257.8	260.2	415.6	232.3	66.7
Oct...	131.4	280.0	295.3	445.4	237.1	66.7
1864, Jan...	142.9	302.2	316.3	504.6	266.6	69.4
April..	154 3	288.9	300.0	475.0	283.8	75.0
July..	165.7	524.4	593.0	831.3	467.7	88.9
Oct...	171.4	568.9	480.0	682.8	307.3	94.4
1865, Jan...	171.4	480.0	537.2	712.5	411.3	88.9
April..	165.7	177.8	188.4	463.1	270.9	100.0
July..	137.1	337.8	360.5	386.0	290.3	111.1
Oct...	151.4	484.4	453.5	397.8	354.8	100.0

Date	Tickings	Alcohol	Alum	Bichrom. of Potash	Blue Vitriol	Brimstone
1860, Jan ..	100.0	100.0	100.0	100.0	100.0	100.0
April.	100.0	85.2	105.6	95.2	97.4	100.0
July..	100.0	81.5	100.0	100.0	97.4	122.2
Oct...	100.0	85.2	100.0	100.0	94.7	128.9
1861, Jan...	95.6	74.1	94.4	100.0	94.7	133.3
April.	95.6	66.7	94.4	100.0	86.8	95.6
July..	98.5	63.0	94.4	100.0	89.5	88.9
Oct...	101.5	74.1	94.4	95.2	94.7	88.9
1862, Jan...	122.1	74.1	94.4	100.0	94.7	133.3
April.	150.0	88.9	100.0	95.2	94.7	95.6
July..	136.8	107.4	100.0	97.6	94.7	97.8
Oct...	211.8	122.2	133.3	95.2	100.0	106.7
1863, Jan...	266.2	142.6	155.6	104.8	121.1	111.1
April.	.....	174.1	166.7	114.3	157.9	122.2
July..	.....	161.1	166.7	114.3	134.2	111.1
Oct...	.....	192.6	133.3	107.1	142.1	116.7
1864, Jan...	416.2	342.6	161.1	114.3	142.1	127.8
April.	.....	379.6	161.1	119.0	168.4	131.1
July..	413.2	657.4	200.0	133.3	189.5	188.9
Oct...	617.6	638.9	266.7	133.3	221.1	166.7
1865, Jan...	451.5	814.8	255.6	142.9	192.1	222.2
April.	411.8	796.3	222.2	133.3	178.9	200.0
July..	469.2	759.3	188.9	104.8	147.4	138.9
Oct...	472.1	833.3	183.3	104.8	142.1	133.3

TABLE 2 — *Continued*

RELATIVE PRICES OF VARIOUS COMMODITIES AT WHOLESALE

Date	Castor Oil	Copperas	Flax Seed	Linseed Oil	Mercury	Muriatic Acid
1860, Jan...	100.0	100.0	100.0	100.0	100.0	100.0
April..	104.8	125.0	98.2	105.3	100.0	100.0
July..	100.0	125.0	103.1	103.5	100.0	100.0
Oct...	104.8	125.0	101.2	101.8	100.0	100.0
1861, Jan...	95.2	125.0	89.0	187.7	100.0	100.0
April..	85.7	125.0	85.8	105.3	100.0	100.0
July..	85.7	125.0	92.0	94.7	100.0	100.0
Oct...	102.9	112.5	92.0	103.5	81.8	100.0
1862, Jan...	119.1	150.0	110.4	149.1	81.8	116.7
April..	152.4	125.0	135.0	149.1	81.8	116.7
July..	150.5	125.0	107.4	150.9	81.8	116.7
Oct...	145.7	150.0	116.6	150.9	109.1	116.7
1863, Jan...	190.5	200.0	171.8	219.3	127.3	100.0
April..	214.3	200.0	245.4	298.2	127.3	100.0
July..	190.5	175.0	147.3	210.5	127.3	100.0
Oct...	176.2	150.0	147.3	236.8	141.8	100.0
1864, Jan...	190.5	175.0	184.0	250.9	150.9	133.3
April..	195.2	175.0	214.7	280.7	200.0	133.3
July..	261.9	187.5	220.9	298.2	281.8	133.3
Oct...	333.3	250.0	199.4	245.6	345.5	133.3
1865, Jan...	319.1	237.5	230.1	271.9	250.9	150.0
April..	342.9	200.0	168.7	245.6	181.8	150.0
July..	323.8	150.0	116.6	207.0	96.4	150.0
Oct...	314.3	250.0	177.9	271.9	96.4	150.0

Date	Opium	Oxide of Zinc	Quicksilv'r	Quinine	Soda Ash	Sugar of Lead: Brown
1860, Jan...	100.0	111.1	100.0	100.0	100.0	100.0
April..	121.7	111.1	112.3	122.7	100.0	93.3
July..	95.7	100.0	113.3	136.4	94.7	93.3
Oct...	104.3	100.0	113.8	159.1	89.5	100.0
1861, Jan...	82.6	100.0	113.3	154.5	89.5	100.0
April..	91.3	100.0	108.7	172.7	89.5	93.3
July..	95.7	100.0	98.5	....	78.9	93.3
Oct...	100.0	100.0	96.4	190.9	105.5	93.3
1862, Jan...	87.0	100.0	96.4	227.3	121.1	126.7
April..	87.0	100.0	88.2	204.5	111.1	113.3
July..	108.7	100.0	114.8	236.4	105.5	113.3
Oct...	125.2	100.0	129.2	259.1	115.8	126.7

TABLE 2—*Continued*

RELATIVE PRICES OF VARIOUS COMMODITIES AT WHOLESALE

Date	Opium	Oxide of Zinc	Quicksilv'r	Quinine	Soda Ash	Sugar of Lead: Brown
1863, Jan...	146.1	100.0	139.5	254.5	126.3	166.7
April..	173.9	144.4	164.1	286.4	142.1	200.0
July ..	147.8	144.4	164.1	263.6	142.1	200.0
Oct...	169.6	138.9	160.0	227.3	142.1	120.0
1864, Jan...	169.6	144.4	184.6	231.8	152.6	186.7
April..	204.3	155.6	256.4	272.7	168.4	213.3
July ..	243.5	188.9	389.7	295.5	221.1	213.3
Oct...	300.0	200.0	307.7	304.6	205.2	640.0
1865, Jan...	121.7	200.0	256.4	295.5	273.7	533.3
April..	116.5	200.0	194.9	231.8	110.5	533.3
July ..	102.6	177.8	153.8	200.0	89.5	493.3
Oct...	126.1	200.0	174.4	268.2	136.8	.....

Date	Sugar of Lead; White	Sulphuric Acid	Candles	Coal		
				Anthracite Chestnut	Anthracite Egg	Anthracite Grate
1860, Jan...	100.0	100.0	100.0	100.0	100.0	100.0
April..	95.7	100.0	100.0	.....	100.0	100.0
July ..	95.7	100.0	96.3	92.1	97.4	97.3
Oct...	95.7	100.0	96.3	107.9	111.8	112.2
1861, Jan...	100.0	109.1	96.3	98.4	105.3	116.2
April..	100.0	109.1	96.3	103.2	93.4	110.8
July ..	100.0	109.1	96.3	95.2	97.4	97.3
Oct...	100.0	109.1	96.3	107.9	97.4	102.7
1862, Jan...	104.3	127.3	92.6	95.2	97.4	108.1
April..	100.0	127.3	88.9	85.7	92.1	91.9
July ..	104.3	127.3	88.9	82.5	93.4	90.5
Oct...	139.1	127.3	88.9	85.7	94.7	86.5
1863, Jan...	156.5	109.1	96.3	92.1	98.7	102.7
April..	226.1	109.1	100.0	187.3	155.3	159.5
July ..	173.9	109.1	100.0	190.5	168.4	168.9
Oct...	139.0	109.1	100.0	190.5	203.9	196.0
1864, Jan...	191.3	109.1	100.0	198.4	230.3	216.2
April..	208.7	109.1	100.0	.....	.....	.....
July ..	287.0	145.5	103.7	293.7	263.1	263.5
Oct...	478.3	172.7	148.1	230.2	223.7	229.7
1865, Jan...	413.0	172.7	148.1	269.8	250.0	243.2
April..	391.3	181.8	148.1	.....	.....	.....
July...	347.8	181.8	111.1	198.4	184.2	186.5
Oct...	434.8	181.8	111.1	309.5	276.3	283.8

TABLE 2 — *Continued*

RELATIVE PRICES OF VARIOUS COMMODITIES AT WHOLESALE

DATE	COAL		MATCHES	BRICK	CEMENT: Rosendale	CHESTNUT Lumber, in the Log
	Anthracite Stove	Bitumi- nous				
1860, Jan...	100.0	100.0	100.0	114.3	80.0	100.0
April..	.....	105.0	100.0	97.1	100.0	100.0
July..	98.7	102.0	100.0	100.0	100.0	100.0
Oct...	102.6	105.0	100.0	102.8	100.0	104.2
1861, Jan...	116.7	108.0	100.0	102.8	100.0	104.2
April..	94.9	96.0	100.0	91.4	90.0	108.3
July..	98.7	92.0	100.0	80.0	90.0	108.3
Oct...	97.4	97.0	100.0	85.7	90.0	108.3
1862, Jan...	98.7	97.0	100.0	85.7	90.0	116.7
April..	92.3	135.0	100.0	91.4	90.0	125.0
July..	93.6	122.0	100.0	91.4	90.0	133.3
Oct....	94.9	180.0	100.0	94.3	90.0	133.3
1863, Jan...	100.0	160.0	100.0	137.1	90.0	133.3
April..	151.3	150.0	100.0	140.0	120.0	133.3
July..	166.7	150.0	100.0	137.1	120.0	133.3
Oct....	201.3	160.0	100.0	148.6	120.0	133.3
1864, Jan...	243.6	173.0	100.0	205.7	120.0	133.3
April..	.....	180.0	100.0	171.4	140.0	133.3
July..	262.8	199.3	208.3	160.0	150.0	133.3
Oct...	224.4	233.2	208.3	217.1	160.0	133.3
1865, Jan...	243.6	256.2	208.3	211.4	160.0	133.3
April..	.....	250.0	395.8	217.1	160.0	133.3
July..	179.5	165.0	395.8	171.4	150.0	133.3
Oct...	275.6	200.0	395.8	262.9	175.0	133.3

Date	Hemlock: Lumber, in the Log	Lime: Rockland	Pine: Lumber, in the Log	Pine Boards: B'rds,1 in.	Putty	Rubber: Para
1860, Jan...	100.0	133.3	100.0	106.4	100.0	100.0
April..	100.0	141.7	100.0	106.4	100.0	109.1
July..	100.0	100.0	100.0	100.0	100.0	122.7
Oct...	133.3	125.0	125.0	106.4	100.0	118.2
1861, Jan...	133.3	133.3	125.0	106.4	116.7	100.0
April..	133.3	133.3	125.0	106.4	116.7	68.2
July..	133.3	133.3	125.0	106.4	116.7	81.8
Oct...	133.3	133.3	125.0	106.4	116.7	77.3
1862, Jan...	166.7	.....	187.5	106.4	133.3	87.3
April..	166.7	137.5	187.5	109.6	133.3	90.9
July..	183.3	91.7	187.5	106.4	133.3	104.5
Oct...	191.7	116.7	193.8	109.6	133.3	121.8

TABLE 2—*Continued*

RELATIVE PRICES OF VARIOUS COMMODITIES AT WHOLESALE

Date	Hemlock: Lumber, in the Log	Lime: Rockland	Pine: Lumber, in the Log	Pine Boards: B'rds, 1 in.	Putty	Rubber: Para
1863, Jan...	200.0	141.7	200.0	109.6	150.0	159.1
April..	200.0	141.7	200.0	132.0	150.0	154.5
July..	200.0	166.7	200.0	132.0	150.0	131.8
Oct...	200.0	191.7	200.0	148.0	150.0	136.4
1864, Jan...	200.0	175.0	200.0	148.0	166.7	145.5
April..	200.0	225.0	200.0	164.0	166.7	150.9
July..	200.0	166.7	200.0	196.0	166.7	172.7
Oct...	200.0	208.3	200.0	196.0	166.7	218.2
1865, Jan...	200.0	250.0	200.0	196.0	183.3	218.2
April..	200.0	266.7	200.0	196.0	183.3	154.5
July..	200.0	200.0	200.0	196.0	183.3	127.3
Oct...	200.0	300.0	200.0	228.0	183.3	136.4

Date	Spruce: Boards	Turpentine	Window Glass			
			American, 10×14, firsts	American, 10×14, thirds	French, 10×14 firsts	French, 10×14, thirds
1860, Jan...	91.7	110.0	91.7	105.8	85.1	106.3
April..	91.7	115.0	91.7	100.0	100.0	106.3
July..	100.0	100.0	100.0	100.0	100.0	100.0
Oct...	100.0	105.0	100.0	100.0	100.0	100.0
1861, Jan...	100.0	87.5	100.0	94.0	93.8	100.0
April..	100.0	90.0	100.0	95.6	108.9	97.7
July..	87.5	205.0	100.0	103.4	96.1	97.7
Oct...	83.3	362.5	100.0	111.2	96.1	109.1
1862, Jan...	83.3	350.0	100.0	118.5	96.1	118.9
April..	83.3	245.0	100.0	159.3	96.1	140.7
July..	79.2	325.0	100.0	159.3	96.1	156.3
Oct...	97.9	562.5	100.0	159.3	96.1	146.6
1863, Jan...	97.9	625.0	133.3	159.3	115.3	140.7
April..	97.9	675.0	133.3	171.5	140.6	156.3
July..	131.3	895.0	153.1	159.3	132.8	156.3
Oct...	127.1	687.5	131.3	159.3	117.2	156.3
1864, Jan...	127.1	750.0	131.3	220.5	125.0	185.3
April..	177.1	800.0	256.9	205.8	146.4	185.3
July..	202.1	900.0	208.3	245.0	223.4	224.7
Oct...	191.7	607.5	250.0	254.8	205.9	254.0
1865, Jan...	191.7	512.5	242.2	274.4	232.0	259.9
April..	168.8	500.0	209.9	240.1	193.4	218.9
July..	168.8	337.5	177.6	161.7	154.7	150.5
Oct...	168.8	262.5	226.0	212.3	180.5	177.8

TABLE 2— *Continued*

RELATIVE PRICES OF VARIOUS COMMODITIES AT WHOLESALE

DATE	BUTTS: Loose-joint, cast 3×3 in.	COPPER: Ingot	COPPER: Sheet	IRON: Wire	LEAD: Drop-shot	LEAD: Pig
1860, Jan...	100.0	100.0	100.0	.....	100.0	100.0
April..	100.0	97.9	100.0	.....	119.1	101.7
July..	93.0	89.4	100.0	100.0	114.9	98.0
Oct...	89.5	90.4	100.0	100.0	110.6	97.8
1861, Jan...	89.5	80.9	100.0	100.0	110.6	95.2
April..	89.5	80.9	93.2	100.0	110.6	95.2
July..	89.5	76.6	93.2	100.0	110.6	84.8
Oct...	89.5	87.2	93.2	100.0	119.1	100.4
1862, Jan...	89.5	112.8	93.2	100.0	144.7	121.2
April..	89.5	93.6	103.4	100.0	144.7	116.9
July..	112.3	97.9	103.4	100.0	144.7	116.9
Oct...	133.3	119.1	103.4	100.0	148.9	123.4
1863, Jan...	133.3	131.9	128.8	105.8	170.2	138.5
April..	133.3	129.8	144.1	232.7	204.3	155.8
July..	140.4	129.8	135.6	169.2	204.3	145.0
Oct...	140.4	138.3	128.8	137.5	187.2	147.2
1864, Jan...	178.9	160.6	162.7	211.5	229.8	186.1
April..	207.0	172.3	178.0	211.5	263.8	201.2
July..	266.7	197.9	194.9	211.5	357.6	251.1
Oct...	308.8	200.0	237.3	285.6	340.4	251.1
1865, Jan...	308.8	208.5	220.3	264.4	340.4	259.7
April..	308.8	144.7	169.5	211.5	272.4	.....
July..	277.2	121.3	152.5	148.1	238.3	173.1
Oct...	277.2	138.3	169.5	169.2	255.4	.....

Date	Lead: Pipe	Shovels	Spelter: Imported	Tin Plates: I. C. Coke	Wood Screws: 1-inch, No. 10, Flat Head, Iron	Zinc: Imported Sheet
1860, Jan...	100.0	100.0	100.0	100.0	100.0	100.0
April..	116.7	100.0	100.0	101.7	100.0	100.0
July..	112.5	100.0	99.0	101.7	80.5	101.8
Oct...	104.2	100.0	95.2	96.5	116.7	96.4
1861, Jan...	104.2	100.0	90.5	94.7	116.7	92.9
April..	108.3	100.0	90.5	98.2	116.7	100.0
July..	108.3	100.0	81.0	98.2	116.7	100.0
Oct...	116.7	100.0	85.7	89.5	116.7	103.6
1862, Jan...	141.7	94.7	109.5	108.9	116.7	103.6
April..	141.7	94.7	95.2	105.3	116.7	103.6
July..	141.7	98.7	114.3	105.3	116.7	103.6
Oct...	145.8	98.7	83.3	122.8	116.7	128.6

TABLE 2—*Continued*

RELATIVE PRICES OF VARIOUS COMMODITIES AT WHOLESALE

Date	Lead: Pipe	Shovels	Spelter: Imported	Tin Plates: I. C. Coke	Wood Screws: 1-Inch, No. 10, Flat Head. Iron	Zinc: Imported, Sheet
1863, Jan...	166.7	102.6	142.9	129.8	135.0	146.4
April..	166.7	.....	161.9	154.4	158.3	178.6
July..	200.0	.....	147.6	136.8	158.3	164.3
Oct...	183.3	122.8	161.9	136.8	118.8	157.1
1864, Jan...	225.0	135.9	176.2	154.4	158.3	171.4
April..	258.3	161.0	238.1	196.5	158.3	214.3
July..	350.0	200.4	333.3	308.8	215.7	357.1
Oct...	333.3	200.4	257.1	210.5	215.7	257.1
1865, Jan...	333.3	184.2	285.7	238.6	215.7	285.7
April..	266.7	184.2	171.4	147.4	215.7	185.7
July..	233.3	134.2	171.4	143.8	215.7	171.4
Oct...	216.7	134.2	202.4	154.4	215.7	207.1

DATE	FURNITURE			PAILS: WOODEN		
	Chairs, Bed-Room	Chairs, Kitchen	Tables, Kitchen	2 Hoops (1)	2 Hoops (2)	3 Hoops
1860, Jan...	100.0	100.0	100.0	100.0	100.0	100.0
April..	100.0	100.0	100.0	100.0	100.0	100.0
July..	100.0	100.0	100.0	100.0	100.0	100.0
Oct...	80.0	100.0	100.0	100.0	100.0	100.0
1861, Jan...	80.0	100.0	100.0	98.2	100.0	100.0
April..	80.0	100.0	100.0	98.2	100.0	100.0
July..	80.0	100.0	100.0	98.2	100.0	100.0
Oct...	80.0	100.0	100.0	98.2	98.1	96.9
1862, Jan...	80.0	100.0	100.0	92.9	92.6	93.8
April..	80.0	100.0	100.0	92.9	92.6	93.8
July..	80.0	100.0	100.0	107.1	107.4	106.3
Oct...	80.0	100.0	100.0	121.4	119.3	118.8
1863, Jan...	85.0	100.0	100.0	121.4	122.2	125.0
April..	105.0	100.0	112.5	150.0	151.9	146.9
July..	105.0	100.0	112.5	139.3	138.5	137.5
Oct...	110.0	111.1	112.5	139.3	138.5	140.6
1864, Jan...	125.0	122.2	112.5	160.7	163.0	156.3
April..	125.0	122.2	125.0	178.6	183.0	176.3
July..	145.0	133.3	137.5	178.6	181.5	176.9
Oct...	180.0	166.7	162.5	178.6	183.0	178.1
1865, Jan...	180.0	166.7	162.5	178.6	183.0	178.1
April..	150.0	155.6	150.0	178.6	181.5	178.1
July..	145.0	144.4	150.0	142.9	146.7	140.6
Oct...	145.0	144.4	150.0	214.3	218.5	203.1

TABLE 2 — *Continued*

RELATIVE PRICES OF VARIOUS COMMODITIES AT WHOLESALE

DATE	TUBS: WOODEN				JUTE	POWDER: Rifle
	(1)	(2)	(3)	(4)		
1860, Jan...	100.0	100.0	100.0	100.0	100.0	100.0
April..	100.0	100.0	100.0	97.8	108.6	100.0
July..	100.0	100.0	96.6	93.3	105.7	100.0
Oct...	100.0	100.0	89.7	88.9	100.0	100.0
1861, Jan...	90.0	93.8	89.7	88.9	114.3	100.0
April..	90.0	93.8	89.7	88.9	91.4	100.0
July..	90.0	93.8	89.7	88.9	91.4	120.0
Oct...	90.0	93.8	86.2	86.7	102.9	120.0
1862, Jan...	90.0	83.8	81.4	80.0	146.3	140.0
April..	100.0	100.0	89.7	98.7	125.7	120.0
July..	110.0	100.0	96.6	95.6	108.6	130.0
Oct...	120.0	112.5	105.2	104.4	148.0	130.0
1863, Jan...	140.0	137.5	124.1	124.4	205.7	130.0
April..	148.0	142.5	127.7	126.7	257.1	135.0
July..	148.0	142.5	131.0	128.9	194.3	135.0
Oct...	152.0	150.0	131.0	128.9	182.8	147.0
1864, Jan...	170.0	162.5	148.3	144.4	251.4	145.0
April..	189 6	168.5	165.5	151.1	320.0	152.0
July..	200.0	175.0	175.9	157.8	354.3	174.0
Oct...	170.0	168.8	148.3	148.9	314.3	172.0
1865, Jan...	180.0	150.0	170.3	154.2	320.0	180.0
April..	140.0	193.8	124.1	126.7	302.8	175.0
July..	160.0	156.3	144.8	140.0	200.0	170.0
Oct...	170.0	162.5	148.3	144.4	171.4	170.0

DATE	ROPE		SOAP: Castile	STARCH		
	Manilla	Tarred, American		Ontario	Pearl	Pure
1860, Jan...	100.0	100.0	100.0	.....	100.0	100.0
April..	100.0	100.0	114.7	100.0	100.0	100.0
July..	97.0	100.0	117.6	100.0	100.0	100.0
Oct...	97.0	100.0	108.8	100.0	100.0	100.0
1861, Jan...	97.0	.....	114.7	100.0	100.0	100.0
April..	106.1	108.1	111.8	100.0	100.0	100.0
July..	93.9	105.1	117.6	100.0	100.0	100.0
Oct...	90.9	.....	141.2	100.0	91.7	92.3
1862, Jan...	121.2	118.9	152.9	100.0	91.7	92.3
April..	130.3	118.9	158.8	100.0	91.7	92.3
July..	124.2	113.5	155.9	100.0	91.7	92.3
Oct...	145.4	129.7	164.7	110.0	100.0	100.0

TABLE 2 — *Continued*

RELATIVE PRICES OF VARIOUS COMMODITIES AT WHOLESALE

DATE	ROPE		SOAP : Castile	STARCH		
	Manilla	Tarred, American		Ontario	Pearl	Pure
1863, Jan...	151.5	143.2	170.6	130.0	116.7	115.4
April..	218.2	164.9	202.9	140.0	125.0	123.1
July..	172.7	162.2	200.0	130.0	116.7	115.4
Oct...	184.8	154.1	194.0	130.0	116.7	115.4
1864, Jan...	197.0	164.9	217.6	160.0	141.7	138.5
April..	230 3	164.9	205.9	180.0	158.3	153.8
July..	254.5	167.6	282.4	200.0	175.0	169.2
Oct...	303.0	205.4	247.1	244.2	191.7	184.6
1865, Jan...	284.8	200.0	294.1	240.0	208.3	200.0
April..	242.4	194.6	247.1	240.0	208.3	200.0
July..	242.4	194.6	194.0	200.0	175.0	169.2
Oct...	272.7	194.6	252.9	200.0	175.0	169.2

DATE	STARCH		DATE	STARCH	
	Refined	Silver Gloss		Refined	Silver Gloss
1860, January..	100.0	100.0	1863, January..	114.3	112.9
April.....	100.0	100.0	April.....	121.4	119.4
July......	100.0	100.0	July......	114.3	112.9
October..	100.0	100.0	October..	114.3	112.9
1861, January..	100.0	100.0	1864, January..	135.7	132.3
April.....	100.0	100.0	April.....	150.0	145.2
July......	100.0	100.0	July......	164.3	158.1
October..	92.9	93.5	October..	178.6	171.0
1862, January..	92.9	93.5	1865, January..	192.9	183.9
April.....	92.9	93.5	April.....	192.9	183.9
July......	92.9	93.5	July......	164.3	158.1
October..	100.0	100.0	October..	164.3	158.1

TABLE 3

RELATIVE PRICES PAID BY FEDERAL GOVERNMENT FOR SUPPLIES, 1860-65 [1]

1. Relative Prices Paid by the Quartermaster General (War Department). Pp. 1596, 1597. Date within Year Not Specified

	1860	1861	1862	1863	1864	1865
Caps, forage...................	100	111	98	102	114	175
Hats, uniform	100	66	69	70	77	96
Great coats..................	100	113	148	117	133	188
Coats, blue flannel, sack	100	102	114	112	126	191
Coats, blue flannel, sack, lined.	100	103	123	122	127	188
Trousers.	100	107	126	89	110	168
Shirts, flannel	100	98	162	170	174	258
Stockings	100	108	133	133	146	200

2. Relative Prices Paid by the Office of the Commissary General of Subsistence (War Department). Pp. 1806-9. Average Prices for Year

		1861	1862	1863	1864	1865
Pork.........................	...	100	89	110	217	238
Bacon........................	...	100	100	100	229	300
Ham.........................	...	100	90	130	190	250
Beef cattle	...	100	100	124	200	232
Fresh beef	...	100	100	100	167	183
Salt beef.....................	...	100	96	94	147	144
Flour	...	100	111	130	175	170
Soft bread	...	100	100	100	133	133
Hard bread	...	100	100	100	150	175
Corn meal....................	...	100	200	300	300	400
Beans........................	...	100	133	167	167	133
Peas	...	100	100	150	150	300
Rice	...	100	86	114	157	143
Hominy......................	...	100	100	150	200	200
Desiccated potatoes...........	...	100	110	100	110	140
Mixed vegetables..............	...	100	109	87	78	109
Green coffee..................	...	100	153	213	293	247
R. and R. and G. coffee.......	...	100	145	190	250	160
Tea..........................	...	100	129	167	239	280
Brown sugar	...	100	111	133	211	167
White sugar..................	...	100	120	160	250	260
Vinegar	...	100	91	146	264	318
Candles......................	...	100	106	122	172	167
Soap.........................	...	100	120	140	220	220
Salt..........................	...	100	117	119	119	119

[1] The data from which the following series of relative prices have been computed are found in the "exhibits" of the *Aldrich Report* on the pages indicated under the several divisions of the table.

TABLE 3 — *Continued*

RELATIVE PRICES PAID BY FEDERAL GOVERNMENT FOR SUPPLIES, 1860–65

3. Relative Prices Paid by Bureau of Provisions and Clothing (Navy Department).
Pp. 1586–93. Date within Year Not Specified

	1860	1861	1862	1863	1864	1865
Beans........................	100	86	100	150	215	215
Beef, fresh...................	100	101	91	86	125	153
Sugar........................	100	94	74	100	281	275
Vegetables...................	100	92	123	84	77	163
Blankets.....................	...	100	99	132	232	329
Flannel.......................	...	100	92	124	232	276
Overshirts, flannel............	100	96	92	103	201	267
Satinet.......................	...	100	94	99	180	238
Trousers, canvas duck........	100	98	97	105	194	350
Trousers, cloth	100	71	68	75	132	207
Shoes, calf skin..............	100	86	74	83	124	149
Socks, woolen................	100	109	102	113	208	234
Mattresses...................	100	97	94	97	244	265
Linseed oil, boiled............	...	100	64	123	190	227
Turpentine...................	100	117	319	576	488	836

4. Relative Prices for Drugs and Chemicals Paid by Surgeon General (War Department). Pp. 1620-24. Average Prices for Year

	1860	1861	1862	1863	1864	1865
Aconite......................	100	107	107	107	200	200
Aloes........................	100	129	167	147	160	160
Alum........................	100	87	91	66	103	103
Ammonia	100	100	100	100	160	160
Arnica	100	115	133	133	167	167
Calomel	100	100	92	112	223	214
Camphor.....................	100	119	222	237	423	420
Castor oil	100	88	90	123	133	105
Chalk........................	100	100	100	100	120	120
Chloroform	100	99	100	100	128	164
Cod liver oil..................	100	71	71	71	77	77
Ether	100	150	54	60	126	131
Extract of ginger.............	100	113	114	114	120	120
Extract of wild cherry bark...	100	100	128	112	200	263
Gum Arabic..................	100	131	134	134	213	213
Ipecac.......................	100	104	116	117	223	265
Laudanum	100	100	100	100	300	300
Magnesia....................	100	89	83	93	208	283
Nitric acid	100	93	75	60	68	95
Olive oil.....................	100	100	100	100	147	147
Opium	100	101	102	115	185	185
Pills, cathartic...............	100	75	75	75	100	100

TABLE 3 — *Continued*

RELATIVE PRICES PAID BY FEDERAL GOVERNMENT FOR SUPPLIES, 1860–65

	1860	1861	1862	1863	1864	1865
Potassium chlorate............	100	104	104	104	200	200
Potassium iodide.............	100	100	100	100	126	126
Quinine......................	100	123	149	187	196	130
Squills, syrup of..............	100	100	100	100	118	118
Sulphur......................	100	111	131	100	100	100
Sulphuric acid	100	81	67	78	111	111
Tartar emetic	100	90	83	120	120	120
Turpentine...................	100	124	163	283	200	211
Zinc, sulphate of	100	100	100	100	267	300

TABLE 4

RELATIVE PRICES OF VARIOUS COMMODITIES AT RETAIL[1]

RELATIVE PRICES OF DRY GOODS AT RETAIL — COTTON FLANNEL, MEDIUM
QUALITY

State	Town	Initial Price per Yd.	1860	1861	1862	1863	1864	1865	1866
Mass. ...	Woburn..........	0.13	100	131	231	269	385	385	346
Conn....	Jewett City......	.15	100	100	113	250	333	387	320
Pa.......	New Castle......	.125	100	120	200	360	440	400	240
W. Va...	New Cumberland	.14	100	179	286	357	429	429	357
W. Va...	Wheeling.........	.125	100	120	200	300	600	480	400
Ohio	Canton...........	.125	100	96	300	400	600	520	400
Ohio	Cincinnati.......	.125	100	100	100	120	200	300	200
Ohio	Zanesville	.10	100	150	200	220	350	370	280
Ind......	Jeffersonville....	.08⅓	100	300	300	300	300	300	300
Ind......	Lawrenceburg...	.125	100	100	200	360	720	600	600
Ind......	New Albany.....	.10	100	125	250	400	500	400	300
Ill.......	Bloomington.....	.125	100	120	200	320	520	720	520

[1] The source of the following series of relative prices at retail is the report prepared by Mr. J. D. Weeks in 1880–83 and published as Vol. XX of the Tenth Census. Not all of the material supplied by Mr. Weeks, however, has been used, for he gives some series of prices at unspecified times of the year and others "on or about June 1." Those series "showing average for the year" alone were used as the basis for the computations in the text, and they alone are given here. The general divisions of the series — dry goods, groceries, provisions, etc. — are the same as in the Census report; but under these heads a classification according to articles was found more convenient than the one according to towns which Mr. Weeks adopted. However, as the state and town from which every series comes are carefully stated, there need be no difficulty in tracing any series to its source. In the case of rent figures are given for 1867 and 1868 for the purposes of Part II, chap. vi.

TABLE 4 — *Continued*

RELATIVE PRICES OF DRY GOODS AT RETAIL — MOUSSELINES DE LAINE

State	Town	Initial Price per Yd.	1860	1861	1862	1863	1864	1865	1866
Mass....	Woburn..........	0.33	100	100	91	91	100	115	106
Conn....	Jewett City......	.25	100	88	100	150	250	268	268
Pa......	New Castle......	.25	100	100	120	140	180	160	140
W. Va...	New Cumberland	.15	100	200	267	400	467	467	267
W. Va...	Wheeling........	.25	100	124	150	160	240	200	150
Ohio....	Canton..........	.25	100	100	120	160	200	150	120
Ohio....	Cincinnati.......	.25	100	100	100	150	160	160	160
Ohio....	Zanesville.......	.15	100	233	267	300	467	267	233
Ind.....	Evansville.......	.20	100	125	175	250	250	250	...
Ind.....	Jeffersonville....	.20	100	175	175	175	175	175	175
Ind.....	Lawrenceburg...	.25	100	100	140	160	260	180	160
Ind.....	New Albany.....	.18	100	111	167	194	222	167	139
Ill......	Bloomington.....	.25	100	100	100	140	140	160	120

PRINTS, MERRIMACK

State	Town	Initial Price per Yd.	1860	1861	1862	1863	1864	1865	1866
Mass....	Woburn..........	0.13	100	115	154	154	154	246	192
Conn....	Jewett City......	.125	100	100	112	176	240	300	264
Pa......	New Castle......	.125	100	100	144	200	300	280	200
W. Va...	New Cumberland	.09	100	222	278	444	556	556	333
W. Va...	Wheeling........	.125	100	120	200	240	400	320	240
Ohio....	Canton..........	.125	100	80	144	240	400	320	240
Ohio....	Cincinnati.......	.125	100	80	100	120	240	300	360
Ohio....	Zanesville.......	.125	100	96	120	176	320	240	200
Ind.....	Evansville.......	.10	100	100	150	250	500	450	300
Ind.....	Jeffersonville....	.125	100	100	100	100	100	120	200
Ind.....	Lawrenceburg...	.125	100	100	160	240	480	280	200
Ind.....	New Albany.....	.10	100	105	200	300	400	250	200
Ill......	Bloomington....	.125	100	100	200	240	360	440	320

SATINETS, MEDIUM QUALITY

State	Town	Initial Price per Yd.	1860	1861	1862	1863	1864	1865	1866
Conn....	Jewett City......	0.75	100	100	133	166	177	177	173
Pa......	New Castle......	1.00	100	100	125	138	150	140	150
W. Va...	New Cumberland	0.11	100	227	364	455	545	545	273
W. Va...	Wheeling........	.75	100	133	167	167	200	200	167
Ohio....	Canton..........	.75	100	100	133	167	200	167	133
Ohio....	Cincinnati.......	.75	100	100	107	113	120	133	133
Ohio....	Zanesville.......	.40	100	100	150	250	213	163	150
Ind.....	Jeffersonville....	.75	100	133	133	133	133	133	133
Ind.....	Lawrenceburg...	.70	100	107	179	179	214	143	143
Ind.....	New Albany.....	.625	100	100	120	172	172	144	144
Ill......	Bloomington.....	.75	100	87	100	133	133	167	133

TABLE 4 — *Continued*

RELATIVE PRICES OF DRY GOODS AT RETAIL—SHEETINGS: BLEACHED, 9 × 8,
STANDARD QUALITY

State	Town	Initial Price per Yd.	1860	1861	1862	1863	1864	1865	1866
Mass....	Woburn.........	0.14	100	114	321	357	250	286	271
Pa	New Castle......	.17	100	118	165	294	353	353	324
W. Va...	New Cumberland	.10	100	200	350	450	500	600	500
W. Va...	Wheeling........	.15	100	107	233	333	533	400	300
Ohio	Canton..........	.15	100	100	250	367	533	467	367
Ohio	Cincinnati	.25	100	110	130	150	160	170	160
Ohio	Zanesville	.13	100	138	169	231	577	346	269
Ind	Lawrenceburg...	.30	100	107	217	317	333	283	300
Ind	New Albany.....	.095	100	111	242	400	579	474	421
Ill.......	Bloomington	.15	100	133	200	300	400	433	300

SHEETINGS: BROWN, 9 × 8, STANDARD QUALITY

Mass....	Woburn.........	0.13	100	115	308	346	308	346	308
Pa	New Castle......	.125	100	120	200	360	440	400	240
W.Va...	New Cumberland	.08	100	225	375	500	625	625	500
W.Va...	Wheeling........	.125	100	120	240	360	600	400	320
Ohio	Canton..........	.125	100	96	280	400	600	520	400
Ohio	Cincinnati.......	.20	100	125	150	175	190	200	190
Ohio	Zanesville	.13	100	138	169	231	562	308	269
Ind	Jeffersonville....	.15	100	167	167	167	167	167	167
Ind	Lawrenceburg...	.28	100	107	214	321	357	304	321
Ind	New Albany.....	.0775	100	135	232	684	877	684	555
Ill.......	Bloomington.....	.15	100	133	233	333	433	500	333

SHIRTINGS: BLEACHED, 4 × 4, STANDARD QUALITY

Mass....	Woburn.........	0.125	100	104	320	360	280	240	240
Conn....	Jewett City......	.16	100	81	100	234	375	419	344
Pa	New Castle......	.15	100	120	167	300	373	367	333
W.Va. .	New Cumberland	.08	100	225	375	500	625	625	500
W.Va...	Wheeling........	.10	100	150	300	400	800	500	400
Ohio	Canton	.125	100	120	240	400	600	480	360
Ohio	Cincinnati.......	.15	100	83	90	133	267	267	300
Ohio	Zanesville	.10	100	150	200	300	650	350	300
Ind	Evansville.......	.10	100	100	125	350	600	650	400
Ind	Jeffersonville	.125	100	120	160	280	440	600	528
Ind	Lawrenceburg...	.125	100	120	176	360	600	360	320
Ind	New Albany.....	.085	100	112	235	412	588	471	412
Ill.......	Bloomington	.125	100	120	200	320	440	480	320

TABLE 4 — *Continued*

RELATIVE PRICES OF DRY GOODS AT RETAIL — SHIRTINGS: BROWN, 4 × 4, STANDARD
QUALITY

State	Town	Initial Price per Yd.	1860	1861	1862	1863	1864	1865	1866
Mass	Woburn	0.11	100	100	318	409	227	227	227
Conn....	Jewett City......	.125	100	88	112	280	400	440	360
Pa	New Castle......	.10	100	120	220	400	500	450	250
W. Va...	New Cumberland	.06	100	250	417	500	667	667	500
W. Va...	Wheeling........	.10	100	125	250	400	750	500	400
Ohio	Canton..........	.09	110	111	222	556	833	556	444
Ohio	Cincinnati.......	.10	100	150	500	600	750	750	650
Ohio	Zanesville.......	.10	100	150	200	350	700	350	300
Ind......	Evansville.......	.085	100	100	118	588	882	824	588
Ind......	Jeffersonville....	.10	100	150	200	300	500	750	600
Ind	Lawrenceburg...	.08	100	113	225	563	813	500	500
Ind	New Albany.....	.0675	100	111	222	741	963	741	593
Ill	Bloomington	.125	100	120	240	360	480	560	360

TICKINGS: GOOD QUALITY

State	Town	Initial Price	1860	1861	1862	1863	1864	1865	1866
Mass	Woburn	0.17	100	118	259	259	259	265	235
Conn....	Jewett City......	.22	100	100	114	150	250	305	273
Pa	New Castle......	.25	100	120	180	220	300	272	260
W. Va...	New Cumberland	.28	100	143	179	250	250	268	143
W. Va...	Wheeling........	.25	100	100	160	200	400	300	240
Ohio	Canton..........	.25	100	100	200	400	500	400	300
Ohio	Cincinnati.......	.225	100	156	167	178	222	333	333
Ohio	Zanesville.......	.25	100	160	200	220	340	220	148
Ind	Jeffersonville....	.25	100	200	200	200	200	200	200
Ind	Lawrenceburg...	.25	100	100	160	200	360	300	320
Ind	New Albany.....	.17	100	118	206	294	441	382	294
Ill.......	Bloomington	.18	100	139	222	278	500	639	500

RELATIVE PRICES OF GROCERIES AT RETAIL — COFFEE: RIO, GREEN

State	Town	per lb.	1860	1861	1862	1863	1864	1865	1866
Mass	Boston	0.13	100	108	172	197	319	254	205
Pa	Philadelphia	.11	...	100	118	155	291	318	309
Md......	Baltimore	.16	100	100	150	219	250	219	188
W. Va...	New Cumberland	.12	100	125	150	167	208	208	167
Ohio	Canton..........	.16	100	94	125	250	313	250	250
Ohio	Springfield	.15	100	80	100	100	167	267	333
Ohio ...	Zanesville.......	.15	100	100	100	133	167	167	200
Ind	Lawrenceburg..	.25	100	100	140	140	160	140	160
Iowa	Cedar Rapids....	.08	...	100	125	313	438	438	375

TABLE 4 — *Continued*

RELATIVE PRICES OF GROCERIES AT RETAIL — MOLASSES: NEW ORLEANS

State	Town	Initial Price per gal.	1860	1861	1862	1863	1864	1865	1866
Pa	Philadelphia.....	0.40	...	100	125	150	175	200	275
W. Va...	New Cumberland	.40	100	125	188	225	250	225	225
Ohio	Canton..........	.40	100	100	250	375	375	313	250
Ohio	Zanesville	.50	100	100	100	150	200	200	250
Ind......	Lawrenceburg...	.60	100	100	100	133	267	250	167
Iowa	Cedar Rapids ...	.50	...	100	100	120	160	220	240

MOLASSES: PORTO RICO

State	Town	Initial Price	1860	1861	1862	1863	1864	1865	1866
Mass	Boston..........	0.26	...	100	123	180	298	245	223
Pa	Philadelphia.....	.40	...	100	100	125	163	200	200
Md......	Baltimore.	.40	100	88	100	125	250	200	200
W. Va...	New Cumberland	.25	100	200	240	320	360	320	360
Ohio	Canton..........	.35	...	100	171	357	357	286	243
Ohio	Springfield	.50	...	100	120	150	150	150	160
Ohio	Zanesville	.55	100	109	109	154	218	227	227
Ind.....	Lawrenceburg...	.40	100	125	125	188	250	250	200
Iowa	Cedar Rapids....	.30	...	100	100	133	133	167	167

SIRUP

State	Town	Initial Price	1860	1861	1862	1863	1864	1865	1866
Pa	Philadelphia	0.50	...	100	110	110	120	160	180
Md.....	Baltimore	.60	100	100	100	117	233	233	167
W. Va...	New Cumberland	.40	100	125	188	250	313	250	250
Ohio	Springfield	.60	100	125	133	167	208	250	250
Ohio	Zanesville	.75	100	80	80	120	167	167	200
Ind.	Lawrenceburg...	.80	100	94	100	125	125	125	150
Ia.......	Cedar Rapids....	.50	...	100	120	120	140	140	200

CODFISH: DRY

State	Town	per lb.	1860	1861	1862	1863	1864	1865	1866
Conn...	Jewett City......	0.05	100	80	100	130	160	160	160
Pa	Philadelphia.....	.04	...	100	100	125	150	175	225
W. Va...	New Cumberland	.06	100	133	167	167	167	167	167
Ohio	Canton..........	.10	100	100	100	100	100	100	100
Ohio	Zanesville	.05	100	100	100	140	160	200	200
Ind......	Lawrenceburg...	.10	100	100	100	100	120	120	100
Iowa	Cedar Rapids....	.06	...	100	117	133	175	208	208

TABLE 4 — *Continued*

RELATIVE PRICES OF GROCERIES AT RETAIL — SUGAR: YELLOW C

State	Town	Initial Price per lb.	1860	1861	1862	1863	1864	1865	1866
Pa	Philadelphia.....	0.07	...	100	114	143	171	214	229
W.Va....	New Cumberland	.07	100	171	200	200	200	200	171
Ohio	Canton..........	.10	100	80	125	150	250	200	160
Ohio	Springfield	.10	100	100	100	150	150	200	250
Ohio	Zanesville.......	.10	100	100	150	200	200	250	200
Ind......	Lawrenceburg...	.12	100	100	100	100	117	117	117
Iowa	Cedar Rapids....	.07	...	100	129	129	157	157	200

SUGAR: YELLOW B

State	Town	Initial Price per lb.	1860	1861	1862	1863	1864	1865	1866
Pa.......	Philadelphia	0.08	...	100	113	138	163	200	213
W. Va...	New Cumberland	.06	100	167	200	200	200	200	200
Ohio	Canton..........	.11	100	73	114	145	227	182	136
Ohio	Zanesville.......	.11	100	109	164	200	200	227	227
Ind.	Lawrenceburg...	.11	100	100	100	100	109	109	109
Iowa	Cedar Rapids....	.08	...	100	125	125	150	150	156

BEANS

State	Town	per qt.	1860	1861	1862	1863	1864	1865	1866
Mass	Boston..........	0.06	100	100	150	167	179	142	175
Conn	Jewett City......	.06	100	117	133	167	167	150	133
Pa	Philadelphia	.06	...	100	133	167	150	200	233
W. Va...	New Cumberland	.07	100	143	171	171	171	171	171
Ohio	Canton..........	.05	100	80	100	160	200	200	160
Ohio	Springfield	.05	100	100	100	100	160	160	160
Ohio	Zanesville.......	.06¼	100	96	112	128	160	160	160
Ind......	Lawrenceburg...	.10	100	100	100	100	100	100	120
Iowa	Cedar Rapids....	.10	...	100	100	120	120	125	125

SOAP: COMMON

State	Town	Initial Price per lb.	1860	1861	1862	1863	1864	1865	1866
Pa	Philadelphia.....	0.06	...	100	117	133	150	167	167
W. Va...	New Cumberland	.06	100	117	133	133	133	117	117
Ohio	Canton..........	.08	100	75	75	125	150	125	113
Ohio	Springfield	.05	100	120	160	160	160	160	160
Ohio	Zanesville.......	.05	100	100	120	200	200	200	200
Ind.	Lawrenceburg...	.12	100	67	83	125	125	125	125
Iowa	Cedar Rapids....	.04	...	100	100	100	150	250	375

TABLE 4 — *Continued*

RELATIVE PRICES OF GROCERIES AT RETAIL —SUGAR: GOOD BROWN

State	Town	Initial Price per lb.	1860	1861	1862	1863	1864	1865	1866
Mass	Boston	0.06$\frac{5}{16}$	100	99	133	175	266	225	183
N. J.	Jersey City	.08	100	100	113	175	250	263	300
Pa	Norristown	.07	100	100	114	157	314	186	186
Pa	Philadelphia	.06	...	100	117	150	183	233	250
Md	Baltimore	.08	100	88	125	156	250	188	175
W. Va...	New Cumberland	.06	100	167	200	200	200	200	200
Ohio	Canton	.08	100	75	100	150	250	250	225
Ohio	Springfield	.09	100	89	89	111	122	167	200
Ohio	Zanesville	.08	100	100	125	150	225	225	225
Ind......	Lawrenceburg...	.10	100	100	100	100	120	110	110
Iowa	Cedar Rapids....	.06	...	100	133	133	167	167	278

COFFEE: RIO, ROASTED

State	Town	Initial Price	1860	1861	1862	1863	1864	1865	1866
Pa	Philadelphia	0.16	...	100	113	138	238	281	281
Md......	Baltimore	.20	100	100	150	210	250	210	180
W. Va...	New Cumberland	.14	100	143	179	179	214	214	179
Ohio	Springfield	.18	100	100	100	100	167	250	333
Ohio	Zanesville	.16	100	94	94	113	125	125	156
Ind......	Lawrenceburg...	.30	100	100	133	133	150	133	150
Iowa	Cedar Rapids....	.10	...	100	120	200	450	450	350

TEA: OOLONG, OR OTHER GOOD BLACK

State	Town	Initial Price	1860	1861	1862	1863	1864	1865	1866
Pa	Philadelphia	0.50	...	100	100	110	130	250	250
Md	Baltimore	.60	100	125	167	167	200	250	208
W. Va...	New Cumberland	.50	100	120	160	160	160	180	160
Ohio	Canton	1.00	100	100	125	150	200	200	180
Ohio	Springfield	0.60	...	100	100	125	250	333	293
Ohio	Zanesville	.925	100	97	97	122	135	149	176
Ind......	Lawrenceburg...	1.00	100	90	100	125	160	160	125
Iowa	Cedar Rapids....	0.30	...	100	233	467	533	667	667

STARCH

State	Town	Initial Price	1860	1861	1862	1863	1864	1865	1866
Pa	Philadelphia.....	0.07	...	100	114	143	171	200	200
W. Va...	New Cumberland	.07	100	114	143	143	143	114	114
Ohio	Canton	.10	100	100	125	150	150	125	100
Ohio	Springfield	.05	100	100	100	160	200	200	200
Ohio	Zanesville	.08	100	125	125	125	188	188	188
Ind......	Lawrenceburg...	.10	100	80	100	120	100	100	100
Iowa	Cedar Rapids....	.05	...	100	100	140	200	360	360

TABLE 4 — *Continued*

RELATIVE PRICES OF PROVISIONS AT RETAIL — BEEF: CORNED

State	Town	Initial Price per Pound	1860	1861	1862	1863	1864	1865	1866
Mass. ...	Boston	0.0775	100	97	97	133	164	200	194
Conn. ...	Jewett City	.08	100	100	88	88	156	150	188
Conn. ...	New London	.10	100	110	110	140	140	140	140
N. J.	Camden..........	.08	100	100	100	125	175	225	225
Pa.	Philadelphia	.09	...	100	100	111	133	156	167
W. Va. ..	New Cumberland	.08	100	125	125	125	125	125	125
Ohio	Canton..........	.06	...	100	133	167	208	200	167
Ohio	Springfield	.065	100	92	92	92	123	123	123
Ohio	Zanesville	.08	100	100	100	125	125	125	125
Ind.	Evansville	.10	...	100	100	100	125	125	125

BEEF: FRESH, ROASTING PIECES

State	Town	Initial Price per Pound	1860	1861	1862	1863	1864	1865	1866
Mass. ...	Boston	0.115	100	100	100	130	166	207	211
Conn. ...	New London	.13	100	123	123	138	154	169	169
N. J.	Camden..........	.14	100	100	100	114	179	250	250
Pa.	Philadelphia	.10	...	100	100	120	140	180	180
W. Va. ..	New Cumberland	.08	100	150	150	150	150	150	150
Ohio	Canton..........	.08	...	100	125	156	188	156	156
Ohio	Springfield	.085	100	94	94	94	147	147	147
Ohio	Zanesville	.09	100	89	100	111	111	111	111
Ind.	Evansville	.075	...	100	100	167	200	200	200

BUTTER

State	Town	Initial Price per Pound	1860	1861	1862	1863	1864	1865	1866
Mass. ...	Boston	0.23⅙	100	86	90	106	159	183	199
Conn. ...	Jewett City	.23	100	96	91	109	122	143	196
Pa.	Philadelphia	.20	...	100	110	120	125	150	140
W. Va. ..	New Cumberland	.16	100	125	125	125	125	125	125
Ohio	Canton..........	.12	100	67	83	150	333	292	292
Ohio	Springfield	.10	100	80	80	100	150	250	300
Ohio	Zanesville	.13	100	96	115	115	231	254	254
Ind.	Lawrenceburg...	.30	100	83	100	83	117	150	100
Ia.	Cedar Rapids....	.06	...	100	200	250	333	417	333

TABLE 4 — *Continued*

RELATIVE PRICES OF PROVISIONS AT RETAIL.— BEEF: FRESH, RUMP STEAKS

State	Town	Initial Price per lb.	1860	1861	1862	1863	1864	1865	1866
Conn. . . .	New London	0.11	100	109	109	127	145	164	164
N. J.	Camden.	.12	100	102	104	133	208	250	250
Pa.	Philadelphia . . .	.14	. . .	100	107	114	143	179	179
W. Va. . .	New Cumberland	.10	100	140	140	140	140	140	140
Ohio	Canton.	.10	100	110	125	150	180	150	150
Ohio	Springfield	.10	100	100	100	100	150	150	150
Ohio	Zanesville	.11	100	91	91	109	109	109	109
Ind.	Evansville.	.075	. . .	100	100	167	200	200	200

BEEF: FRESH, SOUP-PIECES

State	Town	Initial Price	1860	1861	1862	1863	1864	1865	1866
Conn. . . .	New London	0.055	100	127	127	164	164	164	164
N. J.	Camden.	.08	100	100	100	100	175	200	200
Pa.	Philadelphia	.07	. . .	100	100	114	129	171	171
W. Va. . .	New Cumberland	.03	100	233	233	233	233	233	233
Ohio	Canton.	.04	100	100	125	150	200	150	150
Ohio	Springfield	.07	100	86	86	86	143	143	143
Ohio	Zanesville	.06	100	100	100	100	117	117	117
Ind.	Evansville.	.06	. . .	100	. . .	. . .	167	167	167

FLOUR: RYE

State	Town	per bbl.	1860	1861	1862	1863	1864	1865	1866
Mass. . . .	Boston	4.0925	100	92	101	115	172	179	171
Conn. . . .	Jewett City	3.92	100	100	75	75	150	150	150
Pa.	Philadelphia	5.00	. . .	100	120	160	200	220	220
Md.	Baltimore	5.25	100	95	100	119	200	162	129
W. Va. . .	New Cumberland	3.75	100	107	133	147	147	147	127
Ohio	Springfield	3.50	100	129	114	114	200	257	286
Ohio	Zanesville	4.25	100	94	94	141	165	176	188
Ia.	Cedar Rapids . . .	2.00	. . .	100	125	350	350	375	375

FLOUR: WHEAT, EXTRA FAMILY

State	Town	per bbl.	1860	1861	1862	1863	1864	1865	1866
Conn. . . .	Jewett City	8.50	100	91	94	100	124	135	176
Pa.	Philadelphia	8.00	. . .	100	113	150	188	200	200
Md.	Baltimore	8.25	100	103	115	121	161	167	206
W. Va. . .	New Cumberland	6.00	100	125	133	142	142	147	142
Ohio	Canton.	6.00	100	100	108	117	167	167	133
Ohio	Springfield	4.50	100	122	111	111	189	244	289
Ohio	Zanesville	4.75	100	105	105	179	190	200	211
Ia.	Cedar Rapids . . .	2.50	. . .	100	120	300	300	330	330

TABLE 4 — *Continued*

RELATIVE PRICES OF PROVISIONS AT RETAIL — CORN MEAL

State	Town	Initial Price per bbl	1860	1861	1862	1863	1864	1865	1866
Mass. ...	Boston	4.87	100	62	70	97	146	132	101
Conn. ...	Jewett City	3.92	100	100	75	75	150	150	150
Pa.	Philadelphia	3.00	...	100	100	108	133	200	200
W. Va. .	New Cumberland	1.50	100	133	150	167	167	167	150
Ohio	Canton..........	3.00	100	100	117	160	200	200	117
Ohio	Springfield	2.25	100	156	156	156	222	267	356
Ohio	Zanesville	2.25	100	133	133	178	200	200	200
Ind......	Lawrenceburg...	.70	100	114	129	143	150	157	143
Ia.......	Cedar Rapids ...	1.50	...	100	133	200	200	233	233

CHEESE

State	Town	per lb.	1860	1861	1862	1863	1864	1865	1866
Mass. ...	Boston	0.11⅝	100	87	80	117	149	168	160
Conn. ...	Jewett City	.13	100	77	69	92	123	154	177
Pa.	Philadelphia	.12	...	100	125	150	167	208	208
W. Va. ..	New Cumberland	.11	100	136	136	136	136	136	145
Ohio	Canton..........	.10	100	60	80	100	250	250	200
Ohio	Springfield	.08	100	100	100	100	125	150	163
Ohio	Zanesville	.125	100	80	80	120	168	160	200
Ind......	Lawrenceburg...	.18	100	67	83	83	111	150	83
Ia.......	Cedar Rapids ...	.10	...	100	120	120	150	200	280

EGGS

State	Town	per doz	1860	1861	1862	1863	1864	1865	1866
Mass. ...	Boston	0.195	100	87	92	110	144	185	169
Conn. ...	Jewett City	.17	100	82	88	100	135	176	159
Pa.	Philadelphia	.18	...	100	100	111	117	139	144
W. Va. ..	New Cumberland	.10	100	120	140	140	140	140	120
Ohio	Canton..........	.10	100	60	100	120	100	100	100
Ohio	Springfield	.07	100	143	143	171	186	214	229
Ohio	Zanesville	.15	100	40	67	67	100	100	100
Ind......	Lawrenceburg...	.20	100	100	100	75	75	150	150
Ia.......	Cedar Rapids ...	.05	...	100	100	200	200	300	300

TABLE 4—*Continued*

RELATIVE PRICES OF PROVISIONS AT RETAIL—LARD

State	Town	Initial Price per lb.	1860	1861	1862	1863	1864	1865	1866
Mass....	Boston..........	0.12⅚	100	85	77	88	119	199	169
Conn....	Jewett City.....	.14	100	93	89	89	157	200	179
Conn....	New London.....	.12	100	117	117	117	117	117	133
Pa......	Philadelphia.....	.10	...	100	105	105	140	180	190
W. Va...	New Cumberland	.10	100	120	140	140	140	140	150
Ohio....	Canton..........	.09	100	67	89	133	200	222	222
Ohio....	Springfield......	.07	100	114	114	114	143	143	143
Ohio....	Zanesville.......	.10	100	100	120	180	200	220	220
Ind.....	Lawrenceburg...	.15	100	100	100	100	100	100	100

MUTTON CHOPS

State	Town	per lb.	1860	1861	1862	1863	1864	1865	1866
Conn....	New London....	0.16	100	100	100	100	100	113	113
Pa......	Philadelphia.....	.10	...	100	110	120	140	180	180
N. J.....	Camden.........	.12	100	117	117	125	150	208	208
W. Va...	New Cumberland	.08	100	150	150	150	150	150	150
Ohio....	Zanesville.......	.10	100	70	70	80	80	90	100

FLOUR: WHEAT, SUPERFINE

State	Town	per bbl.	1860	1861	1862	1863	1864	1865	1866
Conn....	Jewett City......	7.50	100	93	97	107	127	137	173
Pa......	Philadelphia.....	6.50	...	100	115	138	185	192	192
Md......	Baltimore........	6.00	100	104	129	125	175	167	188
W. Va...	New Cumberland	4.50	100	133	156	167	167	167	156
Ohio....	Canton..........	5.75	100	96	104	113	157	148	122
Ohio....	Springfield......	4.00	100	113	113	113	200	250	300
Ohio....	Zanesville.......	5.25	100	114	114	181	190	200	229
Ia.......	Cedar Rapids....	3.00	...	100	108	267	267	300	300

MILK

State	Town	per qt.	1860	1861	1862	1863	1864	1865	1866
Pa......	Philadelphia.....	0.06	...	100	100	117	117	167	167
W. Va...	New Cumberland	.04	100	200	200	200	250	250	200
Ohio....	Canton..........	.03	100	133	167	200	267	200	200
Ohio....	Springfield......	.05	100	120	120	160	160	160	160
Ohio....	Zanesville.......	.06	100	100	100	133	133	133	167
Ind.....	Lawrenceburg...	.07	100	100	114	143	143	143	143
Ia.......	Cedar Rapids....	.04	...	100	125	125	150	150	150

TABLE 4 — *Continued*

RELATIVE PRICES OF PROVISIONS AT RETAIL— MACKEREL: PICKLED

State	Town	Initial Price per lb.	1860	1861	1862	1863	1864	1865	1866
Conn....	Jewett City......	0.09	100	78	89	89	122	111	111
Pa	Philadelphia.....	.08	...	100	113	125	175	200	225
W. Va...	New Cumberland	.04	100	150	200	200	200	200	200
Ohio	Canton..........	.08	100	75	100	125	125	125	125
Ohio	Zanesville.......	.10	100	50	60	70	80	100	100
Ind	Lawrenceburg...	.08	100	100	100	125	188	125	125
Ia.......	Cedar Rapids....	.07	...	100	114	143	179	179	179

MUTTON: FOREQUARTERS

State	Town	Initial Price per lb.	1860	1861	1862	1863	1864	1865	1866
Mass....	Boston..........	$0.10_{2\frac{7}{4}}$	100	95	61	88	117	124	112
Conn....	New London.....	.10	100	130	130	130	130	140	140
N. J.....	Camden.........	.07	100	114	114	143	157	171	171
Pa	Philadelphia.....	.05	...	100	120	120	160	240	240
W. Va...	New Cumberland	.05	100	140	140	140	140	140	140
Ohio	Zanesville.......	.05	100	100	100	120	120	140	140
Ind	Evansville.......	.075	...	100	100	167	200	200	200

PORK: BACON

State	Town	Initial Price per lb.	1860	1861	1862	1863	1864	1865	1866
Conn....	New London.....	0.12	100	117	117	117	117	117	133
Pa	Philadelphia.....	.09	...	100	100	111	133	200	200
W. Va...	New Cumberland	.08	100	125	150	150	175	175	150
Ohio	Canton..........	.06	...	100	133	250	333	250	...
Ohio	Springfield	.055	100	109	109	109	218	218	218
Ohio	Zanesville.......	.10	100	100	120	140	180	200	200
Ind	Lawrenceburg...	.18	100	78	83	94	97	83	67

PORK: CORNED OR SALTED

State	Town	Initial Price per lb.	1860	1861	1862	1863	1864	1865	1866
Mass....	Boston........ ..	$0.10_{1\frac{1}{3}}$	100	95	89	93	139	212	183
Conn....	Jewett City......	.125	100	100	80	96	176	200	192
Conn....	New London.....	.11	100	109	109	109	109	109	127
Pa	Philadelphia.....	.09	...	100	100	111	133	200	200
W. Va...	New Cumberland	.06	100	117	133	133	133	150	150
Ohio	Zanesville.......	.055	100	164	182	218	291	327	327

TABLE 4—*Continued*

RELATIVE PRICES OF PROVISIONS AT RETAIL—MUTTON: LEG

State	Town	Initial Price per lb.	1860	1861	1862	1863	1864	1865	1866
Conn....	New London.....	0.16	100	100	100	100	100	113	113
N. J.....	Camden.........	.09	100	111	133	133	178	244	244
Pa	Philadelphia.....	.10	...	100	110	120	140	180	180
W. Va...	New Cumberland	.06	100	150	150	150	150	150	150
Ohio	Zanesville.......	.07	100	86	86	100	100	114	129

PORK: FRESH

State	Town	per lb.	1860	1861	1862	1863	1864	1865	1866
Mass....	Boston..........	0.0975	100	87	85	92	128	185	155
Conn....	New London.....	.11	100	109	109	109	109	109	127
Pa	Philadelphia.....	.10	...	100	100	120	140	200	220
W. Va...	New Cumberland	.04	100	125	150	150	150	200	200
Ohio	Canton..........	.045	100	133	133	178	278	278	333
Ohio	Zanesville.......	.06	100	150	150	167	300	300	300

PORK: HAMS, SMOKED

State	Town	per lb.	1860	1861	1862	1863	1864	1865	1866
Mass....	Boston..........	$0.11\frac{1}{8}$	100	93	84	97	154	197	182
Conn....	Jewett City......	.13	100	96	77	96	150	192	192
Conn....	New London.....	.14	100	100	100	100	100	100	114
Pa	Philadelphia.....	.10	...	100	100	120	150	240	250
W. Va...	New Cumberland	.12	100	117	133	133	133	150	150
Ohio	Canton..........	.09	100	139	139	167	222	278	244
Ohio	Springfield......	.075	100	107	107	107	200	200	200
Ohio	Zanesville.......	.11	100	109	136	164	182	227	227
Ind	Lawrenceburg...	.20	100	75	85	90	95	80	75

PORK: SAUSAGES

State	Town	per lb.	1860	1861	1862	1863	1864	1865	1866
Mass....	Boston..........	0.1125	100	97	100	93	113	192	176
Conn....	New London.....	.12	100	117	117	117	117	117	133
Pa	Philadelphia.....	.10	...	100	100	120	150	200	220
W. Va...	New Cumberland	.10	100	120	140	140	140	150	150
Ohio	Springfield	.07	100	100	100	100	114	114	114
Ohio	Zanesville.......	.085	100	118	141	176	212	235	235

TABLE 4 — *Continued*

RELATIVE PRICES OF PROVISIONS AT RETAIL — PORK: SHOULDERS

State	Town	Initial Price per lb.	1860	1861	1862	1863	1864	1865	1866
Conn	New London	0.08	100	150	150	150	150	150	175
Pa	Philadelphia	.07	...	100	100	114	143	214	229
W. Va...	New Cumberland	.07	100	143	171	171	171	200	200
Ohio	Canton..........	.06	100	133	133	167	250	250	208
Ohio	Springfield	.05	100	100	100	100	160	160	160
Ohio	Zanesville	.06	100	167	200	250	300	333	333
Ind......	Lawrenceburg ...	.13	100	100	115	115	123	123	92

VEAL: CUTLETS

State	Town	Initial Price per lb.	1860	1861	1862	1863	1864	1865	1866
Conn. ...	New London.....	0.16	100	113	113	113	113	125	125
N. J.	Camden.........	.14	100	100	100	100	179	179	179
Pa.......	Philadelphia	.15	...	100	100	107	120	167	160
W.Va....	New Cumberland	.10	100	120	120	120	120	120	120
Ohio	Zanesville	.10	100	80	80	90	100	100	120
Ind......	Evansville.......	.20	...	100	100	100	125	125	125

VEAL: FORE QUARTERS

State	Town	Initial Price per lb.	1860	1861	1862	1863	1864	1865	1866
Mass.....	Boston	$0.09\frac{5}{24}$	100	98	63	77	126	153	151
Conn....	New London.....	.10	100	130	130	140	140	150	150
Pa.......	Philadelphia	.06	...	100	100	117	150	200	200
W.Va....	New Cumberland	.04	100	150	150	150	150	150	150
Ohio	Canton..........	.03	100	100	133	200	333	267	267
Ohio	Zanesville	.05	100	100	100	120	140	140	140
Ind.	Evansville.......	.075	...	100	100	167	200	200	200

VEAL: HIND QUARTERS

State	Town	Initial Price per lb.	1860	1861	1862	1863	1864	1865	1866
Conn....	New London.....	0.14	100	107	107	114	114	129	129
N. J.	Camden.........	.10	100	100	100	100	140	140	140
Pa.......	Philadelphia	.10	...	100	100	100	120	150	150
W.Va ...	New Cumberland	.05	100	160	160	160	160	160	160
Ohio	Canton..........	.04	100	100	125	200	300	250	250
Ohio	Zanesville	.06	100	100	100	117	133	133	133
Ind......	Evansville.......	.08	100	100	100	156	188	188	188

TABLE 4 — *Continued*

RELATIVE PRICES OF PROVISIONS AT RETAIL — RICE

State	Town	Initial Price per lb.	1860	1861	1862	1863	1864	1865	1866
Conn. ...	Jewett City	0.06	100	117	150	167	167	250	250
Pa.......	Philadelphia	.08	...	100	113	125	162	175	175
Md......	Baltimore	.06	100	100	150	167	250	250	233
W.Va ...	New Cumberland	.07	100	143	214	214	214	214	214
Ohio	Canton..........	.06	100	100	133	208	333	250	208
Ohio	Springfield	.08	100	100	125	125	125	125	125
Ohio	Zanesville	.0625	100	160	192	240	288	320	320
Ind......	Lawrenceburg ...	.10	100	100	150	200	200	120	120
Ia.	Cedar Rapids....	.05	...	100	200	240	240	250	250

POTATOES

State	Town	per bu.	1860	1861	1862	1863	1864	1865	1866
Mass. ...	Boston	1.02⅔	100	81	94	93	153	117	117
Conn. ...	Jewett City	0.50	100	90	110	100	180	160	120
Pa.......	Philadelphia	.60	...	100	100	125	133	150	167
W.Va ...	New Cumberland	.35	100	143	214	214	214	214	214
Ohio	Springfield	.30	100	133	133	167	250	283	333
Ohio	Zanesville	.60	100	83	83	100	133	167	167
Ind......	Lawrenceburg...	.80	100	94	125	150	94	94	188
Ia.	Cedar Rapids....	.20	...	100	175	200	200	200	350

RELATIVE PRICES OF FUEL AT RETAIL — OIL

State	Town	Initial Price per Gal	1860	1861	1862	1863	1864	1865	1866
Conn....	Jewett City	1.00	100	75	75	75	92	100	90
Conn....	New Haven	1.00	100	75	75	85	75	120	90
N.Y.....	Watertown......	1.12	...	100	45	54	73	107	67
Pa.......	Norristown......	0.70	100	100	100	100	171	171	143
Pa.......	Philadelphia	.25	...	100	100	400	400	400	320
W.Va ...	New Cumberland	.30	100	100	133	133	167	167	133
Ohio	Canton..........	.50	100	80	80	100	120	100	80
Ohio	Zanesville	.60	100	100	100	100	100	100	117
Ill.......	Rock Island	.35	...	100	171	286	286	229	171

TABLE 4—*Continued.*

RELATIVE PRICES OF FUEL AT RETAIL — COAL: ANTHRACITE

State	Town	Initial Price per Ton	1860	1861	1862	1863	1864	1865	1866
Mass....	Boston (1)	6.00	100	98	117	175	217	217	204
Mass....	Boston (2)	5.75	100	121	117	173	220	229	192
Pa	Philadelphia (1) .	5.00	...	100	100	120	130	140	160
Pa	Philadelphia (2) .	3.41	...	100	123	186	277	281	218
Pa	Reading..........	2.50	...	100	100	180	220	260	260
Ohio	Zanesville.......	3.00	100	100	133	167	167	167	167

COAL: BITUMINOUS

W. Va...	New Cumberland	1.40	100	171	179	214	214	196	196
Ohio	Canton..........	2.00	100	88	100	175	175	150	150
Ohio	Springfield	3.50	...	100	100	100	100	100	100
Ohio	Zanesville	1.50	100	100	100	200	200	200	200
Indiana .	Lawrenceburg...	3.50	100	93	114	114	129	114	107
Illinois..	Belleville........	1.82	100	...	...	...	171	171	171
Illinois..	Rock Island.....	3.12	100	80	96	104	104	104	104

WOOD: HARD

		Per C'd							
Mass ...	Boston (1).......	6.50	100	...	150	169	200	200	231
Mass ...	Boston (2).......	6.50	100	123	183	164	192	195	228
Conn . .	Danielsonville ...	4.00	100	100	100	100	119	138	125
Conn ...	Jewett City	3.50	100	100	100	114	114	157	143
Pa	Reading..........	4.00	...	100	100	125	125	150	150
W. Va...	New Cumberland	1.75	100	100	114	143	143	143	143
Ohio	Canton..........	2.50	100	80	100	120	120	180	180
Ohio	Springfield	3.00	100	92	92	100	133	167	167
Ohio	Zanesville.......	1.50	100	133	133	150	183	200	200
Indiana .	Lawrenceburg...	4.00	100	100	138	150	150	138	125
Illinois..	Rock Island.....	4.50	100	89	133	144	144	133	133
Iowa....	Cedar Rapids....	2.50	...	100	100	120	120	200	200
Missouri.	Pilot Knob	2.50	100	120	120	160	160	160	160

WOOD: PINE

Mass....	Boston (1)	4.50	100	...	153	178	233	211	267
Mass....	Boston (2)	4.50	100	133	154	185	230	207	267
Conn ...	Danielsonville ...	3.50	100	100	100	100	121	143	129
W. Va...	New Cumberland	1.50	100	100	117	133	150	150	150
Ohio	Zanesville	1.00	100	175	175	200	225	250	275
Illinois..	Rock Island.....	1.00	...	100	150	200	200	150	150

TABLE 4—*Continued*

RELATIVE PRICES OF MEN'S HEAVY BOOTS, AT RETAIL

State	Town	Initial Price per Pair	1860	1861	1862	1863	1864	1865	1866
Conn	Ansonia...............	2.50	...	100	120	140	150	160	180
Conn	Jewett City	3.00	100	96	92	100	117	133	142
Conn	Waterbury...........	3.25	...	100	108	108	123	123	123
N. Y.......	Homer	3.50	...	100	100	114	143	171	157
N. J	Camden.............	2.50	100	100	115	135	150	160	155
Pa.........	Sharon	3.50	100	100	100	129	200	171	143
W. Va.....	New Cumberland....	3.50	100	129	171	171	171	186	200
W. Va.....	Wheeling	4.00	100	113	125	138	150	150	150
Ohio	Canton...............	3.00	100	100	133	200	267	200	167
Ohio	Cincinnati	6.00	100	67	83	100	100	117	117
Ohio	Ravenna	3.00	100	108	142	158	183	183	183
Ohio	Zanesville	3 50	100	100	114	114	143	143	171
Ind	Aurora	5 00	100	100	100	100	120	120	100
Ind	Evansville	3.00	...	100	100	117	150	150	133
Ind	Fort Wayne..........	3.50	...	100	114	129	157	157	157
Ind	LaFayette	4.00	...	100	100	...	125	150	150
Ind	New Albany (1).....	3.00	100	100	117	1'33	167	167	133
Ind	New Albany (2)......	3 125	100	100	124	144	160	160	160
Ind	Terre Haute	4.00	100	100	150	150	169	181	181
Ind	Vincennes............	3.00	...	100	150	200	267	233	217
Ill	Belleville (1).........	4.50	100	100	100	111	111	111	111
Ill	Belleville (2).........	3.50	100	71	...	...	...	171	157
Ill	Bloomington.........	2.50	100	110	120	140	160	160	160
Ill	Springfield..........	2.00	100	100	88	113	150	175	200	225
Iowa	Cedar Rapids	3.50	...	100	157	157	143	143	143
Mo	Pilot Knob............	4.00	100	100	113	125	125	125	100
Mo	St. Louis.............	2.50	10')	120	140	160	160	160	140

RELATIVE RENT OF HOUSES PER MONTH — FOUR ROOMS

State	Town	Initial Rent per Month	1860	1861	1862	1863	1864	1865	1866	1867	1868
Mass	Boston	5.00	100	100	100	100	140	140	140	140	200
Conn.......	Jewett City.............	2.00	100	100	100	100	100	100	100	100	100
N. J........	Camden................ ...	6.50	100	100	100	92	92	115	115	115	123
Pa	Philadelphia	6.00	...	100	100	100	133	167	200	200	200
W. Va......	New Cumberland.......	4.00	100	100	125	125	138	138	138	125	100
Ohio.......	Canton	6.25	100	64	80	96	96	96	96	96	96
Ohio	Cincinnati	6.00	100	67	67	83	100	100	100	83	83
Ohio.......	Springfield.....	5.00	100	100	100	100	100	100	100	120	120
Ohio.......	Zanesville...............	7.00	100	100	114	114	114	129	129	143	143
Ky........	Louisville.....	12.00	100	125	125	167	208	208	208	167	167
Ind	Indianapolis.............	7.00	...	100	129	129	129	1 9	143	143	143
Ind	LaFayette	6.00	100	100	100	100	108	117	133	142	
Ind	Lawrenceburg...........	7.00	100	114	143	143	143	143	143	143	129
Ind	Terre Haute	8.00	...	100	125	163	175	175	175	175	175
Ill........ ...	Bloomington.............	8.00	...	100	100	113	125	125	125	138	138
Ill..........	Rock Island........	4.00	...	100	100	100	100	125	125	125	125
Iowa	Cedar Rapids............	5.00	...	100	100	100	100	120	120	1:30	130
Mo	Pilot Knob...............	5.00	100	100	120	120	120	120	80	80)	80
Mo	St. Louis.................	10.00	100	100	100	150	150	150	180	180	180

TABLE 4— *Continued*

RELATIVE RENT OF HOUSES PER MONTH — SIX OR SEVEN ROOMS

State	Town	Number of Rooms	Initial Rent per Month	1860	1861	1862	1863	1864	1865	1866	1867	1868
Mass......	Boston..........	6	$ 9.00	100	100	100	100	133	133	133	133	189
Mass......	Boston........ .	7	10.00	100	100	100	100	140	140	140	140	200
Conn..... .	Jewett City......	6	3.00	100	100	100	100	100	100	100	100	100
N. J.......	Camden..........	6	8.00	100	100	100	100	100	125	125	150	188
Pa.........	Hokendauqua ...	6	3.42	100	100	111	117	129	129	129	129	129
Pa.........	Philadelphia.....	6	9.00	...	100	100	100	133	167	200	200	200
W. Va.....	New Cumberland	6	6.00	100	100	133	133	133	133	133	133	117
Ohio......	Canton..........	6, 1st	7.00	...	100	114	129	143	143	143	143	143
Ohio...... .	Canton........ .	6, 2d	7.00	100	71	86	100	114	114	114	114	114
Ohio......	Cincinnati	6	8.00	100	100	100	150	313	313	313	250	250
Ohio......	Zanesville	6	9 00	100	100	100	111	111	111	111	122	122
Ky.........	Louisville	6	15.00	100	133	133	167	233	233	233	167	167
Ind....	Indianapolis.....	6	8.00	...	100	125	125	138	138	138	150	150
Ind........	La Fayette.......	6	18.00	100	100	100	100	100	113	125	138	144
Ind........	Lawrenceburg...	6	10.00	100	110	125	125	125	125	125	125	125
Ill.........	Bloomington.....	6	10.00	...	100	100	120	120	120	120	130	130
Ill.........	Rock Island.....	6	6.00	...	100	100	100	100	100	117	117	117
Ia.........	Cedar Rapids....	6	[6.00	...	100	100	100	117	117	117	125	125
Mo...	St. Louis.........	6	15.00	100	80	80	111	111	111	133	133	133

RELATIVE PRICE OF BOARD PER WEEK — FOR MEN

State	Town	Initial Price per Week	1860	1861	1862	1863	1864	1865	1866
Conn..... ..	Jewett City... ...	$2.00	100	100	100	100	150	150	175
Pa.........	Philadelphia.........	3.00	...	100	117	117	1 3	167	167
Pa.........	Sharon..............	2.50	100	100	100	160	200	200	200
W. Va.....	New Cumberland....	1.50	100	133	167	167	167	167	167
Ohio......	Canton..............	2.50	100	120	180	180	180	180	160
Ohio......	Cincinnati	1.75	100	114	114	171	229	229	229
Ohio......	Springfield..........	2.50	100	120	120	160	200	200	180
Ohio......	Zanesville,..........	2.75	100	109	109	127	127	145	145
Ky........	Louisville	4.00	100	100	100	100	125	175	175
Ind........	Fort Wayne.........	2.00	...	100	100	150	150	150	150
Ind...:....	Indianapolis	3.50	...	100	114	128	143	143	143
Ind........	Lawrenceburg.......	3.50	100	100	114	128	143	143	128
Ill....	Belleville	5.00	...	100	100	100	100	100	100
Ill...	Rock Island.........	2.50	...	100	100	100	100	120	120
Ia.........	Cedar Rapids........	2.50	...	100	100	100	120	120	120
Mo.... ..	Pilot Knob..........	3.00	100	117	133	150	150	150	117

FOR WOMEN

State	Town	Initial Price per Week	1860	1861	1862	1863	1864	1865	1866
Conn.....	Jewett City..........	$1.50	100	100	100	100	133	133	167
Pa.........	Philadelphia	1.75	...	100	114	129	143	171	171
W. Va.....	New Cumberland....	1 25	100	140	160	160	160	160	160
Ohio......	Canton..............	2.50	100	120	180	180	180	180	160
Ohio......	Cincinnati..........	1.50	100	100	100	167	233	233	233
Ohio......	Springfield..........	2.50	100	120	120	160	200	200	180
Ohio......	Zanesville	2.00	100	138	138	150	150	175	175
Ky........	Louisville...........	3.00	100	100	100	133	167	167	167
Ind........	Indianapolis.........	3.00	...	100	133	133	133	133	133
Ill.........	Belleville............	4.00	...	100	100	100	100	100	100
Ill.........	Rock Island.........	2.00	...	100	100	100	100	125	125
Ia.........	Cedar Rapids........	2.00	...	100	100	100	150	150	150
Mo....	Pilot Knob..........	3.00	100	117	133	150	150	150	117

TABLE 5

COMPARISON OF THE RELATIVE PRICES OF TWENTY-THREE COMMODITIES
AT WHOLESALE AND AT RETAIL

		Number of Price Series	1860	1861	1862	1863	1864	1865	1866
Sheetings: brown, 4-4, Atlantic A....	Wholesale	1	100	109	199	407	610	480	299
Sheetings: brown, 4-4, Atlantic A....	Retail	11	100	135	233	352	469	405	328
Shirtings: bleached, 4-4, N. Y. Mills..	Wholesale	1	100	98	131	222	331	332	302
Shirtings: bleached, 4-4, N. Y. Mills..	Retail	13	100	123	207	335	511	447	366
Tickings: Amoskeag, A.C.A...........	Wholesale	1	100	98	151	...	482	451	396
Tickings: Amoskeag, A.C.A...........	Retail	12	100	130	187	237	335	324	271
Flour: Rye..........................	Wholesale	1	100	70	100	117	163	165	142
Flour: Rye..........................	Retail	8	100	102	108	153	198	208	205
Meal: corn, yellow, kiln-dried........	Wholesale	1	100	66	84	91	178	163	122
Meal: corn, yellow, kiln-dried........	Retail	9	100	111	118	143	174	190	183
Beans	Wholesale	1	100	109	143	150	148	133	151
Beans	Retail	9	100	104	122	142	156	156	160
Rice: Carolina prime	Wholesale	1	100	114	163	...	...	244	273
Rice: Carolina prime	Retail	9	100	113	159	187	220	217	211
Sugar: Havana brown., ...	Wholesale	1	100	80	108	138	225	189	153
Sugar: good brown..................	Retail	11	100	102	123	151	213	201	212
Molasses: N. O. prime..............	Wholesale	1	100	89	112	219	251	236	
Molasses: N. O. prime..............	Retail	6	100	104	144	192	238	235	235
Molasses: Porto Rico, best..........	Wholesale	1	100	89	105	133	220	220	185
Molasses: Porto Rico, best..........	Retail	9	100	114	132	192	242	227	220
Starch: ordinary laundry...........	Wholesale	1	100	92	92	115	169	169	154
Starch: ordinary laundry...........	Retail	7	100	103	115	140	165	184	180
Butter	Wholesale	1	100	82	99	124	206	209	237
Butter	Retail .. .	9	100	93	110	129	188	218	215
Cheese	Wholesale	1	100	81	75	125	173	184	190
Cheese	Retail	9	100	90	97	113	153	175	180
Eggs	Wholesale	1	100	83	90	119	150	168	163
Eggs	Retail	9	100	92	103	122	133	167	163
Mackerel: salt, shore, No. 1.........	Wholesale	1	100	53	52	88	188	138	142
Mackerel: pickled, No. 1.....	Retail	7	100	93	111	125	153	149	152
Beef...............................	Wholesale	3	100	95	98	107	146	184	191
Beef...............................	Retail .. .	35	100	108	112	129	158	167	167
Mutton............................	Wholesale	1	100	98	93	112	136	171	160
Mutton............................	Retail	17	100	109	111	122	135	158	158
Pork: hams, sugar-cured	Wholesale	1	100	80	107	195	257	288	298
Pork: hams, smoked................	Retail	9	100	104	107	119	154	185	182
Pork: bacon, clear.................	Wholesale	1	100	64	56	60	119	170	185
Pork: bacon, clear.................	Retail	7	100	104	116	139	179	178	138
Pork: salt mess....................	Wholesale	1	100	92	66	82	182	173	172
Pork: corned or salted..............	Retail	6	100	114	116	127	164	191	197
Lard	Wholesale	2	100	81	69	89	131	179	172
Lard	Retail	9	100	100	106	118	146	169	167
Coal: anthracite, stove.............	Wholesale	1	100	101	94	154	242	232	246
Coal: anthracite, stove...	Retail	6	100	103	115	167	205	216	200
Coal: bituminous..................	Wholesale	1	100	95	130	150	191	211	178
Coal: bituminous..................	Retail	7	100	105	115	151	156	148	147
Average of relative prices...........	Wholesale	..	100	88	105	138	221	222	206
Average of relative prices...........	Retail	..	100	107	129	165	211	214	202

APPENDIX C

RELATIVE WAGES

TABLE 1

WAGE-SERIES FROM TABLE XII OF THE ALDRICH REPORT[1]—
AGRICULTURAL IMPLEMENTS

1. Massachusetts

	FOREMEN WOODWORK'S		LABORERS		MACHINISTS		PAINTERS		WOODWORK'S	
Sex	M.		M.		M.		M.		M.	
Initial wage per day....	$1.64		$1.00		$1.665		$1.25		$1.333	
	No.	Rel. Wages	No.	Rel. Wages	No.	Rel. Wages	No.	Rel. Wages	No.	Rel. Wages
1860, Jan...	1	100	2	100	2	100	1	100	3	100
July..	1	100	2	100	2	100	1	100	2	103
1861, Jan...	1	100	2	100	2	108	1	100	2	103
July..	1	99	2	100	2	108	1	100	1	94
1862, Jan...	1	99	2	88	2	100	1	100	1	113
July..	1	98	1	100	1	84	..	...	1	113
1863, Jan...	1	108	3	90	1	113	..	...	2	113
July..	1	112	5	112	2	101	..	...	2	119
1864, Jan...	1	122	2	117	2	108	3	89	4	124
July..	1	152	3	142	3	123	2	106	3	161
1865, Jan...	1	152	3	150	3	125	2	113	4	169
July..	1	175	7	161	3	138	2	127	4	189
1866, Jan...	1	175	6	163	6	131	3	124	5	191
July..	1	183	5	169	5	134	1	120	5	179

[1] In the following tables the series of relative wages from the "exhibits" of the *Aldrich Report*, used in chap. v of Part II, are reproduced in full. As in the exhibits, the series are classified by establishments, and the establishments by industries. To facilitate references, the same order of arrangement is followed and the number assigned to each establishment in the exhibits and the state in which it is located are given. A change has been made, however, in the arrangement of the series by grouping the foremen, overseers, etc., in any establishment at the beginning and the females at the end. The initial wage from which variations are computed and the number of employees are given because they were made use of in preparing certain of the tables in the text.

TABLE 1 — *Continued*

WAGE-SERIES FROM TABLE XII OF THE ALDRICH REPORT — ALE, BEER, AND PORTER

2 New York

	FOREMEN LABORERS		BREWERS		COOPERS		LABORERS		TEAMSTERS	
Sex............	M.		M.		M.		M.		M.	
Initial wage per day....	$1.34		$6.39		$1.505		$0.85		$1.44	
	No.	Rel. Wages	No.	Rel. Wages	No.	Rel. Wages	No.	Rel. Wages	No.	Rel. Wages
1860, Jan...	1	100	1	100	8	100	26	100	4	100
July..	1	100	1	100	8	101	28	99	3	107
1861, Jan...	1	120	1	100	8	101	32	99	3	107
July..	1	120	1	100	10	100	30	100	3	107
1862, Jan...	1	120	1	150	7	101	26	99	3	107
July..	1	120	1	150	6	101	33	101	3	107
1863, Jan...	1	120	1	150	7	101	26	102	2	107
July..	2	115	1	150	8	103	27	114	2	107
1864, Jan...	3	124	1	150	6	125	29	134	2	107
July..	3	129	2	150	7	131	28	147	2	107
1865, Jan...	3	136	1	150	5	127	23	151	2	107
July..	4	130	1	150	4	148	18	149	2	107
1866, Jan...	4	132	1	250	5	146	30	154	2	107
July..	4	132	1	250	5	143	21	152	2	107

BOOKS AND NEWSPAPERS

4 Md.   5 N. Y.   5 N. Y.   5 N. Y.   5 N. Y.   5 N. Y.

	PRINTERS: Bk. and Job		FOREMEN COMPS.		FOREMEN PRESSMEN		CARPENT'S		COMPOSITORS		COMPS. LEARNERS	
Sex........	M.		M.		M.		M.		M.		M.	
Init. wage per day ..	$1.665		$2.00		$2.00		$1.315		$1.665		$0.695	
	No.	Rel. Wages	No.	Rel. Wages	No.	Rel. Wages	No.	Rel. Wages	No.	Rel. Wages	No.	Rel. Wages
1860, Jan.	..	...	2	100	1	100	2	100	17	100	10	100
July	..	...	2	100	1	100	2	100	11	100	7	81
1861, Jan.	8	100	2	100	1	100	1	95	20	99	8	76
July	8	100	2	100	1	100	..	...	17	99	6	72
1862, Jan.	6	100	2	100	1	100	2	95	16	99	5	81
July	6	100	2	100	1	100	2	95	18	99	7	88
1863, Jan.	6	100	2	100	1	100	1	102	21	99	5	94
July	8	100	..	...	..	...	1	102	..	...	..	...
1864, Jan.	6	120	..	...	..	...	1	102	..	...	..	...
July	9	150	2	138	1	133	1	127	23	150	4	99
1865, Jan.	12	180	2	150	1	133	1	127	27	150	4	108
July	12	180	2	150	1	142	1	127	25	150	4	105
1866, Jan.	12	180	2	150	1	150	1	140	23	150	5	120
July	12	180	2	150	1	150	..	...	26	150	3	132

TABLE 1 — *Continued*

WAGE-SERIES FROM TABLE XII OF THE ALDRICH REPORT — BOOKS AND NEWSPAPERS

5 New York

	MACHIN'TS		PRESSMEN		PRESSROOM HANDS		PORTERS		FOLDERS		PRESSROOM HANDS	
Sex........	M.		M.		M.		M.		F.		F.	
Init. wage per day ..	$1.705		$1.665		$0.612		$0.915		$0.47		$0.465	
	No.	Rel. Wages	No.	Rel. Wages	No.	Rel. Wages	No.	Rel. Wages	No.	Rel. Wages	No.	Rel. Wages
1860, Jan.	2	100	1	100	3	100	2	100	16	100	6	100
July	3	95	..	...	1	41	3	109	7	99	5	104
1861, Jan.	3	95	2	100	3	105	3	115	16	91	8	97
July	4	95	2	100	4	104	3	103	15	94	10	98
1862, Jan.	3	94	2	100	5	113	3	103	11	100	7	84
July	1	88	2	100	3	95	3	109	12	105	9	95
1863, Jan.	2	92	2	100	2	126	3	119	11	104	9	103
July	..	...	..	...	..	...	..	...	..	...	..	...
1864, Jan.	..	...	..	...	..	...	..	...	..	...	..	...
July	3	137	2	150	4	119	5	138	26	119	14	137
1865, Jan.	2	161	1	150	5	139	5	144	41	110	14	133
July	3	156	3	133	4	133	4	146	30	117	13	140
1866, Jan.	2	153	3	130	5	134	5	144	30	119	12	140
July	..	...	3	130	5	115	3	140	22	134	13	145

6 New York

	FOREMEN COMPOSITORS		COMPOSITORS		COMPOSITORS APPRENTICES		PRESSMEN		PRESS-FEEDERS	
Sex............	M.		M.		M.		M.		F.	
Initial wage per day	$2.50		$1.835		$0.755		$2.335		$0.33	
	No.	Rel. Wages	No.	Rel. Wages	No.	Rel. Wages	No.	Rel. Wages	No.	Rel. Wages
1860, Jan...	2	100	2	100	9	100	1	100	..	...
July..	2	100	2	104	9	101	1	93	..	...
1861, Jan...	2	100	3	108	8	88	1	93	..	...
July..	2	100	4	104	7	83	1	93	1	100
1862, Jan...	2	100	6	106	7	93	1	93	1	152
July..	2	100	6	104	8	91	1	93	1	152
1863, Jan...	2	100	6	107	6	89	1	93	1	152
July..	2	100	6	111	6	89	1	93	1	152
1864, Jan...	2	110	9	114	2	121	1	93	2	152
July..	2	117	8	117	3	99	1	93	2	164
1865, Jan...	3	129	11	138	4	98	..	...	2	174
July..	3	129	8	136	3	121	..	...	3	189
1866, Jan...	3	129	10	134	4	97	..	...	4	202
July..	3	129	10	134	3	103	..	...	4	202

TABLE 1—*Continued*

WAGE-SERIES FROM TABLE XII OF THE ALDRICH REPORT—BUILDING TRADES

	7 Conn.		8 Conn.		8 Conn.		9 Conn.		9 Conn.		10 Md.	
	CARPENT'S		CARPENT'S		CARPENT'S HELPERS		HOD CARRIERS		MASONS		PAINTERS	
Sex........	M.		M.		M.		M.		M.		M.	
Init. wage per day ..	$1.50		$1.715		$1.00		$0.80		$1.765		$1.75	
	No.	Rel. Wages	No.	Rel. Wages	No.	Rel. Wages	No.	Rel. Wages	No.	Rel. Wages	No.	Rel. Wages
1860, Jan.	4	100	9	100	1	100	8	100	6	100	2	100
July	6	117	10	99	..	...	17	137	11	116	4	100
1861, Jan.	3	89	9	91	1	138	12	125	12	105	2	86
July	4	100	6	87	2	132	40	125	1	113	1	86
1862, Jan.	3	89	1	87	..	...	15	125	9	113	1	86
July	3	100	7	89	1	134	9	125	9	113	6	86
1863, Jan.	2	100	..	...	..	...	10	188	7	158	1	86
July	3	117	20	112	2	125	7	202	4	131	8	100
1864, Jan.	3	117	19	111	6	125	..	...	..	...	2	114
July	..	...	23	131	9	157	17	199	21	140	9	143
1865, Jan.	3	150	10	127	6	146	..	...	..	...	5	143
July	4	183	..	...	..	...	5	208	7	160	9	143
1866, Jan.	4	171	..	...	..	...	..	...	..	...	5	143
July	4	188	..	...	..	...	13	208	10	170	11	143

12 Massachusetts

	FOREMEN BRICKL'RS		FOREMEN MASONS		BRICKL'RS		BRICKL'RS HELPERS		MASONS		MASONS' HELPERS	
Sex........	M.		M.		M.		M.		M.		M.	
Init. wage per day ..	$2.50		$2.50		$1.765		$1.12		$1.875		$1.055	
	No.	Rel. Wages	No.	Rel. Wages	No.	Rel. Wages	No.	Rel. Wages	No.	Rel. Wages	No.	Rel. Wages
1860, Jan.	1	100	1	100	9	100	5	100	5	100	9	100
July	1	100	1	100	12	86	6	91	11	85	15	100
1861, Jan.	1	100	1	100	12	107	12	100	11	101	9	85
July	1	100	1	120	28	101	35	100	13	96	15	92
1862, Jan.	1	100	1	100	10	106	13	101	10	84	20	97
July	1	100	1	100	11	105	14	110	13	105	17	110
1863, Jan.	1	100	1	100	4	110	9	109	4	93	6	118
July	2	110	1	100	17	105	14	108	9	102	16	114
1864, Jan.	1	120	1	100	15	120	11	122	7	114	11	130
July	..	...	2	120	19	131	13	134	19	102	8	142
1865, Jan.	..	...	1	120	9	139	9	134	7	116	9	142
July	..	...	1	160	20	146	18	134	8	137	8	142
1866, Jan.	1	160	1	160	15	147	11	156	13	143	13	160
July	1	160	1	160	13	167	11	156	15	167	21	166

TABLE 1—*Continued*

WAGE-SERIES FROM TABLE XII OF THE ALDRICH REPORT—BUILDING TRADES

	13 Mass.		13 Mass.		13 Mass.		13 Mass.		13 Mass.		14 Mass.	
	FOREMEN CARPENT'S'		FOREMEN PAINTERS		CARPENT'S		CARPENT'S' HELPERS		PAINTERS		STM. & GAS FITTERS	
Sex........	M.		M.		M.		M.		M.		M.	
Init. wage per day..	$1.67		$1.50		$1.425		$0.83		$1.165		$1.875	
	No.	Rel. Wages	No.	Rel. Wages	No.	Rel. Wages	No.	Rel. Wages	No.	Rel. Wages	No.	Rel. Wages
1860, Jan.	1	100	1	100	7	100	1	100	6	100	4	100
July	1	100	1	100	17	93	4	100	6	102	5	90
1861, Jan.	1	100	1	100	14	93	3	100	6	101	4	105
July	1	100	1	100	21	83	3	100	4	99	..	...
1862, Jan.	1	120	1	100	18	90	..	...	4	107	4	93
July	1	105	..	...	18	95	3	90	4	103	..	...
1863, Jan.	1	120	..	...	20	99	3	120	6	119	3	111
July	1	120	1	111	23	106	5	120	6	107	2	110
1864, Jan.	1	135	1	111	15	110	4	120	7	110	3	115
July	1	135	1	117	20	119	6	120	20	130	6	106
1865, Jan.	1	135	1	133	17	126	3	151	3	150	4	123
July	1	150	1	150	19	147	3	151	5	172	4	120
1866, Jan.	1	165	1	167	30	152	5	181	15	152	6	113
July	1	195	1	183	24	167	6	211	4	182	5	120

	14 Mass.		15 Mass.		16 N. J.		16 N. J.		16 N. J.		17 N. Y.	
	ST'M & GAS FITTERS' HELPERS		PAINTERS HOUSE		PLUMBERS		LABORERS		TINSMITHS		CARPENT'S	
Sex........	M.		M.		M.		M.		M.		M.	
Init. wage per day..	$1.195		$1.10		$2.00		$1.18		$1.52		$1.185	
	No.	Rel. Wages	No.	Rel. Wages	No.	Rel. Wages	No.	Rel. Wages	No.	Rel. Wages	No.	Rel. Wages
1859, July	2	100	..	...	..	...	..	...	...		...	
1860, Jan.	..	...	5	100	1	100	3	100	8	100	2	100
July	..	...	10	101	1	100	3	100	8	104	5	110
1861, Jan.	1	84	5	103	1	100	2	85	6	108	5	112
July	..	...	17	101	1	100	2	85	5	110	5	122
1862, Jan.	2	110	3	114	2	81	3	92	3	113	3	127
July	..	...	6	102	2	84	2	85	3	113	6	127
1863, Jan.	1	105	5	116	2	94	2	95	3	115	5	133
July	1	42	1	102	2	100	2	97	2	107	10	152
1864, Jan.	1	112	2	136	2	113	3	97	4	132	9	152
July	3	77	7	175	2	125	3	117	4	122	14	169
1865, Jan.	3	63	5[1]	164	2	125	4	123	3	128	12	183
July	4	79	9	195	3	150	3	153	3	148	12	174
1866, Jan.	2	84	4	227	3	150	5	151	5	148	10	186
July	3	73	10	198	4	139	2	155	5	155	10	196

[1] Hours reduced January, 1865, from 13 to 10.

TABLE 1—*Continued*

WAGE-SERIES FROM TABLE XII OF THE ALDRICH REPORT—BUILDING TRADES

	17 N. Y.		17 N. Y.		17 N. Y.		17 N. Y.		18 N. Y.		19 N. Y.	
	CARPENT'S APPREN.		CARPENT'S' HELPERS		LABORERS		TEAMSTERS		PAINTERS		CARPENT'S	
Sex........	M.		M.		M.		M.		M.		M.	
Init. wage per day..	$.375		$1.00		$0.88		$0.75		$2.00		$2.00	
	No.	Rel. Wages	No.	Rel. Wages	No.	Rel. Wages	No.	Rel. Wages	No.	Rel. Wages	No.	Rel. Wages
1859, Jan.	..	...	..	...	..	...	1	100	..	...	..	...
1860, Jan.	4	100	1	100	1	100	..	...	15	100	30	100
July	5	123	3	79	1	100	..	...	60	100	65	100
1861, Jan.	4	147	3	79	3	99	..	...	8	100	30	100
July	1	88	4	92	3	109	1	100	40	100	70	100
1862, Jan.	1	112	5	100	1	142	1	100	8	100	15	100
July	1	100	8	111	2	142	1	100	45	100	40	100
1863, Jan.	3	96	5	113	..	...	1	133	10	100	12	100
July	4	133	2	125	2	114	1	167	40	113	60	100
1864, Jan.	4	139	2	125	1	114	1	167	7	113	20	113
July	2	183	..	...	..	...	1	233	45	150	65	150
1865, Jan.	..	...	1	150	..	...	1	233	12	150	25	150
July	..	...	1	150	..	...	1	233	45	175	50	163
1866, Jan.	1	267	..	...	1	142	1	233	10	175	40	175
July	..	...	1	150	2	156	1	233	45	175	80	175

	20 N. Y.		21 N. Y.		22 N. Y.		22 N. Y.		22 N. Y.		23 N. Y.	
	PLUMBERS		ROOFERS SL. & M'T'L		BRICKL'RS		BRICKL'RS' HELPERS		PLAST'R'S		PAINTERS	
Sex........	M.		M.		M.		M.		M.		M.	
Init. wage per day..	$1.875		$1.25		$2.00		$1.25		$2.00		$1.915	
	No.	Rel. Wages	No.	Rel. Wages	No.	Rel. Wages	No.	Rel. Wages	No.	Rel. Wages	No.	Rel. Wages
1860, Jan.	4	100	2	100	8	100	12	100	8	100	..	...
July	4	100	6	125	8	100	10	100	8	100	3	100
1861, Jan.	4	100	3	120	7	100	10	100	7	100	..	...
July	4	100	4	120	7	100	10	100	7	100	5	93
1862, Jan.	5	101	2	160	5	113	8	100	5	100	..	...
July	5	107	3	160	5	113	8	100	5	113	2	91
1863, Jan.	10	107	3	240	4	125	6	130	4	125	..	...
July	12	133	6	240	5	125	6	130	5	125	3	113
1864, Jan.	4	160	5	280	9	125	10	180	9	125	..	...
July	4	187	8	280	9	125	10	180	9	150	4	150
1865, Jan.	4	187	2	320	5	150	3	180	5	150	..	...
July	4	187	5	320	5	150	4	180	5	150	2	185
1866, Jan.	6	195	2	280	5	175	10	180	5	175	..	...
July	6	195	6	280	5	200	10	200	5	200	4	183

TABLE 1 — *Continued*

WAGE-SERIES FROM TABLE XII OF THE ALDRICH REPORT — BUILDING TRADES

24 N. Y.   26 Pa.   26 Pa.   27 Pa.   28 Pa.   29 Pa.

	ROOFERS		BRICKLAY'S		BRICKLAY'S HELPERS		CARPENT'S		CARPENT'S		PLAST'R'S	
Sex........	M.		M.		M.		M.		M.		M.	
Init. wage per day..	$1.835		$2.00		$1.12		$1.75		$1.75		$1.665	
	No.	Rel. Wages	No.	Rel. Wages	No.	Rel. Wages	No.	Rel. Wages	No.	Rel. Wages	No.	Rel. Wages
1860, Jan.	2	100	6	100	3	100	3	100	6	100	9	100
July	2	91	20	100	10	100	8	100	10	100	13	102
1861, Jan.	3	82	..	...	..	...	4	100	5	100	9	98
July	2	82	20	100	10	112	10	100	12	114	16	99
1862, Jan.	4	78	6	113	3	112	4	114	7	114	10	99
July	4	82	20	113	10	112	10	114	16	143	12	100
1863, Jan.	5	84	..	...	..	...	4	114	5	143	8	116
July	4	105	..	...	..	...	10	114	10	171	12	115
1864, Jan.	4	113	10	125	10	134	10	129	6	171	10	114
July	5	131	35	125	18	134	14	129	8	171	14	116
1865, Jan.	4	150	10	150	5	179	20	136	7	171	10	114
July	4	150	30	150	15	179	21	133	12	143	14	137
1866, Jan.	4	163	12	150	12	179	15	151	8	143	8	139
July	4	163	40	150	20	179	19	151	20	143	10	156

CARRIAGES AND WAGONS

33 New York

	BLACKSMIT'S		BLACKSMIT'S' HELPERS		PAINTERS		WHEELWRI'S	
Sex.....................	M.		M.		M.		M.	
Initial wage per day.......	$1.50		$0.835		$1.25		$1.25	
	No.	Rel. Wages	No.	Rel. Wages	No.	Rel. Wages	No.	Rel. Wages
1860, January..........	3	100	3	100	2	100	6	100
July	3	100	3	100	2	100	6	100
1861, January..........	3	100	3	100	2	100	6	100
July	3	100	3	100	2	100	6	100
1862, January..........	3	200	3	180	2	140	6	160
July	3	200	3	180	2	140	6	160
1863, January..........	3	200	3	180	3	140	6	160
July	3	200	3	180	3	140	6	160
1864, January..........	3	200	3	180	3	140	6	160
July	3	200	3	180	2	140	6	160
1865, January..........	3	200	3	180	2	140	6	160
July	3	200	3	180	2	140	6	160
1866, January..........	5	200	5	180	4	140	6	160
July	5	200	5	180	4	140	6	160

TABLE 1— *Continued*

WAGE-SERIES FROM TABLE XII OF THE ALDRICH REPORT— CITY PUBLIC WORKS

	34 Mass.		34 Mass.		35 N. Y.		35 N. Y		35 N. Y.		35 N. Y.	
	FOREMEN LABORERS		LABORERS		FOREMEN LABORERS		BLACKSM'S		BLACKSM'S' HELPERS		BLASTERS	
Sex........	M.		M.		M.		M.		M.		M.	
Init. wage per day..	$1.25		$1.02		$2.00		$1.82		$1.25		$1.25	
	No.	Rel. Wages	No.	Rel. Wages	No.	Rel. Wages	No.	Rel. Wages	No.	Rel. Wages	No.	Rel. Wages
1860, Jan.	1	100	7	100	42	100	16	100	15	100	6	100
July	2	140	24	99	30	100	23	99	12	100	10	100
1861, Jan.	1	140	18	99	25	100	17	99	19	92	15	100
July	2	170	16	99	28	100	25	96	8	84	..	...
1862, Jan.	2	100	21	99	20	100	9	97	4	92	..	...
July	2	160	27	100	22	100	7	99	5	91	..	...
1863, Jan.	2	160	7	107	19	100	4	106	4	100	2	128
July	2	170	12	146	20	110	7	110	5	108	..	...
1864, Jan.	3	147	29	119	17	125	8	137	5	128	..	...
July	4	220	14	131	16	150	7	151	7	152	1	152
1865, Jan.	6	193	75	120	12	150	7	176	5	160	1	160
July	3	167	19	153	11	150	5	179	5	160	1	160
1866, Jan.	5	180	12	147	12	150	2	179	1	160	1	160
July	4	180	32	157	8	150	2	192	1	160	..	...

35 New York

	BRICKLAY'S		CARPENT'S		GARDEN'RS		LABORERS		MASONS		STONECUT'S	
Sex........	M.		M.		M.		M.		M.		M.	
Init. wage per day..	$2.00		$1.72		$1.40		$1.00		$2.00		$2.00	
	No.	Rel. Wages	No.	Rel. Wages	No.	Rel. Wages	No.	Rel. Wages	No.	Rel. Wages	No.	Rel. Wages
1860, Jan.	25	100	36	100	20	100	1225	100	150	100	240	100
July	45	100	18	100	40	93	1500	100	165	100	185	100
1861, Jan.	25	100	28	101	14	93	1200	100	58	100	290	100
July	35	90	38	97	30	82	1100	90	55	90	20	113
1862, Jan.	7	88	14	100	10	79	800	100	8	88	..	...
July	8	88	13	99	15	79	900	100	8	88	16	88
1863, Jan.	7	100	19	114	15	93	800	125	7	100	15	100
July	12	110	8	116	16	100	800	125	12	110	5	113
1864, Jan.	5	125	8	145	16	114	700	150	6	125	5	125
July	8	150	10	158	30	136	650	180	8	150	20	150
1865, Jan.	5	160	9	174	20	143	500	190	5	160	10	160
July	3	150	10	187	22	143	450	190	3	150	1	150
1866, Jan.	2	175	8	189	12	143	420	190	3	175	11	175
July	1	175	11	203	12	143	500	190	2	175	2	175

TABLE 1 — *Continued*

WAGE-SERIES FROM TABLE XII OF THE ALDRICH REPORT—CITY PUBLIC WORKS

	35 N. Y.		36 Pa.		36 Pa.		36 Pa.		36 Pa.		36 Pa.	
	QUARRYM'N		CARPENT'S		ENGINEERS		ENGINEER ASSISTANT		FIREMEN		LABORERS	
Sex........	M.		M.		M.		M.		M.		M.	
Init. wage per day..	$1.10		$2.00		$2.125		$1.25		$1.25		$1.335	
	No.	Rel. Wages	No.	Rel. Wages	No.	Rel. Wages	No.	Rel. Wages	No.	Rel. Wages	No.	Rel. Wages
1860, Jan.	110	100	..	...	4	100	1	100	3	100	23	100
July	340	100	1	100	4	100	1	100	3	100	30	97
1861, Jan.	280	100	1	100	6	99	1	88	6	100	30	97
July	...	...	2	100	6	99	1	88	7	103	34	96
1862, Jan.	...	...	2	100	6	99	1	88	7	103	34	96
July	...	...	2	100	6	99	1	88	7	103	34	96
1863, Jan.	...	...	..	...	6	94	5	92	6	102	8	96
July	...	...	..	...	6	94	5	92	5	99	8	96
1864, Jan.	70	145	..	...	6	96	5	92	10	99	36	112
July	45	173	..	...	6	96	5	92	10	99	36	112
1865, Jan.	70	182	..	...	4	119	5	132	8	132	21	131
July	50	182	2	138	4	119	6	132	8	132	26	131
1866, Jan.	30	182	2	138	4	119	7	132	8	132	15	131
July	..	...	1	138	4	119	6	132	8	132	13	131

	36 Pa.		36 Pa.		36 Pa.		37 Pa.	
	MACHINISTS		PATTERN MAKERS		WATCHMEN		LABORERS	
Sex..........................	M.		M.		M.		M.	
Initial wage per day.......	$1.50		$1.50		$1.50		$1.25	
	No.	Rel. Wages	No.	Rel. Wages	No.	Rel. Wages	No.	Rel. Wages
1860, January..........	1	100	..	...	2	100	28	100
July..............	1	100	..	...	2	100	30	100
1861, January..........	4	121	1	100	4	89	33	100
July..............	4	121	1	100	4	89	37	100
1862, January..........	4	121	1	100	4	89	16	100
July..............	4	121	1	100	3	94	29	100
1863, January..........	1	100	..	...	2	73	20	120
July..............	1	100	..	...	2	73	34	120
1864, January..........	4	146	..	...	2	73	19	140
July..............	1	133	..	...	2	73	38	140
1865, January..........	6	175	1	150	2	100	24	140
July..............	8	183	1	150	2	100	37	140
1866, January..........	12	183	1	150	2	100	15	140
July..............	12	178	1	150	2	100	23	140

TABLE 1 — *Continued*

WAGE-SERIES FROM TABLE XII OF THE ALDRICH REPORT — COTTON GOODS

38 Massachusetts

	M'ST'R MA-CHINISTS		OVERSEERS CARDING DEP'T		OVERSEERS CLOTH ROOM		OVERSEERS DRESSING DEP'T		OVERSEERS SPINNING DEP'T		OVERSEERS WEAVING DEP'T	
Sex......	M.		M.		M.		M.		M.		M.	
Init. wage per day..	$3.33		$3.00		$2.00		$3.00		$3.00		$2.065	
	No.	Rel. Wages	No.	Rel. Wages	No.	Rel. Wages	No.	Rel. Wages	No.	Rel. Wages	No.	Rel. Wages
1860, Jan.	1	100	1	100	1	100	1	100	2	100	4	100
July	1	100	1	100	1	100	1	100	2	100	4	100
1861, Jan.	1	100	1	83	1	84	1	83	2	83	4	85
July	1	100	1	83	1	84	1	83	2	83	4	85
1862, Jan.	1	100	1	83	1	84	1	83	2	83	4	85
July	1	100	1	83	1	84	1	83	2	83	4	85
1863, Jan.	1	106	1	100	1	100	1	100	2	100	4	103
July	1	106	1	100	1	100	1	100	2	100	4	103
1864, Jan.	1	120	1	117	1	125	1	117	2	113	3	129
July	1	120	1	117	1	125	1	117	2	113	3	129
1865, Jan.	1	120	1	117	1	113	1	117	2	117	4	121
July	1	120	1	117	1	113	1	117	2	117	4	121
1866, Jan.	1	150	1	133	1	138	1	133	2	133	4	157
July	1	150	1	133	1	138	1	133	2	133	4	157

	SECOND HANDS		THIRD HANDS		BACKBOYS		BALERS		BEAM-CARRIERS		BELTMEN	
Sex........	M.		M.		M.		M.		M.		M.	
Init. wage per day..	$1.365		$0.97		$0.265		$1.00		$0.835		$1.50	
	No.	Rel. Wages	No.	Rel. Wages	No.	Rel. Wages	No.	Rel. Wages	No.	Rel. Wages	No.	Rel. Wages
1860, Jan.	13	100	17	100	13	100	1	100	2	100	1	100
July	13	100	17	100	13	100	1	100	2	100	1	100
1861, Jan.	13	77	18	71	12	87	1	83	2	83	1	100
July	13	77	18	71	12	87	1	83	2	83	1	100
1862, Jan.	13	78	12	80	13	74	1	83	2	83	1	111
July	13	78	12	80	13	106	1	83	2	83	1	111
1863, Jan.	10	101	9	103	14	136	1	108	1	129	1	111
July	10	101	9	103	14	158	1	108	1	129	1	111
1864, Jan.	12	113	4	155	14	177	1	133	1	150	1	117
July	12	113	4	155	14	177	1	133	1	150	1	117
1865, Jan.	11	139	6	159	13	172	1	133	2	159	1	122
July	11	139	6	159	13	172	1	133	2	162	1	122
1866, Jan.	12	157	13	175	13	187	1	167	2	175	1	150
July	12	157	13	175	13	187	1	167	2	175	1	150

TABLE 1 — *Continued*

WAGE-SERIES FROM TABLE XII OF THE ALDRICH REPORT — COTTON GOODS

38 Massachusetts

	BLACK-SMITHS		BOBBIN MEN		BOILERMEN		B'L'RM'N'S' HELPERS		CARPENT'S		CARD GRINDERS	
Sex........	M.		M.		M.		M.		M.		M.	
Init. wage per day..	$1.79		$1.415		$1.75		$1.08		$1.52		$1.025	
	No.	Rel. Wages	No.	Rel. Wages	No.	Rel. Wages	No.	Rel. Wages	No.	Rel. Wages	No.	Rel. Wages
1860, Jan.	4	100	..	...	1	100	2	100	5	100	7	100
July	4	100	..	...	1	100	2	100	5	100	7	100
1861, Jan.	4	97	2	100	1	86	2	100	6	102	7	90
July	4	97	2	100	1	86	2	100	6	102	7	90
1862, Jan.	3	106	2	106	1	95	2	100	7	113	3	111
July	3	106	2	106	1	95	2	100	7	113	3	111
1863, Jan.	3	106	1	124	2	100	1	116	6	113	3	111
July	3	106	1	124	2	100	1	116	6	113	3	111
1864, Jan.	3	116	1	159	2	98	1	116	6	132	3	120
July	3	116	1	159	2	98	1	116	6	132	3	120
1865, Jan.	3	151	1	153	2	107	2	130	6	168	3	140
July	3	151	1	153	2	107	2	130	6	168	3	140
1866, Jan.	3	158	4	144	1	114	1	139	6	164	3	141
July	3	158	4	144	1	114	1	139	6	164	3	141

	DOFFERS		DOUBLE TENDERS		ENTRYMEN		FILLING CARRIERS		LAP CARRIERS		M'CHINISTS	
Sex........	M.		M.		M.		M.		M.		M.	
Init. wage per day..	$0.315		$0.64		$0.92		$0.83		$0.71		$1.565	
	No.	Rel. Wages	No.	Rel. Wages	No.	Rel. Wages	No.	Rel. Wages	No.	Rel. Wages	No.	Rel. Wages
1860, Jan.	33	100	6	100	1	100	5	100	2	100	7	100
July	33	100	6	100	1	100	5	100	2	100	7	100
1861, Jan.	33	92	4	88	1	82	4	81	2	92	7	97
July	33	92	4	88	1	82	4	81	2	92	7	97
1862, Jan.	33	97	4	110	1	82	4	81	2	126	·7	105
July	33	97	4	110	1	82	4	81	2	126	7	105
1863, Jan.	27	124	4	117	1	109	4	111	2	118	7	109
July	27	124	4	117	1	109	4	111	2	118	7	109
1864, Jan.	26	139	3	113	1	136	4	141	2	146	8	128
July	26	139	3	113	1	136	4	141	2	146	8	128
1865, Jan.	26	186	3	198	1	136	4	155	3	144	9	144
July	26	186	3	198	1	136	4	155	3	144	9	144
1866, Jan.	27	183	3	198	1	163	4	155	3	192	8	166
July	25	187	3	198	1	163	4	155	3	192	8	166

TABLE 1 — *Continued*

WAGE-SERIES FROM TABLE XII OF THE ALDRICH REPORT — COTTON GOODS

38 Massachusetts

	MASONS		OILERS		PAINTERS		PICKERS		ROLLER COVERERS		WASTE HANDS	
Sex........	M.		M.		M.		M.		M.		M.	
Init. wage per day..	$1.48		$0.42		$1.36		$0.71		$1.50		$1.10	
	No.	Rel. Wages	No.	Rel. Wages	No.	Rel. Wages	No.	Rel. Wages	No.	Rel. Wages	No.	Rel. Wages
1860, Jan.	5	100	2	100	3	100	12	100	2	100	3	100
July	5	100	2	100	3	100	12	100	2	100	3	100
1861, Jan.	6	99	2	107	2	104	9	111	2	100	3	91
July	6	99	2	107	2	104	9	111	2	100	3	91
1862, Jan.	7	98	2	107	2	107	9	109	1	111	3	86
July	7	98	2	107	2	107	9	109	1	111	3	86
1863, Jan.	5	115	2	107	2	107	9	146	1	111	2	121
July	5	115	2	107	2	107	9	146	1	111	2	121
1864, Jan.	5	151	2	112	2	113	7	181	1	122	1	136
July	5	151	2	112	2	113	7	181	1	122	1	136
1865, Jan.	3	192	2	131	2	135	9	193	2	142	2	132
July	3	192	2	131	2	135	9	193	2	142	2	132
1866, Jan.	3	225	4	242	2	156	9	200	2	151	2	114
July	3	225	4	242	2	156	9	200	2	151	2	114

	WATCHMEN		WHEELPIT MEN		YARD HANDS		YARN CARRIERS		CARD STRIPPERS		SCRUBBERS	
Sex........	M.		M.		M.		M.		F.		F.	
Init. wage per day..	$1.33		$2.00		$1.10		$0.68		$0.71		$0.45	
	No.	Rel. Wages	No.	Rel. Wages	No.	Rel. Wages	No.	Rel. Wages	No.	Rel. Wages	No.	Rel. Wages
1860, Jan.	4	100	1	100	5	100	3	100	6	100	4	100
July	4	100	1	100	5	100	3	100	6	100	4	100
1861, Jan.	4	81	1	113	4	91	3	74	6	96	4	83
July	4	81	1	113	4	91	3	74	6	96	4	83
1862, Jan.	4	81	1	113	3	82	2	74	6	113	4	83
July	4	81	1	113	3	82	2	74	6	113	4	83
1863, Jan.	4	107	1	113	3	110	3	74	6	141	4	111
July	4	107	1	113	3	110	3	74	6	141	4	111
1864, Jan.	4	113	1	125	3	127	4	92	5	162	4	129
July	4	113	1	125	3	127	4	92	5	162	4	129
1865, Jan.	4	132	2	133	3	114	1	178	5	190	4	149
July	4	132	2	133	3	114	1	178	5	190	4	149
1866, Jan.	2	150	1	150	3	127	4	145	5	190	7	164
July	2	150	1	150	3	127	4	145	5	190	7	164

TABLE 1—*Continued*

WAGE-SERIES FROM TABLE XII OF THE ALDRICH REPORT — COTTON GOODS

	38 Mass.		38 Mass.		39 Mass.		39 Mass.		39 Mass.		39 Mass.	
	SPOOLERS		SWEEPERS		FOREMEN CARPENT'S		FOREMEN MACHIN'TS		FOREMEN YARD		OVERSEERS CARD. DEP.	
Sex........	F.		F.		M.		M.		M.		M.	
Init. wage per day...	$0.50		$0.71		$1.75		$1.75		$2.00		$2.00	
	No.	Rel. Wages	No.	Rel. Wages	No.	Rel. Wages	No.	Rel. Wages	No.	Rel. Wages	No.	Rel. Wages
1860, Jan.	47	100	2	100	1	100	1	100	1	100	1	100
July	47	100	2	100	1	107	1	100	1	100	1	100
1861, Jan.	45	84	1	70	1	107	1	100	1	100	1	100
July	45	84	1	70	1	107	1	100	1	100	1	100
1862, Jan.	45	80	1	85	1	107	1	94	1	100	1	100
July	45	80	1	85	1	114	1	94	1	100	1	75
1863, Jan.	45	105	3	97	1	114	1	114	1	100	1	100
July	45	105	3	97	1	114	1	114	1	100	1	100
1864, Jan.	44	95	3	102	1	114	1	119	1	100	1	100
July	44	95	3	102	1	129	3	129	1	100	1	113
1865, Jan.	..	...	3	102	1	143	1	143	1	100	1	113
July	..	...	3	102	1	143	3	143	1	113	1	113
1866, Jan.	37	200	14	104	1	171	1	171	1	125	1	125
July	37	200	14	104	1	171	1	186	1	125	1	125

39 Massachusetts

	OVERSEERS CLOTH R'M		OVERSEERS DRESS. DEP.		OVERSEERS SPIN. DEP.		OVERSEERS WEAV. DEP.		SECOND HANDS		CARPENT'S	
Sex........	M.		M.		M.		M.		M.		M.	
Init. wage per day...	$2.25		$1.75		$2.00		$2.00		$1.175		$1.42	
	No.	Rel. Wages	No.	Rel. Wages	No.	Rel. Wages	No.	Rel. Wages	No.	Rel. Wages	No.	Rel. Wages
1860, Jan.	1	100	1	100	1	100	1	100	6	100	11	100
July	1	100	1	100	1	100	1	100	7	103	11	96
1861, Jan.	1	100	1	100	1	100	1	100	6	103	9	98
July	1	100	1	100	1	100	1	100	2	103	11	99
1862, Jan.	1	100	1	100	1	100	1	100	3	101	10	98
July	1	78	1	86	1	75	1	75	4	89	12	95
1863, Jan.	1	78	1	114	1	100	1	100	1	99	24	90
July	1	78	1	114	1	100	1	100	1	99	26	92
1864, Jan.	1	78	1	114	1	100	1	100	2	128	14	106
July	1	92	1	114	1	88	1	113	2	106	8	128
1865, Jan.	1	100	1	129	1	88	1	113	2	106	8	143
July	1	100	1	129	2	113	1	113	5	136	14	148
1866, Jan.	1	111	1	143	1	125	1	138	5	149	12	147
July	1	111	1	143	1	129	1	138	4	154	12	150

TABLE 1—*Continued*

WAGE-SERIES FROM TABLE XII OF THE ALDRICH REPORT — COTTON GOODS

39 Massachusetts

	CARD GRINDERS		CARD STRIPPERS		MACHIN'TS		PAINTERS		PICKERS		SECTION HANDS	
Sex........	M.		M.		M.		M.		M.		M.	
Init. wage per day...	$0.83		$0.625		$1.38		$1.14		$0.735		$0.76	
	No.	Rel. Wages	No.	Rel. Wages	No.	Rel. Wages	No.	Rel. Wages	No.	Rel. Wages	No.	Rel. Wages
1860, Jan.	2	100	6	100	24	100	7	100	2	100	5	100
July	2	110	6	103	24	101	7	104	2	102	6	110
1861, Jan.	2	110	3	111	14	104	7	111	2	102	6	106
July	2	110	4	112	13	106	5	111	2	102	6	107
1862, Jan.	3	114	4	112	14	97	4	111	2	102	6	109
July	3	104	2	104	17	99	6	100	1	102	4	103
1863, Jan.	2	110	1	96	7	109	4	95	1	113	3	113
July	2	110	1	96	10	102	6	97	1	113	3	113
1864, Jan.	2	151	5	120	11	112	8	97	1	136	2	109
July	1	160	2	179	10	126	6	119	1	170	3	123
1865, Jan.	1	160	2	179	10	145	6	130	1	204	2	109
July	2	201	4	179	12	136	6	133	2	181	5	147
1866, Jan.	2	202	4	179	16	146	6	132	2	171	7	185
July	2	192	4	179	15	149	5	136	3	165	7	185

	SLASHER TENDERS		WATCHMEN		YARD HANDS		DRAWERS-IN		DRAWING HANDS		SPEEDERS	
Sex........	M.		M.		M.		F.		F.		F.	
Init. wage per day...	$1.08		$0.86		$0.855		$0.475		$0.42		$0.52	
	No.	Rel. Wages	No.	Rel. Wages	No.	Rel. Wages	No.	Rel. Wages	No.	Rel. Wages	No.	Rel. Wages
1860, Jan.	3	100	14	100	17	100	5	100	4	100	4	100
July	4	92	14	100	12	101	3	112	3	119	4	106
1861, Jan.	2	83	14	100	12	101	4	84	3	119	4	104
July	2	83	14	100	14	102	5	113	3	119	4	101
1862, Jan.	1	84	14	100	10	92	4	114	3	119	4	104
July	..	...	13	100	18	101	3	117	2	95	2	96
1863, Jan.	2	97	13	100	14	104	2	114	2	95	1	92
July	2	97	13	100	13	105	2	114	2	95	1	92
1864, Jan.	5	111	15	116	8	119	5	123	3	119	2	106
July	3	131	14	145	9	150	2	143	2	119	3	110
1865, Jan.	2	127	15	145	5	148	2	141	2	119	2	110
July	2	139	14	145	10	152	7	133	4	129	5	121
1866, Jan.	6	148	16	174	14	154	6	189	4	160	4	161
July	4	155	15	174	13	168	5	171	5	160	5	161

TABLE 1— *Continued*

WAGE-SERIES FROM TABLE XII OF THE ALDRICH REPORT — COTTON GOODS

	39 Mass.		39 Mass.		39 Mass.		40 Mass.		40 Mass.		40 Mass.	
	SPINNERS FRAME		WARPERS		WEAVERS		MASTER MACHIN'TS		FOREMEN YARD		OVERSEERS CARD. DEP.	
Sex........	F.		F.		F.		M.		M.		M.	
Init. wage per day...	$0.475		$0.595		$0.46		$2.00		$1.50		$2.50	
	No.	Rel. Wages	No.	Rel. Wages	No.	Rel. Wages	No.	Rel. Wages	No.	Rel. Wages	No.	Rel. Wages
1860, Jan.	28	100	6	100	19	100	1	100	1	100	1	100
July	21	92	6	115	15	103	1	100	1	100	1	100
1861, Jan.	26	97	7	108	25	110	1	113	1	117	1	100
July	29	95	6	105	16	102	1	113	1	117	1	100
1862, Jan.	30	102	7	79	18	112	1	113	1	117	1	100
July	25	102	5	84	19	102	1	113	1	117	1	100
1863, Jan.	23	97	1	67	21	117	1	113	1	117	1	100
July	25	99	1	67	23	118	1	125	1	117	1	100
1864, Jan.	24	114	2	94	20	128	1	150	1	150	1	110
July	25	121	1	109	22	149	1	150	1	167	1	110
1865, Jan.	28	118	1	97	24	140	1	150	1	167	1	110
July	34	131	2	141	25	132	1	150	1	167	1	120
1866, Jan.	34	191	4	132	24	186	1	163	1	157	1	120
July	31	189	1	161	22	198	1	163	1	167	1	120

40 Massachusetts

	OVERSEERS CLOTH R'M		OVERSEERS DRESS.DEP.		OVERSEERS SPIN. DEP.		OVERSEERS WEAV.DEP.		SECOND HANDS		THIRD HANDS	
Sex........	M.		M.		M.		M.		M.		M.	
Init. wage per day...	$1.42		$1.83		$2.50		$2.25		$1.485		$1.265	
	No.	Rel. Wages	No.	Rel. Wages	No.	Rel. Wages	No.	Rel. Wages	No.	Rel. Wages	No.	Rel. Wages
1860, Jan.	1	100	1	100	1	100	2	100	6	100	5	100
July	1	100	1	100	1	100	2	100	6	100	5	100
1861, Jan.	1	106	1	100	1	100	2	111	7	97	5	100
July	1	106	1	100	1	100	2	111	7	97	5	100
1862, Jan.	1	106	1	137	1	100	2	111	6	97	4	100
July	1	106	1	137	1	100	2	111	5	97	2	96
1863, Jan.	1	106	1	137	1	100	1	111	6	97	2	82
July	1	106	1	137	..	...	1	111	3	96	2	82
1864, Jan.	1	106	1	150	1	120	2	98	13	109	2	112
July	1	123	1	150	1	120	2	102	13	112	1	132
1865, Jan.	1	123	1	164	1	110	2	102	14	114	2	122
July	1	123	1	164	1	110	2	111	14	118	2	125
1866, Jan.	1	123	1	164	1	120	2	111	15	119	5	132
July	1	123	1	164	1	120	2	111	11	121	2	128

TABLE 1—*Continued*

WAGE-SERIES FROM TABLE XII OF THE ALDRICH REPORT—COTTON GOODS

40 Massachusetts

	BAND BOYS		CARPENT'S		CARD GRINDERS		CARD STRIPPERS		CLOTH-R'M HANDS		DRAWING HANDS	
Sex........	M.		M.		M.		M.		M.		M.	
Init.wage per day..	$0.79		$1.49		$0.83		$0.755		$0.50		$0.662	
	No.	Rel. Wages	No.	Rel. Wages	No.	Rel. Wages	No.	Rel. Wages	No.	Rel. Wages	No.	Rel. Wages
1860, Jan.	2	100	8	100	11	100	11	100	2	100	5	100
July	4	89	8	100	11	100	11	100	2	100	4	100
1861, Jan.	4	93	7	104	8	105	11	99	2	108	5	95
July	1	105	7	104	8	105	11	99	2	108	5	95
1862, Jan.	1	127	7	105	8	105	14	99	1	116	4	79
July	1	127	9	106	2	96	4	99	1	116	2	94
1863, Jan.	..	...	9	103	1	106	3	100	1	116	..	...
July	..	..	9	107	..	...	..	...	1	116	..	...
1864, Jan.	..	...	13	128	6	181	9	166	..	...	2	106
July	..	...	9	139	7	178	12	175	..	...	3	113
1865, Jan.	1	63	11	128	5	179	10	180	..	...	3	121
July	4	111	11	140	6	189	9	179	..	...	3	129
1866, Jan.	1	127	14	141	6	189	9	180	2	169	5	157
July	..	...	8	159	6	189	9	181	2	169	6	176

	DRESSERS		DOFFERS		ENGINEERS		FIREMEN		HARNESS HANDS		LABORERS	
Sex	M.		M.		M.		M.		M.		M.	
Init. wage per day..	$0.98		$0.303		$3.00		$1.415		$0.38		$0.995	
	No.	Rel. Wages	No.	Rel. Wages	No.	Rel. Wages	No.	Rel. Wages	No.	Rel. Wages	No.	Rel. Wages
1860, Jan.	2	100	27	100	1	100	4	100	2	100	16	100
July	2	100	28	100	1	100	3	102	2	97	16	100
1861, Jan.	3	101	25	102	1	100	3	98	2	121	11	103
July	3	102	15	107	1	100	3	99	2	121	11	103
1862, Jan.	2	88	14	105	1	100	4	100	2	126	9	100
July	2	90	5	114	1	100	4	105	1	132	6	106
1863, Jan.	1	88	9	94	1	100	4	105	..	...	5	107
July	1	92	..	...	1	100	4	99	..	...	4	124
1864, Jan.	2	94	15	124	2	92	4	104	1	197	11	147
July	2	100	15	124	2	92	4	106	1	197	14	173
1865, Jan.	3	73	15	132	2	96	4	107	..	...	8	164
July	4	88	14	132	2	96	4	108	..	...	13	174
1866, Jan.	5	111	10	165	2	96	4	112	2	216	13	176
July	7	117	9	165	2	100	4	118	1	234	8	177

TABLE 1—*Continued*

WAGE-SERIES FROM TABLE XII OF THE ALDRICH REPORT—COTTON GOODS

40 Massachusetts

	MACHIN'TS		MACHIN'TS' APPRENT'S		PICKING ROOM H'DS		ROVING HANDS		SECTION HANDS		SPOOLERS	
Sex	M.		M.		M.		M.		M.		M.	
Init. wage per day	$1.765		$0.875		$0.85		$0.38		$1.25		$0.448	
	No.	Rel. Wages	No.	Rel. Wages	No.	Rel. Wages	No.	Rel. Wages	No.	Rel. Wages	No.	Rel. Wages
1860, Jan.	14	100	2	100	4	100	4	100	4	100	4	100
July	13	102	2	100	4	100	5	101	4	102	5	101
1861, Jan.	10	105	3	114	6	98	4	101	4	107	2	84
July	10	105	3	114	6	98	4	104	4	108	2	96
1862, Jan.	10	105	3	114	7	98	..	...	1	106	3	119
July	10	105	2	114	7	98	1	132	1	106	3	128
1863, Jan.	9	103	2	124	2	106	..	...	..	...	1	62
July	10	102	3	137	2	106	..	...	..	...	2	61
1864, Jan.	14	125	4	119	3	123	7	108	7	108	3	92
July	13	127	4	126	5	165	3	132	7	108	3	98
1865, Jan.	14	126	2	129	2	162	2	145	5	127	7	107
July	15	134	..	...	4	162	2	151	3	131	6	114
1866, Jan.	16	132	1	77	7	181	4	153	4	122	8	144
July	17	142	1	114	8	187	4	168	5	115	5	183

	TEAMSTERS		WATCHMEN		CLOTH-R'M HANDS		DOFFERS		DRAWING HANDS		DRESSERS	
Sex	M.		M.		F.		F.		F.		F.	
Init. wage per day	$1.50		$1.06		$0.61		$0.315		$0.455		$1.059	
	No.	Rel. Wages	No.	Rel. Wages	No.	Rel. Wages	No.	Rel. Wages	No.	Rel. Wages	No.	Rel. Wages
1860, Jan.	1	100	2	100	6	100	2	100	22	100	9	100
July	1	100	2	100	6	100	5	103	23	105	10	105
1861, Jan.	2	92	4	94	5	87	5	103	9	130	8	107
July	2	92	4	94	5	87	3	112	9	134	7	106
1862, Jan.	2	92	..	...	..	82	2	105	8	114	6	69
July	2	92	..	...	..	82	1	105	5	122	6	71
1863, Jan.	3	89	8	94	1	...	4	98	3	101	3	54
July	2	83	8	94	1	...	..	...	1	114	3	55
1864, Jan.	3	94	4	134	3	99	..	...	13	127	5	105
July	3	94	4	158	3	99	..	...	18	125	5	105
1865, Jan.	3	91	4	158	3	130	..	...	20	117	10	92
July	3	91	5	158	3	130	6	127	20	127	11	98
1866, Jan.	2	117	5	165	8	136	6	159	21	139	11	117
July	2	117	3	165	8	136	8	159	19	134	7	138

TABLE 1—*Continued*

WAGE-SERIES FROM TABLE XII OF THE ALDRICH REPORT—COTTON GOODS

40 Massachusetts

	HARNESS HANDS		ROOM HANDS		SPEEDERS		SPOOLERS		STRETCH-ERS		SWEEPERS	
Sex........	F.		F.		F.		F.		F.		F.	
Init. wage per day..	\$0.464		\$0.67		\$0.503		\$0.404		\$0.533		\$0.39	
	No.	Rel. Wages	No.	Rel. Wages	No.	Rel. Wages	No.	Rel. Wages	No.	Rel. Wages	No.	Rel. Wages
1860, Jan.	5	100	1	100	8	100	9	100	3	100	2	100
July	4	103	1	100	8	100	11	95	3	100	2	100
1861, Jan.	1	125	1	112	6	104	15	86	6	110	1	103
July	1	125	1	112	6	105	20	90	6	114	1	103
1862, Jan.	1	140	1	112	6	105	12	98	8	113	..	...
July	1	140	1	112	1	99	12	101	3	118	..	...
1863, Jan.	1	151	1	112	1	99	7	88	8	119	..	...
July	1	151	1	112	..	...	7	103	6	116	..	...
1864, Jan.	2	162	2	93	10	144	10	120	6	117	3	128
July	2	162	1	106	8	154	11	127	6	120	2	147
1865, Jan.	1	162	2	106	8	152	15	118	6	122	2	154
July	1	162	1	149	8	156	17	125	6	124	5	156
1866, Jan.	3	185	8	152	8	155	19	173	6	134	6	182
July	1	192	2	153	8	159	24	200	6	143	7	187

	WARPERS		WEAVERS		WEAVERS	
Sex........	F.		F.		F.	
Initial wage per day	\$0.059		\$0.32[1]		\$0.42[2]	
	No.	Rel. Wages	No.	Rel. Wages	No.	Rel. Wages
1860, January	7	100	12	100	8	100
July	9	100	14	100	7	100
1861, January	11	99	14	106	6	100
July	12	103	15	106	9	100
1862, January	6	100	10	106	5	102
July	5	103	10	106	6	102
1863, January	1	102	3	109	8	107
July	1	102	9	116	9	107
1864, January	3	137	8	116	10	107
July	3	148	6	116	8	107
1865, January	2	127	16	125	10	107
July	3	126	10	125	8	119
1866, January	6	162	45	125	9	119
July	3	202	52	125	6	119

[1] Per cut for sheetings 46 inches wide, 48 yards per cut.
[2] Per cut for sheetings 72 inches wide, 40 yards per cut.

TABLE 1—*Continued*

WAGE-SERIES FROM TABLE XII OF THE ALDRICH REPORT—DRY GOODS

42 New Hampshire

	PORTERS		SALESMEN		SALESWOMEN	
Sex......................	M.		M.		F.	
Initial wage per day......	$1.00		$1.125		$0.80	
	No.	Rel. Wages	No.	Rel. Wages	No.	Rel. Wages
1860, January..	1	100	4	100	5	100
July............	..	...	..	...	..	...
1861, January........	..	...	..	...	..	...
July............	1	100	4	100	5	100
1862, January........	1	100	4	100	5	100
July............	1	100	4	100	5	100
1863, January..	1	125	4	156	5	100
July............	1	125	4	156	5	100
1864, January........	1	125	4	156	5	100
July............	1	125	4	156	5	100
1865, January..	1	125	4	178	4	104
July............	1	125	4	178	4	104
1866, January	1	125	4	178	4	104
July............	1	125	4	178	4	104

GINGHAMS

43 Massachusetts

	OVERSEERS								SECOND HANDS		BACK BOYS	
	Carding Dep't		Dressing Dep't		Spinning Dep't		Weaving Dep't					
Sex........	M.		M.		M.		M.		M.		M.	
Init. wage per day..	$3.00		$3.00		$2.50		$3.00		$1.55		$0.30	
	No.	Rel. Wages	No.	Rel. Wages	No.	Rel. Wages	No.	Rel. Wages	No.	Rel. Wages	No.	Rel. Wages
1860, Jan.	1	100	1	100	2	100	1	100	5	100	16	100
July	1	100	1	100	2	100	1	100	5	100	16	100
1861, Jan.	1	100	1	100	2	100	1	100	5	100	16	100
July	1	100	1	100	2	100	1	100	5	100	16	100
1862, Jan.	1	100	1	100	2	100	1	100	5	100	16	100
July	1	100	1	100	2	100	1	100	5	100	16	100
1863, Jan.	1	100	1	100	2	100	1	100	5	100	16	100
July	1	100	1	100	2	100	1	100	5	100	16	100
1864, Jan.	1	100	1	100	2	100	1	100	5	103	16	100
July	1	100	1	100	2	100	1	100	5	116	16	117
1865, Jan.	1	100	1	100	2	100	1	100	5	124	16	117
July	1	108	1	108	2	110	1	108	5	132	16	123
1866, Jan.	1	108	1	117	2	110	1	133	5	148	16	133
July	1	108	1	117	2	120	1	133	5	152	16	150

TABLE 1—*Continued*

WAGE-SERIES FROM TABLE XII OF THE ALDRICH REPORT—GINGHAMS

43 Massachusetts

	BOILER TENDERS		CARPENTERS		CARD GRINDERS		CARD STRIPPERS		CARD TENDERS		DRESSERS	
Sex........	M.		M.		M.		M.		M.		M.	
Init. wage per day..	$1.165		$1.75		$1.25		$0.83		$0.75		$1.64	
	No.	Rel. Wages	No.	Rel. Wages	No.	Rel. Wages	No.	Rel. Wages	No.	Rel. Wages	No.	Rel. Wages
1860, Jan.	2	100	4	100	2	100	4	100	7	100	14	100
July	2	100	4	100	3	100	4	100	7	100	14	112
1861, Jan.	2	100	2	100	3	100	4	100	7	100	14	110
July	2	100	2	86	3	100	4	100	7	100	9	112
1862, Jan.	2	100	2	86	3	100	4	100	6	100	10	114
July	2	100	2	86	3	100	4	100	6	100	10	120
1863, Jan.	3	100	2	86	3	100	3	100	3	111	10	117
July	3	100	3	100	3	100	3	114	3	111	11	107
1864, Jan.	4	100	4	100	3	107	3	114	6	111	11	110
July	4	129	4	114	3	120	3	135	6	133	9	112
1865, Jan.	4	129	4	114	3	120	3	135	6	149	10	118
July	3	140	4	129	3	140	4	169	6	167	11	131
1866, Jan.	3	140	5	129	4	140	4	181	5	187	14	137
July	4	140	6	134	4	140	5	181	5	187	14	138

43 Massachusetts

	DYERS		LOOM FIXERS		MACHINISTS		PAINTERS		PICKERS		SMASH MENDERS	
Sex........	M.		M.		M.		M.		M.		M.	
Init. wage per day..	$1.00		$1.58		$1.55		$1.75		$1.00		$1.30	
	No.	Rel. Wages	No.	Rel. Wages	No.	Rel. Wages	No.	Rel. Wages	No.	Rel. Wages	No.	Rel. Wages
1860, Jan.	24	100	13	100	6	100	3	100	3	100	3	100
July	24	100	13	99	4	90	2	100	3	100	3	100
1861, Jan.	24	100	13	97	4	90	2	100	3	100	3	100
July	22	100	13	103	4	99	2	100	3	100	3	100
1862, Jan.	22	100	13	94	4	97	2	100	3	100	3	87
July	22	100	13	84	3	92	2	100	3	100	3	87
1863, Jan.	12	100	12	107	3	97	2	100	3	100	3	87
July	12	100	12	96	4	100	2	100	3	112	3	87
1864, Jan.	16	125	13	97	4	100	2	100	4	112	3	87
July	23	150	13	99	6	107	2	103	4	125	3	90
1865, Jan.	24	150	14	128	7	110	2	103	4	125	4	96
July	33	175	17	136	7	128	2	114	5	150	4	106
1866, Jan.	35	175	18	146	7	145	2	120	4	165	3	115
July	35	175	17	147	7	152	2	120	4	165	3	115

TABLE 1—*Continued*

WAGE-SERIES FROM TABLE XII OF THE ALDRICH REPORT—GINGHAMS

43 Massachusetts

	WATCHMEN		WEAVERS		YARD HANDS		DRAWERS-IN		DRAWING-FRAME TENDERS		QUILLERS	
Sex........	M.		M.		M.		F.		F.		F.	
Init. wage per day..	$1.165		$0.93		$1.00		$0.80		$0.49		$0.57	
	No.	Rel. Wages	No.	Rel. Wages	No.	Rel. Wages	No.	Rel. Wages	No.	Rel. Wages	No.	Rel. Wages
1860, Jan.	2	100	85	100	10	100	5	100	10	100	36	100
July	2	100	93	98	10	100	5	100	10	102	35	100
1861, Jan.	2	100	108	100	10	100	4	100	10	102	37	100
July	2	100	100	104	8	100	4	115	9	102	36	96
1862, Jan.	2	100	82	97	6	100	4	118	10	102	34	96
July	2	100	65	104	6	100	4	111	10	102	29	104
1863, Jan.	2	100	23	97	6	100	5	108	8	102	23	104
July	2	100	11	104	6	100	5	104	8	102	20	100
1864, Jan.	2	100	35	99	8	100	5	103	11	112	25	100
July	3	115	40	105	8	125	5	105	14	122	29	128
1865, Jan.	3	115	40	129	10	150	5	103	12	133	29	128
July	4	129	34	135	10	163	6	100	15	163	39	131
1866, Jan.	2	129	85	167	12	163	6	125	10	163	45	153
July	2	129	98	185	12	163	6	150	12	173	45	160

43 Massachusetts

	REELERS		SPEEDERS		SPINNERS FRAME		WARPERS		WEAVERS		WINDERS	
Sex........	F.		F.		F.		F.		F.		F.	
Init. wage per day..	$0.66		$0.60		$0.56		$0.73		$0.72		$0.56	
	No.	Rel. Wages	No.	Rel. Wages	No.	Rel. Wages	No.	Rel. Wages	No.	Rel. Wages	No.	Rel. Wages
1860, Jan.	34	100	12	100	19	100	26	100	115	100	103	100
July	38	100	12	100	17	105	26	100	103	97	101	105
1861, Jan.	33	120	10	100	10	105	27	100	98	99	99	107
July	28	120	13	100	10	105	20	134	97	111	70	121
1862, Jan.	26	120	12	100	10	105	20	133	120	101	61	121
July	19	145	12	100	10	105	19	130	89	114	54	121
1863, Jan.	14	145	6	100	6	105	11	123	88	107	43	121
July	14	132	6	100	8	107	13	108	90	106	37	121
1864, Jan.	21	132	12	108	16	116	18	104	115	101	44	121
July	25	130	11	117	18	125	25	101	160	109	25	141
1865, Jan.	26	130	11	133	20	143	20	110	140	134	49	143
July	39	129	13	158	29	170	28	142	188	151	70	168
1866, Jan.	45	144	17	158	26	170	35	144	196	1654	82	175
July	43	148	17	167	25	170	34	144	172	178	85	186

TABLE 1 — *Continued*

WAGE-SERIES FROM TABLE XII OF THE ALDRICH REPORT—GROCERIES

44 New Hampshire

	SALESMEN		TEAMSTERS	
Sex	M.		M.	
Initial wage per day...	$0.875		$1.50	
	No.	Rel. Wages	No.	Rel. Wages
1860, January......	2	100	1	100
July	2	100	1	100
1861, January......	2	100	1	100
July	2	129	1	100
1862, January......	2	157	1	133
July	2	157	1	133
1863, January......	2	186	1	133
July	2	186	1	133
1864, January......	2	186	1	133
July	2	186	1	133
1865, January......	2	186	1	133
July	2	186	1	133
1866, January......	2	186	1	133
July	2	186	1	133

ILLUMINATING GAS

45 Mass.　46 Mass.　46 Mass.　46 Mass.　47 N. Y.　47 N. Y.

	RETORTM'N		COOL HANDLERS		FIREMEN		LABORERS: STREET		BLACK-SMITHS		BLACKSM'S HELPERS	
Sex........	M.		M.		M.		M.		M.		M.	
Init. wage per day..	$0.955		$1.00		$1.00		$1.00		$1.965		$1.125	
	No.	Rel. Wages	No.	Rel. Wages	No.	Rel. Wages	No.	Rel. Wages	No.	Rel. Wages	No.	Rel. Wages
1860, Jan.	2	100	3	100	7	100	3	100	7	100	4	100
July	2	109	..	...	6	100	12	100	8	98	3	111
1861, Jan.	2	109	4	100	7	100	..	...	10	97	3	111
July	2	109	1	100	6	100	8	100	10	97	6	100
1862, Jan.	2	109	2	100	12	100	2	109	10	97	5	100
July	2	109	1	100	10	113	6	100	9	97	6	100
1863, Jan.	2	109	2	100	14	113	..	...	6	104	5	100
July	2	109	..	...	9	137	5	110	6	140	5	156
1864, Jan.	2	116	5	143	14	137	..	...	7	124	5	133
July	2	136	1	150	10	175	6	125	6	140	5	156
1865, Jan.	2	138	1	150	15	175	2	125	6	151	4	178
July	2	146	..	...	8	175	4	125	6	151	5	178
1866, Jan.	3	138	2	150	11	175	..	...	6	151	5	178
July	3	160	..	...	9	200	4	150	6	153	5	178

TABLE 1 — *Continued*

WAGE-SERIES FROM TABLE XII OF THE ALDRICH REPORT — ILLUMINATING GAS

47 New York

	BRICKLAY-ERS		BRICKL'RS' HELPERS		CARPEN-TERS		ENGINEERS		FIREMEN		LABORERS	
Sex........	M.		M.		M.		M.		M.		M.	
Init. wage per day..	$2.105		$1.335		$1.75		$2.165		$1.34		$1.055	
	No.	Rel. Wages	No.	Rel. Wages	No.	Rel. Wages	No.	Rel. Wages	No.	Rel. Wages	No.	Rel. Wages
1860, Jan.	7	100	3	100	6	100	3	100	80	100	219	100
July	26	97	4	103	6	100	3	100	80	100	208	98
1861, Jan.	11	97	4	103	10	100	3	100	90	100	240	99
July	15	97	5	101	9	100	3	100	90	100	210	98
1862, Jan.	11	97	5	101	9	100	3	100	90	100	220	99
July	4	101	4	103	6	100	3	100	60	100	190	97
1863, Jan.	2	107	3	119	4	100	3	112	60	131	100	142
July	2	131	4	131	4	143	3	123	60	168	80	142
1864, Jan.	4	119	2	131	3	133	6	112	80	149	90	142
July	1	119	2	131	4	143	3	123	80	168	60	142
1865, Jan.	3	127	2	150	5	171	3	135	70	187	75	186
July	7	143	6	150	5	171	3	139	80	187	43	188
1866, Jan.	3	143	3	150	6	171	2	139	80	187	65	188
July	9	160	5	150	8	182	2	162	60	187	55	173

	47 N. Y.	47 N. Y.	47 N. Y.	48 Ohio	48 Ohio	48 Ohio

	PAINTERS		PAVERS		STABLE-MEN		BLACK-SMITHS		BLACKSM'S' HELPERS		BRICKLAY-ERS	
Sex	M.		M.		M.		M.		M.		M.	
Init. wage per day..	$1.50		$1.25		$1.25		$1.50		$1.00		$2.25	
	No.	Rel. Wages	No.	Rel. Wages	No.	Rel. Wages	No.	Rel. Wages	No.	Rel. Wages	No.	Rel. Wages
1860, Jan.	1	100	3	100	3	100	1	100	1	100	2	100
July	1	100	6	100	3	100	1	100	1	100	2	100
1861, Jan.	1	100	6	100	3	100	1	100	1	100	2	100
July	1	117	4	100	3	100	1	100	1	100	2	111
1862, Jan.	1	117	3	100	3	100	1	100	1	100	2	111
July	1	117	4	100	3	100	3	111	1	115	2	111
1863, Jan.	1	117	4	100	3	104	3	128	1	115	2	122
July	1	167	4	140	2	160	3	139	1	125	2	122
1864, Jan.	1	150	1	120	3	140	3	172	1	175	2	133
July	1	167	3	140	1	160	3	178	1	200	2	178
1865, Jan.	1	183	4	160	2	160	3	189	1	200	2	178
July	2	200	3	160	2	160	3	189	1	200	2	178
1866, Jan.	2	200	2	160	2	160	3	217	1	200	2	178
July	1	217	2	160	2	160	3	217	1	200	2	200

TABLE 1 — *Continued*

WAGE-SERIES FROM TABLE XII OF THE ALDRICH REPORT — ILLUMINATING GAS

48 Ohio

	CARPENTERS		FIREMEN		LABORERS		WATCHMEN	
Sex	M.		M.		M.		M.	
Initial wage per day........	$1.525		$1.225		$1.00		$1.10	
	No.	Rel. Wages	No.	Rel. Wages	No.	Rel. Wages	No.	Rel. Wages
1860, January..........	5	100	58	100	40	100	2	100
July	2	103	58	100	40	100	2	100
1861, January..........	2	103	58	100	40	100	2	100
July	2	103	75	100	40	100	2	102
1862, January..........	2	103	75	100	40	100	2	102
July	2	107	75	113	65	113	2	114
1863, January..........	2	115	75	116	65	115	2	114
July	2	131	75	141	65	125	2	136
1864, January..........	2	148	90	204	111	150	2	159
July	1	164	123	169	46	175	2	159
1865, January..........	1	164	123	169	10	175	2	159
July	1	197	123	169	10	175	2	159
1866, January..........	1	197	123	184	10	190	2	159
July	1	180	133	184	10	190	2	159

LEATHER

50 Massachusetts

	BLACKERS		CELLAR HANDS		FINISHERS		FLATTEN-ERS		GLOSSERS		SETTERS-OUT	
Sex........	M.		M.		M.		M.		M.		M.	
Init. wage per day..	$1.00		$1.00		$1.195		$1.165		$1.165		$1.165	
	No.	Rel. Wages	No.	Rel. Wages	No.	Rel. Wages	No.	Rel. Wages	No.	Rel. Wages	No.	Rel. Wages
1860, Jan.	1	100	1	100	6	100	1	100	1	100	1	100
July	1	100	1	100	6	100	1	100	1	100	1	100
1861, Jan.	1	100	1	117	6	109	1	115	1	115	1	115
July	1	100	1	117	6	118	1	129	1	115	1	115
1862, Jan.	1	117	2	125	6	128	1	129	1	129	1	129
July	1	117	2	125	6	137	1	143	1	129	1	143
1863, Jan.	1	117	2	142	6	144	1	158	1	143	1	158
July	1	134	2	150	6	146	1	158	1	143	1	172
1864, Jan.	1	134	2	175	9	141	1	172	2	143	1	186
July	1	134	2	184	9	143	1	172	2	143	1	186
1865, Jan.	2	134	2	200	10	157	1	186	2	143	1	136
July	2	134	2	200	10	160	1	186	2	150	1	186
1866, Jan.	2	159	2	200	7	144	3	162	2	150	1	172
July	2	159	2	192	7	146	3	158	2	158	1	172

TABLE 1— *Continued*

WAGE-SERIES FROM TABLE XII OF THE ALDRICH REPORT—LEATHER

50 Mass.   50 Mass.   50 Mass.   50 Mass.   51 Mass.   51 Mass.

	SPLITTERS		STUFFERS		TABLE HANDS		WHITEN'RS		BARK GRINDERS		BEAMSTERS	
Sex........	M.		M.		M.		M.		M.		M.	
Init. wage per day..	$1.50		$1.085		$1.055		$1.035		$1.50		$1.50	
	No.	Rel. Wages	No.	Rel. Wages	No.	Rel. Wages	No.	Rel. Wages	No.	Rel. Wages	No.	Rel. Wages
1860, Jan.	1	100	2	100	3	100	5	100	2	100	5	100
July	1	100	2	100	3	100	5	100	2	100	5	100
1861, Jan.	1	122	2	107	3	105	5	113	2	111	5	111
July	1	122	2	107	3	105	5	116	2	111	5	111
1862, Jan.	1	133	2	123	3	127	4	133	2	111	5	129
July	1	133	2	123	3	132	4	141	2	111	5	129
1863, Jan.	1	144	3	143	3	142	3	150	2	133	5	140
July	1	144	3	148	3	147	3	161	2	133	5	140
1864, Jan.	1	156	4	150	3	147	2	185	2	144	4	144
July	1	156	4	153	3	147	2	201	2	144	4	144
1865, Jan.	1	156	3	179	4	158	3	188	2	144	4	144
July	1	156	3	179	4	160	3	188	2	144	4	144
1866, Jan.	1	156	3	174	2	158	2	177	2	144	4	144
July	1	156	3	174	2	158	2	169	2	144	4	144

51 Massachusetts

	LEACH TENDERS		LIMERS		SHAVERS		YARD HANDS	
Sex......................	M.		M.		M.		M.	
Initial wage per day.........	$1.50		$1.50		$2.50		$1.165	
	No.	Rel. Wages	No.	Rel. Wages	No.	Rel. Wages	No.	Rel. Wages
1860, January..........	1	100	1	100	2	100	13	100
July..............	1	100	1	100	2	100	13	100
1861, January..........	1	100	1	111	2	100	13	120
July..............	1	100	1	111	1	100	13	129
1862, January..........	1	122	1	111	1	100	9	130
July..............	1	122	1	111	1	100	9	130
1863, January..........	1	133	1	133	1	100	9	133
July..............	1	133	1	133	1	100	9	133
1864, January..........	2	144	1	144	1	120	8	173
July..............	2	144	1	144	1	120	8	173
1865, January..........	2	144	1	144	1	120	8	182
July..............	2	144	1	144	1	120	8	182
1866, January..........	2	139	1	144	1	120	7	186
July..............	2	133	1	144	1	120	7	186

TABLE 1— *Continued*

WAGE-SERIES FROM TABLE XII OF THE ALDRICH REPORT—LUMBER

52 New Hampshire

	LABORERS		LUMBERMEN	
Sex......................	M.		M.	
Initial wage per day......	$0.385 [1]		$0.505 [1]	
	No.	Rel. Wages	No.	Rel. Wages
1860, January........	4	100	19	100
October	4	100	16	104
1861, January........	3	100	23	99
October	3	100	24	100
1862, January........	2	119	17	130
October	3	119	16	126
1863, January........	2	160	12	182
October	2	160	11	186
1864, January........	2	179	14	189
October	1	179	16	194
1865, January........	2	179	15	202
October	2	179	23	201
1866, January........	2	179	21	202
October	3	179	19	208

53 New York

	SALESMEN		TEAMSTERS		YARD HANDS	
Sex.................	M.		M.		M.	
Init. wage per day..	$1.50		$1.125		$1.04	
	No.	Rel. Wages	No.	Rel. Wages	No.	Rel. Wages
1860, January ...	1	100	2	100	9	100
July.......	1	100	2	100	11	104
1861, January ...	1	100	2	115	14	104
July.......	2	92	3	99	14	106
1862, January ...	2	92	2	94	12	101
July.......	2	100	2	94	11	106
1863, January ...	2	114	2	98	11	105
July.......	4	101	2	98	10	119
1864, January...	3	115	3	117	11	123
July.......	3	120	2	111	11	131
1865, January ...	3	139	2	111	15	135
July.......	3	139	2	111	14	135
1866, January ...	3	139	2	122	13	129
July.......	3	139	2	122	12	130

[1] Board supplied.

TABLE 1— *Continued*

WAGE-SERIES FROM TABLE XII OF THE ALDRICH REPORT—METALS AND METALLIC GOODS

54 Connecticut

	FOREMAN BOILER-M'S		FOREMAN MACHINIST		FOREMAN MOLDERS		BLACK-SMITHS		BLACKSM'S' HELPERS		BOILER-M'S	
Sex........	M.		M.		M.		M.		M.		M.	
Init. wage per day..	$3.00		$3.835		$2.875		$2.25		$1.375		$1.77	
	No.	Rel. Wages	No.	Rel. Wages	No.	Rel. Wages	No.	Rel. Wages	No.	Rel. Wages	No.	Rel. Wages
1860, Jan.	1	100	1	100	1	100	1	100	3	100	4	100
July	1	100	1	100	1	104	1	100	3	100	5	99
1861, Jan.	1	100	1	100	1	104	1	100	1	100	3	101
July	1	100	1	100	1	104	1	100	7	101	4	101
1862, Jan.	1	100	1	100	1	104	2	94	6	96	1	99
July	1	100	1	100	1	104	1	100	1	100	1	99
1863, Jan.	1	100	1	100	1	104	1	100	1	100	2	120
July	1	117	1	100	1	122	2	94	3	103	3	141
1864, Jan.	1	133	1	125	1	122	2	111	4	100	3	127
July	1	183	1	167	1	157	2	133	2	121	5	144
1865, Jan.	1	200	1	167	1	157	1	156	1	133	3	141
July	1	200	1	167	1	157	2	130	1	121	10	138
1866, Jan.	1	133	1	98	1	139	1	156	1	121	3	136
July	1	133	1	98	1	139	3	148	..	...	9	149

54 Connecticut

	BOILER-M'S HELPERS		ENGINEERS		MACHIN'TS		MACHIN'TS' HELPERS		MOLDERS		MOLDERS' HELPERS	
Sex........	M.		M.		M.		M.		M.		M.	
Init. wage per day..	$1.15		$1.50		$1.765		$1.16		$1.625		$1.215	
	No.	Rel. Wages	No.	Rel. Wages	No.	Rel. Wages	No.	Rel. Wages	No.	Rel. Wages	No.	Rel. Wages
1860, Jan.	5	100	1	100	12	100	6	100	1	100	7	100
July	5	102	1	100	15	100	4	104	2	112	10	100
1861, Jan.	3	109	1	100	9	102	7	126	1	123	9	100
July	7	101	1	100	6	106	16	110	2	112	8	102
1862, Jan.	3	109	1	100	18	97	26	109	1	123	7	109
July	3	109	1	100	14	98	13	110	1	123	7	112
1863, Jan.	6	100	1	100	6	96	4	125	2	119	6	108
July	8	106	.	...	12	103	1	97	5	126	5	103
1864, Jan.	9	121	1	117	14	111	7	129	3	126	11	109
July	12	143	1	150	21	129	4	130	4	152	7	134
1865, Jan.	8	145	1	167	16	149	5	134	4	152	9	142
July	6	145	1	167	14	144	2	122	4	152	7	123
1866, Jan.	5	152	1	167	20	145	7	123	10	147	10	120
July	6	150	1	167	23	154	7	137	15	168	8	130

TABLE 1 — *Continued*

WAGE-SERIES FROM TABLE XII OF THE ALDRICH REPORT — METALS AND METALLIC GOODS

	54 Conn.		54 Conn.		54 Conn.		55 Conn.		55 Conn.		55 Conn.	
	PATTERN-MAKERS		BLACK-SMITHS		BLACKSM'S HELPERS		BOILER-MAKERS		BOILER-M'S HELPERS		MACHIN'TS	
Sex........	M.		M.		M.		M.		M.		M.	
Init. wage per day..	$1.75		$1.895		$1.00		$1.555		$1.005		$1.645	
	No.	Rel. Wages	No.	Rel. Wages	No.	Rel. Wages	No.	Rel. Wages	No.	Rel. Wages	No.	Rel. Wages
1859.....	..	...	6	100	10	100	11	100	12	100	46	100
1860, Jan.	2	100	..	...	..	...	..	...	..	...	..	...
July	1	100	..	...	..	...	..	...	..	...	..	...
1861, Jan.	2	86	..	...	..	...	..	...	..	...	..	...
July	3	105	..	...	..	...	..	...	..	...	..	...
1862, Jan.	2	100	8	93	9	109	21	108	6	114	65	108
July	1	100	6	96	6	111	19	106	5	115	62	109
1863, Jan.	4	89	10	96	11	113	15	121	10	117	58	122
July	3	102	8	108	20	125	26	129	39	126	86	126
1864, Jan.	2	111	7	118	15	132	42	138	46	121	69	141
July	2	136	7	132	13	147	47	163	60	141	65	158
1865, Jan.	4	138	6	136	11	148	45	172	59	144	52	171
July	3	159	6	136	13	146	45	170	48	147	51	168
1866, Jan.	3	171	6	132	10	147	26	173	24	150	49	173
July	4	152	7	145	14	151	33	178	32	147	79	176

	55 Conn.		55 Conn.		56 Conn.		56 Conn.		56 Conn.		56 Conn.	
	MACHIN'TS HELPERS		PATTERN-MAKERS		PAT'N-M'RS HELPERS		FOREMAN MACHIN'TS		FOREMAN MOLDERS		BLACK-SMITHS	
Sex........	M.		M.		M.		M.		M.		M.	
Init. wage per day..	$1.135		$1.675		$1.00		$4.79		$2.49		$1.75	
	No.	Rel. Wages	No	Rel. Wages	No.	Rel. Wages	No.	Rel. Wages	No.	Rel. Wages	No.	Rel. Wages
1859.....	21	100	10	100	2	100	..	...	..	...	..	...
1860, Jan.	..	...	..	...	..	...	1	100	1	100	1	100
July	..	...	..	...	..	...	1	100	1	100	1	100
1861, Jan.	..	...	..	...	..	...	1	100	1	100	1	100
July	..	...	..	...	..	...	1	100	1	120	1	100
1862, Jan.	20	99	..	...	..	...	1	100	1	120	1	114
July	22	101	14	110	..	...	1	100	1	120	1	114
1863, Jan.	25	110	14	110	..	...	..	...	1	120	1	114
July	37	111	16	117	2	75	..	...	1	128	1	114
1864, Jan.	31	115	18	129	2	75	..	...	1	128	1	129
July	41	121	17	140	2	100	1	68	1	192	..	...
1865, Jan.	31	127	11	147	2	150	..	...	1	192	..	...
July	32	126	8	150	1	150	1	67	1	192	..	...
1866, Jan.	21	130	10	161	2	150	2	101	1	192	..	...
July	29	136	9	173	2	165	2	100	1	257	..	...

TABLE 1 — *Continued*

WAGE-SERIES FROM TABLE XII OF THE ALDRICH REPORT — METALS AND METALLIC GOODS

56 Conn.

	ENGINEERS		MACHIN'TS		MACHIN'TS' APPRENT'S		MACHIN'TS' HELPERS		MOLDERS		MOLDERS' APPRENT'S	
Sex........	M.		M.		M.		M.		M.		M.	
Init. wage per day..	$1.165		$1.715		$0.615		$1.04		$1.53		$0.55	
	No.	Rel. Wages	No.	Rel. Wages	No.	Rel. Wages	No.	Rel. Wages	No.	Rel. Wages	No.	Rel. Wages
1860, Jan.	1	100	12	100	5	100	4	100	12	100	2	100
July	1	100	12	102	5	102	4	106	9	101	1	109
1861, Jan.	1	100	8	98	7	101	4	105	11	102	2	115
July	1	107	10	99	8	109	6	104	15	101	2	119
1862, Jan.	1	107	19	99	9	107	11	106	12	104	2	119
July	..	...	14	105	9	109	9	109	12	104	2	125
1863, Jan.	1	129	9	106	6	96	9	109	9	105	1	121
July	1	129	5	110	4	102	5	117	12	112	1	182
1864, Jan.	1	143	7	119	4	103	5	127	18	113	1	205
July	1	158	12	119	3	106	6	135	25	126	1	145
1865, Jan.	1	172	12	127	11	129	6	141	14	145	1	155
July	1	172	12	137	12	140	10	150	18	149	..	...
1866, Jan.	1	172	27	143	13	145	8	142	17	141	1	182
July	1	186	23	149	12	154	12	149	23	146	1	182

56 Conn.	56 Conn.	57 Md.	57 Md.	57 Md.	57 Md.

	MOLDERS' HELPERS		PATTERN-MAKERS		BLACK-SMITHS		BLACKSM'S' HELPERS		BOILER-MAKERS		LABORERS	
Sex........	M.		M.		M.		M.		M.		M.	
Init. wage per day..	$1.075		$1.875		$1.565		$1.00		$2.085		$0.92	
	No.	Rel. Wages	No.	Rel. Wages	No.	Rel. Wages	No.	Rel. Wages	No.	Rel. Wages	No.	Rel. Wages
1860, Jan.	14	100	2	100	8	100	8	100	2	100	4	100
July	13	100	2	100	8	103	10	100	4	86	4	100
1861, Jan.	11	97	2	100	3	99	3	100	1	120	4	100
July	13	95	2	100	2	96	6	96	1	72	5	82
1862, Jan.	16	95	2	100	4	95	5	97	2	88	4	82
July	13	95	2	100	4	95	8	92	2	94	4	90
1863, Jan.	11	98	2	100	6	109	6	100	6	87	8	109
July	13	110	2	100	6	117	6	125	8	92	8	125
1864, Jan.	18	110	2	109	7	135	10	135	13	107	10	134
July	21	125	2	120	8	170	13	147	8	106	8	156
1865, Jan.	17	132	2	140	7	176	13	159	15	136	14	162
July	13	130	2	140	6	173	8	165	11	138	16	172
1866, Jan.	14	132	3	142	6	184	8	173	12	139	14	176
July	12	138	3	142	8	178	7	172	7	120	12	174

TABLE 1— *Continued*

WAGE-SERIES FROM TABLE XII OF THE ALDRICH REPORT — METALS AND METALLIC GOODS

	57 Md.	57 Md.	57 Md.	57 Md.	57 Md.	58 Mass.
	MACHIN'TS	MOLDERS	PAINTERS	PATTERN-MAKERS	TEAMSTERS	FOREMAN F'RN'CEM'N
Sex........	M.	M.	M.	M.	M.	M.
Init. wage per day..	$1.645	$1.87	$1.56	$1.62	$0.97	$3.00

	No.	Rel. Wages	No.	Rel. Wages	No.	Rel. Wages	No.	Rel. Wages	No.	Rel. Wages	No.	Rel. Wages
1860, Jan.	16	100	5	100	8	100	17	100	4	100	1	100
July	20	100	5	100	3	99	11	102	3	102	1	100
1861, Jan.	12	103	4	103	1	107	7	106	4	100	1	100
July	8	94	2	94	1	75	4	89	4	87	1	100
1862, Jan.	9	98	1	107	1	75	3	99	2	84	1	100
July	12	102	5	98	1	75	6	98	2	94	1	100
1863, Jan.	22	112	4	103	1	107	11	104	2	116	1	100
July	27	116	6	103	4	109	11	116	3	122	1	100
1864, Jan.	24	125	6	114	1	96	17	119	3	131	1	100
July	20	157	18	120	..	...	15	139	2	155	1	117
1865, Jan.	28	164	9	135	1	144	12	153	4	159	1	117
July	22	167	5	136	1	160	12	161	4	169	1	100
1866, Jan.	47	169	15	141	1	160	10	177	4	169	1	100
July	28	169	10	141	3	170	9	181	4	169	1	100

58 Mass.

	FOREMAN MACHIN'TS	FURNACE-MEN	LABORERS	MACHIN'TS	MACHIN'TS' HELPERS	MOLDERS
Sex........	M.	M.	M.	M.	M.	M.
Init. wage per day..	$2.68	$1.445	$0.89	$1.72	$1.28	$1.56

	No.	Rel. Wages	No.	Rel. Wages	No.	Rel. Wages	No.	Rel. Wages	No.	Rel. Wages	No.	Rel. Wages
1860, Jan.	7	100	2	100	30	100	42	100	9	100	19	100
July	8	101	1	100	38	102	74	98	14	97	25	102
1861, Jan.	6	104	1	100	40	101	81	100	21	100	23	102
July	7	105	3	91	88	98	114	97	33	98	58	100
1862, Jan.	9	106	4	90	60	99	110	100	18	100	38	101
July	11	102	3	94	36	103	81	102	14	98	27	102
1863, Jan.	10	97	1	100	42	104	78	103	10	100	15	105
July	14	101	6	110	27	105	70	103	32	93	24	110
1864, Jan.	6	117	4	97	30	110	112	120	53	99	21	120
July	7	117	18	94	9	122	106	125	42	109	20	120
1865, Jan.	12	127	6	92	14	143	78	136	30	112	24	141
July	12	128	2	99	22	153	77	137	20	117	22	147
1866, Jan.	10	127	2	102	28	153	86	141	26	121	25	153
July	5	147	2	121	40	152	98	146	24	121	26	155

TABLE 1— *Continued*

WAGE-SERIES FROM TABLE XII OF THE ALDRICH REPORT — METALS AND METALLIC GOODS

	58 Mass.	58 Mass.	59 Mass.	59 Mass.	59 Mass.	60 Mass.
	TEAMSTERS	TEAMSTERS WITH TEAM	LABORERS	M'CHINISTS	PATTERN-MAKERS	LABORERS
Sex........	M.	M.	M.	M.	M.	M.
Init. wage per day..	$0.94	$2.50	$0.90	$1.50	$1.75	$1.25
	No. Rel. Wages	No. Rel. Wages	No. Rel. Wages	No. Rel. Wages	No. Rel. Wages	No. Rel. Wages
1860, Jan.	5 100	1 100	2 100	17 100	1 100	9 100
July	8 109	1 100	2 100	17 100	1 100	13 100
1861, Jan.	5 106	1 100	2 100	17 100	1 100	12 120
July	10 104	.. ...	2 100	17 100	1 100	10 120
1862, Jan.	8 108	1 100	2 100	17 100	1 100	16 120
July	10 109	1 100	2 100	17 100	1 100	16 120
1863, Jan.	9 112	1 100	3 100	22 100	1 100	18 140
July	12 121	1 100	3 100	22 113	1 100	14 140
1864, Jan.	7 124	1 100	3 100	25 120	1 114	14 140
July	8 139	1 100	3 144	25 153	1 137	12 140
1865, Jan.	8 146	1 100	3 144	25 150	1 137	12 128
July	10 158	1 100	3 144	25 150	1 137	10 140
1866, Jan.	5 160	1 100	3 167	26 157	1 143	14 160
July	9 156	1 100	3 167	26 167	1 143	15 160

	60 Mass.	60 Mass.	60 Mass.	61 Mass.	61 Mass.	61 Mass.
	M'CHINISTS	PATTERN-MAKERS	WATCHMEN	BLACK-SMITHS	LABORERS	M'CHINISTS
Sex........	M.	M.	M.	M.	M.	M.
Init. wage per day..	$1.665	$2.00	$1.50	$2.00	$1.125	$1.635
	No. Rel. Wages	No. Rel. Wages	No. Rel. Wages	No. Rel. Wages	No. Rel. Wages	No. Rel. Wages
1860, Jan.	75 100	3 100	1 100	1 100	4 100	11 100
July	73 100	3 100	1 100	1 88	4 100	11 100
1861, Jan.	72 108	3 105	1 120	1 88	2 111	12 104
July	72 120	3 105	1 120	1 88	2 111	12 107
1862, Jan.	65 132	3 113	1 120	1 88	1 111	12 108
July	75 132	3 113	1 120	1 88	1 118	11 109
1863, Jan.	65 180	3 125	1 120	1 100	2 118	11 108
July	60 180	3 150	1 120	1 100	2 133	11 112
1864, Jan.	54 165	3 150	1 120	1 100	3 133	11 117
July	52 165	3 150	1 140	1 119	3 133	11 133
1865, Jan.	62 180	3 175	1 140	1 119	4 133	16 130
July	59 180	3 175	1 160	1 119	4 133	16 137
1866, Jan.	91 180	4 175	1 160	1 119	2 122	17 143
July	82 180	4 175	1 160	1 119	2 122	17 145

TABLE 1 — *Continued*

WAGE-SERIES FROM TABLE XII OF THE ALDRICH REPORT — METALS AND METALLIC GOODS

	61 Mass.		62 N. H.		62 N. H.		62 N. H.		62 N. H.		62 N. H.	
	WOOD-WORKERS		BLACK-SMITHS		ENGINEERS		LABORERS		M'CHINISTS		M'CH'N'STS' APPRENT'S	
Sex........	M.		M.		M.		M.		M.		M.	
Init. wage per day ..	$1.665		$1.50		$1.17		$1.14		$1.48		$0.485	
	No.	Rel. Wages	No.	Rel. Wages	No.	Rel. Wages	No.	Rel. Wages	No.	Rel. Wages	No.	Rel. Wages
1860, Jan.	3	100	1	100	1	100	3	100	19	100	5	100
July	3	100	1	100	1	100	5	104	23	103	5	106
1861, Jan.	3	110	1	95	1	100	1	88	10	102	8	99
July	3	110	1	95	..	...	1	88	6	104	5	124
1862, Jan.	4	113	1	105	1	100	1	88	13	105	5	134
July	4	116	1	100	1	100	3	97	16	104	3	92
1863, Jan.	3	115	2	106	1	100	3	100	12	110	5	113
July	3	115	2	111	1	107	4	102	12	116	3	108
1864, Jan.	3	125	2	114	1	107	2	117	12	117	5	114
July	3	130	1	150	1	128	1	110	11	125	5	138
1865, Jan.	3	135	2	167	1	128	1	81	11	134	3	166
July	3	150	1	150	1	128	1	81	12	122	4	170
1866, Jan.	3	155	2	167	1	150	5	121	10	144	10	156
July	3	155	3	159	1	150	4	130	12	136	9	160

	62 N. H.		62 N. H.		65 N. J.		65 N. J.		66 N. Y.		66 N. Y.	
	PATTERN-MAKERS		WOOD-WORKERS		FOREMEN M'CHINISTS		M'CHINISTS		CORE-MAKERS		CUPOLA MEN	
Sex........	M.		M.		M.		M.		M.		M.	
Init. wage per day..	$1.67		$1.375		$3.00		$2.00		$1.25		$1.055	
	No.	Rel. Wages	No.	Rel. Wages	No.	Rel. Wages	No.	Rel. Wages	No.	Rel. Wages	No.	Rel. Wages
1859, July	..	...	..	...	1	100	3	100	..	...	..	...
1860, Jan.	1	100	2	100	..	...	..	...	1	100	3	100
July	1	100	1	109	..	...	..	...	1	100	3	100
1861, Jan.	1	95	..	...	..	...	..	...	1	100	3	100
July	1	95	..	...	..	...	..	...	1	100	2	103
1862, Jan.	..	...	1	91	..	...	..	...	1	100	2	103
July	1	90	1	91	..	...	..	...	1	100	2	103
1863, Jan.	..	...	1	121	1	100	9	86	1	100	2	110
July	1	90	1	133	1	100	7	91	1	100	2	110
1864, Jan.	1	120	1	109	1	100	12	94	1	100	2	114
July	1	120	1	133	1	111	17	110	1	120	3	127
1865, Jan.	..	...	1	164	1	139	15	110	1	120	2	136
July	1	120	..	...	1	139	17	113	1	120	2	136
1866, Jan.	1	150	1	158	1	139	17	120	1	120	3	134
July	1	180	..	...	1	139	19	121	1	120	3	134

TABLE 1—*Continued*

WAGE-SERIES FROM TABLE XII OF THE ALDRICH REPORT — METALS AND METALLIC GOODS

	66 N. Y.		66 N. Y.		66 N. Y.		66 N. Y.		66 N. Y.		67 N. Y.	
	ENGINEERS		LABORERS		M'CHINISTS		TEAMSTERS		WATCHMEN		BLACK-SMITHS	
Sex........	M.		M.		M.		M.		M.		M.	
Init. wage per day..	$1.00		$0.835		$1.125		$1.00		$0.855		$1.75	
	No.	Rel. Wages	No.	Rel. Wages	No.	Rel. Wages	No.	Rel. Wages	No.	Rel. Wages	No.	Rel. Wages
1860, Jan.	1	100	6	100	1	100	1	100	1	100	1	100
July	1	100	6	100	1	100	1	100	1	100	1	100
1861, Jan.	1	100	5	100	1	100	1	100	1	100	1	100
July	1	100	..	...	1	100	1	100	1	100	1	100
1862, Jan.	1	100	7	97	1	100	1	100	1	100	1	100
July	1	100	13	98	1	100	1	100	1	100	1	100
1863, Jan.	1	100	11	101	2	137	1	100	1	100	1	105
July	1	100	11	122	1	119	1	100	1	117	1	105
1864, Jan.	1	117	12	125	1	133	1	117	1	100	1	114
July	1	150	13	160	1	163	1	142	1	117	1	157
1865, Jan.	1	150	10	166	1	163	1	142	1	117	1	157
July	1	150	8	166	1	163	1	142	1	117	1	150
1866, Jan.	1	150	6	167	1	163	1	142	1	117	..	...
July	1	150	7	167	1	163	1	142	1	117	1	157

67 New York

	BL'KS'THS' HELPERS		LABORERS		MACHIN'TS		MACHIN'TS' HELPERS		MOLDERS		MOLDERS' APPREN.	
Sex........	M.		M.		M.		M.		M.		M.	
Init. wage per day...	$0.875		$0.89		$1.59		$1.095		$1.66		$0.675	
	No.	Rel. Wages	No.	Rel. Wages	No.	Rel. Wages	No.	Rel. Wages	No.	Rel. Wages	No.	Rel. Wages
1860, Jan.	1	100	8	100	7	100	7	100	7	100	4	100
July	1	107	10	99	8	101	7	100	7	100	3	105
1861, Jan.	1	107	9	99	8	102	7	100	6	102	3	103
July	1	100	7	97	6	100	5	91	6	100	1	93
1862, Jan.	1	100	7	97	6	96	4	95	4	100	1	111
July	1	100	8	97	9	100	4	95	7	97	1	111
1863, Jan.	1	86	7	103	8	101	2	94	6	103	..	...
July	1	143	10	133	12	106	2	105	6	111	..	...
1864, Jan.	1	143	9	134	13	115	2	126	7	119	..	...
July	1	186	12	177	13	151	5	146	8	138	1	111
1865, Jan.	1	186	12	174	12	153	5	146	9	141	2	98
July	1	186	11	169	12	153	4	148	8	145	1	86
1866, Jan.	2	179	12	170	14	153	5	139	9	142	1	111
July	1	186	15	166	13	152	5	144	10	143	2	106

TABLE 1—*Continued*

WAGE-SERIES FROM TABLE XII OF THE ALDRICH REPORT — METALS AND METALLIC GOODS

	67 N. Y MOLDERS' HELPERS		67 N. Y. PATTERN-MAKERS		67 N. Y. PATTERN-MAKERS' APPREN.		67 N. Y. WATCHMEN		68 N. Y. FOREMEN BL'KSM'S		68 N. Y. FOREMEN BOILERM'S	
Sex	M.		M.		M.		M.		M.		M.	
Init. wage per day...	$1.125		$1.50		$0.33		$0.81		$2.00		$2.00	
	No.	Rel. Wages	No.	Rel. Wages	No.	Rel. Wages	No.	Rel. Wages	No.	Rel. Wages	No.	Rel Wages
1860, Jan.	3	100	3	100	..	...	1	100	..	...	..	...
July	4	97	3	100	..	...	1	100	..	...	..	...
1861, Jan.	4	97	3	100	..	...	1	103	..	...	..	...
July	3	101	3	94	1	100	..	...	1	100	1	100
1862, Jan.	4	98	3	94	1	100	..	...	1	100	1	100
July	3	96	3	94	1	152	1	102	1	100	1	100
1863, Jan.	4	95	3	94	1	152	1	115	1	100	1	125
July	4	108	3	103	..	...	1	115	1	125	1	125
1864, Jan.	3	108	3	106	..	...	1	115	1	175	1	125
July	3	126	3	136	1	152	1	132	1	175	1	163
1865, Jan.	3	126	3	136	1	189	1	123	1	225	1	163
July	3	130	3	136	1	189	1	123	1	225	1	163
1866, Jan.	3	144	4	135	1	227	1	132	..	...	1	167
July	3	144	4	135	1	227	1	132	1	150	1	167

68 New York

	BLACK-SMITHS		BOILER-MAKERS		BOILERM'S' APPREN.		BOILERM'S' HELPERS		MACHIN'TS		MACHIN'TS' APPREN.	
Sex	M.		M.		M.		M.		M.		M.	
Init. wage per day...	$1.25		$1.21		$0.375		$0.84		$1.375		$0.545	
	No.	Rel. Wages	No.	Rel. Wages	No.	Rel. Wages	No.	Rel. Wages	No.	Rel. Wages	No.	Rel. Wages
1860, Jan.	1	100	3	100	1	100	12	100	8	100	4	100
July	1	110	2	98	2	116	8	90	4	100	2	115
1861, Jan.	..	...	..	...	..	...	..	...	..	...	..	...
July	..	...	5	132	2	133	4	119	3	119	5	89
1862, Jan.	1	100	7	127	3	133	9	109	9	107	6	89
July	..	...	6	131	3	111	5	110	12	115	7	108
1863, Jan.	3	103	5	116	1	100	3	114	13	117	8	102
July	5	114	14	137	2	105	5	89	12	128	4	69
1864, Jan.	5	120	17	152	1	112	10	98	14	131	7	90
July	5	140	30	162	4	123	9	98	11	162	10	100
1865, Jan.	5	164	27	173	4	151	5	107	12	158	11	116
July	5	164	21	174	3	156	3	124	9	144	11	118
1866, Jan.	6	155	18	174	..	...	4	108	11	156	10	122
July	5	158	5	149	..	...	1	119	13	169	7	122

TABLE 1—*Continued*

WAGE-SERIES FROM TABLE XII OF THE ALDRICH REPORT — METALS AND METALLIC GOODS

	68 N. Y.		68 N. Y.		68 N. Y.		68 N. Y.		69 N. Y.		69 N. Y.	
	MOLDERS		MOLDERS' APPRENT'S		MOLDERS' HELPERS		PATTERN-MAKERS		M'CHINISTS		M'CH'N'STS' APPRENT'S	
Sex........	M.		M.		M.		M.		M.		M.	
Init. wage per day..	$1.315		$0.50		$0.72		$1.29		$1.49		$0.855	
	No.	Rel. Wages	No.	Rel. Wages	No.	Rel. Wages	No.	Rel. Wages	No.	Rel. Wages	No.	Rel. Wages
1860, Jan.	8	100	2	100	12	100	3	100	25	100	7	100
July	11	116	1	125	8	128	2	107	17	96	9	74
1861, Jan.	..	...	..	...	1	122	1	126	18	99	13	86
July	11	117	2	84	8	130	1	136	20	102	6	91
1862, Jan.	11	117	2	84	10	120	2	116	35	103	7	99
July	16	115	2	117	14	131	3	116	22	115	4	95
1863, Jan.	13	117	1	117	16	135	7	116	15	115	5	89
July	23	122	4	113	10	162	8	133	2	109	..	...
1864, Jan.	23	123	6	106	12	162	8	143	1	235	..	...
July	39	137	6	129	..	...	9	158	63	154	12	83
1865, Jan.	41	149	4	148	1	139	5	169	65	157	12	85
July	29	147	2	157	2	191	4	179	61	159	9	77
1866, Jan.	35	149	1	84	2	153	5	180	43	168	3	94
July	26	152	3	97	2	174	5	186	54	172	8	81

	69 N. Y.		70 N. Y.		71 N. Y.		71 N. Y.		71 N. Y.		71 N. Y.	
	M'CH'N'STS' HELPERS		M'CHINISTS		FOREMEN BL'KS'THS		BLACK-SMITHS		BL'KS'THS' HELPERS		CARP'NT'RS	
Sex........	M.		M.		M.		M.		M.		M.	
Init. wage per day..	$1.25		$1.90		$3.00		$2.075		$1.15		$1.915	
	No.	Rel. Wages	No.	Rel. Wages	No.	Rel. Wages	No.	Rel. Wages	No.	Rel. Wages	No.	Rel. Wages
1860, Jan.	3	100	7	100	1	100	12	100	11	100	9	100
July	4	92	8	98	1	100	12	100	11	100	9	100
1861, Jan.	5	98	4	99	1	100	10	100	13	100	8	101
July	8	95	2	103	1	100	9	101	11	100	8	101
1862, Jan.	7	102	6	97	1	100	9	103	5	100	8	103
July	5	92	5	102	1	100	9	104	13	104	8	103
1863, Jan.	2	80	4	104	1	111	9	113	5	120	8	108
July	..	...	5	107	1	111	10	117	12	124	9	121
1864, Jan.	..	...	4	125	1	133	11	132	15	141	8	130
July	7	98	4	144	1	167	11	160	17	174	6	135
1865, Jan.	7	98	5	155	1	167	17	155	18	172	6	136
July	8	104	5	159	1	167	13	164	13	177	6	136
1866, Jan.	1	110	5	162	1	167	14	164	15	176	6	140
July	3	110	5	169	1	167	13	167	15	176	6	145

TABLE 1 — *Continued*

WAGE-SERIES FROM TABLE XII OF THE ALDRICH REPORT — METALS AND METALLIC
GOODS

71 N. Y. 71 N. Y. 71 N. Y. 71 N. Y. 72 N. Y. 72 N. Y.

	DRAUGHTS-MEN		LABORERS		MOLDERS		PATTERN-MAKERS		BLACK-SMITHS		BL'KS'THS' HELPERS	
Sex........	M.		M.		M.		M.		M.		M.	
Init. wage per day..	$2.165		$1.00		$1.885		$1.96		$1.515		$0.875	
	No.	Rel. Wages	No.	Rel. Wages	No.	Rel. Wages	No.	Rel. Wages	No.	Rel. Wages	No.	Rel. Wages
1860, Jan.	3	100	12	100	14	100	3	100	9	100	7	100
July	3	100	12	100	14	100	3	100	8	97	10	105
1861, Jan.	4	98	10	100	13	102	4	97	5	92	6	100
July	4	98	10	100	13	102	4	97	4	93	5	103
1862, Jan.	3	100	10	102	11	104	5	94	5	96	9	103
July	3	100	10	103	12	102	5	94	4	109	5	111
1863, Jan.	4	106	11	111	11	107	5	99	5	102	6	114
July	5	115	11	121	12	115	5	111	4	122	7	118
1864, Jan.	7	127	13	130	15	132	7	125	3	121	10	129
July	7	137	19	152	16	158	8	146	5	144	7	165
1865, Jan.	7	155	10	150	10	164	6	145	3	149	8	171
July	8	154	15	152	15	160	7	144	5	152	12	170
1866, Jan.	6	171	19	152	17	170	5	147	4	165	11	177
July	9	183	18	152	15	171	5	148	3	165	9	176

72 New York

	CARP'NT'RS		CARPENT'S HELPERS		COAL WHEELERS		M'CHINISTS		MASONS		MASONS' HELPERS	
Sex........	M.		M.		M.		M.		M.		M.	
Init. wage per day..	$1.625		$0.815		$0.895		$1.375		$2.50		$0.965	
	No.	Rel. Wages	No.	Rel. Wages	No.	Rel. Wages	No.	Rel. Wages	No.	Rel. Wages	No.	Rel. Wages
1860, Jan.	..	...	..	...	11	100	3	100	1	100	5	100
July	2	100	1	100	6	102	6	101	1	100	4	104
1861, Jan.	1	92	..	...	9	103	9	102	1	100	5	100
July	1	92	..	...	5	109	7	108	1	100	5	100
1862, Jan.	..	...	..	...	10	104	6	103	2	87	4	89
July	..	...	3	148	9	131	4	104	6	83	7	107
1863, Jan.	..	...	6	161	6	126	..	...	8	82	7	109
July	1	123	9	171	10	148	..	...	3	87	5	114
1864, Jan.	1	135	6	202	16	164	..	...	3	92	7	121
July	5	126	2	107	13	170	5	160	3	104	6	138
1865, Jan.	5	135	3	210	15	198	8	181	3	104	10	148
July	4	134	4	215	..	...	4	166	4	96	5	149
1866, Jan.	7	134	4	211	15	197	6	174	4	109	4	149
July	7	130	3	204	14	197	8	176	3	109	7	149

TABLE 1—*Continued*

WAGE-SERIES FROM TABLE XII OF THE ALDRICH REPORT—METALS AND METALLIC GOODS

73 Pennsylvania

	BLACK-SMITHS		BL'KS'THS' HELPERS		CORE-MAKERS		LABORERS		M'CHINISTS		MOLDERS	
Sex	M.		M.		M.		M.		M.		M.	
Init. wage per day..	$1.89		$1.00		$1.335		$1.00		$1.705		$1.635	
	No.	Rel. Wages	No.	Rel. Wages	No.	Rel. Wages	No.	Rel. Wages	No.	Rel. Wages	No.	Rel. Wages
1860, Jan.	3	100	2	100	1	100	13	100	12	100	5	100
July	3	103	4	100	2	100	16	100	9	102	8	94
1861, Jan.	4	100	2	100	2	100	16	100	9	102	8	97
July	3	103	3	100	3	100	17	100	8	103	9	98
1862, Jan.	2	108	3	100	4	100	20	100	11	103	9	96
July	3	106	2	113	3	100	22	100	13	103	8	94
1863, Jan.	3	112	2	113	3	100	18	106	13	103	8	97
July	2	126	2	121	4	112	21	114	13	112	7	101
1864, Jan.	2	139	3	125	4	125	20	123	13	116	5	112
July	5	139	3	150	4	137	22	148	13	144	4	122
1865, Jan.	3	159	3	167	3	150	20	159	14	162	3	132
July	3	153	2	167	4	150	24	159	8	159	4	132
1866, Jan.	4	152	3	167	5	150	18	159	8	173	4	153
July	5	148	4	167	5	150	23	159	16	165	8	153
	73 Pa.		74 Pa.		74 Pa.		74 Pa.		74 Pa.		74 Pa.	

	PATTERN-MAKERS		BLACK-SMITHS		BL'KS'THS' HELPERS		CORE-MAKERS		DRAUGHTS-MEN		ENGINEERS	
Sex........	M.		M.		M.		M.		M.		M.	
Init. wage per day..	$1.585		$2.20		$1.40		$1.20		$2.50		$2.40	
	No.	Rel. Wages	No.	Rel. Wages	No.	Rel. Wages	No.	Rel. Wages	No.	Rel. Wages	No.	Rel. Wages
1860, Jan.	4	100	2	100	2	100	8	100	..	....	1	100
July	2	110	2	100	3	107	8	100	2	100	1	100
1861, Jan.	3	112	2	100	3	107	10	100	2	100	1	100
July	3	112	2	91	3	107	10	100	2	100	1	100
1862, Jan.	3	112	2	91	3	107	9	117	2	100	1	100
July	3	112	2	100	3	107	8	117	2	100	1	100
1863, Jan.	3	119	2	100	3	114	10	117	2	100	1	100
July	3	126	2	114	3	114	12	117	2	100	1	110
1864, Jan.	3	152	2	114	3	114	7	117	2	108	1	110
July	2	174	2	114	3	121	7	125	2	108	1	125
1865, Jan.	3	175	2	114	3	121	7	142	2	108	1	125
July	3	175	2	114	3	121	7	142	2	108	1	125
1866, Jan.	5	173	3	114	4	121	10	167	2	108	1	125
July	5	173	3	114	4	121	8	167	2	108	1	125

TABLE 1 — *Continued*

WAGE-SERIES FROM TABLE XII OF THE ALDRICH REPORT — METALS AND METALLIC GOODS

74 Pennsylvania

	LABORERS		M'CHINISTS		MILL-WRIGHTS		MOLDERS		PATTERN-MAKERS		P'T'N-M'K'S HELPERS	
Sex	M.		M.		M.		M.		M.		M.	
Init. wage per day..	$1.00		$1.65		$2.00		$1.70		$1.535		$1.30	
	No.	Rel. Wages	No.	Rel. Wages	No.	Rel. Wages	No.	Rel. Wages	No.	Rel. Wages	No.	Rel. Wages
1860, Jan.	15	100	16	100	2	100	12	100	3	100	2	100
July	15	110	17	101	2	100	12	100	4	101	2	100
1861, Jan.	15	110	15	101	2	100	10	118	4	101	2	100
July	12	110	14	100	2	100	8	118	4	101	2	100
1862, Jan.	14	110	14	112	2	100	10	118	4	107	2	100
July	13	120	16	112	2	100	10	129	4	114	2	100
1863, Jan.	14	140	16	112	2	100	10	129	4	121	2	115
July	12	140	15	112	2	100	6	147	4	127	2	115
1864, Jan.	13	140	16	124	2	115	6	147	4	130	2	115
July	15	140	16	124	2	125	10	176	5	143	2	115
1865, Jan.	17	150	16	138	2	150	8	176	5	159	2	154
July	18	150	16	138	2	150	8	176	5	159	2	154
1866, Jan.	18	150	15	158	2	185	10	176	4	176	3	123
July	18	150	14	157	2	185	10	176	4	176	3	123

PAPER

75 Massachusetts

	ENGINEERS		FINISHERS		LABORERS		MACHINE HANDS	
Sex	M.		M.		M.		M.	
Initial wage per day	$1.165		$1.25		$1.00		$1.335	
	No.	Rel. Wages	No.	Rel. Wages	No.	Rel. Wages	No.	Rel. Wages
1860, January	2	100	1	100	22	100	2	100
July	2	100	1	100	20	100	2	100
1861, January	2	100	1	100	17	100	2	100
July	2	100	1	100	16	100	2	100
1862, January	2	100	1	87	15	80	2	100
July	2	100	1	87	15	80	2	112
1863, January	2	115	1	107	12	100	2	112
July	2	115	1	107	12	100	2	112
1864, January	2	115	1	107	12	100	2	125
July	2	129	1	140	12	134	2	150
1865, January	2	143	1	160	12	150	2	169
July	2	143	1	160	12	167	2	169
1866, January	2	143	1	200	10	150	2	187
July	2	143	1	200	9	150	2	187

TABLE 1 — *Continued*

WAGE-SERIES FROM TABLE XII OF THE ALDRICH REPORT — PAPER

75 Massachusetts

	M'H'NE H'S HELPERS		PAPER CUTTERS		RAG SORTERS	
Sex....................................	M.		F.		F.	
Initial wage per day	$1.00		$0.50		$0.50	
	No.	Rel. Wages	No.	Rel. Wages	No.	Rel. Wages
1860, January........................	2	100	6	100	6	100
July	2	100	6	100	8	100
1861, January........................	2	100	6	100	9	100
July	2	100	6	100	10	100
1862, January........................	2	100	6	80	10	80
July	2	117	6	80	10	80
1863, January........................	2	117	6	100	12	100
July	2	117	6	100	12	100
1864, January........................	2	117	6	100	9	100
July	2	150	6	117	10	117
1865, January........................	2	150	6	117	10	117
July	2	150	6	130	10	117
1866, January........................	2	150	4	130	14	117
July	2	150	4	150	14	130

RAILWAYS

76 Massachusetts

	BAGGAGE-MEN		BRAKEMEN PASS'G'R		BRAKEMEN FREIGHT		CONDUCT'S PASS'G'R		CONDUCT'S FREIGHT		ENGINEERS LOCOMO'VE	
Sex........	M.		M.		M.		M.		M.		M.	
Init. wage per day...	$1.915		$1.25		$1.165		$3.195		$1.61		$2.30	
	No.	Rel. Wages	No.	Rel. Wages	No.	Rel. Wages	No.	Rel. Wages	No.	Rel. Wages	No.	Rel. Wages
1860, Jan.	6	100	10	100	22	100	16	100	20	100	56	100
July	6	100	12	100	6	100	12	100	19	102	41	100
1861, Jan.	6	100	18	100	14	100	12	100	23	109	33	100
July	6	100	18	100	10	100	12	100	22	108	46	100
1862, Jan.	8	100	18	100	12	100	10	100	23	111	46	100
July	10	100	18	100	12	100	12	100	16	110	40	100
1863, Jan.	4	100	12	100	13	100	12	100	17	111	43	105
July	10	100	9	100	13	120	22	100	17	113	47	105
1864, Jan.	6	100	17	100	16	120	22	100	30	110	43	106
July	10	100	6	100	9	120	16	100	22	110	46	106
1865, Jan.	10	110	12	100	10	120	10	120	26	163	50	125
July	10	110	18	153	10	120	13	120	17	165	56	130
1866, Jan.	10	110	32	140	10	146	12	120	21	172	46	130
July	3	110	18	153	16	146	12	120	23	159	48	131

TABLE 1—*Continued*

WAGE-SERIES FROM TABLE XII OF THE ALDRICH REPORT — RAILWAYS

76 Massachusetts

	FIREMEN LOCOMOTIVE		FOREMEN MASONS		CARPENTERS		MASONS		PAINTERS	
Sex	M.		M.		M.		M.		M.	
Initial wage per day...	$1.145		$2.50		$1.30		$2.00		$1.425	
	No.	Rel. Wages	No.	Rel. Wages	No.	Rel. Wages	No.	Rel. Wages	No.	Rel. Wages
1860, Jan...	42	100	1	100	79	100	..	...	11	100
July..	24	114	1	100	..	...	4	100	1	117
1861, Jan...	38	114	1	100	..	...	..	...	1	140
July..	22	114	1	100	49	111	7	91	..	...
1862, Jan...	22	114	1	100	65	107	..	...	..	...
July..	50	114	1	100	24	87	..	...	4	96
1863, Jan...	38	117	1	100	29	98	..	...	..	...
July..	56	117	1	100	68	108	8	113	8	105
1864, Jan...	36	117	1	100	49	131	3	125	..	...
July..	36	117	1	100	27	118	6	125	9	140
1865, Jan...	36	153	1	140	58	170	3	125	8	145
July..	42	153	1	140	61	165	5	140	6	142
1866, Jan...	40	153	1	160	50	135	16	105	6	160
July..	42	153	1	100	54	156	19	147	11	177

SIDEWALKS

77 New York

	SIDEWALK LAYERS		SIDEWALK LAYERS' HELPERS		STONE CUTTERS		TEAMSTERS	
Sex	M.		M.		M.		M.	
Initial wage per day	$2.00		$1.00		$2.00		$2.00	
	No.	Rel. Wages	No.	Rel. Wages	No.	Rel. Wages	No.	Rel. Wages
1860, January	12	100	6	100	12	100	1	100
July	15	100	7	100	15	100	1	100
1861, January	10	100	5	100	10	100	1	100
July	12	100	6	100	12	100	1	100
1862, January	8	100	4	100	8	100	1	100
July	9	100	4	100	8	100	1	100
1863, January	6	113	4	125	6	113	1	100
July	6	113	4	125	6	113	1	100
1864, January	8	138	3	175	8	138	1	100
July	8	138	4	175	8	138	1	100
1865, January	7	175	3	250	7	175	1	100
July	8	175	4	250	7	175	1	100
1866, January	8	175	3	275	8	175	1	100
July	8	188	4	275	8	188	1	100

TABLE 1 — *Continued*

WAGE-SERIES FROM TABLE XII OF THE ALDRICH REPORT — SPICE

78 Pennsylvania

	GRINDERS		LABORERS		TEAMSTERS		PACKERS	
Sex	M.		M.		M.		F.	
Initial wage per day	$1.00		$1.05		$1.50		$0.12[1]	
	No.	Rel. Wages	No.	Rel. Wages	No.	Rel. Wages	No.	Rel. Wages
1860, January...........	..	...	5	100	1	100	2	100
July	..	...	5	100	1	100	2	100
1861, January...........	1	100	9	101	..	...	5	100
July	1	100	2	103	..	...	5	100
1862, January...........	2	92	8	103	..	...	7	100
July	1	84	10	106	..	...	15	100
1863, January...........	1	84	9	112	..	...	15	100
July	1	84	5	116	..	...	11	100
1864, January...........	3	111	8	115	1	100	12	100
July	2	142	5	149	1	122	12	100
1865, January...........	1	134	5	152	1	122	11	100
July	1	134	4	167	1	122	9	100
1866, January...........	..	...	4	167	2	117	12	100
July	..	...	4	167	2	117	12	100

STONE

	79 Conn.		79 Conn.		80 Conn.		80 Conn.		81 Md.		81 Md.	
	FOREMEN QUARRYM'N		QUAR'YM'N[2]		FOREMEN[3] QUARRYM'N		QUAR'YM'N[4]		CARPENT'S		CARVERS	
Sex........	M.		M.		M.		M.		M.		M.	
Init. wage per day.	$1.435		$0.80		$1.465		$0.82		$1.375		$2.50	
	No.	Rel. Wages	No.	Rel. Wages	No.	Rel. Wages	No.	Rel. Wages	No.	Rel. Wages	No.	Rel. Wages
1860, Jan.	4	100	89	100	3	100	86	100	1	100	2	100
July	2	98	267	100	4	100	117	100	1	100	2	100
1861, Jan.	2	113	50	113	4	126	109	149	1	100	1	100
July	6	126	138	97	1	84	83	80	..	...	..	...
1862, Jan.	..	...	37	100	..	...	..	...	..	...	..	...
July	3	120	140	91	2	79	80	87	..	...	..	...
1863, Jan.	3	137	26	100	..	...	5	110	1	121	..	...
July	6	137	268	114	3	105	126	111	1	121	1	100
1864, Jan.	2	98	162	136	3	126	130	165	1	121	2	95
July	5	140	213	135	7	114	162	130	2	115	2	125
1865, Jan.	5	142	143	159	6	133	81	152	1	121	2	130
July	8	169	208	155	5	132	162	144	1	121	2	130
1866, Jan.	5	167	247	177	6	145	148	174	1	121	2	145
July	9	178	300	158	6	138	195	156	1	121	2	140

[1] Per gross.

[2] Because of difference between the summer and winter wages of quarrymen, the relative wages for January of each year are computed as percentages of the wage in January, 1860 ($0.80), and those for July as percentages of the wage in July, 1860 ($1.18).

[3] See note concerning quarrymen, Stone 79; wages Jan., 1860, $1.465; July, 1860, $1.90.

[4] See note concerning quarrymen, Stone 79; wages Jan., 1860, $0.82; July, 1860, $1.22.

APPENDIX C   511

TABLE 1 — *Continued*

WAGE-SERIES FROM TABLE XII OF THE ALDRICH REPORT — STONE

81 Maryland

	ENGINEERS		LABORERS		MARBLE CUTTERS		MARBLE POLISHERS		MARBLE RUBBERS		TEAMSTERS	
Sex........	M.		M.		M.		M.		M.		M.	
Init. wage per day	$1.50		$1.125		$2.00		$1.15		$1.085		$1.125	
	No.	Rel. Wages	No.	Rel. Wages	No.	Rel. Wages	No.	Rel. Wages	No.	Rel. Wages	No.	Rel. Wages
1860, Jan.	1	100	2	100	7	100	5	100	6	100	2	100
July	1	100	2	100	7	113	5	100	4	101	2	100
1861, Jan.	..	...	2	100	6	104	4	98	4	101	..	...
July	..	...	..	...	4	100	1	87	3	100	..	...
1862, Jan.	..	...	..	...	..	...	..	...	2	104	1	100
July	..	...	..	...	..	...	..	...	1	92	1	89
1863, Jan.	1	89	2	89	..	...	2	87	5	92	1	89
July	1	111	3	111	7	113	3	109	5	115	1	100
1864, Jan.	1	111	3	111	6	113	3	120	5	118	1	111
July	1	145	2	141	8	145	3	140	10	151	1	133
1865, Jan.	1	145	3	148	9	163	4	149	9	154	1	148
July	1	145	3	148	9	163	4	149	11	153	1	148
1866, Jan.	1	145	3	158	8	163	3	155	9	149	2	163
July	1	145	3	158	8	163	3	155	9	150	2	163

81 Md.   82 N. Y.   82 N. Y.   82 N. Y.   83 N. Y.   84 Pa.

	WATCHM'N		MARBLE CUTTERS		MARBLE POLISHERS		MARBLE RUBBERS		GRANITE CUTTERS		LABORERS	
Sex........	M.		M.		M.		M.		M.		M.	
Init. wage per day	$1.00		$2.00		$1.315		$1.155		$2.25		$1.25	
	No.	Rel. Wages	No.	Rel. Wages	No.	Rel. Wages	No.	Rel. Wages	No.	Rel. Wages	No.	Rel. Wages
1860, Jan.	1	100	5	100	2	100	8	100	1	100	1	100
July	1	100	8	102	2	100	14	99	1	100	1	100
1861, Jan.	1	100	6	87	3	92	12	95	2	83	1	100
July	1	72	8	78	3	79	12	88	1	89	1	100
1862, Jan.	..	...	5	74	2	81	6	88	2	89	1	100
July	..	...	6	86	3	83	9	88	2	83	1	100
1863, Jan.	1	100	4	88	3	89	10	98	2	89	1	100
July	1	100	9	98	5	106	10	133	2	94	1	120
1864, Jan.	1	100	9	108	4	112	7	119	4	97	1	120
July	1	125	9	131	5	156	11	160	6	133	1	120
1865, Jan.	1	125	9	136	7	156	7	166	6	133	1	120
July	1	125	11	149	15	166	6	181	8	133	1	120
1866, Jan.	1	125	13	146	12	157	5	195	7	133	1	120
July	1	125	21	148	9	153	7	200	7	157	1	120

TABLE 1 — *Continued*

WAGE-SERIES FROM TABLE XII OF THE ALDRICH REPORT — STONE

84 Pennsylvania.

	Stone Cutters			Stone Cutters	
Sex..............	M.		Sex........................ ..	M.	
Initial wage per day	$1.50		Initial wage per day.......	$1.50	
	No.	Rel. Wages		No.	Rel. Wages
1860, January.........	1	100	1863, July	5	133
July	3	117	1864, January.........	4	158
1861, January.........	2	100	July	8	179
July	4	117	1865, January.........	3	206
1862, January.........	2	100	July	5	203
July	6	117	1866, January.........	4	217
1863, January.........	2	133	July	7	217

WHITE LEAD

85 Pennsylvania

	Engineers		Laborers		Laborers, Boys		Watchmen	
Sex	M.		M.		M.		M.	
Initial wage per day........	$1.50		$1.12		$0.635		$1.145	
	No.	Rel. Wages	No.	Rel. Wages	No.	Rel. Wages	No.	Rel. Wages
1860, January..........	1	100	13	100	5	100	1	100
July ,............	1	100	15	100	5	105	1	100
1861, January..........	1	100	16	101	3	105	1	100
July	1	100	15	102	2	92	1	100
1862, January..........	1	111	15	104	1	105	1	100
July	1	111	14	104	1	105	1	100
1863, January..........	1	111	9	112	1	92	1	125
July	1	111	8	112	3	101	2	125
1864, January..........	1	133	6	110	2	118	..	...
July	ʼ	133	4	143	1	105	1	150
1865, January.........	1	117	1	150	2	98	1	150
July	1	117	5	156	4	105	1	150
1866, January..........	1	117	8	156	4	105	1	150
July	1	117	6	156	3	96	1	150

TABLE 1 — *Continued*

WAGE-SERIES FROM TABLE XII OF THE ALDRICH REPORT — WOOLEN GOODS

86 Connecticut

	Overseers Card. Dep.		Overseers Dye House		Overseers Finish. Dep		Overseers Fulling & Gigg. Dep.		Overseers Weav. Dep.		Card Cleaners	
Sex........	M.		M.		M.		M.		M.		M.	
Init. wage per day..	$2.00		$1.80		$1.375		$1.375		$1.50		$0.69	
	No.	Rel. Wages	No.	Rel. Wages	No.	Rel. Wages	No.	Rel. Wages	No.	Rel. Wages	No.	Rel. Wages
1860, Jan.	1	100	1	100	1	100	1	100	1	100	1	100
July	1	100	1	100	1	100	1	109	1	100	2	100
1861, Jan.	1	125	1	100	1	100	1	109	1	100	1	112
July	1	125	1	100	1	100	1	109	1	117	1	112
1862, Jan.	1	88	1	83	1	100	1	109	1	117	1	138
July	1	125	1	83	1	109	1	109	1	117	1	100
1863, Jan.	1	150	1	83	1	218	1	109	1	117	4	103
July	1	150	1	83	1	218	1	95	1	117	5	104
1864, Jan.	1	150	1	125	1	218	1	84	1	133	4	109
July	1	150	1	128	1	218	1	98	1	173	5	112
1865, Jan.	1	180	1	167	1	262	1	145	1	177	2	154
July	1	190	1	167	1	262	1	120	1	175	3	115
1866, Jan.	1	190	1	167	1	262	1	120	1	200	3	138
July	1	190	1	167	1	262	1	120	1	200	6	121

86 Connecticut

	Card Tenders		Carpent's		Fullers & Giggers		Loom Fixers		Second-Hands		Shearers	
Sex........	M.		M.		M.		M.		M.		M.	
Init. wage per day..	$0.60		$1.50		$0.84		$1.25		$0.90		$0.75	
	No.	Rel. Wages	No.	Rel. Wages	No.	Rel. Wages	No.	Rel. Wages	No.	Rel. Wages	No.	Rel. Wages
1860, Jan.	6	100	1	100	4	100	..	...	2	100	..	...
July	4	104	1	100	8	88	..	...	2	100	..	...
1861, Jan.	5	107	..	...	3	107	..	...	2	98	1	100
July	5	105	..	...	6	93	1	100	2	98	..	...
1862, Jan.	8	106	..	...	10	94	1	100	2	106	1	100
July	8	101	..	...	8	95	3	93	1	100	4	117
1863, Jan.	4	108	1	108	3	107	2	110	2	119	4	107
July	7	105	..	...	12	86	3	113	2	98	2	103
1864, Jan.	6	113	..	...	9	87	2	125	2	107	2	133
July	6	99	1	108	3	149	2	176	2	111	3	149
1865, Jan.	7	143	2	108	6	168	2	192	2	144	2	187
July	7	137	1	108	6	151	2	160	2	158	3	193
1866, Jan.	9	123	1	150	9	152	1	160	2	150	4	183
July	6	130	1	150	10	154	2	150	2	189	5	160

TABLE 1 — *Continued*

WAGE-SERIES FROM TABLE XII OF THE ALDRICH REPORT — WOOLEN GOODS

86 Connecticut

	SPINNERS JACK AND MULE		SORTERS		WATCHMEN		WEAVERS		YARN CARRIERS		DRAWERS-IN	
Sex........	M.		M.		M.		M.		M.		F.	
Init. wage per day..	$1.05		$1.50		$1.00		$0.925		$0.69		$0.62	
	No.	Rel. Wages	No.	Rel. Wages	No.	Rel. Wages	No.	Rel. Wages	No.	Rel. Wages	No.	Rel. Wages
1860, Jan.	12	100	1	100	1	100	13	100	1	100	1	100
July	10	101	1	100	1	100	16	104	..	...	2	89
1861, Jan.	9	100	1	100	1	100	15	125	..	...	..	...
July	7	110	1	100	1	100	16	119	..	...	1	100
1862, Jan.	10	95	1	100	1	100	16	121	..	...	1	119
July	13	106	3	122	1	100	22	119	..	...	1	119
1863, Jan.	11	124	1	120	1	100	23	146	..	...	1	119
July	12	117	1	142	1	100	26	120	..	...	2	119
1864, Jan.	15	129	2	150	1	125	25	133	..	...	..	...
July	14	129	2	150	1	140	24	145	1	120	1	134
1865, Jan.	11	160	1	157	1	150	27	173	2	133	1	202
July	15	170	1	160	1	175	22	151	2	133	1	202
1866, Jan.	13	171	1	167	1	175	27	159	1	181	1	222
July	12	184	1	160	1	175	37	175	2	172	..	...

	86 Conn.		86 Conn.		86 Conn.		86 Conn.		87 Mass.		87 Mass.	
	HANDERS-IN		SPECKERS		SPOOLERS		WEAVERS		OVERSEERS CARD. DEP.		OVERSEERS DYE HOUSE	
Sex........	F.		F.		F.		F.		M.		M.	
Init. wage per day..	$0.50		$0.50		$0.65		$0.81		$2.00		$2.50	
	No.	Rel. Wages	No.	Rel. Wages	No.	Rel. Wages	No.	Rel. Wages	No.	Rel. Wages	No.	Rel. Wages
1860, Jan.	1	100	1	100	2	100	4	100	1	100	1	100
July	..	...	2	100	3	92	5	119	1	100	1	75
1861, Jan.	..	...	..	...	2	114	4	136	1	115	1	75
July	1	60	4	100	2	114	4	131	1	115	1	75
1862, Jan.	1	60	2	100	4	102	4	132	..	...	1	113
July	1	60	..	...	2	114	5	130	1	115	1	113
1863, Jan.	1	60	2	108	3	128	4	160	1	115	2	119
July	2	60	6	108	4	103	6	117	1	115	1	125
1864, Jan.	..	...	..	...	7	102	7	141	..	...	2	138
July	1	90	4	132	8	106	5	148	2	138	1	150
1865, Jan.	1	96	2	140	6	82	5	180	2	138	1	150
July	1	120	..	...	5	128	7	152	1	125	1	150
1866, Jan.	1	90	1	126	6	117	4	151	1	150	1	175
July	..	...	2	166	3	123	4	184	1	150	1	175

TABLE 1 — *Continued*

WAGE-SERIES FROM TABLE XII OF THE ALDRICH REPORT — WOOLEN GOODS

87 Massachusetts

	Overseers Weav. Dep.		Carders		Card Tenders		Dye-House Hands		Loom-Fixers		Card Tenders	
Sex	M.		M.		M.		M.		M.		F.	
Init. wage per day..	$1.75		$0.795		$0.378		$0.65		$1.25		$0.418	
	No.	Rel. Wages	No.	Rel. Wages	No.	Rel. Wages	No.	Rel. Wages	No.	Rel. Wages	No.	Rel. Wages
1860, Jan.	1	100	8	100	6	100	22	100	1	100	4	100
July	1	100	6	120	14	137	16	94	1	100	2	115
1861, Jan.	1	100	9	108	7	135	16	101	1	100	..	...
July	2	107	4	95	14	143	23	99	..	...	..	...
1862, Jan.	1	114	3	103	19	136	29	98	1	140	5	128
July	1	114	7	109	22	148	29	102	1	140	13	120
1863, Jan.	1	114	8	109	30	146	19	119	3	122	8	123
July	1	171	5	123	12	152	22	119	..	...	20	130
1864, Jan.	..	...	5	122	13	155	24	119	6	127	14	128
July	1	171	12	113	5	144	18	132	5	148	15	136
1865, Jan.	1	171	8	116	7	160	12	155	13	164	16	146
July	1	229	6	135	4	173	15	156	9	184	15	147
1866, Jan.	1	229	7	148	6	179	16	195	7	192	18	165
July	1	229	8	147	5	179	15	195	7	192	17	165

88 Rhode Island

	Overseers Card. Dep.		Overseers Dye House		Overseers Finish. Dep		Overseers Spinn. Dep.		Overseers Weav. Dep.		Second-Hands	
Sex	M.		M.		M.		M.		M.		M.	
Init. wage per day..	$1.75		$1.67		$1.50		$1.33		$1.33		$1.145	
	No.	Rel. Wages	No.	Rel. Wages	No.	Rel. Wages	No.	Rel. Wages	No.	Rel. Wages	No.	Rel. Wages
1860, Jan.	1	100	1	100	1	100	1	100	1	100	3	100
July	1	100	1	100	1	100	1	110	1	107	3	102
1861, Jan.	1	100	1	105	1	100	1	110	1	107	3	102
July	1	100	1	105	1	100	1	113	1	107	3	103
1862, Jan.	1	100	1	105	1	100	1	113	1	107	3	104
July	1	100	1	120	1	100	1	113	1	107	3	104
1863, Jan.	1	143	1	120	1	100	1	126	1	113	3	119
July	1	143	1	120	1	100	1	126	1	113	3	119
1864, Jan.	1	157	1	120	1	111	1	150	1	126	3	132
July	1	157	1	120	1	111	1	150	1	126	3	132
1865, Jan.	1	200	1	120	1	111	1	150	1	138	3	132
July	1	200	1	120	1	111	1	150	1	138	3	132
1866, Jan.	1	200	1	120	1	111	1	150	1	150	3	132
July	1	229	1	120	1	136	1	201	1	150	3	128

TABLE 1 — *Continued*

WAGE-SERIES FROM TABLE XII OF THE ALDRICH REPORT — WOOLEN GOODS

88 Rhode Island

	ALLEY BOYS		CARD FEEDERS		CLEANERS		DRESSERS		DYERS		FILLING CARRIERS	
Sex........	M.		M.		M.		M.		M.		M.	
Init. wage per day..	$0.63		$0.58		$0.83		$1.00		$1.10		$1.12	
	No.	Rel. Wages	No.	Rel. Wages	No.	Rel. Wages	No.	Rel. Wages	No.	Rel. Wages	No.	Rel. Wages
1860, Jan.	3	100	5	100	2	100	2	100	1	100	1	100
July	3	100	5	100	2	90	2	100	1	100	1	100
1861, Jan.	3	100	5	100	3	90	2	92	1	109	1	100
July	3	100	5	100	3	90	2	92	1	114	1	100
1862, Jan.	3	100	5	100	4	90	2	92	1	114	1	112
July	3	79	5	86	5	90	2	92	1	114	1	112
1863, Jan.	3	79	1	86	5	90	2	92	1	109	1	112
July	3	79	1	86	5	90	2	92	1	114	1	112
1864, Jan.	3	92	1	122	4	100	2	92	1	114	1	112
July	3	92	1	122	4	100	2	92	1	114	1	119
1865, Jan.	3	100	1	143	2	86	2	100	1	114	1	119
July	3	100	1	143	2	86	2	117	1	114	1	127
1866, Jan.	2	100	1	152	2	88	2	125	1	114	1	127
July	3	113	1	159	3	80	2	150	1	118	1	127

88 Rhode Island

	FILLING SORTERS		FINISHERS		FULLERS		GIGGERS		LABORERS, DYE HOUSE		PICKERS	
Sex........	M.		M.		M.		M.		M.		M.	
Init. wage per day..	$1.21		$0.79		$1.17		$0.79		$0.96		$1.21	
	No.	Rel. Wages	No.	Rel. Wages	No.	Rel. Wages	No.	Rel. Wages	No.	Rel. Wages	No.	Rel. Wages
1860, Jan.	1	100	2	100	1	100	2	100	2	100	1	100
July	1	100	2	100	1	100	2	100	2	100	1	100
1861, Jan.	1	100	2	100	1	100	2	100	1	100	1	100
July	1	100	2	100	1	100	2	95	1	100	1	100
1862, Jan.	1	103	2	100	1	100	2	95	1	100	1	100
July	1	103	3	95	1	103	2	105	1	100	1	100
1863, Jan.	1	110	3	95	1	103	2	105	1	100	1	110
July	1	110	3	95	1	107	2	105	1	96	1	110
1864, Jan.	1	110	3	116	1	107	2	127	1	96	1	117
July	1	110	3	116	1	107	2	127	1	100	1	117
1865, Jan.	1	110	3	127	1	107	2	127	1	104	2	124
July	1	110	3	127	1	114	2	127	2	104	2	124
1866, Jan.	1	114	3	127	1	114	2	142	3	104	2	124
July	1	117	3	137	1	114	2	148	3	104	2	131

TABLE 1— *Continued*

WAGE-SERIES FROM TABLE XII OF THE ALDRICH REPORT — WOOLEN GOODS

88 Rhode Island

	PRESS-MEN		SCOUR-ERS		SECTION HANDS		SHEAR-ERS		SPINNERS JACK		WASHERS		WASTE SORTERS	
Sex	M.		M.		M.		M.		M.		M.		M.	
Init. wage per day..	$1.00		$0.83		$1.00		$1.00		$0.95		$0.92		$0.92	
	No.	Relative Wages	No.	Relative Wages	No.	Relative Wages	No.	Relative Wages	No.	Relative Wages	No.	Relative Wages	No.	Relative Wages
1860, Jan..	1	100	1	100	2	100	1	100	7	100	2	100	1	100
July.	1	100	1	100	2	100	1	100	7	100	2	100	1	100
1861, Jan..	1	100	1	106	2	100	1	100	7	100	2	100	1	100
July.	1	100	1	106	2	100	1	100	7	100	2	109	1	100
1862, Jan..	1	100	1	106	2	100	1	100	7	100	3	109	1	100
July.	1	100	1	106	2	100	1	100	9	100	4	109	1	100
1863, Jan..	1	100	1	106	2	113	1	100	9	105	5	101	1	109
July.	1	100	1	111	2	113	1	100	9	105	5	111	1	109
1864, Jan..	1	104	1	111	2	100	1	104	9	125	4	127	1	109
July.	1	104	1	111	2	125	1	104	9	125	4	127	1	122
1865, Jan..	1	108	1	111	2	125	1	108	16	123	4	132	1	122
July.	1	117	1	111	2	125	1	117	16	123	4	132	1	136
1866, Jan..	1	117	1	111	2	133	1	117	19	126	4	136	1	136
July.	1	121	1	116	2	150	1	117	19	126	5	145	1	136

88 Rhode Island

	WATCH-MEN		WEAVERS		BURLERS		DRAW-ERS-IN		HAND-ERS-IN		TWISTERS		WEAVERS	
Sex	M.		M.		F.		F.		F.		F.		F.	
Init. wage per day..	$1.05		$0.94		$0.54		$1.00		$0.46		$0.67		$0.70	
	No.	Relative Wages	No.	Relative Wages	No.	Relative Wages	No.	Relative Wages	No.	Relative Wages	No.	Relative Wages	No.	Relative Wages
1860, Jan..	1	100	10	100	4	100	1	100	2	100	1	100	12	100
July.	1	100	11	98	5	100	1	100	2	100	1	100	9	103
1861, Jan..	1	100	11	101	5	100	1	100	2	100	1	100	10	104
July.	1	100	10	102	5	100	1	100	2	100	1	100	11	107
1862, Jan..	1	100	7	104	6	100	1	104	2	100	1	100	13	117
July.	1	100	8	106	6	100	1	104	2	109	1	100	12	120
1863, Jan..	1	100	10	110	7	100	1	104	2	109	1	100	11	116
July.	1	100	10	105	8	100	1	104	2	109	1	100	10	127
1864, Jan..	1	100	10	106	9	100	1	104	2	109	1	106	12	130
July.	1	100	9	115	10	107	1	104	2	109	1	124	11	143
1865, Jan..	1	105	7	117	14	107	1	104	2	109	1	124	13	140
July.	1	105	10	119	14	117	1	104	2	109	1	124	9	147
1866, Jan..	1	114	6	126	16	124	1	104	2	109	1	137	20	151
July.	1	119	18	129	16	131	1	104	2	109	1	137	20	149

TABLE 2[1]

WAGE-SERIES FROM VOL. XX OF THE TENTH CENSUS

AGRICULTURAL IMPLEMENTS

Massillon, O., 9

Occupation	Initial Wage p'r Day	1860	1861	1862	1863	1864	1865	1866
	$							
Blacksmith.......	1.50	...	100	100	117	133	140	150
Finisher	1.62	...	100	100	115	123	123	154
Laborers	0.90	...	100	111	122	133	139	167
Molder...........	1.50	...	100	117	133	150	150	150
Painter	1.50	...	100	100	117	133	133	133

BOOTS AND SHOES

Lafayette, Ind., 16, 17

	$							
Overseer........	66.66⅔[2]	100	125	125	125	150	150	225
Cutter, Sole	3.00	100	100	100	100	100	100	100
Cutter, Upper...	4.00	100	100	100	100	100	100	100
Fitter..........	2.50	100	100	100	100	100	100	100

Baltimore, Md., 19

	$							
Overseer........	60.00[2]	100	100	107	107	120	120	133
Buttoner or lacer	0.75	100	100	100	100	100	100	100
Cutter..........	1.50	100	100	100	117	133	133	150
Fitter..........	1.00	100	100	100	125	125	125	150
Packer	1.50	100	100	100	100	100	100	100
Treer	1.25	100	100	100	120	120	120	140

[1] In this Appendix the series of relative wages computed from the material in Mr. WEEKS's "Report on the Statistics of Wages in Manufacturing Industries" (*Tenth Census of the United States*, Vol. XX) are given at length. The order of arrangement under industries and establishments is that of the source, and the number following the name of the town and state in which each establishment is located shows the page of the "Report" on which the original data may be found. As in the preceding Appendix, the initial wage is recorded, but the sex and number of employees are not, because they are not stated by Mr. Weeks.

[2] Per month.

TABLE 2—*Continued*

WAGE-SERIES FROM VOL. XX OF THE TENTH CENSUS

BOOTS AND SHOES

Mass., 20, 21

Occupation	Initial Wage p'r Day	1860	1861	1862	1863	1864	1865	1866
	$							
Cutter..........	1.33	100	100	132	132	150	150	201
Edge-setter.....	2.00	...	100	130	125	138	163	163
Fitter..........	0.50	100	100	200	200	250	250	400
Finisher........	1.16⅔	...	100	143	143	172	172	243
Treer..........	1.50	100	133	133	167	167	183	183
Packer.........	1.50	100	100	117	133	133	167	167
Trimmer........	2.00	...	100	130	125	138	163	163

BREWERIES

Columbus, O., 25

	$							
Cellarman......	1.15	100	100	117	133	167	200	200
Laborers.......	0.76	100	100	126	151	201	228	228
Maltster........	1.15	100	100	117	133	167	200	200
Teamster.......	0.96	100	100	120	140	159	180	180

BRICK

St. Louis, Mo., 31

	$							
Boy............	0.7825	100	...	80	111	105	168	207
Engineer.......	1.66	100	100	...	120	196	211	301
Laborers (1st)...	1.00	100	88	113	138	175	200	200
Laborers (2d)...	1.25	100	60	60	80	120	120	140
Molder.........	1.50	100	75	133	117	199	212	218

Trenton, N. J., 33

	$							
Burner.........	1.62	100	100	100	100	100	154	154
Carrier.........	0.75	100	100	100	100	100	133	133
Molder.........	1.375	100	100	100	100	100	127	164
Pit-filler........	1.25	100	100	100	100	100	120	160
Presser.........	1.25	100	100	100	100	100	120	140
Off-bearer......	0.60	100	100	100	100	100	142	167
Setter..........	1.62	100	100	100	100	100	154	170
Sorter..........	1.10	100	100	100	100	100	118	136
Teamster.......	1.00	100	100	100	100	100	125	150
Wheeler........	1.10	100	100	100	100	100	114	136
Wh'l'r and tosser	1.10	100	100	100	100	100	136	159

TABLE 2—*Continued*

WAGE-SERIES FROM VOL. XX OF THE TENTH CENSUS

BRICK

Philadelphia, Pa., 34

Occupation	Initial Wage p'r Day	1860	1861	1862	1863	1864	1865	1866
	$							
Foreman	1.92	100	117	117	149	156	156	167
Burner	2.00	100	100	100	125	138	175	200
Carrier off......	0.62	100	100	100	121	121	161	161
Carter..........	1.00	100	100	100	112	125	150	150
Carver up......	0.50	100	100	100	100	124	124	124
Driver..........	1.00	100	100	100	112	125	150	150
Engineer	1.50	100	100	117	133	150	167	167
Laborer	1.00	100	100	100	112	125	150	150
Molder	1.375	100	91	91	118	136	182	200
Off-bearer	0.75	100	100	100	133	133	167	167
Presser	1.50	100	100	83	93	100	108	150
Press-sorter.....	1.50	100	100	100	133	133	150	200
Setter	1.75	100	86	86	114	129	171	186
Watchman......	1.00	100	100	112	112	125	150	150
Wheeler	1.20	100	100	104	104	104	125	167
Wh'l'r and tosser	1.12	100	100	112	112	112	134	156

CIGARS AND TOBACCO

Washington, D. C., 41

	$							
Cigarmaker.....	0.83⅓	100	125	142	186	196	299	289

St. Louis, Mo., 44

	$							
Caser...........	2.66	100	100	150	162	188	188	216
Cutter..........	1.85	100	100	127	162	178	178	178
Laborers	1.00	100	100	130	166	185	185	185
Packer	1.30	100	100	142	181	192	192	192
Sorter	2.66	100	100	150	162	188	188	216
Stripper	0.70	100	100	143	186	186	186	186

New Jersey, 45

	$							
Caser...........	1.00	100	100	100	100	100	100	100
Cutter..........	2.00	100	100	100	100	100	100	100
Laborer	0.70	100	100	100	100	129	129	160
Packer	1.37	100	100	100	100	100	100	100
Sorter	2.00	100	100	100	100	125	125	150
Stripper	1.00	100	100	100	100	100	100	100

TABLE 2—*Continued*

WAGE-SERIES FROM VOL. XX OF THE TENTH CENSUS

CIGARS AND TOBACCO

Wisconsin, 50

Occupation	Initial Wage p'r Day	1860	1861	1862	1863	1864	1865	1866
	$							
Maker	1.33⅛	100	100	125	150	175	175	162
Packer	1.75	100	100	114	126	143	171	152
Stripper.........	0.25	100	100	120	133	133	133	133

CLOTHING

Kentucky, 51

	$							
Cutter..........	3.84	100	100	125	125	125	125	125
Salesman	2.56	100	150	150	150	150	150	150
Tailor	1.75	100	129	129	171	171	171	157
Tailoresses	1.16⅝	100	129	129	172	172	172	158

Newark, N. J., 51

	$							
Cutter..........	2.00	...	100	125	117	138	142	167
Man............	1.25	...	100	100	100	100	120	130
Tailor...........	1.25	...	100	100	100	100	120	130
Tailoresses......	0.375	...	100	100	100	100	133	167
Woman	0.375	...	100	100	100	100	133	167

Syracuse, N. Y., 52

	$							
Foreman........	80.00[1]	100	100	125	125	150	150	150
Apprentice	0.33⅛	100	122	122	122	149	149	149
Cutter..........	1.83	100	123	146	146	160	160	160
Machine woman.	0.66⅝	100	113	126	126	126	126	126
Presser	1.00	100	116	133	150	150	150	133
Tailor..........	1.50	100	100	111	122	122	122	122
Tailoress	0.66⅝	100	100	126	126	126	126	126
Trimmer........	0.66⅝	100	126	126	126	150	150	150

FLOUR MILLS

Stanton, Del., 58

	$							
Assistant miller .	1.73	...	100	100	100	100	100	100
Miller	2.50	...	100	100	100	100	100	100
Packer	1.73	...	100	100	100	100	100	100

[1] Per month.

TABLE 2—*Continued*

WAGE-SERIES FROM VOL. XX OF THE TENTH CENSUS

FLOUR MILLS

Belleville, Ill., 59

Occupation	Initial Wage p'r Day	1860	1861	1862	1863	1864	1865	1866
	$							
Assistant miller..	1.73	100	89	100	133	166	178	200
Engineer	1.54	100	75	100	125	162	186	249
Firemen	1.00	100	75	100	125	175	175	200
Laborers	1.00	100	75	100	125	150	150	150
Miller	1.92	100	90	100	160	200	250	300
Packer	1.00	100	100	125	125	200	200	200
Teamster	1.00	100	75	100	125	150	150	175

Fort Wayne, Ind., 60, 61

	$							
Assistant miller.	1.75	100	100	114	114	114	114	114
Laborer	1.00	100	125	125	150	150	150	125
Miller	2.50	100	120	120	140	140	140	120
Millwright	3.00	100	100	100	117	117	117	100
Packer	1.25	100	100	104	108	116	120	88
Stone dresser	1.75	100	114	114	129	129	129	129
Teamster	1.25	100	120	120	140	140	140	140

Lafayette, Ind., 62

	$							
Assistant miller.	1.15	100	117	117	152	217	217	181
Laborers	0.875	100	100	100	129	153	153	181
Miller	1.44	100	116	116	139	174	174	174
Millwrights	3.00	...	100	117	117	117	117	117
Stone dressers	2.00	...	100	100	113	113	125	125
Teamster	1.15	100	100	100	130	174	174	174

De Soto, Ia., 64

	$							
Assistant miller.	0.60	...	100	167	167	208	200	250
Laborer	0.55	...	100	150	178	201	218	160
Miller	1.15	...	100	150	250	250	235	200
Millwright	1.50	...	100	117	133	167	167	150
Teamster	0.60	...	100	167	167	208	200	167

TABLE 2—*Continued*

WAGE-SERIES FROM VOL. XX OF THE TENTH CENSUS

GAS AND GAS COKE

Indianapolis, Ind., 76

Occupation	Initial Wage p'r Day	1860	1861	1862	1863	1864	1865	1866
	$							
Laborer	1.00	100	100	100	150	150	175	175
Stoker..........	1.00	100	100	100	150	150	200	200

East Boston, Mass., 77

	$							
Foreman	16.00[1]	100	100	100	100	100	100	100
Laborer.........	14.00[1]	100	100	100	100	100	100	100

FLINT GLASS

Cambridge, Mass., 81

	$							
Manager........	125.00[2]	100	100	100	100	120	120	120
Blower	3.00	100	100	100	100	100	100	100
Carrying-in boy.	0.62	100	100	100	100	161	161	161
Clay-tramper ...	1.50	100	100	100	100	100	100	100
Clearing-off boy.	0.62	100	100	100	100	161	161	161
Cutter..........	2.00	100	100	100	100	138	138	138
Driver..........	1.50	100	100	100	100	117	117	117
Engineer........	2.00	100	100	100	100	125	125	125
Engraver........	2.00	100	100	100	100	138	138	138
Finisher	2.52	100	99	99	99	119	119	119
Gatherer........	1.00	100	100	100	100	200	200	200
Laborers	1.50	100	100	100	100	117	117	117
Machinist.......	2.00	100	100	100	100	138	138	138
Mixer	1.50	100	100	100	100	133	133	133
Mold-holder	0.62	100	100	100	100	161	161	161
Mold-maker	2.00	100	100	100	100	138	138	138
Packer	1.50	100	100	100	100	117	117	117
Pot-filler.......	1.50	100	100	100	100	133	133	133
Pot-maker	2.00	100	100	100	100	100	100	100
Presser	1.50	100	100	100	100	133	133	133
Sticker-up	0.75	100	100	100	100	167	167	167
Teaser..........	1.50	100	100	100	100	133	133	133

[1] Per week.   [2] Per month.

TABLE 2—*Continued*

WAGE-SERIES FROM VOL. XX OF THE TENTH CENSUS

FLINT GLASS

Pittsburg, Pa., 84, 85

Occupation	Initial Wage p'r Day	1860	1861	1862	1863	1864	1865	1866
	$							
Foreman cutter.	21.00[1]	100	100	100	100	100	100	143
Carrying-in boy.	0.60	100	100	100	100	100	100	133
Clay-tramper ...	6.50[1]	100	100	100	108	108	108	169
Cutter, j'yman ..	7.37[1]	100	100	100	105	105	105	170
Driver..........	7.00[1]	100	100	100	100	100	100	186
Finisher........	2.58	100	100	100	131	131	131	196
Gatherer	1.12	100	100	100	136	136	136	176
Laborer	5.00[1]	100	100	100	120	120	120	200
Mixer	6.50[1]	100	100	100	123	123	123	215
Mold-m'k'r, ass't	11.70[1]	100	100	100	114	114	114	194
Packer	6.25[1]	100	100	100	120	120	120	232
Pot-maker	13.00[1]	100	100	100	131	131	131	146
Presser.........	2.62	100	100	100	126	126	126	193
Sticker-up	0.90	100	100	100	100	100	100	178
Teaser..........	6.50[1]	100	100	100	115	115	115	262

Pennsylvania, 86, 87

	$							
Blower	2.00	...	100	109	113	175	245	245

Pennsylvania, 87, 88

	$							
Manager........	76.00[2]	100	100	100	100	100	100	158
Cutter..........	2.50	100	80	80	80	80	100	100
Driver..........	1.00	...	100	133	167	200	200	200
Engineer	1.50	100	100	111	133	133	167	178
Furnaceman	1.50	100	100	117	117	117	133	150
Laborer	1.33⅓	100	100	100	100	100	125	125
Mixer	1.66⅔	100	70	70	70	70	80	80
Mold-cleaner....	0.75	100	100	100	120	120	120	120
Mold-maker	3.00	100	100	100	100	100	111	111
Packer	1.16⅝	100	94	94	100	100	129	129
Top-filler	1.66⅔	100	70	70	70	70	80	80
Leerman........	1.10	100	136	155	155	159	182	182
Teaser..........	1.42 6/7	100	100	100	100	100	120	120

1 Per week.   2 Per month.

TABLE 2—*Continued*

WAGE-SERIES FROM VOL. XX OF THE TENTH CENSUS

FLINT GLASS

Wheeling, W. Va., 89

Occupation	Initial Wage per Day	1860	1861	1862	1863	1864	1865	1866
	$							
Manager	120.00¹	100	100	100	100	100	100	100
Clay-tramper ...	0.83¾	100	99	89	119	159	159	159
Driver	1.16	100	100	86	115	158	158	158
Eng'r and blksm.	1.75	100	100	76	133	152	171	171
Laborer	0.83⅓	100	100	90	120	160	160	160
Mixer	0.91⅝	100	127	109	127	145	145	154
Moldm'kr,j'yman	2.08	100	90	96	108	163	132	130
Packer	1.125	100	100	89	119	148	160	148
Pot-filler........	0.83⅓	100	100	90	120	160	160	169
Pot-maker	1.50	100	100	83	83	122	133	144
Teaser..........	1.00	100	100	100	100	200	200	200

ICE

Peoria, Ill., 108

	$							
Carpenter	1.50	100	100	117	133	200	167	183
Hook-carrier	1.00	100	125	125	125	150	150	175
Laborer	0.75	100	133	133	133	167	133	167
Packer	1.00	100	125	125	125	150	150	150
Peddler	1.25	100	100	100	100	120	120	140
Plower	1.00	100	125	125	125	150	150	175
Sawyer	1.00	100	125	125	125	150	125	150
Spudder........	1.00	100	125	125	125	125	125	150
Teamster	0.60	100	125	125	167	167	167	208

IRON BLAST FURNACES—ANTHRACITE

New York, 115

	$							
Manager........	125.00¹	100	100	100	100	100	140	140
Blacksmith	1.375	100	91	100	119	145	164	182
Bl'ksmith'shelp'r	1.25	100	85	90	100	130	120	140
Bottom-filler	1.00	100	88	94	125	175	164	164
Carpenter	1.25	100	100	100	140	160	170	200
Cinderman	1.125	100	89	95	122	167	156	156
Engineer	15.00²	100	96	100	117	167	167	125
Founder........	1.50	100	89	94	118	142	142	144
Keeper	1.25	100	90	95	120	160	150	150
Keeper's helper .	1.125	100	89	95	122	167	156	156
Laborer	1.00	100	88	94	125	163	150	150

¹ Per month.   ² Per week.

TABLE 2—*Continued*

WAGE-SERIES FROM VOL. XX OF THE TENTH CENSUS

IRON BLAST FURNACES — ANTHRACITE

Catasauqua, Pa., 116

Occupation	Initial Wage p'r Day	1860	1861	1862	1863	1864	1865	1866
Foreman, ma hine shops	$ 2.50	100	100	100	114	130	130	127
Blacksmith, boss	1.55	100	100	97	113	145	145	145
Carpenter, boss .	1.75	100	100	106	114	129	135	143
Boss laborer	2.00	100	100	100	113	125	125	138
Boss mason.....	1.60	100	97	97	125	172	156	172
Bl'ksmith helper	0.80	100	100	125	144	200	200	200
Bl'ksmith j'yman	1.35	100	100	93	111	130	130	137
Bottom- and top-filler	1.43	100	100	104	108	154	149	148
Brakeman	1.00	100	90	100	120	160	175	185
Carpenter j'yman	1.25	100	100	108	120	160	160	168
Engineer	7.91[1]	100	93	106	124	164	159	177
Engineers, loco-motive........	1.65	100	97	106	106	121	141	145
Fireman	1.12	100	94	98	121	156	161	170
Founder........	2.25	100	100	100	100	133	133	133
Keeper	2.01	100	95	102	107	135	130	129
Keeper's helper..	1.69	100	101	103	100	137	136	135
Laborer	0.80	100	100	113	141	181	178	191
Machinist	1.40	100	100	104	118	150	161	143
Mason	1.40	100	96	96	125	161	161	161

Pennsylvania, 119

	$							
Blacksmith	1.25	100	86	100	146	186	203	200
Bl'ksmith helper	1.00	100	88	100	114	200	200	200
Engineer, j'yman.	8.04[1]	100	100	110	139	160	187	149
Bottom-filler	0.90	100	111	125	151	222	222	222
Cinderman	1.50	100	117	75	86	133	133	133
Founder........	1.30	100	103	103	175	219	296	296
Keeper	1.15	100	100	116	150	198	192	192
Keeper's helper .	1.00	100	100	113	143	200	207	207
Laborer	0.875	100	100	114	130	229	171	171
Metal-weighman.	0.90	100	100	111	127	190	199	199
Top-filler	1.00	100	113	113	143	214	207	200

[1] Per week.

TABLE 2—*Continued*

WAGE-SERIES FROM VOL. XX OF THE TENTH CENSUS

IRON BLAST FURNACES — BITUMINOUS

Youngstown, O., 122

Occupation	Initial Wage p'r Day	1860	1861	1862	1863	1864	1865	1866
Manager........	$100.00[1]	100	100	100	100	100	100	100
Blacksmith	1.50	100	100	100	110	167	292	292
Bottom-filler and top-filler......	1.125	100	100	100	122	222	200	188
Carpenter	1.50	100	100	100	118	175	150	167
Cinderman	1.00	100	100	100	138	238	225	212
Engineer	1.12	100	100	100	120	210	210	220
Founder........	4.81	100	100	100	100	100	100	100
Keeper	1.50	100	100	100	127	192	175	167
Keeper's helper.	1.125	100	100	100	133	222	200	188
Laborer	0.875	100	100	100	143	229	200	200
Metal-carrier....	1.00	100	100	100	140	250	225	225

IRON BLAST FURNACES — CHARCOAL

Baltimore, Md., 128

Manager........	$32.00[1]	...	100	...	113	139	175	...
Coal-raker	0.85	...	100	...	134	155	218	...
Collier..........	0.95	...	100	...	116	133	165	...
Engineer........	6.00	...	100	...	121	150	192	...
Filler...........	0.96	...	100	...	111	131	164	...
Keeper..........	0.85	...	100	...	126	146	193	...
Keeper's helper..	0.78	...	100	...	128	146	182	...

Boiling Springs, Pa., 132

Blacksmith	$1.25	100	100	100	100	100	100	100
Carpenter	1.25	100	100	100	100	100	100	100
Cartman........	1.00	100	100	100	100	100	100	100
Coal-raker	1.00	100	100	100	100	100	100	100
Collier..........	1.10	100	100	100	100	100	100	100
Filler...........	1.10	100	100	100	100	100	100	100
Founder........	1.50	100	100	100	100	100	100	100
Gutterman	1.10	100	100	100	100	100	100	100
Keeper..........	1.30	100	100	100	100	100	100	100
Keeper's helper..	1.10	100	100	100	100	100	100	100
Laborer.........	1.00	100	100	100	100	100	100	100
Ore miner.......	1.00	100	100	100	100	100	100	100
Teamster........	1.00	100	100	100	100	100	100	100

[1] Per month.

TABLE 2—*Continued*

WAGE-SERIES FROM VOL. XX OF THE TENTH CENSUS

IRON BLAST FURNACES — CHARCOAL

Pilot Knob, Mo., 129

Occupation	Initial Wage p'r Day	1859	1860	1861	1862	1863	1864	1865	1866
Filler.....	$1.00	100	...	...	...	110	120	150	140
Keeper....	1.35	100	...	...	...	85	93	111	148
Laborer ..	1.00	100	...	...	...	100	115	140	140

Amenia, N.Y., 130

Filler.....	$0.875	100	...	...	86	129	137	171	...

IRON AND STEEL FOUNDRIES — STOVE

Quincy, Ill., 141

	$								
Foreman	80.00[1]	100	113	113	125	125	125	125	
Blacksmith	1.50	100	117	117	133	133	133	133	
Carpenter	1.50	100	117	133	133	150	167	167	
Cleaner.........	1.25	100	120	120	120	140	140	140	
Cupola man	2.25	100	100	111	111	111	111	111	
Engineers	1.75	100	114	114	114	129	129	129	
Filer	1.25	100	120	140	160	180	180	180	
Finisher	1.25	100	100	120	120	140	140	140	
Grinder	1.25	100	100	100	100	100	100	100	
Laborer	1.25	100	100	100	120	120	120	120	
Melter	2.00	100	113	125	125	125	125	125	
Melter's helper..	1.75	100	100	114	114	114	114	114	
Molder	3.00	100	117	150	158	167	167	167	
Molder's ap'rent.	0.50	100	200	200	200	200	200	200	
Mounter........	1.50	100	117	117	133	133	150	150	
Pattern-dresser..	1.50	100	117	117	117	117	100	100	
Pattern-maker ..	2.00	100	113	125	138	150	150	150	
Teamster	1.25	100	100	120	120	120	140	140	

Philadelphia, Pa., 148

	$								
Engineer........	1.50	100	133	133	133	133	139	156	
Finisher	1.15⅜	100	80	101	94	207	170	188	
Laborers........	1.08	100	84	81	100	121	132	136	
Molder.........	1.545	100	93	128	71	128	218	184	
Molder's helper..	1.24⅝	100	81	81	52	90	78	85	

[1] Per month.

TABLE 2 — *Continued*

WAGE-SERIES FROM VOL. XX OF THE TENTH CENSUS

IRON AND STEEL FOUNDRIES — STOVE

Taunton, Mass., 142, 143

Occupation	Initial Wage p'r Day	1860	1861	1862	1863	1864	1865	1866
	$							
Foreman	66.66⅔[1]	...	100	100	100	100	113	113
Carpenter	1.75	...	100	100	86	100	114	143
Cleaner..........	1.50	...	100	100	83	93	100	117
Engineer........	1.75	...	100	100	86	86	129	157
Filer	1.50	...	100	100	83	93	100	117
Finishers	1.75	...	100	100	86	91	114	143
Grinder	1.50	...	100	100	83	93	100	117
Laborer	1.25	...	100	100	80	96	120	140
Melter..........	3.00	...	100	100	67	75	92	83
Melter's helpers.	1.50	...	100	100	83	93	100	117
Molder	2.50	...	100	100	80	90	110	140
Mounter........	2.00	...	100	100	75	95	113	138

St. Louis, Mo., 143, 144

Occupation	Initial Wage	1860	1861	1862	1863	1864	1865	1866
	$							
Foreman........	150.00[1]	100	133	133	133	133	133	167
Carpenter	2.30⅔	100	100	160	160	160	147	147
Cleaner	1.50	100	100	100	100	100	100	100
Cupola man.....	1.54	100	110	180	180	180	180	165
Engineer........	2.885	100	100	120	120	120	120	107
Filer...........	2.00	100	100	150	150	200	200	200
Laborer	1.50	100	133	133	150	150	147	...
Melter..........	1.54	100	110	180	180	180	180	165
Molder..........	2.00	100	100	100	250	250	250	200
Mounter........	2.00	100	100	100	100	100	111	113
Teamster	2.50	100	100	100	100	100	100	77

HARDWARE

Connecticut, 159

Occupation	Initial Wage	1860	1861	1862	1863	1864	1865	1866
	$							
Foreman........	65.00[1]	100	100	100	100	100	100	108
Blacksmith	1.50	100	107	107	107	107	110	110
Galvanizer......	1.25	100	112	112	112	112	112	120
Grinder	1.00	100	100	100	100	100	110	110
Packer	2.00	100	113	113	113	113	125	125

[1] Per month.

TABLE 2 — *Continued*

WAGE-SERIES FROM VOL. XX OF THE TENTH CENSUS

HARDWARE

Connecticut, 157

Occupation	Initial Wage p'r Day	1860	1861	1862	1863	1864	1865	1866
	$							
Foreman	60.00 [1]	100	100	125	125	125	125	125
Blacksmith	2.00	100	100	113	125	138	138	150
Engineer	2.00	100	100	113	113	113	125	125
Forger	2.125	100	100	118	129	141	141	153
Grinder	1.75	100	100	114	129	143	143	157
Helper	1.50	100	100	117	117	133	133	150
Packer	1.50	100	100	117	117	133	133	133
Laborer	1.00	100	100	125	125	125	125	150
Machinist	2.00	100	100	113	113	113	125	125
Polisher	1.75	100	100	114	114	129	129	129
Temperer.......	1.50	100	100	117	117	133	133	150

Chicopee, Mass., 159

	$							
Foreman	71.50 [1]	100	109	109	109	127	145	145
Blacksmith	2.00	100	100	100	113	125	138	138
Forger..........	1.60	100	100	100	109	125	141	141
Grinder	1.90	100	100	100	105	145	158	158
Helper	0.90	100	100	100	111	139	167	167
Laborer	0.90	100	100	100	111	139	167	167
Machinist	1.75	100	100	100	114	129	143	143
Polisher	1.25	100	100	100	120	140	160	160
Temperer	2.15	100	100	100	116	140	163	163

Massachusetts, 161

	$							
Foreman	52.00 [1]	100	100	100	113	125	125	138
Blacksmith	2.00	100	100	100	125	150	150	175
Forger	1.25	100	120	140	140	180	180	180
Grinder	1.75	100	100	114	114	114	114	114
Laborer	1.00	100	100	100	125	125	125	140
Machinist	2.17	100	104	104	104	115	127	138
Packer	1.50	100	100	117	117	133	167	200
Polisher	1.50	100	100	117	117	117	117	117
Temperer.......	1.00	100	100	125	125	150	167	167

[1] Per Month.

TABLE 2—*Continued*

WAGE-SERIES FROM VOL. XX OF THE TENTH CENSUS

HARDWARE

Massachusetts, 160, 161

	$							
Forger	3.00	100	100	100	117	117	117	125
Laborer	1.00	100	100	100	100	100	100	125
Machinist	1.75	100	100	100	114	114	114	129
Packer	1.25	100	100	100	100	100	100	100
Polisher	1.50	100	100	100	117	117	117	117
Temperer.......	2.50	100	100	100	110	110	110	110

Fisherville, N. H., 162

Occupation	Initial Wage p'r Day	1860	1861	1862	1863	1864	1865	1866
	$							
Foreman	52.00 [1]	100	100	100	100	125	125	150
Forger..........	3.84$\frac{3}{8}$	100	100	100	100	75	75	75
Laborer	1.125	100	100	100	100	111	111	133

New York, 164

	$							
Forger	3.50	100	100	100	100	100	100	100
Grinder	2.25	100	100	100	100	100	100	100
Helper, first	1.50	100	100	100	100	100	100	100
Helper, second..	1.00	100	100	100	100	100	100	100

MACHINERY

Lafayette, Ind., 171

	$							
Blacksmith	2.00	100	100	100	125	138	150	150
Bl'ksmith helper	1.25	100	100	100	120	120	160	160
Laborer	1.00	100	100	100	125	125	150	150
Machinist	1.75	100	100	100	129	157	171	171
Molder	1.75	100	100	100	143	157	171	171
Pattern-maker ..	1.75	100	100	100	129	143	143	143

Paterson, N. J., 173

	$							
Blacksmith	1.075	100	108	108	140	131	180	186
Laborer	0.75	100	100	100	131	131	179	186
Machinist	1.3125	100	100	84	132	124	171	193
Molder	1.3125	100	100	95	114	124	222	209

[1] Per Month.

TABLE 2 — *Continued*

WAGE-SERIES FROM VOL. XX OF THE TENTH CENSUS

MACHINERY

St. Louis, Mo., 172

Occupation	Initial Wage p'r Day	1860	1861	1862	1863	1864	1865	1866
	$							
Apprentice	0.525	100	100	100	100	114	124	124
Blacksmith	1.60	100	83	100	125	179	188	219
Bl'ksmith helper	1.00	100	90	125	133	166	200	200
Engineer	1.25	100	100	100	100	120	120	140
Draughtsman...	1.60	100	83	94	125	172	188	219
Laborer	1.00	100	90	100	125	125	160	160
Machinist	1.60	100	83	100	125	172	188	219
Machinist helper	1.00	100	90	100	120	133	167	200
Melter	1.00	100	90	100	125	150	200	200
Molder	1.60	100	94	100	125	168	188	219
Molder's helper.	1.00	100	90	100	120	133	167	180
Patternmaker...	1.60	100	83	94	125	172	188	219

Albany, N. Y., 173, 174

	$							
Blacksmith	1.34⅜	100	98	98	115	163	163	172
Engineer	1.16⅜	100	100	100	100	139	139	150
Laborer	1.00	100	97	97	125	175	156	163
Machinist	1.3125	100	95	100	114	162	162	167
Molder	1.625	100	98	98	93	131	135	138
Patternmaker...	1.50	100	142	142	146	158	158	158

Akron, O., 175, 176

	$							
Apprentice	0.48	100	100	100	100	100	100	100
Blacksmith	1.75	100	114	129	143	143	143	143
Bl'ksmith helper	1.25	100	120	120	120	120	120	120
Draughtsman ..	1.75	100	114	129	143	143	143	143
Engineer	0.64	100	100	100	100	100	100	100
Machinist	1.75	100	114	129	143	143	143	143
Machinist helper	1.125	100	111	111	111	111	111	111
Melter	1.20	100	108	108	113	113	113	113
Molder	1.75	100	114	129	143	143	143	143
Molder's helper.	1.125	100	111	111	111	111	111	111
Patternmaker...	1.75	100	114	129	143	143	143	143

TABLE 2—*Continued*

WAGE-SERIES FROM VOL. XX OF THE TENTH CENSUS

MACHINERY

Detroit, Mich., 177, 178

Occupation	Initial Wage p'r Day	1860	1861	1862	1863	1864	1865	1866
	$							
Blacksmith.....	1.50	100	100	107	117	157	167	183
Boiler-fitter.....	1.50	100	100	100	108	200	200	183
Boiler-helper....	1.00	100	100	100	120	175	175	180
Boiler-maker....	1.50	100	100	100	108	200	200	183
Boiler-riveter....	1.50	100	100	100	108	200	200	183
Engineer........	1.375	100	109	109	127	127	127	127
Laborer.........	0.875	100	100	100	114	171	200	186
Machinist.......	1.50	100	100	107	127	167	175	183
Machin't's helper	0.875	100	100	100	114	171	186	186
Molder..........	1.25	100	130	130	140	240	200	220
Molder's helper..	0.875	100	109	109	120	171	200	186

New York, 182

	$							
Apprentice	0.60	100	100	100	100	100	100	100
Blacksmith.....	1.50	100	100	100	117	167	167	167
Boiler-maker....	1.50	100	100	100	117	167	167	167
Riveter	1.25	100	100	100	120	180	180	200
Engineer	1.50	100	100	100	100	100	100	100
Machinist	1.50	100	100	100	117	167	167	167
Melter..........	1.25	100	100	100	120	120	120	120
Molder	1.50	100	100	100	117	133	133	133
Patternmaker...	2.00	100	100	100	100	125	150	150

New Albany, Ind., 185

	$							
Blacksmith	2.00	100	125	125	138	138	138	138
Blacks'th helper.	1.00	100	125	125	125	125	125	125
Cleaner.........	1.00	100	125	125	125	125	125	125
Coremaker......	1.50	100	100	100	100	117	117	117
Laborer	1.00	100	125	125	125	125	125	125
Machinist	2.00	100	125	125	138	138	138	138
Molder	2.00	100	113	113	138	138	138	138
Molder's helper..	1.00	100	125	125	150	150	150	150
Patternmaker...	2.00	100	100	100	150	150	150	150
Teamster	1.25	100	120	120	120	120	120	120

TABLE 2—*Continued*

WAGE-SERIES FROM VOL. XX OF THE TENTH CENSUS

MACHINERY

Buffalo, N. Y., 179, 180

Occupation	Initial Wage p'r Day	1860	1861	1862	1863	1864	1865	1866
Blacksmith	$ 1.50	100	117	117	117	117	117	133
Blacks'th helper	0.75	100	133	133	133	133	133	167
Boiler-fitter	1.25	100	120	140	160	180	180	180
Boiler-flanger . . .	1.50	100	117	133	150	167	167	167
Boiler-helper. . . .	0.50	100	150	150	200	200	200	200
Boiler holder-on.	0.75	100	133	167	167	167	167	167
Boiler-maker. . . .	1.25	100	120	140	160	180	180	180
Boiler-riveter . . .	1.25	100	120	140	160	180	180	180
Engineer	1.12	100	179	179	179	179	179	179
Machinist	1.12	100	134	156	156	179	179	201
Melter.	1.10	100	100	100	100	114	136	114
Molder	1.50	100	109	109	109	117	133	183
Molder's helpers	0.85	100	102	102	102	129	147	176
Machin't's help..	0.75	100	100	100	100	117	117	133
Patternmaker. . .	1.60	100	156	156	156	156	156	172
Joiner	1.50	100	100	100	100	100	100	117
Joiner's helper. .	1.00	100	100	100	100	100	100	100

Worcester, Mass., 187

Girl.	$ 0.80	100	100	100	113	125	150	188
Machinist	1.50	100	93	93	143	150	217	267
Skilled workman	2.10	100	95	95	143	155	238	333
Unskilled work..	1.10	100	91	91	136	159	227	273

Evansville, Ind., 191

Blacksmith	$ 1.75	. . .	100	114	124	176	181	133
Boilermaker	1.575	. . .	100	127	149	214	222	222
Engineer	2.025	. . .	100	118	123	146	146	146
Laborer	1.025	. . .	100	112	132	183	183	185
Machinist	1.55	. . .	100	126	135	176	194	194
Painter	1.625	. . .	100	129	138	200	169	192
Patternmaker. . .	1.50	. . .	100	133	183	244	250	250
Tinner.	1.50	. . .	100	150	160	227	233	210

TABLE 2—*Continued*

WAGE-SERIES FROM VOL. XX OF THE TENTH CENSUS

NAIL FACTORIES

Pittsburg, Pa., 231

Occupation	Initial Wage p'r Day	1860	1861	1862	1863	1864	1865	1866
Carpenter	$1.125	100	100	100	156	211	233	272
Engineer	1.25	100	100	100	200	200	250	250
Hook-up	1.00	100	100	100	113	194	225	225
Laborer	0.835	100	100	110	135	155	202	225
Machinist	1.375	100	100	127	164	182	227	245
Teamster	1.16⅜	100	100	100	115	115	158	200

TIN AND SHEET IRON WORKS

Newark, N. J., 234

	$							
Coppersmith....	1.75	100	100	114	157	171	200	200
Gasfitter........	1.75	100	100	114	157	171	200	200
Helper	1.50	100	133	133	150	167	200	200
Laborer	1.25	100	140	140	160	160	200	200
Plumber........	1.75	100	100	114	157	171	200	200
Pump-maker....	2.00	100	138	138	150	175	175	175
Tinsmith	1.75	100	100	114	157	171	200	200

MARBLE WORKS

Lafayette, Ind., 235

	$							
Carver	2.50	100	...	...	160	160	160	160
Cutter..........	1.50	100	...	...	167	167	167	167
Letterer	2.50	100	...	...	160	160	160	160
Rubber.........	1.50	100	...	...	133	133	133	133

Troy, N. Y., 236

	$							
Cutter..........	2.00	100	100	100	113	113	113	125
Carver	2.25	100	100	100	111	111	111	133
Engineer	1.50	100	111	133	150	150	133	133
Letterer	2.00	100	100	100	100	113	113	125
Polisher	1.33⅛	100	112	112	112	125	131	125
Rubber.........	1.33⅛	100	112	112	112	112	125	125
Teamster	1.25	100	100	107	120	120	120	120

TABLE 2—*Continued*

WAGE-SERIES FROM VOL. XX OF THE TENTH CENSUS

IRON-MINING

Amenia, N. Y., 253

Occupation	Initial Wage p'r Day	1860	1861	1862	1863	1864	1865	1866
Laborer	$ 0.96	100	96	96	98	120	159	164

Hokendauqua, Pa., 254

	$							
Engineer	1.00	100	...	115	115	175	166	166
Miner	0.80	100	...	125	125	200	188	188

PAPER

Unionville, Conn., 266, 267

	$							
Foreman	4.00	100	100	100	100	167	167	167
Overseer in rag-room...	1.47	100	90	90	114	136	136	170
Back-tender	0.92	100	100	100	109	163	163	163
Bleacher........	1.00	100	100	100	100	150	150	167
Box-maker......	1.17	100	171	171	171	171	171	171
Calenderer, girl.	0.58	100	100	100	100	116	129	159
Carpenter	1.17	100	100	100	100	143	143	171
Counter, girl....	0.67	100	100	100	100	100	124	149
Cutter, girl.....	0.58	100	100	100	100	116	155	155
Engineer's helper	0.92	100	100	100	109	163	163	182
Finisher........	1.50	100	100	100	111	167	167	167
Finisher's helper	1.33	100	100	100	113	169	169	169
Fireman	0.92	100	100	100	109	163	163	217
Folder, girl	0.67	100	100	100	100	134	124	149
Machinist	1.50	100	100	100	117	167	200	200
Machine-tender .	1.50	100	100	100	111	111	133	150
Machine-tender's help..	0.92	100	100	100	109	163	163	163
Millwright......	1.50	100	100	100	117	167	200	200
Laborer	1.00	100	100	100	100	150	150	150
Loftman	1.42	100	118	118	118	158	158	211
Rag engineer ...	1.50	100	100	100	100	111	133	150
Rag-sorter, girl..	0.58	100	100	100	100	108	129	155
Sealer	1.33	100	107	126	126	126	126	150

TABLE 2—*Continued*

WAGE-SERIES FROM VOL. XX OF THE TENTH CENSUS

PAPER

New Jersey, 279

Occupation	Initial Wage p'r Day	1860	1861	1862	1863	1864	1865	1866
	$							
Foreman	2.00	...	100	100	100	100	200	225
Asst. bleacher ..	1.25	...	100	100	100	100	100	100
Back-tender	1.50	...	100	100	100	100	100	100
Bleacher........	1.50	...	100	100	100	100	100	160
Calenderer	1.50	...	100	100	100	100	100	100
Carpenter	1.50	...	100	100	100	100	100	100
Cutter, girl	0.75	...	100	100	100	100	100	100
Finisher	1.50	...	100	100	100	100	100	100
Finisher's helper	1.00	...	100	100	100	100	100	100
Fireman	1.50	...	100	100	100	100	100	100
Laborer	1.25	...	100	100	100	100	100	100
Machinist	1.50	...	100	100	100	100	100	100
Machine-tender .	2.00	...	100	100	100	100	100	100
Machine-tender's helper	1.50	...	100	100	100	100	100	100
Millwright	1.75	...	100	100	100	100	100	100
Rag engineer ...	1.66⅔	...	100	100	100	100	100	100
Rag engineer's helper	1.50	...	100	100	100	100	100	100
Teamster	1.50	...	100	100	100	100	100	100

Niagara Falls, N. Y., 280

Occupation	Initial Wage p'r Day	1860	1861	1862	1863	1864	1865	1866
	$							
Foreman	5.00	100	100	100	100	100	100	100
Overseer in rag-room...	1.75	100	100	100	114	114	114	114
Asst. bleacher ..	1.00	100	100	100	100	100	100	100
Bleacher........	1.50	100	100	100	100	100	100	100
Carpenter	1.75	100	100	100	100	100	100	100
Cutter, girl	0.75	100	100	100	100	100	100	100
Finisher	1.50	100	100	100	117	117	117	117
Fireman	1.50	100	100	100	117	117	117	117
Folder..........	0.75	100	100	100	100	133	133	133
Laborer	1.00	100	100	100	100	100	125	125
Loftman	1.00	100	100	113	125	125	125	125
Machinist	1.75	100	100	114	114	114	114	114
Machine-tender .	1.50	100	117	117	133	133	133	133
Machine-tender's helper	1.00	100	113	113	125	125	125	125
Millwright	1.75	100	100	114	114	114	114	114
Rag engineer ...	1.25	100	100	100	100	100	100	100
Rag engineer's helper	0.875	100	100	100	100	100	100	100
Teamster	1.75	100	100	100	100	100	100	100

TABLE 2—*Continued*

WAGE-SERIES FROM VOL. XX OF THE TENTH CENSUS

PAPER

Evansville, Ind., 272

Occupation	Initial Wage p'r Day	1860	1861	1862	1863	1864	1865	1866
	$							
Engineer	1.50	100	100	100	100	100	100	111
Fireman	1.16⅔	100	100	100	100	100	100	115
Laborer	1.00	100	117	117	117	117	117	117
Machine-tender .	1.66⅔	100	100	100	100	100	100	120
Rag engineer ...	1.50	100	100	100	100	100	100	111
Teamster	1.00	100	100	100	100	100	100	117

Watertown, N. Y., 281, 282

	$							
Overseer in rag-room ...	1.00	100	100	100	113	125	150	150
Calenderer	0.50	100	100	120	130	140	140	160
Finisher, female	0.50	100	100	120	130	140	140	160
Finisher, male ..	1.25	100	100	100	106	120	140	140
Fireman........	1.00	100	100	100	113	125	150	150
Folder..........	0.50	100	100	120	130	140	140	160
Laborer	1.00	100	100	100	113	125	150	150
Loftman........	1.13	100	89	100	111	133	177	155
Machine-tender .	1.50	100	83	100	100	133	167	167
Rag engineer ...	1.13	100	89	111	118	133	166	155
Rag engineer's helper	1.00	100	100	100	113	125	150	150
Rag-sorter	0.40	100	125	150	163	175	175	175

Pennsylvania, 287

	$							
Overseer in rag-room ...	1.16⅔	100	100	100	115	172	172	172
Asst. bleacher ..	0.91⅔	100	100	109	137	182	201	201
Back-tender	0.83½	100	110	100	140	180	200	220
Bleacher........	1.16⅔	100	100	100	143	172	186	172
Calenderer	1.25	100	100	93	133	160	173	160
Cutter, girl	0.50	100	100	100	117	133	167	167
Finisher	1.33½	100	100	100	125	150	162	150
Fireman........	1.00	100	100	100	117	167	183	167
Laborer	0.83⅓	100	100	100	80	130	130	180
Machine-tender .	1.50	100	100	100	144	167	183	167
Rag engineer ...	1.33½	100	100	100	131	150	175	159
Rag-sorter	0.66⅔	100	100	100	126	126	126	126

TABLE 2 — *Continued*

WAGE-SERIES FROM VOL. XX OF THE TENTH CENSUS

PAPER

Wisconsin, 288

Occupation	Initial Wage p'r Day	1860	1861	1862	1863	1864	1865	1866
Foreman........	5.00	100	100	100	100	100	100	100
Bleacher........	1.00	100	100	100	150	150	175	175
Carpenter.......	1.25	100	100	100	120	120	120	140
Cutter, girl......	0.50	100	100	100	100	125	125	125
Finisher	1.50	100	100	100	100	133	133	133
Fireman	1.00	100	100	100	100	150	150	175
Folder..........	0.75	100	100	100	100	133	133	133
Laborer.........	1.00	100	100	100	150	150	150	175
Machine-tender..	1.75	100	100	100	100	100	114	114
Rag engineer....	1.25	100	100	100	140	140	140	140
Rag engineer's helper.........	1.00	100	100	100	150	150	175	175
Rag-sorter.......	0.50	100	100	100	100	100	125	125
Teamster	1.00	100	100	100	150	150	150	175

PIANOS AND ORGANS

Westfield, Mass., 289, 290

Occupation	$	1860	1861	1862	1863	1864	1865	1866
Action-maker....	2.00	100	100	100	100	100	125	125
Misc. (all others)	1.75	100	100	100	100	100	129	129
Tuner..........	3.50	100	100	100	100	100	114	114
Voicer	3.50	100	100	100	100	100	114	114

New York, N. Y., 292

Occupation	$	1860	1861	1862	1863	1864	1865	1866
Foreman........	3.66⅔	100	100	109	114	136	284	284
Action-maker ...	2.16⅔	100	92	100	108	115	115	123
Action-regulator.	2.16⅔	100	92	100	108	115	115	115
Carver..........	1.83⅓	100	91	100	118	127	127	127
Case-maker	1.83⅓	100	91	100	118	127	127	127
Clerk..........	3.33⅓	100	100	110	125	125	125	150
Finisher	2.16⅔	100	92	100	108	115	115	115
Fly finisher	2.16⅔	100	92	100	108	115	115	115
Key maker......	2.00	100	92	100	108	117	117	117
Laborer.........	1.50	100	89	100	111	111	122	122
Salesmaker......	3.33⅓	100	110	150	200	200	200	225
Sound-board maker.........	2.16⅔	100	92	100	115	123	123	123
Tone regulator..	2.50	100	93	100	107	113	113	113
Top-maker......	2.50	100	93	100	107	113	113	113
Tuner..........	2.33⅓	100	93	100	107	114	114	114
Varnisher.......	1.88⅓	100	91	100	109	127	127	127

TABLE 2 — *Continued*

WAGE-SERIES FROM VOL. XX OF THE TENTH CENSUS

PIANOS AND ORGANS

Concord, N. H., 291

Occupation	Initial Wage p'r Day	1860	1861	1862	1863	1864	1865	1866
	$							
Action-maker ...	1.75	100	114	114	114	143	143	143
Case-maker	1.75	100	100	100	100	114	114	114
Finisher	1.75	100	100	100	100	114	114	114
Mill hand.......	1.65	100	106	106	106	121	121	121
Tuner	2.00	100	113	113	113	138	138	138
Varnisher.......	1.75	100	100	100	100	114	114	114

PINS

Waterbury, Conn., 293

	$							
Girl	0.58½	100	100	100	143	143	156	156
Laborer	1.00	100	100	100	125	125	150	150
Mechanic	1.50	100	100	100	133	133	150	150

POTTERY

East Liverpool, O., 300

	$							
Boy	0.30	100	100	...	167	167	167	167
Clay-maker	1.50	100	100	...	133	133	133	133
Dipper	1.50	100	100	...	133	133	133	133
Dish-maker.....	1.50	100	100	...	150	150	150	150
Fireman	1.50	100	100	...	167	167	167	167
Girl	0.30	100	100	...	167	167	167	167
Jiggerman	2.00	100	100	...	125	125	125	125
Kilnman........	1.25	100	100	...	160	160	160	160
Laborer	0.75	100	100	...	250	250	250	250
Mold-maker.....	2.00	100	100	...	150	150	150	150
Packer	1.50	100	100	...	167	167	167	167
Presser	1.50	100	100	...	133	133	133	133
Sagger-maker...	1.50	100	100	...	167	167	167	167
Woman.........	0.40	100	100	...	163	163	163	163

Liverpool Township, O., 303

	$							
Foreman........	52.00[1]	...	100	100	100	100	113	113
Brick-molder ...	1.50	...	100	100	100	113	117	117
Carpenter	1.25	...	100	120	120	120	140	140
Engineer	1.10	...	100	100	100	114	114	114
Laborer	1.00	...	100	100	120	125	140	150
Miner	1.00	...	100	100	110	125	135	135

[1] Per month.

TABLE 2 — *Continued*

WAGE-SERIES FROM VOL. XX OF THE TENTH CENSUS

POTTERY

East Liverpool, O., 301, 302

Occupation	Initial Wage p'r Day	1860	1861	1862	1863	1864	1865	1866
	$							
Boy.............	0.33	100	100	...	152	152	182	182
Clay-maker.....	1.50	100	100	...	133	133	167	167
Dipper.........	1.50	100	100	...	150	150	167	167
Dish-maker.....	2.00	100	100	...	113	113	125	125
Fireman........	1.50	100	100	...	167	167	200	200
Girl............	0.33	100	100	...	121	121	152	152
Handler.........	2.00	100	100	...	113	113	125	125
Kilnman........	1.25	100	100	...	160	160	180	180
Laborer.........	1.00	100	100	...	150	150	175	175
Mold-maker	2.00	100	100	...	125	125	175	175
Packer..........	1.50	100	100	...	150	150	167	167
Presser.........	1.50	100	100	...	133	133	150	150
Sagger-maker...	1.50	100	100	...	167	167	183	183
Thrower........	3.00	100	100	...	117	117	133	133
Turner..........	2.00	100	100	...	113	113	125	125
Warehouseman..	1.25	100	100	...	160	160	160	160
Woman.........	0.50	100	100	...	150	150	160	160

Newark, N. J., 302

	$							
Laborer.........	1.00	...	100	100	150	150	150	150

TANNERIES

Binghamton, N. Y., 312

	$							
Beam hand......	1.00	100	100	100	125	150	165	175
Currier	1.70	100	118	129	141	153	153	153
Finisher........	1.25	100	120	128	140	160	140	140
Handlerman.....	1.00	100	100	112	150	160	160	160
Shaver..........	1.70	100	118	129	141	153	153	153
Striker..........	1.25	100	120	128	140	160	140	140
Teamster........	0.88	100	100	114	127	148	142	142
Yard hand	1.00	100	100	112	150	160	160	160

New York, N. Y., 313

	$							
Foreman........	125.00[1]	100	100	100	100	100	100	100
Laborer.........	1.375	100	100	100	100	100	100	100

[1] Per month.

TABLE 2—*Continued*

WAGE-SERIES FROM VOL. XX OF THE TENTH CENSUS

TANNERIES

Lancaster, N. Y., 314

Occupation	Initial Wage p'r Day	1860	1861	1862	1863	1864	1865	1866
	$							
Bark-grinder....	0.75	100	100	167	183	183	200	200
Beam hand.....	0.875	100	100	171	186	186	200	200
Engineer.......	0.875	100	100	171	186	186	200	200
Handlerman....	0.81	100	100	169	185	185	201	201
Laborer........	0.75	100	100	167	183	183	200	200
Roller..........	0.81	100	100	185	201	201	216	216
Teamster.......	0.875	100	100	171	186	186	200	200
Watchman......	0.875	100	100	171	186	186	200	200
Yard hand......	0.81	100	100	154	170	170	185	185

Sanford, N. Y., 316

	$							
Foreman........	2.24	100	100	100	107	107	107	121
Bark-grinder....	0.75	100	100	107	133	133	133	133
Beam hand.....	0.77	100	104	104	149	164	175	...
Currier.........	0.72	100	100	104	132	139	139	153
Engineer.......	1.00	100	100	108	135	142	154	157
Handlerman.....	0.76	100	100	100	132	132	164	164
Laborer........	0.73	100	100	105	158	169	173	185
Roller..........	0.88	100	102	108	125	142	159	159
Teamster.......	0.70	100	100	107	107	121	136	136
Watchman......	0.90	100	100	111	139	139	167	194
Yard hand......	0.76	100	100	100	132	132	164	164

Pike Pond, N. Y., 316

	$							
Foreman........	25.00[1]	...	100	100	100	160	180	180
Beam hand.....	0.77	100	...	100	...	130	149	...
Handlerman....	0.73	100	...	105	...	137	158	...
Laborer........	0.69	...	100	100	100	145	167	167
Roller..........	0.85	100	...	113	...	118	135	...
Teamster........	0.73	100	...	105	...	137	158	...
Watchman......	0.65	100	...	...	...	154	177	...
Yard hand......	0.69	100	...	112	...	145	167	...

[1] Per month.

TABLE 2—*Continued*

WAGE-SERIES FROM VOL. XX OF THE TENTH CENSUS

TANNERIES

Wellsville, N. Y., 318

Occupation	Initial Wage p'r Day	1860	1861	1862	1863	1864	1865	1866
	$							
Foreman	50.00[1]	100	100	150	150	150	200	200
Bark-grinder	0.75	100	100	133	133	167	167	200
Beam hand	1.00	100	100	100	100	125	125	150
Engineer	1.25	100	100	100	100	100	120	120
Handlerman	0.75	100	100	100	133	167	167	200
Laborer	0.75	100	100	133	167	167	200	200
Roller	1.00	100	100	100	100	125	125	150
Teamster	1.00	100	100	100	125	125	150	150
Watchman	1.25	100	100	100	100	100	120	120
Yard hand	1.00	100	100	100	100	125	125	150

Oneida, N. Y., 315

Occupation	Initial Wage	1860	1861	1862	1863	1864	1865	1866
	$							
Foreman	40.00[1]	100	100	100	113	113	105	113
Bark-grinder	0.92½	100	100	100	124	124	124	145
Beam hands	1.15	100	100	100	117	117	107	117
Engineer	1.15	100	100	100	117	117	107	117
Laborer	0.92½	100	100	100	124	124	124	124
Yard hand	0.92⅜	100	100	100	124	124	124	124

Cincinnati, O., 318, 319

Occupation	Initial Wage	1860	1861	1862	1863	1864	1865	1866
	$							
Bark-grinders	1.00	100	100	83	116	133	183	183
Beam hand	1.25	100	100	93	120	160	166	173
Currier	1.50	100	111	100	117	133	144	155
Finisher	1.33	100	113	106	113	162	150	162
Handlerman	1.08	100	100	100	116	185	185	216
Engineer	1.58	100	105	116	137	147	158	168
Laborer	1.00	100	100	83	100	166	166	166
Shaver	1.66	100	110	100	110	140	151	160
Watchman	1.16	100	100	72	115	158	172	172
Yard hand	1.08	100	100	100	116	185	185	185

[1] Per month.

TABLE 2—*Continued*

WAGE-SERIES FROM VOL. XX OF THE TENTH CENSUS

CARPETS

Massachusetts, 324

Occupation	Initial Wage p'r Day	1860	1861	1862	1863	1864	1865	1866
Carder	$ 0.39	...	100	103	105	133	177	187
Carpenter	1.50	100	89	100	100	117	133	133
Dyer	1.38	100	100	87	109	115	127	127
Finisher (earnings for Dec.)..	0.57	...	100	100	102	123	191	181
Laborer.........	0.83	100	100	90	111	171	181	181
Loom-fixer	1.38	100	100	91	100	127	139	163
Machinist.......	1.50	100	89	100	109	133	150	150
Pickerman......	0.83	100	100	90	100	161	171	181
Reeler	0.45	...	100	98	109	156	202	216
Spinner.........	0.49	...	100	100	98	127	198	204
Spinner jack....	0.73	...	100	100	110	144	160	159
Spooler	0.43	...	100	88	102	140	237	226
Teamster	1.25	100	100	100	106	120	134	134
Twister	0.46	...	100	109	107	135	196	207
Warper	0.51	...	100	127	122	163	241	249
Weaver	0.52	...	100	115	125	165	229	229
Winder	0.37	...	100	100	103	132	224	230
Wool sorter (wages for Dec.)	1.10	100	105	114	127	168	182	182

COTTON MANUFACTURE

Willimantic, Conn., 333

	$							
Carding overseer	50.00[1]	100	100	120	120	130	266	266
Spinn'g overseer.	50.00[1]	100	100	100	110	130	156	182
Back boy	0.33⅛	100	100	100	100	175	175	175
Card-stripper ...	0.83⅛	100	100	100	100	150	150	150
Carpenter	1.50	100	100	100	100	133	167	167
Drawer	0.58⅛	100	100	100	100	123	143	143
Grinder.........	1.25	100	100	100	100	100	113	120
Laborer	1.00	100	100	100	125	150	150	150
Machinist.......	1.50	100	100	100	133	150	167	183
Mule-spinner....	0.83⅛	100	100	100	100	150	150	160
Painter	1.50	100	100	100	100	100	117	133
Picker	0.83⅛	100	100	100	100	140	140	150
Second hand....	1.25	100	107	120	140	140	147	147
Speeder.........	0.50	100	100	100	100	133	144	178
Yard hand......	1.00	100	100	100	125	150	150	150

[1] Per month.

TABLE 2—*Continued*

WAGE-SERIES FROM VOL. XX OF THE TENTH CENSUS

COTTON MANUFACTURE

Connecticut, 336

Occupation	Initial Wage p'r Day	1860	1861	1862	1863	1864	1865	1866
Overseers, card'g, spinn'g, weav'g	$54.00 [1]	100	100	100	106	106	111	128
Back boy	0.25	100	100	100	108	108	108	133
Baler	0.83⅓	100	100	100	120	120	120	140
Card-stripper	0.75	100	100	100	100	100	100	155
Carpenter	1.50	100	100	83	83	100	117	150
Cloth trimmer	0.41⅔	100	100	100	108	120	133	151
Doffer	0.475	100	100	112	123	123	123	149
Drawer	0.41⅔	100	100	108	120	120	120	160
Dresser	1.29	100	100	100	87	116	136	174
Folder	0.875	100	100	100	133	133	153	171
Frame-spinner	0.33⅓	100	100	104	133	133	133	179
Grinder	1.16⅔	100	100	100	100	100	100	136
Laborer	1.00	100	100	100	83	100	125	133
Machinist	1.50	100	100	100	94	117	150	167
Mule-spinner	1.05	100	84	84	89	110	127	167
Painters	1.33⅛	100	100	100	100	100	106	125
Picker	0.75	100	100	100	89	89	89	155
Second hand	1.00	100	100	100	100	100	125	150
Speeder	0.50	100	100	100	100	120	150	200
Spin'g section h'd	1.08⅛	100	100	100	115	138	161	184
Spooler	0.45	100	100	100	100	100	100	122
Warper	0.54	100	100	100	108	108	108	139
Weaver	0.77	100	100	97	91	119	130	162
W'v'g section h'd	1.33⅛	100	94	87	87	112	131	150
Web-drawer	0.80	100	94	88	83	94	115	130
Yard hand	0.83⅛	100	100	100	100	120	150	160

Evansville, Ind., 341

In cloth r'm, fem.	1.00	....	100	100	100	100	100	100
In cl. room, male	1.50	....	100	100	100	100	100.	100
Repairer	1.75	....	100	100	100	100	100	100
Weaver, female	1.05	....	100	100	100	100	143	143

[1] Per month.

TABLE 2 — *Continued*

WAGE-SERIES FROM VOL. XX OF THE TENTH CENSUS

COTTON MANUFACTURE

Connecticut, 338

Occupation	Initial Wage p'r Day	1860	1861	1862	1863	1864	1865	1866
Overseers, card'g, spinn'g, weav'g	$ 41.00[1]	100	100	104	99	102	124	134
Back boy	0.25	100	100	100	100	100	112	116
Baler	1.08$\frac{1}{3}$	100	100	100	107	107	115	123
Card-stripper ...	0.83$\frac{1}{3}$	100	100	100	100	130	130	140
Carpenter	1.16$\frac{2}{3}$	100	100	115	115	121	172	186
Cloth-trimmer ..	0.46	100	100	109	109	109	127	182
Doffer	0.37	100	100	101	101	107	124	146
Drawer	0.41$\frac{2}{3}$	100	100	120	120	141	160	181
Folder	1.08$\frac{1}{3}$	100	100	100	100	100	115	115
Laborer	1.00	100	100	100	100	108	125	125
Machinist	1.66$\frac{2}{3}$	100	100	95	95	95	125	125
Painters	1.16$\frac{2}{3}$	100	100	107	107	107	121	136
Picker	0.83$\frac{1}{3}$	100	100	100	100	120	130	140
Speeder	0.66$\frac{2}{3}$	100	100	100	100	113	113	138
Spinner	0.70$\frac{5}{6}$	100	100	106	111	123	148	153
Spin'g section h'd	0.66$\frac{2}{3}$	100	100	113	126	150	188	226
Spooler	0.45	100	100	100	100	111	148	148
Warper	0.75	100	100	100	100	122	133	167
Weaver	0.91$\frac{2}{3}$	100	100	100	100	100	109	119
W'v'g section h'd	1.16$\frac{2}{3}$	100	100	143	107	107	115	143
Web-drawer	0.83$\frac{1}{3}$	100	100	100	100	100	120	140

Christiana Hundred, Del., 340

Carpenter	$ 1.50	100	100	100	100	123	167	167

Chicopee Falls, Mass., 347

Overseers, card'g, spinn'g, weav'g	$ 42.81[1]	....	100	100	103	117	126	145
Card-stripper ...	0.64	....	100	100	117	176	179	195
Drawer	0.41	....	100	98	121	121	129	178
Grinder	0.97	....	100	99	114	136	148	169
Picker	0.72	....	100	90	104	144	175	175
Slasher	1.08	....	100	96	127	144	156	181
Spinner, female .	0.51$\frac{1}{3}$	....	100	100	115	126	135	195
Spin'g section h'd	0.82	....	100	121	141	178	188	212
Warper, girl	0.52	....	100	103	114	126	135	178
Weaver, girl	0.565	....	100	86	104	136	155	219

[1] Per month.

TABLE 2— *Continued*

WAGE-SERIES FROM VOL. XX OF THE TENTH CENSUS

COTTON MANUFACTURE

Maine, 343

Occupation	Initial Wage p'r Day	1860	1861	1862	1863	1864	1865	1866
Overseers, card'g, spinn'g, weav'g	$ 65.00[1]	100	100	102	102	110	120	120
Back boy	0.30	100	83	83	83	110	110	110
Card-stripper ...	0.75	100	100	100	100	133	167	167
Carpenter	1.33	100	125	102	102	119	159	159
Dresser	1.00	100	100	83	83	88	115	115
Frame-spinner ..	0.54	100	107	96	96	107	135	135
Grinder	1.08	100	100	93	93	108	146	146
Machinist	1.50	100	100	90	90	110	155	155
Mule-spinner ...	1.22	100	99	82	82	119	116	116
Painter	1.50	100	...	58	58	...	139	139
Picker	0.75	100	100	100	100	133	167	167
Second hand ...	1.50	100	100	77	77	112	133	133
Spooler	0.54	100	96	100	100	109	143	143
Weaver	0.75	100	80	84	84	107	120	120
Web-drawer	0.63	...	100	102	102	121	108	108
Warper	0.65	100	108	92	92	98	108	108
Yard hand	1.00	100	100	80	80	106	140	140

Concord, N. H., 355, 356

	$							
Carding overseer	32.00[1]	100	100	94	94	113	150	225
Spinning overse'r	34.00[1]	100	94	88	88	124	147	176
Weaving overse'r	38.00[1]	100	95	84	84	116	126	158
Back boy	0.25	100	100	100	100	100	120	120
Card-stripper ...	0.70	100	100	95	95	119	179	179
Cloth-trimmer ..	0.46	100	100	100	100	109	136	163
Day watchman..	1.00	100	100	92	92	116	133	150
Doffer	0.25	100	100	100	100	100	120	120
Drawer	0.45	100	100	100	100	111	148	148
Dresser	1.33½	100	100	100	100	106	125	150
Frame-spinner ..	0.46	100	100	100	100	109	117	182
Grinder	0.95	100	100	96	96	123	158	175
Laborer	1.00	100	100	92	92	100	100	125
Loom-fixer	0.96	100	100	86	86	130	156	182
Machinist	1.58½	100	105	105	105	116	142	158
Machinist (wood)	1.33½	100	112	112	112	119	131	187

[1] Per month.

TABLE 2—*Continued*

WAGE-SERIES FROM VOL. XX OF THE TENTH CENSUS

COTTON MANUFACTURE

Massachusetts, 350-52

Occupation	Inital Wage p'r Day	1860	1861	1862	1863	1864	1865	1866
	$							
Carding overseer	3.00	100	100	100	100	100	104	117
Spin'ing overseer	3.00	100	100	100	100	100	104	108
Weav'ng overseer	3.00	100	100	100	100	100	104	133
Back boy	0.29	100	109	109	109	112	136	147
Card-stripper ...	0.83	100	100	100	100	135	163	187
Carpenter	1.75	100	86	86	100	114	129	134
Cloth-trimmer ..	0.47	100	100	100	100	100	100	100
Doffer	0.475	100	100	84	87	105	132	158
Drawer..........	0.53	100	96	96	96	113	127	156
Drawer-in	0.80	100	115	111	104	103	225	150
Dresser.........	1.74	100	106	113	101	105	124	130
Dyer	1.00	100	100	100	100	132	160	175
Frame-spinner..	0.53	100	108	104	109	111	130	168
Grinder	1.25	100	100	100	100	112	128	140
Laborer	1.00	100	100	100	100	125	150	163
Lap-head tender	0.75	100	100	100	100	133	167	200
Machinist	1.40	100	110	102	111	119	142	168
Mule-spinner ...	0.40	100	125	130	118	145	153	203
Painters	1.75	100	100	100	100	103	114	120
Picker..........	1.085	100	88	88	98	122	134	152
Quiller	0.57	100	96	104	100	128	131	160
Ruler...........	0.66	100	120	145	132	130	129	149
R.W. head tender	0.75	100	100	100	100	120	167	187
Second hand....	1.625	100	100	100	92	115	138	162
Scrubber	0.55	100	100	105	105	115	109	152
Speeder	0.60	100	98	98	98	113	129	154
Sweeper	0.55	100	100	105	105	115	109	152
Warper.........	0.73	100	134	130	108	101	142	144
Watchman	1.16⅜	100	100	100	100	107	115	134
Weaver	0.94	100	106	96	72	97	118	153
W'v'g sect'n hand	1.52	100	109	95	96	111	116	126
Winder.........	0.59	100	115	136	115	134	159	176
Yard hand......	1.00	100	100	100	100	125	150	163
Yardman	1.00	100	100	100	100	125	150	163

TABLE 2—*Continued*

WAGE-SERIES FROM VOL. XX OF THE TENTH CENSUS

COTTON MANUFACTURE

Concord, N. H., 355, 356

Occupation	Initial Wage p'r Day	1860	1861	1862	1863	1864	1865	1866
	$							
Mule-spinner ...	1.08⅛	100	100	100	100	115	153	184
Night watchman	1.16⅔	100	100	93	115	115	129	143
Picker..........	0.83⅛	100	100	100	100	140	160	160
Second hand....	1.00	100	100	92	92	100	125	125
Speeder	0.50	100	100	100	100	117	142	167
Spin. section h'd	0.92	100	100	100	100	109	136	136
Spooler.........	0.41⅔	100	111	111	111	120	141	160
Warper.........	0.50	100	117	133	133	150	167	200
Weaver.........	0.625	100	106	106	106	120	134	174
W'v'g section h'd	0.92	100	100	100	100	109	136	136
Web-drawer	0.62⅛	100	100	94	94	120	146	154
Yard hand......	1.00	100	100	92	92	100	100	125

Dover, N. H., 356, 357

Occupation	Initial Wage	1860	1861	1862	1863	1864	1865	1866
	$							
Carding overseer	66.00[1]	100	89	73	...	91	109	127
Spin'ing overseer	66.00[1]	100	73	73	...	91	109	127
Weavi'g overseer	48.00[1]	100	88	100	...	125	150	163
Back boy	0.26	100	104	104	...	115	146	192
Card-stripper ...	0.83	100	81	90	...	151	151	160
Carpenter	1.50	100	89	93	117	133	133	158
Doffer	0.32	100	84	78	...	103	94	172
Drawer.........	0.24	100	88	88	...	104	96	125
Dresser.........	0.56	100	89	80	...	95	104	179
Frame-spinner ..	0.35	100	89	71	...	94	94	160
Grinder	1.08	100	82	93	...	139	139	155
Machinist	1.50	100	89	93	117	133	133	158
Mule-spinner ...	0.85	100	100	87	...	101	124	176
Painters	1.42	100	94	94	94	141	141	141
Picker..........	0.75	100	89	100	...	167	167	177
Second hand....	1.25	100	90	100	...	120	120	160
Speeder	0.39	100	95	85	...	103	100	131
Spooler.........	0.19	100	121	84	...	137	253	247
Warper.........	0.42	100	95	69	...	81	107	138
Weaver.........	0.36	100	86	75	...	94	100	258
Web-drawer	0.39	100	92	87	...	87	113	164
Yard hand	0.83	100	100	100	120	151	151	181

[1] Per month.

TABLE 2—*Continued*

WAGE-SERIES FROM VOL. XX OF THE TENTH CENSUS

COTTON MANUFACTURE

Massachusetts, 352, 353

Occupation	Initial Wage p'r Day	1860	1861	1862	1863	1864	1865	1866
	$							
Overseer, spinn'g	45 00¹	100	100	100	100	100	122	122
Dresser.........	1.5575	100	104	104	104	104	123	123
Machinist	1.73¼	100	100	100	100	100	122	122
Spinner	0.615	100	100	100	100	106	106	106
Spooler.........	0.5575	100	110	110	110	110	117	117
Warper..........	0 5575	100	110	110	110	110	117	117
Yard hand......	1.15⅓	100	100	100	100	100	100	100

New Hampshire, 358

Occupation	$	1860	1861	1862	1863	1864	1865	1866
Overseers, card'g, spinn'g weav'g	65.00¹	100	100	100	100	100	120	120
Back boy	0.35	100	100	100	100	100	117	117
Baler...........	1.00	100	100	100	100	117	133	137
Card-stripper ...	0.83	100	96	96	96	100	160	160
Carpenter	1.58	100	100	100	100	100	111	111
Cloth-trimmer ..	0.56	100	100	100	100	120	134	141
Doffer	0.50	100	100	100	100	120	170	200
Drawer.........	0.50	100	100	100	100	108	150	184
Dresser.........	0.83	100	100	100	100	121	121	193
Folder..........	1.00	100	100	100	100	117	125	133
Frame-spinner ..	0.54	100	100	100	100	100	185	185
Grinder	1.16⅔	100	100	100	100	107	129	136
Laborer	1.08	100	100	100	100	100	116	116
Machinist	2.25	100	100	100	100	100	89	89
Mule-spinner ...	1.00	100	100	100	100	100	142	142
Painters	1.33	100	100	100	113	126	126	126
Picker..........	0.87	100	103	109	109	129	153	153
Second hand....	1.50	100	100	100	100	100	100	133
Speeder	0.83	100	66	72	72	96	120	133
Spin. section ha'd	1.125	100	100	100	100	111	126	126
Spooler.........	0.54	100	130	130	130	130	170	170
Warper.........	0.54	100	100	111	111	111	207	207
Weaver.........	0.92	100	100	89	89	114	138	138
W'v'g section h'd	1.33	100	100	100	100	100	119	132
Web-drawer	0.83	100	84	84	84	90	120	139

¹ Per month.

TABLE 2—*Continued*

WAGE-SERIES FROM VOL. XX OF THE TENTH CENSUS

COTTON MANUFACTURE

Cohoes, N. Y., 361, 362

Occupation	Initial Wage p'r Day	1860	1861	1862.	1863	1864	1865	1866
Overseer, carding	$58.50[1]	100	100	100	100	122	133	178
Overseer, cloth-room	1.125	100	100	100	100	100	133	156
Overseer, spin'g..	55.25[1]	100	100	100	100	112	112	129
Overseer, weav'g.	65.00[1]	100	100	100	100	110	120	140
Back boy	0.30	100	100	100	100	150	167	183
Baler	0.80	100	100	100	100	110	118	125
Card-stripper....	0.70	100	100	100	104	108	125	125
Carpenter	1.62	100	100	100	100	108	123	139
Cloth-trimmer...	0.50	100	100	100	100	108	116	125
Drawer	0.625	100	100	100	104	106	106	133
Doffer	0.50	100	100	100	112	112	112	124
Dresser	2.00	100	100	100	100	113	125	125
Folder	0.50	100	100	100	100	108	116	125
Frame-spinner...	0.56	100	100	100	111	111	111	125
Grinder	0.875	100	100	100	100	111	135	157
Laborer	0.75	100	100	100	133	150	167	167
Lap-boy	0.33	100	100	100	115	127	136	152
Lapper	0.70	100	100	100	100	107	143	196
Machinist	2.00	100	100	100	100	113	125	138
Painters	1.50	100	100	100	100	117	133	150
Pressman	1.00	100	100	100	100	113	125	138
Piecer-mule	1.00	100	100	100	100	155	170	180
Picker	.7875	100	100	100	100	111	142	174
Mule-spinner ...	1.00	100	100	100	100	155	170	180
Second hand....	1.3125	100	100	100	106	138	133	157
Slubber	.65	100	100	100	115	115	115	154
Spreader	.50	100	100	100	125	140	150	200
Speeder	.65	100	100	100	115	115	115	173
Spinning section-hand	1.50	100	100	100	100	117	133	133
Spooler	.62	100	100	100	110	110	110	121
Watchman	.8375	100	100	100	112	123	145	164
Warper	.70	100	100	100	89	107	114	131
Weaving section-hand	1.375	100	100	100	100	118	127	145
Yard hand	.75	100	100	100	133	150	167	167

[1]Per month.

TABLE 2—*Continued*

WAGE-SERIES FROM VOL. XX OF THE TENTH CENSUS

COTTON MANUFACTURE

Philadelphia, Pa., 364, 365

Occupation	Initial Wage p'r Day	1860	1861	1862	1863	1864	1865	1866
	$							
Overseer, carding	80.00[1]	100	100	100	100	100	100	100
Overseer, spinn'g.	60.00[1]	100	100	100	100	100	100	100
Overseer, weavi'g	60.00[1]	100	100	100	100	100	100	100
Folder..........	1.50	100	100	100	100	100	100	100
Grinder.........	1.50	100	100	100	100	100	100	100
Laborer.........	1.50	100	100	100	100	100	100	100
Machinist.......	2.50	100	100	100	100	100	100	100
Mule-spinner....	2.50	100	100	100	100	100	100	100
Picker..........	1.50	100	100	100	100	100	100	100
Second hand	1.50	100	100	100	100	100	100	100
Spinning section-hand	1.66⅔	100	100	100	100	100	100	100
Weaver	1.50	100	100	100	100	100	100	100
Web-drawer	1.50	100	100	100	100	100	100	100

WOOLEN INDUSTRY

Indianapolis, Ind., 385, 386

	$							
Overseers, different departm'ts	39.00[1]	100	111	133	133	167	200	200
Carder	1.75	100	114	114	129	143	143	143
Carder, boy	.75	100	100	100	100	100	100	100
Dyer	1.50	100	100	133	133	200	200	200
Dyer's helper....	1.00	100	100	125	125	150	150	150
Engineer	1.50	100	100	100	100	133	133	167
Finisher	1.50	100	108	108	108	167	200	200
Fuller	1.50	100	111	133	133	150	150	150
Gigger..........	1.25	100	100	120	120	120	120	120
Laborer	1.00	100	100	100	100	150	200	200
Loom-fixer	1.66	100	100	120	120	120	151	151
Picker, boy......	.75	100	100	100	100	100	100	100
Scourer.........	1.25	100	100	120	120	120	120	120
Shearer.........	1.50	100	111	133	133	150	150	150
Spinner.........	1.25	100	120	160	160	160	200	200
Warper	1.25	100	100	100	100	100	100	100
Weaver, girl	.66⅔	100	100	100	150	150	150	150
Wool-sorter	1.25	100	120	120	120	133	133	133

[1]Per month.

TABLE 2—*Continued*
WAGE-SERIES FROM VOL. XX OF THE TENTH CENSUS — WOOLEN INDUSTRY
Massachusetts, 392, 393

Occupation	Initial Wage p'r Day	1860	1861	1862	1863	1864	1865	1866
	$							
Overseer, carding No. 1	1.75	100	100	100	71	143	200	180
Overseer, carding No. 2	1.75	100	100	100	143	114	157	142
Overseer, carding No. 3	3.00	100	100	100	133	133	133	133
Overseer, dressing No. 1	1.75	100	100	100	114	157	214	··214
Overseer, dressing No. 2	1.75	100	100	100	114	157	214	214
Overseer, dyeing.	1200.00¹	100	100	100	150	150	150	150
Overseer, finish'g	3.00	100	100	100	108	117	133	133
Overseer, fulling.	2.00	100	100	100	125	150	150	150
Overseer, gigging	3.00	100	100	100	108	117	133	150
Overseer, repairs No. 1	2.00	100	100	100	138	175	175	200
Overseer, repairs No. 2	2.00	100	100	100	125	150	150	175
Overseer, spinning No. 1	1.75	100	100	100	114	157	157	157
Overseer, spinning No. 2	1.75	100	100	100	114	129	171	171
Overseer, spinning No. 3	1.75	100	100	100	129	171	171	200
Overseer, waste sorting No. 1	1.00	100	100	100	120	150	150	150
Overseer weaving No. 1	2.25	100	100	100	111	133	167	167
Overseer weaving No. 2	2.25	100	100	100	111	133	167	167
Overseer, yard	2.50	100	100	120	65	80	90	100
Carder	1.75	100	100	100	71	114	143	157
Carder, boy	0.68	100	79	81	96	113	132	138
Dyer	0.91	100	100	100	108	145	164	165
Finisher, female.	0.48½	100	106	115	113	123	124	180
Finisher, male	0.88	100	103	102	105	135	153	161
Fuller	0.81	100	98	99	107	152	154	157
Gigger	0.84	100	100	102	110	151	164	168
Laborer	1.75	100	100	114	77	95	109	115
Picker	0.81	100	91	100	105	142	164	168
Repairer	1.38	100	98	101	116	138	159	159
Spinner	0.78	100	109	121	122	154	199	221
Teamster	1.75	100	100	114	77	95	108	115
Warper	.8025	100	119	114	117	118	143	214
Waste-sorter	0.34	100	100	103	126	156	144	159
Watchman	1.00	100	100	100	106	132	154	154
Weaver, female..	0.69⅜	100	109	103	100	102	133	179
Wool-sorter	1.17	100	99	101	113	138	157	171

¹Per year.

TABLE 2 — *Continued*

WAGE-SERIES FROM VOL. XX OF THE TENTH CENSUS

WOOLEN INDUSTRY

Dover, Me., 389

Occupation	Initial Wage p'r Day	1860	1861	1862	1863	1864	1865	1866
Foreman	$ 39.00[1]	100	100	100	115	141	154	154
Overseers, different departm'ts.	39.00[1]	100	100	100	100	141	150	150
Carder, boy.....	0.50	100	100	110	120	150	180	180
Carpenter	1.33	100	100	113	113	150	169	169
Dyer	1.33	100	100	113	113	132	141	141
Dyer's helper ...	1.00	100	100	110	115	125	150	150
Fuller	1 00	100	100	105	110	125	150	175	175
Laborer	1.00	100	100	100	110	133	150	150
Loom-fixer......	1.00	100	110	133	133	133	150	150
Machinist	1.33	100	100	113	113	150	169	169
Picker..........	0.86	100	100	105	116	116	116	116
Scourer	1.00	100	100	110	115	125	150	150
Spinner	1.30	100	100	100	115	135	140	138
Spooler	0.46	100	100	100	109	163	174	163
Teamster	1.00	100	100	100	110	133	150	150
Warper, female..	0.67	100	100	100	100	137	149	149
Weaver, female..	0.70	100	107	107	114	136	143	143
Wool-sorter	1.00	100	100	100	125	140	155	160

Fitchburg, Mass., 390

	$							
Superintendent ..	83.33[1]	100	100	100	100	100	100	100
Overseers of different dep'tm'ts.	42.25[1]	100	100	108	115	128	136	138
Carder..........	1.25	100	106	106	112	120	120	120
Carder, boy......	0.60	100	100	108	117	133	133	133
Dyer's helper....	0.75	100	100	127	133	177	177	177
Fuller	0.92	100	100	100	100	145	145	145
Gigger	0.75	100	100	127	133	177	177	177
Loom-fixers	1.25	100	100	100	100	120	120	120
Picker, boy......	0.60	100	100	108	117	133	133	133
Spinner	0.85	100	100	104	129	176	206	206
Spooler, girl	0.58	100	103	103	103	108	122	122
Warper	1.25	100	112	112	110	140	140	140
Weaver, female..	0.75	100	100	100	107	107	120	127
Wool-sorter	1.80	100	100	100	125	138	138	138

[1] Per month.

TABLE 2 — *Continued*

WAGE-SERIES FROM VOL. XX OF THE TENTH CENSUS

WOOLEN INDUSTRY

Illinois, 384

Occupation	Initial Wage p'r Day	1860	1861	1862	1863	1864	1865	1866
Superintendent .	$65.00[1]	100	100	100	100	120	120	160
Foreman	58.50[1]	100	100	111	111	111	111	111
Carder	0.50	100	100	100	100	100	120	120
Engineer	2.25	100	100	100	100	100	100	100
Spinner	0.50	100	100	100	100	100	120	120
Spooler	0.50	100	100	100	100	100	100	100
Weaver	1.00	100	100	100	100	100	125	125
Wool-sorter	2.00	100	125	125	125	125	125	125

New York, 398, 399

Occupation	Initial Wage	1860	1861	1862	1863	1864	1865	1866
Superintendent .	$160.00[1]	100	100	100	100	100	188	188
Foreman	100.00[1]	100	100	100	100	100	200	200
Overseers, different departm'nts	53.56[1]	100	100	100	100	100	149	149
Carder	1.25	100	100	100	100	100	120	120
Carder, girl	0.42	100	100	100	100	100	137	137
Carpenter	1.25	100	100	100	100	100	140	140
Dyer	1.50	100	100	100	100	100	133	133
Dyer's helper....	0.70	100	100	100	100	100	179	179
Engineer	2.00	100	100	100	100	100	200	200
Finisher........	.5375	100	100	100	100	100	182	182
Fuller	0.75	100	100	100	100	100	200	200
Gigger..........	0.70	100	100	100	100	100	179	179
Laborer	0.75	100	100	100	100	100	167	167
Loom-fixer......	1.50	100	100	100	100	100	117	117
Machinist	1.25	100	100	100	100	100	140	140
Picker..........	0.625	100	100	100	100	100	200	200
Scourer.........	0.75	100	100	100	100	100	200	200
Shearer	0.75	100	100	100	100	100	100	100
Spinner	1.13	100	100	100	100	100	142	142
Spinner, boy or girl...........	0.56	100	100	100	100	100	82	82
Spooler, girl.....	0.30	100	100	100	100	100	140	140
Teamster	0.75	100	100	100	100	100	167	167
Watchman	0.85	100	100	100	100	100	147	147
Warper.........	0.75	100	100	100	100	100	230	230
Weaver.........	0.94	100	100	100	100	100	133	133
Weaver, boy or girl...........	0.40	100	100	100	100	100	135	135
Wool-sorter.....	1.10	100	100	100	100	100	145	145

[1] Per month.

TABLE 2 — *Continued*

WAGE-SERIES FROM VOL. XX OF THE TENTH CENSUS

WOOLEN INDUSTRY

Manchester, N. H., 396

Occupation	Initial Wage p'r Day	1860	1861	1862	1863	1864	1865	1866
Overseers, different departm'nts	$ 66.56[1]	100	106	96	100	118	129	142
Carder..........	0.92	100	100	103	100	136	136	145
Carpenter	1.47	100	97	101	110	144	133	139
Laborer	1.00	100	100	100	117	125	125	133
Loom-fixer.......	1.25	100	100	100	106	120	134	140
Machinist	1.36	100	105	104	122	118	143	137
Picker...........	0.92	100	100	103	109	136	136	145
Shearer	1.00	100	100	125	125	112	117	128
Spinner	0.52	100	123	112	112	121	127	175
Spooler	0.60	100	100	102	128	127	127	183
Teamster	1.17	100	100	100	107	128	128	128
Warper..........	0.60	100	100	102	128	127	127	183
Weaver	0.78	100	90	79	90	109	112	171
Wool-sorter.....	1.48	100	95	95	116	116	124	139

Dresden, O., 400]

Occupation	Initial Wage p'r Day	1860	1861	1862	1863	1864	1865	1866
Overseers, different departm'nts	$ 58.50[1]	100	100	100	100	100	100	100
Carder	2.25	100	100	100	100	100	100	100
Carder, boy......	0.60	100	100	125	125	125	125	125
Dyer............	1.25	100	100	160	160	160	160	160
Dyer's helper....	1.25	100	100	120	120	120	120	120
Fuller	1.25	100	100	100	120	120	120	120
Gigger	1.25	100	100	120	120	120	120	120
Loom-fixer.......	2.00	100	100	100	100	100	100	100
Picker, boy......	0.60	100	100	125	125	125	125	125
Shearer	2.00	100	100	100	100	100	100	100
Scourer	1.25	100	100	160	160	160	160	160
Spinner	1.25	100	100	120	120	120	120	120
Teamster........	1.00	100	100	100	100	100	100	100
Warper	1.00	100	100	125	125	125	125	125
Weaver	1.00	100	100	100	100	100	100	100

[1] Per month.

TABLE 2—*Continued*

WAGE-SERIES FROM VOL. XX OF THE TENTH CENSUS

WOOLEN INDUSTRY

Springfield, Ill., 382, 383

Occupation	Initial Wage p'r Day	1860	1861	1862	1863	1864	1865	1866
	$							
Overseers of different dep'ts ..	36.25 [1]	100	122	122	126	152	197	206
Carder..........	1.50	100	87	87	100	167	183	183
Carder, boy	0.75	100	80	80	100	107	107	107
Dyer............	2.00	...	100	100	100	125	150	150
Engineer........	1.25	100	128	128	140	160	200	200
Finisher	1.50	100	100	100	117	150	133	150
Laborer.........	1.00	100	100	100	100	125	125	150
Picker	0.75	100	133	133	133	167	200	200
Spinner.........	1.40	100	93	93	100	143	179	179
Weaver	1.25	100	120	100	120	140	200	160
Wool-sorter	1.25	...	100	100	120	160	220	220

New Hampshire, 396, 397

Occupation	Initial Wage	1860	1861	1862	1863	1864	1865	1866
	$							
Overseers in different dep'ts ..	42.25 [1]	100	100	100	100	100	138	138
Carder..........	0.50	100	100	100	125	125	150	150
Carpenter.......	1.75	100	100	100	100	100	143	143
Dyer............	1.00	100	100	100	100	100	130	130
Engineer........	1.375	100	100	100	109	109	145	145
Fuller	0.875	100	100	100	114	114	149	149
Laborer.........	0.875	100	100	100	114	114	157	157
Machinist.......	1.25	100	100	100	108	108	160	160
Spinner.........	1.10	100	100	100	114	114	148	148
Spooler	0.50	100	100	100	100	100	100	100
Teamster	0.875	100	100	100	114	114	149	149
Weaver	1.10	100	100	100	107	107	125	125

CARRIAGE AND WAGON WORKS

Belleville, Ill., 413

Occupation	Initial Wage	1860	1861	1862	1863	1864	1865	1866
	$							
Apprentice......	0.33⅓	100	100	149	149	149	149	149
Blacksmith	2.00	100	100	125	125	150	150	150
B'lksmith, helper	1.00	100	100	125	125	150	150	150
Bodymaker	2.00	100	100	125	125	150	150	150
Painters	2.00	100	100	125	125	150	150	150
Striper..........	1 75	100	114	143	143	171	171	171
Trimmer........	2.00	100	100	125	125	150	150	150
Varnisher.......	2.00	100	100	125	125	150	150	150
Wood-worker ...	2.00	100	100	125	125	150	150	150

[1] Per month.

TABLE 2—*Continued*

WAGE-SERIES FROM VOL. XX OF THE TENTH CENSUS

CARRIAGE AND WAGON WORKS

Indianapolis, Ind., 414

Occupation	Initial Wage p'r Day	1860	1861	1862	1863	1864	1865	1866
	$							
Apprentice......	0.50	100	100	100	100	100	150	150
Blacksmith......	2.25	100	100	89	89	89	111	111
Bl'ksmith, helper	1.00	100	100	75	75	100	125	125
Body-maker.....	2.25	100	100	78	78	111	111	111
Laborer.........	1.00	100	100	100	100	100	125	125
Painters.........	2.00	100	100	75	75	88	88	88
Stitcher.........	1.00	100	100	100	100	100	125	125
Striper..........	1.50	100	100	100	100	117	117	117
Trimmer........	2.00	100	100	100	88	88	100	100
Varnisher.......	2.00	100	100	100	88	88	100	100
Watchman	1.00	100	100	100	100	100	125	125
Wheelright......	1.75	100	100	100	86	86	100	100
Wood-worker....	2.00	100	100	75	75	75	88	88

Dubuque, Ia., 416

	$							
Blacksmith......	1.25	100	120	160	200	220	220	220
Painter	1.25	100	120	160	200	220	220	220
Trimmer........	1.25	100	120	160	200	220	220	220
Wood-worker....	1.25	100	120	160	200	220	220	220

Portland, Me., 417

	$							
Foreman	1.75	100	100	114	143	171	171	171
Apprentice	0.60	100	100	100	108	108	108	108
Blacksmith......	1.75	100	100	114	143	171	171	171
Bl'ksmith, helper	1.25	100	100	100	100	120	120	120
Body-maker.....	1.75	100	100	114	143	171	171	171
Finisher	1.25	100	140	120	120	140	140	140
Laborer.........	1.25	100	100	100	120	120	120	120
Painter	1.75	100	100	114	143	171	171	171
Stitcher.........	1.25	100	100	120	160	160	160	160
Striper..........	1.75	100	100	114	143	171	171	171
Teamster........	1.25	100	100	100	100	120	120	120
Trimmer	1.75	100	100	114	143	171	171	171
Varnisher.......	1.75	100	100	114	143	171	171	171
Watchman	1.00	100	100	100	125	150	150	150
Wheelwright	1.50	100	100	117	150	183	200	200
Wood-worker....	1.50	100	100	117	167	200	200	200

TABLE 2—*Continued*

WAGE-SERIES FROM VOL. XX OF THE TENTH CENSUS

CARRIAGE AND WAGON WORKS

Massachusetts, 420, 421

Occupation	Initial Wage p'r Day	1860	1861	1862	1863	1864	1865	1866
	$							
Foreman	2.875	100	109	109	109	109	109	109
Apprentices	0.75	100	117	117	117	117	117	117
Body-maker	1.33	100	100	100	132	132	132	188
Finisher	2.50	100	120	120	120	120	120	120
Painter	1.58	100	100	...	116	116	116	158
Stitcher.........	1.50	100	108	108	108	108	108	108
Striper..........	1.875	100	117	117	117	117	117	117
Teamster........	1.50	100	83	83	83	83	83	83
Trimmer	1.58	100	100	100	142	142	142	206
Varnisher	2.00	100	113	113	113	113	113	113
Watchman	1.00	100	113	113	113	113	113	113
Wheelwright	1.33	100	100	100	132	132	132	188
Wood-worker....	1.25	100	160	160	160	160	160	160

New York, 423

	$							
Helpers	0.875	100	115	121	116	116	129	146
Mechanics	1.365	100	111	111	111	115	140	149

Ravenna, O., 424

	$							
Blacksmith......	1.50	100	100	117	167	183	200	200
Bl'ksmith, helper	1.00	100	100	125	150	150	150	150
Body-maker	1.50	100	100	126	167	183	183	183
Painter	1.375	100	100	127	164	164	164	164
Trimmer	1.375	100	100	127	164	182	182	182
Wheelwright	1.50	100	100	133	133	167	167	167

Whitewater, Wis., 426

	$							
Blacksmith......	1.25	100	110	120	120	140	150	180
Bl'ksmith, helper	0.80	100	125	125	125	156	188	188
Engineer	1.00	100	113	113	125	138	150	175
Laborer.	0.75	100	107	133	133	167	183	200
Machinist	1.25	100	100	120	120	120	160	180
Teamster........	0.76	100	132	132	132	164	197	197

TABLE 2— *Continued*

WAGE-SERIES FROM VOL. XX OF THE TENTH CENSUS

CARRIAGE AND WAGON WORKS

Louisville, Ky., 416

Occupation	Initial Wage p'r Day	1860	1861	1862	1863	1864	1865	1866
	$							
Blacksmith	2.33	100	64	71	129	172	186	215
Painter	2.00	100	96	92	108	125	150	158
Trimmer.........	2.00	100	83	92	108	121	150	158
Wood-worker....	1.66	...	100	110	120	140	151	181

FURNITURE

New Haven, Conn., 435

Occupation	Initial Wage	1860	1861	1862	1863	1864	1865	1866
	$							
Foreman.........	65.00[1]	100	108	115	123	123	123	131
Cabinet-maker..	2.00	100	100	100	113	113	125	125
Carver..........	2.00	100	100	113	113	113	113	125
Chair-maker	1.80	100	100	100	100	111	111	111
Engineer	2.00	100	100	100	113	125	125	138
Finisher	1.80	100	100	111	111	111	125	125
Laborer	1.25	100	100	120	120	120	120	120
Machine hand ..	2.00	100	113	125	125	125	125	125
Packer	1.75	100	100	114	114	114	129	129
Turner	2.00	100	100	113	125	125	125	125
Upholsterer.....	2.00	100	100	100	100	100	125	125
Varnisher.......	2 00	100	100	100	113	113	125	125

Chicago, Ill., 438

	$	1860	1861	1862	1863	1864	1865	1866
Cabinet-maker..	1.10	100	100	114	148	205	227	250

Kentucky, 446

Occupation	Initial Wage	1860	1861	1862	1863	1864	1865	1866
	$							
Foreman.........	75.00[1]	100	100	113	113	113	113	133
Cabinet-maker..	1.40	100	107	125	179	179	196	196
Carver..........	1.50	100	100	133	133	133	200	200
Engineer	2.00	100	100	100	100	100	100	100
Laborer	1.00	100	100	125	125	125	150	150
Machine hand ..	1.25	100	120	140	160	160	200	200
Packer	1.25	100	100	100	120	120	120	160
Turner	1.50	100	100	100	167	167	183	183
Upholsterer.....	1.25	100	120	140	200	200	200	220
Varnisher.......	1.25	100	100	120	140	140	160	160

[1] Per month.

TABLE 2 — *Continued*

WAGE-SERIES FROM VOL. XX OF THE TENTH CENSUS — FURNITURE

Indiana, 441, 442

Occupation	Initial Wage p'r Day	1860	1861	1862	1863	1864	1865	1866
	$							
Foreman........	40.00[1]	100	125	125	138	150	163	175
Boy	0.33⅓	100	100	100	100	100	100	175
Carver..........	2.00	100	100	100	113	113	113	125
Chair-maker	1.66⅔	100	100	100	100	100	120	120
Engineer	1.50	100	100	100	117	117	117	117
Finisher	1.50	100	100	100	117	117	117	117
Laborer	0.75	100	100	100	100	100	101	111
Machine hand ..	1.00	100	100	100	100	100	100	100
Packer	1.00	100	100	150	150	150	150	150
Painter	1.16⅔	100	100	100	100	100	100	100
Turner	1.25	100	100	120	120	140	140	160
Varnisher.......	1.25	100	100	100	120	120	120	120

Louisville, Ky., 444

Occupation	Initial Wage p'r Day	1860	1861	1862	1863	1864	1865	1866
	$							
Foreman........	150.00[1]	...	100	100	100	100	100	100
Cabinet-maker..	1.80	...	100	100	100	100	100	100
Carver..........	1.90	...	100	100	100	100	100	100
Engineer	2.00	...	100	100	100	100	100	100
Finisher	1.75	...	100	100	100	100	100	100
Laborer	1.50	...	100	100	100	100	100	100
Machine hand...	1.80	...	100	100	100	100	100	100
Packer	1.80	...	100	100	100	100	100	100
Turner	1.75	...	100	100	100	100	100	100
Varnisher.......	1.55	...	100	100	100	100	100	100

Louisville, Ky., 445

Occupation	Initial Wage p'r Day	1860	1861	1862	1863	1864	1865	1866
	$							
Foreman........	80.00[1]	100	100	100	100	100	100	100
Cabinet-maker..	2.00	100	100	100	100	100	100	100
Carver..........	2.50	100	100	100	100	100	100	100
Chair-maker	2.00	100	100	100	100	100	100	100
Engineer	2.25	100	100	100	100	100	100	100
Finisher	2.50	100	100	100	100	100	100	100
Laborer	1.25	100	100	100	100	100	100	100
Machine hand ..	1.75	100	100	100	100	100	114	114
Packer	1.50	100	100	100	100	100	100	100
Turner	2.00	100	100	100	100	113	113	113
Varnisher.......	2.00	100	100	100	100	100	100	100

New York, N. Y., 450

Occupation	Initial Wage p'r Day	1860	1861	1862	1863	1864	1865	1866
	$							
Foreman........	48.00[1]	100	100	104	125	167	229	229
Cabinet-maker..	1.16⅔	100	100	143	172	229	286	315
Carver..........	1.33⅓	100	75	112	137	162	187	200
Finisher	1.16⅔	100	86	115	129	186	200	200
Packer	1.00	100	100	133	167	200	217	217
Upholsterer.....	1.50	100	78	111	133	167	189	211
Varnisher.......	1.00	100	100	133	167	200	233	217

[1] Per month.

TABLE 2 — *Continued*

WAGE-SERIES FROM VOL. XX OF THE TENTH CENSUS

FURNITURE

Rochester, N. Y., 450

Occupation	Initial Wage p'r Day	1860	1861	1862	1863	1864	1865	1866
	$							
Cabinet-maker..	1.50	100	100	100	100	117	117	133
Carver..........	2.50	100	100	100	100	100	100	100
Chair-maker	1.50	100	100	100	100	117	117	133
Finisher	1.25	100	100	100	120	120	120	160
Machine hand ..	1.50	100	100	100	100	100	100	100
Packer	1.00	100	100	100	125	125	150	150
Upholsterer.....	2.00	100	100	100	100	113	113	113
Varnisher.......	1.25	100	100	100	120	120	120	160

New York, 452

	$							
Foreman........	60.00[1]	100	100	100	100	120	120	120
Cabinet-maker..	1.50	100	100	100	100	167	167	167
Carver..........	1.75	100	100	100	100	143	143	143
Chair-maker	1.50	100	100	100	100	150	150	150
Engineer	2.00	100	100	100	100	150	150	150
Finisher	1.50	100	100	100	100	150	150	150
Laborer	1.25	100	100	100	100	120	120	120
Machine hand ..	1.50	100	100	100	100	150	150	150
Packer	1.00	100	100	100	100	175	175	175
Turner	1.50	100	100	100	100	150	150	150
Upholsterer.....	1.75	100	100	100	100	143	143	143
Varnisher.......	1.50	100	100	100	100	150	150	150

Columbus, O., 454

	$							
Foreman........	100.00[1]	100	100	100	100	100	100	100
Carver...:......	3.50	100	100	100	100	100	100	100
Cabinet-maker..	2.50	100	100	100	100	100	100	100
Chair-maker	2.50	100	100	100	100	100	100	100
Engineer	3.00	100	100	100	100	100	100	100
Finisher	2.00	100	100	100	100	100	100	100
Turner	2.50	100	100	100	100	100	100	100
Laborer	1.50	100	100	100	100	100	100	100
Machine hand ..	3.00	100	100	100	100	100	100	100
Packer	2.25	100	100	100	100	100	100	100
Upholsterer.....	2.40	100	100	100	100	100	100	100
Varnisher.......	2.00	100	100	100	100	100	100	100

[1] Per month.

TABLE 2— *Continued*

WAGE-SERIES FROM VOL. XX OF THE TENTH CENSUS

FURNITURE

New Hampshire, 448

Occupation	Initial Wage p'r Day	1860	1861	1862	1863	1864	1865	1866
	$							
Foreman	36.40[1]	100	100	100	125	125	125	125
Cabinet-maker..	1.15	100	109	117	117	130	139	139
Machine hand ..	1.00	100	110	125	125	140	150	150
Turner	1.25	100	100	100	120	120	140	140

Philadelphia, Pa., 456, 457

	$							
Foreman	48.00[1]	100	100	100	125	125	125	125
Cabinet-maker..	1.67	100	100	100	120	120	120	120
Carver	2.00	100	100	100	113	113	113	113
Chair-maker	1.50	100	100	100	117	117	117	117
Packer	1.50	100	100	100	117	117	117	117
Upholsterer.....	2.00	100	100	100	125	125	125	125
Varnisher.......	1.32	100	100	100	126	126	126	126

Wisconsin, 459

	$							
Foreman	33.33⅛[1]	...	100	150	250	250	250	250
Cabinet-maker..	1.50	...	100	...	117	117	117	117
Carver	1.50	...	100	...	117	117	117	117
Chair-maker	1.50	...	100	...	117	117	117	117
Engineer	1.50	...	100	...	117	117	117	117
Finisher	1.50	...	100	...	117	117	117	117
Laborer	1.25	...	100	...	120	120	120	120
Machine hand ..	2.00	...	100	...	125	125	125	125
Packer	1.50	...	100	...	117	117	117	117
Turner	2.00	...	100	...	125	125	125	125
Varnisher.......	1.50	...	100	...	117	117	117	117

SAW- AND PLANING-MILLS

Carrollton, Mich., 473, 474

	$							
Engineer	2.37	100	100	74	84	148	148	148
Filer	2.00	100	100	100	119	103	175	175
Laborer	1.00	100	100	100	150	200	175	188
Sawyer	1.345	100	102	114	139	180	182	202
Teamster	1.00	100	94	100	150	225	200	200

[1] Per month.

TABLE 2 — *Continued*
WAGE-SERIES FROM VOL. XX OF THE TENTH CENSUS
SAW- AND PLANING-MILLS
Kentucky, 468, 469

Occupation	Initial Wage p'r Day	1860	1861	1862	1863	1864	1865	1866
Foreman, dress'g department ...	$ 80.00[1]	100	63	81	100	156	208	125
Foreman, sash department ...	70.00[1]	100	71	86	143	179	143	143
Bench hand, sash department ...	1.50	100	83	83	167	183	200	200
Laborer	1.00	100	125	150	175	175	175	160
Machine hand, sash departm't	1.75	100	80	86	157	171	186	186
Matcher, dress'g department ...	1.375	100	91	91	127	164	218	218
Molder, dressing department ...	1.80	100	83	89	111	153	181	181
Planer, dressing department ...	1.375	100	91	91	127	164	218	218
Sawyer, dressing department ...	1.375	100	91	91	127	164	218	218
Surfacer, dress'g department ...	1.375	100	91	91	127	164	218	218
Steamboat joiner	1.60	100	94	109	125	172	203	188
Teamster	1.00	100	100	100	138	167	150	200

Traverse City, Mich., 477

Occupation	Initial Wage p'r Day	1860	1861	1862	1863	1864	1865	1866
Foreman	$ 153.83[1]	100	100	100	100	100	100	...
Engineer	5.81⅔	100	100	100	100	100	100	...
Filer	1.00	100	100	100	150	173	261	...
Laborer	0.385	100	119	140	200	260	300	...
Sawyer	0.77	100	100	100	130	175	200	...
Setter	0.77	100	100	100	130	175	200	...
Teamster	0.385	100	119	140	200	260	300	...

Wisconsin, 496

Occupation	Initial Wage p'r Day	1860	1861	1862	1863	1864	1865	1866
Foreman, sawing department ...	$ 52.00[1]	100	100	100	125	150	200	200
Engineer	1.50	100	100	100	117	150	167	167
Filer	1.50	100	100	100	133	150	200	200
Laborer	1.00	100	100	100	113	150	150	175
Sawyer, sawing department ...	1.50	100	100	100	133	150	183	200
Setter	1.25	100	100	100	120	120	160	160
Teamster	1.00	100	100	100	113	150	150	175

[1] Per month.

TABLE 2— *Continued*

WAGE-SERIES FROM VOL. XX OF THE TENTH CENSUS

SAW- AND PLANING-MILLS

Utica, N. Y., 481, 482

Occupation	Initial Wage p'r Day	1860	1861	1862	1863	1864	1865	1866
Foreman, dress'g department ...	$ 83.33⅓[1]	100	100	100	100	100	100	100
Foreman, sash department ...	83.33⅓[1]	100	100	100	100	100	100	100
Bench hand	1.875	100	100	100	100	100	100	100
Engineer	2.00	100	100	100	100	100	100	100
Laborer	1.25	100	100	100	100	90	90	90
Machine hand ..	1.75	100	100	100	100	86	86	86
Matcher	1.75	100	100	100	100	100	100	100
Molder	1.75	100	100	100	100	86	86	86
Planer	1.75	100	100	100	86	86	86	86
Sawyer	1.75	100	100	100	86	86	86	86
Surfacer	1.75	100	100	100	100	86	86	86
Teamster	1.625	100	100	100	100	100	100	100

Ohio, 485, 486

	Initial Wage p'r Day	1860	1861	1862	1863	1864	1865	1866
Foreman, dress'g department ...	65.00[1]	100	120	140	160	200	200	200
Foreman, sawing department ...	65.00[1]	100	120	140	160	200	200	200
Foreman, sash department ...	65.00[1]	100	100	100	140	160	200	200
Bench hand	1.50	100	100	117	133	183	233	233
Engineer	1.75	100	100	100	114	143	171	171
Laborer	1.00	100	100	100	150	200	200	200
Machine hand ..	1.75	100	100	114	143	200	229	229
Matcher	1.50	100	100	133	167	200	233	250
Molder	1.75	100	114	114	143	171	200	229
Planer	1.50	100	100	133	167	200	200	200
Sawyer, dressing department ...	1.50	100	117	133	167	200	200	200
Sawyer, sawing department ...	1.75	100	100	114	143	200	229	229
Teamster	1.25	100	100	100	140	200	200	200

Menomonee, Wis., 495

	Initial Wage p'r Day	1860	1861	1862	1863	1864	1865	1866
Filer	$ 3.00	...	100	100	100	117	117	117
Laborer	1.08	100	106	114	128	150	150	128
Sawyer	2.00	...	100	100	100	125	125	125
Setter	1.50	...	100	100	107	133	133	113
Teamster	1.30	100	104	110	123	146	146	131

[1] Per month.

TABLE 2—*Continued*

WAGE-SERIES FROM VOL. XX OF THE TENTH CENSUS

SHIP-CARPENTRY

St. Louis, Mo., 499

Occupation	Initial Wage p'r Day	1860	1861	1862	1863	1864	1865	1866
	$							
Calker..........	2.50	100	120	120	120	170	200	180
Carpenter	2.50	100	120	120	120	170	200	180
Engineer	2.885	100	100	133	133	167	200	200
Laborer	1.00	100	125	125	125	200	250	225

Ohio, 500

	$							
Carpenter	1.75	100	143	143	143	200	200	200
Laborer	1.125	100	111	118	111	140	140	140
Dock hand......	2.00	100	125	125	125	188	188	188
Sawyer	2.25	100	111	111	111	156	156	156

TABLE 3

RELATIVE SALARIES OF SCHOOL-TEACHERS [1]

Baltimore, Md.

Grade	Init. Sal. pr.Yr.	Sex	1860	1861	1862	1863	1864	1865	1866
	$								
Principals, high schools, boys..........	1,500	M.	100	100	100	100	120	120	147
Assistants, high schools, boys..........	1,100	M.	100	100	100	100	127	127	164
Principals, grammar schools, boys	900	M.	100	100	100	100	144	144	167
Principals, grammar schools, girls	500	F.	100	100	100	100	140	140	180
First assistants, grammar schools, boys	350	F.	100	100	100	100	171	171	200
First assistants, grammar schools, girls	300	F.	100	100	100	100	167	167	233
Principals, primary schools, boys and girls	300	F.	100	100	100	100	167	167	233
Highest grade, primary schools, boys and girls.................	200	F.	100	100	100	100	175	175	250
Assistants, beginners, primary schools, boys and girls	100	F.	100	100	100	100	250	250	400

Boston, Mass.

Head masters, high schools [2]	2,800	M.	100	100	100	100	107	125	125
Masters, high schools [2]..................	2,000	M.	100	100	100	100	110	125	125
Masters, grammar schools [2]............	2,000	M.	100	100	100	100	110	125	125
First assistants, grammar schools.....	500	F.	100	100	100	100	120	140	140
Assistants, lowest, primary schools [3] ..	300	F.	100	100	100	100	133	150	150

[1] From the *Aldrich Report*, Part IV, Table XIV.
[2] After four years' service.   [3] First year of service.

TABLE 3—*Continued*

RELATIVE SALARIES OF SCHOOL-TEACHERS

Cincinnati, O.

Principals, high schools................	1,750	M.	100	86	86	100	114	114	138
Principals, intermediate schools	1,320	M.	100	87	87	100	121	121	159[1]
Principals, district schools	1,200	M.	100	89	89	100	125	125	158[1]
Assistants, highest, intermediate sch'ls	450	F.	100	90	90	100	100	100	100
Assistants, highest, district schools ...	420	F.	100	91	91	100	100	100	167[2]
Assistants, lowest, district schools	300	F.	100	92	92	100	100	100	133

St. Louis, Mo.

Assistants, high schools................	1,200	M.	100	67	83	...	125	125	142
Principals, district schools	1,250	M.	100	64	80	...	120	120	136
Head assistants, district schools	425	F.	100	82	94	...	141	141	153
Third assistants, district schools, minimum salaries	375	F.	100	73	87	...	120	120	133

Barnstable County, Mass.

Teachers of country schools............	40.73[3]	M.	100	101	100	102	105	122	132
Teachers of country schools............	19.12[3]	F.	100	94	99	94	98	109	118

Franklin County, Mass.

Teachers of country schools............	27.44[3]	M.	100	102	99	100	106	134	141
Teachers of country schools............	15.91[3]	F.	100	96	99	100	103	120	133

[1] After three years' service. [2] After six years' service. [3] Per month.

INDEX